A Warrior's Gateway

A Warrior's Gateway

Durban and the Anglo-Boer War 1899–1902

Edited by
Johan Wassermann
and
Brian Kearney

Hazel England, Graeme Fuller, Brian Kearney, Dave Matthews,
JL McCracken, Ian Swanepoel, Paul Tichmann
Johan Wassermann, Annette Wohlberg, John Yelland

Protea Book House
Pretoria
2002

Hazel England was educated at St Thomas Aquinas Convent and General Hertzog High School in Witbank, the University of the Witwatersrand and the Johannesburg College of Education. She worked for the South African Institute of Race Relations before moving to Durban. She became involved in various aspects of the history of Pinetown, ranging from genealogy to oral history. Since 1991 she has been employed in the Pinetown Museum, of which she is currently the curator.

Graeme Fuller was born in Durban and educated at St Andrew's College in Grahamstown and the University of Cape Town, from which he graduated as a medical doctor in 1971. He has been involved for many years in medical matters and the military, and still serves actively in these capacities both locally and in Britain. He is a practising neurosurgeon in Durban.

Brian Kearney was born and went to school in Pietermaritzburg. He taught architecture at the University of Natal and practised architecture from 1966 to 1993, thereafter retiring as Emeritus Professor of Architecture. He has lectured and published on the history and conservation of South African and Natal architecture and local history.

Dave Matthews was born in Edgeware, Middelsex, England in 1941. He was educated at Lyndhurst School and Rickmansworth Grammar School, both in Hertfordshire. He emigrated to South Africa in 1982 to join a motor manufacturing plant in Durban and became a member of the Natal branch of the South African Military History Society where he developed a long-standing interest in the Anglo-Zulu and Anglo-Boer Wars.

JL McCracken was born in County Down and educated at Queens University, Belfast. He was a lecturer in history at the University of the Witwatersrand (1947–1950), and was the Sir Robert Wood research lecturer at Trinity College, Dublin, 1950–1952. He was a senior lecturer and subsequently professor of history at Magee College, Londonderry, 1950–1969, becoming a professor of history, New University of Ulster, 1969–1979. He held the Hugh le May research fellowship from Rhodes University, 1980–1981.

Ian Swanepoel was born in Durban and educated at Glenwood High School. He joined the South African Transport Services where he worked until his retirement in 1987. He is intensely involved in the Natal and South African Numismatic Societies and is a very keen amateur historian.

Paul Tichmann was born in Ixopo in 1959 and educated at the Little Flower High School and the University of Natal. He joined the Durban Local History Museum as a research officer in 1994 and is currently the acting director of the said museum.

Johan Wassermann was born in Amersfoort in 1962. He was educated at various Dundee schools, the PU for CHE, Rhodes University and the University of the Free State. He taught at schools in Durban from 1989 to 1993, and lectured in history and geography at the Durban College of Education from 1993 until the closure of the institution in 2000. He currently lectures in history education at the University of Natal.

Annette Wohlberg was born in Pietermaritzburg in 1957. She was educated at various Dundee schools, the University of Pretoria, Unisa and the University of the Free State. She taught at Ladysmith and Dundee up to 1996. From 1996 to 2000 she lectured history and geography at the Durban College of Education. She currently teaches history at Westville Girls High.

John Yelland was born in Kimberley in 1931 and educated at Kimberley Boys' High School and the University of the Witwatersrand. He worked as an architect in various African countries, Australia and England and retired in 1989 as head of the Durban office of Boutek of the CSIR. He is a leading member of numerous societies including the South African Military History Society and the Genealogical Society of South Africa.

Published by
Protea Book House
PO Box 35110, Menlopark
0102

ISBN 1-919825-85-1

Design and reproduction by PrePress Images, Pretoria.
Printed by ABC Press, Cape Town.

Errata:

The dedication should be to *George Allan Chadwick (27.8.1914–25.8.2002)*.

On the content pages Josh McCracken should read *JL McCracken* – this correction includes the resultant errors on pages 12, 349 and 350.

On page xv 31.3.1990 should read *31.3.1900*.

On page 41 the 99% in the 4th last line should read *95%*.

On page 43 the last sentence of the third paragraph should read: *This was because even the army's best guns were within range of the Boer's mausers and the 6-inch guns would have been far more effective against the Boers entrenched along the Tugela.* In the next paragraph Peter's Hill should read *Pieter's Hill*.

On page 301 endnote 6 should refer to *Wohlberg*.

On page 357 white in the 6th line should read *European*.

Dedication

The authors wish to dedicate this publication to
George Alan Chadwick (27.8.1924 – 26.8.2000),
a remarkable inspiration and driving spirit in the
commemoration of the Anglo-Boer War who, through
his multilingual skills, set an example of reconciliation.

Contents

PREFACE

The origins of the book

Under the remarkable leadership of the late George Chadwick, a committee was formed in Durban in 1997 to organise and administer various ways of commemorating the centenary of the Anglo-Boer War locally. The various activities of this committee included several special and memorable public functions and re-enactments. Thirty-five plaques were erected around the city to inform the public where particular events had taken place. An information brochure on Durban and the war was also published with maps and illustrations. This brochure was the result of joint authorship by a number of the members of the committee. It was relatively easy to persuade this group of authors to take the process much further, and to research many more dimensions and collectively write up the fascinating story of Durban and the Anglo-Boer War. Sadly George died in August 2000 before he could make any further contribution to the publication.

Co-authorship

The book is the result of an enthusiastic spirit of co-authorship, and the contributions have not only been made in individual chapters and sub-chapters but in vigorous debate and dialogue which characterised numerous meetings over the past two years. The authors of the book emanate from a wide variety of backgrounds, including the academic world, museums, the medical profession and industry, but all are bound together by their love of history. Such varied expertise and experience made for fertile discussions which we believe have served only to enrich the publication.

The debate has been about the war, about the people involved, about Durban, about writing style and format, and about the nature of historical research, criticism and description. While there has been a concerted effort to present the material in a consistent and holistic way, there has also been a deliberate attempt to allow freedom of individual thought and presentation by each author. In particular, it will be noted that endnote styles vary slightly from author to author to mirror their own individual philosophies. Nevertheless the co-editors must share the final responsibility for the balance between the two ideals of consistency and individuality.

Sources and references

At the time of the preparatory meetings of the commemorative committee, a number of people began to research aspects of the war in the context of Durban. George Chadwick wrote to a large number of local and overseas individuals and organisations asking for clues, ideas and information. Some members were already well advanced in terms of their own personal research, and others began working through the local archives, historical collections and the newspapers of the period. Many questions were raised and many remained unanswered at that stage.

However since the idea of putting together a book took firm root, an enormous amount of information has come to light from a wide range of sources. In particular the colonial office and war office records in the Public Record Office in London have revealed many dimensions of the Durban story. Some of those sources even led back to local archive repositories. However, it has also been frustrating for the authors to meet with the strange ways of some curators and conservators who, in their enthusiasm for the conservation of collections, split up the component documentary parts of a story. Thus maps and photographs have often been removed from written texts in reports, probably to be archived elsewhere (who knows where), and so the whole cannot be understood – the pieces cannot be read together as they were originally intended. This kind of conservation certainly does not appear to have use and research as an objective.

It has been a deliberate publication strategy to use as many illustrations as possible to provide contextual richness to the essays. These illustrations have come from a wide variety of origins, both local and elsewhere. They are also of diverse quality and thus there is an unevenness in presentation. But the variations in themselves provide another level of interest by illustrating a complex weave of events.

While there are some issues and items that are covered in more than one chapter of the publication, the authors have decided to eliminate obvious cross-referencing between chapters and to leave it to the discernment of the reader to establish the connections.

The authors have been particularly conscious of the fundamental importance of using primary source materials and of the distinct dangers of using published secondary material. They have been specially concerned with the voices of the past – personal and official narratives to be listened to as historic pictures are viewed. Many questions have been answered, but many remain unanswered and it is the hope of the authors that the process in which they have been engaged in will excite others to continue.

Commemoration of war and the celebration of peace

This publication has been subsidised by the Durban Metro Committee for the centenary commemoration of the Anglo-Boer War and through the waiving of royalties by the authors.

The centenary of the Anglo-Boer War has been commemorated throughout South Africa since 1999. The re-enactments and public commemorations have themselves now faded into the past, but it is hoped that this publication will be a lasting memorial of the war and its impact on Durban. The date of publication has been timed to coincide with the centenary of the proclamation of peace on the 31 May 1902, and thus to shift the act of commemorating a war to a celebration of peace.

Spellings and placenames

The authors have had to face the usual dilemma of the spelling of Zulu-based place names. Many of these were corrupted from the original Zulu in colonial writings and on maps which were written or compiled by persons with little or no knowledge of the Zulu language. This unfortunate legacy still dwells with us and archaic spellings are generally still used to identify geographical features such as rivers like the Umgeni and Umbilo which ran through Durban. As no standard placenames or spellings thereof have yet been decided upon, this work, for pragmatic reasons and for the ease of reading, perpetuates the past spellings as found on most maps and in the majority of secondary works.

Monetary values are expressed in the imperial units used at the time under review, namely pounds – £, shillings – s, and pence – p, simply because of the impossibility of converting these realistically into present-day values. As far as units of weight and measure are concerned, the metric system has been applied, often in brackets following imperial units.

Wreath laying at the Wyatt Road Military Cemetery, Sunday 17 October 1999 (Editors' collection).

Acknowledgements

In the course of writing the book numerous people in various libraries and archival repositories, and elsewhere have assisted the authors. As it is impossible to name them all, we would like to record our deep indebtedness to all who rendered friendly and professional assistance. A special word of thanks and congratulations should go to the Durban Metro Council, who were farsighted enough, despite pressures to the contrary, to support financially the commemoration of the war in Durban and therefore this book.

DIE ANGLO-BOEROORLOG
DURBAN -DIE POORT

JOIN OUR COMMEMORATION
ANGLO-BOER WAR
1899 **100** 1999
ANGLO-BOEREOORLOG
DEEL IN ONS HERDENKING

Hierdie brosjure is saamgestel onder beskerming van die Durban Metro Subkomitee vir die Herdenking van die Eeufees van die Anglo-Boeroorlog. Dit vervat die verhale van die verdediging van die dorp en beskryf die belangrike rol van die hawe en die spoorweg met betrekking tot die vervoer van duisende man en perde, sowel as tonne proviand, na die oorlogsfront; dit beskryf die vrywillige regimente; die perdedepots en die Indiese ambulanskorps; die hospitaaltreine en - skepe. Ook ingesluit is die verhale van die vier Boere-konsentrasiekampe en die kamp van die Boere-krygsgevangenes; vlugtelinge van buite Natal; die maatskaplike toestande in die dorp terwyl krygswet geheers het; sensuur; die staptog van 7 000 Zoeloes vanaf die Witwatersrand, onder leiding van Muhle; liefdadigheidsverenigings; Winston Churchill; en 'n buitengewone hond met die naam Jack. Daar is kaarte met die ligging van die spesiale gedenkplate in die stad om terreine en plekke, wat van belang is vir die Anglo-Boeroorlog, aan te dui.

IMPI YAMANGISI NAMABHUNU

Leli bhukwana lilungiswe ngokohlelo lwekomidi le Durban Metro lilungiselelwa umqubo weminyaka eyikhulu wempi yaMaNgisi namaBhunu. Lilanda ngezindaba zokuvikelwa kwedolobha nangeqhaza elabanjwa yichweba nololiwe ekuthutheni izinkulungwane zamadoda namahhashi kanye nokunye okwakuyizidingo zempi; lichaza ngamabutho Qyezinikele; izikhumulo zokuphumula nokuhlonyiswakanye noMbutho wama-Ambulensi Amandiya isitimela esiyisibhedlela kanye nemikhumbi eyezibhedlela. Liqukethe imininingwane yezinKambi ezine zamaBhunu angabaThunjwa kanye, nenkambu okwakugcinwe kuyo iziboshwa zempi ezingama Bhunu ababaleki ababevela ngaphandle kwemingcele yelaseNatali; izimo zenhlalo ngaphansi kombuso wamabutho empi ukucindezelwa kwezoshicilelo; uhambo lwamaZulu abalelwa ezinkulungwaneni eziyisikhombisa (7 000) esuka eWitwatersrand eholwa nguMhle (nguMuhle) izinhlangano ezingxubevange ezithintekayo uWinston Churchill kanye nenja engejwayelekile eyayibizwa mgokuthi uJack. Leli bhukwana linamabalazwe akhombisa izindawo ezinezingqwembe ezinqala heziyisipesheli eziwuphawu lweza nezindawu ezithize ezizungeze idolobha; Okuyizindawo ezibalulekile ngokwempi yamaNgisi namaBhunu.

This brochure has been prepared under the auspices of the Durban Metro Sub-Committee for the Commemoration of the Centenary of the Anglo-Boer War. The Durban Metro Council and Kwa Zulu Natal Tourism are gratefully acknowledged for their financial support. The Urban Design Unit of the City Council provided technical assistance for the maps. The following persons have contributed: **George Chadwick, Ian Swanepoel, Johan Wassermann, Annette Wohlberg, Hazel England, Paul Tichmann, and Col. Graeme Fuller.** Professor Brian Kearney, Editor.

ACKNOWLEDGEMENTS: Photographs are taken from the private collections of the authors and the Durban Local History Museums; The Campbell Collections of the University of Natal; the Pietermaritzburg Depot of the National Archives; the War Museum of the Boer Republics, Bloemfontein and the National Cultural History Museum, Pretoria.

KINGDOM OF ZULU
KWAZULU NATAL

A page from the commemorative brochure, 1999.

INTRODUCTION
DURBAN: A WARRIOR'S GATEWAY

'In the study of warfare much emphasis is often laid on the glamour and tragedy of the various battles, while scant attention is paid to the importance of facilities and infrastructure in the base areas and the fortunes of the people living in them. Such was the case of Durban in the records of the Anglo-Boer War. Had it not been for the developments in the area, the tide of war might have been profoundly influenced.' These words were written by George Chadwick in the commemorative brochure published in 1999.

An urban historical study

The publication may be viewed as an urban history of Durban during the time of the Anglo-Boer War which lasted from 1899 to 1902. Within this time frame the emphasis is on the impact which the war had on Durban. As a result of a somewhat limited focus, certain aspects of the history of Durban at the time are merely alluded to, or excluded totally, since they have been deemed to be outside the context of the work and on the fringes of its impacts. Recreation and religious life are such aspects. On the other hand, the authors have also been especially conscious of the nature of 'Durban' and of how far its boundaries extended as a geographical, rather than a political or economic entity. In this regard it has been considered appropriate to have a somewhat flexible or fluctuating boundary depending on the nature of the subject. Thus, for example, the subject of medical services inevitably reaches well beyond Durban since the town was one component in a comprehensive chain of medical arrangements. And, too, the story of the seizure of ships and contraband as prizes, though focussed on the town of Durban itself, extends well out into the Indian Ocean and up the east coast of Africa, certainly to include the port of Lourenço Marques.

Urban histories of the Anglo-Boer War period are not an entirely unknown entity. Theron has produced a study of Pretoria and the early phases of the war (*Pretoria at War 1899–1900*, Protea, 2000), while Joubert completed an MA on Port Elizabeth and the Anglo-Boer War (*Port Elizabeth en die Anglo-Boere Oorlog*, UPE, 1985). Generally this is a neglected area in the historiography of the war and one which is often dwarfed by the military campaigns and the sufferings in the concentration camps.

The book, then, is about the city of Durban (or the town as it then was) and the war; and it addresses a number of questions concerning the impact of the war on the town and all its peoples, and the way it influenced the course of events. What difference did the war make to Durban? What impact did it have on the political, military, social and economic life of the town? And how, for example, did the new experience of martial law affect its peoples and their interrelationships?

Several themes are presented with Durban viewed as a gateway: a gateway to be defended; a gateway for warriors to pass through from both sides; a gateway for animals and machines; a gateway to the outside world and to the hinterland of the country; and a gateway for the easy movement of goods military and goods contraband – at times a gateway is open and at other times it is closed; a gateway joins and a gateway separates; and a gateway may have opportunities and costs attached.

Gateways compared

The authors have been specially conscious of the reality that Durban was one of several gateways of the Anglo-Boer War – Cape Town, Port Elizabeth, East London and Lourenço Marques were others. Each of these had its own unique patterns of events and people and things, but Durban's pattern, within its own historical and geographical context, is indeed a rich one involving subjects as diverse as guns and cattlemen, ambulance trains and contraband, concentration camps and volunteer regiments, benevolence and prize courts.

Consider some of the famous and leading role-players like Hely-Hutchinson, Hime, Milner and Chamberlain; Princess Christian of Shleswig-Holstein, Lady Randolph Churchill, Mohandas Gandhi, Parsee Rustomjee, Winston Churchill, Sir Percy Scott and Sir Roger Casement. The pattern presented is all the richer for having such persons woven in, but indeed is much more meaningful with the inclusion of the 'little local people' like the widows and orphans, the African suspects and refugees like Hilda Bowesa, the semi-literate sergeant, the Boer women and children, the train drivers and nurses, the police and the charity workers, the prostitutes and thieves.

Overlapping phases

What appears to be clear from the records is that Durban and the Anglo-Boer War can be understood in several overlapping phases. Initially the stage was one of impending war and military preparations (though often the wrong ones); this was followed by a phase of unbridled military and patriotic enthusiasm which spilled over into waves of volunteering; then there was a phase of administrative order under martial law, and a logistical period of moving men and women and animals and guns and machines in vast numbers – of refugees and benevolence; then finally a phase dominated by economic interests in the returns of war and the benefits to be gained or lost. Whose war was it – South Africa's or Britain's or the empire or Natal's or Durban's?

Conflicts

Within each of these phases and within the 'gateway' themes, we can also detect sets of conflicts – 'wars within wars': the inevitable conflicts between the military and civilian authorities, be they the commandants or naval transport officers on the one hand, and civilian society on the other; the conflicts between the colonial government and the military; the municipal government and the military; the port and transport authorities and the military; and the commercial world and the military. In many respects these conflicts reopened wounds from the past political skirmishes between the colony and the mother country. One specifically British characteristic which coloured the events of the time was a highly developed bureaucratic system of administration which pervaded all sections of society.

The essays in the book attempt to unravel a complex web of superimposed layers of interest, authority and control. The bureaucratic hierarchies stretched from Chamberlain and other ministers of state in London, through Milner, the high commissioner in Cape Town, to Hely-Hutchinson and McCullum, the colonial governors in Pietermaritzburg, down to the local commandants, civil servants, councillors and the ordinary populace.

Culture and society

Over and above the effects of the war on the local inhabitants of the town, the period of the war provided a whole new set of circumstances which would change various components of society forever. The arrival of large numbers of refugees and Uitlanders in the port would in itself initiate a pattern which has continued up to the present when the inhabitants of the hinterland of the country still descend on Durban – but now as holiday-makers for vacations. Ironically close on 18 000 Boer men, women and children actually did arrive to live around the town and port which their political and military leaders had aspired to take by force, but they came as prisoners of war or as inmates of concentration camps. And for many of these people from the rural hinterland this would not only have been their first experience of the coast and the sea, but also their first experience of a form of urban life in the camps themselves.

For the men and boys who lived in the Umbilo prisoner-of-war camp the greatest irony would have been that they were only a stone's throw away from the site of one of the earliest Voortrekker settlements in Natal at Congella. The advantages of temporary employment were to be many for the growing number of African refugees who came into the town from surrounding areas, but the temporary nature of the military employment offered would in itself prefigure the way life would work out in the future – an existence based largely on temporary opportunities for work and thus conditions beyond any form of personal control.

A scene at the Point (*The Illustrated London News,* August 1899).

Orderlies from HMS *Terrible* with bicycles (Newnes).

A railway traveller with *jotis* and turban at the Greenwood Park Railway Station (KCL).

xi

Technology and modernity

Given the specific time period of the war – at the end of a century which had seen the unleashing of the industrial revolution on the world and particularly in Britain – it is not surprising that there were a number of instances which involved the application of new technologies to human circumstances. Many of these were of military importance: the development of state-of-the-art naval cruisers like HMS *Powerful* with their enormous capacities and voracious appetite for coal; the naval guns and the innovations which Captain Scott introduced for use on land; the modification of guns and the provision of armoured trains in the local railway workshops; the Natal railway system itself; the adaptation of steam-driven trains for ambulances and ships as hospitals complete with electricity, ventilating fans and refrigeration; the rapid despatch of a pre-fabricated wood and iron hospital from Britain to Pinetown Bridge; the use of X-ray apparatus and the electrification of hospitals from adjacent railway generators; advances in medical and surgical treatments; the developed use of tinned foods and extracts; the extensive uses of the telephone and telegraph (with encrypted codes) alongside pigeon post; the extraordinary attitude to the use of steam traction engines by an army steeped in the traditions of the horse; the development and use of large searchlights for communicating signals, to be hauled on ox wagons.

The use of many of these technological advances in transport, communication, energy and food thus has to be viewed against the social and cultural background of the semi-agrarian character of the Natal colonists on the one hand, and an almost eighteenth century Afrikaner culture on the other. Several different worlds in confrontation – consider, for example, the simultaneous existence in Durban of HMS *Terrible*, the jin-rickshas and ox wagons in the streets and Boer women in quasi-medieval serge dress.

Other new technologies were of a non-military nature: the fascinating saga of the Transvaalsche Koelkamers – a large meat refrigeration facility which was almost presented on a plate to the Natal government by the outbreak of war and which could provide a method for controlling and refining the trade in meat; the ongoing construction of harbour piers and quay walls with pre-cast concrete production sites; teams of divers working underwater; a flotilla of dredgers to allow the passage of ships into the bay.

The techniques of photography were so highly advanced by the time of the war that an enormous number of photographic illustrations were fed to the local and British public, eager for a visual sense of the day-to-day events. But publications such as *The Illustrated London News* and *The Graphic* also relied on drawings or retouched images which gave more dramatic effect. Sometimes the exaggerations bordered on the absurd. The war was also the first to be filmed in moving pictures, or 'biographs' as they were called at the time.

A highly exaggerated graphic of the volunteers marching past a gigantic town hall. They are also going the wrong way (*The Illustrated London News*).

The graphic below was based on the photograph above (*The Illustrated London News* and Newnes).

Economics and commerce

In many other ways life went on normally or at least many tried to have it that way. The complex commercial interconnections between the various parties who were involved in the war and especially the transit port role which characterised Durban's commercial world were distinctly affected. The closures of business gateways – gateways of opportunity denied through martial law, the seizure of goods and declarations of contraband – forced new opportunities and new gateways.

One hundred years ago the country of South Africa, the colony of Natal and the town of Durban moved into a new century steeped in a war between the two ruling European groups. Between 1899 and 1902 Durban was a warrior's gateway as the twentieth century dawned.

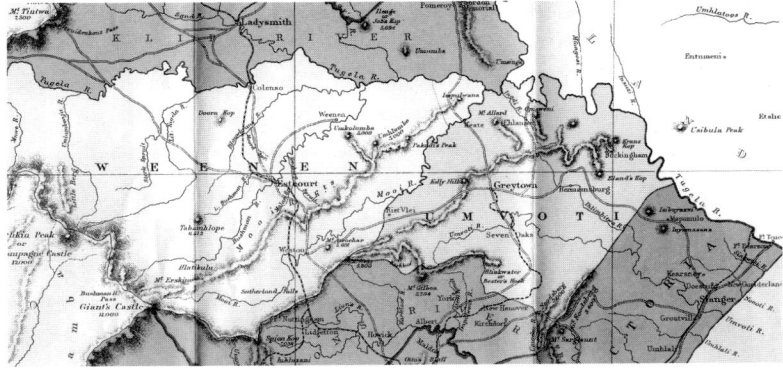

A portion of Russell's school map of Natal (Russell).

Merchant houses and banks tower over the town gardens with statues of Robinson and Escombe flanking the Volunteer Memorial (LHM).

In 1896, after the Jameson Raid, Lieutenant Colonel Grant of the Royal Engineers had been tasked by the British intelligence unit to prepare accurate maps of the north of Natal as there was 'no efficient map'. Grant had worked clandestinely on this project from August until December 1896, so as not to arouse the suspicions of the local population and because he had found little support from the colonial government. Unfortunately, the project ran out of funding and he was only able to work on the area north of Ladysmith towards the Biggarsberg and Laing's Nek. Thus there was no accurate map of the region to the south of Ladysmith. When Harry Escombe visited London in 1897 for the Diamond Jubilee celebrations, he met with Sir John Ardagh, the head of the intelligence section of the British army. Ardagh had arranged the meeting to request Escombe to facilitate the completion of maps of Northern Natal, which the intelligence unit had been unable to finish.

So Ardagh sought the assistance of Escombe and the Natal colonial government to arrange for Royal Engineers from the Cape to complete the mapping with the same degree of accuracy. Escombe assured him that the colony would be able to find £800 for the project. However, on his return to Natal, Escombe lost the elections and a new prime minister was elected. Therefore nothing more was done to complete the map.

In his evidence to the Royal Commission on the war in South Africa, Grant explained that the only map of any use for the area south of Ladysmith was that prepared by WH Nott for the office of the superintendent inspector of schools, Robert Russell, in 1893. (This same map was published in Russell's *Natal The Land and its Story*.) The issue raises many questions. Why did Escombe not ask Binns, his successor, to arrange for the continuation of the work? Did Escombe simply forget all about the request? Does this imply that the British generals went to war in Natal with substantially comprehensive topographical maps of the region to the north of Ladysmith, but with a schoolchild's map of the area to the south, a map so naively incorrect that it showed caterpillar-like mountain ranges across the interior? Did persons like Escombe consider that there would never be any need for proper maps further south? Could this not partially explain some of the problems associated with the various campaigns to the south of Ladysmith and especially along the Tugela River and at Spioenkop? It is interesting to note that in the case of Spioenkop, the Royal Engineers were frantically preparing topographical maps of the Tugela at the time of the battles and many of these were also inaccurate.

TIME LINE FOR THE ANGLO-BOER WAR

	EVENTS IN SOUTH AFRICA	EVENTS IN DURBAN OR RELATED TO DURBAN
8.9.1899	British government decides to send 10 000 soldiers to Natal.	
27.9.1899	Orange Free State joins the Transvaal (ZAR).	
9.1899		Bethune appointed Durban commandant. Ambulance Train No. 1 prepared in NGR workshops.
29–30.9.1899		Durban volunteer regiments called out and depart.
10.1899		Large numbers of Uitlanders and refugees arrive.
3.10.1899		Princess Christian Hospital initiated.
7.10.1899	British mobilise on a large scale.	White arrives in Durban.
9.10.1899	Boer ultimatum issued.	
11.10.1899	Boer ultimatum expires; Boers invade Natal and Cape.	Chamberlain instructs authorities to search all British ships for contraband.
12–13.10.1899	First action of the war at Kraaipan.	Chamberlain revokes contraband ruling. Muhle marchers arrive in Dundee.
14.10.1899	Inception of the siege of Mafeking.	Censorship office opened.
15.10.1899	Inception of the siege of Kimberley.	
16.10.1899		Gandhi advocates Indian support of British against Boers.
18.10.1899		*Avondale Castle* seized.
20.10.1899	Battle of Talana.	
21.10.1899	Battle of Elandslaagte.	
23–24.10.1899	British retreat from Dundee.	Hely-Hutchinson commences raising recruits.
25–26.10.1899		First Boer POWs arrive in Durban.
28.10.1899		Martial law proclaimed. National Bank of the ZAR searched. Nathan Marks arrested as a spy.
29.10.1899		Bethune detains Balwe.
30.10.1899	Mournful Monday: British defeats at Nicholson's Nek, Modderspruit.	Naval brigade and naval guns reach Ladysmith.
11.1899		British troops from all over the empire arrive in Durban.
3.11.1899		Durban under martial law. Scott appointed as commandant. Durban rifle associations called out.
2.11.1899	Inception of the siege of Ladysmith.	
6.11.1899		HMS *Terrible* arrives in Durban.
7.11.1899		Scott appointed commandant. His first defence report.
8.11.1899		Guns placed in position around Durban.
9.11.1899		Armoured trains run to the north and south of Durban.
14.11.1899	Boers take Colesberg.	
15.11.1899		Armoured train incident at Chieveley.
21.11.1899	Battle of Willow Grange.	

23.11.1899	Boer retreat at Belmont. End drive southwards towards Durban.	
25.11.1899	Boer retreat at Graspan.	Prize court proclaimed. Advertising for colonial scouts.
26.11.1899	Battle of Derdepoort.	
28.11.1899	Battle of Modder River.	Naval gun crews stand down.
12.1899		All tinned goods and portable rations to be viewed as contraband.
10–15.12.1899	Black Week: British defeats at Stormberg, Colenso and Magersfontein.	
9.12.1899		Ambulance train No. 2 completed.
14.12.1899		Indian Ambulance Corps arrives at Estcourt.
16.12.1899		*Regina* seized.
18.12.1899	Roberts replaces Buller as commander-in-chief. Army reserves called out.	
22.12.1899		First steam traction engines arrive.
28.12.1899		*Bundesrath* seized.
1.1900		Casement posted to British consulate in Lourenço Marques.
1.1900		Proclamation on contraband.
6.1.1900	Boers defeated at Platrand.	*Herzog* seized.
7.1.1900		Indian Ambulance Corps return to the front.
10.1.1900	Arrival of Roberts and his chief-of-staff, Kitchener.	Barton asks Scott for a 4.7" gun on a railway truck.
23–24.1.1900	Battle of Spioenkop.	
29.1.1900		Hospital ship *Maine* arrives.
2.1900		*Review and Critic* closed.
5.2.1900	Battle of Vaalkrans.	
8–12.2.1900		Naval guns modified, tested at the beach and dispatched.
11.2.1900	Roberts starts massive advance.	
15.2.1900	Relief of Kimberley.	
18.2.1900	Battle of Paardeberg.	
21–23.2.1900	Battle of Tugela Heights.	
27.2.1900	Massive Boer surrender at Paardeberg; Boers beaten at Tugela Heights and siege of Ladysmith lifted.	
6.3.1900		Princess Christian ambulance train arrives.
7.3.1900	Boers flee at Popular Grove.	
10.3.1900	Boers defeated at Driefontein, last stand before fall of the Orange Free State capital.	
13.3.1900	British enter Bloemfontein.	
14.3.1900		Scott's final report on the defence of Durban.
15.3.1900	Roberts offers terms to hendsoppers.	
17.3.1900	Boer conference at Kroonstad decides on guerilla war.	
19.3.1900		Princess Christian ambulance train departs.
26.3.1900		*Assaye* arrives with Princess Christian Hospital.
27.3.1900	Death of General Piet Joubert.	Scott sails for China.
31.3.1990	De Wet's success at Sannaspos. First blockhouse.	Removal of able-bodied men from charity.

4.1900	British delayed at Bloemfontein owing to typhoid.
4.4.1900	Royal Irish surrender at Reddersburg.
3.5.1900	British advance from Bloemfontein.
14.5.1900	British advance in the Biggarsberg as Boers retreat.
17.5.1900	Mafeking relieved.
24.5.1900	Durban Uitlander Committee formed.
25.5.1900	Princess Christian Hospital opened.
28.5.1900	Orange Free State annexed, now Orange River Colony.
31.5.1900	British enter Johannesburg. British defeated at Lindley.
5.6.1900	Roberts enters Pretoria, ZAR capital moves east.
6.6.1900	Select committee report on compensation for widows and dependants of volunteers.
7.6.1900	Action of De Wet at Roodewal.
11–12.6.1900	Battle of Donkerhoek.
12.6.1900	Buller enters the ZAR.
16.6.1900	First threat by Roberts to burn farms.
26.6.1900	NNV volunteers disbanded.
4.7.1900	Buller and Roberts join hands.
31.7.1900	Massive Boer surrender in Brandwater Basin. Pursuit of De Wet starts.
14.8.1900	Pursuit of De Wet continues.
27.8.1900	British win final set-piece battle at Bergendal.
30.8.1900	2 000 British POWs released from Nooitgedacht.
19.9.1900	Royal commission of enquiry into medical matters related to the war meets in Durban.
24.9.1900	Komatipoort, last town on the Delagoa railway, falls.
10.1900	Holland succeeds Van Koughnet as NTO.
2.10.1900	Durban volunteers return home.
8–9.10.1900	Durban volunteer regiments disbanded.
19.10.1900.	President Kruger sails for Europe. Schalk Burger acts as president.
24.10.1900	Buller leaves for Britain.
25.10.1900	ZAR annexed by the British.
6.11.1900	De Wet and Steyn almost captured at Bothaville.
29.11.1900	Kitchener becomes commander-in-chief.
16.12.1900	Kritzinger and Hertzog invade Cape.
27.12.1900	Emily Hobhouse visits concentration camps.
27.1–26.3.1901	Major drive by General French.
31.1.1901	Smuts occupies Modderfontein.
7.2.1901	30 000 additional British mounted troops despatched.
10.2.1901	De Wet's invasion of the Cape fails.
28.2.1901	Botha and Kitchener meet at Middelburg to discuss peace.
10.4.1901	Drive in the northern Orange Free State starts.

6.4.1901		King-Hall replaces Holland as NTO.
8.5.1901	Milner departs for London on leave.	
16.5.1901	Kritzinger's second invasion of the Cape.	
14.5.1901	British opposition to the war increased owing to efforts of Campbell-Bannerman.	
7.1900	Fawcett Commission constituted.	
18.7.1901	Drive in Cape Colony starts.	
7.8.1901	Proclamation of Kitchener that captured Boer leaders to be deported.	
3.9.1901	Smuts invades the Cape.	
7.9.1901	Smuts defeats 17th Lancers.	
13.9.1901		First inhabitants of Merebank arrive.
17.9.1901	Boer victory at Blood River.	
26.9.1901	Botha attacks Itala and Prospect.	
1.10.1901		Natal concentration camps handed over to civil authorities.
6.10.1901	Botha escapes north.	
11.10.1901	Lotter executed.	
7.12.1901	National Scouts formed.	Fawcett Commission visits Merebank.
11.12.1901	Kritzinger's third invasion of the Cape.	
16.12.1901	Kritzinger captured.	
25.12.1901	De Wet's victory at Tweefontein.	
17.1.1902.	Gideon Scheepers executed.	
2.1902	Various drives in the eastern Free State.	Umbilo POW camp created.
17.2.1902		First inhabitants of Jacobs concentration camp arrive.
27.2.1902	Breaker Morant executed for shooting Boer POWs.	
25.3.1902		First inhabitants of Wentworth concentration camp arrive.
29.3–11.4.1902		Pinetown concentration camp inhabitants arrive.
7.3.1902	De la Rey's victory at Tweebos.	
9.4.1902	Boer conference at Klerksdorp to discuss peace.	
12–18.4.1902	Peace negotiations start in Pretoria.	
4.5.1902	Siege of O'kiep relieved.	
6.5.1902	Battle of Holkrantz.	
29–31.5.1902	Vereeniging peace conference.	
31.5.1902	Peace treaty signed.	
2.6.1902		Thanksgiving service for peace in town hall.
7.6.1902		Schalk Burger explains terms of peace to concentration and POW camps.
22.9.1902		Wentworth concentration camp closes.
10.8.1902		Pinetown concentration camp closes.
10.12.1902		Merebank concentration camp closes.
15.11.1902		Post of commandant abolished.
6.6.1902–3.1903	POWs and concentration camp inhabitants return home.	
1.1903		Jacobs concentration camp closes.
2.1903		Umbilo POW camp closed.

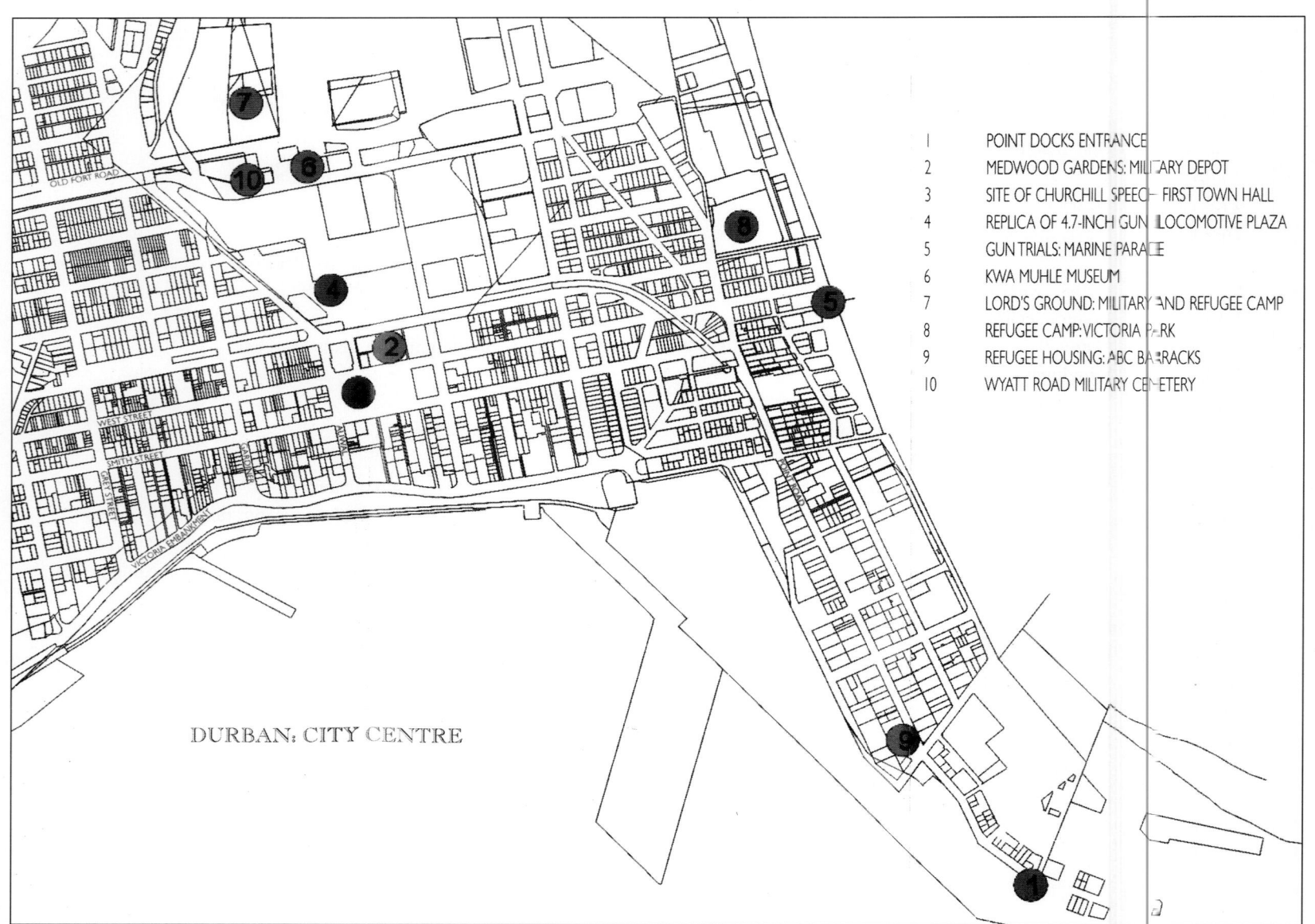

1   POINT DOCKS ENTRANCE
2   MEDWOOD GARDENS: MILITARY DEPOT
3   SITE OF CHURCHILL SPEECH: FIRST TOWN HALL
4   REPLICA OF 4.7-INCH GUN: LOCOMOTIVE PLAZA
5   GUN TRIALS: MARINE PARADE
6   KWA MUHLE MUSEUM
7   LORD'S GROUND: MILITARY AND REFUGEE CAMP
8   REFUGEE CAMP: VICTORIA PARK
9   REFUGEE HOUSING: ABC BARRACKS
10   WYATT ROAD MILITARY CEMETERY

DURBAN: CITY CENTRE

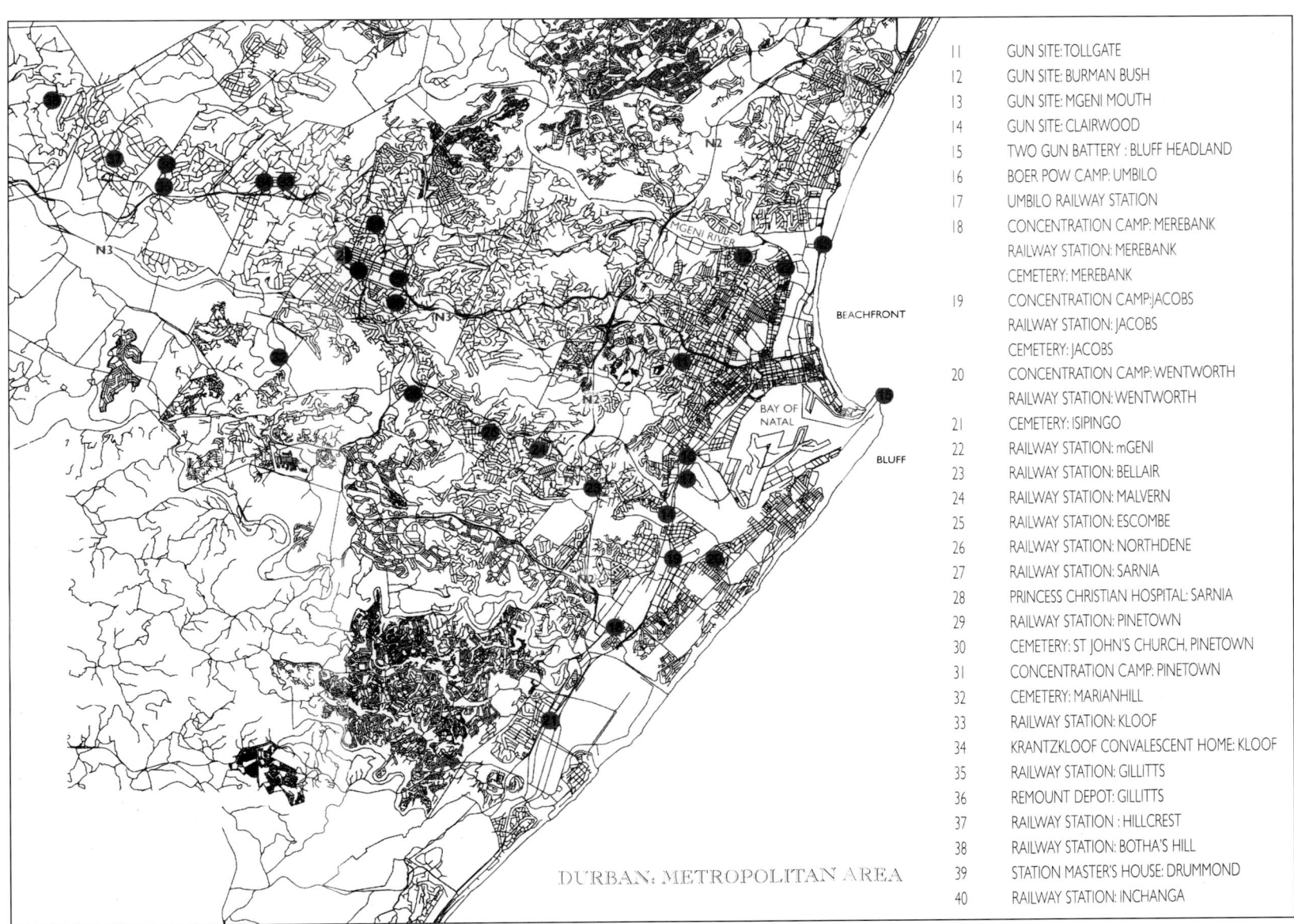

11	GUN SITE: TOLLGATE
12	GUN SITE: BURMAN BUSH
13	GUN SITE: MGENI MOUTH
14	GUN SITE: CLAIRWOOD
15	TWO GUN BATTERY : BLUFF HEADLAND
16	BOER POW CAMP: UMBILO
17	UMBILO RAILWAY STATION
18	CONCENTRATION CAMP: MEREBANK
	RAILWAY STATION: MEREBANK
	CEMETERY: MEREBANK
19	CONCENTRATION CAMP: JACOBS
	RAILWAY STATION: JACOBS
	CEMETERY: JACOBS
20	CONCENTRATION CAMP: WENTWORTH
	RAILWAY STATION: WENTWORTH
21	CEMETERY: ISIPINGO
22	RAILWAY STATION: mGENI
23	RAILWAY STATION: BELLAIR
24	RAILWAY STATION: MALVERN
25	RAILWAY STATION: ESCOMBE
26	RAILWAY STATION: NORTHDENE
27	RAILWAY STATION: SARNIA
28	PRINCESS CHRISTIAN HOSPITAL: SARNIA
29	RAILWAY STATION: PINETOWN
30	CEMETERY: ST JOHN'S CHURCH, PINETOWN
31	CONCENTRATION CAMP: PINETOWN
32	CEMETERY: MARIANHILL
33	RAILWAY STATION: KLOOF
34	KRANTZKLOOF CONVALESCENT HOME: KLOOF
35	RAILWAY STATION: GILLITTS
36	REMOUNT DEPOT: GILLITTS
37	RAILWAY STATION : HILLCREST
38	RAILWAY STATION: BOTHA'S HILL
39	STATION MASTER'S HOUSE: DRUMMOND
40	RAILWAY STATION: INCHANGA

DURBAN: METROPOLITAN AREA

xix

PART ONE

DURBAN:
A GATEWAY TO THE WAR

Berea Road, Durban, ca 1900 (KCL).

Panoramic view of Durban from the Berea, ca 1900 (KCL).

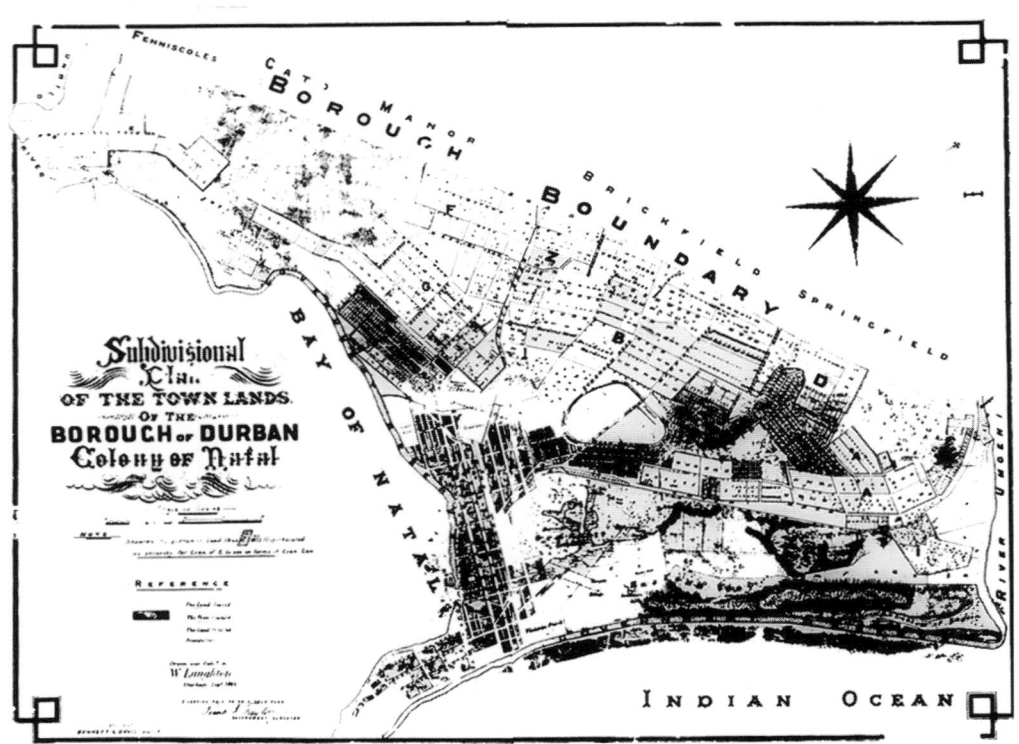

Map of the town lands of Durban by Laughton and Taylor, 1896 (LHM).

The Natal one penny stamp symbolising the rule of Queen Victoria.

CHAPTER 1

DURBAN: THE GATEWAY CONTEXT

Brian Kearney and Ian Swanepoel

A view of life in Durban (*The Graphic*, 30 September 1899).

The settlement

At the time of the war, between 12 October 1899 and 31 May 1902, Durban was an emerging colonial settlement which was beginning to shrug off its limited Victorian past, but which carried many of the structures of that past into the new century. These included strong racial attitudes which underpinned local discrimination and the segregation responsible for separating its constituent peoples. The population of the town was made up of various groups: the Europeans who were predominantly from Britain and Ireland and who constituted the ruling class; the Africans, mostly male, and many of whom were migrant workers, who had been drawn into an urbanising process over the previous 40 years. The Africans constituted the working classes with no political rights or representation. Indians had also come to the region as migrant workers, primarily for the developing sugar industry and, after the expiry of their employment contracts, became another sector of the urbanised working classes – also without proper rights or representation. As early as 1867, town councillors were calling for a separate 'Coolie Village' and this was laid out in 1874 on the Eastern Vlei behind the beachfront.[1] The smallest group were the so-called 'coloureds', who shared few of the social characteristics of either the Africans, Indians or Europeans. Though the patterns of spatial settlement were complex, each of these groups lived apart, many outside the actual borough boundaries as they were then.

The spatial complexity was also based on an unusual urban morphology – a structural system which was derived from the town's origin around the Bay of Natal as a place for hunters and frontiersmen who lived like tribal chiefs in distinct kraals. Thus the urban landscape was made up of discrete pockets of settlement which existed around the town. In the mid-nineteenth century small settlements were to be found at Congella (a Voortrekker village), the Point (with its rudimentary docks), and at the crossings of the Umbilo and Umgeni Rivers, where small villages appeared. These all existed in addition to the formal town centre. By 1899, this pattern had been extensively repeated and extended over a topography where the drainage of water provided both opportunities and problems – such as, for example, the Western and Eastern Vleis. These pockets of settlement were discrete and only in the first part of the twentieth century were they to become connected to make up an urban whole. This disjointed physical environment was, in many ways, admirably suited to a fractured society.[2]

'Woodlands', the Berea home of the Dacomb family (KCL).

Indian shacks along the Umgeni River (KCL).

Hindi temple, Somsteu Road, 1901, designed by J P Mumford (Kearney collection).

Mosque and Grey Street ca. 1895 (LHM).

Topographical altitude reflected social and political status and power. Europeans therefore occupied veranda houses on the higher ground such as the slopes of the Berea, Greyville and Glenwood. In the story of Breaker Morant and the Bushveldt Carbineers, *Scapegoats of Empire*, George Witton described these suburbs as: '. . . picturesque and pleasing, much of the country being covered with sugar plantations and orange groves. The Berea, a chain of hills at the back of the town, is the "Toorak" of Durban; splendid mansions and pretty villas peep from gardens of luxuriant tropical growth, and look out upon the town, the harbour, the Bluff and the open sea beyond.'[3]

Indians settled either in the vicinity of Grey Street, with its own commercial centre, or in scattered pockets on lower or steeper ground around the edges of the borough, such as Clairwood, South Coast Junction, Puntan's Hill or Umgeni Village. Many who worked for the Natal Government Railways (NGR) or the municipality were housed in large barracks. Africans who did not occupy servants' rooms on the properties of their employers or the various worker barracks and compounds around the town, found accommodation in the growing shacklands beyond the edges. Marginalised groups, such as St Helenites, Tsongas and Chinese, found temporary homes in Bamboo Square at the Point.[4] Freed Zanzibari slaves occupied land on the Bluff.

Here, therefore, was a British colonial town set around an African bay with distinct elements of British influence in its suburbs, railway system, docks, commercial enterprises, architecture, schools and social customs. And yet there was much that was African in terms of its climate and lush vegetation and its peripheral worker population including the *togt* workers and contract labourers, domestic servants and ricksha pullers. There also existed a strong sense of a place, set, as it was, on the Indian Ocean resonating with Asian images such as the temples and mosques and other cultural manifestations of both Hindus and Muslims. Even without an Anglo-Boer War there were sufficient local ingredients to produce a gateway of spice, drama and contrast.

Culture and society

Besides being a gateway to the hinterland, Durban was also the largest town in the Colony of Natal. In July 1899, its population was 41 259, made up of 19 762 Europeans (6 922 men and 5 370 women and 7 470 children); 9 562 Indians (6 024 men and 3 538 women) and 11 935 Africans, of whom only 601 were women. As it was a crown colony, the British government was still responsible for Natal's affairs, both internal and external, and its people were British subjects. Though it had had a responsible government since 1893, any act passed by the legislature required the approval of the British parliament, which was locally represented by the governor, Sir Walter Hely-Hutchinson. Anyone coming to Natal could not fail to notice the British trappings – the Union Jack flying over public buildings, a British currency, and the prevalence of British persons in the civil service and local government. In common with most expatriates, the loyalty and patriotism of the British increased in direct proportion to the distance they were away from their motherland. So, for most Europeans, Britain was still referred to as 'home' or the 'old country'.

The Indian population also retained strong linkages with their mother country. An example of such patriotism during the war was the establishment of 'The Central Indian Famine Relief Committee'. This committee had been set up with representation from the town council and the colonial government, and MK Gandhi served as the honorary secretary. Its objective was to collect donations for the relief of famine, plague and cholera in India.[5]

There were two principal newspapers at the time: the *Natal Mercury* was the morning paper, while the *Natal Advertiser* ran an afternoon edition. Being under separate ownership, they often reflected different views on daily life and popular issues, but both were modelled on their British counterparts and carried numerous news items and editorial comment from 'home' sources.

In addition to the public library, museum and art gallery, the town also provided opportunities for recreation, though primarily for Europeans, at the public and Turkish baths in West Street, and in the form of numerous sporting facilities which had been developed in the last decades of the nineteenth century. These included polo, rugby, cricket, bowls and golf. Some of these games were provided for by the municipality leasing a portion of the ordinance land, which came to be known as Lords Ground. African football commenced informally at about the time of the war, with the first teams originating at the Point, close to the large Bell Street *togt* barracks. Horseracing was also a popular pastime and regular race meetings were held at the Greyville Racecourse on the Western Vlei.

In 1899, before the outbreak of the Anglo-Boer War, Durban had witnessed a period of continued development and growth. New buildings for two girls schools had been opened: the new Durban Girls' Model School in Gale Street,[6] and the Maris Stella day and boarding school on the Berea which was opened by Bishop Jolivet on 23 May 1899.[7] Plans for the Durban Club were invited for a new building on a site on the Victoria Embankment at a cost of not more than £16 000. The large number of buildings under construction around the town kept the building inspectors' section of the borough engineer's department busy. Amongst the projects was a major new municipal market, situated adjacent to the central railway station, but a shortage of building materials, owing to the war, prevented the construction from proceeding smoothly. Vacant land was becoming scarce on the Berea, though a six-acre fruit farm with easy access to the Mitchell Park/Florida Road tram terminus was advertised for sale.

Besides the effects of the war on the local inhabitants of the town, the period of conflict gave rise to a whole new set of circumstances which would change various components of society forever. The arrival of large numbers of refugees and Uitlanders in the port would in itself initiate a pattern which has continued up to the present. The inhabitants of the hinterland of the country still descend on Durban, but now, seasonally, as holidaymakers on vacation. Ironically, close on 17 000 Boer men, women

Pine Street with the railway station to the right and the new municipal market building, both designed by Street Wilson (LHM).

Durban Girls' Model School, Gale Street, designed by FM Kent (LHM).

Public baths, West Street, designed by W Powell, 1893, (LHM).

Coaling at the Point docks, 1902 (LHM).

The Durban borough seal at the time of the war.

Ernest Leslie Acutt, mayor from 1901 to 1902 (Henderson).

and children actually did arrive in the town and port which their political and military leaders had aspired to take by force, but now they came as prisoners of war (POWs) or as inhabitants of concentration camps. For many of these people from the rural hinterland, their arrival in Durban would not only have been their first experience of the coast and the sea, but also their initiation into a form of urban life in the camps themselves. For the men and boys who lived in the Umbilo POW Camp the greatest irony would have been that they were only a stone's throw away from the site of one of the earliest Voortrekker settlements in Natal at Congella.

The growing number of African refugees who came into the town from the surrounding region fairly easily found work, but the temporary nature of the military employment offered would in itself cast the mould for their future lives, where an urban existence would be based largely on short-term work opportunities, and thus create conditions beyond any form of personal control.

Local government

Durban had achieved borough status in 1854 and, from that time the town was governed by a European town council. At the outbreak of the Anglo-Boer War, a number of prominent local businessmen held office as councillors. These included John Nicol, who had taken over from BW Greenacre as mayor in August 1897, and who was to continue to serve in that capacity until 31 July 1901, when he was succeeded by EL Acutt.[8] On his resignation, Greenacre had presented the borough with a mayoral chain. This was made of 18-carat London hallmarked gold and was composed of 29 shields with the arms of Natal at the centre. The shields on either side bore the imperial crown symbolic of a British possession. A pendant suspended from the centre carried the borough crest.[9]

Other councillors who served during the period of the war included WR Poynton, R Jameson, HR Collins, CC Clarke, C Henwood, JF Hitchins, E Pickering, D Taylor and W Middleton. The town was administered through several municipal departments such as those of the town clerk, town treasurer, market, borough engineer and surveyor, police force and fire brigade. Their day-to-day work was supervised by standing committees of the council.

The fire brigade was kept busy during 1899 attending to a large number of fires in the town. On 18 April, a disastrous fire swept through three stores in Pine Street and it took Captain Morgan from 23:00 until 3:00 to bring it under control. The spectacle was witnessed by a fairly large crowd, some of whom made themselves comfortable on the seating afforded by old stacks on the railway track. On 30 April 1899, there were two more fires: on the premises of Alcock, the saddler, and at Mrs Lawrie's Tea Room in central West Street. No sooner had these fires been doused than another broke out at the timber yard of Hunt, Leuchars & Hepburn, in Mazeppa Street at the east end of town. These fires brought the total in a ten-month period to 30.[10]

In December 1896, the mayor at the time, George Payne, put a resolution to the town council which initiated a memorial to mark the 1897 diamond jubilee of Queen Victoria. The Royal Academy in London was consulted about a suitable person to execute a sculpture and, on their recommendation, Hymo Thorneycroft was commissioned in February 1897. By July, Thorneycroft had submitted tracings of the design for the statue and its surrounds to the council for approval. After examining numerous alternative locations for the memorial, a site was eventually chosen in the town gardens opposite the town hall (now the main post office). On 1 March 1899, the five and a half ton statue arrived on the SS *Engeli*, shipped freight free by JT Rennie & Sons.

The governor, Hely-Hutchinson, performed the unveiling ceremony on 19 April 1899 before an estimated crowd of 15 000. The assembly included several thousand school children and the men of the local volunteer units: the Natal Mounted Rifles (NMR) and the Durban Light Infantry (DLI), together with sailors from HMS *Philomel*. The bands of the DLI and the NMR were also in attendance, as were the guns of the Natal Field Artillery (NFA). After the unveiling there were outbursts of enthusiastic cheering; the governor read out a message from the queen; the NFA fired a 21-gun salute, and then the procession of dignitaries and school children made its way up West Street to Albert Park for a grand children's fete. This was the first public statue to be erected in Durban, and was to become the rallying point for many patriotic meetings.[11]

So representative was the town council of British convictions that they were ready to alter their business in reaction to the critical events of the war. For example, shortly after the outbreak of war, on 26 October 1899, the mayor, John Nicol, announced to a full meeting of the council that he had just been informed of the death of Major General Penn-Symons at Dundee. He continued that: 'he was certain they would all feel the sense of loss which the Colony and the cause had sustained in the death of the gallant general, and he moved as a mark of regret that the council do now adjourn.'[12] In the latter part of 1900, the town council became imbued with a spirit of optimism about the course of the war and, in September, elected a special committee for the sole purpose of arranging a programme for the celebration of peace.[13] Unfortunately, this was somewhat premature, since it was to be just less than two years before such celebrations could be seriously considered. In November of the same year, after the local volunteer units had returned from action, the council voted to erect a memorial to those volunteers who had died in the war.[14] The commission was also carried out by the British sculptor, Hymo Thorneycroft, and sited in the town gardens opposite the town hall, close by the statue of Queen Victoria.

Technology

The war took place at the end of a century which had witnessed the impact of the industrial revolution on the world. Since the revolution had such far-reaching consequences in Britain, it was not surprising that its

HMS *Powerful* (Kearney collection).

Gathering wood at Merebank concentration camp (NCHM).

ripples were felt in the application of new technologies to human circumstances in Natal and in Durban. Many of these were of military importance and included the development of state-of-the-art naval cruisers such as HMS *Powerful*, with enormous capacities and a voracious appetite for coal, and which were to encourage interstate competition amongst major world powers for the naval control of the seas. New military technology also included the development of accurate naval guns and the innovations which Captain Scott introduced for their use on land, and the provision of armoured trains which were equipped in the local railway workshops. The Natal railway system itself was based extensively on British technology and administration; and so it could facilitate the adaptation of steam-driven trains for ambulances. Local building construction skills, also being modelled on British systems, could be used for the speedy conversion of ships to hospitals complete with electricity, ventilating fans and refrigeration.

The British also made use of other technological advances such as the prefabricated wood and iron building systems for hospitals, camps and remount depots. Thus, for example, a complete hospital was rapidly despatched from Britain to Pinetown Bridge early in the war. They also used X-ray apparatus and provided electricity to hospitals from adjacent railway generators. In addition, there were advances in medical and surgical treatments; the utilisation of factory-produced tinned foods and extracts as rations for far-flung troops; and the extensive employment of the telephone and the telegraph with encrypted codes, though used together with pigeon post and messengers on bicycles. Large searchlights for communicating signals over long distances and lighting night works were locally developed but ironically hauled on ox wagons. However, the degree of acceptance of such new technologies probably reached its limit when an army steeped in equestrian traditions was confronted with steam traction engines as an alternative transport medium.

The application of many of these technological advances to transport, communication, energy and food has to be viewed against the social and cultural background of the semi-agrarian character of the Natal colonists on the one hand, and an almost eighteenth century Afrikaner culture on the other. Here were several different worlds in confrontation. Consider, for example, the simultaneous existence in Durban of HMS *Powerful*, the jin-rickshas, ox wagons in the streets, and Boer women in quasi-medieval serge dress.

The mechanical production of cold storage was well advanced by the time war broke out. Thus a large meat refrigeration facility, the Transvaalsche Koelkamers Beperk, was available for use by the colonial government to provide a method for controlling and refining the trade in meat with a technology which superceded the traditional ice trade.

The period of the war also witnessed a series of changes in transportation which were profoundly to affect life and urbanisation during the following century. Rickshas had become a common means of personal transport and bicycles were very much in vogue. By July 1899, the *Natal Mercury* noted a considerable increase in traffic in West Street, with 164 vehicles passing Mark Lane in 15 minutes. Bicycle riders 'were scorching' down the street at speeds estimated at 16 to 20 kilometres per hour, and accidents did take place. In Point Road, a woman cyclist collided with a vehicle and was thrown into the middle of a naval parade.[15]

The railway system, which had been in use in the town from the 1860s, provided some local benefits to the inhabitants with a line running from the Point to the centre and from there outwards towards the Umbilo and Umgeni Rivers. By the end of the nineteenth century the system would encourage the growth of a suburban layout, even as far as the 'old main line' settlements of Seaview, Bellair and Hillary. From 1879, however, horse-drawn trams encouraged the growth of the inner suburbs of the town such as Greyville and the Berea. These lines also spread out in several directions from the town centre, much like the rail system. After the municipality took over the Durban Tramways Company in the 1890s, the tram routes were electrified with an overhead trolley system. In turn this required a major increase in electricity generation and the Alice Street power station was built in 1902 to replace the earlier one at Bamboo Square. In 1897, the first motor car had appeared in Durban and, by 1900, when Police Superintendent Alexander requested the town council to commence the licensing of bicycles, he suggested that they might just as well include motor vehicles.[16]

A comprehensive new water supply system for the town had been built in 1887 along the Umbilo River some 14 kilometres away and, from 1894, work had begun on the new Umlaas waterworks to supplement the supply of water to reservoirs along the Berea. From 1893, the borough engineer commenced work on a water-borne sewerage disposal system with a treatment plant sited at Bamboo Square from where the effluent was pumped out to sea.[17]

The ongoing construction of harbour piers made use of advances in marine engineering technology. Quay walls and piers were constructed of pre-cast concrete blocks manufactured on large production sites; teams of divers worked underwater, positioning and grouting the blocks in place. By 1900, a flotilla of 15 state-of-the-art dredgers sucked up sludge and sand within the Bay of Natal and at the entrance channel to allow the passage of ships into the harbour. Electric cranes took over from the problematic hydraulic ones at the dockside. Though there were still numbers of sailing vessels calling for the timber trade, shipping had become predominantly steam powered, which necessitated the processing of coal at the wharfside.

Economics, commerce and industry

In numerous ways life went on normally during the war, or at least many attempted to conduct their affairs in the usual manner. But the commercial interconnections between the various parties who were involved in the conflict were complex and the transit port role which characterised Durban's commercial world was distinctly affected. The closures of business possibilities, gateways of opportunity, were denied through martial law. But the seizure of goods and declarations of contraband created fresh opportunities; new business connections were formed

Rickshas at the corner of Pine and Gardiner Streets (LHM).

Horse-drawn trams in West Street between Field and Grey Streets, ca 1895 (LHM).

Electric trams in Gardiner Street. Note the town hall to the right and the enlarged railway station in the background (LHM).

Alice Street power station (LHM).

A small bucket dredger in the entrance channel to the bay (KCL).

The construction of quay walls and reclamation work at the Point docks (LHM).

Loading wool at the Point docks (LHM).

and new gateways opened.

While most of the local Durban merchants of British origin had probably been tied patriotically to the imperial apron strings at the commencement of the war, the closure of trading possibilities during its course led them to an understanding of a business world which was wider and more embracing than the British empire. It probably also made them question the value of patriotism. The change would have been precipitated by the immense concentration of foreign shipping which used the port during the war with the sole purpose of feeding the British military machine.

The main focus of trade in Durban was retail business, but there were a limited number of secondary industries, which were mainly concerned with the port. The war raised an old colonial controversy. Should local goods and products for the war effort be bypassed in favour of imported ones? Was the local economy really so inadequate in providing for this military machine ?

Certainly many made money as a direct result of the war and its new requirements in terms of goods and services. Undoubtedly many lost business. One particular issue, however, which probably had a disastrous impact on certain local merchant houses, was the way the British and military authorities, in the later stages of the war, favoured the Cape merchants in respect of the wool trade. But this was more probably through fear of the consequences of a Cape rebellion, rather than a deliberate attempt to deny economic opportunity to Natal merchants.

This then was Durban, a loyal gateway for the Anglo-Boer War.

1. *Natal Mercury*, 14.8.1867; DAR, 3 DBN, 5/2/7/1/1: town council sanitary committee, 11.11.1874.

2. Kearney, BT, *A Revised listing of Important Places and Buildings in Durban*, pp.21–22.

3. Witton, G, *Scapegoats of Empire*, p.31.

4. DAR, 3DBN 5/2/7/1/2: 7.6.1876; 5/2/5/5/1. 26.5.1875.

5. PAR, 1/Melmoth 3/2/8: notice by MK Gandhi, 11.8.1900.

6. *Natal Mercury*, 3.5.1899.

7. *Natal Mercury*, 23.5.1899.

8. Henderson, WPM, *Durban, Fifty Years' Municipal History*, p.175.

9. Ibid., p.181.

10. *Natal Mercury*, 1.5.1899.

11. Henderson, p.181.

12. DAR, TC 5/2/6/1/14: town council minutes, 26.10.1899.

13. DAR, TC 5/2/6/1/15: town council minutes, 9.1900.

14. DAR, TC 5/2/6/1/15: town council minutes, 26.11.1900.

15. *Natal Mercury*, 9.11.1899.

16. DAR, 3DBN 5/2/5/3/6: police report, 5.11 1899.

17. Henderson, pp.226–290.

Umgeni iron works, Briardene (NSL).

Lamport's steam-driven sugar mill at Merebank, ca 1870 (LHM).

Sir Walter Hely-Hutchinson, governor of Natal from 1893 to 1901
(War Pictures).

Government House, Longmarket Street, Pietermaritzburg
(*Natal Mercury Pictorial*, 1912).

CHAPTER 2

THE POLITICAL SCENE IN WARTIME DURBAN
Josh McCracken

On 28 December 1899, a fortnight after the battle of Colenso, the editorial in the *Natal Mercury* began with the ominous words 'a great blow has stricken the colony'. This was not news of another military reverse, however, it was a political disaster that had stricken the colony. Harry Escombe had died. He was, by consensus, Natal's ablest politician and Durban's 'most eminent and gifted citizen'.[1] Natal could ill afford to lose such a man. There was no great reserve, either of experience or talent, to draw from in the political sphere.

The colony and its institutions had come into being during the lifetime of many people still alive. Natal had been annexed as an adjunct of the Cape colony only 56 years before, and it had been a separate colony for 43 years, but had not achieved self-governing status until 1893, six years before the outbreak of the Anglo-Boer War. The disparity in numbers between the small European settler population and the vast African and Indian majority had not only retarded constitutional development, but had clouded relations with the imperial government and had dominated colonial politics. Since not all Europeans had the inclination, the talent or the means to participate in politics, membership of parliament was confined to a prosperous elite. Thirty-nine members of parliament were elected to the legislative assembly and 12 were nominated to the legislative council. The six members of the cabinet were responsible to the Natal parliament but the governor, representing the crown, was appointed from Britain.

The first governor under the new constitution, Sir Walter Hely-Hutchinson, remained in office until 1901. As the crisis unfolded, he identified himself more closely with the imperial authorities than with his own colonial ministers. The first three prime ministers of Natal had come from coastal constituencies, two of them from Durban, but the wartime government was headed by Colonel, later Sir, Albert Hime, a retired colonial engineer, and was dominated by Pietermaritzburg and up-country farming constituencies. Durban's parliamentary representatives consisted of four members elected to represent Durban, and three to represent Durban County in the legislative assembly, plus two members nominated by the governor in council to represent the Durban area in the legislative council. The two Durban nominated councillors, who enjoyed the title Honorable, Hon Archibald Mitchell Campbell and Hon Robert Jameson, sat for the whole duration of the war, but no member of the lower house did. In all, 16 men occupied the seven seats in the constituencies of Durban and Durban County during the course of the war. Escombe was one of them.

Two politicians of stature

A Londoner who came to Natal in 1859, Escombe was a lawyer by profession, he was town solicitor and standing councillor for Durban for 30 years, a member of the Natal legislature on and off from the early 1870s, a member of Natal's first cabinet, a privy councillor and the second prime minister of Natal. He served as a volunteer in the Anglo-Zulu War and was a founder of the Natal Naval Volunteers, and their first commander. He was much admired for his impressive presence, his forensic skills, his oratorical ability and his enthusiastic advocacy of causes. His dislike of formality commended him to many. He refused a knighthood, preferred being called Harry rather than the more formal Henry, and he had no use for pomp and ceremony. When, as a representative of the colony at Queen Victoria's jubilee in 1897, he had to don court dress, he held up the short-legged pants and scornfully remarked 'Fancy a big fellow like me getting into these things.'[2] But his impatience with opposition, or even criticism, exposed him to charges of arrogance and stubbornness, and his tendency to change his mind on major issues to allegations of inconsistency, self-seeking and dishonesty. His impatience and hot temper aggravated such hostile reactions. He once slapped a fellow member across the face for calling him a liar. Escombe's political mission was to provide Durban with a deep-water harbour by conquering the sandbar which blocked the entrance to the bay. Here, as on other issues, controversy arose because Escombe had strong views on what should be done, regardless of what professional engineers advised.

Only one other Natal politician ever enjoyed a reputation comparable to that of Escombe and he was also a member for Durban in a wartime legislative assembly. Sir John Robinson was an even more long-standing member than Escombe, going back to 1863, when he was elected for Durban at the unusually young age of 24. He had come as a child from Yorkshire with the first influx of settlers in 1850. The son of the founder of the *Natal Mercury*, he succeeded his father as owner-editor. He was a member of the Natal parliament for 33 years. After years of campaigning for responsible government, he became the first prime minister of Natal in 1894. He was a much less colourful, but more pragmatic politician than Escombe. He eschewed confrontational politics, was invariably courteous, some even said unctious, and was more successful than Escombe in avoiding the animosity of other politicians. He was, as one of his admirers admitted, 'extremely frothy',[3] but this facility with words had a positive side in his literary output: in addition to writing most of his paper's editorials himself, he contributed articles to English magazines and published a guide book to Natal, a collection of verse, a novel, a study of British colonies and an autobiography. Escombe and Robinson were the only elected members of the Natal parliament whom contemporaries saw fit to honour with statues, both in Durban.

Harry Escombe (NSL).

Sir John Robinson and family at home at 'Withersea', North Ridge Road (KCL).

Statues of Robinson and Escombe flanking the Volunteer War Memorial, town gardens (LHM).

Birds of a feather: the political oligarchy

These two Durban politicians were atypical of the general run of Natal parliamentarians in their ability and dedication; otherwise they had much in common with their fellow members. Only three of the 18 Durban members had been born in Natal; the rest came from Britain, at various times, in search of health or prospects and, although without inherited wealth, they had not been driven to emigrate by dire poverty. Nearly all of them were in their forties or fifties before they entered politics because, although there was an allowance of £1 a day and travelling expenses for members who did not live in or near Pietermaritzburg, only a well-established man could afford to be away from his business or farm for six or eight weeks every year. For the great majority of these men the war years were only part of their parliamentary service. Some, like Robinson, had been members for many years before. Others, like Frank Oliver Fleetwood Churchill, remained members until Natal was merged in the Union, and then reappeared in the Union parliament. Over half of them served from four to nine years, but another third served for ten years or more. Five of the 18 Durban members were in volunteer units during the war and another eight had seen military service at one time or another. But what characterised them most markedly was the uniformity of their social and economic status. They were all self-made men, products of that much-prized Victorian virtue, self-help. Most of them were engaged in commerce, wealthy men, most of them, with numerous business interests.

The two legislative councillors were role models of the type. Hon AM Campbell was managing director of Parker Wood & Co, general merchants, importers and shipping agents, with branches all over South Africa, and Hon Robert Jameson was a jam manufacturer. Of the members of the legislative assembly, Sir BW Greenacre, who started as a shop assistant, was the founder of Durban's leading department store, Harvey Greenacre & Co and served on the board of many companies; William Palmer controlled William Palmer & Son, accountants, agents and trustees, and was the founder of the Natal Building Society; Maurice S Evans was in charge of a department in Randles Bros & Hudson; JW Payn was a corn merchant, and Harry Sparks was a farmer, butcher and founder of the first cold storage business in Durban; John Fyfe King, originally a gunsmith with a packing case as his first counter, founded a firm supplying all sorts of sporting equipment; CG Smith was a sugar estate agent, an auctioneer and subsequently a leading figure in the sugar industry, with interests in gold, coal and other commercial activities. Dan Taylor was the leading haulage contractor in Durban. George Payne founded Payne Bros which grew to rival Greenacres. JG Maydon was a leading figure in the shipping world, and Charles Henwood had been a subcontractor to the NGR and a transport rider.

Greenacres department store, West Street (LHM).

Conflict of interests

The war with the Boer republics was not the making of men like these. As the crisis intensified there was strong pressure for conciliation. Henry Binns, who succeeded Escombe as prime minister, told his fellow sugar planter, Marshall Campbell, that the dream of his political life was a union with the Orange Free State.[4] He let it be known to Kruger that he was an admirer of his and when Kruger was re-elected president in 1897 he sent him a telegram of congratulations.[5] Escombe supported the demand of two of Hime's cabinet, Frederick Moor and Charles Smythe, that the imperial government should consider the views of South African ministers before resorting to war. Milner and Hely-Hutchinson were angered by this intrusion into imperial affairs by these 'wobblers and mugwumps', as they called them, and they agreed on the need to combat this spirit of compromise by, as Milner put it, separating the sheep from the goats. To that end they encouraged the South African League, whose aim was the maintenance of British supremacy in South Africa.[6]

Adjusting to war

The Boer invasion of the colony routed the mugwumps. Apart from some farmers of Boer extraction in the northern counties, there were no pro-Boers in Natal during the war. Men who had striven to avoid war accepted the inevitable. Escombe, for example, on the eve of the war, set off with his wife for Newcastle on a confidence-building expedition and was among the last to leave in the face of the advancing Boers. He then went to Dundee and Estcourt at Hime's request and, having been re-gazetted to his volunteer unit, was present with them at Colenso.[7] The war was the one absorbing subject, according to Frank Churchill, the son of a former Durban parliamentary member and a successful candidate himself in the 1901 general elections. Normal political activity was disrupted. With martial law proclaimed, the role of the colonial ministers was reduced to more or less an advisory one and the military authorities showed little inclination to accept their advice. Durban members were even more powerless, for none of them were Hime supporters.[8] The war did not, however, bring about any fundamental change in colonial politics: the personnel of politics remained the same, political activity, such as there was, followed the traditional pattern and the few indications of change that may be discerned during the course of the war cannot be attributed to the conflict itself. Indeed, some long-standing attitudes and convictions were reinforced by exposure to wartime experiences: the homage paid to military personalities boosted the authoritarian spirit so strongly entrenched in colonial society, jingoistic fervour invigorated the old loyalty to Britain and, on the other hand, impatience with military incompetence confirmed the belief that they were better qualified than the imperial authorities to manage the affairs of Natal.

Impact of war

Two by-elections had to be held in Durban during the opening months of the war. At the first, the veteran, Sir Benjamin Greenacre, was elected by an overwhelming majority after a muted campaign in which he addressed only three meetings. The result of the election was overshadowed by the news of the battle of Colenso which appeared in the same issue of the *Natal Mercury*.[9] The return of Sir John Robinson on 7 February 1900 to replace Escombe was very much a stopgap arrangement. He had already retired from the premiership for health reasons, he took no part in debates during the session and at its end he was granted leave of absence.[10]

The parliamentary session of 1900 reflected the impact of the war in several ways. It was unusually short, transacting only essential business. The assembly met in the supreme court building because the parliament building has been taken over as a military hospital. Eight members of the assembly, including JS Wylie and H Sparks of Durban, were absent on war service for all or most of the session, and the opening ceremony was stripped of its glitter. The *Natal Mercury* described it as sordid and shabby, a secondhand sort of affair, and the amount of public interest in it was not worth mentioning. A guard of honour with a fragment of a band arrived at 11:30, and a crowd of small boys and a few others gathered. The bishops of Natal and Pretoria and a group of staff officers were the only distinguished visitors. At noon the governor arrived in his brilliant court uniform, wearing the brightly coloured sash of the Order of St Michael and St George, and that was the only spot of colour in the whole ceremony.[11]

The wartime general election

Parliament did not meet again for a year when the session of 1901 lasted from 17 May to 7 August. The main political event of the year was the general election held in September 1901, in accordance with the terms of the constitution. With eight candidates contesting the four Durban seats and four the three Durban County seats, there was a good deal more vigour in this election campaign than there had been in the recent by-elections. Two of Durban's existing members, Evans and Wylie, declined requisitions to stand again. Robinson had already retired and so now did Greenacre, so the last of the old guard had gone, and the outcome was that only one of the sitting members, JG Maydon, was re-elected. More than double the number of votes were cast in this Durban election than had been in the previous one of 1897, a fact which reflects the impact of the war on Durban's population.

In Durban County, all the sitting members were replaced by new men. With the end of the war in sight, local political issues were being debated, such as the growing competition from Indians in the labour market and whether the railway line from Durban to the interior should be doubled or whether an alternative route should be chosen for a new single line. There was still apathy, at least at the beginning of the campaign. When William McLarty was selected as a candidate at a meeting in the Princess Café, only about 40 people were present, and his first campaign meeting in Greyville hall on 18 September 1901 was sparsely attended. Ancketill's meeting in the masonic hall at Addington attracted only a few, though that was attributed to a heavy downpour of rain and, when all the candidates for Durban County except Henwood, who was at the front, addressed a meeting at Malvern, the hall was only 'semi filled'. On the other hand, McLarty was able to muster a crowd of 400 to 500 at the bandstand in the town gardens. As had been the case during the by-elections, very little was said about the war at any of the election meetings.

The customary electioneering stratagems were unaffected by the war. The number of candidates, each with his own colours, ensured that the town had a festive air on election day. Ancketill had a large banner stretched across West Street bearing the words 'Vote for Ancketill' and his posters in red, white and blue were prominent throughout the town. Taylor had four drays, each depicting one of his activities: 'Dan as a yachtsman', 'Dan as a volunteer', 'Dan as a cricketer', 'Dan as a boating champion' and 'Vote for Taylor' was stenciled on the pavement. McLarty had cartoons displayed in shop windows, one depicting the race for the election stakes, showing McLarty, having cleared the liquor hurdle, coming in first with Ancketill just behind him. In another, Natalia is telling McLarty she will not vote for candidates like the last ones (a bunch of whom are shamefacedly standing around) who had promised much and what had they done? She is shown pointing to a crowd of Indians.

The usual spate of doggerel appeared in the press. One effort entitled 'Only a dream' began:

I dreamt I stood in a Durban Hall
Where a battle fierce was raging
For there the Durban candidates
In conflict were engaging.

There Henry fought with a Maydon tall
And Ellis fought with a Taylor
And Labistour's face was white with Payne
And as he fought grew paler.[12]

Brightly coloured rosettes were much in evidence and ladies doing the rounds of the shops 'added to their other attractions the ribbons of their favourite candidates'.[13] In Durban County, CG Smith had a 'festive' African at the Toll Bar, carrying a sandwich board proclaiming on one side 'Vote for CG Smith' and on the other, 'He is the man to make the native work'. All the candidates except McLarty had carriages to convey supporters to the polling places.[14]

New faces and new ideas

While there was much that was familiar in the personnel and practices of wartime Durban politics, there was discernible also the hint of impending changes. Among the new generation of politicians and aspiring politicians were a few who did not conform to pattern. William McLarty, who stood unsuccessfully for Durban in 1901 and was returned unopposed in 1903, was a prosperous businessman, but he had spent some years in New Zealand, New South Wales and Queensland, where he had been impressed by some of the social welfare and industrial legislation he encountered there. He described himself as a tradesman who had worked on the Clyde. He was the official candidate of the Durban trades council, but he never joined the Natal Labour Party when it came into being or, for that matter, any of the bodies that preceded it. Nonetheless, his championship of the white working man and his anti-Indian stance was to win him support from organised labour.

A strange phenomenon on the Durban political scene was Dr CH Haggar who also came to Natal via Australia. He was a colourful figure, squat, bald headed and with an enormous black beard. He could 'talk the leg off an iron pot', and he had a somewhat mysterious background. He had been a teacher – 'professor' – of languages and of chemistry in Queensland and a preacher, and he claimed to have taken some medical courses. He was referred to as 'doctor', but of what and from where is not clear. He had stood for parliament unsuccessfully in Queensland and he was unsuccessful again in the by-election in Durban in 1899. As a correspondent in the *Natal Mercury* put it, his 'candidature came upon the electors like a bombshell'. He lost his £25 deposit, much to the satisfaction of the *Natal Mercury*, which expressed the hope that this would probably deter the doughty champion of 'people's rights' from once again throwing down the gauntlet, and it rejoiced that Durban had been saved 'from having the masses separated from the classes – as in Australia'. But in 1906, Haggar was to win a seat in the Natal parliament as a Labour representative and, in 1909, he became the first general secretary of the South African Labour Party and editor of its official newspaper, *The Worker*.[15]

The third newcomer with a new approach, Henry Ancketill, was as different from the other two as he was from the majority of his fellow members. He was of Irish landed gentry stock, the Anketells of Ancketells Grove, County Monaghan, but he broke with the family, and changed the spelling of his name, when they rejected his suggestion that they should hand over the land to the 400 tenants on the estate. He had spent a spell in the navy as a boy and then read for holy orders, but he declined ordination because of the church's indifference to social problems. In America he became an enthusiastic admirer of Henry George's writings on economic and political subjects, especially of his ideas on land taxation.

Ancketill came to Natal in 1896 and founded the Natal Progressive League and its monthly journal called *The Torch*, which he edited and wrote to propagate his views, many of which were, as he put it, 'advanced things'. He was a vegetarian, a non-smoker, a teetotaler and a believer in natural healing. He was also, in addition to his political writings, a poet and a songwriter. He held that all gambling of whatever kind was wrong. While not in favour of enfranchising Africans, he supported their right to proper representation in parliament and the same justice and access to land as Europeans. He opposed Indian immigration in the interest of European workers, but championed the cause of local Indians. He could be relied on to come to the aid of way-out causes, like favouring the recognition of Yiddish as a European language, or presenting a petition on behalf of the Christadelphians of Durban, who were opposed to military service. And it was he who, in 1904, introduced a bill to grant the vote to women, the first proposal of its kind in any South African parliament.

Ancketill was surprisingly popular, both with working men and with his fellow members. He got a warmer reception from the crowd than any of the other successful candidates when the election results were announced, and most of the men who later became prominent in the Natal Labour Party were members of his league. The fact that he was twice offered the speakership of the legislative assembly shows that he was equally well thought of by his peers. But Ancketill was not a wealthy man; that was his greatest oddity in the Natal parliament of his day. In 1905 he retired from parliament, saying it was no place for a poor man. If working men were to send one of them to represent them, as he hoped they would, they would have to find him the wherewithal to make it possible.[16]

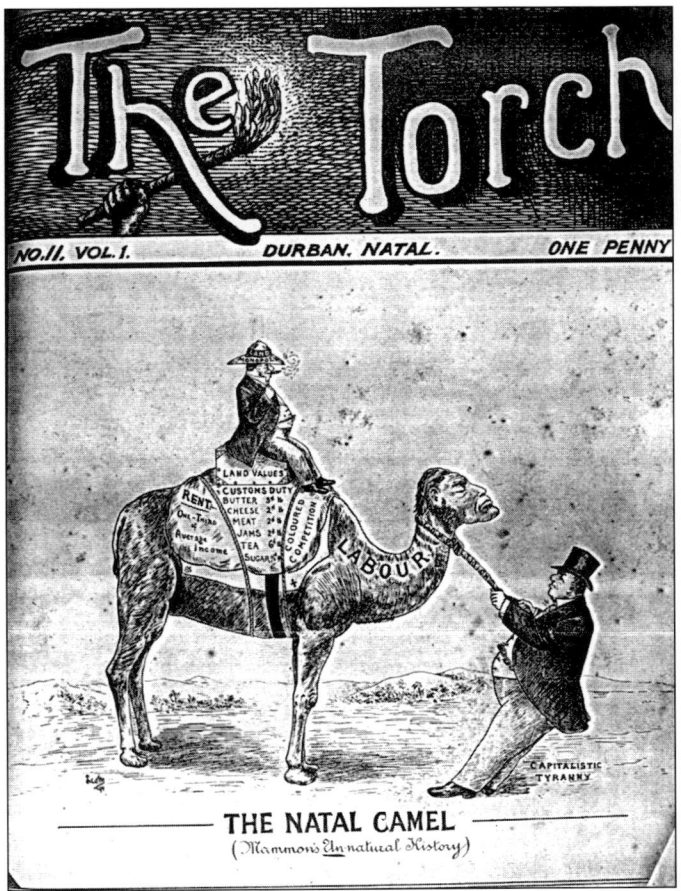

Indian aspirations and frustrations

Ancketill's bill foreshadowed a change in the status of women, but for the other excluded sections of the population there was little to suggest political developments. European anti-Indian feeling had been growing since the 1880s, and the Natal parliament lost no time in using its newly acquired powers under responsible government to impose fiscal and commercial constraints designed to force as many as possible to return to India, and to obstruct Indian merchants in competing with European business interests. Tighter immigration requirements were designed to check the flow of 'passengers' or 'Arabs', non-indentured merchants and traders who came at their own expense, and an act of 1896 denied Indians the right to be registered as parliamentary electors in the future.

The enmity towards Indians led to the formation of extra parliamentary bodies. On the one side, the Working Men's Association was founded in 1887 to protect the interests of white artisans and, on the other, the Indian merchant class formed the Durban Indian Committee and then in 1894 the better organised Natal Indian Congress, with Abdulla Hadji Adam, a leading merchant, as president and MK Gandhi as honorary secretary. Neither the Natal Indian Congress's petitions and appeals to Britain, India and the Natal government, nor Gandhi's organisation of an Indian ambulance corps during the war won the Indians any goodwill among Durban politicians. In the by-election of 1899, CH Haggar was vehement in his attacks and in the general election of 1901 other candidates still played the anti-Indian card.[17]

Abdulla Hadji Adam, the first president of the NIC (Bhana).

The unveiling of the queen's statue in the town gardens, 19 April 1899 (LHM).

The African role

Since they were not regarded as being so immediate a threat, Africans were less the focus of hostile attention by white politicians, but were even more rigidly excluded from political life than Indians. Although in theory Africans could qualify for the vote, the process was so complicated that virtually none did: the first voter to qualify was Jabez Molife from Edendale in 1893 and by 1903 there were two.[18] In Natal African political frustration manifested itself in two ways – among the Kholwa, the Christian, mission-educated Africans, and in the Ethiopian movement. Frustration at white obstruction of Kholwa aspirations had resulted in the formation of the Funamalungelo (those who had rights) society in 1888 by John Kumalo from Estcourt, and in the broader-based Natal Native Congress in 1900. The first resolution passed by this body declared that the time had come when the 'native people of the colony' should be directly represented. The *Natal Witness* considered the founding of the congress inopportune because of the war, but found nothing extravagant in its demands.[19]

Some Natal politicians like GH Hulett, who actually addressed the inaugural meeting of the Natal Native Congress, believed that Africans were inadequately represented in parliament, but it was generally accepted that direct representation was a distant prospect. FR Moor, minister for native affairs in several ministries, believed that whites were the dominant race and must remain so. Consequently, the fewer opportunities African leaders had of meeting together the better; so he opposed the governor's proposal to call a meeting of chiefs to celebrate the visit of the Duke and Duchess of Cornwall and York to Natal in 1901.[20]

The popular contribution

The war may not have dramatically changed the political scene in Durban, but it did enliven it. A spectator interest in politics had always been a feature of white society in the two urban centres, but Pietermaritzburg enjoyed all the advantages. 'Going to the house', attending meetings of the legislative council, had long been a fashionable evening activity in the capital. Formal parliamentary occasions provided colourful spectacles; to watch the social activities of members interested a wider circle than those involved. By contrast, all Durban had was the excitement of parliamentary elections, the occasional visit of the governor and political meetings. Now, as a gateway to the war, Durban citizens had abundant opportunities to indulge their curiosity and demonstrate their enthusiasm for the war. Thanks to the efforts of the South African League, supported by High Commissioner Lord Alfred Milner and Hely-Hutchinson, the ground had been well prepared before the war began. In July 1899, a crowd estimated at from three to four thousand, gathered around the queen's statue in Durban one Saturday in support of the Uitlanders.[21] When the troopships began to arrive, 'The people of Durban greeting Tommy' became a theme for the photographers' art. A crowd

West Street decorated for the relief of Ladysmith (*The Illustrated London News*, 7 April 1900).

turned out to see General Penn-Symons landing at the Point; General Buller had a hero's welcome on his way to Britain after his replacement; there was a crowd on the balcony of the Central Hotel and outside in West Street when Colonel Baden Powell passed through Durban in December 1900, and West Street was densely packed with people, with some on the roofs, to greet Lord Roberts on his way home in November 1900.[22]

Celebrating the relief of Ladysmith and other British victories occasioned other mass demonstrations. Lord Salisbury's statement in March 1900 that the future independence of the Boer republics was unacceptable was enthusiastically endorsed at a mass meeting presided over by the mayor, and at public meetings at Bellair, Sydenham and Pinetown, with members of the legislative assembly and ex-members of the legislative assembly participating.[23] A group of leading citizens called the Durban Vigilance Committee was set up to monitor the eventual settlement.[24] The members of the local debating society, the 'Durban Parliament', added their voices to the popular clamour. At the first meeting of the 1900 session, motions of loyalty to the queen and of support for the imperial government's decision were vigorously supported.[25] Durban emphatically rebutted the attacks on Milner and the charges of genocide made at the pro-Boer People's Congress at Worcester in the Cape, as well as the denunciation of the British army by Boer sympathisers at home and abroad towards the end of the war.[26]

On three occasions in the course of the war Durban's patriotic fervour was brought to fever pitch by the visit of a high-profile public figure from Britain. Winston Churchill's arrival on 23 December 1899, so soon after the disasters of Black Week, was a great fillip to morale. His exploits in escaping from the Boers had earned him worldwide publicity, and his rapid return to the scene of the fighting won him hero status in Natal. When the coaster on which he had travelled from what was then Lourenço Marques arrived in Durban harbour, congestion compelled it to treble berth. But, undeterred, an admiral, a general and the mayor of Durban scrambled over the two intervening ships to greet Churchill, followed by a crowd who bore him shoulder high ashore where he 'favoured them with a speech'. His admirers then proceeded to haul him in a ricksha to the town hall where they sang 'Rule Britannia', and listened to another short speech which they cheered to the echo. Then, after briefing reporters on his escape, he was hauled off to the station by the crowd in a frenzy of patriotic enthusiasm.[27]

The second occasion was a royal visit when the Duke and Duchess of Cornwall and York, the future King George V and Queen Mary, included South Africa in a tour of the empire that lasted nearly eight months. Initially, both the king and the duke were opposed to a South African visit fearing a threat of danger from the war and from the outbreak of plague at Cape Town. Chamberlain had to point out that 'no member of the royal family ought to be supposed to be afraid'.[28] The visit to Durban was a brief one, 53 hours in Natal, four of them in Durban.

The town was lavishly decorated for the occasion, but torrential rain the night before the royal arrival, on 13 August 1901, destroyed many of the decorations. A crowd, estimated by the *Natal Mercury* at 50 000, lined the route of the royal procession. The main ceremony, which lasted

Celebrations at the Point docks for the relief of Ladysmith (KCL).

Churchill's arrival in Durban, 23 December 1899 (War Pictures).

The arrival of Chamberlain by tug at the Point, 26 December 1902 (*The Illustrated London News*, 24 January 1903).

only about a quarter of an hour, was held in Albert Park, in a pavilion containing two models of the coronation chair and a stand to accommodate 2 000 of the town's elite. Addresses were presented by members of the town council and other bodies and the duke replied briefly. After a lunch at the Royal Hotel, presided over by the mayor, an elaborate table gong was presented to the duchess by the women of Durban before the pair proceeded to the station to board the train for Pietermaritzburg. The celebrations continued for the rest of the day, however, and the *Natal Mercury* believed that the visit would 'ever be remembered as an historic landmark'.[29]

The third visit was by far the most important and significant occasion. Joseph Chamberlain, the colonial secretary, and his wife, arrived in state on board the cruiser, *Good Hope,* on 26 December 1902, and they were received by the governor and the prime minister of Natal. They were driven through crowded streets to the town hall to receive an address of welcome. At the lunch which followed, the veteran politician, Sir John Robinson, struck a wrong note by comparing the sentiment he had detected when he interviewed the then colonial secretary, Lord Kimberley, after Majuba, with what he imagined was the attitude of the colonial office of the day. Chamberlain, however, had come, not to promise retribution, but to preach reconciliation and the fusion of the two white races.

The theme of the second speech emphasised the obligations, as well as the privileges of empire. In addition to these formal occasions, Chamberlain had a series of private meetings with a variety of people anxious to forward some cause: the Durban chamber of commerce, the coastal planters, groups seeking war damage compensation or shipping subsidies, champions of African or Indian rights, even members of the Birmingham association. A government dinner, a mayoral garden party and 36 floral presentations to Mrs Chamberlain were witnessed by throngs of people all frantic with joy and enthusiasm.[30]

Chamberlain leaving the town hall with Hely-Hutchinson and Hime, 26 December 1902 (*The Illustrated London News*, 24 January 1903).

1.   *Natal Mercury*, 28.12.1899.

2.   *Review of Reviews*, pp.561–562.

3.   PAR, A 113: CG Smith to J. Henderson, 27.7.1923.

4.   KCL, KCM 30465: Campbell papers.

5.   Marais, JS, *The Fall of Kruger's Republic*, p.206; Headlam, C, *The Milner Papers*, Vol.1, p.212.

6. Marais, pp.260–261, 271–272, 287–288; Headlam, Vol.1, pp.359, 398; *The Natal Mercury*, 3.7.1899.

7. Tower, C, *Harry Escombe and Natal*, pp.240–243.

8. KCL, KCM 52: C Smythe to (probably) his mother, 26.10.1899.

9. *Natal Mercury*, 7, 12, 16, 18, 23.12.1899.

10. PAR, *Legislative Assembly debates*, 1900, p.8.

11. *Natal Mercury*, 7.5.1900; PAR, votes and proceedings, legislative assembly, 1900, p.3.

12. *Natal Mercury*, 21.9.1901.

13. *Natal Mercury*, 27.9.1901.

14. *Natal Mercury*, 11, 19, 20, 21, 23, 24 and 27.9.1901.

15. McCracken, JL, Irishmen in Southern African colonial parliaments, in *Southern African-Irish Studies*, 1, 1991, p.80; *Natal Mercury*, 15.9.1905.

16. McCracken, JL, Irishmen in Southern African colonial parliaments, in *Southern African-Irish Studies*, 1991, p.80; Natal Mercury, 15.9.1905.

17. Bhana, S, *Gandhi's Legacy, The Natal Indian Congress 1894–1994*, pp.1–2, 9–22; Pachai, B, (ed), *South Africa's Indians: The Evolution of a Minority*, pp.13–21, 68–89; Swan, M, *Gandhi, The South African Experience*, pp.46, 65, 67; Henning, CG, *The Indentured Indians in Natal*, 1860–1917, pp.81, 94, 185, 192–193.

18. Lambert, J, White dominance and control of the Kholwa petty bourgeois elite to the franchise and authority in late colonial Natal, in *Kleio, XXVII*, 1995, p.77.

19. *Natal Witness*, 15.8.1900.

20. Mesthrie, U, White dominance and control in Natal, 1893 to 1903, in *Journal of Natal and Zulu History*, VII, 1988, pp.41–44.

21. *Natal Mercury*, 3.7.1899.

22. KCL, KCM photographs: D1/1006, D1/010, D1/012, D2/075, D2/076, D2/158, D2/171.

23. PRO, CO 179/211: pp.525–528, 535–536, 22.3.1900; PAR, CSO 2589: 9.4.1900; *Natal Mercury*, 5, 7, 10.4.1900.

24. PAR, PM 17/1900/730: 17.4.1900.

25. *Natal Mercury*, 22.3.1900.

26. PRO, CO 179/215/203, 12.12.1900; CO 179/217/1054; DAR, 3DBN, 2/1/1/166: 11.7.1902.

27. Sandys, C, *Churchill: wanted dead or alive*, pp.133–138.

28. For the royal visit see, Buchner, P, The royal tour of 1901, the construction of an imperial identity in South Africa, in *South African Historical Journal*, 41, 1999, pp.324–348.

29. *Natal Mercury*, 14.8.1901.

30. *The Natal Mercury*, 27 and 29.12.1902; Amery, J, *Life of Joseph Chamberlain*, V, pp.204 and 296–298, *The Graphic*, 24 and 30.1.1903.

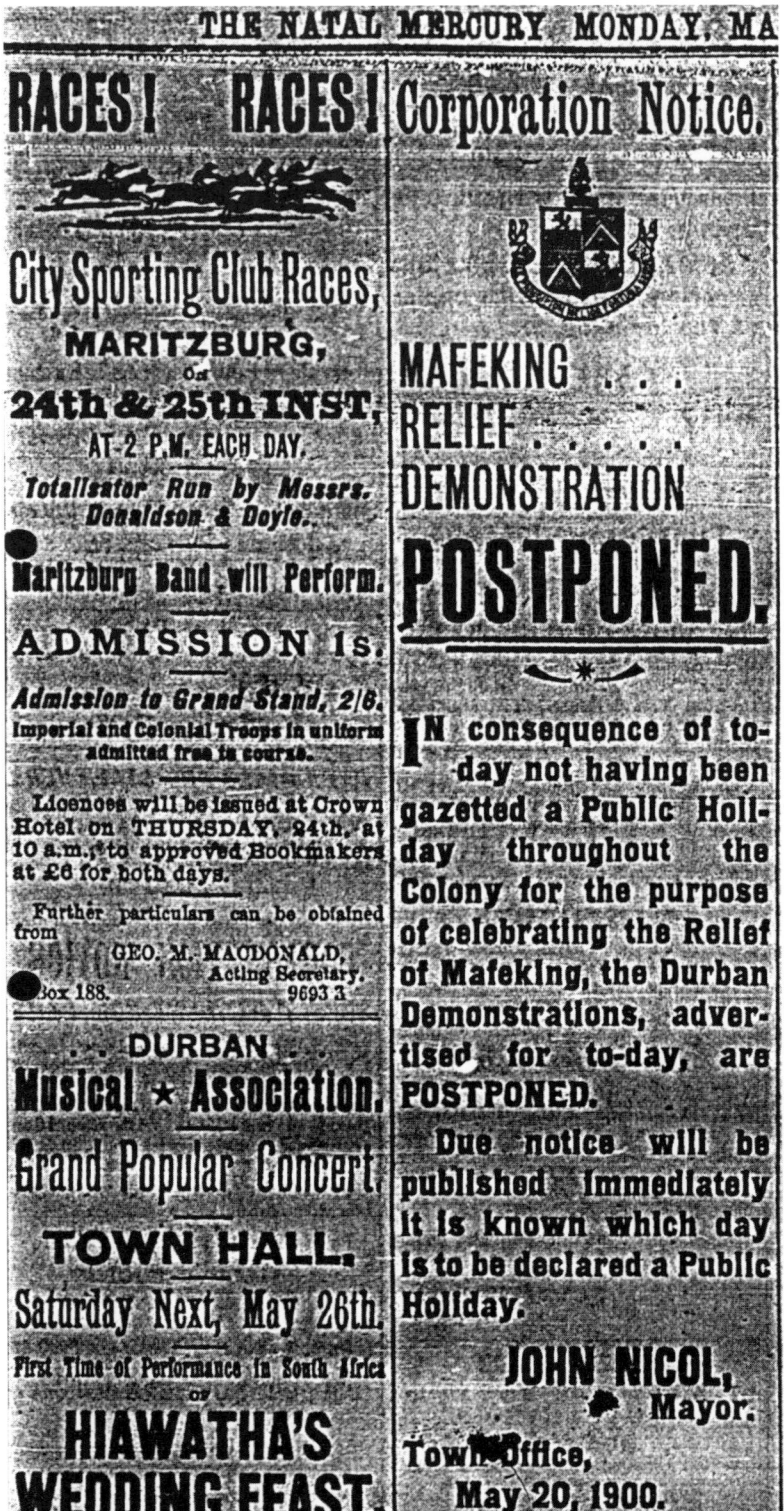

The earliest fort which preceded the establishment of Durban was a strangely sited structure built by Francis Farewell in 1825 close to the present centre of the town and described by Nathaniel Isaacs as: 'Mr Farewell has commenced building a fortress, which he proposes calling Fort Farewell. This is situated on the flat. It will cover a surface of about two hundred yards, and is to be constructed in the form of a triangle. A ditch by which it will be encompassed was in progress; and palisades were being planted. A mud fort had been commenced, at each angle designed to mount three 12-pound cannonades, which were lying there dismounted.[1] This fort, which was never completed, was probably sited more for purposes of defence from possible attack by Shaka and his Zulu impis rather than for protection from an overseas foe.'

The arrival of the British troops at the Point, 1838 by Bowler (LHM).

The arrival of HMS *Southampton* on 26 June 1842 (Russell).

CHAPTER 3

DURBAN: A DEFENDED GATEWAY
Brian Kearney and John Yelland

The early defences

Before 1898, the town of Durban had never had a comprehensive plan of defence. Traditionally, defence and fortifications in Durban appear to have been primarily concerned with ensuring military control, in terms of access to the Bay of Natal through the entrance channel, by mounting defences on either side on the two pieces of land which abutted the channel, that is, on the Point and on the Bluff.

In 1839, after the first British occupation of Natal, a small fort was built on a high sand dune at the Point by detachments of the 72nd High-landers and the Royal Artillery under Major Charters. Fort Victoria, as it came to be called, was a rudimentary palisade strengthened by earth-works which overlooked the harbour entrance. Charters considered the entire situation, including a stone store near the beach, to be highly suit-able for defence.

> [From] a military point of view, the position is ex-tremely favourable for defence by a small number of men. Our left flank is protected by the sea, which at high water reaches to within a few yards of Maynard's store. This is a substantial stone building, and will be a good barrack, capable of containing about sixty men. At low water the sea retires to a considerable distance, leaving a firm sandy flat, but the whole of it can be swept by the artillery of the port. Our right flank is also protected by the open sea, which rolls a lofty surge on the beach, and is, I believe, unapproachable by boats In front of ... Maynard's store rises a com-manding sandhill of inconsiderable surface and from 60 to 80 feet above it. It looks into the ravines and gullies; and many parts of the sea beach are exposed to its view.
>
> My present intention is to construct a stockade round the buildings – to stockade the sandhill strongly, and mount a field piece on it ... On the sea shore on our right ... the two heavy guns will be placed in bat-tery: they will command the anchorage, the entrance to the harbour, and range along the sea beach in every direction.[2]

This force was withdrawn a year later and the flag of the Republic of Natalia was hoisted by the Boers. Bearing in mind that the stated intention of Britain in embarking upon its defence strategy was to provide a British presence in a land which had been ravaged by conflicts between Zulus and Voortrekkers, this particular pattern of defence was probably based on a textbook view about where the potential threat of attack lay. It is also possible that such a view may have developed in the military minds of those who came from an island kingdom and who thus had a fixed opinion about invasions from the sea. So all energies were directed against an enemy approaching from the Indian Ocean, in spite of the highly mobile group of mounted Boers who occupied the surrounding countryside and who could quite easily have attacked and besieged Fort Victoria from the land.

It is extraordinary that this concept of defence was to be maintained during the subsequent occupation by the British in 1842, during the Anglo-Zulu War of 1879, and that it also became an essential part of the 1898 defence plan for Durban. Obviously the military guarding of the entrance channel would protect friendly shipping arriving and departing via that route, but it is difficult to understand how Charters and subsequent commanders thought that their defence measures would in any way be effective against horsemen. Unless, of course, one considers the absurd possibility that they genuinely believed that a group of wandering, mounted Boers would have had powerful international friends with battleships and cruisers.

When Captain Smith led the second occupation in May 1842, he inspected Fort Victoria and decided to split his forces between this location on the Point, and a new fort which he commenced on a site adjacent to the town centre. A slight rise in the marshy soil was selected, a deep surrounding trench dug and an earthen parapet formed. Gun emplacements were constructed at the corners and hutments were built inside. As it turned out this fort was to be besieged for 45 days after the disastrous attempt by Smith to attack Congella on the 23 May 1842. However, two nights later, the Boers easily overran the post at the Point, taking 35 British prisoners.[3]

After the formal annexation of Natal to the Cape and the resulting withdrawal of the Boers from Congella and around Durban into the hinterland of the country, the British forces, under Lieutenant Gibb of the Royal Engineers, completed the main fort, and also commenced the building of a substantial blockhouse on a sandhill at the Point, close to the earlier Fort Victoria. Once again the objective was to protect the entrance channel to the bay. In addition, the 27th regiment built a magazine of dry stone close by. The loopholed blockhouse was constructed by the 45th regiment and the Royal Engineers. It was two-storied and could hold about 80 men and, for many years afterwards, was occupied by a detachment of the 45th and a few artillerymen.

Even during the Anglo-Zulu War of 1879, and amidst the rumours of a Zulu invasion, other than a rudimentary laager in the centre of the town and a redoubt built on the Western Vlei to complement the old fort, the Point was again the main base chosen by the Durban defence committee as a place for a 'last-ditch' stand, and for securing white women and children and Indian and African refugees of the town. For this purpose a timber stockade was built from the bay to the sea.[4]

The blockhouse at the Point, 1849 (Watercolour, LHM).

The bay, Bluff and Point from the Berea, by West, 1859 (LHM).

Anglo-Zulu War stockade at the Point, 1879 (KCL).

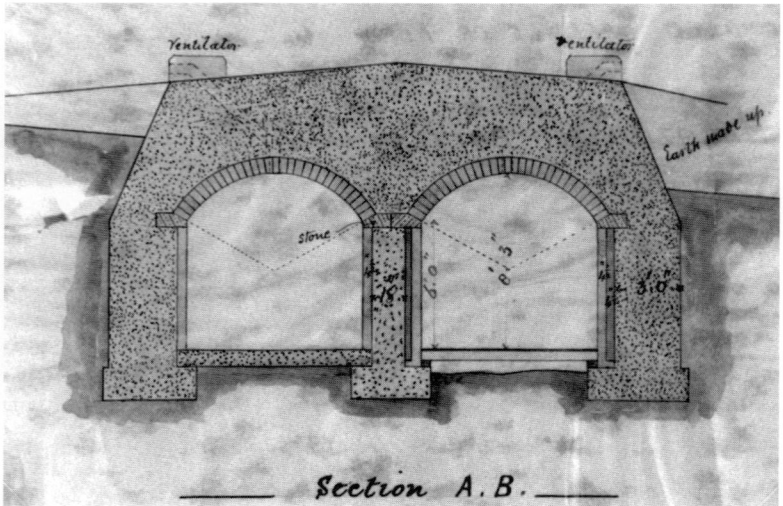

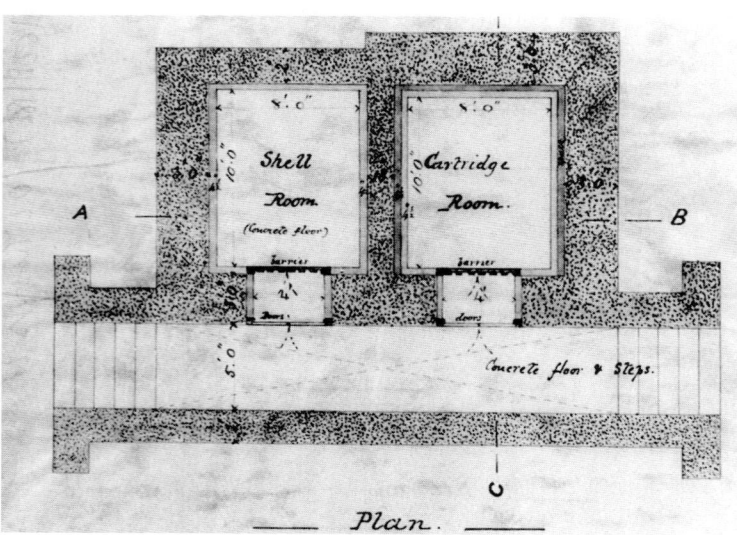

Plan and section of Two Gun battery, Bluff, Major Rathbone, 11 June 1887 (PAR).

By 1903, the 6-inch BL Mark IV guns were replaced by one 12-pounder QF gun located close to the original site but more towards the entrance channel, and two new 6-inch, BL Mark VII guns replaced the original one on the eastern side. An additional part of the revised seaward defence was to move the two original guns to a new battery to be built north of Back Beach battery towards the Umgeni River. This plan was never carried out. In 1910, the Natal Militia reported on the poor state of Bluff battery, with almost every one of 32 items of equipment being condemned as useless.[7]

The Bluff and Back Beach batteries

Thus, historically, Durban had no real plans for defence against an attack from the hinterland: virtually the only defences that had been established were for the possibility of warding off an attack from the sea. British fears of Russian expansionist movements during the 1830s into Bulgaria and towards Afghanistan caused concern about the possible invasion of India and perhaps other British colonies. The colonial office thus instructed all Indian Ocean colonies to improve their defences, particularly their seaward ones. Major Rathbone of the Royal Engineers, stationed at Fort Napier in Pietermaritzburg, was requested to prepare designs for coastal batteries.[5] Two gun battery sites were chosen. One would be on the beach facing the Indian Ocean to the north of the town, and the other would be positioned on the top of the Bluff. The theory was that a foreign navy would attack from the sea, whereafter they might capture and destroy the telegraph cable station which was located on the beachfront near the Umgeni River mouth, thereby isolating the two South African colonies from the rest of the British empire. This thinking prevailed right up to the outbreak of the Anglo-Boer War in October 1899.

The drawings for Two Gun battery depict its design as being an extensive concrete and earth fortification positioned at the crest of the Bluff, complete with central magazines for shells and cartridges. The colonial engineer utilised the services of the harbour engineer, Cathcart Methven, for the supervision of the construction of this battery and for the design and construction of its partner, northwards along the beach. In 1890, two 6-inch breech-loading Mark IV coastal defence guns were emplaced on top of Two Gun battery. To reach the summit of the Bluff, these guns would have been hauled up an old Voortrekker pathway which led from the beach on the bay side.

Their arc of fire was approximately 115° covering an area from 225° to 80°, and with a particular focus on the region of the outer anchorage off Durban. Their range was in the order of 15 000 yards (13,7 km), depending on the type of shell fired. For example, if shrapnel was used, the range was reduced, owing to the fact that the shell exploded while still in the air, scattering lead balls over the target area. However, although these guns were mounted *en barbette*, they could be turned around to fire inland in which case their range would have covered areas almost as far as Westville. In contrast to their use at sea where uninterrupted visibility would have been the norm, their inland range was limited. As there was no provision for forward artillery observation posts, they would only have been accurate within direct line-of-sight range, namely, as far as the Berea Ridge. In 1890, the completed battery was handed over to the volunteer department.[6]

By 1892, work had commenced on the Back Beach battery and, in 1894, two 6-inch BL Mark IV coastal defence guns were emplaced on specially constructed embrasures. The work entailed the building of a branch rail line off the Umgeni rail to facilitate the supply of materials and the guns. These guns had an arc of fire of approximately 130°, from 40° to 170°, with a similar range to those on the Bluff and again were to be trained on the outer anchorage, but without the advantage of elevation,

Two Gun battery, Bluff (PAR).

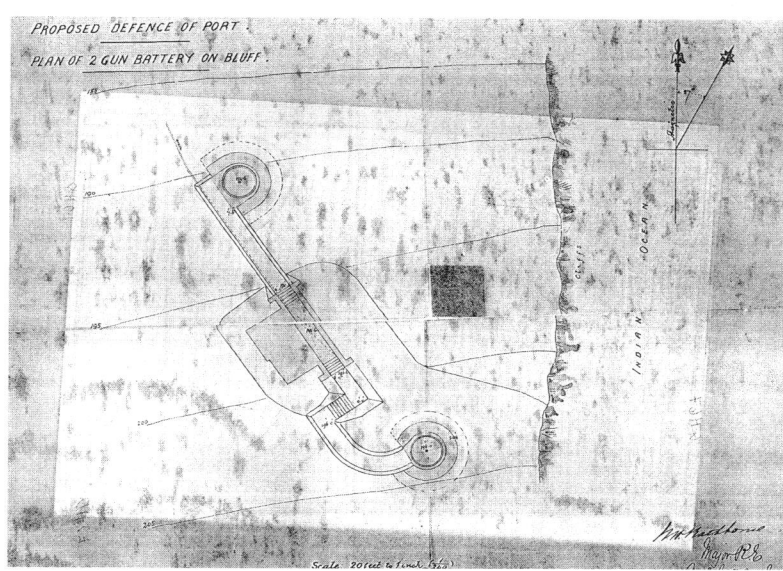
Plan of Two Gun battery, Bluff, Major Rathbone, 11 June 1887 (PAR).

since they were virtually at sea level. Similarly, these guns could be turned around to fire inland, but with the same range limitations. In practical terms, the maximum distance would also have been as far as the Berea Ridge. Both of these batteries were to become essential components of the 1898 defence plan for Durban, and for the radical revisions to that plan which were made in November 1899 to defend the gateway.

The 1898 defence scheme

In November 1898, in response to a secret circular dated 26 July 1898 from the secretary of state, and a circular from Lord Knutsford dated 22 October 1898, the Natal governor, Hely-Hutchinson, instituted a plan preparing for the defence of Durban. The plan was outlined in a secret document printed for the colonial office in February 1899.[8] The printed copy of the report was accompanied by a despatch from the governor describing it as 'the scheme of Defence for this Colony'. The beach off Durban was considered to be the only part of the coast which needed defending. It was not considered likely that it would be attacked by a fleet, but rather by roving cruisers which would take possession of the shore end of the telegraph cable which linked all of the southern African colonies with Europe. Such an attack might also result in the coal in the harbour being appropriated (the Natal government had already offered 12 000 tons to the Royal Navy); possibly the town and ships in the inner harbour could be held to ransom; and ships in the outer anchorage could be sunk. Durban was thus considered to be vulnerable to torpedo boats or launches and it might have had to withstand bombardment.

Contingency plans suggested that a garrison required for protection could be supplied by volunteers stationed in the district so that the imperial forces inland could be retained. If necessary an inland corps of volunteers could be mobilised. In addition, this arrangement was also considered to be the best 'with which to deal with any Native disturbances, always most likely to break out in times of difficulty'.[9]

Signal station, Point, ca. 1895 (KCL).

The plan enumerated the broad distribution of troops in Natal and outlined the numbers of volunteers required for each of the four posts plus the signal station. Durban would have at its disposal a total of 4 490 troops, most of whom would have to be drawn from their posts in Pietermaritzburg and Ladysmith. Of these, some 600 would be regular cavalry; 2 500 regular infantry with 400 volunteers and 300 regular mounted infantry supported by 600 local volunteers. Moreover, the Natal Naval Volunteers (NNV) could provide 90 men for a Garrison Artillery at the two coastal batteries, of whom 53 would be stationed at Two Gun battery on the Bluff. A comprehensive table of the distribution of armaments and ammunition in the colony was included, with Durban having access to four 6-inch BL guns, four 7 pounders, two .45 Maxims, two .303 Maxims. Reserves included four 9-pounder guns, two 7 pounders, two RBL Armstrongs, and four 3-pounder Hotchkisses. In addition Durban possessed 594 rifles and tens of thousands of rounds of ammunition of various types.

The plan embodied a full description of the command division: the commandant was to be the commandant of volunteers, Colonel Royston with his headquarters in the Point signal station where he would be backed by a large contingent of the Natal Mounted Infantry (NMR), the Natal Field Artillery (NFA) and the Durban Light Infantry (DLI). Other stations for the various role-players would include the mayor at the town hall; the commissariat and transport officer in the town solicitor's office; the medical command at Addington Hospital; and sanitary administration based at the police station. All artillery was to be directed from Two Gun battery at the Bluff.

Communications between these headquarter stations and the four posts at the Bluff battery, the Point, the Back Beach battery and the cable house at the Umgeni River would be via telegraph and telephone. In addition signals, semaphores and hand post would also be used as a means of communication. A branch telephone under construction along the Bluff rail line would supply a line to the Bluff battery. Another line would be provided to the Back Beach battery and cable house. Various signal stations were also selected north and south of Durban, and were positioned on the north coast just beyond the Tugela and Tongaat Rivers, and on the south coast beyond the Umbogintwini River, at the Aliwal Shoal lighthouses and at Port Shepstone. Local signal stations were identified to provide alarms should the need arise. These included the town hall clock tower, the Point and the Bluff signal stations. The hoisting of the colonial flag would be a signal for the Durban volunteers to mobilise, and the raising of the Union Jack would signal the arrival of a hostile cruiser. The alarm would be cancelled by flying the colonial flag under the Union Jack.

Methods of meeting various forms of attack in various places and of assistance from up country by rail were fully described. Descriptions of

One of the first local innovators in the use of the telephone was George Ireland who offered his system to the Natal Harbour Board in 1883. They initially declined his offer but were eventually persuaded to accede. Ireland's telephone wires which were draped across the entrance channel between the Point and Bluff became a hazard to shipping. In 1886 TN Price established a switchboard with 12 subscribers, which increased to 50 about two years later. In 1889 the Natal Telephone Company was formed. When the Durban Municipal Telephone system was inaugurated in 1901 there were 598 subscribers.[10]

Right: 1898 Plans for the defence of Durban showing Back Beach and Bluff (Two Gun) batteries (PRO).

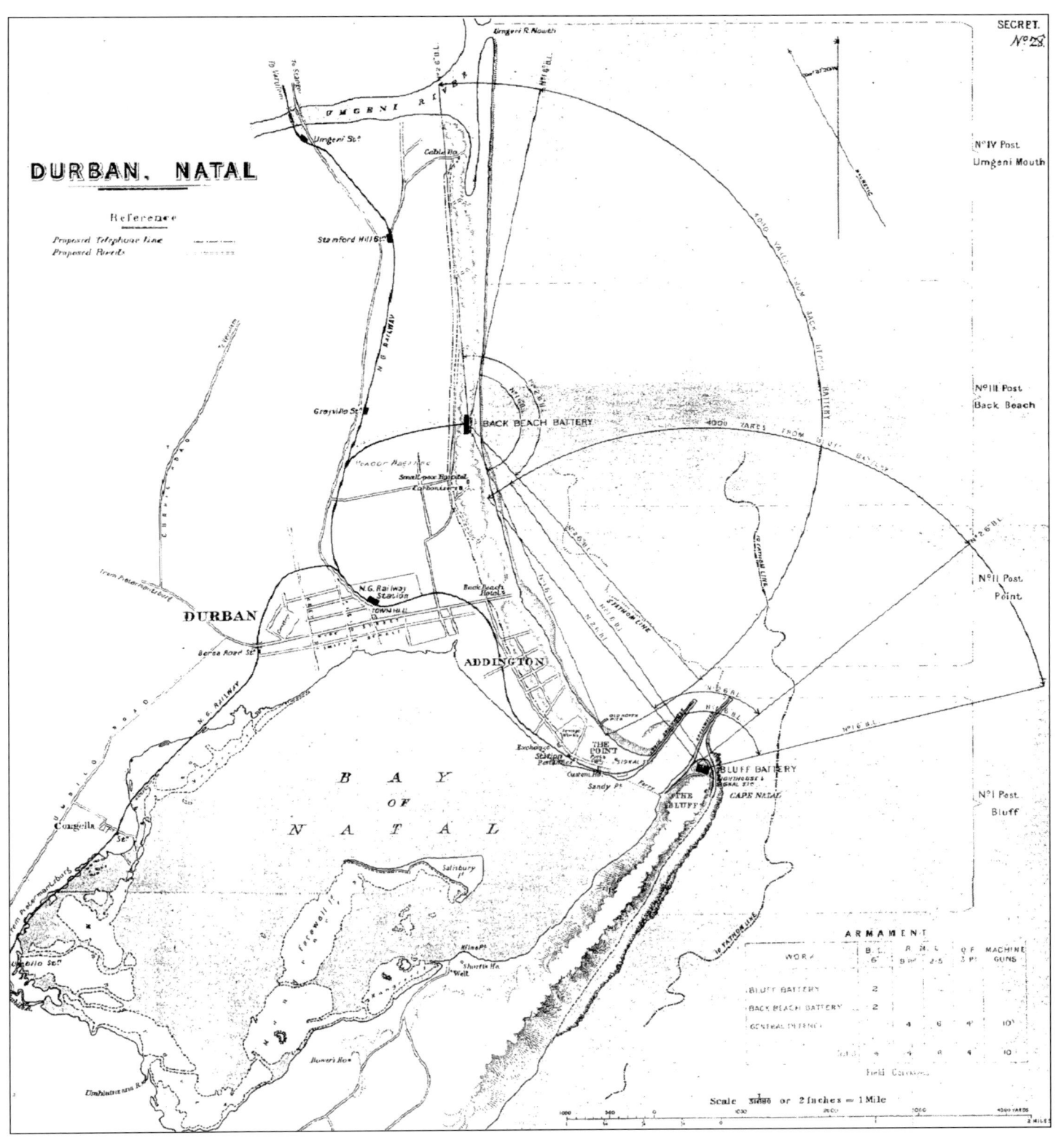

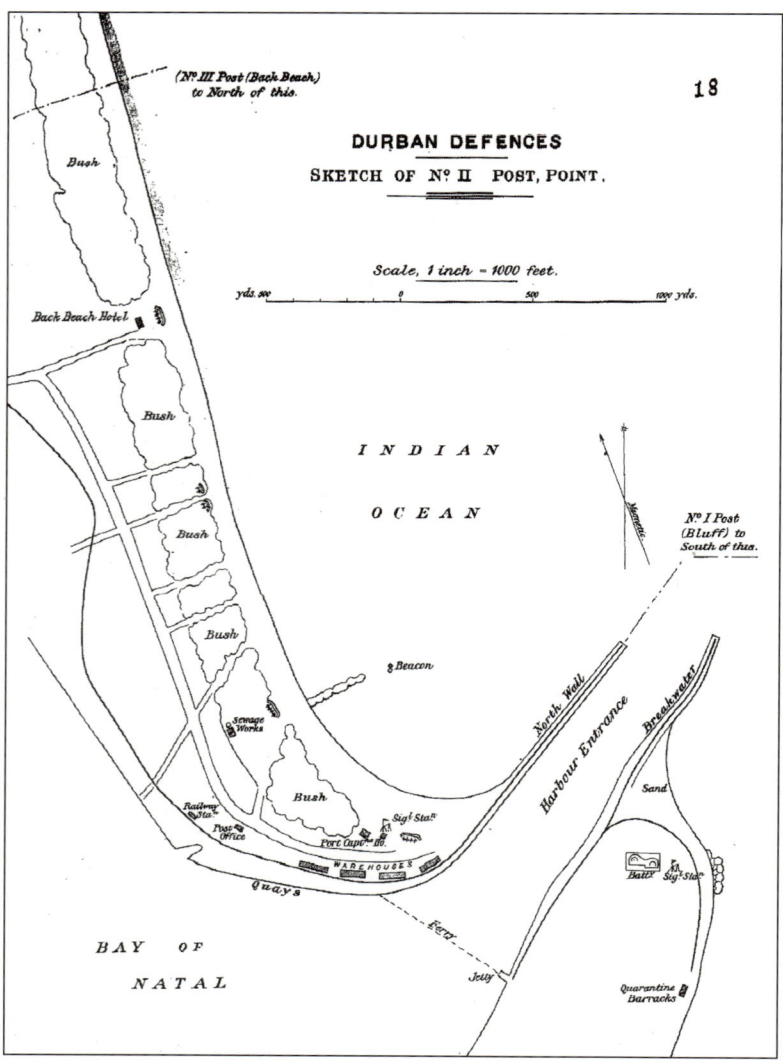

the proposed sequence of actions were provided for various levels of staff and departments including details relating to military press censorship; instructions regarding alarmist publications; and administrative requisites for rail and other forms of transport which would be regulated by the mayor. The mayor would also arrange for supplies to be despatched to various posts and for the delivery of picks, shovels and empty sugar bags. The post at the Point would need 70 picks, 70 shovels and 400 empty sugar bags, while the post at the mouth of the Umgeni River only required 20 picks and shovels and 100 sugar bags. Railway sleepers for the defence works could be requisitioned from the NGR. Volunteers at the Point would use No. 2 shed on the quayside as barracks and all others were to use tents. The commanding Royal Engineer would proceed to Durban to supervise the strengthening of posts, while hospital arrangements would be made by the mayor, including the appointment of local doctors and the appropriate provision of stores.

Instructions were given to officers commanding each post and for a town commandant to implement all the above orders. Details included specifications for artificial covers to be constructed for guns at the Point, the Back Beach battery and the Umgeni Mouth, and a map which showed various new gun posts to be established along the beach.

Orders were attached for the various officers commanding the volunteer corps, namely the NMR, NFA, DLI, the NNV and a group of 101 reserves who were to be stationed at the Point signal station. After a public proclamation had been made by the mayor, arrangements for civil administration were to be left in the hands of the municipal authorities. Further details concerned the necessary sanitary arrangements which would be the responsibility of 'the inspector of nuisances'. The municipality would also arrange for the early closing of hotels and canteens; the swearing in of special police; establishing various headquarter stations; the appointment of civilians for duties; administering railway arrangements for those wishing to leave; and selecting suitable buildings to be used as hospitals (amongst which were the masonic halls in Smith Street and at Addington, Rennie's and the Union Company's stores). Resident doctors would be required and ladies would also be needed to act as matrons and nurses. Special harbour regulations were to be implemented. The expected line of enemy fire was to be down West Street.

The plan of defence was thus fairly extensive and detailed and sensibly, though optimistically, relied largely on close co-operation between military, volunteer and civil authorities. The plans had been formulated by a local defence committee, with strong military representation, although it also included Harry Escombe, who would have served the interests of the municipal government and the harbour authorities. It is, however, interesting to note how few of the elements of the scheme actually came into being and how many components were to be rapidly abandoned in the face of the reality of an enemy coming not from the sea, but from the hinterland.

Apparently, both the colonial defence committee and the Durban defence committee made certain remarks about the published proposals, and because prior comments had not been taken into account the scheme was deemed to require considerable alterations. The Admiralty agreed

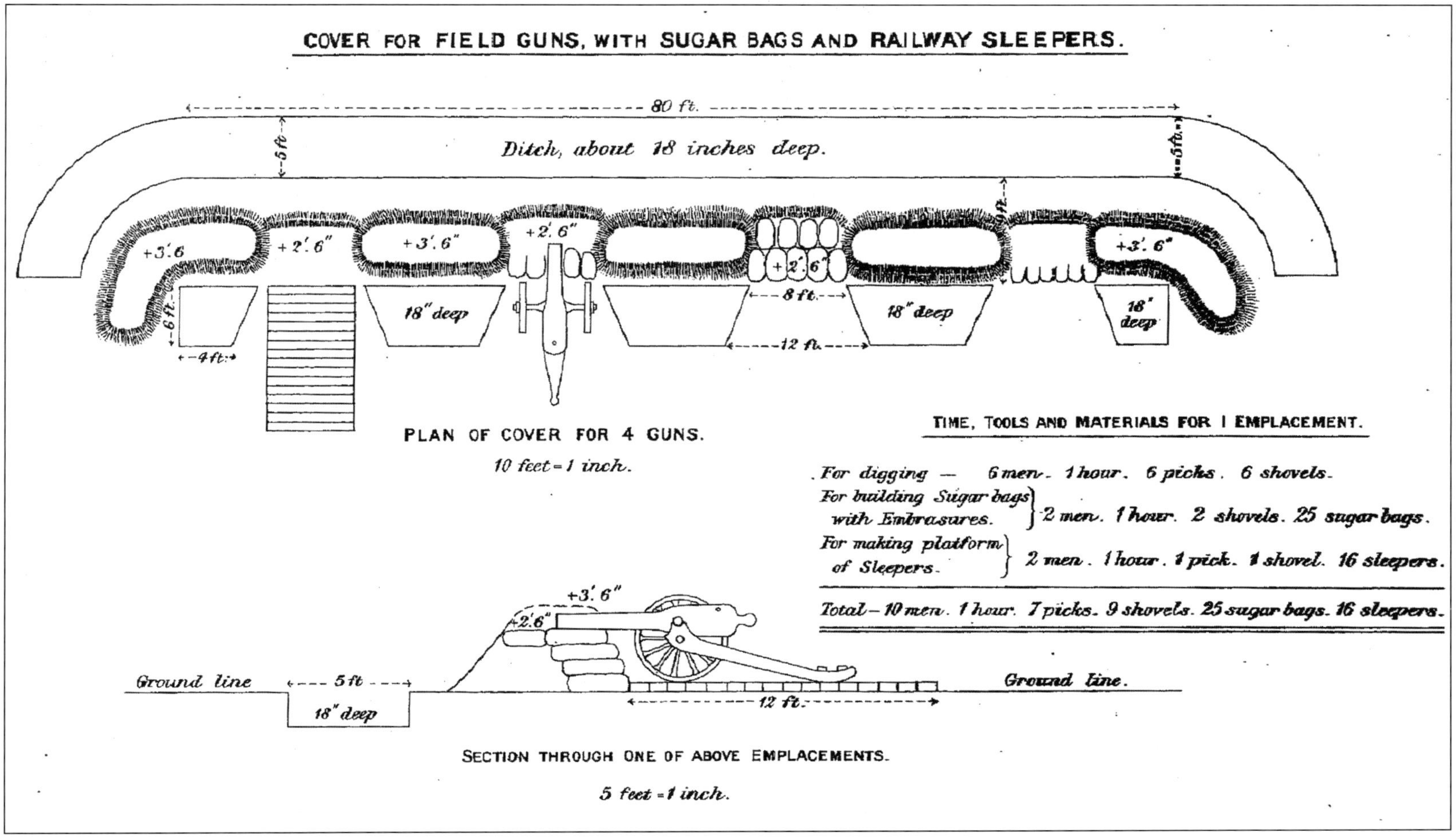

COVER FOR FIELD GUNS, WITH SUGAR BAGS AND RAILWAY SLEEPERS.

← - - - - - - - - - - - - - - - - 80 ft. - - - - - - - - - - - - - - - - →

Ditch, about 18 inches deep.

5 ft.   5 ft.

+3'.6"   +2'.6"   +3'.6"   +2'.6"   +2'6"   +3'.6"

6 ft.

18" deep   18" deep   18" deep

4 ft.   ← - 8 ft. - →

← - - 12 ft. - - →

PLAN OF COVER FOR 4 GUNS.

10 feet = 1 inch.

TIME, TOOLS AND MATERIALS FOR 1 EMPLACEMENT.

For digging —   6 men. 1 hour. 6 picks. 6 shovels.
For building Sugar bags
  with Embrasures.   } 2 men. 1 hour. 2 shovels. 25 sugar bags.
For making platform
  of Sleepers.   } 2 men. 1 hour. 1 pick. 1 shovel. 16 sleepers.

Total — 10 men. 1 hour. 7 picks. 9 shovels. 25 sugar bags. 16 sleepers.

+3'.6"
+2'.6"

Ground line   ← - 5 ft. - →   *Ground line.*

18" deep   ← - - - 12 ft. - - - →

SECTION THROUGH ONE OF ABOVE EMPLACEMENTS.

5 feet = 1 inch.

with the objections made. In May 1899, the secretary of state for war suggested that these remarks be forwarded to the general officer commanding the troops in South Africa, and that Natal be advised to revise the scheme annually.[12] One revision, which was made in October 1898 and which hinted at an attack from the hinterland, was an amendment to the plan that allowed for a temporary fort to be established on the flat ground in front of Claremont Station.

West Street, looking towards the town from the beach (LHM).

Durban: a defended gateway   **51**

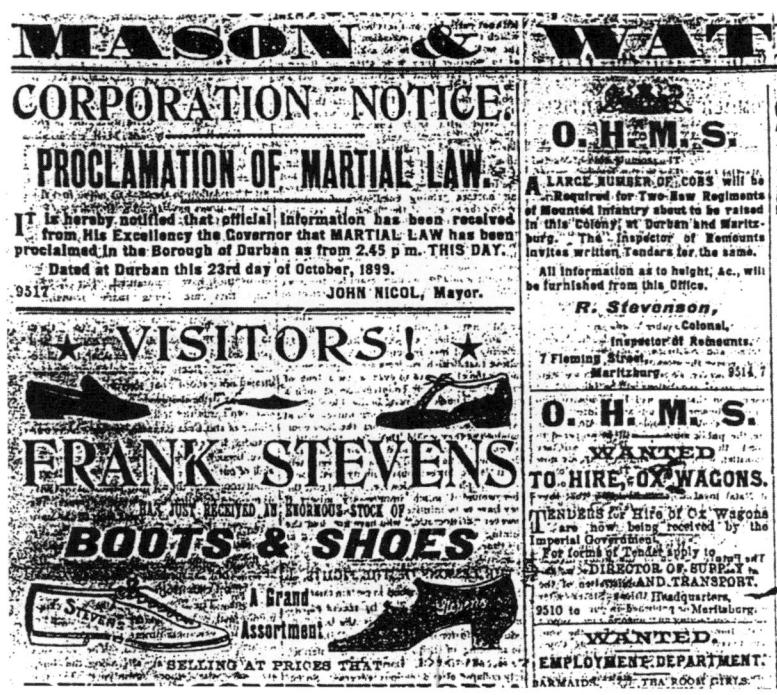

The first commandant, Colonel EC Bethune and the declaration of martial law

Brigadier General Wolfe-Murray and the governor chose to proclaim and commence martial law at 14:45 on 23 October 1899 at precisely the same time that the National Bank of the ZAR in Durban was to be occupied. This was probably a matter of convenience – he needed to have martial law in place before the seizure of the bank. Instructions were issued to the newly appointed commandant, Colonel Bethune.

On 30 October 1899, Colonel Bethune, who evidently supplied the governor with a daily report, recorded that Durban was quiet: 'I have a patrol on the Berea every night ... I have found it necessary to put a guard on the Umgeni Bridge, about four miles away, as the road over it corresponds directly with Zululand and strange men have been seen riding from the town on several occasions.'[26]

The following day Hely-Hutchinson was informed that he could raise further forces for the defence of Durban. General White in Ladysmith had more or less accepted standing a siege there and Pietermaritzburg and Durban would have to look after themselves. The general officer commanding, lines of communication, had the idea of preparing a fortification at Fort Napier and arming it with long range 12-pounder guns from the Royal naval cruisers *Powerful* and *Terrible*. The main difficulty the governor foresaw was the problem of women and children, 'as although we should not defend the town itself Boers are capable of shelling it'. He also noted that Durban was crammed: '... the Prime Minister estimates number of women and children at 10 000 including refugees. Have you any room at Cape ports and can you help in the event of one having to ask them to go?' He also recorded that the commandant in Durban had ordered the submission of proposals for the defence of the town.[27]

At the end of October 1899, Captain Lambton of the Royal Navy, who was on his way to Ladysmith with two 4.7-inch guns and three long-range 12 pounders taken from HMS *Powerful*, called on Hely-Hutchinson and informed him that HMS *Terrible* at Cape Town could make a similar contribution to the defence of Durban and Pietermaritzburg. Then Hely-Hutchinson told General Wolfe-Murray, Colonel Hinde of the Border Regiment and Major Gaisford, the commandant of Pietermaritzburg, about the idea, and they agreed to wait for the initial results from Ladysmith. On the 3 November 1899, Hely-Hutchinson also noted that he had been in touch with the senior naval officer regarding the defence of Durban. HMS *Tartar* and *Philomel* were in port, and HMS *Forte* and *Terrible* were expected, while HMS *Powerful* was in the roadstead. Bethune's Mounted Infantry had been enrolled with about 116 horses, while a regiment of Uitlander infantry was being formed to assist with defence.

At this time the governor also appears to have been prepared to abandon Pietermaritzburg: 'No attempt will be made to defend the town itself against anything more than a raid. Any attempt to defend the town against an attack in force supported by guns would be useless, and would involve the slaughter of many non-combatants.'[28] He was also making arrangements to send all the confidential papers from his office to

HMS *Terrible*, 1899 (Newnes).

Captain Lambton, RN (Newnes).

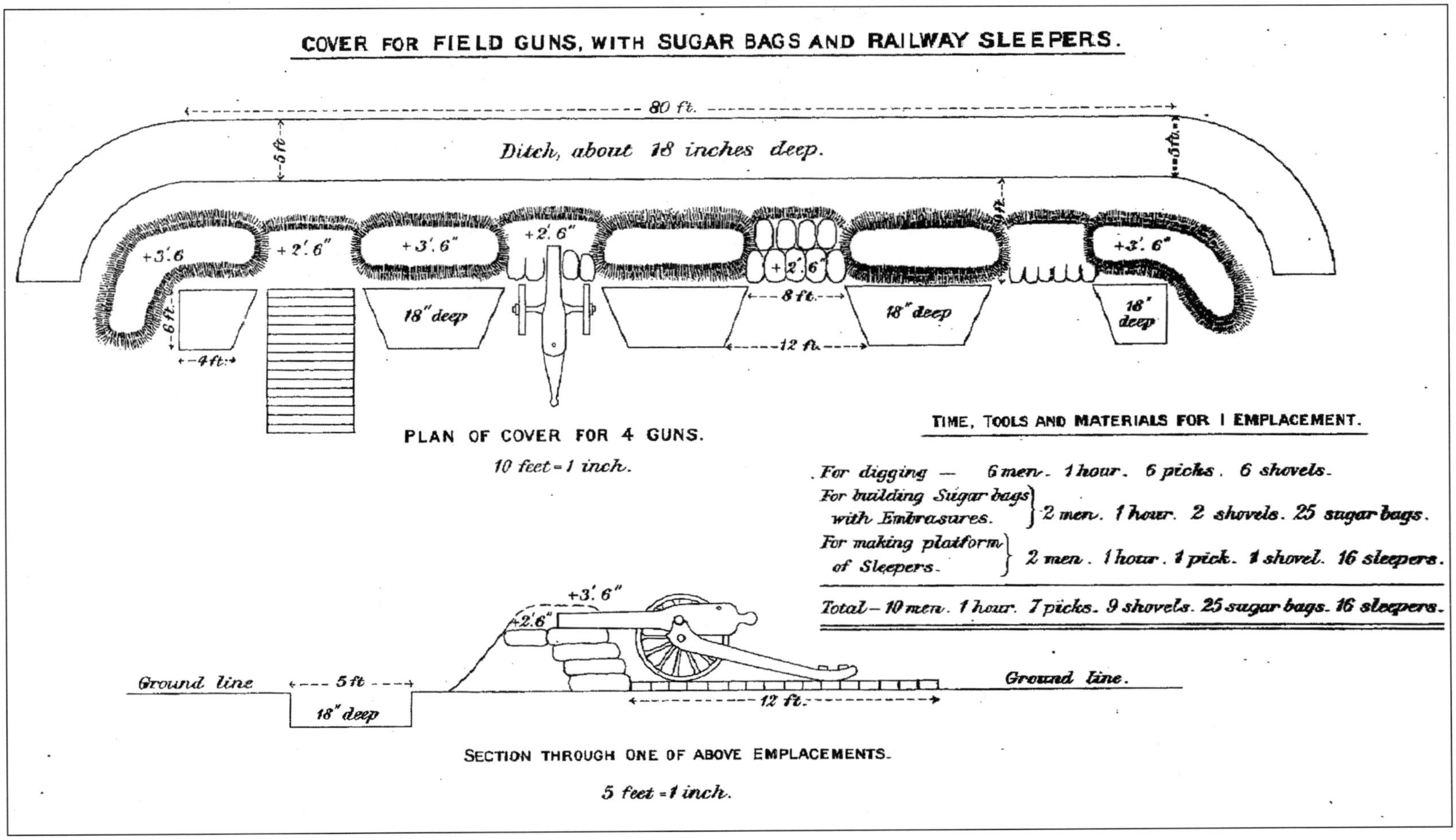

COVER FOR FIELD GUNS, WITH SUGAR BAGS AND RAILWAY SLEEPERS.

— 80 ft. —

5 ft.

Ditch, about 18 inches deep.

5 ft.

+3'.6   +2'.6"   +3'.6"   +2'.6"   +2'.6"   +3'.6"

6 ft.   18" deep   18" deep   18" deep

4 ft.   8 ft.

12 ft.

PLAN OF COVER FOR 4 GUNS.

10 feet = 1 inch.

TIME, TOOLS AND MATERIALS FOR I EMPLACEMENT.

. For digging —   6 men. 1 hour. 6 picks. 6 shovels.
For building Sugar bags
with Embrasures.   } 2 men. 1 hour. 2 shovels. 25 sugar bags.
For making platform
of Sleepers.   } 2 men. 1 hour. 1 pick. 1 shovel. 16 sleepers.

Total — 10 men. 1 hour. 7 picks. 9 shovels. 25 sugar bags. 16 sleepers.

+3'.6"
+2'.6"

Ground line   — 5 ft —   *Ground line.*

18" deep   — 12 ft. —

SECTION THROUGH ONE OF ABOVE EMPLACEMENTS.

5 feet = 1 inch.

with the objections made. In May 1899, the secretary of state for war suggested that these remarks be forwarded to the general officer commanding the troops in South Africa, and that Natal be advised to revise the scheme annually.[12] One revision, which was made in October 1898 and which hinted at an attack from the hinterland, was an amendment to the plan that allowed for a temporary fort to be established on the flat ground in front of Claremont Station.

West Street, looking towards the town from the beach (LHM).

Why defend Durban?

As early as June 1896, Major Altham, an officer of the British Intelligence, had forecast that 'the increase in the military strength of the Boers – their political aspirations – and especially their desire to possess Natal and a sea-port at Durban, rendered it not impossible that the two Boer states may make a dash at Natal'.[13] But the preparations for war by the British authorities which preceded the actual invasion of October 1899 completely disregarded this advice and relied on the view that 'the Boers would make no serious advance into either Natal or the Cape Colony during the month or six weeks which must elapse before troops sufficient for our advance can be concentrated in South Africa'.[14] The British also wrongly assumed that the 1899 picture would be a repetition of the 1881 Anglo-Transvaal War and dangerously ignored the political reality that 'the Boers regarded Natal as theirs by right of first occupation, and that Durban would give them a seaport which they greatly coveted'.[15] In addition, of course, the capturing of the various ports in southern Africa, particularly Durban, would deny the British disembarkation facilities along the southern African coast. It was common knowledge that visitors to the Boer republics had heard open boasts that the Boers would be in Durban and Cape Town by Christmas. As was the case with most military intelligence of that time, very few people took Major Altham's warning seriously.

In addition, with the build-up of the British forces along the northern border of the Colony of Natal, it was inconceivable to both the politicians and the military authorities that the Boers, who appeared to be a poorly equipped rabble of undisciplined farmers with very little military training, could defeat the might of the British empire in battle. Unfortunately, the British army had not fought any battles against a white army since the time of the Crimean War of 1853–56. All their battles had been of a colonial nature against poorly armed indigenous people. Not even the defeats suffered at Isandhlwana and Majuba alerted them to the possibility of yet another defeat. And thus it was that nobody was overly concerned about the threat to the port of Durban.

Notwithstanding, realisation that a major threat could come from the hinterland began to dawn with the outbreak of war, when the commandos of the Boer republics invaded Northern Natal in a seemingly unstoppable advance along the main railway line southwards. Newcastle was abandoned in favour of Dundee, but after the disastrous battle of Talana and the ignominious retreat by the British forces to Ladysmith, doubts began to form, although even then it was still felt that the British forces were virtually unconquerable, and that the Boers would be held at Ladysmith.

Nonetheless some had considered an alternative possibility. As early as August 1898, the mayor of Durban, John Nicol, expressed a serious concern about the defence of the town to the colonial secretary, writing: 'a communication has been made to me to the effect that in the event of hostilities all the Volunteers will be withdrawn from the Coast Districts for the protection of the upper Districts of the Colony. If this information is correct, I shall be glad to be informed what steps the Government propose to take for the protection of Durban and the surrounding districts.'[16]

Hime requested Colonel Royston, the Commandant of Volunteers, to comment and received the following response:

> ... I am at a loss to understand in what way Durban requires protection by troops. After taking away the Volunteers there will remain within the Borough over 6,000 white males over 18 years of age. After deducting those physically incapable, foreigners etc., it is estimated there will remain some 4,000 able-bodied Britishers who will be able to bear arms. Let these men enrol themselves under the local Rifle Associations. If the purchase of a Rifle is a stumbling block, I suggest that the merchant princes of Durban, who have most at stake, should each guarantee the payment of so many rifles ...[17]

In the minute papers, Hime added that he too was surprised that the mayor should have requested such information. The colonial secretary responded to the mayor, tactfully omitting the reference to the 'merchant princes' – a barbed reference to persons like Nicol himself.

In September 1899, the colonial secretary addressed a memo to all the Natal and Zululand magistrates, warning them to be particularly careful about fulfilling the provisions of Sections 28, 41 & 42 of Law No. 11 of 1862, which controlled the registration of firearms. Given the fact that, simultaneously, there were reports of the distribution of arms among the Boers of Northern Natal who were thought to be preparing themselves to cross over the border to join the Transvaal Boers, this step appears to have been warranted.

The magistrate of Durban was personally notified to employ strict measures of control and to communicate with the government before authorising the registration of any firearm if he had any doubt as to the purchaser being a fit and proper person to hold one. It would thus seem that sedition and treachery were suspected from within the home ranks.

Once the invasion of Northern Natal had commenced on 12 October 1899, the unease displayed by the authorities almost turned into panic. Five days later the governor requested a Naval Brigade, not exceeding 100 men with one machine gun, to be sent to Pietermaritzburg, as 'he ha[d] reason to believe that disloyal Dutchmen [might] rise and try to rush the town'.[19] The following week an alarmed governor telegraphed the general officer commanding asking: 'Do I understand that you have determined to keep all troops at Ladysmith? If you have I ought to be informed at once, as there seems no doubt now that part of Joubert's force will come in by Greytown, and both in Durban and here we are practically defenceless'.[20] Suddenly the elaborate defence plan of 1898 appeared redundant and Nicol's request for protection must have been viewed differently!

On the 22 October 1899, martial law was proclaimed in Durban. Two days later, the Natal governor, Hely-Hutchinson, telegraphed Chamberlain in the colonial office again notifying him of the measures which had been taken and informing him that Colonel Bethune had been appointed commandant of Durban. Hely-Hutchinson continued: '... There is always danger of raid being attempted and there seems no doubt it was part of Boers plans but recent events seem to have given them pause ... we are carefully watching borders of Zulu (land) and the Tugela River ...'.[21] On the same day Hely-Hutchinson communicated with the general officer commanding, assuring him that he would not exert pressure 'to weaken the force at Ladysmith', and saying that he thought they were able to meet any small raid, 'but a raid in force, especially if supported by guns, will be a serious matter'. He continued: 'With the Rifle Brigade and Border Regiment, if they come, and the guns and the maxims from the "Powerful", and the corps now being raised here, we ought to make a fair show against any ordinary raid both in Maritzburg and Durban'.[22]

A few days later, Hely-Hutchinson again expressed the opinion that Pietermaritzburg and Durban were practically undefended. He had expected the military authorities at least to leave the Border Regiment or the Rifle Brigade in response to his request. The secretary of state, in a note to Chamberlain, complained of the governor interfering in matters which belonged to the general command, and that Hely-Hutchinson should be told to organise the males of the two towns and that the necessary arms would be supplied from the Cape. The secretary of state for war duly authorised Hely-Hutchinson to enrol men from Durban, with the assurance that 2 000 magazine rifles would be despatched to Cape Town and 1 000 to Durban. The correspondence suggests that there was no clear idea about the availability and nature of arms in Durban, and indicates that the detailed lists included in the 1898 defence scheme were already gathering dust.

Buller later explained that the parlous situation in Natal had arisen because the colonies of the Cape and Natal had not been 'garrisoned according to a systematic scheme of defence, as [he had] recommended in July 1899...'.[23] In the event of a coastwards thrust by the Boers, the commander had been instructed not to make a prolonged defence either of Colenso or of Pietermaritzburg, but to make sure, at all costs, of protecting Durban, and to destroy the railways as he retreated. Buller confessed that he would have had extreme difficulty in preventing the enemy from pressing their advantage in the fortnight which followed 30 October, since the British forces which arrived around 20 November were 'sadly deficient in mounted men; and so the situation in Natal was far from comfortable; our want of mounted men made it impossible to deal with so mobile an enemy as the Boers'.[24] Buller's original intention had been to send the colonial troops through Zululand to Helpmekaar, but this proved to be impossible as the number of colonial volunteers raised was less than expected; and there were inadequate oxen for wagons owing to the rinderpest. Moreover, in Natal, even before crossing the Tugela, the 'entire staff equipment of an army had to be created'.[25]

John Nicol
John Nicol was a prominent merchant in Durban who ran a large building and timber company. He was born in 1838 at Ramstone, Scotland, and had come to Natal in 1860. He served in the NFA and on the town council from 1885, with four successive terms of office as mayor.

Evidently, a certain Aurel Schulz, who was a Natal citizen living on the Transvaal border, believed that between 700 and 1 000 young Boers from Natal would cross the border in time of war; he suggested that the Natal authorities should arrange for young farmers to report every day, in order to prevent them from slipping over the border unnoticed; he also observed that ammunition and rifles had been sent to the Natal Boers.[18]

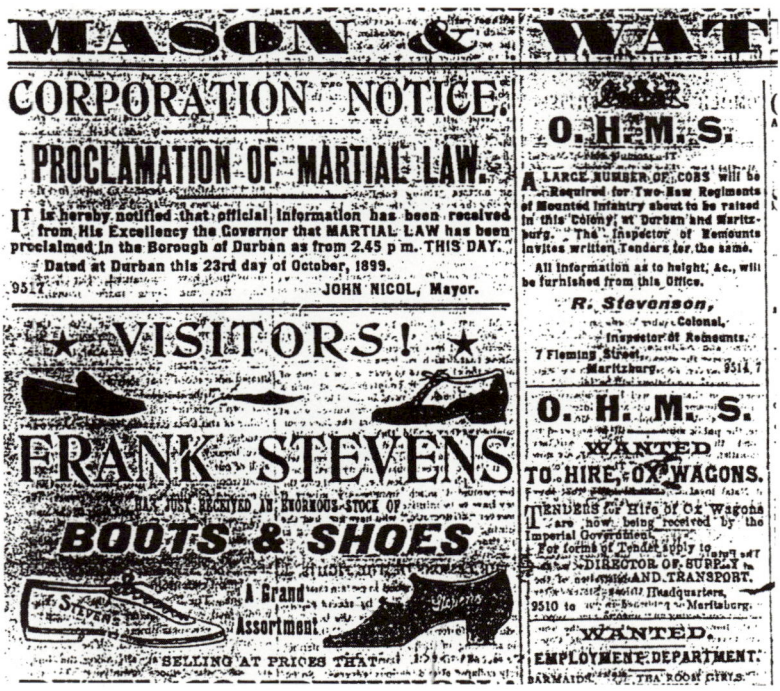

The first commandant, Colonel EC Bethune and the declaration of martial law

Brigadier General Wolfe-Murray and the governor chose to proclaim and commence martial law at 14:45 on 23 October 1899 at precisely the same time that the National Bank of the ZAR in Durban was to be occupied. This was probably a matter of convenience – he needed to have martial law in place before the seizure of the bank. Instructions were issued to the newly appointed commandant, Colonel Bethune.

On 30 October 1899, Colonel Bethune, who evidently supplied the governor with a daily report, recorded that Durban was quiet: 'I have a patrol on the Berea every night ... I have found it necessary to put a guard on the Umgeni Bridge, about four miles away, as the road over it corresponds directly with Zululand and strange men have been seen riding from the town on several occasions.'[25]

The following day Hely-Hutchinson was informed that he could raise further forces for the defence of Durban. General White in Ladysmith had more or less accepted standing a siege there and Pietermaritzburg and Durban would have to look after themselves. The general officer commanding, lines of communication, had the idea of preparing a fortification at Fort Napier and arming it with long range 12-pounder guns from the Royal naval cruisers *Powerful* and *Terrible*. The main difficulty the governor foresaw was the problem of women and children, 'as although we should not defend the town itself Boers are capable of shelling it'. He also noted that Durban was crammed: '... the Prime Minister estimates number of women and children at 10 000 including refugees. Have you any room at Cape ports and can you help in the event of one having to ask them to go?' He also recorded that the commandant in Durban had ordered the submission of proposals for the defence of the town.[27]

At the end of October 1899, Captain Lambton of the Royal Navy, who was on his way to Ladysmith with two 4.7-inch guns and three long-range 12 pounders taken from HMS *Powerful*, called on Hely-Hutchinson and informed him that HMS *Terrible* at Cape Town could make a similar contribution to the defence of Durban and Pietermaritzburg. Then Hely-Hutchinson told General Wolfe-Murray, Colonel Hinde of the Border Regiment and Major Gaisford, the commandant of Pietermaritzburg, about the idea, and they agreed to wait for the initial results from Ladysmith. On the 3 November 1899, Hely-Hutchinson also noted that he had been in touch with the senior naval officer regarding the defence of Durban. HMS *Tartar* and *Philomel* were in port, and HMS *Forte* and *Terrible* were expected, while HMS *Powerful* was in the roadstead. Bethune's Mounted Infantry had been enrolled with about 116 horses, while a regiment of Uitlander infantry was being formed to assist with defence.

At this time the governor also appears to have been prepared to abandon Pietermaritzburg: 'No attempt will be made to defend the town itself against anything more than a raid. Any attempt to defend the town against an attack in force supported by guns would be useless, and would involve the slaughter of many non-combatants.'[8] He was also making arrangements to send all the confidential papers from his office to

HMS *Terrible*, 1899 (Newnes).

Captain Lambton, RN (Newnes).

Durban, and commented that he would stay and take his chances with the troops in the fort and see that his cyphers were burnt in case of disaster.

Captain Percy Scott: the second commandant

It was at this stage that the reality of the war struck home to Durban. The possibility that Boer commandos would reach and capture the port of Durban by Christmas was no longer an idle boast. Captain Percy Scott of the Royal Navy, who was on his way from Cape Town at that stage, was appointed military commandant of Durban, thereby succeeding Colonel Bethune. Between 2 November and 7 November 1899, a barrage of 21 telegrams passed between the governor in Pietermaritzburg, the Royal Navy in Durban and Simonstown and the general communications in Estcourt regarding the appointment. What precipitated this was the arrival of Royal naval vessels in Durban with officers senior to Colonel Bethune. Hely-Hutchinson requested Captain Bearcroft of HMS *Philomel* to 'take charge, for the present of defence arrangements at Durban ...'. In turn, Bearcroft informed the governor that HMS *Forte* had arrived and stated that 'she is senior to me'. Bearcroft thought that Bethune should remain commandant and that he would work with him. HMS *Terrible*, a cruiser, was due to arrive within days, however, and her captain was senior to both those present in Durban. Hely-Hutchinson then sought the views of Admiral Harris in Simonstown. The Admiral recommended that Captain Percy Scott of the *Terrible* should take over. Hely-Hutchinson then requested Scott to take charge of defences and take over as commandant, but not before General Wolfe-Murray pedantically pointed out that the veteran commander, Colonel Stevenson was also senior to Colonel Bethune.[29] On the 7 November, Scott's appointment came into force and Colonel Bethune thereafter devoted his time to the training of his mounted infantry corps.

NOTICE.

NOTICE is hereby given that I have appointed Captain PERCY SCOTT, R.N., H.M.S. "Terrible," to take charge of the defence of Durban, and have also appointed him Commandant of Durban.

(sd.) WALTER HELY-HUTCHINSON, Governor.

Government House,
Pietermaritzburg, Natal.
7th November, 1899.

_____

NOTICE.

Commandant's Office is at New Buildings in West Street, opposite Court House.

By order

HMS *Racoon* in the Bay of Natal, 1899 (KCL).

Captain Percy Scott (Industries).

Umgeni River valley looking northwards (LHM).

Scott wasted no time. Having arrived on board the HMS *Terrible* on 6 November 1899, and having been appointed from 7 November, he could report on the same day to the governor by special messenger on details of the defence of Durban: 'everything is now in place and I consider the town safe against an attack by the enemy.'[30] Within 48 hours, the entire traditional defence pattern for the town had been completely altered, since Scott now turned his attentions to the control over the immediate hinterland of Durban and specially the two major river valleys which formed its outer boundaries. The details of his defence measures included the following:

To the Northward.
One 4.7" and six twelve-pounders are in positions on the Berea Ridge, commanding all the main roads and approaches from the Northward.
To the Eastward.
Six twelve-pounders are in position to command the Umgeni Bridge and Valley: this valley is also commanded by guns at the entrance to the Umgeni River.
To the Westward.
Six twelve-pounders are in position to sweep the open country west of Clairmont.
Two 6" guns in the Bluff Fort are manned and can command both the Eastern and Western approaches to the town.
Two armoured trains are on the line with three-pounders mounted on them; one train works to Claremont, the other to Umgeni.

Her Majesty's Ships '*Forte*' and '*Thetis*' are anchored in position to command the Umgeni Valley.

Should the enemy force this cordon three hundred seamen with maxims and rifles are in readiness to land and dispute the streets, which will be barricaded.

Colonel Bethune has kindly undertaken the patrolling and scouting with his cavalry.

'A feathered postman', one of 160 pigeons trained by Mr Hirst of the Durban and Coast Poultry Club (Wilson).

The mouth of the Umgeni River received particular attention from both land and sea, since the telegraph station was located there, and the government of Natal had been reminded of its significance as recently as 5 November 1899 in a general directive from Chamberlain. The events of the next two months, however, were to give precedence to other matters, and only on 27 December 1899 did Hely-Hutchinson respond that 'the landing place for the present cable is protected by the permanent defences of Durban'.[31]

On 17 November 1899, Lord Landsdowne, the secretary of state for war, enquired of Chamberlain as to Scott's jurisdiction and whether it extended to control over the military forces either stationed in Durban or passing through.[32] It is not known what the response was, but it must be assumed that he did not control the military forces.

In addition to these defences, Scott also instituted a pigeon postal system between Durban and Ladysmith. This was ingenious, but must have had some political consequences as the pigeons overflew Pietermaritzburg, and Scott would have therefore been the first to receive important news and information which he would then relay by telegraph to the governor in the capital.[33]

An important component of Scott's defence plan for Durban was the use of two armoured trains which ran north and south from the railway station in the centre of town. These were armed with 3-pounder guns on an open truck. The northwards patrol went as far as the Umgeni Station close to the Umgeni River, while the other went south on the main line as far as Clermont Station (now Clairwood). Both of these trains were under the charge of the Naval Brigade and were in service by 9 November 1899.[34] At Clermont, Scott had established a strong battery of six 12-pounder guns which commanded the Umbilo and Umhlatazana valleys and this site came to be known as Fort Terrible. The position also protected the main rail line to the interior where it crossed the Umbilo River. It is likely, however, that the original position chosen did not have a particularly good line of sight and the 'fort' was later shifted eastwards to higher ground at Wentworth.

Four days after the system was commenced, an experimental armoured train was despatched from Durban up the north coast as far as the Tugela River, departing from Durban at 6:30 and reaching its terminus at 12:25.[35] Scott probably tried this out as a mechanism to thwart any likely movement of Boers down through the north coast from Zululand. The trial was not repeated.

Two days after his arrival, Scott formed up some 450 men on the Market Square where Medwood Gardens is today and, to the strains of 'A life on the Ocean Wave', marched them out of the town to their various defence positions. There were two 4.7-inch guns, 16 12-pounder guns (thereafter to be known as 'Long 12's'), two 12-pounder 8-cwt guns, two 3-pounder guns, two Nordenfelts (Pom-poms) and four Maxims. By 16:00 all the main approaches to Durban by road or rail were covered by these makeshift weapons with two armoured trains in readiness.

Scott's reputation had preceded him and the people of Durban provided him with every assistance. He was most impressed having come from Cape Town, where an almost carnival atmosphere prevailed with

Armoured train (Kearney collection).

Armoured train (Newnes).

Armoured train on the Zululand line (Edwards).

Unloading naval guns at the Point (KCL).

Naval gun park at Medwood Gardens (KCL).

military and naval authorities spending much time in social gatherings; and this in spite of the rumoured threat of the local Afrikaners rising up in rebellion to assist the Boer republics against the British forces. Now, to be in charge of a loyal civilian population was most encouraging to Scott and led him to record: 'It was a great pleasure to work in loyal Natal.'[36]

The seven gun positions were marked on a map prepared under Scott and four of these have been positively identified. The Bluff and Back Beach batteries were, of course, those which had been in existence since the late 1880s and now they were added to with five others strung out along the western boundary of the town from the Umgeni Mouth in the north, along the ridge of the Berea, to Clermont in the south. Two sites were chosen to overlook the Umgeni valley and the approaches from Zululand. The site for one of the 4.7-inch guns marked 'C' on Scott's map, was located on the property of the Greaves family overlooking Mayville and the main western approach road from Pietermaritzburg. Presently this site is a public park off Charles Henwood Avenue between Tollgate and Nazareth House. The other identified site, 'D', was in Hartley Road in the grounds of Overport House, the property of the Hartley family. Six 12-pounder guns were located here between the house and the stables, to overlook the valleys west of the Berea Ridge.

Once the guns had been emplaced and the defence of Durban secured, Scott set about the training of the gun crews. He is reputed to have been a strict disciplinarian and often drove his men to the maximum. On one occasion he gave an order to the commander of one of the gun crews: 'Take a 4.7-inch gun without oxen to the Umgeni River and fire one round; report time of leaving and time of return.' Five minutes later Scott was informed that they had left, and four hours later Scott rode out to meet the returning squad. They had marched nearly 20 kilometres on a typically hot and humid November day. Nevertheless, when the men, 'who were marching magnificiently' saw Scott, 'they broke into a run'. Scott later admitted that he had never seen a finer sight.[37]

Naval gun at Medwood Gardens (Edwards).

Hauling a gun from HMS *Terrible* up Smith Street, with young ladies catching a ride (KCL).

Naval gun outside the Old Court House in Smith Street (Newnes).

Hauling guns from HMS *Terrible* up Berea Road (Richards).

Naval gun in position on the Berea (KCL).

An apocryphal story exists concerning the gun crews stationed on the grounds of Overport House. Mrs Brandt, William Hartley's granddaughter, recalled that the crews manning the guns used to drag the guns along Hartley Road down to Essenwood Road and back to Overport Drive as a daily exercise. It must be remembered that the roads of the time were mainly sand, in fact when the guns were positioned on one particular site, a team of horses could not drag them through the heavy sand and a large crew of bluejackets was required to move them. The daily routine was evidently to stand the men in good stead when they moved up to the Colenso front a month later. According to Mrs Brandt, Scott also tested the vigilance of the sentries himself by posing as a night prowler. On one occasion he was arrested by his own men for not having any identity documents and had to be bailed out of the Musgrave Road police cells the following morning.[38]

After Ladysmith had been encircled, the Boers decided to press on with their original plan of advancing on Durban in order to drive the British into the sea. On 13 November 1899, a commando force of 2 000 men, led by Commandant-General Piet Joubert and General Louis Botha, left their main laager near Colenso and moved down the railway line, bypassing the remaining 2 300 British troops encamped at Chieveley, who were awaiting reinforcements from the coast. After the various actions at Willow Grange, the Boers realised just how vulnerable their position was between the two British forces at Estcourt and Mooi River, and decided to retire, but via Weenen to hide their intentions from the enemy. To the British, it appeared as if the Boers were heading in a south-easterly direction towards the coast and possibly even on to Durban.

This had a marked effect on the citizens of Durban, as they now realised that Boer boasts of having Christmas in their city could become a reality. Because of the possibility of enemy spies in their midst, Captain Scott placed an 23:00 to 5:00 curfew on all the town's residents.[39]

Ironically, at this time there occurred an event that changed the entire direction of the war and relieved the pressure on Durban. On one of the Boer commando incursions, Commandant-General Piet Joubert fell off his horse and suffered severe internal injuries. He immediately withdrew his attacking force and finalised his defence line along the Tugela River. General Botha and some of the younger and more ardent Boer leaders wanted to continue their drive towards Durban, but Joubert denied them the opportunity. Joubert eventually had to hand over command to General Louis Botha and was invalided out of the Natal battle area by train, to a hospital in Pretoria where he later died. But the damage had been done. The Boers had lost the advantage and there was nothing General Botha could do to restore the momentum, because in the meantime British troops, horses and equipment had been pouring into Natal through the port of Durban, and the threat to its capture by the Boer commandos had all but disappeared.

Towards the end of November, General Sir Redvers Buller arrived in Natal to replace General Sir George White, who at that stage was languishing in the besieged town of Ladysmith. When Buller heard of the preparedness and the capabilities of Scott's naval guns and their crews, he immediately ordered two 4.7-inch guns and four 'Long 12's', as the 12-pounder guns were now called, to be sent to the front. By the next morning they were with Buller's army, which was encamped at Chieveley, north of Estcourt.

By 28 November, the main threat had passed and, although martial law was still in operation in Durban, most of the troops and gun crews were stood down. The guns were released for active service at the front and played an active part in the battle of Colenso, which was one of the disastrous battles fought in what became known as 'Black Week'. There were no less than two 4.7-inch guns and 16 'Long 12's' in action at that battle.

Overport House (KCL).

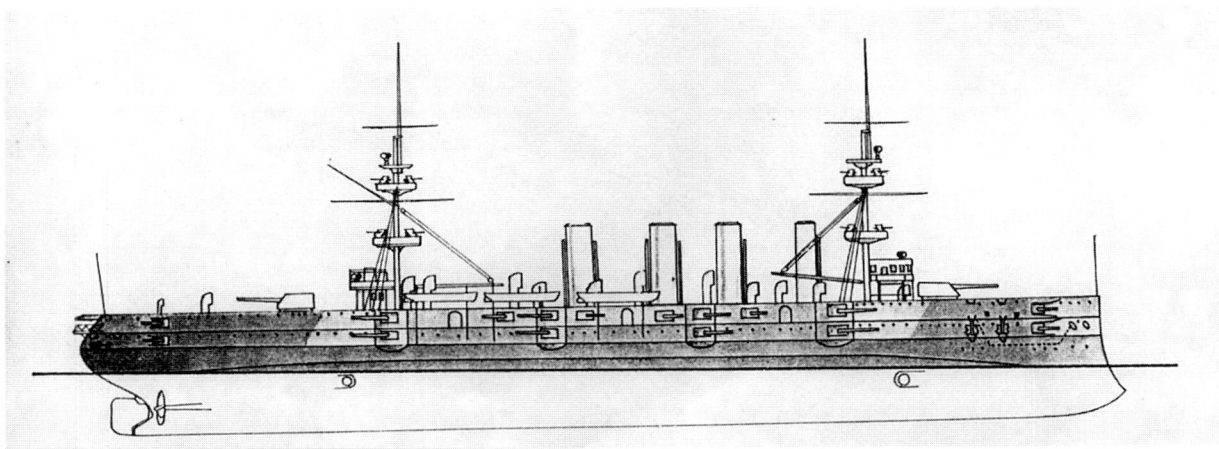

Royal naval ships

One of the most extraordinary elements of the Natal theatre of the Anglo-Boer War was the participation of the Royal Navy in a conflict which was completely based on land. In 1903, Vice-Admiral Sir Robert Harris was called to give evidence and be examined by the Royal Commission of Enquiry into the War.[40] He had prepared his scattered squadron during the three months preceding hostilities and testified that: 'Every one was docked and repaired before the war.' At Simonstown he had the *Doris, Forte, Magicienne, Philomel, Tartar, Barrosa, Barracouta, Monarch, Widgeon, Partridge, Thrush* and the *Dwarf*. After the outbreak of war this fleet was complemented by the *Powerful, Terrible, Niobe, Fearless, Pelorus, Racoon* and the *Thetis*. The first use of naval guns from these ships took place in the defence of Stormberg and then Queenstown in the Eastern Cape where 140 marines and bluejackets manned two short 12-pounder guns.

Harris believed that defending Cape Town and Simonstown, at Milner's request, with a Naval Brigade of 500 men, and ships in Table Bay and False Bay, severely handicapped him in assisting with the war in other places. After the ultimatum he had been ordered by the Admiralty to consider it 'his principal duty to protect the seaports of the coast'. Harris recounted :

> The position at Durban began to get critical. It was not so much at Durban first; it was most critical at Pietermaritzburg. The Governor of Natal, Sir Walter Hely-Hutchinson, was very apprehensive that the Boers might leave Ladysmith and approach by the Greytown road, and come down and carry Pietermaritzburg very easily ... I thought it was quite indefensible, and so it was arranged in the event of any difficulties to retire on Durban, and put all the archives and things on board a man-of-war stationed there ... we lent him two long 12-pounders to mount on Signal

HMS *Terrible* (War Pictures).

HMS *Terrible* and *Powerful* were built in 1894 as Royal Navy cruisers in response to the existence of the Russian cruisers *Rurik* and *Rossia*. They were the first battleships to use the large tube Bellville boiler, eight boiler rooms having 48 such boilers. They had a displacement of 14 200 tons; and were 152.3 m in length; the triple expansion engines developed over 25 000 hp for the twin screws. Each vessel carried twelve 6-inch and two 9.2-inch guns. In addition they were armed with four submerged torpedo tubes, 14 18-inch tubes and four 14-inch tubes. During her visit to South African waters, HMS *Terrible* had a company of 50 officers, 99 petty officers, 277 seamen, 44 ship's boys, 97 marines and an engine room establishment of 294 men, totalling 861 in all.

HMS *Thetis* (Newnes).

Hill at Maritzburg by way of deterring the Boers from approaching ... then the burden of protecting Durban was thrown upon my shoulders by the Admiralty by a telegram ... so I despatched the '*Terrible*' there, and asked that the Captain ... might assume complete control of the place as Military Governor.[41]

The 12 pounders were to join an earlier group of 25 men with a 9-pounder gun and maxim which had been sent from HMS *Tartar* on 29 October 1899.[42] On receipt of another telegram from the Natal governor, Harris then decided to send to Ladysmith a Naval Brigade from HMS *Powerful* with two 4.7-inch guns and four 12-pounders. 'These left Simon's Town in the 'Powerful' forty-eight hours afterwards. I telegraphed to have everything clear at Durban for sending them straight into Ladysmith, and they arrived forty-eight hours afterwards at Durban, and twelve hours after that they were in Ladysmith.'[43]

Harris explained that his reason for deploying men from the two large cruisers – HMS *Terrible* and *Powerful* – to Ladysmith and for the defence of Durban was that the two ships had very large crews and 'they burnt so much coal that they were absolutely beyond my power to keep them complete if I had used them as cruisers ... every time they coaled they required 2 000 tons nearly and sometimes more ... when the '*Terrible*' men were landed for the defence of Durban she was simply tied up useless'. Thus the irony of the awe-inspiring HMS *Terrible*, supposedly lying in guard off Durban, was that she had no coal, few guns and a skeleton crew. Eventually the navy had in the region of 1 400 men and some 22 large guns ashore.

The naval guns

Although the ships were rendered virtually useless, their guns were of great importance. How had such a situation come about; how had it happened that there was such a demand for naval guns while the British army had despatched its artillery to the front? Why were the army's guns outclassed by the guns of a motley collection of farmers, and furthermore, why were the Royal Navy's guns regarded as superior?

Up until the Anglo-Boer War the British army had only been pitted against poorly armed tribesmen in various colonial wars and their guns had to be light and easily transportable. Consequently, their heaviest gun was the 15-pounder (6.8 kg) QF (quick-firing) field gun. It had a range of 5 600 yards (5 km), but it had the advantage of being easily transportable in that it could be brought into battle by a team of horses.[44] There had also been a long-standing argument within the British army, regarding the use of breech-loading (BL) as opposed to muzzle-loading (ML) guns which dated back to the Crimean War. The more conservative echelon in the army preferred the muzzle loaders, because it was felt that a greater muzzle pressure and consequently velocity could be built up in the latter. However, from the Royal Navy's point of view, this argument

Naval 12-pounder gun with a shore mounting on HMS *Terrible* (PAR).

had been settled in 1879 when one of their first turret battleships, HMS *Thunderer*, had its front turret destroyed by a double-loaded muzzle loader, which had exploded, killing all the members of the gun crew. Thereafter, the navy concentrated on improving muzzle velocity by increasing the length of the barrel and by using breech loading. Weight was not a problem as these guns were mounted in battleships, where extra displacement was of little consequence. Thus it was that the navy was years ahead of the army when it came to the development of long-range guns.

The Boers had embarked upon a major rearming drive as a result of the ill-fated Jameson Raid of 1896. They had realised that war with Britain was inevitable and had sent their military leaders to Europe to purchase as many guns as possible. Their choice of rifle was the high-powered, low-trajectory Mauser, which in the hands of a skilled marksman was a deadly weapon and was used to devastating effect against the British.

When it came to artillery, they opted for the 75mm Creusot QF and the 75mm Krupps QF field guns, which were generally regarded as the best in the world at that stage. Both these guns had ranges in excess of 6 000 yards (5.5 km) for percussion shells and their shell weights were 11.5 lbs (5.2 kg) and 13.5 lbs (6.1 kg) respectively. As their defensive or fortress guns, they chose the famous 155mm Creusots which were to be known as the 'Long Toms'. They had a range of 11 000 yards (10 km) and a shell weight of 94 lbs.(42 kg)[45] However, these guns were originally intended for use in the various forts constructed around Pretoria and it was never anticipated that they would be used as field guns.

The 155mm Creusot had been developed as a result of the Franco-Prussian War of 1870 and was designed to be used as a defensive siege gun in the siege of Paris. In fact, the French regarded these guns as obsolete when they were sold to the Boer republics as they had already been in service for 25 years by that stage. The Boers, nonetheless, turned them into very effective weapons by using them as field guns. They were transported into action by means of oxen and manpower.

Thus it was that on 24 October 1899, General Sir George White sent his desperate plea from Ladysmith to Hely-Hutchinson, who then forwarded it to Harris in Simonstown: 'In view of heavy guns being brought by General Joubert from the north, I would suggest that the navy be consulted with the view to sending here detachments of bluejackets with guns firing heavy projectiles at long ranges.'[46]

It was shortly before this that Captain Percy Scott arrived in southern African waters as commander of HMS *Terrible*, the first of a line of cruisers which placed Britain at the top of the field in naval technology. Together with its sister ship, HMS *Powerful*, they were the two most powerful cruisers afloat at that time. What was even more significant was that Scott was the Royal Navy's top expert on naval gunnery. In fact, he was almost fanatical on the subject and was known as 'The man who taught the navy to hit the target!'[47] When he joined his first ship in the Royal Navy as a midshipman in 1868, naval gunners had a 99% miss rate and most naval captains regarded gunnery as a waste of time and money. Thirty years later, while in command of HMS *Scylla*, Scott's ship scored an incredible 80% hit rate of the target in a fleet floating-target shooting competition.[48]

Taking a naval gun across the Tugela (Wilson).

Naval guns in action at Colenso (Burne).

Captain Scott superintending the despatch of the guns on HMS *Terrible* at Simonstown (Newnes).

Captain Scott had served in South African waters during the Anglo-Transvaal War in 1881, so he knew what conditions were like. In addition, Scott took cognisance of the fact that the Boer republics had no navies of their own and that there was not likely to be much of a threat from the sea. But he also realised that the Boer republics were superior when it came to artillery, both in range and rate of fire. While in Cape Town, and on his own initiative, he immediately set about resolving the problem. He took the gun barrel off one of his 12-pounder (5.4 kg) QF anti-torpedo boat guns and mounted it on a pair of gun trails made out of 12-inch (30 cm) square timber baulks from his patent target drogue. This was then mounted on a pair of Cape wagon wheels which he had bought in Cape Town, thereby transforming the gun into a very effective field weapon. It fired the same size shell as the army's 12-pounder gun, but had a range of 8 000 yards (7.3 km).[49]

Scott then approached Rear-Admiral Harris with a suggestion that such guns could play a major role in the war against the Boer republics. While they were talking, Harris, who, on the advice of his gunnery lieutenant thought General White's request for long-range naval guns impossible to fulfil, handed to Scott White's desperate plea for help. Scott felt that there was no difficulty in carrying out White's request and, by the following evening, had succeeded in mounting two 4.7-inch (12 cm) pedestal guns onto two fixed timber platforms comprising several baulks of timber, (possibly railway sleepers) bolted together at right angles to each other. Holding-down bolts were fitted with nuts at the top to facilitate loosening and thereby allowed mobility.[50] These guns were successfully test fired on the hills overlooking Simonstown and, together with the 12-pounder (5.4 kg) field guns Scott had already constructed, were despatched post-haste on HMS *Powerful* to Durban, so that they could be used to assist General White in Ladysmith.

Naval 6-inch gun mounted on a railway truck (Wilson).

Detail of gun mounting and wheels, naval gun park, Medwood Gardens (NSL).

During the voyage to Durban in the first week of November 1899, Scott had designed and fabricated the mountings for a 4.7-inch field gun, much along the lines of the 12-pounders. He had used the barrels from the coastal defence guns at the Cape and mounted them on 12-foot long timber baulk trailers, which may have been part of the floating drogue. The wheels were made out of four-foot (121 cm) diameter steel plates with mild steel angle spokes rivetted to them. These were then fitted with four-inch (10 cm) wide steel rims and tyres, and mounted on a four-inch square wrought-iron crosstree by means of a standard wagon wheel hub. Unfortunately, the wheelbase was too narrow and tended to overturn when used on uneven ground.

In addition to the 4.7-inch and 'Long 12' field gun modifications, Scott also designed a timber carriage for a 6-inch (15 cm) field gun. This time he took a 6-inch gun barrel off the HMS *Terrible* and, as before, mounted it onto a pair of 12-inch x 12-inch timber baulk trails, possibly from one of his patent floating target drogues, and the whole contraption was mounted onto a pair of spare 4.7-inch gun wheels, but reinforced with 6-inch wide iron tyres to take the heavier load.

When Buller was asked if he would like one of these 6-inch guns, he replied that Admiral Harris had said that he (Buller) was not to denude the Royal Navy's ships of their guns and therefore he could not accept one. Afterwards, Scott maintained that if Buller had had half a dozen of his 6-inch guns at the Tugela, Ladysmith would have been relieved three months earlier. This was because even the army's best weapons were within range of overhead shrapnel bursts from the Boers' mausers and the 6-inch guns would have been far more effective against the Boers entrenched along the Tugela.

However, when Buller was away at Spioenkop on 10 January 1900, General Barton asked Scott if he could provide a 4.7-inch gun mounted on a railway truck in order to shell a new Boer position. Scott had a pedestal 4.7-inch gun mounted on a platform, similar to those which had been sent to Ladysmith, but he cut the cross members short to allow it to pass through the numerous railway tunnels en route. The whole device was secured to the railway truck with chains. This gun was named the 'Lady Randolph Churchill' after Winston Churchill's mother. With this particular gun, Scott kept the recoil cylinder under the barrel as it was used on board ship. As the cylinder was intended to absorb most of the recoil, the gun could be fired at right angles to the railway track without overturning. Three more guns were constructed along these lines and were used to great effect at Peter's Hill, where they laid a creeping barrage ahead of the advancing British troops. Buller actually preferred these guns to the wheeled field gun version, because the recoil system absorbed most of the firing stresses, and, being rigidly mounted, the gun did not move on firing, thereby allowing a greater rate of fire.

Notwithstanding Buller's original refusal to take a modified 6-inch gun, at 16:00 on Thursday 8 February 1900, he urgently signalled for such a weapon on a wheeled carriage for the final attack on Pieter's Hill: 'Have you any 6in guns on carriages that I could move a mile or so across the flat in Durban. If you have telegraph in my name to the admiral and ask him if I may have them for a few days. Utmost importance. If pos-

The problem of recoil proved to be a major difficulty with all the Scott designs in that they had to be held in position with chains and then re-laid after each firing. In addition, the enormous stresses were splitting the timber rails. In the words of Lieutenant Burne:

... the hastily improvised gun-carriage of the 12 pounders had, on account of this very haste, the following defects:

(1) Too weak generally in all parts, particularly wheels and axles, for any long campaign.
(2) Wheels and axles being a scratch lot, none in any of the batteries were interchangeable, which caused many times later in the campaign when wheels began to give out, much anxiety.(sic) Several times we had only guns ready for action or trekking by the 'skin of one's teeth', and it must be borne in mind that any new wheels wired-for sometimes took two months to arrive on the very overcrowded railway – a single line.
(3) The system of checking the recoil of the field carriage was a bad one.

In particular the gun trail consisted of a timber block some 12 feet long, and when the gun was laid for a range of over 7 000 yards (6.4 km), the oil cylinder would 'bring up against this trail and so prevent laying'. This necessitated digging special pits for the trails. Burne noted that the real solution was to make a carriage with a steel trail of two plates with a space between. After the relief of Ladysmith, a number of the guns were modified in the locomotive workshops of the NGR in Durban, channel iron trails and hydraulic spade restraints being fitted. Despite observing the additional problems of narrow axles and high wheels, which resulted in a number of accidents, and the lack of a braking mechanism, Burne clarified his criticisms:

I simply wish to point out details that, if more time had been available, would certainly have been avoided in them by their very clever designer, Captain Percy Scott, R.N., to whom the service in general (and I personally) owe a debt of gratitude; for assuredly not a Q.-F.gun or a single one of us with the batteries would ever have been landed unless it had been for him and his brains and his determination to have the Royal Navy represented in the campaign ... [51]

4.7-inch gun mounted on a railway truck (KCL).

The 6-inch gun with wheeled carriage at the NGR workshops (KCL).

sible I want them Monday 12th instant and you to work them.'[52]

A 6-inch barrel was brought ashore from HMS *Terrible* and some unwanted 4.7-inch gun wheels were delivered from Pietermaritzburg. Under the supervision of GW Reid, the locomotive superintendent of the railway workshops in Durban, the gun was fitted to a carriage with wider tyres to withstand the heavier weight. The gun was ready by midnight on Saturday. It was then dragged to the Back Beach by bluejackets and test fired on Sunday. By that evening it was loaded onto a train at the Durban Station and delivered to Buller at Chievely at dawn on Monday 12 February 1900 in time for the battle of Tugela Heights.

In 1909, when Scott met Louis Botha at the Pre-Union Conference in Durban, Botha is purported to have said to Scott, '... that but for the Naval guns, the *Vierkleur* would have flown over Durban's Town Hall'.[53]

A sequence of illustrations showing the test firing of the 6-inch gun at the beachfront on Sunday 11 February 1900 (LHM and KCL).

A mobile searchlight mounted on a railway truck at the Durban Station (Edwards).

A mobile searchlight in action (Newnes).

Scott's mobile searchlights

Besides his ingenious modifications of naval guns and his effective defence plan for Durban, Scott contributed another useful device for assisting with communications: the mobile searchlight. In 1898 he had already taken out a British patent for a venetian-blind type of signalling lamp and, while he was in Cape Town in October 1899, he adapted it for use with a ship's searchlight mounted on an open truck powered by a motor and dynamo on an adjacent truck. The system was known as 'the Natal blind' and, with some modifications, the idea has been used by the Royal Navy up to today.

From Pietermaritzburg, and later from Estcourt, the British troops could communicate at night with the besieged forces in Ladysmith by reflecting morse messages off high clouds. Later, more powerful projectors were added to the system, which overcame the Boers' attempts to interfere with messages by using their own lights. Buller required one late in November 1899 and requested 'a vertical compound engine from the Pietermaritzburg corporation' to be railed to him at once.[54]

The Royal Engineers were to report fully on the employment of searchlights in Natal.[55] The first, arranged by Scott, was initially used at Fort Napier in Pietermaritzburg, and was cobbled together with a direct-driven dynamo and engine from a tug in the Durban harbour, and a projector loaned from the Natal Harbour Board. It was mounted on an ox wagon and worked by an 8 hp boiler. Four civilians – FF Parker, H McMurtrie, C Porter and E Bell – were engaged to work the light, while Lance Corporal Bradley of the King's Royal Rifles was trained as the signaller. General Hildyard claimed that they could read the messages from Estcourt some 60 miles (96 km) away, while there were also similar claims from Ladysmith, 35 miles (56 km) further on. When the light was pushed forward, a 'Rustin Proctor' 8 hp portable boiler was substituted. The remainder of the plant consisted of a Siemens compound dynamo and engine; a projector with signalling shutter; a 60 cm parabolic glass mirror, a lamp, carbons and 1-inch negatives. On 19 November 1899, the plant was used from Estcourt to establish direct communication with Ladysmith. When Estcourt itself became silenced, a second and duplicate light was ordered from Durban. This light was manned by two officers of the Royal Navy and five bluejackets, and was fixed to a rail truck. Eventually the signalling teams found that the best system was to reflect off the edges of clouds, but the slow rate at which the cypher messages were sent caused problems in reading them accurately.

Evidently, the zig-zag sweeps made by the Boer searchlights, sometimes for up to three hours, did not seriously interfere with the transmission as the different lights could be easily identified. In addition, the searchlights were used to detect Boer positions and trenches. Once the British forces moved off the rail line, the advantages of the first ox-drawn model became obvious. Twenty oxen pulled the portable engine and by then it was manned by a staff of 21 including 15 African assistants. The 'wagon did its own foraging for fuel', with coal being carried on a second wagon, while water was hauled on a third in a 2 270 litre tank. A fourth wagon carried the dynamo and engine and the projector was placed on a fifth, with a grand total of 80 oxen involved – a wonderful example of mixed technologies !

On 20 January 1900, the light was taken across the Tugela, where it was used every night until 5 February 1900, when it was shelled by the Boers and forced to retire. As much as 362 kg of coal, 1800 litres of water and 2½ pairs of carbons were used in nine to ten hours work each night. Later the lights were also found useful in illuminating night work on the Tugela bridge repairs.

After the war, Captain Lloyd Owen of the Royal Engineers detailed a list of searchlight stores left over. This included numerous portable plants, dynamos and several projectors of different types.[56] He noted projectors with diameters varying from 90 cm to 30 cm and that the four extant, portable plants were only capable of running projectors smaller than 60 cm.

Captain Scott's last report

Before leaving Durban, Captain Scott submitted a comprehensive report to Governor Hely-Hutchinson on his term of office as commandant of Durban between November 1899 and March 1900. He outlined the various sections of his work and the details of his office. In this work he had been primarily assisted by Major HR Bousfield, a local attorney and a reserve officer of the Natal Volunteer Force. Bousfield was specifically appointed for his local knowledge, not only of Durban, but about the complex web of colonial administration and government. Scott recorded:

> He was appointed by Your Excellency at the beginning of my term of office and has been my right hand throughout: his local knowledge was of great assistance to me in the disposition of the guns for the defence of Durban; his legal knowledge has been invaluable to me in dealing with many of the intricate matters which have come before me.[57]

Cullinan, the assistant paymaster of the *Terrible*, had served as his secretary. Scott also acknowledged the help he had received from Sergeant EN Brooke of the Natal Police; TO Fraser, the censor; Superintendent RC Alexander of the Borough Police; Harrison, the government inspector of the National Bank of the ZAR and Commander AH Limpus of HMS *Terrible*, who had obviously taken over command of the vessel on Scott's appointment as commandant.

The report included matters relating to 'spies and suspected persons, of whom there are at present several still under detention in the gaol at Durban; numbers of others having been examined and dealt with ...', and Scott added that: 'There are still a large number of suspects detained in Durban on parole or under supervision.' He then reported on the supervision of passenger traffic up and down the coast and dealing with travel applications to Delagoa Bay and other east coast ports. Censorship also fell under his control, as did the detention of goods 'intended for the enemy, and preventing trade with the enemy ...'.

A naval 4.7-inch gun from HMS *Philomel* at Peter's Hill, 27.2.1900 (Riall).

Major Henry Bousfield

Henry Ritchings Bousfield had a long and distinguished career in the local militia, the colonial civil service and as an advocate of the supreme courts of both Natal and the Cape. He had been born at Winchester, England, the eldest son of Bishop Henry Brougham Bousfield who became the first Anglican Bishop of Pretoria and who was expelled from there by the Boers in January 1900. During the Sekukuni Wars in the Transvaal (1880) Henry Ritchings had been in charge of the advanced field depot at Lydenburg; then acted as a clerk in the Natal administration of the Transvaal in 1881; he was appointed to the colonial secretary's office in Pietermaritzburg in the same year; then the resident magistrate's office in Durban in 1883. In 1885 he was chief clerk and clerk of the court in Durban and in 1889 and 1890, acting magistrate of Durban. He resigned from the civil service in 1890 to practise as an advocate and notary public, being made a barrister-at-law of the Inner Temple in London in 1892. He had served as a lieutenant in the Royal Durban Rifles and later as the commanding officer of their successor regiment, the DLI, from 1893. He retired from the DLI as an honorary colonel in 1902. Bousfield married Coral, the second daughter of Harry Escombe in 1890.[58]

Scott went on to China in March 1900 where the guns were used in the Boxer Rebellion. He returned to Durban as admiral of a Royal Naval squadron on the cruiser *Good Hope* in 1908. He and 40 officers travelled to Johannesburg where they were given a civic luncheon by the mayor and feted by the town. He returned again in 1909 to attend the opening of the Union Convention in Durban: 'It was not the first time that its commander had hurried to Durban in view of an anticipated visit from General Botha and his colleagues.' Scott predicted the dangers posed by U-boats and aerial bombing before World War 1 broke out. He retired in 1913 and was knighted for his services to the navy. However, he was brought back to the navy as an adviser on naval gunnery and is credited with the establishment of the Anti-Aircraft Corps in 1915. His memoirs were published in 1919 and he died in 1924. The 'running of the guns' was introduced into the Royal Tattoo in 1907 and became an entrenched exercise until 1999.

HMS *Good Hope* at the Point docks, 1908 (KCL).

It was specifically in these two areas that he revealed a degree of high-handedness. The very energetic and decisive qualities which he had brought to bear in matters concerning the military defence of the town, and the quite remarkable way he had established a clear and effective plan in a very short time, together with his technical ingenuity, could not so easily be observed of his dealings with civil and commercial society. A matter in case was the seizures of various 'prizeships'. And when Hely-Hutchinson, in a glowing tribute to Scott, said that he had 'discharged his duties with tact and firmness',[59] he might have later regretted the use of the word 'tact', for it was to be the unfortunate lot of the commandants who succeeded Scott to repair the damage which this 'firmness' had caused; firmness, yes – but tact, not quite.

Over and above these matters the other facets of his administration of the town had included the general 'supervision and maintenance of law and order'; the introduction of night passes and a curfew; regulating the work of the banks, specifically in terms of economic issues concerned with the Boer republics; supervising the recruitment of local volunteers; and working with the port authorities leading to his special praise for the port captain – Ballard.

Scott appended an updated version of his November 1899 explanation of the defence plan for the town to this report. His directives had included the protection of the main water supply by mounting two 12-pounder guns on the hill which overlooked the Umlaas water works. The position was entrenched and held by a party of seamen and marines. Harry Escombe had made arrangements for the patrolling of the conduits and the surrounding countryside. In November 1899, Cathcart Methven, a former harbour engineer, had offered his services to the governor, specifically in connection with the protection of the water supply which he considered to be 'our weak point'. The commandant and the mayor rejected his offer of assistance, claiming that: 'our Borough Engineer [is] quite able to deal with the water supply'.[60]

Scott concluded his report with a detailed precis, together with photographs, of the various modifications which he had made to the naval guns. On the 14 March 1900, he submitted the report to the governor. Some two weeks prior to this, the Admiralty had informed Hely-Hutchinson that the *Terrible* was urgently required at the China station and asked him to replace Scott as commandant. Scott resumed command of the *Terrible* and departed from Durban on 21 March 1900.

Notwithstanding the abrasive aspects of his administration, the municipality gave him a civic banquet before his departure and for his services he became a Companion of the Order of the Bath. He was also showered with further praise by both Chamberlain and Hely-Hutchinson, and on his return to England in October 1902, he was made a Companion of the Royal Victorian Order, upgraded in 1906 to Knight Commander.

The later commandants

Scott was replaced by Colonel AW Morris, who had been a member of the 'old Northamptonshire Regiment – the Steelbacks', and had already served in the British forces in Natal in 1879 and 1881. Despite the fact that any real threat to the town had passed with the changing face of the war, he nevertheless had the difficult task of patching up problem areas left behind by his predecessor, which he appears to have carried out with success. One of his duties was to initiate some recognition for Major Bousfield, who returned to his professional life in September 1900. Morris thought him: 'an officer of exceptional abilities, far sighted and hardworking, and in losing his services, I am losing an excellent staff officer. He has always been ready to give his professional advice, (he being a barrister) which on numerous occasions has been most valuable.'[61] However, one is left with the question as to why Scott did not make greater use of Bousfield's legal skills, especially in his dealings with the commercial and shipping world. Morris went on to serve for nine months, until January 1901, and in turn was succeeded by Lieutenant Colonel WHS O'Neil who served until February 1902, and then Colonel Simpson before the post of commandant was abolished on 15 November 1902.[62]

1. Isaacs, N, *Travels and Adventures in Eastern Africa*, p.25.

2. Bird, C, *Annals of Natal*, pp.432–432.

3. Ibid., p.728.

4. Van Zyl, DA, *The Anglo-Zulu War of 1879 and its Economic Consequences for the Colony of Natal*, p.97.

5. PAR, M2/492/2: *Design for Two Gun Battery*, Bluff, Major Rathbone, 11.6.1887.

6. PAR, *Bluebook for Natal*, Vol. 2, PWD report, p.4.

7. PAR, NDR 5/11: *Report on Bluff battery*, 7.9.1910.

8. PRO, CAB 11/34/2: *Defence scheme for Durban*, February 1899, p.4.

9. PRO, CAB 11/34/2: *Defence scheme for Durban*, February 1899, p.5.

10. Henderson, C, Durban: *Fifty Years of Municipal History*, pp.328–333.

11. DAR, 3/DBN 5/2/7/1/1: town council sanitary committee, 1867–1875.

12. PRO, CO 179/208: documents relating to Durban defences, 18.5.1899.

13. *Royal Commission on the War in South Africa*, p.131.

14. Ibid., p.131.

15. Ibid., p.131.

16. PAR, CSO 1623: mayor to colonial secretary, 19.8.1899.

17. PAR, CSO 1623: Colonel Royston to prime minister, 24.8.1899.

18. PRO, CO 179/208: documents relating to arms in Natal, 18.9.1899.

19. PRO, CO 179/208: Hely-Hutchinson to Admiralty, 18.9.1899.

20. PRO, CO 179/208: Hely-Hutchinson to general officer commanding, 17.10.1899.

21. PRO, CO 179/207: Hely-Hutchinson to Chamberlain, 26.10.1899.

22. PRO, CO 179/207: Hely-Hutchinson to general officer commanding, 26.10.1899.

23. PRO, WO 132/24: Buller: notes on the war, 8.11.1899.

24. Ibid.

25. Ibid.

26. PRO, CO 179/210: Bethune to Hely-Hutchinson, 30.10.1899.

27. PRO, CO 179/209: Hely-Hutchinson to Milner, 31.10.1899.

28. PRO, CO 179/207: Hely-Hutchinson to Chamberlain, 3.11.1899.

29. PRO, CO 179/207: governor to secretary of state, 9.11.1899.

30. PRO, CO 179/207: governor to secretary of state, 7.11.1899.

31. PRO, CO 179/208: governor to colonial office, 27.12.1899.

32. PRO, CO 179/208: secretary of state for war to Chamberlain, 17.11.1899.

33. PRO, CO 179/207: governor to colonial secretary, 9.11.1899.

34. PAR, MJPW 116: general manager NGR to prime minister, 8.11.1899.

35. PAR, MJPW 71: general manager NGR to minister of lands and works, 11.11.1899.

36. Hall, DD, et al., The Naval Guns in Natal 1899–1900, *SA Military History Journal*, V4/3, June 1978, p.78.

37. Ibid.

38. SABC Radio interview with Mrs Brandt, 17.3.1936.

39. Bridgeland, T, *Fieldgun Jack versus the Boers: The Royal Navy in South Africa*, p.51.

40. *Royal Commission on the War in South Africa*, pp.382–384.

41. Ibid., p. 384.

42. PRO, CO 179/208: Admiralty to secretary of state, 29.10.1899.

43. *Royal Commission on the War in South Africa*, p.384.

44. Hall, p.81.

45. Ibid., p.6.

46. PRO, CO 179/207: Hely-Hutchinson to Chamberlain, 24.10.1899.

47. Gray, E, Sir Percy Scott – The man who taught the Navy to hit the target, *Military History*, 11/8/115, August 1983, p.350.

48. Ibid.

49. Padfield, P, *Aim Straight*, p.95.

50. Brooks, R, *The Long Arm of Empire*, p.217.

51. Burne, CRN, *With the Naval Brigade in Natal*, p.104.

52. PRO, CO 179/210: governor to colonial secretary, 16.3.1900.

53. Ibid., Hall, p.78.

54. PAR, GH 563: commandant, Durban to mayor, Pietermaritzburg, 28.11.1899.

55. PRO, WO 108/296: report of the work of the Royal Engineers in Natal, 1899–1902, pp.16–21.

56. PAR, GH 536: general officer commanding to the governor, 23.2.1903.

57. PRO, CO 179/210: governor to colonial secretary, 16.3.1900.

58. *Natal Who's Who*, p.20.

59. PRO, CO 179/210: Hely-Hutchinson to Chamberlain, 13.3.1900.

60. PAR, MJPW 71: Methven to prime minister, 10.11.1899.

61. PRO, CO 179/214: Commandant Morris to colonial secretary, 4.10.1900.

62. PAR, IRD 12: commandant to IRD, 6.11.1902.

PART TWO

DURBAN: A WARRIOR'S GATEWAY

The arrival of the Prince of Wales and West Yorkshire Regiments (Riall).

A sergeant of the 2nd battalion of the Royal Lancaster Regiment (Matthews collection).

CHAPTER 4

NARRATIVES OF THE ARRIVAL AND DEPARTURE OF BRITISH TROOPS

Dave Matthews

'Durban is a very pretty place from the sea'

It was reported in the *Natal Mercury* of 6 June 1899 that rumours of the mobilisation of British troops in South Africa had been emphatically denied by both the war office and the colonial office. It was also reported in the same issue that, on 5 June 1899, the USS *Gascon* had arrived in Cape Town with 500 troops on board to relieve British troops whose period of duty had expired.

This denial was soon proved to be incorrect. By September 1899 the war office, which was expecting a war, had requested additional forces to be sent to South Africa to protect the colonies of Natal and the Cape. The military authorities in India were especially prompt in responding to this request, and troops and equipment started to arrive in Durban on 3 October 1899. The movement of these troops to the Transvaal border triggered the start of the war on 11 October 1899. The Boers attacked the British forces on several fronts and inflicted a number of severe defeats. By the end of October, the Boers had besieged Mafeking, Kimberley and Ladysmith. Britain was thus obliged to send in further troops in order to relieve those under siege and to ease the embarrassing situation they found themselves in.

These and many more troops were subsequently to pass through the port of Durban en route to the interior. It was thus not surprising that Durban played a significant role as a gateway for the arrival and departure of British troops from many different units and regiments from all corners of the British empire. Besides the statistics and details relating to these 'warriors', a number of personal narratives have survived, which provide accounts of travel experiences and of their arrival in Durban.

When the war began, there were 27 054 imperial troops in South Africa, compared to the more than one million troops armed and available throughout the empire. These were of many different religions, races and classes. Subsequently, on 28 July 1899, the British prime minister made a declaration, which would exclude a vast body of men from the campaign, announcing that only white soldiers would be employed for the forthcoming engagement. Even though this declaration was not strictly adhered to, it meant that the distribution of available white men outside the United Kingdom was 67 921 in India, 3 699 in Egypt, 7 496 in Malta, 5 104 in Gibraltar, 738 in Barbados, 170 in Jamaica, 1 599 in Canada, 1 896 in Bermuda, 962, in Mauritius 1 589 in China and Hong Kong, and 1 407 in the Straits settlements.[1]

Thousands of these available men were sent to South Africa, and eventually the British forces in South Africa were reinforced by no fewer than 448 495 officers and men. Of these, 584 officers and 17 950 men came from British garrisons in India. Most of the soldiers who landed in Durban were from India and exceeded troops from other colonies such as Canada, the Australian colonies and New Zealand, although the 337 219 servicemen sent from Britain still outnumbered any other group by far.

Arrangements for conveying troops to South Africa

During the invasion of the Falkland Islands in 1982, the general public expressed astonishment not only in Britain, but in other quarters, that such a massive operation, involving the movement of vast quantities of troops, equipment and supplies to such a remote part of the world had been possible in such a short space of time.

More than 100 years before, in 1876, the army sea transport department was so well organised that a considerable force could be shipped overseas at short notice.[2] Full particulars of all suitable ships for the transport of men and materials were recorded and frequently updated. Equipment and supplies for the conveyance of 55 000 men and 10 000 horses were permanently available.[3]

All army sea transport work was carried out by the Admiralty through its transport department, with the following exceptions: arrangements for the Indian contingent, the remounts and anything else sent from India, were made by the director of Indian Marine for the outward voyage, and by the Admiralty for the return voyage. For the colonial contingents, passage was provided partly in freight ships, locally engaged by the colonial governments, and partly in Admiralty transports sent from the Cape. The return voyage in all cases was regulated by the Admiralty. Remounts from ports abroad were conveyed in freight ships hired by the remount department up until February 1901. Thereafter they were transported by the Admiralty.[4]

It is necessary to differentiate between freight ships and transports. Troops were carried either in a freight ship or in a transport. A freight ship is one in which the whole or a portion of the accommodation is engaged at a rate per head or for a lump sum for a specific voyage. A transport is a vessel wholly taken up by the government on a time charter.[5]

The method by which the government carried out the sea transport of the army was as follows: the Board of Admiralty, as agents for, and on the requisition of, the secretary of state for war, undertook all the work, except coastwise conveyance in the United Kingdom. From 1 April 1888, army sea transport had been always charged to the army instead of the navy, but the control of the Admiralty over the transport service remained unaffected. The Admiralty had always held that the work could only be efficiently and satisfactorily carried out by a naval department. For convenience sake, the director of transports was placed in direct communication with the war office in respect of all ordinary matters. An officer of the quartermaster-general's department visited the transport department frequently, whether in peacetime, or in times of war. He was placed at the Admiralty to assist the director of transports in military matters. The transport department examined all claims chargeable to the

army before they were passed to the war office for payment. The system by which one department did the work while another provided for the cost seems somewhat anomalous, but the experience of the Anglo-Boer War, in which the system was put to a test of some magnitude, conclusively proved that it worked well and demonstrated the necessity of the sea transport service remaining, as it had always been, under the control of the Admiralty.[6]

When, in November 1899, Sir Redvers Buller first decided to divert a large part of the expeditionary force to Natal for temporary work there, it was arranged that sufficient transports should be held empty and in readiness at the various ports to transfer troops back to Cape ports or to reinforce them, mainly from Cape Town. Enough ships to carry a complete army corps had, consequently, to lie idle up and down the coast, in some cases adding to the existing congestion. The reservation of these transports was a very costly affair and, in the end, they were never needed for the intended purpose, but the precaution was one that was perhaps worth paying dearly for, since the time factor was vitally important during the critical weeks of the campaign.[7]

A constant handicap to the work of the embarkation staff and to that of the transports was the loss of men by desertion from the crews. The worst cause of this was the illegal recruiting of the irregular corps, which offered the temptation of high pay and the excitement of active service. As a result transports were often so short handed that only the most strenuous efforts and offers of extravagant rates of pay enabled them to get to sea at all. This evil was dealt with by martial law, though in one instance an officer of an irregular corps was deprived of his commission for recruiting among the crews of the transports.[8]

Landing at Durban

When the British government decided to impose its suzerainty over the South African Republic (Transvaal), the troops already in South Africa were augmented by a further 10 000. The majority of these troops were sent from India and landed at Durban. On 3 October 1899, the *Lalpoora* arrived in Durban from India with troops and equipment of the 21st Field Artillery and the 26th Field Hospital. This was the forerunner of an armada of freight ships which brought troops, equipment and animals to augment the British forces already stationed in South Africa. In one week alone, between 2 and 9 October 1899, 13 ships brought groups from seven different regiments to the war from the subcontinent.

One of the units which came from India was the second battalion of the Gordon Highlanders. They had been warned on 7 September 1899 that they would be leaving for service in Africa and by 11 September the battalion had moved down from Solon to Umballa, north of Delhi, where all the preliminary measures for mobilisation took place. This included fitting new shoes to the horses, the completion of kits and medical inspections. While they were there, 'one hundred and eight of the finest mules arrived from Peshawar'. By 18 September, the unit was entrained

Ships Carrying British regiments from India in 1899[9]		
Date of arrival	**Ship**	**Regiment**
2.10.1899	*Lalpoora*	21st Btn Royal Field Artillery
4.10.1899	*Secundra*	42nd Btn Royal Field Artillery
5.10.1899	*Purnia*	2nd Btn Kings Royal Rifles
5.10.1899	*Booldana*	53rd Btn Royal Field Artillery
5.10.1899	*City of london*	1st Btn Devonshire Regiment
5. 10.1899	*Sutlej*	1st Btn Devonshire Regiment
5.10.1899	*Pundua*	19th Hussars
7.10.1899	*Vadala*	19th Hussars
7.10.1899	*Palitana*	2nd Btn Gordon Highlanders
9.10.1899	*Wardha*	9th Lancers
9.10.1899	*Nurani*	1st Btn 1st Gloucester Regiment, 2nd Btn KRR.
9.10.1899	*Sirsa*	2nd Btn Gordon Highlanders
9.10.1899	*Warora*	19th Hussars

Transport officers at the Bombay docks
(*Black and White Budget*).

Troops boarding transports at the Bombay docks
(*Black and White Budget*).

Guns and munitions shipped to Natal at Bombay
(*Black and White Budget*).

with its baggage, ammunition and transport under extremely hot conditions. Crossing the great Indian desert the Highlanders travelled 'mostly by night and halting in grilling rest-camps by day ...' and the battalion reached Bombay by 23 September from where it sailed on the *Palitana* and the *Sirsa*. It took 16 days to reach Durban where:

> the swell was too heavy for any ship to cross the bar, and both vessels tossed giddily till afternoon ... Many a Briton and many a Boer knew that sickening scend and heave of the Durban swell during the next two years. Many ships remained outside the overcrowded harbour and discharged personnel into lighters; if it was rough, men were shut into a wicker cage, swung overboard by the derrick, and dumped with a crash into the swaying lighter. Boer prisoners who had never seen the sea thought their last hour was come when subjected to this ordeal.[10]

By that evening, the whole battalion had entrained in open trucks for Ladysmith, 'receiving a great ovation – immense enthusiasm all along the line, inhabitants chucked cigarettes, bananas, lemonade, to the men, and cheered like blazes. Much better going on service here than in India, where there are no fellow-countrymen to add the touch of Romance to the departure'.[11]

The port of Durban was extremely busy in the first weeks of October 1899. More than 26 vessels arrived with the majority coming from India. On one day alone, 5 October, no less than five ships arrived from Calcutta and Bombay, carrying over 2 000 men and hundreds of horses and mules. Four days later, a further five ships arrived with equal numbers of troops and animals. Of the 36 ships to arrive in Durban from India between September 1899 and January 1900, 30 came from Bombay. Many of them carried Indian 'followers', at times as many as 378. Ships carrying large numbers of horses and mules, such as the *Nurani*, the *Sirdhana* and the *Nerbudda*, also brought many Indians, probably attendants and members of the initial remount department, though a number would have been the servants of British officers.

However, towards the latter part of October, the numbers began to incorporate ships from further afield. These included the *Avoca*, which disembarked on 12 October, having transported 26 officers and 848 men of the 1st Battalion Royal Irish Fusiliers from Egypt. The first vessel from England, the *Kinfauns Castle*, arrived on 26 October with the 2nd balloon section of the Royal Engineers. Of the ships from places other than India, 11 carried more than 1 000 troops each, with the *Pavonia* having 1 639 on board and the *Bavarian* 1 870.

The arrival of ships in Cape Town, predominately from England, began in earnest on 7 October 1899 with the docking of the *Gaul* from Southampton, carrying the 1st Battalion Northumberland Fusiliers and the Army Ordinance Corps. During the course of the war, the total number of voyages to and from South Africa with troops, animals and stores was about 1 500, representing over 9 000 000 miles (14 480 000 km) of steaming, exclusive of coastal movements.[12]

The Gordon Highlanders entraining at the Point (*The Illustrated London News*, 25 November 1899).

Troops embarking at the customs house quay, Malta for Durban (Newnes).

2nd Rifle Brigade on parade in Cairo before leaving for Durban (Newnes).

British troops embarking at Southampton (Brown).

Life on a troopship

An article appeared in the *Natal Mercury* on Thursday 23 May 1901 which gave local readers some idea of life on a troopship:

The P&O liner S.S. Assaye, transport No.15, left Southampton on April 11th. At about 5 o'clock in the afternoon, bound for South Africa. We had over 1,100 men on board, in command of Lieut-Col. Boyne. Over 500 of these were Metropolitan Mounted Rifles and Imperial Yeomanry, and the rest were South African Constabulary. They were nearly all young men in prime condition. The S.A.C's especially being good specimens of England's young manhood. It was a beautiful sunny afternoon when we left. Crowds were at the pier to see us off. The ladies were throwing oranges for the men to catch.

The inevitable photographers were there also, but the one who enlivened the scene most was an enterprising trumpeter, who played us off with such airs as "The boys of the Old Brigade," "Soldiers of the Queen," and "Old Lang Syne" and so with perpetual cheering, singing and showers of coppers, we got safely out to sea. The pilot left us in the early afternoon with the words "all clear", we gave him a parting cheer, and off we went.

We had a good swell on in passing through the bay, and most of us, officers and men, kept below. The sickness soon wore off, and we were all moving about to enjoy the bright sunshine and the fresh sea breeze, and to engage in our various duties. All on board was perfect order and discipline. We had our hospital, with several doctors, taking their daily turns of duty to look after any who were sick. We had in Captain Grant, our Adjutant, one who guided and controlled all under the Colonel with a kindly and firm hand. In Captain Browne, the Master of the ship and his officers, with our Chief Engineer and his staff, we had men more than equal to their great duties and responsibilities. To travel in such a ship as the "Assaye", with such men to look after us, was a rare treat and experience which few of us will ever forget.

The Chief Steward and his staff looked after our physical wants and our sleeping comforts in a way above all praise. The food, the serving, the sleeping accommodation, both for officers and men, were in the first order. There was plenty for all without any extravagant luxury or waste.

Where such large bodies of men are cooped up in such limited space, with the sea as a continual barrier, some outlets for energies and activities are necessary and, in fact, indispensable. When daily drilling and parading and sword exercise were over then the men would scatter about on the poop decks, some to play cards, some to indulge in friendly boxing matches, and some to play at quoits. We had sports on board on a large scale after crossing the line. The officers provided the prizes, and the men entered into the various competitions with all their heart. We had boxing matches, potato races, sack races, and tugs of war. In the latter the S.A.C'.s carried all before them. It was noticeable how our tough, brawny, Scotch (sic) boys pulled like grim death, and never stopped until the opposing pullers were almost dragged off their feet. Then we had several concerts on a large scale, sometimes among the men themselves, and sometimes with both officers and men taking part.

Cartoons of life on a transport (Newnes).

With so many vessels arriving in South African waters at a time of year when high winds and gales are not uncommon, it is not surprising that some mishaps occurred. One such incident was reported by the governor, Sir Hely-Hutchinson, to Joseph Chamberlain. The *Wardha* from India having disembarked troops at Durban, continued on to Cape Town with two squadrons of the 9th Lancers, but had to put back into Durban having damaged her rudder and lost all her boats, deck gear and 90 horses in a storm off East London.[3] This, of course, would not be the last incident to occur during the conflict.

The troops' mess on the *Braemar Castle* (Dickson).

Congestion and conflict at the Durban docks

When the initial effort of landing the army corps was completed, the work of marine transport became a matter of steady, though laborious routine. From the beginning of 1900, a stream of troops, remounts and stores poured into all South African ports from every corner of the empire, but at no single period was there a repetition of the extreme effort of the first few weeks. With so many troops and mountains of military supplies arriving, problems were bound to arise, and as a result, by the beginning of 1900, congestion at the Durban docks became a serious problem. Two causes in particular contributed to this. The break up of the army corps brought confusion to all the arrangements previously made. Divisions and brigades were split up and their units sent in different directions as they arrived piecemeal at Cape Town. Troops disembarked at Cape Town were hurriedly re-embarked for Durban. Half the cargo of a ship was wanted here, and the remainder there. Store ships had to be emptied, the stores for different destinations sorted out on the quay, and then reloaded and despatched. In these circumstances, a complete break-down at the docks would have been understandable. As it was, owing to the positive attitude and energy of all involved, the docks were cleared of the backlog and the campaign was hardly affected.[14]

It should also be mentioned that ships which had been badly loaded in England owing to bad judgment, overworked staff and a great desire to get troops off in the quickest possible time did cause considerable delays at their destinations. Rapid unloading depended mainly on the forethought and methods used in loading. In the freight ships, private cargo was sometimes found piled on top of government stores, which had to remain for a day or two before they could be reached. In many cases artillery material (guns and wagons) had been dismantled and their parts stowed separately. When they were unloaded piecemeal, the wharves would be encumbered by the heavy articles, which could not be moved away until the wheels had been offloaded and attached to them.[15]

The *Braemar Castle* landing troops at the Point
(*The Illustrated London News*, 23 September 1899).

Royal Field Artillery at the Point docks (KCL).

Particulars of ships conveying troops and supplies from India

Vessel	Tonnage	Port	Departure	Arrival	Officers	Troops	Horses	Mules	Followers
Lalpoora	3 209	Bombay	8.9.1899	2.10.1899	11	190	160	–	116
Secundra	2 610	Bombay	17.9.1899	4.10.1899	7	181	167	–	22
Purnia	3 306	Calcutta	18.9.1899	5.10.1899	24	718	5	–	9
Booldana	2 860	Bombay	19.9.1899	5.10.1899	7	176	154	–	23
City of London	3 229	Bombay	21.9.1899	5.10.1899	20	304	30	108	75
Sutlej	4 164	Bombay	21.9.1899	5.10.1899		20	572	1	3
Pundua	3 305	Bombay	22.9.1899	5.10.1899	17	176	199	12	17
Vadalla	3 331	Bombay	21.9.1899	7.10.1899	9	159	203	12	3
Ellora	1 996	Bombay	20.9.1899	7.10.1899	2	37	7	11	378
Palitana	2 098	Bombay	23.9.1899	9.10.1899	19	516	6	54	30
Wardha	3 976	Bombay	24.9.1899	9.10.1899	5	160	169	12	1
Nurani	4 432	Calcutta	20.9.1899	9.10.1899	6	274	2	261	31
Sirsa	2 610	Bombay	23.9.1899	9.10.1899	12	342	1	54	1
Warora	3 980	Bombay	23.9.1899	9.10.1899	9	161	145	12	31
Lindula	3 316	Bombay	26.9.1899	11.10.1899	8	172	183	12	29
Nowshora	3 024	Bombay	24.9.1899	11.10.1899	9	163	180	12	30
Nevassa	2 998	Bombay	27.9.1899	12.10.1899	7	105	151	–	23
India	4 074	Calcutta	24.9.1899	13.10.1899	26	709	6	–	6
Sirdhana	2 720	Calcutta	25.9.1899	16.10.1899	1	4	2	250	123
Nerbudda	3 025	Calcutta	27.9.1899	18.10.1899	1	2	–	250	127
Upada	5 257	Bombay	4.10.1899	20.10.1899	6	157	257	–	18
Patiala	2 998	Bombay	8.10.1899	22.10.1899	12	154	147	12	–
Virawa	3 333	Bombay	8.10.1899	25.10.1899	7	154	190	12	–
Palamcotta	3 413	Bombay	8.12 1899	22.12.1899	7	557	45	–	–
Lindula	3 346	Bombay	6.1.1900	21.1.1900	23	190	177	12	29
Fazika	4 152	Bombay	6.1.1900	19.1.1900	8	181	192	12	–
Nairung	4 425	Bombay	6.1.1900	21.1.1900	7	186	183	12	–
Muttra	4 644	Bombay	8.1.1900	22.1.1900	3	28	273	–	78
Urlana	5 253	Bombay	8.1.1900	23.1.1900	5	183	298	–	42
Pekin	3 957	Bombay	9.1.1900	25.1.1900	2	29	284	–	80
Lawada	3 269	Bombay	10.1.1900	26.1.1900	6	25	211	–	62
Ujina	5 310	Bombay	11.1.1900	26.1.1900	7	194	301	–	42
Umta	5 366	Bombay	13.1.1900	27.1.1900	3	34	324	–	97
Uganda	5 366	Calcutta	8.1.1900	28.1.1900	2	31	274	–	78
Pandua	3 305	Bombay	14.1.1900	28.1.1900	6	17	207	–	59
Nankin	3 960	Bombay	15.1.1900	30.1.1900	3	28	278	–	76

Ships engaged in the conveyance of troops, horses and guns from Britain and the Mediterranean to Durban

Vessel	Departure	Arrival	Officers	Troops	Horses	Guns
Avoca	24.9.1899	12.10.1899	26	848	5	–
Jelunga	20.9.1899	26.10.1899	26	835	5	–
Kinfauns Castle	30.9.1899	26.10.1899	2	33	–	–
Gaika	30.9.1899	29.10.1899	8	202	120	–
Roslin Castle	20.10.1899	12.11.1899	37	1047	6	1
Hawarden Castle	23.10.1899	12.11.1899	29	946	3	1
Yorkshire	20.10.1899	14.11.1899	26	1064	3	1
Moor	21.10.1899	14.11.1899	11	8	4	–
Manila	20.10.1899	15.11.1899	24	1041	3	1
Armenian	24.10.1899	17.11.1899	24	654	519	18
Oriental	23.10.1899	17.11.1899	35	1130	6	1
City of Cambridge	23.10 1899	22.11.1899	26	939	3	1
Cephalonia	24.10.1899	23.11.1899	36	978	6	1
Pavonia	22.10 1899	23.11.1899	54	1639	5	2
Briton	4.11.1899	24.11.1899	29	875	3	1
German	28.10.1899	25.11.1899	29	1082	3	1
Manchester Port	30.10.1899	27.11.1899	27	562	520	1
Kildonian Castle	4.11.1899	27.11.1899	10	245	–	–
Servia	4.11.1899	28.11.1899	37	1166	3	1
Idaho	3.11.1899	1.12.1899	10	293	232	6
Urmston Grange	1.11.1899	2.12.1899	9	182	153	6
Templemore	2.11.1899	5.12.1899				
Montfort	13.11.1899	8.12.1899	25	558	499	1
Ismore	4.11.1899	27.12.1899	5	170	137	6
Catalonia	5.11.1899	5.12.1899	35	1048	6	1
Bavarian	10.11.1899	1.12.1899	54	1870	3	2
Narrung	16.11.1899	12.12.1899	6	276	18	6
Victorian	13.12.1899	6.1.1900	30	559	634	7
Atlantian	5.12.1899	1.1.1900	19	381	376	2
Canada	30.11.1899	23.12.1899	33	1390	7	1
Simla	24.11.1899	21.12.1899	22	944	3	1
Dilwara	2.12.1899	30.12.1899	25	1049	3	1
Majestic	13.12.1899	2.1.1900	24	838	4	1

Ammunition, supplies and equipment

It is interesting to note that during the course of the conflict the following items were shipped to South Africa in addition to the war equipment taken out by each unit: 354 000 water bottles, 1 246 600 blankets, 93 500 tents, 595 000 waterproof sheets, 175 tons of wagon grease, 119 000 sets of mule harnesses, 76 100 sets of saddlery, 3 772 000 pairs of horse and mule shoes, 351 300 rounds of 15-pounder breech-loading ammunition, 105 100 12 pounder breech-loading, 137 000 000 rounds of small arms ammunition exclusive of that taken out by the troops, of which 66 000 000 were expended. With the exception of the ammunition, which was chiefly made in the ordnance factories, the majority of these items was supplied by contractors from the trade. The following are a few items of clothing despatched up to May 31, 1902: 1 997 000 pairs boots, 510 000 riding breeches, 748 000 underpants, 497 000 field dressings, 1 152 000 helmets, 545 000 jerseys, 971 000 putties, 1 714 400 shirts, 2 743 800 pairs socks. A good number of these articles will have passed through Durban.[16]

Difficulties of another nature were caused by the attitude of part of the civil administration at some ports. At Cape Town, East London and Port Elizabeth, the ports were under the control of harbour boards, the members of which were composed partly of elected merchants and partly of government nominees. The occupation of so much harbour and quay accommodation by government ships naturally caused inconvenience to the civil work of the ports, though the naval staff often showed great consideration in freeing their special berths for civil purposes whenever it was temporarily possible.

This exclusion from their accustomed berthing accommodation caused much grumbling on the part of merchants and shippers. They often seemed to forget, or to ignore, the fact that the army was arriving for the defence of British South Africa and, in their eagerness to make the greatest use of their opportunities for generating profit out of the work brought by the war, offered the most irritating opposition to the task of landing and supplying the troops.

In some cases, lack of sympathy with the British cause may have contributed to their obstructive attitude. It was not until October 1901 that martial law was enforced at the ports of the Cape and, until that time the principal transport officer had to appeal for help to the high commissioner to enable him to override the obstacles raised by the harbour boards. At all the ports, unscrupulous and even dishonest dealing, which so often accompanies civilian work during military operations, was strongly in evidence. The country's need was the contractor's and merchant's opportunity, and considerations of patriotism seemed to have small restraining power in the face of such temptations.

The embarkation staff at Durban were more fortunate than those at the Cape ports, since martial law had been in force from the beginning. Thus the harbour was more directly under the control of the Natal government and a loyal spirit of co-operation met the transport staff in their work. There, too, they were splendidly served by the pilot staff of the port, whose courage, skill and loyalty helped to overcome the natural deficiencies of Durban as a landing place for troops and stores.[17]

Troops landing by basket at the outer anchorage (Newnes).

Royal Field Artillery landing guns at the Point docks (Newnes).

Troops waiting to be entrained at the Point (Edwards).

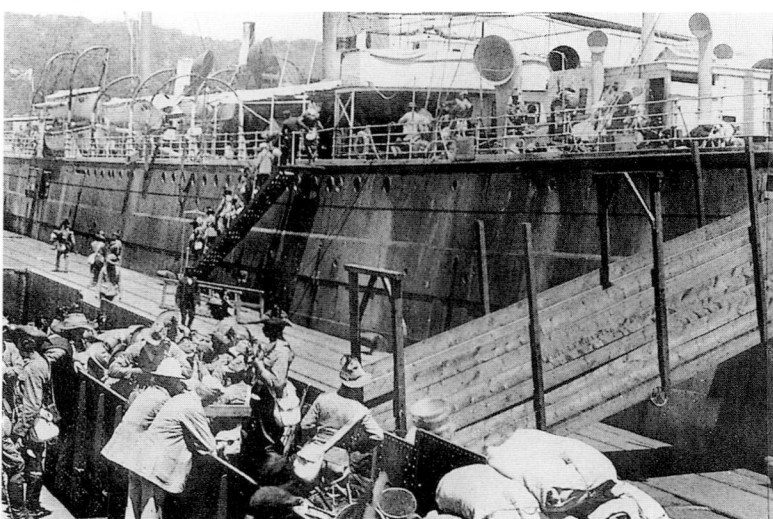

South African Light Horse disembarking at the Point (Edwards).

Following the wake, track and spoor of some regiments

To gain an understanding of the process involved in transporting soldiers from far-flung corners of the world to the battlefields via Durban, it is necessary to follow in the wake of some regiments.

The King's Royal Rifle Corps

Many of the regiments had been widely dispersed prior to the threat of hostilities in South Africa, and arrived in the country from many parts of the world, none more so than the King's Royal Rifle Corps (KRRC). Regimental records for the KRRC show that they had four battalions involved in the conflict.[20] Movements by ship and train were as follows:

1st Battalion: On 21 March 1899, battalion headquarters and four companies with nine officers and 424 other ranks arrived from Mauritius and disembarked in Durban on the *Clive*. This half battalion left for Pietermaritzburg, and was joined there on 11 May 1899 by another four companies from Cape Town, comprising seven officers and 499 other ranks.

2nd Battalion: Battalion headquarters and seven companies (17 officers and 711 other ranks embarked in India on the *Furnia* on 18 September 1899, while G Company and Transport Company (two officers and 122 other ranks) sailed from India on 20 September 1899 on the *Nurami*. The 2nd Battalion subsequently departed from Durban on 23 July 1900 aboard the *Orient* and the *Mishawk*, having been assigned the task of escorting Boer POWs to Ceylon and guarding them there. After a few months, the 2nd Battalion returned to Rawalpindi in India.

3rd Battalion: 28 officers and 1 073 other ranks left Queenstown (Cork) in Ireland on the *Servia* on 4 November 1899 and arrived in Durban on 28 November 1899.

4th Battalion: 25 officers and 814 other ranks arrived in Durban from Cork on board the *Roslin Castle* on 3 January 1902, entraining for Harrismith on 4 January 1902.

The British Regiments which arrived via Durban

By the outbreak of war on 11 October 1899, the British forces, including those recently arrived from India and elsewhere, and the colonial volunteer units were distributed in a number of centres in Natal, with the majority based in Dundee and Ladysmith[18].

Dundee
18th Hussars
One squadron Natal Carbineers
M.I. coy 1st Btn Leicestershire Regiment
M.I. coy 1st Btn King's Royal Rifle Corps
M.I. coy 2nd Btn Royal Dublin Fusiliers
Detachment Natal Police
13th, 67th, and 69th Batteries, Royal Field Artillery
1st Btn Leicestershire Regiment
1st Btn King's Royal Rifle Corps
2nd Btn Royal Dublin Fusiliers

Colenso
Durban Light Infantry
Detachment Natal Naval Volunteers
One sqdn Natal Carbineers

Estcourt
Natal Royal Rifles

Pietermaritzburg
2nd Btn King's Royal Rifle Corps
Imperial Light Horse

Durban
One sqdn 5th Dragoon Guards.

Ladysmith
5th Lancers
10th Lancers
21st, 42nd, and 53rd Batteries, Royal Field Artillery
10th Mountain Battery
23rd coy Royal Engineers
1st Btn Liverpool Regiment and M.I. coy
1st Btn Devonshire Regiment
1st Btn Manchester Regiment
2nd Btn Gordon Highlanders
Natal Mounted Rifles
Natal Carbineers
Border Mounted Rifles
Natal Field Artillery
Detachment Natal Police
Natal Naval Volunteers
Natal Corps of Guides

Helpmekaar
Umvoti Mounted Rifles.

Eshowe
One mounted coy 1st Btn King's Royal Rifle Corps.

During the remainder of 1899, officers and men of the following units arrived at Durban.[19]

Royal Army Medical Corps
Army Service Corps Nos. 25,27,and 32 Companies
Nos. 4, 8, 9 and 12 Bearer Companies
1st Btn Connaught Rangers
1st and 2nd Btns Devonshire Regiment
2nd Btn Dorset Regiment
5th Dragoon Guards
1st Royal Dragoons
1st, 2nd Btns Royal Dublin Fusiliers
1st Btn Durham Light Infantry
2nd Btn East Surrey Regiment
Royal Engineers 2nd balloon section, No.1 telegraph section
Nos. 1, 2, 3, 9, 15 and 17 Field Hospitals
Royal Field Artillery ammunition column
64th and 73rd Btns Royal Field Artillery

Gloucestershire Regiment
2nd Infantry Division
4th and 6th Infantry Brigade staff
13th, 14th, 18th, 19th Hussars
1st Btn Royal Inniskilling Fusiliers
1st and 2nd Btns Royal Irish Fusiliers
2nd Btn Royal Irish Fusiliers
1st, 2nd 3rd Btns King's Royal Rifle Corps
1st Btn South Lancashire Regiment
2nd Btn Royal Lancaster Regiment
1st and 2nd Btns Rifle Brigade
2nd Btn Royal Scots Fusiliers
2nd Btn Scottish Rifles
1st Btn Royal Welsh Fusiliers
2nd Btn West Surrey Regiment
2nd Btn West Yorkshire Regiment

The major's 'mummy'.

Major William (Molly) Myers was a member of the 7th Battalion of the KRRC. He had served with the corps during the Anglo-Zulu War of 1879, in the Egyptian campaigns of 1885–1886 and in the Hazara expedition in India in 1891. While in Egypt in 1882, he met Emile Brugsch, reputedly the illegitimate son of Kaiser Wilhelm 1 and the assistant curator of the Boulaq Museum, who introduced him to the idea of collecting antiquities, particularly items from Egypt's rich past. Having retired from the army in 1894, he made several more trips to the Middle East and built up a substantial collection of antiquities representing Egyptian, Saracenic and Persian culture.

When war with the Boers appeared to be imminent, Myers rejoined his regiment and departed from Egypt for Durban. He probably brought with him a recently acquired item of considerable Egyptian importance: a mummy, and possibly left it with the Durban Museum for safe keeping before moving on to Dundee and Ladysmith. The war was not three weeks old, when Myers was killed on Monday 30 October 1899, while attacking the Boers at Farquar's farm, a short distance outside of Ladysmith.

The mummy has been in the museum since then and has been identified as being that of an Egyptian priest, Peten-Amun, who lived in about 300 BC in Akhmim in Upper Egypt. The only firm link which can be established with Myers is the original label on the sarcophagus which bore his name. Myers had developed such a substantial collection that the Persian and Saracenic items are now housed in the Victoria and Albert Museum in London, and his Egyptological antiquities were bequeathed to his former school, Eton College. This has been said to be one of the finest private collections in existence.[21]

Major William Joseph Myers (Steve Watt Collection).

The mummy of Peten-Amun (Durban Natural Science Museum).

The 1st battalion of the Manchester Regiment (the 'Garth Manchesters') arriving to a large public welcome at Alexandra Square at the Point (KCL).

The arrival of the Devonshire Regiment (KCL).

The Royal Fusiliers entraining at the Point (Edwards).

British regimental troops d sembarking (*The Illustrated London News,* 9 September 1899).

British regimental troops at Alexandra Square (LHM).

The Royal Inniskilling Fusiliers

Another of the many regiments who distinguished themselves in Natal was the Royal Inniskilling Fusiliers. It was only after 9 October 1899, when the Transvaal ultimatum was delivered to Britain, that the reservists were ordered to rejoin the colours. Four hundred and sixty-eight men were called up and, by October 19, all but four of them had given up their employment in civil life, said farewell to their families and reported to the headquarters of the battalion. Throughout the whole of Ireland the response of the reservists was equally good.

The mobilisation of the battalion was completed by 19 October. Eleven days later it was inspected by Field Marshall Lord Roberts, who was then commanding the forces in Ireland, with 29 officers and 997 other ranks on parade. Five days later, at midnight, the battalion entrained at Mullingar, after being escorted to the station by enthusiastic crowds who carried torches made of turf soaked in paraffin oil. The men were in wild spirits and, after cheering for the queen and the Inniskillings, a soldier in the ranks suddenly called out, 'Three cheers for Krooger'. When asked why he wanted to cheer the enemy, the man replied, 'Sure, if it hadn't been for that old devil there would niver have been any fighting at all.'[22]

A few hours later the Inniskillings arrived at Queenstown with 55 sergeants, 916 rank and file, and 29 officers. The embarkation on the *Catalonia* which, including the Inniskillings, carried 40 officers, two warrant officers and 1 128 other ranks, was so steadily and smartly carried out that it won high praise from Major General A Fitzroy Hart, CB, who commanded the 5th (or Irish) Brigade, of which the battalion formed part. The general also sailed in the *Catalonia* and, a few days after leaving England, wrote as follows:

11th November 1899.

To Lt. Colonel Thackeray
Comg. 1st Batt. Royal Inniskilling Fusiliers.

I desire to express my great approval of the manner in which the 1st Batt. Royal Inniskilling Fusiliers under command of Lt.Colonel Thackeray embarked in this ship at Queenstown on the 5th Nov. 1899. I am of opinion that the degree of quiet and good order and speed in which a battalion embarks and settles down on board ship is a very keen test of its soldierly discipline and readiness to work in the field. I watched the embarkation at Queenstown attentively, and I am glad to inform the Royal Inniskilling Fusiliers that it met with my approval at all points, and is a pleasant promise of good work to come when we meet the Boers. The send off from Ireland was a hearty demonstration that none of us will ever forget and it will remind us in camp, and on the march and in battle, how many friends there are at home who will mark the pro-

An illustration of troop arrivals for the English public (*The Black and White Budget*).

gress of the Irish Brigade and will cheer when they read as the war proceeds what we endure and what we do.

(signed) A. FITZROY HART,
Major-General Comg. the Irish Brigade'.[23]

At about 16:00 on 5 November, the ship got under way amidst a scene of wild enthusiasm. Dense crowds on the quay cheered vociferously. The crews of HMS *Howe* and *Black Prince*, at anchor in the harbour, manned ship. The bands played national airs, and the inhabitants of Queenstown, determined to give the Inniskillings a good send off, illuminated the town. A few hours later, the 27th were facing the stern realities of a storm at sea. The *Catalonia* ran into very bad weather, which convinced the young soldiers of the battalion that if guard duty and 'sentry-go' are objectionable on land, 'they are simply abominable at sea'. In the gale, several of the officers' chargers perished. On the 12th, the ship coaled at Las Palmas, the capital of the Spanish island of Grand Canary. Here the Inniskillings heard the first of the lying rumours about the war, which became a frequent occurrence during the course of the campaign. The troops were constantly regaled with tales such as: 'White had gained a victory at Ladysmith. We had captured Colenso, but it had again fallen in to the hands of the enemy.'

From the Canaries onwards the voyage was quiet and prosperous. By noon on November 30 the *Catalonia* had anchored in Table Bay, and Major General Hart learned that, owing to the activity of the Boers in Natal, his brigade was ordered to the eastern theatre of war, and that one of his battalions, the Second Royal Irish Rifles, which had already arrived in Cape Town, had been sent to form part of the column with which Major General Sir W Gatacre was holding back the invaders in the eastern part of the Cape Colony. As the ship did not leave Cape Town until the evening of 1 December, the Inniskilling Fusiliers were taken on a route march of eight miles in the morning of that day. Early on 5 December, the *Catalonia* reached Durban, and the fears of the Inniskillings that they would be too late to take part in the relief of Ladysmith were laid to rest by the news that the advance guard of the Natal army was still at Frere, a village and railway station 161 miles (260 km) north of Durban, and 28 miles (45 km) south of Ladysmith.

No time was lost in the disembarkation, and about nine hours after the ship arrived in port, the first of the three trains required to transport the battalion was on its way up-country. The soldiers sat in open trucks, a mode of locomotion which appeared primitive to troops fresh from home, but later in the campaign they would look back to with nostalgia when they had travelled for hundreds of miles clinging to the tops of trucks loaded with coal, forage and stores. The people of Natal warmly welcomed the Inniskillings, as they had served in the colony in its earliest days, and had participated in hostilities against the Boers as early as 1842. At every station along the line, ladies were waiting to press upon officers and men offerings of fruit, tobacco and cigars, and to wish them Godspeed on their way to the front.[24]

Tales of other regiments which arrived via Durban

The 1st Battalion of the South Lancashire Regiment arrived in Durban aboard the SS *Canada* on 23 December 1899, and at once entrained for the area at Estcourt where the 5th Division was concentrated. They subsequently fought at Spioenkop and on the Tugela Heights, with their efforts culminating in the final charge up Peter's Hill when, in the words of General Buller's despatch, the main position 'was magnificently carried by the South Lancashire Regiment about sunset'. The commanding officer, Lieutenant Colonel McCarthy O'Leary, was amongst those who fell in this assault, his last words being, 'Remember, men, the eyes of Lancashire are watching you today.'[25]

A romanticised illustration of troop arrivals at the Point (Ridpath and Ellis).

The following article appeared in the *Natal Witness* on 3 May 1900, concerning the arrival of the Durham Artillery, the Edinburgh Militia and the Gloucesters.

Considerable commotion was occasioned in Durban yesterday afternoon by the announcement that a number of troops – some of the details, which arrived by the troopship "Umbria" on Sunday – were to march through the town and be officially welcomed by the Mayor, Mr. John Nicol. It was rumoured that the troops which comprised Edinburgh Militia numbering five officers and 153 men, the Durham Artillery with 7 officers and 156 men and 2 officers and 100 men of the Gloucesters would reach the Town Hall at 3.30. Owing however to the delay in disembarkation they did not arrive until 5.15.

Meantime the crowd gradually augmented and before the arrival of the troops, the steps of the Town Hall and the Queens statue enclosure was well occupied. The band of the Gloucester Regiment, now in Durban, proceeded to the Point to head the troops to town. The Mayor, who waited their arrival on the Town Hall steps, was accompanied by the deputy Mayor, Mr. J Ellis-Brown, the Town Clerk, Mr. W Cooley, the Borough Engineer Mr. J. Fletcher and more of the Town officials. Superintendent Alexander arranged for a clear space in front of the Town Hall for the men to be drawn up to receive the Mayor's welcome.

The Mayor, in addressing the officers and men of the Edinburgh Militia and the Durhams, offered them a hearty welcome to Durban. That was, he said, the first occasion the Militia had ever been in South Africa, and also the first time during the present war that the inhabitants of Durban had had the opportunity of seeing soldiers, landed at the port, march through the town. Although there had been something like 60,000 or 70,000 troops landed at Port Natal, these had been sent forward by train direct from the harbour, and the citizens had not had the privilege of seeing them march through the Borough. They were to be stationed at Durban in the meantime, and although they had not a garrison in Durban in which to quarter them, they had picked out as nice a camping ground for them as they could. He again offered them a hearty welcome. During their stay in Durban they would not see any active service, nor did the inhabitants wish to see them engaged in active service here (laughter).

Addressing the men of the Gloucester's, the Mayor said, the Gloucester regiment which had been to the front had done good service in this Colony, and had suffered severely. To the officers and men of their

contingent he also gave on behalf of the residents of the Borough a hearty welcome, and he hoped that their stay in Durban would be a pleasant one.

The troops then gave three cheers for the Mayor. Under the direction of the Commandant they came to attention and saluted the Mayor. "God save the Queen" was played, and then headed by the band they marched up West Street en route to their camping ground.

The camping ground selected for the troops is on the Congella flats about half a mile on the town side of the Congella railway station.

The Gloucester's afterwards proceeded to join the camp of their regiment on the Berea.

The Royal Welch Fusiliers

The Royal Welch Fusiliers (RWF) were involved in many of the well-recorded actions of the war and the following is a chronological record of the experiences of the 1st Battalion.

1899

8 October	Order received at Pembroke Dock to mobilise for active service in South Africa.
9–20 October	Reservists mobilised and joined.
22 October	Left Pembroke dock for Southampton.
23 October	Sailed aboard SS *Oriental*. Called at St Vincent, Cape Verde islands (31 Oct) and Cape Town (13–14th Nov).
17 November	Disembarked at Durban. Entrained to Mooi River.
22–26 November	In action at Mooi River area.
26 November	Marched from Mooi River to Estcourt, 23 miles in 7 hours.
9 December	Marched to Frere, 11 miles.
11 December	Night march with 2nd btn Royal Fusiliers and half 2nd btn Royal Scots Fusiliers to seize a ridge beyond Chieveley.
15 December	Battle of Colenso. Attempt to cross the river Tugela at Colenso commenced. 6 Brigade moved in direction of Hlangwane to protect the right flank. Vain attempt to rescue guns of Royal Artillery, three men wounded.
17 December	Brigade encamped near Chieveley Station.

1900

January	Base in Chieveley Camp. Constant demonstrations against Colenso.
14 February	Advance on and capture of Hussar Hill. One killed, eight wounded.
15 February	RWF seized a wooded spur about one mile east of Hussar Hill.

18 February	Further advance. One killed, six wounded. Severe water shortage led to the drinking of contaminated water, causing, later on, a severe outbreak of enteric fever (typhoid) killing Lt. Salt and several men.
19 February	Hlangwane Hill occupied unopposed.
21–22 February	At night Lt-Colonel CH Thorold, Lieutenant FA River.
23 February	RWF and RF occupied Horse-Shoe Hill in darkness.
24 February	In daylight the exposed position was completely overlooked by Boers. Btn pinned down by enemy fire all day and all that night. Colonel CH Thorold, Lieutenant FA Stebbing and seven men killed. Lieutenant. CC Norman and 31 Ors wounded. Lieutenant GES Salt recommended for the DSO for gallantry.
27 February	Boers withdraw from the Tugela.
3 March	Btn took part in the formal entry into Ladysmith.
12 March	Now in 10th Division, the Fusilier Brigade marched to Modder Spruit, 5 miles north east of Ladysmith.
15 March	Two officers and 100 reservist reinforcements arrived. Also 114 all ranks of the (1 st) Volunteer Company. Btn strength now 31 officers and 1200 Ors.
14 April	Btn left Ladysmith by train for Durban. Embarked for Cape Town 15 April arriving 19th. Disembarked 25 April and entrained for Kimberley. Arrived 28 April, Dronfield Camp, six miles north. Draft of 100 arrived. Strength 27 and 1 099. 255 sick left in Natal and Cape Town – mostly enteric fever and dysentery. Flying column formed for the relief of Mafeking.
1 May	Captain PR Mantell to command Btn. Vice-Captain A Gough – sick.
4 May	Advance northward started. Action at Rooidam 5 May. RWF and RF attack and capture Boer position. Captain RGB Lovett and 7 men killed. Capts Mantell (commanding) and WG Braithwaite (Adjutant) and 14 Ors wounded.
7–14 May	Btn remained at Fourteen Streams.
15 May	Advance on Christiana, Transvaal. Town surrendered 16th May.
22–25 May	Btn marched North to Tuangs, North again by train to Vryburg.
27 May–4 June	Btn marched from Vryburg, north-east to Lichtenburg.
7 June	2nd Lieutenant Kyrke's detachment rejoined, having taken part in the relief of Mafeking.
10–14 June	Btn marched to south-east to Potchefstroom.
22 June	Btn moved north-east by train to Krugersdorp as part of the garrison.
24 June	Lt-Colonel Sir Robert Colleton arrived to command Btn – Vice-Captain Gough.
6–12 July	D and C Coys to Potchefstroom.[26]

Royal Welch Fusiliers with their long-haired regimental mascot (Newnes).

The goat 'in action' (Wilson).

Troops waiting to entrain at Alexandra Square, Point (KCL).

Troops entraining at the Point. The electrical and hydraulic generating station is in the background (KCL).

Soldiers' narratives of the Berea and beyond

How then did the arriving British troops, mere faceless soldiers, view Durban, and the areas immediately beyond the city. The following extracts are images from the personal writings of two British soldiers who passed through Durban en route to Ladysmith:

The letters of Lieutenant HVV Kyrke

The records in the museum of the Royal Welch Fusiliers include letters written by Lieutenant HVV Kyrke, which run to 20 November 1899.[27] Kyrke described the voyage on the *Oriental* as it travelled along the South African coast to Durban during the latter part of November 1899, and noted many details including the expectations of his regiment. He also provided interesting comments relating to Durban's reception of such units before they departed for the war front. This, incidentally, was the last war in which soldiers were able to write uncensored letters.

> S.S. *Oriental*
> November 16th. 1899
> My dearest Mother,
> We did not leave Cape Town until 11am next morning on account of the gale that prevented us from getting out of harbour. It was a perfect day, and we went quite close to the coast, about three quarters of a mile off, so it was awfully jolly especially after only seeing water every day.
>
> The mountains rise sharp up from the water for a very long distance along the Coast here and the colour was just like the limestone of the Mediterranean ... We passed the Cape about 12 o'clock, there is nothing very striking about it as the promontory is fairly low. We passed Agulhas about 6pm. where there is a lighthouse, as there is on every cape here.
>
> Yesterday, Wednesday, we passed Port Elizabeth just at dusk so could not get a good look at it. It was a lovely day yesterday, the wind having gone down but we were not quite so close to the coast which was more level near the water though there were big mountains behind ... I should think that my next address would be Colenso, but it may be anywhere, Pretoria perhaps, so you will have to say Royal Welsh Fusiliers, South Africa.
>
> We were to have gone to East London and through the Orange Free State via Bloomfontein (sic) and so on to Pretoria, but they seem to want us too much at Ladysmith. You probably know a great deal more at home than they know at Cape Town, as news there is very scanty, but I don't expect that we shall have the

triumphal march through that you expected. It is 9 hours journey from Durban to Estcourt, and 2 days march from there to Colenso where we shall probably concentrate before we join Sir George White. We passed East London about an hour ago, but I could not see it for the rain, which was a pity. There have been a lot of beautiful white gulls with about 6 inches quite black at the end of the wing, and there are also a lot of perfectly black gulls and other sorts flying after the ship ... We shall probably get to Durban at 6pm. tomorrow Friday 17 th. If there is much swell we shall have to get out in baskets and shall not be able to cross the bar which will waste a lot of time.

Best love your loving son,
Vernon.

P.S. We have arrived at Durban but too late to get in at high tide, so have to wait till 2pm. We hear that Estcourt whither we are bound is invested, and that the bridge over the Tugela, a huge one, will probably have to be blown up. Durban is a very pretty place from the sea. You cannot see all the town proper but all around for about 2 miles on the hills are nice villas of rich people. The port is a river only about 60 yards across which goes around a bend inland and you can only see the masts of the ships inside. The soil is red. There are two men-of-war, the Terrible and another, and two Castle liners and another liner and some big sailing ships outside with us. I caught a butterfly on the ship which I send you. It is funny as we must be three quarters of a mile out at sea.

Repeating best love
Ever your loving son,
Vernon.

Five days later, Lieutenant Kyrke wrote another letter, this one addressed to his father and repeated some of the news of the previous letter which was written to his mother:

Mooi River Camp
November 21st.1899
My dearest Father,
I got to the place I think where we were just outside Durban. We were just too late for the morning tide and had to wait until 2 pm. It is a very pretty town with broad streets with grass at the sides and trees between the houses, and at least 10 yards of beautiful palms.

We got an awfully good reception – different from Cape Town. Hundreds crowded round the station and, though they could hardly see us, threw a perfect hail of bananas, bread buns, and other luxuries to the men. Along the line for several miles all the blacks turned

out with torches and "hurrahs". We passed a passenger train with white people in the first class carriages, apparently of good birth, and they shook hands with the Tommies as our train stopped beside theirs.

All passenger traffic is stopped now up here. It took three trains to take us and our baggage up. The men went in open trucks, it was pretty cold for them I expect. We started from Durban at 6 pm. And had dinner at 10 at a station, an hours journey from Pietermaritzburg, and as I had nothing since 11 o'clock in the morning I felt pretty hungry. It was a very good dinner. The next stop we made was at Pietermaritzburg, about 12 pm., where we left our heavy baggage, and we got here at 4 am(18th). The scenery on the way up was rather hidden as it was night but there was a full moon. In the lowlands and up to a certain distance the scenery was lovely, and little valleys and hills covered with palms and various shrubs and trees, this later changed to grass land. There was not a single tunnel the whole way as we dodged round the hills and fearful curves which you would not think the train could turn, and very steep gradients. Mooi River is where we have stopped as there is an important bridge here to protect. It is not a pretty place, there are hills all round, and the river in the bottom ...

Lieutenant Kyrke's letter to his father continued and described day-to-day events at the camp including swimming in the river, various false alarms and the occasional long-range sighting of Boer patrols by piquets and outposts. It was said in the camp that the Boers had looted and burnt a farm only three miles from the camp. The arrival of reinforcements was mentioned including the arrival of the Devonshires, Queens, and a great quantity of supplies. Kyrke also noted that the officers no longer carried swords but wore a 'Tommies' kit instead, consisting of a white belt, a water bottle, a haversack and a pugaree off-helmet. Officers, however, were allowed to wear their revolvers.

Private Edward Stanton of the Somerset Light Infantry

The 2nd Battalion of the Somerset Light Infantry disembarked from the *Briton* at Durban harbour on 24 November 1899. Private Edward Stanton, in his diary, gives an account of their arrival.[28]

We arrived in Durban at an early hour on the 24th November 1899. Our welcome into Natal was a good one. The jetty being simply packed with all classes. Getting into Durban we had another hard task, to unload everything, but we set to work with a will, and soon accomplished our somewhat difficult task.

In Durban it seemed as if the people had got a hobby of collecting soldier's badges, such as are worn in caps and coats. For these badges the people would give you nearly anything in exchange, and in many instances offered to buy them. I think in most cases they were given, as it's no good of being smart on the battlefield, at all events in dress, and bright things as a rule make a very good target.

The people were giving the troops (free of charge) pipes, tobacco, cigars, cigarettes, well in fact everything they thought would be of use during the hardships of which they were about to endure. All the people of the Town seemed to be pleased to get into conversation with the soldiers, asking them where they had come from, where they were bound for, and several other questions.

During the time we were waiting for our trains, we were in want of nothing, people bringing refreshments, in fact we got a great deal more than we could carry. We had got all the luggage off the boat, and were waiting now for the train.

There was a lady, and two gentlemen in particular on the jetty who were taking down addresses and promised to write home, and let the friends know we had arrived safely, also send money home for us if desirous of them doing so.

The railway authorities were well up to their work for it was not long before the trains were waiting to convey us up country. Durban is a nice seaport Town, and the only one in Natal. When we arrived in Africa, it was nearly the middle of summer so naturally would look at its best. We all thought we had come to a beautiful country, and so it was then especially Natal, as the Colony is called the garden of Africa.

As soon as the trains arrived upon the scene, some kind people made it their business to put bread and meat in addition to several kinds of fruit into each carriage before their departure. No doubt these people knew how long it would take before we got to our journeys end, and lucky for us they did, because we didn't get out of the train till a couple of hours before midnight.

The first of the trains (of which there were three) steamed out of Durban at 8am. The others following quickly afterwards. It was not long after we were seated in the train than we began to move but at a very slow rate. All the places for some distance however looked magnificent, every kind of flower apparently in its splendour, and the grass all over the country nice and green. Several large flowers caught our eyes that we had never looked upon in England, and which we did not gaze upon again after leaving Durban and its outskirts, some of the houses being situated in the centre of all good things, and a war raging only a hundred miles or so away. We all felt quite comfortable travelling in such a fine country, while our friends at home were shortly expecting snow.

The people all along the line would wave their handkerchiefs to us, and in several places the words were written, "Remember Majuba Hill". Flags were flying everywhere and it looked quite peaceful, more like a rejoicing, than what was really taking place. About one hour's ride from Durban we began to lose sight of the beautiful flowers but in their place came the enormous large veldt, and mountains. No doubt the latter was something we had not seen before, but we got quite enough before we had been in Africa many months. It takes some time after you leave one station, before you get to another, as the stations are much farther apart than what they are in England, and the speed of the trains not half so fast.

Some would hardly recognize some of the stations, if it was not for the sign board informing one of the name of the station. Most of the stations are only two houses, one the station, the other the station masters residence and apart from being the station master, he is the porter, ticket collector, clerk, in fact master of all, with one or two kaffirs to do the hard work.

Entrained troops and local well-wishers at the Point (NSL).

Naturally, not all soldiers or enlisted troops found that they had the perseverance and other characteristics required for wartime service. It is significant that in the period immediately before the outbreak of war, there were more deserters advertised in the pages of the Natal Government Gazette than during the war itself. Ten were advertised for the period from 1 July to 11 July 1899. Among these were five men from the 6th Dragoons, three from the North Staffordshire Regiment and two from the Royal Scots. Another ten were listed the following week. At the time of the war 15 men deserted. These included:

Pte JW Stewart of the 2nd Btn Scottish Rifles (2 October 1899);

Pte Jas Baker of the 1st Btn Manchester Regiment (10 October 1899);

Pte Arthur King of the 1st Btn Kings Liverpool Regiment (16.10.1899);

Pte Thomas Murrock of the 5th Lancers. Murrock was described as aged 24–6 months, height 5ft 8in with a fresh complexion, dark brown hair and hazel eyes. His trade was that of a bleacher; he had enlisted on 23.10.1894 and had come from Belfast.

Gnr Doran of the Mountain Battery of the Royal Garrison Artillery deserted on 21 November 1899. He was 5ft 8-in tall with a fresh complexion and brown hair.

Corp Merton of the Royal Engineers, aged 28 years, also of 5ft 8in height with fair, light brown hair and grey eyes, deserted around the 27 March 1900.

Driver Francis John of the ASC who was described as a labourer by trade, deserted on 8 April 1900. He could be recognised by his short height – 5ft 3in, dark complexion, dark brown hair and blue eyes. He bore a small scar on his right forearm and a tattoo of clasped hands and hearts on his right forearm in red and blue. The back of this arm had another tattoo of a cross in blue.

Trooper C Moran, alias Corp C Turner of the Queen's Royal Lancers was 24 years old and had brown eyes and a fresh complexion and was also 5ft 8in tall. He had deserted nearly five years before the war on 22 May 1895 and was apprehended at Inchanga on 2 April 1900.

Not all problems and deserters were regular British army men and the number also included local volunteers. Among these were: **Gunner Thomas Powell** of the Natal Naval Volunteers who was dismissed for disobedience and disgraceful conduct on 16 January 1900. Two troopers of the Imperial Light Horse deserted – **William Swain**, with a fair complexion and hair and brown eyes, deserted on 18 March 1900, while **Donald McArthur** went absent about 29 March 1900 at the end of his leave. He was described as blue-eyed with fair hair and complexion. He had last been seen at the Central Hotel in Pietermaritzburg. **Corp S Smith** of Thorneycroft's Mounted Infantry deserted on 31 May 1900. He wore a moustache, had dark eyes and a dark complexion and had last been seen dressed in a black coat and vest with brown breeches, gaiters, a straw hat, boots and spurs. **Trooper R Burford** of the Border Mounted Rifles went absent on 21 July 1900. He was described as being of fair complexion with dark blue eyes and dark hair.[29]

Government Notice No. 214, 1900.

THE following descriptive reports of an absentee without leave and of a deserter from Her Majesty's Forces in Natal, are published for general information.

C. BIRD,
Principal Under Secretary
Colonial Secretary's Office, Natal,
9th May, 1900.

———

Description of Trooper Booth, S.A.L. Horse, who was granted leave until the 27th April, 1900, to proceed to Maritzburg, and has not yet returned.

Height.— 5 feet 6 inches.
Complexion — Dark.
Moustache. —Dark.
Eyes.—Dark.
Hair.—Black.

Dressed in the Uniform of the S.A.L. Horse.

G. P. APPLEBY, Captain,
Garrison Adjutant
Pietermaritzburg,
6th May, 1900.

——— —

No. 22 COMPANY ARMY SERVICE CORPS.

Report of a deserter from the above Regiment :—

Number, Rank, and Name.—6630, 2nd Corpl. Bateman George.
Age.—33 years 9 months.
Height.—5ft. 4¾ins.
Colour of Complexion.—Fresh.
„ Hair.—Brown.
„ Eyes.—Grey.
Trade.—Baker and Confectioner.
Date of Enlistment.—26th January, 1886.
Place of Enlistment.—Exeter.
Parish and County in which Born.—Plymouth, Devon.
Date of Desertion or Absence. — 6th November, 1899.
Place of Desertion or Absence. — Ladysmith, Natal.
Marks.—Tattooed 5 dots on the back of left wrist.
Service.—Under 14 years. On active service.

T. K. TULL, Lieut. and Q.M.
Commanding No. 22 Depot and Comp.,
Army Service Corps.

Pietermaritzburg,
27th April, 1900

Ricksha puller and ricksha in Point Road (KCL).

The biograph in action (Wilson).

The arrival of the 1st Liverpool Regiment (Richards).

WKL Dickson, a biographer, or film maker

The Anglo-Boer War was probably the first war to be filmed by pioneering film makers or 'biographers'. In his book, *The Biograph in Battle*,[30] Dickson gives a first-hand account of his arrival and subsequent experiences in Durban.

Friday 10th November. We arrived at Durban, one month after our departure from London, and were greeted with the news that Ladysmith was still being bombarded. The Natal Dutch were disloyal, and that there was a possibility of the Boers coming to Durban. A very sea-sick tug came alongside and we were lowered in a basket, spending a wretched forty-five minutes until all got safe on board. Finally the tug departs, and with many a cheer for the Captain and crew we leave the good ship *Dunottar* behind, cross the bars safely and rush through the surf which is swarming with porpoise. The harbour reached, we pass through the customs without difficulty, for the simple reason that we had no baggage with us. We intended returning for the horses, cart and other things as soon as we had secured our rooms. Rooms however, are not easily found. With much difficulty we secure a small one with three cots which we gladly take as a makeshift. We are well received by the manager of Curries Line, Mr. Wisely, and Mr. Curry promised every assistance.

Saturday 11th. Next morning we rose at 4.30 and made our way down to the jetty, just in time to catch the only tug going out that day to the *Dunottar Castle*. There was not much time to lose in bringing away our horses, Cape cart and baggage, the ship having received orders to sail at noon that day. The sea by this time had calmed down, although not sufficiently to allow the tug to go alongside. We had to go through the bar and out to sea on the huge flat-topped lighters intended for the horses. With skillful handling the little tug succeeded in hauling our two lighters alongside the *Dunottar* and while we were bumping about, the Captain appeared on deck in his dressing gown. He greeted us with a smile and ordered a basket to be lowered for us. By this time I was conscious of an indescribable disagreeable sensation and found myself intoning dismally, "I love thee not, uncomfortable sea." But after a cold water bath and a good breakfast, I soon forgot my troubles and was discussing the latest war news with the Captain and his officers. After breakfast the Captain insisted on putting on his shore clothes, and after our belongings had been lowered to the lighters, we were swung out to the sea in the inevitable basket and rapidly let down to the little tug as it rose on a huge wave. The approach to Durban over this truly terrifying bar of boiling, seething waves ought to deter any adventurer who has not got a good pilot on board. Added to the unrest of the water is the rather alarming aspect of the hundreds of porpoises which guard the harbour entrance, and which by the uninitiated might easily be taken for sharks. Once past the breakwaters we approach the cosy and admirably protected harbour, well patronized with various craft, ranging from large ocean steamers to gunboats, sailing vessels and fishing smacks.

All this time my good friend, Captain Rigby, who had come purposely on shore to introduce me to his numerous friends, was delivering a most learned disquisition on the growth of Durban. Noon came and the Captain returned to his vessel having thoroughly paved the way for us.

On our return to the Customs, our weapons were given back to us. These I had declared for the purpose of stamping and registration. A charge of five shillings being made on each, to be refunded upon our leaving the country. Passing out of the sheds where our things had been stored, we were arrested by an extraordinary sight. Fifty or more savage looking rickshaw runners came racing towards us for our patronage, each one more grotesquely decorated than the other. Horned, winged, feathered and dressed in every conceivable garb to attract the visitor. This attire was set off by fiendish yells and capers, and I felt that in all my travels, I had never seen anything so unique.

Sunday 12th. At 5am. We found ourselves on the wharf prepared for action, having learned late the night before that the *Roslin Castle* filled with troops would be in at 6am. So with the assistance of twelve turbaned chaps, we had our flat wagon wheeled into position and all got in readiness. Not until nine, however, were we rewarded by a sight of the ship, crowded from one end to the other and far up into the rigging with khaki-coloured uniforms and helmets. Eleven hundred troopers and ninety officers all told. No words can describe the thrill of the moment as the huge vessel slowly and majestically rounded the wharf and was gently drawn in amidst the deafening hurrahs of the thousands on the shore and on the surrounding decks of the harbour boats. We were busy with a vengeance, all our cameras at work, and before the day was out and the troops gone we had many pictures, covering the various scenes enacted that sunny, happy Sunday, when the faithful and loyal people of Durban rejoiced and their anxieties passed away. To add to

their joy, a message was received from General Buller to the people of Durban and Natal, highly commending them for their fidelity and loyalty.

Among the snap shots taken on this eventful Sunday will be found several views of the *Roslin Castle's* approach to the pier, showing a mass of helmeted troopers hanging on the sides, many having clambered up the riggings. After the landing, some of the snaps showed Colonel Kitchener talking to one of the officers. The rest were views of the stacked accoutrements of the troops.

Monday 13th. Today was spent preparing ourselves for the plunge into the interior, and it was as much as we could do to keep on our feet as we were driven here and there by a terrific wind which carried clouds of fine sand through the air. We fastened the Biograph to the back of the seat of the cart so that we could fire at a moment's notice.

Tuesday 14th. The hospital ship *Spartan* next had our attention and many good pictures were obtained showing the wards and the convalescents on deck. The patients told us some marvelous tales of hair-breadth escapes. One man was shot through his helmet, the ball just skimming his head and rendering him unconscious for hours.

Wednesday 15th. Rain, rain, rain, so we continue our preparations for the great trek, arranging also for the transport of our cart and horses, a very difficult matter as all the railroads are under military control. However, after explaining the purpose of our trip to Mr. David Hunter, General Manager, Natal Government Railway, that gentleman acceded most graciously to all my wishes, namely to give us all railway facilities as well as transport for our cart and horses. It was therefore arranged that whenever we could not go any further by train, we could drive to the next spot of unbroken rail.

Another big load of soldiers came in today and the docks and railways are kept busy, the people of Natal never seeming tired of the sight and shouting themselves hoarse with delight. Durban is overwhelmingly happy. Troops by the thousand are pouring in daily and the warships are ready for action. Each morning the marines from the man-of-war *Terrible* may be seen near the town hall drilling round their cannons, which are painted khaki colour, and which were brought on shore the day we arrived.

Thursday 16th. The *Armenian* has just come in with 604 horses, eighteen guns, and 900 men, cavalry and artillery. Great excitement prevails, while the cars

on the landing are being loaded up with guns and horses, which are slung out of the ship and lowered on the wharf and cars. A biograph picture shows a train load of these guns en route for Estcourt, drawing into Durban station from the Point (where they have been loaded). In less than twelve hours every horse had been sent to the front.

Troops disembarking from the *Roslin Castle* (KCL).

Returning home from Durban: troublesome troops

When the British troops had first arrived in Durban, their stay had been too brief for them to land in any trouble. Returning home or to bases in other parts of the empire was an entirely different matter. Troops then spent some time in Durban and some managed to get themselves into serious trouble. In August 1900, George Marshall, a military man with a wife and children, who was stationed at Congella, was charged in the Durban Circuit with 'Assault with intent to Rape' on an eight-year-old white girl named Florence Dickinson. Although Marshall pleaded guilty, he believed that the sentence of three year's imprisonment with hard labour was too harsh. In his defence he claimed that, despite the fact that he had committed the crime while 'absent without leave', he had been drinking excessively, and was unaware of his deed. In mitigation his commanding officer, Major Lee, claimed that Marshall was a good soldier! The judge, however, felt that Marshall had not been so drunk at the time of the offence that he was unaware of what he was doing, and found Marshall was guilty of deliberately enticing the girl to the railway yard opposite the military cemetery where he tried to rape her. Had he not been noticed by a passerby who called the police, Marshall would probably have succeeded in his hideous deed, and for this reason, the presiding judge, JM Beamont, did not find the sentence too harsh.[31]

Death in a ricksha

Private George McDowell of the 1st Argyle and Sutherland Highlanders was charged, tried and convicted for culpable homicide in Durban by J Stuart, the assistant magistrate on 2 May 1902. McDowell stood trial for the murder of the 27-year-old Isaac Elstein, an unmarried white gentleman who was known to drink heavily. McDowell had apparently hit Elstein, who was found dead in a ricksha, with his fist, on the left side of the face. After a post-mortem, the district surgeon, Dr Birtwell, found that Elstein had died from a haemorrhage of the lungs, which may have been accelerated by the shock of the blow. He also said that although it was possible that a blow had been struck, there were no marks or bruises. The ricksha puller also gave evidence in the trial, stating that he had taken the deceased to the police station, while another ricksha boy stated that on the night of the disturbance he had seen several soldiers upset a ricksha near Bingham's corner and strike the ricksha puller. A white man was thrown out of the ricksha and got 'mixed up with the soldiers'. He had then heard the deceased call out as if he had been hurt, but did not recognise the accused as one of the soldiers involved in the incident. On 9 July 1902 McDowell was eventually sentenced to one month's imprisonment, the magistrate taking into account the fact that he had already been in jail for two months.[32]

Canadian and Australian troops

While the soldiers in general behaved in an exemplary manner, not only individuals but also entire units made life difficult for Superintendent Alexander and his men. In early July 1902, trouble started first in Tattersall's Bar when the police had to arrest two Canadian soldiers. At 21:00 the police were again called to Tattersall's where a picket from the Canadian forces had arrested one of their men. The bar eventually had to be cleared. At 22:00 the Central Hotel was rushed, liquor was demanded and revolvers were pointed at the nightwatchman. The men were removed after great difficulty. Sunday was fairly quiet but, on Monday night, about 100 Canadians and Australians broke out from Lords Grounds where they were camped. They proceeded in a body to Queen Street and Victoria Street where they wrecked several brothels and houses occupied by Indians. They then tore up a fence and armed themselves with pieces of it. A small number of police present arrested two of the men, and two others were taken into custody, but one was rescued by the Canadians. When the police were reinforced, the men dispersed. The next night brought even more trouble when several drunken Canadian soldiers were making a nuisance of themselves in West Street. When the police tried to arrest them, more soldiers arrived and soon the street was a mass of drunken troops shouting, overturning rickshas and generally causing havoc. When more police arrived on the scene the crowd gradually moved towards the police station and several soldiers were arrested. The crowd demanded the release of the prisoners and, on being refused, they started to attack the police station. Many of the soldiers were armed with revolvers and they lined up over one hundred strong in front of the station, where someone ordered them to prepare to fire. Superintendent Alexander was busy marshalling the local police force, both whites and blacks, the latter armed only with sticks. Because of the hubbub the fire brigade was alerted, and, before the soldiers could make a charge the brigade turned a fire hose on them. This tactic proved most effective and soon the soldiers were out of range of the hoses, but then someone shouted 'Canadians fire!' and two shots rang out, the bullets smashing the police station window. The riot abated temporarily and the officers tried to persuade the men to go away. However, many of them still shouted for revenge. Superintendent Alexander stepped out and tried to reason with the mob, but again someone shouted 'Fire, fire!' and two shots rang out. The bullets missed the superintendent and hit the inside wall of the office. Messengers had been despatched to call for reinforcements from the Point, and not long after they arrived order was restored.[33]

Further departures

As the war progressed, numerous troops and officers continued to arrive in Durban, while others began to depart through the town. On Saturday 20 October 1900, two weeks after relinquishing his command, General Sir Redvers Buller arrived in Durban to depart from the port at which he had arrived months before. He was received at the Berea Station by the mayor, the members of the corporation, the commandant and the senior naval officer.

An address was presented to Buller at the town hall, and the streets and ships were decorated with bunting. Sir Redvers embarked from the Point at 15:45 where a guard of honour was provided from HM ships *Philomel* and *Partridge*. Under Lieutenant AB Hughes a salute of 17 guns was fired by the *Philomel* as the general embarked, and the ships companies cheered as the tug steamed out of the harbour.

The next important British officer to depart via Durban was Lord Roberts. By 29 November 1900, he was ready to hand over his command to Kitchener, convinced that he was leaving Kitchener little more than the mopping up of scattered guerilla activities. Lord Roberts would then succeed Wolseley as Commander-in-Chief of the army in Britain. The *Natal Mercury* recorded his departure from South Africa:

> Lord Roberts left Pietermaritzburg at 10am on the 5th December 1900 having been seen off at the railway station by his Excellency the Governor (Sir Walter Hely-Hutchinson), the Prime Minister (Sir Albert Hime), His Worship the Mayor (Cr. G.J. Macfarlane), the Deputy Mayor (Cr. P.F. Payn), the Commandant (Col. Martin), the Commandant of Volunteers (Gen. Dartnell) and several other leading citizens.
>
> At about 2 o'clock the train arrived at the Berea Station, which was decorated with as fine taste as that displayed on the occasion of the arrival of General Sir R. Buller. The Commander-in-Chief was met on the platform by the Mayor and Town Council, General Hildyard and staff, and all the other principal officers in town, together with the deputations from the Irish and Indian Associations. The town presented a very gay appearance, every building, practically speaking, in West Street, being bedecked with flags, streamers, bunting, or inscriptions. The pillars of the Town Hall were swathed with red, white and blue, and garlanded.
>
> On Lord Roberts' arrival a ringing cheer was set up and continued until he left the station, and the procession was on its way to the Town Hall. The horses of the Mayor's carriage had been taken away, and the vehicle was drawn by the crowd all the way thither.
>
> The scene at the Town Hall was a memorable one. As early as 1 o'clock the hall was crowded, those in the body of the hall standing, and the gallery, which was reserved for ladies and children was packed. On the platform about 150 specially favoured ladies were seated. Mr. Macdonald, the Borough Organist, relieved the monotony of weary waiting by playing a number of selections, a few classical, but the majority popular. The decorations in the hall were not very elaborate. All the gallery pillars were garlanded and surmounted with clusters of palm leaves. From the Mayor's gallery hung the Royal Standard, with a Union Jack on either side. The front of the platform was festooned.
>
> The guns of the N.F.A. fired a salute as the procession reached the building, and the Mayor led the way onto the platform. Lord Roberts was followed by his staff, General Hildyard and staff. Col. Morris, Commander Tatum, N.N.V., the deputy Mayor, Major Dick and officers of the D.L.I., Town Councillors, etc.
>
> Cheers greeted the distinguished General as he mounted the platform, and the assembly, with great enthusiasm, sang, "For he's a jolly good fellow".

W Cooley, the town clerk, then read an address on behalf of the corporation, and this was followed by an address from the Natal Indians delivered by MK Ghandi. Lord Roberts in his reply said:

> He did not know how to thank them for the kindly welcome accorded him. He rejoiced at the change of plan which enabled him to carry out his wish of over twenty years of visiting the great port of Natal. He wished to say that there was a great future in store for Durban. In the future the inhabitants of Durban would realize how much they were owed for the excellent way the Boroughs affairs had been conducted, and as to what it did for the soldiers during the war. He did not wish to take up their time by quoting statistics, but would like to refer to a few just handed to him. The number of troops despatched from the Point, Durban, from September 20th 1899 to October 31st 1900, was 2,450 officers, 68,374 men, 26,789 horses and 117 guns. (applause) They had also brought down the poor wounded and invalided, no less than 31,935 officers and men. He was delighted that Sir Redvers Buller had borne testimony to the help he received from one and all at Durban. Many amongst them hurried to join the Imperial troops, and covered themselves with honour and glory.
>
> They had shown the world that the fighting power of the Englishmen was as good as in the days of yore, whether they come from Great Britain or Greater Britain. The Empire was founded by the energy and perseverance of their forefathers, whose sons in times of danger were found fighting alongside the sons of

the mother country (cheers) especially the Imperial Light Horse and the Natal Carbineers.

Lusty cheers were then given for the Commander-in-Chief and Lady and Misses Roberts. As the train moved away, the National Anthem was sung. The station was tastefully decorated by Mr. Prior, and the hotel and other buildings were decked with flags, etc.

The address which was handsomely framed in gold and plush, was executed by Mr. J. Dunlop, a Scotch (sic) artist at present sojourning in the neighbourhood, and is a work of art. The Royal arms appear at the head of the address, whilst those of Lord Roberts occupy the left side, with the Natal arms directly beneath. On the right-hand side is a well drawn sketch of Tommy Atkins standing with fixed bayonet. The address proper is in gold and blue, and the shamrock is entwined with the gilt bordering.[34]

So efficient was the Durban harbour that Lord Roberts heaped praise on it as can be gleaned from the following extract from the report of Port Captain Ballard for the year 1900, as printed in the *Natal Mercury* of 18 December 1900:

When Lord Roberts came to Durban on his way home to the Mother Country on December 5th 1900, after having so triumphantly crushed the Mahdi of South African Dutch Republicanism, speaking at the Town Hall in reply to the address of welcome and congratulations which had just been presented to him, he said:
– I had wished to see Durban because I believe there is a great future in store for this part of South Africa. The future inhabitants of Durban will then be able to realize how much they were owed to the present generation for the able and intelligent manner in which they conducted the affairs of this port, and for the great aid they gave to the soldiers of the Queen.

In one aspect the *Natal Mercury* was wrong, the Boers had not yet been defeated and the war continued for another 15 months, culminating in surrender terms being signed at Vereeniging on 31 May 1902. No British war since 1815 had been so prodigal of money and lives. The cost to the British taxpayer was in excess of £200 000 000. There were over a 100 000 casualties of all kinds among the 364 693 imperial and 82 742 colonial soldiers who had fought.[35]

General Buller entraining at Alexandra Square, November 1899 (LHM).

When the war did end, the desire of the authorities to return the troops to their homes with the utmost speed placed an immense strain on the transport staff. By this time, the number of transports had been reduced to some 30 vessels, and no others were engaged. Every available ship had to be taken into service and the mail and passenger steamers were called upon to carry troops. As all animals were to be left in South Africa, the horse and mule ships were rapidly adapted to carry troops by alterations being made to their internal fittings. These measures were carried out so energetically that by the end of October 1902, 148 000 officers and men had left South Africa and been safely landed in Great Britain, India, Canada, Australia and New Zealand, These numbers were embarked in the proportion of Cape Town 50%, Durban 25%, the other 25% being divided between Port Elizabeth and East London.

A few figures will eloquently show the magnitude of the task of moving British troops accomplished by the transport service during its three years of work. From July 1899 to the end of 1902, 423 373 officers and men were embarked for South Africa from all parts of the empire and 370 225 embarked in South Africa for Britain and other parts of the empire. Of these 329 251 officers and men were taken out and 278 284 brought back by 117 transports of a total tonnage of 719 837 tons; 79 855 were sent out, and 83 991 sent back by freight ships; 8 300 of the Indian contingent were sent in 41 transports from India, while 5 967 of the colonial contingents were sent out and 8 050 sent back by ships hired in the several colonies or in Cape Town. The full cargo store freight ships engaged by the Admiralty numbered 210, and the amount of cargo engaged amounted to 974 257 tons and 3 745 mules. Besides these, 57 ships, making 117 voyages, were chartered by the remount department for the transport of horses and mules from foreign countries up to March 1901, when the duty was taken over by the Admiralty. During the same period, many thousands of officers and men were brought back as invalids from South Africa, partly in the hospital ships, and partly in the ordinary transports. The work was carried out at the cost of only two ships wrecked, the transport *Ismore* and the freight ship *Denton Grange*.[36]

The credit for this accomplishment is due, primarily, to the transport department of the Admiralty. The organising and directing officials carried the chief responsibility for success and failure alike and, by common consent, the department proved itself ready and capable for the task it had to face.

The departure of the Gloucestershire Regiment (Newnes).

1. Amery LS, (ed.), *The Times History of the War in South Africa 1899–1900*, Vol. VI, p.89.

2. Amery, p.99.

3. Amery, p.100.

4. Amery, p.97.

5. Amery, p.98.

6. Amery, p.99.

7. Amery, p.201.

8. Amery, p.291.

9. Maurice, F, *A History of the War in South Africa 1899–1902*, Vol. I, p.453.

10. Greenhill, G, *The Life of a Regiment*, Vol. 3, pp.10–15.

11. Ibid., p.11.

12. Maurice, p.470.

13. PRO, CO 179/206: Hely-Hutchinson to Chamberlain, 12.10.1899.

14. Amery, p.288.

15. Amery, p.289.

16. Amery, p.452.

17. Amery, p.291.

18. Maurice, p.456.

19. Ibid.

20. Correspondence, Colonel IH McCausland to G Chadwick, 11.3.1999.

21. Bennett, DR, Strange Bedfellows: The Anglo-Boer War and the Mummy at the Museum, *Palmnut Post*, 3, (1). March 2000, pp.16–17.

22. *Regimental History*, Museum of the Royal Inniskilling Fusiliers, Enniskillen.

23. Ibid.

24. Ibid.

25. Correspondence, Lieutenant Colonel EJ Downham to G Chadwick, 17.3.1999.

26. Correspondence, Lieutenant Colonel RJM Sinnett to G Chadwick, 1.12.1999.

27. Kyrke, HW, Mus.4812: *Letters from the Front*, Royal Welch Fusiliers Museum.

28. Stanton, E, *Diary*, Light Infantry Office, Somerset.

29. Natal Government Gazettes, 2.10.1899 to 7.8.1899.

30. Dickson, WKL, *The Biograph in Battle*, pp.30–47.

31. PAR, CSO, 1687: G Marshall to Major Lee, 25.9.1901; CSO, 1687: P O'Hea to the governor, 26.9.1901; CSO, 1687: report by JM Braumont, 3.1.1901

32. PAR, AGO, 1/8/85: various notes in minute paper – Ref 272A/1902; *Natal Witness* 15.5.1902.

33. *Natal Mercury*, 4.7.1902.

34. *Natal Mercury*, 6.12.1900.

35. Packenham, T, *The Boer War*, p.287.

36. Amery, p.452.

CHAPTER 5

VOLUNTEERS, RECRUITS AND SCOUTS
Brian Kearney

The Durban volunteers called out

With war impending, advertisements had appeared in the local press on 29 and 30 September 1899 ordering all members of the four part-time volunteer regiments to parade at the drill hall at 13:00 on Saturday the 30th for entraining.

> Durban Light Infantry
> Special Order
> The Regiment with buglers and all detachments (Bandsmen in the ranks) will parade today Saturday at 1p.m. to entrain for up country. Uniform khaki serge, helmets with covers, waterbottles, mess tins, haver-sacks, leggings, great coats rolled, field service order, belts and two pouches, rifles and side arms. All absen-tees from this parade will be regarded as deserters. Kit bags must be handed in at the Drill Hall not later than 11 a.m. today Saturday.
> By Order,
> James Dick, Capt. & Adjt.
> DLI Headquarters, September 29, 1899 [1]

At 10:00 on Saturday morning, the Natal Field Artillery (NFA) loaded six of their seven-pounder guns, saddles, harnesses and ropes onto two rail trucks at the station across Pine Street. These guns were described as being 'of the latest pattern for field work, and are adapted more particularly for moving about the country. They are painted a slate colour after the fashion which has come into vogue for arms of all kinds ...'.[2] The Natal Naval Volunteers (NNV) also paraded that morning and three nine-pounder gun detachments were ordered out. After being kitted out, each man received 90 rounds of ammunition and was then told to stand down. At 13:00 the 400 men of the Durban Light Infantry (DLI) re-sponded to the bugle call at the drill hall and formed up to receive 150 rounds of ammunition and their rations for the journey consisting of biscuits and cheese. Sir John Robinson, Harry Escombe and his wife, Mayor John Nicol and other dignitaries arrived to offer their best wishes. When all the units had assembled, the march to the station commenced. The *Natal Mercury* recorded the events:

VOLUNTEERS CALLED OUT – A THOUSAND DEPART TODAY

In the street, extending along the length of the Town Gardens, on by the back of the Town Hall, by the side of the Public Library, around the Market House and in front of the Railway Station buildings, dense crowds of people had assembled to give the departing men a hearty send-off. Shortly before 2 o'clock orders were given for them to march. The Durban Light Infantry marched out to the number of 430 rank and file. Lieutenant-Col. McCubbin was in command ... The Natal Naval Volunteers marched out to their full strength under Commander Tatum. The band of the Natal Mounted Rifles, under Bandmaster Gibb, played the men to the station, and with the gun detachments of the Navals at the head, and the remainder of the corps at the rear, the infantrymen marched out. There was a drizzling rain prevailing at the time and a cold wind, which made it somewhat uncomfortable for the spectators, but there was, nevertheless, great enthu-siasm in the crowd. As the volunteers marched along the street, they were greeted with tremendous cheer-ing, which increased as they neared the station, hats and handkerchiefs being waved by the crowd, and every feeling of pride and good-will being manifested. Yet among all the signs of enthusiasm and good cheer, there were not a few touching scenes. Among the crowd were mothers, wives, sisters, and sweethearts to whom the departure of the men was anything but a matter for kindly regard, a fact to which the tear-stained faces of many eloquently testified ... At the main entrance to the railway station the men wheeled and entered the old station platform by the back entrance ... the platform was closed to the general public and only those armed with special permits were allowed to see the men entrain ... the crowd outside made frantic efforts to gain admittance to the platform, and the police had the greatest difficulty in keeping back the people. Many, including several ladies, took advantage of the goods office windows to climb through. There was a considerable amount of cheering, and at 2.30 the train steamed out amid the strains of 'God Save the Queen'.[3]

The men scrambled into open trucks and at 14:10 the first train departed while the band played 'Soldiers of the Queen'. Twenty minutes later, the next train departed. And so, with equally large crowds in attendance, a further seven special trains departed during that afternoon and evening and well into the next day. Detachments of the Natal Mounted Rifles (NMR) from Verulam and Stanger were to travel on the last four trains

The Durban volunteer regiments marching up West Street from the drill hall to the railway station on Saturday 30 September 1899 (KCL).

The Natal Field Artillery (NFA) had been formed in September 1862 as the artillery company of the Durban Rifle Guard, under Captain AW Evans. In 1892 the name of the unit was changed to the Natal Field Artillery. In 1904 it was joined by the Pietermaritzburg Battery of the Natal Royal Regiment.[4]

The Natal Mounted Rifles (NMR) also originated from a mid-nineteenth century militia unit – the Royal Durban Rangers (1852). A royal charter was received in 1855 and the Rangers existed until 1871. The unit was succeeded by the Victoria Mounted Rifles (1862) who amalgamated with the Stanger Mounted Rifles in 1887. By 1888 these units had been joined by the Alexandra Mounted Rifles (1865) and the Durban Mounted Rifles (1875) collectively to form the Natal Mounted Rifles with their headquarters in Durban.[5]

The Natal Naval Volunteers (NNV) were initiated by Harry Escombe in April 1885, at a public meeting held at the Point, where 100 men volunteered. Their principal objective was to defend the port of Durban. Escombe himself commanded the corps until 1897, thus conferring on the unit the distinction of being the only volunteer force to be commanded by a prime minister.[6]

The largest of the four local volunteer regiments was the Durban Light Infantry (DLI) which had originated as the Durban Volunteer Guard in 1854. In turn, it was replaced by the Durban Rifle Guard which existed from 1859–1869. The Royal Durban Rifles was formed in 1873 and joined with the Natal Royal Rifles in 1889. Major HR Bousfield was officer commanding in 1893. The remaining half of the battalion of the Royal Rifles became the DLI in January 1895.[7]

The regiments turn into Church Street from West Street (KCL).

The DLI departing from the Durban Railway Station (War Pictures).

Volunteers off to the front, by FC Dickinson (Supplement to *The Graphic*, 18 November 1899).

and entrained at the siding between the station and the Prince Edward Bridge.

The troops were accommodated in 'seated trucks', that is specially adapted rail trucks with temporary wooden seats. Officers naturally had the luxury of 'composite carriages'. 'Donkey' trucks were used for horses and guns.[8] Their route took them through the southern part of the town alongside the bay, past the Umbilo and South Coast Junction Stations, then up through the old main line suburbs of Seaview, Bellair and Hillary; then on to Malvern, Northdene, Pinetown Bridge and Pinetown itself; and afterwards up into the hills through Krantzkloof, Gillitts, Botha's Hill and across the viaduct to Inchanga, where there was a stop of 16 minutes. The first train which had left at 14:10 on Saturday reached Pietermaritzburg by 19:55 that evening, and Colenso the following afternoon at 14:57. The remaining six trains were to go as far as Ladysmith, with the last of the 1 000 odd troops arriving on Monday at 8:40. At every station, large groups of inhabitants had assembled to cheer them on and wish them well, offering refreshments and cigarettes. At Bellair 'young ladies handed out parcels they had made up to the troops'.[9]

Writing to a friend in Durban a young naval volunteer captured the atmosphere:

We were nearly overwhelmed with the grand send-off.

The enthusiasm was the same all along the line till midnight, crowds, great & small according to the station and how they cheered and we cheered and sang Rule Brittania. We had a merry journey, the best to Maritzburg I have had. Open trucks are far nicer than closed carriages to my mind, in spite of rain which did not penetrate our none too warm overcoats. It was cold after the City, bitter at Nottingham Road & Mooi River. But the warm enthusiasm from every white soul we saw made the weather mild. I had not a few minutes sleep, few got a wink. It is anything but quiet here. Crowded trains from Johannesburg create great excitement but we have no news. We are here surrounded by hills on two of which our two guns are to be placed. Our position is a responsible one – on the alert for attack. It is an exciting experience, rather different from the Bluff. Goodbye to comfort for some weeks but I will not miss it at all. May we prove our worth ere we return. Must starve for some days ere I relish this bully beef. So far I have lived on excitement. However this life will make us giants soon. Not like Sunday at all here, the peaceful Berea Sabbath is

Bellair Railway Station (PAR).

Botha's Hill Railway Station (PAR).

The railway viaduct at Inchanga under construction (NSL).

The drill hall and police station in central West Street (LHM).

The drill hall, West Street (LHM).

like a dream today. We are an excellent party and of course such experience will make us all brothers. [10]

The departure of the four local volunteer regiments from Durban was accompanied by great pomp and ceremony. Here were the local lads stepping out into the unknown for queen, empire and colony. But it could also be construed that the occasion was deliberately elaborate to instill a sense of community patriotism and to arouse emotions, not only in the observing women and children, but in other young men who might be inspired to volunteer. The very public display of departure, including the march from the drill hall to the station down West Street, was a serious public relations exercise intended to prick the consciences of those young men who had chosen to remain behind, for the reality was that the actual number of volunteers was relatively small compared to the availability of able-bodied persons. [11] There must have been many questions in the minds of the volunteers and the public: were they departing to defend Durban or the colony or the British empire? Whose war was it: Britain's or Natal's?

The sense of order which accompanied the call-up and the quick departure from Durban of the volunteer troops with all their equipment and guns also emphasises that the call-up had been anticipated for some time, and that the ranks of the volunteers were in a state of readiness. One need only consider the careful organisation required for the special trains with their complex timetables to realise how prepared the military had been prior to the event. [12] In fact, the actual reorganisation of the volunteer's home base in the preceding year further underlines the fact that planning and preparation for war had long been in effect for those of imperial military enthusiasm.

Already in March 1899, plans and designs had been prepared for a new and enlarged drill hall and other accommodation for the various volunteer regiments. [13] This accommodation was located within a kind of government 'compound', next to the Durban borough police station and at the end of the block bordered by Aliwal, West and Pine Streets, utilising a portion of the originally much larger market square. Since the chief government functions were positioned in Pietermaritzburg, the capital town, the colonial authorities had consolidated their local Durban presence in a group of wood and iron structures and set up their excise offices, a Transvaal customs office, a bonded warehouse and various facilities for the public works department, such as plumbers' and carpenters' shops. There was also a harness room, a gun shed and armoury, a fire-engine room, stables and staff quarters. The new 'volunteer stores and offices' were put out to public tender and built by WF Johnstone.

Located with the documents describing this compound, which were probably prepared for insurance purposes, was a pattern for a new heraldic design for the various volunteer regiments. The design consisted of a flanking lion and unicorn, with a smaller British lion mounted on a crown. This was designed for the front of the new premises and symbolically displayed the role of these groups who represented a gathering of local forces on behalf of the greater empire. Thus the regiments, freshly housed and united in heraldic strength, were well prepared for war!

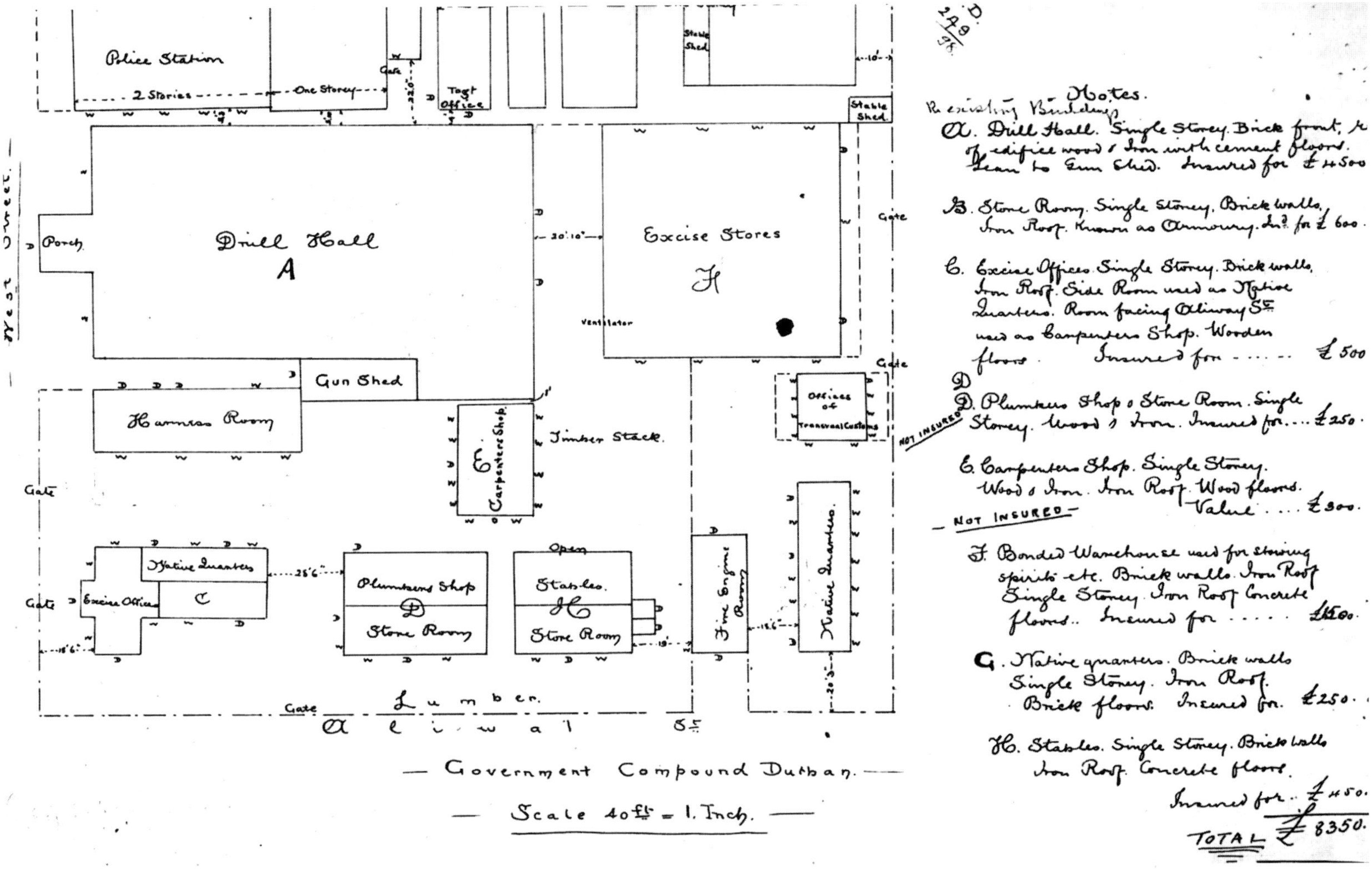

Government compound, Market Square (PAR).

Notes.

Re existing Buildings

A. Drill Hall. Single Storey. Brick front, re of edifice wood & Iron with cement floors. Lean to Gun Shed. Insured for £4500

B. Stone Room. Single Storey. Brick walls, Iron Roof. Known as Armoury. Ins⁄d for £600.

C. Excise Offices. Single Storey. Brick walls, Iron Roof. Side Room used as Native Quarters. Room facing Aliwal St. used as Carpenters Shop. Wooden floors. Insured for £500

D. Plumbers Shop & Stone Room. Single Storey. Wood & Iron. Insured for ..... £250.
NOT INSURED

E. Carpenter Shop. Single Storey. Wood & Iron. Iron Roof. Wood floors. Value .... £300.
— NOT INSURED —

F. Bonded Warehouse used for storing spirits etc. Brick walls. Iron Roof Single Storey. Iron Roof Concrete floors. Insured for ..... £1500.

G. Native quarters. Brick walls Single Storey. Iron Roof. Brick floors. Insured for £250.

H. Stables. Single Storey. Brick walls. Iron Roof. Concrete floors. Insured for £450.

TOTAL £8350.

Heraldic design for the volunteer units (PAR).

The Durban volunteer regiments

Members of the volunteer regiments were drawn from every quarter of white Durban society, with the officer corps coming from the established elite – either civil or government – and the rank and file drawn from business and trades. Movement between the lower orders and the commissioned ranks was highly unlikely since the two orders were as sealed as the respective classes they reflected. Some information is at hand which suggests that volunteers coming from certain businesses were influential in encouraging others in their firms to join up; but there is probably a more complex set of historical, traditional and social reasons for individuals volunteering.

NMR officer in service dress (Goetzsche).

Most of the recruits gave up their weekends and evenings to attend parades and even included recent arrivals in the colony such as Private Z Espeland of the DLI, who was a Norwegian. We know that numbers of recruits came from the Durban municipality: the council initially agreed in November 1899 to grant all volunteer staff full pay up to 11 January 1900, and thereafter to make up their military pay to their normal municipal level.[14] Twenty-six staff members of the Natal Harbour Board also volunteered and were allowed to draw the difference between the volunteer rate of pay and their normal wages.[15] There appears to have been a considerable amount of interest in the question of remuneration. Those on horse received a shilling more than those on foot, as an individual allowance for their mount. Officers received between 14 and 15 shillings per day, while men in the ranks received between 5 and 8 shillings.[16]

Durban supplied four of the eight volunteer regiments which participated in the Natal theatre of the war, representing a total of just under 50% of the total number of regimental volunteers from the colony (1 031 of a total of 2 077 men).[17] The other regiments that participated from Natal were the Natal Carbineers (NCO), the Border Mounted Rifles (BMR), the Umvoti Mounted Rifles (UMR) and the Natal Royal Rifles (NRR). Most of the NNV, NFA and NMR went on to Ladysmith to see action as well as the inaction of siege during the several months that followed, but their colleagues in the DLI and some of the NNV stopped at Estcourt and Colenso. By 6 October, Colonel Royston, the commandant of volunteers, could report that the NNV had 88 men in Ladysmith, 31 at Colenso, and 16 at Estcourt. The NMR and the NFA were all consolidated in Ladysmith with the DLI all in Colenso .

After Ladysmith, the NFA went on to serve at Elandslaagte, Lombard's Kop, Colenso, Estcourt, Willow Grange, Pomeroy, Helpmekaar, Babanango and then through Laing's Nek where they were the first guns and volunteers to enter the Transvaal. They also took part, with General Hildyard column, in taking the town of Vryheid in September 1901. One of their numbers died of disease and another from injuries sustained in being thrown from a horse.

The NNV also served at Colenso in December 1899, and at Caesar's Hill and Spioenkop in January 1900, as well as at Vaal Krantz and Peter's Hill in February. Some of the original 123 officers, NCOs and men were disbanded on 17 April, and the remainder went on to fight in the border actions at Botha's Pass, Allerman's Nek and Sand Spruit in June 1900.

Some 20 men of the NMR under Captain Tatham formed Sir George White's bodyguard at Ladysmith with all its members taking part in every one of White's campaigns and skirmishes. In total four were wounded and two killed; one member of the picket, Trooper AW Evans, was awarded the Distinguished Service Order for conspicuous bravery at Besters on 23 November 1899. During 1899 and the early part of the war, the regiment participated in the various actions at Elandslaagte, Tinta Inyoni, Lombard's Kop, and Besters, and then during 1900 at Draai Hoek, Willow Grange, Colenso, Acton Homes, Spioenkop, Trichardt's Drift, Monte Cristo and Peter's Hill. Of the original number of 217 who set out from Durban, some 104 were invalided with some 32 remaining in the field after Ladysmith. It is significant to note that this regiment succeeded in recruiting a further 93 men for service after the siege.

By far the largest number of local regimental volunteers belonged to the DLI, which initially contributed 476 men and officers, and they also sustained the largest number of casualties with 18 deaths occurring. Having taken part in the armoured train incident at Chievely on 16 November 1899, they went on to fight at Colenso and Willow Grange, and thereafter the corps was stationed at Mooi River, Estcourt, and Frere, and then as part of Buller's slow northward drive, at Elandslaagte, Waschbank and Dundee 'rendering great aid to the Imperial forces and performing most arduous and excellent duties'.

In March 1900, after Ladysmith was relieved, the prime minister, Albert Hime, asked the military authorities why the DLI, who were still stationed at Estcourt, and the NNV, who were attached to the Royal Navy Field Force, should be kept on active service. The general officer commanding replied that he would be glad to let them go, but if the DLI were to be dismissed they would have to be replaced, and there was still a need for the NNV.[18] The NNV were completely disbanded on 26 June and, eventually, on 8 and 9 of October, the remaining Durban volunteer units were also disbanded and returned home to a heroes' welcome, having been on service for a little over a year. Some 300, however, did volunteer for further service and were to serve for the remainder of the war.

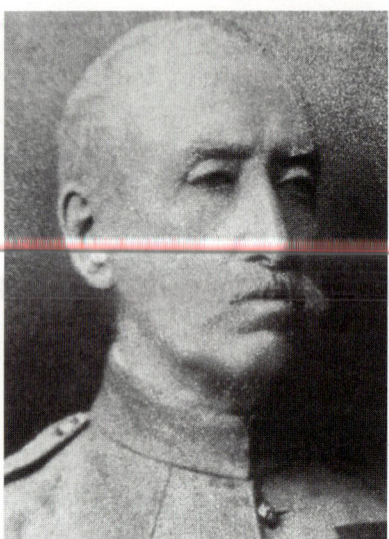

Henry Buxton-Browne

Buxton-Browne was a member of the Scottish Corporation of accountants. He had been born in Derbyshire, England, in 1845, and had served in the fourth battery of 'The Kings Regiment' for 23 years, from which he retired as a major. As a commanding officer of the volunteers, he received the Volunteer Officer's Decoration. Buxton-Browne also played a major role in the local masonic movement.

To Scotchmen.

IT is proposed to form a SCOTTISH COMPANY of MOUNTED INFANTRY for Service at the Front, under Major Thornycroft ; Men of Scottish Descent who can ride and shoot are invited to provisionally enrol their names with

MR. A. DICKSON,
Hon. Secretary, Caledonian Society of Johannesburg
308 Smith Street (opposite the Club) ; or to

MR. HAROLD J. STUART,
Hon. Secretary, Natal Caledonian Society,
Field Street Buildings.

9518 ?

IMMEDIATE APPLICATION ALSO INVITED

The rifle associations

On 3 November 1899, the governor called out the local rifle associations with the statutory two days' notice. Those in the Durban area, including Malvern, Isipingo and Krantzkloof, were to report to Colonel E Bethune, who had been appointed as the first commandant of the town.[19] Bethune had obviously included these volunteers in his rudimentary defence plan which he described as 'a scheme for the defence of Durban against a possible inroad of the enemy. In conjunction with the senior naval officer I have already thought out a plan but will now elaborate a full scheme'. The rifle associations had been formed in the various magisterial districts of Natal from 1862 and they provided the next layer of available recruits from the local white community. Bethune also wished to include the rifle association from Victoria County, north of the Umgeni River, but rule 37 of the association regulations forbade their inclusion. The others were all to work within their various magisterial districts and to communicate with their respective magistrates.

Major H Buxton-Browne was the president of the Durban Rifle Association. When he reported his muster roll to the commandant of Durban on 16 January 1900, the personal details of the men listed showed that they were drawn from a variety of backgrounds, occupations and different areas of the town. Six of their members had transferred either to the irregular corps or to Bethune's Mounted Infantry.[20] Besides Buxton-Browne, there were at least two other officers, Lieutenants Puntan and Voysey. On 4 November 1899, Buxton-Browne acknowledged the receipt of a telegram, and confirmed that he had already reported to the magistrate and Colonel Bethune and was awaiting their instructions.[21]

On 14 November 1899, Prime Minister Albert Hime, asked if any of the Durban associations had turned out. Captain Scott, who had taken over from Bethune as commandant on 7 November, reported back on the 16th that none had yet 'turned out for active service'. The colonial ministers considered that, as the Durban associations had not yet been called upon by the authorities to perform any duties, there should be no authorisation for uniforms. On 20 November 1899, Buxton-Browne wrote to the commandant of volunteers and argued on behalf of his Durban association that his members needed uniforms to march through the streets: 'I am unable to carry out any extended drills as I feel unwilling that the members should march thro' the streets of Durban in civilian clothes.'[22]

On 27 November 1899, the association, which met in the drill room at the corner of Commercial Road and Field Street, still had no uniforms, and Buxton-Browne explained that Bethune had called them out for service and told them to be on stand by so as not to interfere with the men's 'civil avocations'. He had been instructed to commence drills and this he had done. Already some 22 drills of one and a half hours each and ten ball-firing practices had been held; 'the members freely giving both time and money to make themselves efficient, which I think they have fairly succeeded in doing'. On the previous Saturday, he had organised an extended order drill which lasted five hours on the Eastern Vlei, in which the men practised attack movements, ball firing and advancing on head-

and-shoulder targets. In any event Buxton-Browne thought it was grossly unfair that the Pietermaritzburg rifle group already had their uniforms and he could not see the object of calling up his association if they were to present themselves as a kind of ragtag army. It is interesting to note that the major did not see much danger from invading Boers, but thought that the chief threat to the safety of Durban was to come from 'our enormous refugee population, very many of them are known undesirables, they have been quiet so far but there is no knowing how long they may continue when their resources become exhausted'.[23]

Recruits and scouts

In addition to the local regiments which had gone off to Northern Natal, a number of men from Durban must also have counted among those who served in the medical and veterinary volunteer corps. But the next large wave of volunteers were soon to follow. By 23 October 1899, Hely-Hutchinson had obtained General White's approval for raising two corps of mounted men, each 500 strong, for the respective defences of Durban and Pietermaritzburg in order to fill the large vacuum formed by the departed regiments. This was not without the usual conflict between civil and military authorities and the secretary of state for war altered White's approval, though belatedly, and recommended that these should be half infantry and half mounted. Hely-Hutchinson sensibly argued for all to be mounted: 'Mounted men are much more needed than infantry against the Boers; and infantry would be almost useless against a Boer raid without mounted men ...'[24] On 4 November 1899, Hely-Hutchinson also explained to Joseph Chamberlain, the colonial secretary, that the original request was for a corps of 1 000 to defend Durban. Instructions had accordingly been issued and it was too late to alter arrangements.

However, by 12 November, Hely-Hutchinson appears to have altered his original ideas, probably because of the shortage of horses, and he told Chamberlain: 'the General of Communications however informs me in any case any considerable increase in numbers of mounted infantry previously authorised would have necessitated separate organisation. Infantry is cheaper than mounted corps and could be organised much more rapidly. Situation was urgent and Infantry regiment therefore adopted.'[25]

The recruits were chosen to serve under Bethune, Thorneycroft or in the newly formed Imperial Light Horse, all of which were to be eventually formed into the Volunteer Composite Regiment by the second half of 1900. The latter corps was the first regiment to be raised of South African colonials and had been informally organised by Colonel Wools-Sampson even before hostilities commenced. The Uitlander committees in Natal had facilitated these recruiting procedures with registers of suitable men and horses.

Who would pay for this arrangement? The war office agreed that equipment and horses would be paid for out of a royal warrant, while the colony would need to foot the bill for the volunteers. In turn, the question was also raised regarding how much the volunteers should be paid. The

Recruiting for the volunteer units

Boscawen-Wright described the formation of two volunteer units: 'Offices were opened in various parts of the town and the enrolment of volunteers proceeded with pace. The mounted corps had no difficulty in getting their full complement of men, the only difficulty being in the selection of candidates, so many offering their services; the want of mounts also proved somewhat of a drawback, however they did their utmost with the material at their command and within a week or so, two fine corps, commanded respectively by Colonels Thorneycroft and Bethune, were ready to take the field. On account of the scarcity of horses, the authorities decided to raise an infantry battalion, to be known as the Imperial Light Infantry, and offices were opened in Pine Street, at the premises of the well-known Rand ex-detective A Trimble. One week in Durban was sufficient to imbue all our party with martial ardour, and in company with about fifty others we found ourselves in the enrolling office, where three clerks were hard at work taking down the names of all those who wished to join. All day a constant stream of recruits poured in, who after signing their names were told that they would have to repair the next day to the race-course, and there undergo a medical examination, and get sworn in. Early next morning we set out for the appointed rendezvous, which was not difficult to find, a long procession of all sorts and conditions of men winding their way thitherwards, and by the time we arrived, there must have been close on six hundred men on the ground. We were all marshalled in long lines, and Colonel Nash, who inspected us, asked each individual what kind of marksman he was, and if their replies were in any way correct, he would have had under him absolutely the finest fighting regiment in the world, but unfortunately a trial at the butts a few weeks later proved that their capacity for lying was far in advance of their shooting abilities. On the conclusion of this cursory inspection, we were informed that all would have to pass the doctor, who had a room underneath the Grand Stand. This meant another weary wait ... at length our turn arrived, and in company with a number of others we were ushered into a dim and dingy apartment and ordered to strip. Two doctors were hard at work and subjected each candidate to a minute and rigid examination to discover any hidden ailment. This ordeal passed, a move was made into another room where Adjutant Jackson presided over a huge board with lettering of various sizes. There each recruit, standing at a distance of ten paces from it, had to decipher and if successful passed out into the open to wait around until sworn in. The swearing-in process was a very simple affair, the men filed into a room until it resembled the Black Hole of Calcutta, and when it was found impossible to introduce another man Colonel Nash started reading the oath, everyone repeating it after him, the only intelligible portion being, however, the end – 'So help me God'. This business being satisfactorily disposed of, nothing now remained to be done but to settle down to camp life.'

war office proposed they be paid 1s per day but Colonel Thorneycroft observed that most of them would not serve for that sum, though he went on to explain that some enthusiastic volunteers were even willing to serve without pay. Thorneycroft also considered that for the majority of the men 5s would be a reasonable amount since:

> ... when a Colonial is asked to volunteer to fight he knows from previous experience that if he is disabled or killed he has got no Government pension, and if he is married, as many of them are, he has to keep up his home during the time he is away at the front, and from the expensive nature of living and house-rent in the colonies it is impossible for a trooper to keep his wife and family even on 5s a day.[26]

For most recruits, like Boscawen-Wright and his friends, the principal duties of camp life included learning the goose-step and other elementary drill under drill instructors, which included an old colour-sergeant who 'had a voice of thunder ... and [was] wonderfully smart in detecting a false step, being, in fact, like a musician whose sense of harmony has been disturbed by a jarring note'.[27] The volunteers found it difficult to adjust to the loss of privacy with 16 men to a bell tent and Bosca-wen-Wright described how 'men used to roll up late at night full of whiskey and fight, and clamber into their places by making a doormat of your body ... campaigning is not all sunshine'. During the time they were camped in Durban, a steady drizzle fell continuously and the marshy conditions of the racecourse and the 'sickening effluvium emanating from the damp blankets' made conditions most unpleasant. Other volunteer units had been granted free access to the public baths, but the Imperial Light Infantry had to bathe in the bay, close to where 'one of the main sewers of the town discharged its malodorous contents'. Needless to say they were pleased when, after two weeks, the battalion was ordered to proceed to Pietermaritzburg.

The grand stand at the Greyville Racecourse (LHM).

Colonial scouts

On 21 November 1899, some government ministers suggested in a minute to the governor the idea of raising an irregular corps of 'horsemen for checking Boer raids' and, on 24 November, the military undertook to pay for this corps of 'Colonial Scouts'.[28] On 25 November, a newspaper notice called for volunteers for a corps of mounted men. This was to be a special Durban troop and the pay would be the same as the other volunteers.

Arrangements were made for the Durban magistrate, Broome, to commence recruitment, and some 300 volunteered locally. Of these, 195 could provide their own horses. By 5 December, some 538 men had been recruited and they were formed into five squadrons made up of four troops of 25, with a leader for each troop and a head leader for each squadron. It was reported in the selection that great care had been exercised in terms of the character, physique and general efficiency of the men. It is probable that a fair number would have been drawn from the surrounding farming community. Before the end of 1899, Durban residents had raised £928 10s for the purchase of horses for these scouts. Sir Benjamin Greenacre donated £100 to this fund and most other businessmen contributed £30 each. Thirteen horses were also donated.[29] By January 1900, the borough police were engaged in recruiting volunteers, which they appear to have continued doing for the duration of the war.[30]

Evidently, Durban merchants also contributed towards the equipping of these recruits. In May 1900, a certain J Wood of Pietermaritzburg wrote to the colonial secretary:

> I have the honour to inform you that the equipment supplied by Mr. Acutt to the members of the Colonial Scouts recruited in Durban was not a gift from the Durban Merchants as stated by you ... Every member of the Corps has either been paid or credited with 30/– for equipment, and the amount so allowed ... has accordingly been debited in the men's accounts and deducted from their pay.[31]

In his response to the colonial secretary, Magistrate Broome explained that when he had been requested to raise the recruits he had called on Ernest Acutt of the Mart, Durban, to assist as a subagent, since his 'court and office duties' kept him busy. The understanding at the time was that Acutt would supply the equipment 'and that he would be repaid by the government to the extent of 30s per man'. This had also been done with the approval of the government and Captain Huneberg of the scouts. Broome went on to point out that Wood's letter was in the same handwriting as another he had received under a pseudonym which 'in most offensive terms, suggest[ed] that my support of Mr. Acutt was due to an expectation of sharing in ill-gotten gain'.[32] In addition, he also expressed the surprising possibility that Wood had somehow had sight of their previous correspondence in the matter.

The issue had become more complicated in that some recruits had left before the 30s could be deducted from their pay. Moreover, the lists prepared by Acutt differed from those of Captain Huneberg; Acutt's lists also included the names of those actually rejected as scouts while some recruits claimed that the clothing was unserviceable. What became clear when Acutt presented a bill for £612 was that the clothing had actually cost 35s per head and Acutt had only claimed 30s and, as Broome observed, for the government 'to refuse payment would be a great discouragement to one whose assistance has been very useful in a time of emergency, and who is already a good deal out of pocket' and he added that the 'formation of the Durban contingent was largely due to his efforts'.[33]

As late as January 1901 the recruiting process was still going on, but it now involved the very young such as John Orman Burne, who joined the volunteers around 7 January. He joined Menne's Scouts, a corps which had been specifically raised for the defence of Zululand, without his father's knowledge or consent, which would have been required as he was only 15 years old. His father, William Burne, was a local advocate and partner in the firm of W Burne & Benningfield and he lost no time in writing to the colonial secretary to express his request for the return of his son:

> I learned of this last evening, and this morning I reported to the recruiting officer that the boy had joined without my knowledge or consent and that he is under 16 years of age, but notwithstanding this I find that the boy has been partly equipped and is being sent forward tonight. I therefore report the matter to you and trust you will be good enough to take such steps as may be necessary to cause this boy to be sent back. I have had other sons serving through the greater part of this war and I should let this one go if he were fit to endure the hardships to be encountered but a lad of under 16 years is unfit for the work ...[34]

The colonial secretary passed on the request to the military and young John was located and discharged in Newcastle. It appears that at that stage of the war, recruits were sent directly to Sandspruit, close to Volksrust in the Transvaal. It is interesting to compare the case of John Burne with the large number of child soldiers or *penkoppe* employed by the Boers.

Acutt's Saturday morning mart, Gardiner Street (LHM).

The return of the volunteers

Of the original number of 938 volunteers from the local Durban regiments which had set out under those triumphant conditions on that weekend at the end of September 1899, 105 did not return, 29 having been killed in action and 76 having died of disease. In a despatch to Chamberlain, Hely-Hutchinson noted that eight of the fatalities were officers.[35]

In a detailed notice dated 29 September 1900, addressed to the NGR staff, the general manager, David Hunter, set out the arrangements for special trains to be consigned to convey the volunteer troops home. The route down along the main line from Dundee was prepared to maximise public participation at each of the railway stations en route with attention being focussed on the coastal and Durban detachments scheduled to arrive in Pietermaritzburg by breakfast on Tuesday 2 October, so that all the volunteer regiments could be addressed by the governor before their disbandment. Units from the south coast were to be conveyed in No. 1 train to South Coast Junction 'where a small Engine and Guard will be in readiness to take over the train and run [it] as a ... South Coast Line special ...'.[36]

The remaining troops were not to proceed into the centre of Durban, but to the Umbilo and Congella Stations. Once again this was a major public relations exercise as the returning soldiers would now march through the main streets of the town to the jubilant cheers of the people. A special commemorative *Natal Volunteer Record* was produced by the Durban publishers of the *Natal Mercury*, Robinson & Co., to mark the return of the volunteers, in which the welcome was vividly described:

> The corps left the City between 8.30 and 9.30. At Camperdown some folk gathered bucketfuls of hail, and as the trains moved in greeted the volunteers with showers of ice. A veritable 'snowball' match ensued, the victory resting with the ladies, who got many a handful of ice between collar and neck of discomfited troopers. At Pinetown the inhabitants turned out to shower flowers upon the men; at Pinetown Bridge the convalescents and nurses from the Princess Christian Hospital came out to cheer. Enthusiasm spread from one end of the line to the other; and Durban, dressed in her best, was expectant – waiting for the coming of her sons. The Natal Mounted Rifles and Natal Field Artillery detrained at Umbilo, whose residents regaled them with tea and cake. At 3.45 the men of bronzed faces and much-worn khaki marched on to Congella – Captain Henwood riding his siege horse, the town already pouring out to meet them. At Congella Station the Durban Light Infantry detrained amid the growing crowd. The Mayor (Mr. J. Nicol) wore his chain of office ... the party were also met by Mr. David Hunter, C.M.G., the Deputy Mayor (Mr J. Ellis Brown) and the Natal Naval Volunteers. A move was at once made through Mr. Brown's grounds to the lawn, where laden

tables stood. Heavily equipped in full marching order, the bulk of the men found a convenient seat on a grassy sward, and they were charmingly ministered to by dainty maids in white, over whom Mrs. Brown exercised a matronly supervision. At 5 o'clock the Durham Artillery, commanded by a non-com., headed the cavalcade followed by the Natal Naval Volunteers, the Natal Mounted Rifles, the Natal Field Artillery with guns, and the Durban Light Infantry – all preceded by members of the Town Council. The men brought their pets with them – lambs, goats and birds. The Navals' 'Jack' marched as usual at the head of his corps.

Meanwhile West Street, Durban was packed from kerbstone to roof and ridge, all the windows bowers of beauty, all the street one line of colour and one smile of joy. Along Berea Road came the Natal Naval Volunteers with swinging step, chanting a nautical chorus ... ladies on discovering their relations, burst through the crowd and proudly took their arms, and walked along in quickstep. Cheering and flag-waving, with mutual recognition, the meeting of father and babe, of lover and sweetheart, all moved onward to the Town Hall and Gardens where round some 20,000 people pressed below Her Majesty's Statue.[37]

The usual mayoral and military speeches followed and the celebrations continued long into that night and through to the following Sunday, when a special thanksgiving service was held in the town hall.

As late as mid-1902, newspapers were still carrying advertisements for various types of recruits. Since the local population had probably been almost depleted as a resource, attentions were now turned to new arrivals such as cattlemen. Another option was to return to those who had volunteered many months before and had since been demobilised. Thus the *Natal Mercury* of March and May 1902 carried advertisements for recruits for, among others, the Volunteer Composite Regiment, Steinaecker's Horse, the Utrecht Mounted Police, and a Cape Colony Cyclists' Corps. One bold advertisement called on the 'Boys of the Old Imperial Light Horse to come and fight for your King and Country ... and take 5s a day'.[38]

The brindled bull terrier 'Durban' (Treves).

The dogs of war

Many regiments, even some companies, had mascots during the war and two deserve special mention. A bull terrier, named Jack, first appeared in public through a letter to the editor of the *Natal Mercury* on 10 October 1899:

Jolly Tars and the Dog
Camp of the Naval Volunteers
Ladysmith, October 6
Sir, You can't imagine how we cheered the advertisement contained in your issue of yesterday announcing the fact that Mr. A B Smart had missed his bull terrier. Please let Mr. Smart know through the medium of your valuable paper that 'Jack' is all right with the boys in blue. He came and joined us on Sunday night, just before we left Durban, and has now been sworn in for special service, with a rating of A.B. Mr. Smart would not know him now. 'Jack' has an anchor on his starboard bow and NNV on his stern. He seems as anxious as ourselves to meet Oom Paul and we will march him in front of us when we go through the chains. His owner will be very proud to see his dog return leading the boys down to the Drill Hall. We shall then claim the reward in the shape of a barrel of beer. We are all grateful to our old friend Mr R Jameson for sending us the papers ... I am etc. Harness Cask.'

Smart took this letter in good part and gladly allowed the naval Volunteers to keep Jack, even sending a parcel of bones to the camp as a ration for the mascot. Jack quickly adapted to life in the Navy and camp routine. In the mornings he would 'fall in' on parade for his emergency rations as unconcernedly as everyone else. Jack became very well known at the front and several regiments tried to lure him away, but he would politely but firmly decline and only followed the men in naval uniform. Jack would turn in whenever he liked, lights out had no special significance for him. He would select a tent and then throw himself on the fattest man or the one with the most blankets, make himself comfortable and go to sleep. When the camp came under Boer fire, he would wait to see a small shell bury itself, then dig furiously until he found it, pick it up in his mouth and then deposit at the feet of the nearest officer.

The other dog was believed to have been brought down to Durban by a refugee family. He attached himself to No. 4 field hospital when they were in Durban, and for the want of a better name was called 'Durban'. He was a brindled bull terrier of exceptional physique and intelligence, placid and of good temper. On the railway platform in Pietermaritzburg, he took his place amongst the ranks of the orderlies and boarded the train for Frere. Durban had a special collar on which was emblazoned the red cross of the medical corps. Before the field hospital left for Chieveley, someone made him a pair of putties which he wore on his forelegs and showed off proudly to the camp. No doubt, encouraged by this he was presented with a travelling kit at Spearman's camp. This consisted of a waterproof cape and two small panniers marked with a red cross. The outfit was difficult to secure and early in a march would be found dangling beneath his massive chest. Durban was inordinately fond of bathing and when the corps was camped close to the Little Tugela River he would join any party going to the river and bathe for as long as there was someone to bathe with. He also did his duty as a watch dog, at times choosing the commissariat. One day the hospital was given some sheep which were left to graze in the veld, but no one was able to catch one for the kitchen. The problem was explained to Durban and thereafter he would accompany the cook to the flock and never failed to pull down a sheep. Then he would follow cook and the sheep back to the camp with the air of one who had done his duty for his country.[39]

The Uitlander committee in Durban developed its own, somewhat high-handed and optimistic style of volunteering as the following telegram from A Percy Field at the Durban Club shows:
Dec.1st urgent. Deputation from a Committee of discharged irregulars and other refugees waited upon us asking us to transmit the following statement. *Begins* we have requisitions signed by about 300 discharged irregulars who have objections to joining any of the existing corps but wish to form a new regiment to be called the Johannesburg Mounted Rifles for service in the field anywhere under the following conditions *stop*. 1) Officers with Colonial experience to be appointed in consultation with our Committee *stop*. 2) 3 months service with option of further extension *stop*. 3) disbandment in Johannesburg provided the war is over *stop*. 4) pay five shillings per day all found *stop*. We have already asked the Commandant Durban to transmit our offer to Chief of Staff who referred us to Colonel Capper Cape Town ... if any time is lost numbers of these useful men will be leaving for their homes *stop*. but if immediate sanction is obtained there will not be the slightest difficulty in raising regiment of 500 or more *stop*...[39]

Scouts of Bethune's Mounted Infantry (Wilson).

1.   *Natal Mercury*, 30.9.1899.

2.   *Natal Mercury*, 2.10.1899.

3.   *Natal Mercury*, 2.10.1899.

4.   The Natal Field Artillery, *Centenary Brochure*, p.10.

5.   Hurst, GT, *History of the NMR*, pp.8–9.

6.   *Natal Mercury*, 10.3.1938.

7.   Dick, J, *Historical Record of the Durban Volunteer Infantry Corps*, p.61.

8.   PAR, NGR 26: notice to staff, 29.9.1899.

9.   *Natal Mercury*, 14.11.1899.

10. *Natal Mercury*, 3.10.1899.

11. Brookes, EH, and Webb, C de B, *A History of Natal*, p.202.

12. PAR, NGR 26: notice to staff, 29.9.1899.

13. PAR, PWD 2/73: volunteer stores and offices, und.

14. DAR, 3/DBN 5/2/6/1/14: finance committee, 7.11.1899 and 5.1.1900.

15. PAR, NHD II/1/25:correspondence relating to volunteers, 28.4.1900.

16. PAR, MJPW 70: paylist for Natal volunteers, und.

17. PAR, GH 498: Natal volunteers, regiments etc., 1.10.1900.

18. PAR, MJPW 116: prime minister to general officer commanding, 17.3.1900.

19. PAR, MJPW 71: calling out the rifle associations, 3.11.1899.

20. PAR, NDR 2/2: muster rolls, 16.1.1900.

21. PAR, MJPW 71: Buxton-Browne to colonial secretary, 4.11.1899.

22. Ibid.

23. PAR, MJPW 72: Buxton-Browne to minister of lands and works, 27.11.1899.

24. PRO, CO 179/207:governor to Chamberlain, 23.10.1899.

25. PRO, CO 179/207: governor to Chamberlain, 12.11.1899.

26. Royal Commission on the War in South Africa, p.191

27. Boscawen-Wright, C, *With the Imperial Light Infantry through Natal*, pp.5–9.

28. PRO, CO 179/208: colonial secretary to prime minister, 8.12.1899.

29. PRO, CO 179/208: list of contributions for horses etc. und.

30. DAR, 3/DBN 5/2/5/3/6: report of superintendent of police, 4.1.1900.

31. PAR, CSO 1644: J Wood to colonial secretary, 9.2.1901.

32. Ibid.

33. Ibid.

34. PAR, CSO 1668: W Burne to colonial secretary, 9.2.1901.

35. PRO, CO 179/214: governor to Chamberlain, 2.11.1900.

36. PAR, GH 498: manager NGR to Staff, 29.9.1900.

37. Robinson and Co, *Natal Volunteer Record*, pp.3–4.

38. *Natal Mercury*, March to May 1902.

39. Treves, F, *The Tale of a Field Hospital*, p7.

40. PAR, A 1538: Field to Colonel Capper c/o high commissioner, 1.12.1899.

CHAPTER 6

CATTLEMEN: INVOLUNTARY VOLUNTEERS FOR QUEEN AND KING
Johan Wassermann

At no other time did the words of the country and western song by Willie Nelson, 'Mamas don't let your babies grow up to be cowboys', seem more appropriate than during the Anglo-Boer War. During the voyage to and after docking at Durban, cattlemen experienced a variety of adventures.

Cattlemen were not an uncommon sight in Durban prior to the war, with roughly ten cattleships docking in Durban per annum. These ships arrived from ports all over the globe, including Madagascar, South and North America and Australia. The cattlemen on board these ships were generally a motley bunch consisting of many nationalities: Italians, Americans, Austro-Hungarians, Spaniards, Argentinians, Somali Arabs, Britains, Canadians, Australians and New Zealanders amongst others. They were closer to 30 than 20 years of age, but sometimes even older than 50. In reality, very few of the cattlemen knew much about working with animals. Most, but not all, were adventurers, drifters, petty criminals and troublemakers who roved from port to port. As a result, many, especially during the early part of the war, arrived in Durban on a one-way passage, sometimes as 'extra hands' or stowaways, who were prepared to work their way to the next port. If they found employment and anything else they considered worthwhile, they would remain and settle. If not, they departed on the next cattleship. The officers were therefore the only permanent and experienced staff on cattleships. The constant turnover of staff, difficult working conditions, unpleasant weather and travelling conditions, and alleged abuse of temporary staff often made the journey to their destination uncomfortable.

An extreme example of such experiences occurred on board the *Yarrowdale*, a cargo ship which had been hastily converted into a cattleship and had left Melbourne, Australia on 8 August 1900, en route to Durban. It carried 928 sheep, 50 bulls, 24 cows and some horses. On its journey it ran into a severe storm that wreaked havoc. The livestock in stalls on the deck had to bear the brunt of the elements. During the storm the frail railings quickly gave way, and animals became impaled on the broken spars. Sheep were washed overboard, the cattle were knocked about and consequently had limbs broken, and the deck 'was literally strewn with maimed, moaning, dying and dead cattle, presenting a spectacle sickening to the heart and repulsive to sight'. In total 493 sheep and between 50 and 60 cattle were lost. The verdict of the cattlemen on this ship was that they never again wished to undergo such an experience, or witness such horrible scenes.[1]

The captains of these cattleships were in the habit of signing up cattlemen on a one-way passage, and then leaving them in their port of call. This dumping of cattlemen in ports was a global problem. In Liverpool, cattlemen from the USA and Italian cattlemen from Argentina were left stranded. After complaints by the Italian ambassador regarding this practice, the British prime minister instructed Joseph Chamberlain to act, which led to the Liverpool Chamber of Shipping being severely reprimanded. The Australian colonies went even further and decreed that the captain of a cattleship had to provide security for each cattleman landed.[2] The Natal government, to prevent this and other forms of illegal immigration, passed the Immigration Restriction Act, to be administered by the immigration restriction department (IRD), headed by the immigration restriction officer (IRO), Harry Smith.

At the time of the Anglo-Boer War, the term cattleman referred to any person that worked with livestock, be it horses, sheep or cattle on board a ship. Similarly, the term cattleship was used to describe ships that carried livestock, regardless of the animals they contained.

The Immigration Restriction Act, Act 1 of 1897, defined a prohibited immigrant as:

(a) Any person who, when asked to do so by an officer appointed under this act, shall fail to himself write out and sign, in the characters of a language of Europe, an application to the Colonial Secretary in the form set out in schedule B of this act.
(b) Any person being a pauper, or likely to become a public charge.
(c) Any idiot or insane person.
(d) Any person who suffers from a loathsome or a dangerous contagious disease.
(e) Any person who, not having received a free pardon, has within two years been convicted of a felony or other infamous crime or misdemeanour, involving moral turpitude and not being a mere political offence.
(f) Any prostitute, and any person living on the prostitution of others.

Feeding and watering horses on board ship (*The Graphic,* 14.10.1899).

To ensure that prospective cattlemen knew about the change in legislation in Natal, memos were forwarded to Buenos Aires, Argentina, one of the foremost ports for shipping livestock to Durban. Under the new act, it was extremely difficult to enter Natal, and the British consul in Buenos Aires reported that the act had given 'rise to further complaints being made by cattlemen here ... about the way in which they are sometimes treated by shippers'.[3] The act, which was applied in an almost draconian manner, infuriated the cattlemen immigrants and shipowners to such an extent that HM Pritchard, the master of the *City of Lincoln*, a regular visitor to Durban, wrote a letter to *The Standard*, in Buenos Aires. In an extremely caustic manner, Pritchard related details pertaining to the journey from Argentina to Durban to deliver 650 mules and 560 asses, describing the treatment they had received on arrival in Durban:

> My peons received every attention from polite Natalians, who had a labour committee to meet them, and a fine body of black guides in blue uniforms and silver buttons to escort them around the public buildings, and kindly house them in one of the most formidable, with free quarters and food for a week, when the same honourable escort brought them back on board with the request I would take them back to the Plate, as they had no uses for them. German, French, Italian, and Austrian Consuls stormed at the treatment of their countrymen. It was no use. Natal for the Natalians their policy, they have the Rinderpest and want no other. So my thirty peons have come back sadder and wiser men.[4]

The Immigration Restriction Act did not solve the problems the authorities in Durban faced with cattlemen, especially those who were forced off the ship by the captain, and then abandoned. With the Anglo-Boer War in full swing and the demand for livestock, both for slaughter and transport purposes, growing so did the number of cattleships. These increased from seven in 1899 to 54 in 1900, bringing in no less than 1 689 cattlemen. Of these, 133 on board the *Manchester* were landed at the request of the military authorities who enlisted almost all the men.[5] The first dumping casualties were the 48 cattlemen brought to Durban by the *Sussex*, who were illegally landed in Durban, leaving them destitute. The men should have earned a fair salary on the trip, but instead they were left behind in Durban without being paid their salaries. This left them at the mercy of the Natal authorities, who received them with open arms under the Immigration Protection Act, since they were artisans needed by the colony.[6] Within days of these cattlemen being dumped, the *City of Lincoln* also abandoned men, clearly indicating that, although well aware of the law, as revealed by the letter written to *The Standard* by its master, HM Pritchard, it had no intention of abiding by the regulations. It was during mid-June 1900, that the *City of Lincoln* had docked in Durban, and the 30 Italian cattlemen on board had been landed illegally. The excuse given by the captain, which turned out to be nothing more than a devious scheme to rid his ship and himself of the cattlemen, was that the

City of Lincoln needed to make a short trip up the coast. The cattlemen were to be collected again within a few days. In reality, the *City of Lincoln* steamed for Australia and, being well aware of the strict Australian laws regarding cattlemen, the captain got rid of the men in Durban where it was easier. As a result, there was no need to pay salaries or sustain the cattlemen during the trip to Australia. New workers could simply be hired in Australia. The destitute Italian cattlemen somehow made their way, possibly as cheap labour, to the Stainbank's premises at the Umgeni River. As the men spoke no English, they were regarded as a danger by the surrounding residents, and reported to the police. The superintendent of the Durban borough police, RC Alexander, ordered them to return to their ship, which was impossible. With the intervention of Stainbank, the cattlemen were removed to the refugee camp at Lords Ground, where they were provided with food and looked after by a certain Saunders who spoke Italian. As the men were not responsible for what transpired, they could not be prosecuted. It was thus decided to keep these cattlemen at Lords Ground until the *City of Lincoln* returned or another ship could take them back to Argentina.[7]

One of the main reasons for cattlemen disembarking, both legally and illegally, in Durban lay in the newspaper advertisements which appeared on a daily basis calling for volunteers. In a single edition of the *Natal Mercury*, Bethune's Mounted Infantry, Thorneycroft's Mounted Infantry, Steinaecker's Horse, 1st and 2nd Scottish, Johannesburg Mounted Rifles, South African Light Horse, Kitchener's Fighting Scouts, Damant's Horse, Pietersburg Light Horse, the Canadian Scouts, Driscoll's Scouts and the Railway Pioneer Regiment advertised for recruits. In addition to this, advertisements occasionally appeared in the *Natal Mercury* for farriers, saddlers, smiths, wheelwrights, hospital staff and sub-conductors for ox or mule wagons.[8]

As a result of the ongoing demand for recruits and artisans, the cattleships became a prime target for the recruiting officers of the various units. In the words of IRO, Harry Smith: 'The Recruiting Officer has played an important part in the disposal of these men, of the majority of whom it may be said that in him they met the very individual they had journeyed to South Africa to see. He has not kept them waiting either, but with a keenness on being early that would have done credit to a newspaper man, has commonly gone outside to do business from the pilot boat, and even in some instances traveled down the coast to board vessels bound for this port.' The British military, regardless of how desperate they were, could not enlist all the cattlemen recruited. Some cattlemen were bound to be rejected on medical or other grounds. Since these men, who under normal circumstances would have been prevented from entering Natal by the Immigration Restriction Act, were unable to return to their ship, they were subsequently on the loose in Durban.[9]

The rejection by the military of certain cattlemen, and the dumping of others soon became a bone of contention. In a letter of complaint sent from the secretary of the Durban Refugee Relief Fund, WO Cook, to the Natal government, he complained that a large number of cattlemen, especially from Australia, were constantly knocking on their door for assistance, as they had no other means of supporting themselves. The Durban Refugee Relief Fund indicated that they could not provide for these men from their fund as the city was already overcrowded and unemployment was rife. They felt that ships should be compelled to take the cattlemen back 'rather than land them here in a penniless condition'. The complaint was referred to the IRO, Harry Smith, for comment. In his answer, Smith outlined the procedure which was followed: military recruiting agents went on board each cattleship to inform the men about local conditions and what they could expect, and then the cattlemen were allowed to decide for themselves if they wanted to land and enlist in the British army. According to Smith 'in the exercise of his duties he has not interfered with the entry into the Colony of men from Australia and other Colonies, whose journey to South Africa has been undertaken from patriotic motives'. A very large proportion of these cattlemen were employed by the military authorities, and those that were not successful in this regard were, according to him, 'not of the stamp of undesirable immigrants'. Viewing the letter from Cook as a reflection on him personally and the manner in which his department dealt with cattlemen, Smith launched a retaliatory attack on Cook and the Durban Refugee Relief Fund, reminding them that 'there may be a little strain here and there' but he felt that this did not allow Cook the liberty, in his private capacity or as a member of the committee, to suggest that ships should be compelled to take cattlemen back rather than leave them behind, as they claimed, in a state of poverty.[10]

Harry Smith

Harry Smith was born in 1864 in Southsea in the United Kingdom. He came to Natal in 1880 and by the time of the Anglo-Boer War he had risen to the rank of principal immigration restriction officer. Smith was also the secretary of the Natal harbour department and the Durban branch of the Navy League.

Harry Smith on the veranda of his house, Somerhill, Escombe Terrace, Point (KCL).

The criticism by the Durban Refugee Relief Fund did, however, serve its purpose and resulted in a stricter enforcement of the Immigration Restriction Act. To prevent the captains of ships from dumping cattlemen in Durban, or refusing to take the men back on board once they had disembarked, each captain of a ship which docked in Durban was issued with a reminder that he was responsible for the men who, according to the Immigration Restriction Act, were considered illegal immigrants, and that they should be taken back on board ship. The captain of the *Langton Grange*, however, took no notice of this reminder. Instead, he landed 50 cattlemen: 22 British, 12 Italian, 6 Austro-Hungarians, 4 Spaniards, 2 Germans, 2 Frenchmen, 1 Belgian and 1 Swiss after they had been 'paid off'. Under the stricter application of the act, only one of the Frenchmen, Marriel Claudius, who was on route to Madagascar and who had the financial means to do so, was allowed to stay. Three of the Austro-Hungarians called upon the help of their consul, W Munder, as unfortunately for them their promised employment with Vincent Viscovich did not materialise, and they were escorted back to the *Langton Grange*, where the captain was informed that the men were his responsibility.[11]

The simultaneous and vigorous recruiting of subjects of the empire for irregular units, and the attempts by the IRD to exercise more stringent control over the landing of cattlemen soon came under the spotlight. GA Crouch, an Australian residing in Pietermaritzburg, wrote to Prime Minister Albert Hime enquiring if the following were true: 'Australians, passengers from Australian ports to Natal, I am informed, have been denied the right to land at Durban except on the sole condition of their enlisting and being prepared to serve at the front. This is in some cases against the will of the men desiring to land. These men are writing to their home friends, and the matter will be most probably discussed in the Melbourne and Sydney daily press; and it is quite possible that our Commonwealth would then discuss and enquire into the question.' Crouch followed this up with a letter to Alfred Deakin, the attorney-general of the Australian Commonwealth. This letter provided the full details regarding Private George Rawlings, No. 543, who had served with his unit, the New South Wales Bushmen for seven months in the war. He was injured and disabled when his horse was shot and killed under him. Rawlings was transported per *Mendic* to Sydney where he made a full recovery. In the middle of March 1901 Rawlings had returned to Natal on board the *Southern Cross* to take up a position he had been promised before his injury. According to Crouch, as informed by Rawlings, the latter and several other men were denied permission to land by the IRO, except on the sole condition that they enlisted and agreed to serve at the front. As a result, Rawlings enlisted in Kitchener's Fighting Scouts. The same lot had apparently befallen several other Australians. To Crouch this was unacceptable and he stated: 'I feel strongly and warmly that our Australian manhood should be subjected to such indignity at the hands of the buffer colony of Natal whose sole existence and prosperity depends on the Transvaal, where our Australian manhood desire to go.'

IRO Harry Smith, when confronted with the accusation of Crouch, rejected the idea that cattlemen from Australia were dealt with in such a forceful manner. Of the 956 cattlemen prohibited from landing in the 14 months since the war had started, only six were Australian. Smith made it clear: 'As a matter of fact, beyond the usual inspection, there has been little interference under the Immigration Restriction Act with the extra hands of Australian Cattle boats ... It is however a fact that the requirements of this Department are subordinate to those of the Military Authorities and if the latter want men whose landing I have stopped they take them. As an example, Smith referred to the case of the *Mount Royal* which arrived on 10 March 1901 from New Orleans with 72 cattlemen on board. Applying the law rigorously, Smith refused these men the right to land. On mustering the men prior to the departure of the *Mount Royal*, it was found that the military had recruited 20 of them. These men, as far as Smith was concerned, could not claim that they were denied the right to land on the sole condition that they enlist. The position was simple, the military was the superior power in these matters and had the power to state: 'We want men whom you would send away and if those men are willing to serve us we set your order aside.' When the enquiry from the attorney-general of Australia arrived, Albert Hime could respond by quoting the report of IRO Smith and prove that the complaints made by Crouch were groundless.[12]

Under the stricter application of the Immigration Restriction Act, 72 cattlemen, mainly Americans, but also Germans, Dutch and eight Britains on board the *Politician*, were prohibited from disembarking. The stricter application this time round was requested by the commandant of Durban, Colonel O'Neill, in an attempt to restrict the recruiting of cattlemen to members of the British empire only, and thus prevent foreigners from coming ashore merely to become part of the poverty-stricken population. When the American cattlemen became aware of this, many changed their nationality to become Canadians. This complicated matters, as they were now subjects of the British empire. Smith was, therefore, prepared to wave the Immigration Restriction Act if the chief recruiting officer could provide him with the names of the (Canadian?) cattlemen on board the *Politician* he wished to enlist. The recruiting office not only provided such a list, but added a further 24 names of cattlemen on board the *Glanton* that had been recruited. The majority of the recruited cattlemen immediately went to the drill hall, ready to be enlisted later in the day in various corps.[13]

With apparent chaos reigning in dealing with cattleships and cattlemen, Harry Smith wrote to the commandant of Durban, Colonel O'Neill, to gain some clarity on the co-operation with the military recruiting officers. Smith wanted to know what steps the military had taken to ensure an improved observation of the orders issued against the vessels specified under the Immigration Restriction Act. As an example of the overriding of this law by the recruitment officers, Smith cited the example of the *Mount Royal* which had arrived from New Orleans with 72 cattlemen on board who were employed for the round voyage. These men were prohibited by Smith from coming ashore by law, and the chief recruiting officer of the day was informed accordingly. On a roll-call of the cattlemen prior to the departure of the *Mount Royal*, it was found that 20 were absent. When the captain was asked why he should not be prosecuted under the law, he declared that the absentees had been recruited and produced several letters to prove this. Smith made it clear that he did not want to interfere with the work of the recruiting officers, but that he had a colonial law to uphold and was bound by certain instructions. He therefore suggested that the recruiting officer should ascertain whether any restriction had been placed upon the landing of the crew before boarding the cattleship. He ordered that no recruiting of prohibited immigrants should take place until he himself had had the opportunity of enquiring into the propriety of varying the restriction order. He stressed that, where cattlemen were originally prohibited from landing and were released to the recruiting officer, the said officer should be responsible for the return to the ship of those who had failed the medical test. The suggestions of Smith carried favour with the commandant, who agreed that recruiting officers should see to the return of cattlemen to their ships if they were medically rejected. Colonel O'Neill also agreed that recruiting officers should only board a ship once it had been cleared by the IRO. In the case of the *Mount Royal*, this rule was adhered to. The captain of the ship, however, disregarded the regulations by bringing some of the cattlemen to the drill hall, saying that the restrictions had been removed and the men could be enlisted.[14]

Between October 1899 and March 1901, 70 cattleships, of which 35 had originated in Australia, docked at Durban. Together they carried 2 223 cattlemen, an average of 31 per ship. Altogether 956 or 43% were prohibited from landing.[15] Despite the restrictions, many of these prohibited cattlemen found it relatively easy to go ashore. The right of the military to override the Immigration Restriction Act, the ever-decreasing number of guards at the harbour as the war progressed, and the staff shortages in the police facilitated this relatively easy access. What made the bureaucratic inefficiency even worse was the fact that the IRD had no control over the police, while the captains of cattleships thought their responsibility to the law ended once they had asked for a police guard. This bureaucratic maze made it easy for a prohibited cattleman to slip undetected into Durban.[16] By 1901, the control of the landing of cattlemen, whether by law or otherwise, had become ineffectual, as the vast number of cattleships arriving, apart from all the other ships, strained the system and resources beyond its capacity.

By now the Natal government had also joined the struggle to curb the landing of cattlemen in an already overcrowded Durban. One way to achieve this was to ensure that cattlemen, when they signed up for a ship, were given a return passage in the contract. The British consul in New Orleans, AG Vansittart, was therefore asked to explain to the governor of Natal, Walter Hely-Hutchinson, how the recruiting of cattlemen for British ships worked. According to Vansittart, cattlemen, when signed on at the consulate or on board ship, were given a careful explanation of every term of the agreement. This was, however, where the duty of the consulate staff ended, as they had nothing to do with the contract signed between the owner of the ship and the cattleman enlisted. By 1901, almost all contracts included a return passage as part of the clause, which was not the case in the early stages of the war.[17]

The legacy of the earlier system whereby cattlemen came to South Africa on a one-way passage soon made itself felt. An American, John McPetree, was enlisted from a cattleship in Cape Town. After completing his six-month contract, he proceeded to Durban, via Port Elizabeth, to link up with some friends, who had in the meantime moved on. As he had £15 in cash, he was given permission to disembark. McPetree soon ran into trouble with the police and, in the process, caused a judicial stalemate. He was not an illegal immigrant, and the Natal government, who did not want to go to the extremity of deporting him, allowed McPetree to stay. The only route left was to secure a passage home for McPetree with the aid of the USA consul. This was accomplished, and Durban was relieved of at least one unwanted cattleman.[18]

In an attempt to control the influx of people into South Africa, including cattlemen, permit regulations were implemented under martial law on 1 January 1902. This meant that only passengers issued with a valid permit were allowed to disembark. In reality, this hardly altered matters, because on 8 March 1902, a telegram received by Colonel MW Simpson, the commandant of Durban, from the commanding officer in Pretoria ordered him to take immediate steps to prevent any hindrance to men arriving on cattleships from the colonies of the British empire or America who wished to land, provided they were prepared to enlist for a year. Simpson immediately acted to ensure that all cattlemen, and not only British subjects, could now be enlisted. In a message to the divisional transport officer for Durban, Captain H King-Hall, he outlined the new procedure to be followed when a cattleship arrived in Durban: on arrival the recruiting officer would be informed; when the IRO considered the ship cleared, the recruiting officer, medical officer and orderly officer of the irregular corps for the day would board. A list of the various irregular corps requiring recruits would then be handed to the cattlemen. Once they had selected their corps, the cattlemen would be examined by the medical officer and, if found fit, would be taken by non-commissioned officers of the relevant corps to the drill hall. On the days when the cattleships were dealt with, there would be no medical inspection of recruits at the drill hall.

Captain King-Hall supported the recruiting process, on condition that the cattleships vacated their berths at the wharf timeously. Colonel R McCormack of the Royal Army Medical Corps, however, did not agree with the suggested arrangements for medical examinations. Quietness, a prerequisite for such an examination, could not be assured on board a cattleship, and he therefore suggested that the cattlemen be marched to the drill hall, examined, and then marched back. Those passed 'fit' would thereupon receive their pay certificates and papers of discharge from their ships. This suggestion was, however, overruled, and the process of recruiting cattlemen from all nations for the war against the Boers could proceed.

The IRD, nonetheless, had reservations about the process. Captains of cattleships had in the past refused to give an undertaking that they would re-ship men who had failed the necessary tests, while in other instances they had been unwilling to grant men passed as 'fit' a discharge from their ship. The possibility of a cattleman escaping while ashore also worried the IRD. Bringing additional men ashore made little sense to the IRD, especially when taken into account the number of unemployed men in Durban and the needs of the labour market account. With these complications in mind, the IRD suggested that it was 'better, for all concerned, for all cattleships to be dealt with entirely under Martial Law and not under the Immigration Restriction Act'.[19]

The concerns of the IRD fell on deaf ears and a recruiting frenzy was unleashed on every cattleship that entered the harbour of Durban. In an attempt to keep control of the movements of the cattlemen enlisted, a report was requested from the Durban commandant. This report for the period 29 March 1902 to 16 April 1902 is summarised in the table below,

and provides an indication of the recruiting that took place in a period slightly longer than a fortnight.

These new regulations left room for abuse and misunderstanding. To prevent exploitation of the enlistment opportunities opening up in Durban, Colonel Simpson ordered ships' captains not to sign any discharge papers for employees, regardless if they were cattlemen, fireman, stokers, stewards or seamen, without obtaining such an order from himself or from the chief recruiting officer. Special reference was reserved for stowaways who, if not prosecuted, were available for enlistment. Otherwise the responsibility for stowaways would remain with the captain of the ship. The order that as few obstacles as possible be placed in the way of cattlemen who wanted to enlist soon caused other immigration problems. Men who arrived without permits, with the idea of seeking work, were landed by the deputy shipping master. He was reminded that no one without a permit was allowed to go ashore. To ensure any further abuse of the Immigration Restriction Act, the commandant of Durban instructed Superintendent GE Tatum of the Water Police that every ship was to be visited before departure to ensure that all crew were accounted for. If any crew member was found to be absent, a description was to be provided. Furthermore, if men were landed without permits, and an attempt was made to leave Durban without them on board, a fine of £100 per head was to be levied on the ship, through its agents if necessary. In each such case a report needed to be forwarded to the commandant. On

Cattlemen enlisted in Durban between 29.3.1902 and 12.4.1902.		
Cattleship details	**Profile of cattlemen**	**Irregular corps joined**
NAME: Maori King CAPTAIN: ? ORIGIN: Sydney, Australia ARRIVAL: 29.3.1902.	11 men. Ages not stated.	7 employed by J Cotton. 1 – Bethune's Mounted Infantry 1 – NSW Imperial Bushmen
NAME: Langton Grange CAPTAIN: CSC Crichton ORIGIN: Sydney, Australia ARRIVAL: 5.4.1902.	39 men. All British subjects. Youngest -J Sclimon (18). Oldest -W Wolstercroft (50).	14 – NSW Imperial Bushmen 6 – Driscoll's Fighting Scouts 2 – Steinaecker's Horse 1 – Kitchener's Fighting Scouts
NAME: Pinfield CAPTAIN: HJ Holland ORIGIN: Australia ARRIVAL: 11.4.1902.	13 men. All British subjects. Youngest-HC Butler (18). Oldest-J Goodjer (40).	6 – NSW Imperial Bushmen 2 – South African Constabulary
NAME: Hortensius CAPTAIN: ? ORIGIN: New Orleans, USA ARRIVAL: 12.4.1902	61 men. 59 Canadians and 2 West Indians. Ages not stated.	5 – Kitchener's Fighting Scouts 1 – Canadian Scouts 1 – NSW Imperial Bushmen
NAME: Zingara CAPTAIN: W Jones ORIGIN: Buenos Aires, Argentina ARRIVAL: ?	56 men mentioned, log only contained 54 names. 29 British, 9 French, 7 Italian, 6 German, 2 Belgians, 1 Spaniard. Youngest ED Hens (18) of Belgium. Oldest A Sheridan (49).	8 – Steinaecker's Horse 4 – IMR 3 – South African Light Horse 1 – Canadian Scouts ED Hens the only non-Brit to join.

5 May 1902, even stricter orders were given to the deputy shipping master by Colonel Simpson, namely that only bona fide South Africans were allowed to land in Durban, but that a permit would be issued once their domicile was proved in writing.[20]

By March 1902, cattlemen were thus a sought-after commodity. In the context of the shortage of artisans in Durban at the time, the acting IRO, GW Dick, had issued permits to six Britains, including a machinist, tailor, gardener, steam fitter, erector and fireman giving them permission to seek employment during the final week of February 1902. But owing to their short stay in the harbour and their onboard duties, they were unable to find suitable employment. Dick asked the Natal government whether he had to follow any special procedures to land British tradesmen who arrived at the port as cattlemen. The answer from the government was simple: 'The Immigration Restriction Officer should not prevent the landing of any white skilled workmen who may arrive at the port.'[22] This ruling would soon lead to a conflict between civil and martial law.

When the Anglo-Boer War ended on 31 May 1902, the recruiting for the various irregular corps who needed men from cattleships ceased. This left the IRD uncertain of who might and who might not disembark. Dick therefore asked Colonel Simpson of Durban to clarify the position. The answer from Simpson was simple: 'Apply Martial Law Permit Regulations.'[23] This in itself created a new set of problems. Fifty-eight cattlemen on board the New Zealand ship, *Aparima*, belonging to the Union Steamship Company, had arrived in Durban from Glasgow and wanted to land. All these men were artisans and British subjects and each had approximately £5 in hand. They had made the journey with the aim of settling in Durban, and had therefore worked on the ship in exchange for their passage. Some of them had family in Durban, while others had been offered work by bona fide employers. The IRO had no problem in granting these cattlemen the right to disembark, as under law they were not regarded as undesirables. This assurance did not mean much to the shipping master of the *Aparima* who, bearing the Martial Law Permit Regulations in mind, refused to pay the men off without orders from the commandant of Durban giving him permission to do so. With the men allowed to enter Natal under civil law, but prevented from doing so by martial law, the shipping agents of the *Aparima*, William Coutts & Co., decided to take the matter to the Natal government. They telegraphed the colonial secretary on 19 June 1902, requesting him to notify the commandant as to whether consent was granted for the landing of the 58 cattlemen, as the *Aparima* wanted to go to sea. The Natal government could, however, not interfere in the matter, as the landing of cattlemen and passengers was a matter in which the military had the superior position. The government suggested that the IRO negotiate matters with the commandant. This was done to the benefit of all as the commandant allowed the 58 cattlemen to land. The relieved William Coutts and Co. could not neglect passing on some advice to the commandant, the IRO and the Natal government, namely to prevent a repetition of such events. This advice was taken to heart by the government, and the IRO was ordered to talk to the commandant to ascertain whether anything could be done to minimise future inconveniences of this nature. The IRO did

not regard this as enough, and, in looking for a more permanent solution, suggested that the only way in which such inconvenience could be avoided was by securing the sanction of Lord Milner to relax the permit regulations.[24]

The episode involving the *Aparima* served to highlight the tension between civil law and martial law, which was fast running its course, in the period immediately after the war. While civil law and administration needed to function if market forces, such as allowing artisans to land, were to be addressed, the military still controlled matters as if a war were raging. Despite the *Aparima* debacle, a similar incident happened again soon afterwards. The cattleships, *Bouverie* and *Angle Canadian*, arrived in Durban with some cattlemen on board who could offer trades that were in short supply in post-war Durban. As a result, they were cleared by the IRD for landing, under the Immigration Restriction Act. These cattlemen were, however, again debarred from landing by the commandant of Durban, under the permit regulations stipulated by martial law. In a compromise attempt to solve the clash between martial and civil laws the matter was referred to the Natal government. With the rule of martial law losing impetus the Natal government saw its way open to make an overriding decision – the cattlemen were allowed to land.[25]

When martial law was repealed, and the IRD could again take control of the destiny of the arriving cattlemen under the Immigration Restriction Act, the process had come full circle. This brought an end to the anarchy that surrounded the arrival of cattlemen in Durban during the war, with the overriding concern of the military being recruitment of men and not the maintenance of law and order in a seriously overcrowded city. Up against the power of martial law, the IRD bravely attempted to uphold civil law, while at the same time trying to please the military by keeping track of its ever-changing orders and machinations, while also

The prospect of adventure enticed 17-year-old Max Gordon to run away from his home in New Orleans to join a cattleship, the *America*, bound for South Africa. Although Max provided his correct name, he lied about his address. Instead of 1207 Baronne Street, New Orleans', he gave his address as 14 Bauer Avenue, Cincinnati. In a moving plea the boy's father, Reverend S Gordon, wrote to Magistrate HC Koch in Durban asking him to 'Kindly use your influence to have him safely returned to his home and thus save his mother and father untold anguish'. Magistrate Koch's response seemed almost unsympathetic. He asked the IRO to stop '... the lad's landing should he come within the provisions of the Act. The master of the *American* might be induced to take him back'.[21]

Godfrey Watson Dick

Dick came to Natal in 1882 and at first worked for auctioneers and then merchants before entering the Natal Civil Service in 1895. He rose rapidly through the ranks and acted as the IRO from June 1901 to June 1902. During the Anglo-Boer War he was initially sent to Lourenço Marques and afterwards was appointed to render special services to military commandants and naval transport officers.

keeping an eye on the cunning cattleship captains. To appreciate the enormity of the task faced by the IRD, it should be remembered that cattleships constituted but a small percentage of the vessels that docked in Durban during the war.

Profile of a cattleship — mutiny and murder on board the *Milwaukee*

One of the cattleships that called regularly at Durban was the *Milwaukee*. The first time this ship came to the attention of the authorities, for the wrong reasons, was in November 1900, when the Austro-Hungarian consul, E Munder, informed the IRD that 43 Austro-Hungarian cattlemen and 14 stowaways were proceeding from Cape Town to Durban on board the *Milwaukee*. The captain of the ship had promised the cattlemen and stowaways a free return passage to Cape Town should they be unable to find employment in Durban. As these Austro-Hungarian subjects could not claim a passage home from their government, and as there was little likelihood of the men finding work in Durban, the consul wanted the IRD to ensure that the captain of the *Milwaukee* kept his promise. To prevent the men from landing on his doorstep, as had happened before, Consul Munder wrote four letters to the IRD concerning the matter. In the end he received a promise from the IRO, Harry Smith, that the matter would be dealt with[26].

The second time the *Milwaukee* brought trouble to Durban it was of a much more serious nature, namely, in the form of a mutiny. On arrival in Durban from New Orleans, on 14 May 1901, with 73 cattlemen on board, eight of which were British, and the rest American, 31 of these cattlemen were classified as alleged mutineers and were promptly marched off to prison, on the charge that they had 'neglected their duties so as to imperil the ship, and limbs and lives of officers, men, and animals by combining in disobeying lawful commands of the captain'. This caused the first controversy when the court case opened on 16 May 1902 in front of Magistrate James Stuart, with JS Wylie prosecuting. From the outset, the IRO, Harry Smith, viewed the trial as illegal. In addressing the court at the preliminary hearings, Smith informed Stuart that the court had no authority to try the cattlemen, as they had been brought ashore illegally by a guard of marines. Smith expanded and explained that on arrival of the *Milwaukee* he had gone on board and declared all the cattlemen prohibited immigrants. As this attempt to im-pose the law had been ignored in bringing the alleged mutineers ashore, the men should be returned to their ship and taken to a harbour where they could be legally landed. Elaborating further, Smith maintained that if the cattlemen were tried and sentenced to a term in prison, they would, on release, become dependent on charity in an already overcrowded Durban, as the captain of the *Milwaukee*, out of fear, would not take them on board. The cattlemen would also struggle to find employment on any other ship. The prosecutor did not agree with Smith as the cattlemen had joined the *Milwaukee* on contract for a round voyage, and the court was

obliged, at the very least, to draw up a bond to enforce the terms that had been agreed upon. The magistrate did not share his view and saw no reason why the case should not proceed, suggesting that the bond could be settled afterwards. At this stage, the alleged mutineers demanded the protection of the American consul, AH Rennie, with whom they had not yet had any communication. They also asked for an opportunity to prepare their defence. Permission was granted.[27]

The following day, the case against the cattlemen reopened, with Eugene Renaud acting in their defence. At the outset, Magistrate Stuart enquired if a bond had been drawn up that would provide for the alleged mutineers to be taken back to the USA as prohibited immigrants. The reply of Prosecutor Wylie was that the captain of the *Milwaukee*, Horace E Shaltis, and its agents, W Dunn & Co., refused to bind themselves to a bond of thousands of pounds without the authority of the owners. Wylie failed to see why the men were declared prohibited immigrants by the IRO as they were part of the crew of a British ship. To this Stuart replied that he had no doubt that the cattlemen were prohibited immigrants, but this was not his main concern, as the men had been landed and therefore needed to be tried. His main concern was what would happen after the trial? Stuart therefore wanted to fix a bond of £200 for their return passage. This was challenged by Wylie who regarded such a step beyond the jurisdiction of Stuart. At this point of the proceedings the American consul interjected. According to him the men, as part of the crew of a British steamship, were not undesirables and would therefore have to stand trial. This settled the matter for Stuart and he decided that the trial should continue without the security of a return voyage for the men.[28]

When Smith read of the magistrates decision in the *Natal Mercury* he acted instantly. He had two interviews with Stuart, but failed to convince him that the accused were prohibited immigrants. Having no luck with his petition, Smith in an effort to ensure that justice would be done and that the authority of his department to land people would not be undermined, wrote to the colonial secretary, who in turn referred the matter to the attorney-general. For Attorney-General Bale the central issue was the conflict of laws, and he posed the question whether the captain of the *Milwaukee* could land the cattlemen for trial under section 220 of the Merchant Shipping Act if they were prohibited immigrants within Act 1 of 1897 of the Colony of Natal. To him the answer was straightforward – imperial acts were paramount, and the master was therefore correct in landing the men for trial. The fact that the men were landed illegally in the first place did not impress him, and he concluded it to be a matter of indifference how the cattlemen came ashore.[29]

The court case started on 29 March 1901, with the 31 cattlemen being charged with contravening subsection C and D of sections 225 and 220 of the Merchant Shipping Act during the trip between New Orleans and Durban. The hearing lasted 15 days. From the evidence given by the crew and the 31 alleged mutineers the following account emerged: on 2 April trouble started when the cattlemen complained about the salt meat, certified by the United States department of agriculture to be sound, with the way in which it was dished up being a specific issue. Captain HE Shaltis investigated the matter with the assistance of the medical officer,

Joseph George Stubbs, a doctor from Texas. Stubbs, after 'a biological analysis' which was limited to the effect the meat produced on human beings, found nothing wrong with the meat, despite its smell. He had come to this conclusion as he believed that he 'had such an acute smell that he could determine different diseases by it'. The solution to this complaint was to serve each cattleman's rations separately and to cut the meat in smaller pieces to make it more palatable. This seemed to have pacified the cattlemen for the time being.

On 20 April, there was another dispute. This time the cattlemen complained that the bread was sour and brought it to the captain. The captain agreed, and explained that the storm the previous night had turned the yeast sour, and ordered out extra tea, biscuits, bread, butter and jam. This did not solve the problem. Instead, Lalor, who emerged as the ringleader, demanded, according to the captain, a second course for breakfast, puddings and tarts for dinner, and jam and meat to be added to the tea rations. The captain refused, but he had the salt meat ration increased from twice to three times a week. Lalor was, however, still unhappy and demanded the 'board of trade rations' until he and his companions saw the ration scale.

Further trouble erupted on 22 April, once again over the salt meat. A group of cattlemen went to the bridge and complained to the captain and the other officers that they could not eat the salt meat. Again Dr Stubbs investigated, and again he pronounced the meat good. On informing the cattlemen of his verdict, they swore at and cursed him and started to throw the meat overboard passing comments such as: 'We can't eat your d___ British meat; we are United States citizens.' By 16:00 Lieutenant Thompson of the remount section and the chief foreman reported a virtual mutiny. The more than 30 dissatisfied cattlemen refused to work and intimidated others to join them by 'dumping them' or knocking the 'stuffing' out of them.

The captain called each cattleman in individually, and those who refused to work were sent to the lower forecastle. This group consisted of the 31 men on trial. The other cattlemen were sent to work, 19 of whom would only go if the crew would promise to protect them from their fellow cattlemen. The ladder was removed from the lower forecastle and the hatch secured to imprison the unhappy cattlemen. The law of the jungle soon reigned supreme in the forecastle. It was hot and stuffy in the '510 cubic feet' area, despite the windows and portholes, and those who did not submit, like Ferdinand Pardon of New Orleans, were violently brought into line. When Pardon knocked on the hatch of the forecastle asking to be let out, he was dragged before a 'kangaroo court' which meted out the following punishment: each of the 31 men was to strike him on the jaw as hard as he could with the fist and 'give him 40 licks' with a rope. Pardon was punished as per verdict and starved for four days. Stubbs was later called upon to attend to Pardon and found him in a critical state, only managing to revive him after almost an hour. His report stated that Pardon suffered from contusion of the neck, buttocks and sides and was unable to open his mouth more than one centimetre. It took four days before he could eat again, and eight days before he was pronounced fit. Asked by Renaud whether he was afraid during his

ordeal Pardon replied: 'Eh, waal, I dunt knaw of you would caal it fright, but you would have been on the same side if tew 'der bin theer'. [*sic*]

Prompted by his officers, Captain Shaltis docked at Ascension Island seeking protection. After consultation with Captain Pollard, the *Milwaukee* resumed its journey, this time with a guard consisting of a sergeant, a corporal and eight marines. With the mutineers locked up and a guard on board, Durban was reached.

The quality of the salt meat served on board, but also the other food like the potatoes and oatmeal which were allegedly of a bad quality and insufficient quantity, seemed to be the central issue of the mutiny. While the 31 alleged mutineers complained about the food, the 58 other crew members and the remainder of the cattlemen were satisfied. What the alleged mutineers also agreed on was that 'the strike on board the ship was not the result of a combined movement, but was individually resolved upon'. In other words, individual displeasure was expressed rather than it being a co-ordinated mutiny. With the evidence at his disposal, Stuart had to pass judgement.

Magistrate Stuart did not regard the assault on Pardon as endangering anybody's 'life or limb', especially as he recuperated within eight days. On the charge of disobeying orders and neglecting duty, Stuart found that there was some combined effort by the cattlemen 'to make a determined stand about their food, which in their opinion, was not good enough, or sufficient'. In this, however, no definite order was disobeyed. Instead, the men merely neglected their duty. Matters were exacerbated by the fact that the cattlemen were not experienced seamen but mere novices who did not know that they could have availed themselves of rulings in subsections 1 and 2 of section 199 of the Merchants Shipping Act of 1894, which allowed them to call for compensation at the end of the voyage. Instead, ill-informed men such as Lalor, Farley, Griffiths and John McCarthy, who were lacking in experience and common sense, led the others into trouble by striking at sea, as well as by adopting a defiant attitude while failing to complete their allotted duties. The reaction of the captain to confine the men to the forecastle and to take an armed guard on board did not in any way constitute a breach of contract. Considering the punishment the men had already endured the magistrate acquitted them on the charge of assault on Pardon, but found them guilty of not performing their duties. All the cattlemen were sentenced to two months' imprisonment, except Lalor and Farley who received a sentence of three months.[30]

With the riotous cattlemen of the *Milwaukee* sentenced, one issue remained unresolved: what would happen to them on their release from prison? The only means left to Harry Smith whereby he could force the owners and agents of the *Milwaukee* to fulfil their contract to provide return passages for the imprisoned cattlemen was to prevent the ship from departing. When the captain applied for clearance to leave Durban, Smith, who insisted that the ship remained until the men in prison were released, turned down the application. This did not please the captain and he promised to take action. To Smith the matter was simple – under the Merchant Shipping Act, subsection 4 of section 233, the captain of a ship had the right to ask for the return of any of his imprisoned crew – Smith was prepared to approve such clearance without delay, should Captain Shaltis make such a request. This noble attempt by Smith to see justice done was, however, thwarted. Captain King-Hall, the divisional transport officer, wanted the *Milwaukee* to sail as soon as possible for it had part of the garrison of the island of Ascension on board. Furthermore, the captain had done no wrong, and therefore felt that his vessel should not be detained, nor inconvenienced for the sake of a return passage for the mutineers. For this reason the attorney-general recommended securing a bond for the return of the prisoners. As a result, Smith was ordered to hand the necessary documents to the ship's agents so that the *Milwaukee* could leave. With the ship ready to depart, Smith played his last card. He instructed Sergeant Edwards of the Water Police to board the *Milwaukee* to see which men were not on board. The captain was able to account for 42 cattleman, two of whom were imprisoned for offences committed while in port. For each cattlemen unaccounted for there would be a fine of £100.

With the departure of the *Milwaukee*, the main concern of how the owners of the *Milwaukee* were going to honour their contract of a return passage to the USA for the jailed cattlemen still remained. The USA consul, AH Rennie, asked for a guarantee of a return passage from the agents of the *Milwaukee*. The response of the agents, W Dunn & Co., was emphatic: 'We are not prepared to give such a guarantee.' According to the agents, the matter was argued before the magistrate and his ruling appeared to indicate that the *Milwaukee* was not called upon to undertake such a responsibility. The bitterly disappointed Rennie approached the Natal government, pleading with them to insist that the owners of the *Milwaukee* honour their agreement. In a thinly veiled threat, the consul made it clear that if no assistance was forthcoming, the USA government would report the matter to the imperial government. Rennie also made it clear that if the Natal government failed to act, and the men were stranded in Durban, on their release from prison the USA government would not assume responsibility for their maintenance.

In an attempt to solve the issue which was now heading towards a diplomatic incident, the Natal government telegraphed the IRD for comment. The response from Harry Smith was unceremonious: 'I regret to inform you that no guarantee has been obtained either by myself or by the shipping master.' As the clearance to depart had already been handed over to the *Milwaukee*, the only power to keep the ship in the harbour, apart from a direct appeal to the law to compel the ship to perform its obligations, had been relinquished. On receiving Smith's message, the Natal government informed Rennie that '... the circumstances were brought to the notice of the Agents of the vessel, (Messrs Dunn & Co), who were asked to undertake that the men should be deported to the United States on the completion of their sentence: this they refused to do, and the Government is advised that it has no power to insist upon such an undertaking.' A disgruntled Rennie was not satisfied by this lukewarm response which he failed to understand, especially as contracts had been signed with the men that guaranteed them return passages. Rennie, who had himself worked for a shipping company, believed that such contracts had to be adhered to. His own company had paid £500 in return passages for cattlemen brought from the USA earlier in 1901. As he could not see how the owners of the *Milwaukee* could escape their responsibility, Rennie reported the matter to the USA consul in Cape Town requesting him to take the matter up with the USA government.

What Harry Smith feared at the outset of events became a reality on 25 July 1901, when 29 of the cattlemen mutineers were released from prison with 20s each in their pockets and with nowhere to go. Again the matter was referred to the IRD who was asked for advice. Fortunately the IRD was spared from making any recommendations, as the various volunteer units were quick to enlist the ex-cattlemen. Lieutenant T Hart, the recruiting officer for Kitchener's Fighting Scouts, operating from 11 Central Buildings in West Street, recruited 18 cattlemen, 16 of whom were Americans, whom he, by order, was not really allowed to recruit. The men were: FJ Collins (British, 22) J Griffiths (British, 32) WA Downing (22), H Diehl (36), J Hall (25),W Russell (21), J McCarthy (40), W Carey (25), C Gillies (?), J Halt (25), F Moore (20), Cowie (?), Collins (22), Tipton (22), NA Kearney (21), Marrow (?), Bechack (?) and Baumback (24). Captain G Roseshine, the recruiting officer of Bethune's Mounted Infantry, recruited the following four mutineers, all USA citizens: J Parrott (25), AL Poray (23), C Baumback (24) and E Robille (21).

The seven remaining ex-prisoners had no intention of joining the military and approached their lawyer, Eugene Renaud, to ask for help. Renaud, in turn, referred them to Harry Smith. The men who were by now penniless, could not find employment. To keep themselves from starvation, they worked for the Durban corporation, breaking stone in exchange for free beds and meals. The only option open to Smith was to refer these men to the USA consul, who unsuccessfully tried to persuade the agents of the *Milwaukee* to agree to a return passage for the men. Finally they also signed up with the irregular forces.

After completing their contract of six months at the front, five of the cattlemen returned to Durban hoping to secure a passage home. Despite efforts by the IRD to force the Natal government to deport them as undesirable immigrants, Stuart refused, notwithstanding the fact that the men had 'volunteered for the front'. He maintained that 'ships are

---

Boer POWs on board the *Milwaukee*

The mutineers were not the only prisoners on board the *Milwaukee*. On 31 March 1900, the *Milwaukee* sailed from Cape Town for St Helena with 211 Boer POWs, 22 officers and 189 men, on board. The vessel arrived at St Helena on 10 April 1900.

frequently coming to this port and surely with a little care, ... able bodied men as they are can get away'. All the disgruntled IRD could add to the continuous gallant efforts to assist these men was to point out that they 'had not volunteered but only joined once all protests had failed'.[31]

The third time the *Milwaukee* caused trouble for Durban, murder was involved. The *Milwaukee* steamed from New Orleans for Durban on 15 December 1901, with the usual ragtag bunch of cattlemen aboard, including one Pietro Raymondi, an Italian who spoke no English. Two days after leaving, Raymondi committed a murder. What had provoked him to commit such a heinous crime? According to Raymondi, he was feeding the horses, when John Long, assistant cattleman-foreman, spoke to him in English. The accused indicated that he did not understand the language and continued with his work. This caused Long to become so vexed that he punched Raymondi all over his body. Raymondi responded by hitting Long with a bucket in self-defence. In the ensuing brawl, Long punched Raymondi and also struck him with his whip, while the Italian retaliated by striking Long with the small axe he carried in his belt. Long then went away and returned with John Williams, the cattleman-foreman. Together the two men dragged Raymondi to the bridge, punching him continuously with screws on his face and on his back. At the bridge Raymondi was put in irons and fastened to the bridge. Later that day he was removed to the engine room, while continuously being punched by Long and Williams, eventually causing Raymondi to fall. When he got up, the punching continued, and when he fell again they started kicking him in full sight of greaser, Matthew O'Brien. By now Raymondi had had enough, and he took his knife from his pocket, opened the blade with his teeth and stabbed Williams and Long. The latter pushed him down to the engine room in the process. According to Raymondi, he did not want to kill John Williams, but merely wanted to protect himself from the torments of Long and Williams.

As could be expected, the statement of the officers involved was completely different. According to Owen Williams, the chief officer, Raymondi was brought before him by John Long and John Williams for assaulting Long with a bucket and an axe, and apparently the accused had refused to do his work. Owen Williams ordered that Raymondi be handcuffed to the bridge. Later in the day the captain ordered Raymondi to be brought down to a room near the engine room so that he could be locked up temporarily. Raymondi had at first struggled, then, when he reached the ladder to the engine room, he quietened down. Suddenly Raymondi whipped out a knife and stabbed Long in the stomach and Williams in the chest. Owen Williams grabbed Raymondi, and with the help of O'Brien, overpowered him. At no stage did Owen Williams see John Williams and Long assault Raymondi with screws or their fists. John Williams died on Christmas Day, leaving a wife and children in New Orleans. John Long verified the evidence of Owen Williams, adding that the problems with Raymondi started when he refused to attend to more than 20 horses.

Afterwards Raymondi was handcuffed and incarcerated in a cabin, except when he was brought out daily for exercise on deck. One day he broke away and threw himself overboard. A lifebelt was thrown to him and the *Milwaukee* stopped. Four men under the command of Owen Williams lowered a boat and rescued Raymondi. As a result of this suicide attempt, Raymondi was put under stricter surveillance. In the daytime, one of his arms was chained to the wall, and at night-time both his arms and feet were chained. This did not stop Raymondi. One morning his throat was found to be purple and blue from a botched attempt to strangle himself with twine he acquired by unravelling a portion of his canvas bedding.[34] This was the evidence that confronted Assistant Magistrate J Colenbrander in Durban.

After a preliminary hearing, the case took a new turn. An ordinance, applicable in Natal, determined that all witnesses giving evidence in the colony would have to appear in court in Durban. If such witnesses were unwilling or unable to enter into bond, £500 in this case, they could be jailed. In the case against Raymondi, the medical officer, Chief Officer Owen Williams, a fireman, and John Long would have to remain behind. This proved problematic for Owen Williams as he would lose his billet if he stayed. The cattlemen brought out by the *Milwaukee* were informed that they were free to leave and were taken on board by the *Montreal*, but not before five were recruited by the military.[35]

The fact that several of the crew had to remain behind in Durban for the trial of Raymondi, which was scheduled to start only on 15 March 1902 created problems, and Governor HE McCallum was petitioned to intervene. McCallum was very sympathetic, especially to the plight of Owen Williams, and suggested that his evidence be taken in commission and that he be allowed to accompany the *Milwaukee* on its voyage.

Riots or mutinies on ships bound for Durban during the Anglo-Boer War were not uncommon. The captain of the *Atlantian* had problems with an insubordinate crew on its voyage from Liverpool to Durban. As a result the vessel docked at Beira to have the three ringleaders tried. Even with the main troublemakers imprisoned, matters did not improve, and five fireman still refused to obey orders. On arrival in Durban, the captain had them charged under section 21 of the Merchant Shipping Act. To the disgust of the captain, the men were let off with a warning, despite their admission of guilt and the magistrate informing the prisoners that they had violated the law. As a result, they returned to the ship more defiant than ever, and the captain had to struggle to maintain the 'discipline necessary to keep the ship in a state of efficiency'.[32]

In another incident involving the cattleship *Montreal*, problems arose during its journey from New Orleans to Durban. Albert Roberts, a cattleman, refused to work, faking various ailments, including diarrhoea. When his superiors realised he was merely pretending to be ill to avoid work, he was incarcerated. On arrival in Durban, he was tried for insubordination and sentenced to two months' imprisonment. In a separate incident aboard, a group of British cattlemen broke into a storeroom stealing 'three gallons of port wine and claret and quantities of whisky and brandy'. In the ensuing spree the officers had to draw their pistols to restore order. The main culprit, Gleeson, was put in chains but later released by a mob of cattlemen. Order was never again really restored. Magistrate Millar showed little sympathy with the ringleaders and sentenced them to six months in prison with hard labour.[33]

The attorney-general would not agree to this and made it clear that the witnesses were required to be 'kept' in Durban as their evidence could not be taken in commission. This did not mean that the *Milwaukee* was impounded and so she could leave, provided the chief officer remained behind. To ensure that he stayed, the IRO was informed that the chief officer was to be jailed should he attempt to slip out of the harbour. Captain King-Hall disagreed with the verdict of the attorney-general, as it inconvenienced any shipowners or officers that might be involved in such an incident. To him it also sounded as if the attorney-general wanted to deter ships from bringing their criminals to trial in Natal. King-Hall was afraid that, when merchant navy ships brought their insubordinate crew to book in Durban, as had happened in the past, the accused would be sentenced to three months' imprisonment and returned to the ship, and thus often escaped punishment. As a result, King-Hall directed a ship to retain an insubordinate crew member on board until it reached India 'in preference to charging him at Durban, where he would to all intents and purposes not be punished'. The views of King-Hall did not endear him to the civil establishment, and the attorney-general called it unwarranted, claiming that decisions were made without any knowledge of circumstances and facts. Prime Minister Albert Hime was to comment that King-Hall 'writes as a naval officer which makes his opinion gratuitous'.[36]

What happened to Pietro Raymondi remains a mystery. His case was to start on 15 March 1902, but no report could be found on the case.

1. *Natal Witness*, 15.9.1900.

2. PRO, CO 179/208: documents concerning Italian cattlemen on British vessels, 21.9.1899.

3. PAR, GH 838: memo on restrictions placed on immigration to the colony of Natal, letter to the British consul at Buenos Aires, 8.1.1898.

4. *The Standard*, 19.10.1897.

5. PAR, NHD II/5/16: annual report Natal Harbour Department, 1899.

6. PAR, IRD 3: memo magistrate of Durban regarding the illegal landing of 48 cattlemen from *Sussex*, 22.6.1900.

7. *Natal Witness*, 29.6.1900.

8. *Natal Mercury*, 13.5.1901–24.5.1902.

9. PAR, NCP 7/4/7: report from IRO on cattlemen arriving, 1900.

10. PAR, CSO 1655: letter Durban Refugee Relief Fund complained about the landing of large number of cattlemen without visible means of subsistence, 2.8.1900.

11. PAR, IRD 3: document regarding the landing of 50 cattlemen from *Langton Grange*, 10.10.1900.

12. PAR, PM 21: enquiry if it is true that Australians are only allowed to land if they agree to enlist, 18.3.1901.

13. PAR, IRD 4: document concerning enlistment of cattlemen from the *Politician*, 27.3.1901.

14. PAR, IRD 4: letter IRO H Smith to Commandant O'Neil.

15. PAR, PM 21: enquiry if it is true that Australians are allowed to land if they agree to enlist, 18.3.1901.

16. PAR, IRD 10: report by IRD on the issue of cattlemen, 1901.

17. PAR, GH 838: letter W Hely-Hutchinson to AG Vansittart, 10.12.1900.

18. PAR, IRD 6: documents asking that John McPetree be deported as an undesirable, 12.12.1901.

19. PAR, IRD 4: documents concerning the recruitment of cattlemen, 8.3.1902–13.3.1902.

20. PAR, IRD 8: documents concerning landing and enlisting of men who arrive without permits, 16.4.1902.

21. PAR, IRD 8: letter S Gordon to HC Koch, 14.4.1902.

22. PAR, IRD 8: documents on a special course in dealing with British artisans, 4.3.1902.

23. PAR, IRD 4: letter acting IRO GW Dick to Commandant Simpson, 5.6.1902.

24. PAR, CSO 1706: documents on the landing of 58 cattlemen from *Aparima*, 30.6.1902.

25. PAR, IRD 9: documents on cattlemen on *Bouverie* and *Canadian* debarred from landing, 9.7.1902.

26. PAR, IRD 3: documents on Austro-Hungarian horse attendants and stowaways arriving per *Milwaukee*, 5.11.1900.

27. *Natal Mercury*, 17.5.1902.

28. *Natal Mercury*, 18.5.1902.

29. PAR, IRD 4: documents on the mutineers from *Milwaukee*, 17.5.1901.

30. *Natal Mercury*, 18.5.1901, 21.5.1901, 23.5.1901, 30.5.1901, 31.5.1901.

31. PAR, IRD 4: documents on the mutineers from *Milwaukee*, 17.5.1901.

32. PAR, PM 18: letter of complaint from the captain of the *Atlantian*, 12.7.1900.

33. *Natal Mercury*, 14.3.1901.

34. *Natal Mercury*, 27.1.1902, 28.1.1902, 30.1.1902.

35. *Natal Mercury*, 28.1.1902; PAR, IRD 7: documents concerning the case of murder on the *Milwaukee*, 27.1.1902.

36. PAR, PM 26: documents on the detention of the chief officer of the *Milwaukee*, 1.2.1902.

Prison ships in the harbour of Durban

Arriving at the Point unleashed a new set of emotions and concerns for the POWs. CP van Zyl found the port of Durban frightening and large and the prospect of leaving his fatherland traumatic. Those who had never seen the ocean before experienced the conflicting emotions of fear and amazement. On disembarking from the train, the POWs would either board a tug which took them to their prison ship anchored in the outer anchorage, several kilometres offshore, or be incarcerated in a shed, or at the Point Police Station until the following day. The short sea cruise which followed to the prison ship generally evoked great consternation. Numerous POWs were seasick, while others were terrified. When the tug reached the prison ship, the POWs were hoisted aboard in a basket, containing six to eight men at a time, where they invariably would be united with old friends and family members.[7]

The prisoners remained on these ships until they were sufficient in number to warrant transfer to a transport ship for their removal to one of the permanent camps in either St Helena, Bermuda, India or Ceylon (present day Sri Lanka). The first prison ship to be used in Durban was the *Catalonia*. On 19 April 1900, it was reported that six Boer POWs had been placed on the *Catalonia*.[8] Thereafter, the frequency of POWs sent to Durban increased, and included groups such as the motley crew of 19 Boers and one African who arrived on 21 June 1900. This party, which originated from either Volksrust or Pretoria, declared that only some of them had been taken under arms. Others had been residing on their farms when they were arrested.[9] By 20 July 1900, 162 POWs were aboard the *Catalonia*. On 24 August 1900, the POWs were removed to the *Bavarian*, which took them to Ceylon.[10] Between 15 and 17 August 1900, the *Catalonia* received a further 50 POWs from Harrismith. Prior to boarding the ship, the prisoners were quartered in the war office agency premises in shed A, until arrangements were made for their transfer. The *Natal Mercury* described this party as having a more respectable appearance than the majority of Boer prisoners who had been brought to Durban, with only a few looking like 'typical Boers'.[11] At this stage Boer POWs frequently arrived in Durban in small numbers with, for example, a group of 41 reaching the city on 1 September 1900. The inhabitants of the city no longer even found any spectator value in the arrivals. According to the *Natal Mercury*, Africans were an exception as they did not let the opportunity pass to make some uncomplimentary remark.[12]

Owing to the rapid increase in the number of prisoners arriving in Durban, a second prison ship, the *Chicago*, docked on 5 October 1900. This vessel received its first load of 39 prisoners, consisting of Germans, Frenchman, Irishman, Russians and two Boers, soon afterwards. The *Columbian* left for Cape Town with its cargo of prisoners on 18 October 1900, and was replaced by the *Yorkshire* which immediately took 102 POWs on board. Two weeks later, the *Yorkshire*, transhipped her prisoners to the *Manilla*, and embarked British invalid soldiers to be returned to England. On 9 December 1900, the *Catalonia*, which had been at the outer anchorage since 2 November 1900, steamed for Colombo, Sri Lanka, carrying 632 POWs.[13]

The cosmopolitan nature of the Boer POWs coming into Durban was exemplified by two groups that arrived in July 1900. These groups contained prisoners of all five classes, and included men, women and children, Natal and Cape rebels, Hollanders, and other foreigners and employees of the Netherlands Railway Company. Some of the Dutch subjects were handed over to the Netherlands consul, Balwe, who was to arrange for their passage home. The women and children were taken to various hotels, boarding houses and the drill hall. The remaining men were taken by train, under guard of the Edinburgh Militia, and accompanied by Commandant Morris and Major Bousfield, to the Point. Here they boarded the tug, *Panther*, which took them to the *Catalonia*. Although not all these men were regarded as POWs, it was deemed necessary to imprison them on the *Catalonia* until other arrangements could be made for those against whom there was no charge. A large crowd watched these proceedings and several well-dressed ladies conversed with the men in Dutch and German. When the *Panther* left, a section of the crowd cheered and the detainees responded. Several others then began to jeer, but this was promptly repressed by the wharf master, who explained that the men were not prisoners in the ordinary sense of the word. Within a couple of days, the fate of these prisoners was determined. The Cape rebels were to be sent to the Cape Colony for trial, while the Dutch subjects who had not participated in hostilities were to be sent to the Netherlands, along with their families.[14]

With the creation of the POW camp in Ladysmith, Tin Town, in late 1900, the need for prison ships diminished as class A prisoners were no longer deported or imprisoned on the ships, but were despatched to Ladysmith. Prison ships, however, did not disappear from the outer anchorage of the Durban harbour. Vessels such as the *City of Vienna* and the *Armenian* waited in the outer anchorage until they had enough prisoners on board and then took them to Bombay (Mumbai) or Madras (Chennai) in India.[15] The busiest period was early in 1902 when, in ten weeks, 4 000 prisoners were deported by 12 ships, including the *Roslin Castle* on 6 January,[16] the *Bavarian* on 4 March,[17] and the *Aurania* a week later.[18] This mass deportation coincided with the creation of the Umbilo POW camp. POWs who were to be deported now waited in the camp until a transport ship such as the *Tagus*, *Armenian*, *Mohawk*, *Aurania* or *Templemore* arrived. Only then did the Boer POWs embark for India or Sri Lanka.

For landlubbers such as the Boers, life on board the prison ships was strange and it took some time to get used to it. Almost all the 21 Natal rebels held on the *Catalonia* complained in their letters home about being seasick. Their letters generally requested clothes, money, needles and cotton and tobacco to ease their lives on the ship.[19] Furthermore, conditions were sometimes extremely crowded, as was the case with the *Armenian*, which had more than 1 000 POWs on board in October 1901. Food consisted of meat, bread, potatoes and curried rice, with tea or coffee to drink. Many prisoners felt that the portions were too small and tasteless. The prisoners slept in hammocks beneath the deck, a scenario that reminded many of giant weavers' nests. They complained that the blankets they were given were dirty and infested with lice, which

26. PAR, IRD 3: documents on Austro-Hungarian horse attendants and stowaways arriving per *Milwaukee*, 5.11.1900.

27. *Natal Mercury*, 17.5.1902.

28. *Natal Mercury*, 18.5.1902.

29. PAR, IRD 4: documents on the mutineers from *Milwaukee*, 17.5.1901.

30. *Natal Mercury*, 18.5.1901, 21.5.1901, 23.5.1901, 30.5.1901, 31.5.1901.

31. PAR, IRD 4: documents on the mutineers from *Milwaukee*, 17.5.1901.

32. PAR, PM 18: letter of complaint from the captain of the *Atlantian*, 12.7.1900.

33. *Natal Mercury*, 14.3.1901.

34. *Natal Mercury*, 27.1.1902, 28.1.1902, 30.1.1902.

35. *Natal Mercury*, 28.1.1902; PAR, IRD 7: documents concerning the case of murder on the *Milwaukee*, 27.1.1902.

36. PAR, PM 26: documents on the detention of the chief officer of the *Milwaukee*, 1.2.1902.

CHAPTER 7

BOER PRISONERS OF WAR

Johan Wassermann and Annette Wohlberg

The first Boer POWs in Durban

In an article entitled, 'An Uncommon Scene', the *Natal Mercury* of 27 October 1899 described the arrival of the first Boer POWs in Durban. The event was witnessed by less than ten people:

> A special train arrived from Maritzburg containing 183 prisoners of war, chiefly of the Johannesburg Commando, there being generally 12 to each compartment, special first class accommodation being provided for the captive officers. A guard of 18 British cavalrymen, with loaded carbines occupied the brake van. At the Point the train was met by one or two officers of Imperial troops, a lieutenant of Royal Horse Artillery accompanying the prisoners. The train proceeded to near the end of the wharf where the *Patiala*, lately used as troopship No. 14, was in readiness. The prisoners were soon handed over to the Naval authorities and the soldiers "fell out" for breakfast. The Boer officers were the first to be taken out, and mustered on the wharf, where a strong detachment of Bluejackets and a few Marines, all with fixed bayonets, were drawn up in open order. The spectacle was a picturesque one, and the red coats of the Marines gave a touch of colour certainly not supplied by the sombre, not to say dingy, garb of the prisoners, who saw British soldiers in red coats for the first time since hostilities commenced. The commander of the *Tartar* was in command of the Marine detachments. Among the officers were Mr. De Witt Hamer, Member of the Volksraad; Captain Figulus, various German mercenaries and the Vrederechter of Fordsburg. Capt. Schiel is understood to have arrived by an ordinary train in charge of Detective Lees-Smith. The burly German officers were rather better equipped than the others, and their upright character showed that they had seen some military service. Both officers and men peered anxiously out of the carriage windows, as if apprehensive of danger, but their fears should soon have been put to rest, for they were most courteously and gently treated. The officers walked in twos to the gangway, with no attempt to keep in step, or any display of military smartness. About a dozen of the Staats Artillery followed; then came carriages full of a mixed brigade of Hollanders, Germans, a few of the more civilised looking Boers, one young fellow in a cycling suit, others in khaki. Boots and spurs seemed at a discount. Then came a number of true 'sons of the soil,' whose enormous footgear, shabby dress and slouching gait, dark hair and small peering eyes, to say nothing of expansive grins, which seemed to spread over their entire faces, proclaimed the real Boer. One and all meekly obeyed the command to throw down the boxes of matches with which they have been provided, and all realised the gravity of the situation to the extent of putting out their pipes which they had been smoking incessantly all the way down. Most of the men had only what they stood in, a few had saddle bags, and one or two rugs, bundles and occasional paper parcels. The officers appeared to have thrown away all their belongings in the flight, during which they were made prisoners. By threes they ascended the gangway between the files of Marines, and burly Jack Tars rubbed them down for contraband – all alike underwent the ordeal. They were then taken to their quarters below, and told to remain there until further orders. The last batch of prisoners to go on board numbered two Cape boys and three blacks, who between them carried sackfuls of luggage. When all were safely stowed away, a guard of British Bluejackets with fixed bayonets paced the deck, the detachment of Marines went forward, and the *Patiala* was swung around into the channel, to await a further draft of prisoners.[1]

The *Patiala*, hired by the Admiralty, took the Boer POWs, who had been captured at Elandslaagte, to Simonstown, where they arrived on 2 November 1899, before being transferred to the *Penelope*.[2] The treatment of this first group of Boer POWs to arrive in Durban was considered to have been first class by Lieutenant Adolf Schiel of the German Corps and De Witt Hamer of the Hollander Vrywilliger Korps. Both handed over letters to the commander of the *Tartar*, FRW Morgan, expressing their sincere appreciation for the kind treatment extended to officers and men, and particularly the wounded. These kind words were appreciated by the British authorities, especially as charges of ill-treatment of POWs aboard the *Penelope* were starting to surface at this time.[3]

Very few prisoners were brought down to Durban in the months following the arrival of this first batch of Boer POWs. This was largely owing to the setbacks suffered by the British forces in Northern Natal. Once the tide of war turned in favour of the British with the relief of Ladysmith and the subsequent driving out from Natal of the Boers, followed by the collapse of the republican capitals, the arrival of POWs in Durban became a familiar sight. These prisoners were divided into five categories:

A. Prisoners to be detained in South Africa
B. Prisoners to be deported overseas
C. Prisoners on parole
D. Undesirables – including foreigners and women
E. Indigents who were foreigners who were granted a free passage to Europe[4]

The POW route to Durban

The largest number of Boer POWs that came to Durban were those falling into category B, that is, prisoners to be deported overseas. They generally arrived after a lengthy train journey from the interior. Several of these journeys are vividly described in various prisoner-of-war diaries. Up to 50 men were bundled into an unwashed coal truck in which they had to adopt a low body position for the duration of the journey. They received loaves of bread and canned meat as rations. The toilet facilities comprised an Indian-style toilet, a slit in the floor. Generally no blankets or tarpaulins were made available to shield them from the heat, cold or rain. To protect themselves against the climatic hazards, the prisoners needed to huddle together. The prisoners did, however, receive some comfort from journeying past battlefields associated with famous Boer victories over the British such as those at Amajuba, Spioenkop and Colenso. At the stations where the train sometimes halted for hours, for example, Newcastle, Ladysmith and Pietermaritzburg, the reception was generally hostile. Africans and Europeans alike would jostle for a position to get a better view of the prisoners, while inside the carriages the POWs were experiencing a wide range of emotions ranging from anger and melancholy to disgust at their dirty surroundings. Outside, while ogling this human zoo, the spectators would hurl constant abuse at the prisoners. When a prisoner dared to respond by calling the spectators cowards, he was told to be quiet by the guards who escorted them. On arrival in Durban, sometimes up to 60 hours after the journey had commenced, they were taken on board their prison ships, be it the *Manilla*, *Armenian* or the *Aurania*.[5] Prison ships such as these were lying in the outer anchorage of the Durban harbour and acted as replacements for conventional POW camps.

Orders for escorts convoying POWs by train

1. Not more than 20 prisoners to be loaded in a single truck, or more than 40 in a double truck.
2. The train should be made up in such a way that all trucks taking POWs and escort should be together, and not separated by horse trucks, stores, or guard's van.
3. The POWs should be in the centre trucks, and the escort in the first and last trucks, when there are not more than six trucks altogether; when there are more than six trucks, the central truck or trucks should also be occupied by part of the escort.
4. An NCO or old soldier will be placed in charge of each truck; he will have under his orders two or three privates, who will fall in on each side of the truck to which he has been allocated, at the train halts.
5. For travelling by day, it will not be necessary for any of the escorts to be in the trucks with POWs.
6. When entraining POWs, the officer in charge will see to it that sentries are posted 6 feet (1.82 m) to each side of the train.
7. Every POW, on entering the truck, should be made to sit or lie down, and warned that if he rises he is liable to be shot. After dusk, POWs must lie down.
8. A proportion of the men in the trucks containing escorts only, should be on sentry duty in two hours' relief. These men will keep a general look-out, and will all fire at any man endeavouring to escape.
9. On no account should any spare ammunition be in the same truck as the POWs.
10. After dusk, two sentries should be on duty in each truck. They should stand together at one end of the truck, and POWs should be made to leave that end clear. In two contiguous trucks, these sentries should stand back to back.
11. When a train halts, an NCO. will visit each truck, and if any POW wishes to fall out he will then have facility for doing so, under proper escort.
12. After a halt, it should be ascertained that all POWs are present before the train is allowed to go on.
13. Men off duty must not sleep or even lie down in trucks containing POWs.
14. Great vigilance must be shown when the train slows down to such speed that men are able to jump off.
15. The men must be warned that in the event of any POW trying to escape, they must watch their own truck loads and leave it to the remainder of the escort to fire at the fugitive.[6]

Boer POWs at the Newcastle Station, en route to Durban during early 1902 (de Villiers en Kriel).

Prison ships in the harbour of Durban

Arriving at the Point unleashed a new set of emotions and concerns for the POWs. CP van Zyl found the port of Durban frightening and large and the prospect of leaving his fatherland traumatic. Those who had never seen the ocean before experienced the conflicting emotions of fear and amazement. On disembarking from the train, the POWs would either board a tug which took them to their prison ship anchored in the outer anchorage, several kilometres offshore, or be incarcerated in a shed, or at the Point Police Station until the following day. The short sea cruise which followed to the prison ship generally evoked great consternation. Numerous POWs were seasick, while others were terrified. When the tug reached the prison ship, the POWs were hoisted aboard in a basket, containing six to eight men at a time, where they invariably would be united with old friends and family members.[7]

The prisoners remained on these ships until they were sufficient in number to warrant transfer to a transport ship for their removal to one of the permanent camps in either St Helena, Bermuda, India or Ceylon (present day Sri Lanka). The first prison ship to be used in Durban was the *Catalonia*. On 19 April 1900, it was reported that six Boer POWs had been placed on the *Catalonia*.[8] Thereafter, the frequency of POWs sent to Durban increased, and included groups such as the motley crew of 19 Boers and one African who arrived on 21 June 1900. This party, which originated from either Volksrust or Pretoria, declared that only some of them had been taken under arms. Others had been residing on their farms when they were arrested.[9] By 20 July 1900, 162 POWs were aboard the *Catalonia*. On 24 August 1900, the POWs were removed to the *Bavarian*, which took them to Ceylon.[10] Between 15 and 17 August 1900, the *Catalonia* received a further 50 POWs from Harrismith. Prior to boarding the ship, the prisoners were quartered in the war office agency premises in shed A, until arrangements were made for their transfer. The *Natal Mercury* described this party as having a more respectable appearance than the majority of Boer prisoners who had been brought to Durban, with only a few looking like 'typical Boers'.[11] At this stage Boer POWs frequently arrived in Durban in small numbers with, for example, a group of 41 reaching the city on 1 September 1900. The inhabitants of the city no longer even found any spectator value in the arrivals. According to the *Natal Mercury*, Africans were an exception as they did not let the opportunity pass to make some uncomplimentary remark.[12]

Owing to the rapid increase in the number of prisoners arriving in Durban, a second prison ship, the *Chicago*, docked on 5 October 1900. This vessel received its first load of 39 prisoners, consisting of Germans, Frenchman, Irishman, Russians and two Boers, soon afterwards. The *Columbian* left for Cape Town with its cargo of prisoners on 18 October 1900, and was replaced by the *Yorkshire* which immediately took 102 POWs on board. Two weeks later, the *Yorkshire*, transhipped her prisoners to the *Manilla*, and embarked British invalid soldiers to be returned to England. On 9 December 1900, the *Catalonia,* which had been at the outer anchorage since 2 November 1900, steamed for Colombo, Sri Lanka, carrying 632 POWs.[13]

The cosmopolitan nature of the Boer POWs coming into Durban was exemplified by two groups that arrived in July 1900. These groups contained prisoners of all five classes, and included men, women and children, Natal and Cape rebels, Hollanders, and other foreigners and employees of the Netherlands Railway Company. Some of the Dutch subjects were handed over to the Netherlands consul, Balwe, who was to arrange for their passage home. The women and children were taken to various hotels, boarding houses and the drill hall. The remaining men were taken by train, under guard of the Edinburgh Militia, and accompanied by Commandant Morris and Major Bousfield, to the Point. Here they boarded the tug, *Panther*, which took them to the *Catalonia*. Although not all these men were regarded as POWs, it was deemed necessary to imprison them on the *Catalonia* until other arrangements could be made for those against whom there was no charge. A large crowd watched these proceedings and several well-dressed ladies conversed with the men in Dutch and German. When the *Panther* left, a section of the crowd cheered and the detainees responded. Several others then began to jeer, but this was promptly repressed by the wharf master, who explained that the men were not prisoners in the ordinary sense of the word. Within a couple of days, the fate of these prisoners was determined. The Cape rebels were to be sent to the Cape Colony for trial, while the Dutch subjects who had not participated in hostilities were to be sent to the Netherlands, along with their families.[14]

With the creation of the POW camp in Ladysmith, Tin Town, in late 1900, the need for prison ships diminished as class A prisoners were no longer deported or imprisoned on the ships, but were despatched to Ladysmith. Prison ships, however, did not disappear from the outer anchorage of the Durban harbour. Vessels such as the *City of Vienna* and the *Armenian* waited in the outer anchorage until they had enough prisoners on board and then took them to Bombay (Mumbai) or Madras (Chennai) in India.[15] The busiest period was early in 1902 when, in ten weeks, 4 000 prisoners were deported by 12 ships, including the *Roslin Castle* on 6 January,[16] the *Bavarian* on 4 March,[17] and the *Aurania* a week later.[18] This mass deportation coincided with the creation of the Umbilo POW camp. POWs who were to be deported now waited in the camp until a transport ship such as the *Tagus*, *Armenian*, *Mohawk*, *Aurania* or *Templemore* arrived. Only then did the Boer POWs embark for India or Sri Lanka.

For landlubbers such as the Boers, life on board the prison ships was strange and it took some time to get used to it. Almost all the 21 Natal rebels held on the *Catalonia* complained in their letters home about being seasick. Their letters generally requested clothes, money, needles and cotton and tobacco to ease their lives on the ship.[19] Furthermore, conditions were sometimes extremely crowded, as was the case with the *Armenian*, which had more than 1 000 POWs on board in October 1901. Food consisted of meat, bread, potatoes and curried rice, with tea or coffee to drink. Many prisoners felt that the portions were too small and tasteless. The prisoners slept in hammocks beneath the deck, a scenario that reminded many of giant weavers' nests. They complained that the blankets they were given were dirty and infested with lice, which

Boer POWs arriving at the Point under the watchful eyes of the bluejackets (KCL).

Boer POWs awaiting deportation, ironically at the Natal Harbour Department public waiting room (WM).

fumigation failed to remove.[20] The subtropical climate of Durban, coupled with the muggy conditions below deck, forced many prisoners to sleep outside, which also helped them to escape the constant noise caused by people walking on the wooden floors of the upper decks.[21]

Equally difficult for the prisoners was the monotony of daily life on board ship. Some would constantly write letters, others would gaze at the shore thinking about their personal predicament, while some took to fishing. Under these circumstances, A O'Neill of Cookhouse in the Cape Colony even found himself enjoying the British celebrations and thought that the *Catalonia* 'looked quite nice the last two days, having been decorated all over with flags on account of the relief of Mafeking'.[23] At times, concerts were organised, in which POWs and the military participated to alleviate the boredom,[24] while a French Benevolence Society provided the POWs in Durban with gifts to console them.[25] A welcome relief occurred when Reverend WP Rousseau of the Pietermaritzburg Dutch Reformed Church visited a vessel to conduct services. Unfortunately this privilege was withdrawn when Rousseau was accused of inciting the prisoners and acting as a spy.[26] Solace also came in the form of women visitors. From the inception of the first concentration camp in Durban, Merebank, the women in these camps were allowed to proceed to the wharf to say goodbye to their loved ones. A point in case was Miem Fischer, Lettie Steenkamp and Jettie Sluiter who received passes for 11 February 1902 to visit the *Tagus* for an hour to speak to a family member, Oswald Doyer.[27] The intended visits to prisoners were not always of a friendly nature. Buchanan, Forsyth & Co., merchants of Durban, desperately wanted to get hold of Field-Cornet AJ Kock of Frankfort before he was deported, as he was deeply indebted to them.[28]

For some POWs, such as Bernardus Johannes Badenhorst, a Transvaal citizen who had resided in the Dundee district for two years, and who was of an advanced age and ill, the ordeal aboard the prison ship became just too much and, on 29 May 1900, he requested the commandant of Durban to allow him to take the oath of allegiance. Unfortunately for Badenhorst his request was not granted, and he, together with other Natalians suspected of rebellious activities, was transferred from the *Catalonia* to the Durban goal, to await trial by the civil authorities.[29] Others were more fortunate in their requests. JFC Bosse, a German from Wakkerstroom, who was a prisoner for a month on board the *Yorkshire*, was allowed to join his brothers at New Hanover in the Natal Midlands, on condition that he had to report to the local magistrate at regular intervals.[30]

POWs crowding the top deck of the SS *Montrose* in an attempt to escape the heat and humidity below deck (WM).

POWs on board the SS *Montrose* (WM).

Boer POWs hoisted by basket on board a prison ship, the SS *Montrose* at the outer anchorage (WM).

A GRAND CONCERT WILL BE HELD ON BOARD[22]
H.M.T. AURANIA

Bound for Bombay from Port Natal with Boer POWs
On Saturday, September 28, 1901
Patron: Captain N.J. McCarthey, R.F.A., O.C. Troops
Chairman: Captain J. King

Glee	"Wie ein stolzer Adler"	German Burghers
Song	"Patsy Fegan"	Sergeant Albutt
Pianoforte Solo		Doctor Harrop
Song	"De Maile Baan"	Burgher Lanting
Recitation	"Paddy the Valiant"	Sergeant-Major Glasgow
Song	"Long Tom"	Burgher H. Quin
Recitation	"The Burgher who almost was wounded"	Burgher H. Quin
Glee	"Morgenroth"	German Burghers
Song	"Whisper and I shall hear"	Gunner Rochester
Recitation	"The eve of Waterloo"	Captains Reeders, Burgh
Song	"The lady guide"	Gunner Gordon
Banjo Solo	"Brandy and Soda"	Captain Healy
Song	"The ship that never returned"	Burgher Enslin
Glee	"Setztzusammen die Gewehre"	German Burghers

Boer POWs boarding the *Roslin* Castle bound for Ceylon (Sri Lanka) (WM).

Boer POWs who were allowed to remain in Durban

Besides those aboard the prison ships, various other classes of POWs started to arrive in Durban or were arrested in the city. The biggest group was those who were on parole, that is class C prisoners. One of the most prominent in this group was Gerard Mari Johann Van Dam, commandant of the police in Johannesburg. According to the *Natal Witness*, which dedicated a whole column to him, Van Dam had an exceptional war record, both in Northern Natal and in the Eastern Transvaal. He was captured on the Swaziland border and arrived in Durban on board the *König*.[31] Numerous other Boer POWs were also on parole in Durban as is evident from the lists of POWs published in the daily broadsheets.[32] The numbers increased when class A prisoners were paroled from Tin Town. Such prisoners could then reside in any district of Natal, on condition that the local officer commanding approved of their presence. Colonel O'Neill, the commandant of Durban at the time, accepted such prisoners into the area under his jurisdiction, as long as they did not reside north of Verulam. As a result, POWs such as LF Drake of Vrede, and his two sons, moved to Pinetown and WJ Robertson of Vrede, and CJ Odendaal and PJ Odendaal of Harrismith took up residence in Durban.[33]

To qualify for parole, a burgher had to be able to support himself, which immediately excluded the less affluent. The parole conditions also determined that such a burgher could not take up arms against Britain during the Anglo-Boer War, that he had to reside in Durban and that he was to present himself to the authorities regularly. He had to refrain from participating in political discussions and demonstrations, might not use improper language when referring to the British forces, and was not permitted to have communication with residents of the Transvaal or Orange Free State, except via censored letters. Furthermore information on the war would be furnished to British officers only.[34]

Persons such as the four Transvaal burghers, HAW Wickert, HFC Prigge, AFH Wenhold and CH Kassier, travelling on neutral vessels and suspected of being in the service of the republics, were, however, arrested on board, in this case on the *Bundesrath* and detained as POWs. The four men mentioned were returning from Europe with the intention of joining the Boer forces via Lourenço Marques (Maputo). In due course they were released on parole, but their presence on board the *Bundesrath* provided impetus for the seizure of the vessel as a prize.[35]

At the same time, numerous individuals suspected of being in Boer service were arrested in Durban. A German subject, CT Schmidt, who had been born in Durban, and who was employed by Wilcken & Ackerman in Lourenço Marques, a company which reputedly traded with the republics, was arrested when he wanted to return after a business trip. The fear existed amongst the military in Durban that Schmidt could take comprehensive details of what he had seen and heard in Durban back to Lourenço Marques. Complaints from the German consul about this arrest were ignored.[36] Even deserting the Boer forces and heading for Durban provided no safeguard as Paul Ordolf Nissen, a shop assistant from Reddersburg in the Orange Free State, found out. Nissen was arrested, because he was viewed as either a spy or as being sent down by the Boers to arrange for stores.[37]

Various other groups or individuals were also deported to Durban by the military under the convenient term of 'undesirables'. Amongst the first of such prisoners were Pastor E Harms, a missionary, and Mr Struck, both of the Lutheran Church near Colenso in the Natal Midlands, who arrived in Durban on 17 February 1900. Both were accused of assisting the Boers during their invasion of Natal, and were subsequently arrested and imprisoned in Estcourt. Initially Harms refused to go to Durban on account of his health, but later he relented. On arrival in Durban, Harms and Struck had to sign an agreement whereby they undertook to remain in Durban and to report to the police twice a week.[38] On 5 March 1900, Harms and Struck were allowed to return home without any restrictions being placed on them. Harms then applied for, and received permission to leave for Europe, citing ill health as his reason for wishing to go. Commandant Morris, however, believed that the real reason for Harms' departure for Europe was to make a case through the German foreign office against, what he regarded as, illegal arrest.[39]

Political prisoners of the Transvaal and the Orange Free State, generally either people of social standing and key members of the republican administration, or those suspected of subversion, were likewise banned to Durban. One such group from the Orange Free State included P Botha – landdrost, Phillipolis; Rev Donges – Bultfontein; W Breues – railway clerk; MA Blignaut – landdrost clerk, Bultfontein; JW van Zyl – landdrost, Winburg; JWL Ortlepp – law agent, Dewetsdorp; JJ Swanepoel – farmer; Wepener, J. Bromley – assistant landdrost, Senekal; HO de Vos – landdrost clerk, Heilbron; A Baumann – landdrost, Hoopstad; ? Velds – assistant landdrost, Bultfontein and Dr Hollander, Smaldeel. These gentlemen were sent down to Durban on parole without their families, with the blessing of the Natal government who made it clear that they would not be held responsible for them.[40] With time the military apparently relented towards such prisoners, as PJ Burger successfully petitioned for his wife and two children to be united with him in Durban.[41] The above group were joined in November 1901 by 21 burghers and foreign subjects who were accused of plotting the so-called 'November Conspiracy'. According to the information supplied by a British spy, Daniel Jacobus du Toit, Boer commandos intended to attack Johannesburg while the accused would, as part of the plan, storm the houses of the Rand Rifles and seize arms and ammunition.[42]

These political prisoners were joined by 14 Boers (see above) who were found guilty by a military court for plundering. They were sentenced at Harrismith, on 12 and 13 September 1900.

Two Years	One Year	6 Months
PJ Joubert	Jacobus Viljoen	JA Kok (snr)
PJ du Preez	C Nel	JA Kok (jnr)
Piet Viljoen	HG Cilliers	FJ Kok
DJ Blignaut	E Kruger	TL Kok
	MN Kruger	W Brink

After their conviction, the men were sent to the Durban goal to serve their sentences. Five months into their sentence, the military requested that the prisoners be removed from Durban to the Ladysmith goal. Major JHB Foster, the staff officer for prisoners of war (SOP), Natal, based then at Tin Town, Ladysmith, found it unacceptable that prisoners guilty of civil offences and sentenced by the military were to serve the remainder of their time in the civil goal in Ladysmith, while a POW camp was available. In this he had the full support of the Natal government and, under their combined pressure, the military rescinded the original order, and as a result the prisoners were removed from the Durban goal and sent to Tin Town as POWs, with the possibility of being deported to Sri Lanka.[43]

Others were sent down for various military reasons, as is evident from the following examples: An extended family consisting of JJ Bosman, his wife, E Bosman (neè Von Backstrom) their two children, PJ von Backstrom and Miss F von Backstrom were sent down on parole to Durban from Standerton. Their continued residence in Standerton was regarded as undesirable from a military point of view. The accusations levelled against these surrendered burghers and their families included their being notoriously anti-British, as they had signed a petition prior to the British occupation of Standerton calling for the eviction of all British subjects from the Transvaal. They were also related to a family who supplied commando members with clothes. Eight months after their arrival they unsuccessfully petitioned to be allowed to return to the Standerton concentration camp.[44] The 49-year-old Jean Dongoumoo, a French-born citizen of the Transvaal, along with his wife, four children and stepchild, the latter the daughter of a late private in the Gordon Highlanders, was deported to Durban. The reason given was that ammunition was dug up near their house in Standerton, for which they could provide no explanation. This family arrived in Durban on 3 August 1901 and was paroled a week later.[45]

It is clear from the above that Boer women did not escape deportation as POWs. Classifying the wives and daughters of burghers provided the military in Durban with a headache, for as soon as they left a concentration camp on parole, they were technically POWs. According to Commandant Morris, they could not be classified as class C prisoners on parole, as they were not regarded as POWs in the true sense of the word. Therefore they were regarded as category D prisoners – undesirables.[46] Examples of such women were Mrs Roetz, Miss Aletta Roetz and Mrs Potgieter of the Christiana district. All three of these women had relatives on commando and were incarcerated in the Vryburg concentration camp. For assisting seven Boers to escape and rejoin the commandos, the ladies were deported to Durban as undesirables.[47]

One prisoner who was classified under class D, was JHD Kruyshaar, a Dutch citizen. He complained to the acting consul-general of the Netherlands that he was being kept as a POW in Pretoria, despite the promise by the military that he would be allowed to join his family in Durban. The acting consul-general believed Kruyshaar had the right to feel aggrieved for, as a medical official, he should have been treated under article five of the Geneva Convention which guaranteed his liberty. This letter had an immediate impact and, the following day, 19 November 1901, the military governor of Pretoria allowed Kruyshaar to leave on a second class free ticket to join his family in Natal.[48]

The diverse reasons for deporting people to Durban proved to be a problem to the local commandant, for he struggled to determine who were POWs and who were not. The picture was complicated by surrendered Boers such as E Boshoff, who requested to be sent down from Standerton to Durban, believing that he could live more cheaply there. The problem was that Boshoff arrived without any documentation.[49] The final straw, which lead to an enquiry, was a letter from AL Badenhorst, a surrendered burgher, to O'Neill. Badenhorst, who was allowed to reside at Cato Ridge, complained that he was regarded as a POW on parole. As a result the police at Camperdown would not grant him a pass to proceed to Durban to buy food. He therefore requested O'Neill to rectify the situation. Badenhorst was not the only surrendered burgher who complained of becoming classified as a paroled POW which compromised the conditions of surrender. TP Lauwrens and RF Wentzel arrived in Durban from Harrismith with passes from the military, and with the assurance that they would have freedom of movement. Their requests for permits to proceed to destinations outside of Durban were, however, refused by O'Neill, who viewed them as POWs on parole. Such requests and complaints forced O'Neill to seek guidelines from Major HB Foster.

The problem confronting O'Neill was that no specific charges existed against surrendered burghers, and since they were not on parole, it was impossible to keep them under surveillance or to prevent them from leaving Durban. To the commandant the solution was simple – all subjects of the republics should, on arrival in Durban, be paroled and made to report at intervals, regardless of whether or not they were belligerent, or had surrendered voluntarily, had taken the oath of neutrality or had come to Durban on their own request. This point of view had the support of Major Foster, on condition that the arrangements did not hamper the economic activities of the people in question and that burghers who had taken the oath of allegiance should be excluded from the ruling. When consulted, the provost marshal went a step further, stating that the commandant of Durban had the authority to issue any orders necessary pertaining to these men, and that he had the right to send them to reside in concentration camps.[50]

The powers now vested in the commandant to deal with surrendered burghers of the republics were soon exhibited. Andries Theodorus Tol-

may surrendered after the fall of Potchefstroom. Subsequently he, along with his three brothers, enlisted in the imperial transport service in November 1900, and he was discharged on 28 January 1901, apparently because of ill health and his inability to speak an African language. According to Tolmay, he was then sent to Durban against his wishes. This was refuted by the military, who insisted that he had asked for the transfer. In the Interim, Tolmay, who took the oath of allegiance on 20 April 1901, had become destitute and found himself in a similar position to thousands of other refugees in Durban. He therefore requested to be allowed to return to Potchefstroom to reside in the concentration camp. His application was denied by the provost marshal, and Commandant O'Neill despatched Tolmay to the newly created Merebank concentration camp.[51]

Most Boer POWs, regardless of their classification, were either deported via Durban, imprisoned in Durban or were on parole in the city. A small group of prisoners did, however, arrive from overseas camps. These prisoners were allowed to return to South Africa as they had signed the oath of allegiance to Britain. Eighteen such prisoners arrived in Durban on board the *Atlantian* from Sri Lanka, ten of whom were allowed to disembark and who were subsequently paroled. Seven of these prisoners were allowed to proceed to the Irene concentration camp, one to the Johannesburg concentration camp, one to the Standerton concentration camp and one to the Winburg concentration camp.[52] This group was followed at intervals by smaller groups such as the three who arrived from Sri Lanka and who were sent to the Merebank concentration camp.[53]

With the closure of the Tin Town POW camp in Ladysmith in December 1901, most of its inhabitants were paroled by the provost marshall on behalf of Lord Kitchener. Simultaneously, the intentions towards those Boers still in the veld were made clear: all burghers fit enough to hold a rifle were to be deported, including all boys over the age of 12. No one would be regarded as a non-combatant. Only burghers who relinquished their horses, arms and ammunition or who were instrumental in convincing other burghers to submit to British authority would be considered as voluntarily having surrendered.[54] In line with these orders it was decided to create a camp for POWs in Durban.

The Tin Town POW camp which became the Ladysmith concentration camp in January 1902, upon the opening of the Umbilo POW camp (KCL).

released on parole to reside in Natal, but outside the concentration camps, while only fourteen were to remain in South Africa as class A prisoners. Having surrendered and captured burghers in the same camp caused problems, because the psychological influence of the Boers awaiting deportation on the surrendered Boers was likely to be injurious. For Forster it was difficult to separate the two groups without opening up the second camp enclosure, which would require more troops for guard duty and all the logistics associated with an increase in manpower, which in turn would be detrimental to the war effort.

To Major Forster, the solution for Boers awaiting expatriation was that the SOP of Cape Town should send sufficient staff to Durban to establish a deportation office at the Point, which would both receive and embark Boer POWs. The tasks of this team would include taking the particulars of Boer prisoners, providing them with numbers and reporting on each batch to the SOP of Ladysmith as they arrived from the Transvaal and/or the Free State. To make this process work, a prison ship was to be kept in Durban with a guard of two officers and 60 men on board. This ship would depart to the fixed destination as soon as it had its complement of prisoners, and would then immediately be replaced by another ship and team of guards.

THE UMBILO POW CAMP

The closure of Tin Town and the creation of the Umbilo POW camp

The problem with the location of the Tin Town POW camp in Ladysmith was that it was far up the main railway line from Durban, making it both difficult and costly to transport goods, stores and products to the camp. Transporting goods to and prisoners from the camp also meant that valuable space was taken up on the trains, which hampered the war effort and frustrated the Durban business community. A further problem with Tin Town was that it was next to a military camp, and fears existed that the Boer prisoners could spread diseases to soldiers and vice versa.[55] For the British military, with the war dragging on and the guerilla phase being extremely costly, one way to minimise expense was to reduce transportation costs by train. Moving the prisoner-of-war camp from Tin Town in Ladysmith to Umbilo therefore made both logistical and financial sense.[56]

Major Forster was also developing serious doubts about the accuracy of his records. According to him, only 100 of the 600 POWs in his camp were awaiting deportation. The rest were surrendered burghers who were under orders to be deported under parole to the concentration camps at Volksrust, Standerton and various camps in Natal. Fifty were to be

Three Potgieters and an O'Connor (back, right) in front of the camp fence and onlooking guards (WM).

Prisoners would therefore not be sent to Ladysmith, but directly to the prison ship in Durban. Such a step would save the Tin Town administration manpower, time and logistical layout, as it would no longer be necessary to provide POWs with blankets, utensils and so forth, when they were to be moved on to Durban a few days later anyway. Furthermore, it would also solve the difficulty of finding large groups of escorts from the small garrison at Ladysmith to take large groups of POWs down to Durban. The escorts who brought the Boer prisoners down from the Free State and the Transvaal would then also accompany them to Durban. According to Major Forster, the suggestions he had put forward seemed the most suitable way to control POWs and the situation at Tin Town. Forster, however, also proposed that once his camp was cleared of surrendered burghers it would be possible to assemble Boer prisoners at Tin Town in Ladysmith and only despatch them to Durban when a full trainload was ready.[57]

Forster's argument for the dispensing of Tin Town was given more impetus by the order that all prisoners were to be sent to Ladysmith as plague had broken out in Cape Town. As before, Forster pointed out that Tin Town had originally been established for surrendered burghers or class A prisoners who were to be detained in South Africa, and that prisoners for deportation were now being temporarily housed at his camp before being sent to Durban for direct deportation or for transfer to Cape Town. Major Forster therefore repeated his previous suggestion that a prison ship with guards should be in Durban ready to receive prisoners. This would mean that Tin Town with its expensive attendant garrison and staff would be allowed to die out and be dispensed with within a month.[58] The sending down of Boer prisoners to the Princess Christian Hospital at Pinetown, close to Durban, for hospitalisation, substantiated the arguments of the SOP.

This logical argument by Major Forster on why Tin Town should be replaced by an alternative establishment in Durban did not come into effect immediately, because the creation of an establishment for Boer prisoners in Durban needed approval and a fair amount of planning. The approval eventually came when Commander-in-Chief Kitchener ordered the formation of a POW camp in Durban to replace the Tin Town establishment.[59]

To carry out Kitchener's order, a suitable spot needed to be located for a POW camp. This proved to be challenging, and the solution lay in transactions which had taken place between the Durban corporation and the military in the past. The ordinance land of 324 hectares in size, in the centre of Durban, had been allocated to the military for defence purposes. Gradually, the original defence requirements for the land changed and, in January 1894, this whole area, with the exception of 31 hectares, was handed over to the Durban corporation for the sum of £21 487, arrived at by an independent valuator appointed jointly by the military and civilian authorities. The Durban corporation, however, needed the additional 31 hectares for the further development of the growing city and therefore suggested that an area of town lands at Congella, outside the borough, should be placed at the disposal of the military, and that the corporation should pay the difference in value between the two sites

which was estimated at £80 300. The offer by the Durban corporation was supported by the local military authorities, and the proposed exchange transaction seems to have proceeded.[60] The land in the Congella area was deemed the ideal spot for the proposed Boer prisoner-of-war camp, and so the Umbilo POW camp was erected on this site approximately one and a half kilometres from the Umbilo Station.[61]

The site was on a gentle rise between the foreshore of the harbour and Umbilo Road. It lay approximately 13 metres above sea level and ran along the course of the main road. The soil was very sandy and needed to be systematically drained, levelled and trenched to make it clean and dry before the POWs could be brought in. Furthermore, the bush needed to be cleared away, not only to facilitate the erection of tents to house the POWs, but also to allow for some 32 metres clearance between the bush and the prison enclosure.[62]

For the military this location was ideal. It was close to the site of the Boer camp during the Battle of Congella on 24 May 1842.[63] Although not intended, the position must have had a psychological effect on the Boer prisoners, reminding them of their eventual defeat in 1842. The site also had other important features needed for such a camp. It had enough water, while electricity and sanitary requirements were to be supplied by the Durban corporation. The proposed camp was also close to Umbilo Road as well as to the main railway line leading into Durban for the transportation of both prisoners and the necessary equipment, stocks and material.[64]

The site of the Umbilo camp did have some drawbacks. It was prone to winds, and it was not unusual for the camp inhabitants to experience very strong gusts which destroyed everything in their path. On one Wednesday night in June 1902, the wind was so strong that it blew most of the tents down, including those of British soldiers such as Camp Corporal Wills. As a result, breakfast was served ten minutes late the following morning and the entire next day was spent putting up tents![65] Another irritation faced by the inhabitants of the Umbilo POW camp was the discomfort caused by the ever-present fleas and ticks. They made such an impression that the camp's weekly publication was even named *The Tick*![66]

The choice of the Umbilo site for a prisoner-of-war camp did not please the health officer of Durban, who, after inspection, declared it unfit for human habitation, because of the swampy conditions. Despite his reservations, the health officer did not take any action because he was afraid that suggestions by the corporation would not carry any weight as the terrain was under military control. However, at least one concerned Durbanite suggested that the borough engineer might be approached to see if the drainage could not be improved, since a heavy storm had washed all the drains of the old Boer camp away.[67] These concerns did make an impression on the military and an extensive system of drainage furrows was dug to improve the swampy conditions, and to render the camp habitable.[68]

The process of creating a Boer prisoner-of-war camp in Durban was now underway and during early January 1902 the camp at Tin Town in Ladysmith was transferred to Umbilo in Durban. The Tin Town camp in

Ladysmith with all its buildings was given over to Sir TK Murray, the director for burgher camps in Natal, for the purpose of creating a concentration camp to house the inhabitants of the Harrismith concentration camp which had closed down. As from 14 January 1902, the new office for the SOP for Natal would be at the Point in Durban in facilities rented from the African Boating Company at £10 per month.[69] The process of erecting the Umbilo camp could now begin.[70]

With Tin Town in the hands of the Natal burgher camps department, work on the Umbilo camp needed to commence, as Boer prisoners of war were constantly arriving in Durban for deportation. The estimated provision for the Umbilo camp was for 1 400 prisoners. This figure included prisoners of classes who were to be imprisoned in South Africa and prisoners of the classes who were in transit to the overseas camps.

With little time at his disposal, the SOP Umbilo, Lieutenant Colonel HTW Allatt, put in a requisition for articles necessary for setting up the Umbilo camp to be sent to the Umbilo Station by 20 March 1902. The camp authorities were also to be notified by 27 March 1902 which requested articles were not available. The transportation of the requested articles was to be organised by the officer commanding, Army Service Corps, in Pietermaritzburg.[71]

The requisition of Allatt was now at the mercy of military bureaucracy. After receiving the request, the chief ordnance officer for Natal, Lieutenant Colonel HDE Parsons, forwarded it to the ordnance officer in Pietermaritzburg for processing where a lack of tents for accommodation was identified as a major problem. Parsons therefore suggested that 100 marquees should be provided, rather than the 220 circular tents ordered, since the marquees were more practical for arranging messes with tables for the Boer prisoners. Such tents could accommodate 15 prisoners and would then form a mess. Allatt's proposal that huts should be used if marquees were not available was not acceptable, because Lord Kitchener had ordered that only tents should be supplied. To solve the problem, Parson's suggestion was referred to the general officer commanding, Natal, and the principal ordnance officer, Pretoria, for consideration and until they responded no despatches were to be carried out.[72]

On receiving the orders, Chief Ordnance Officer Parsons proceeded with the execution of the requisition and he informed Allatt that he could supply all the items requested immediately or by 20 March 1902, except for the following items: brooms-bas, waterproof sheets and the full quota of soup cans. The reason why the 140 brooms-bas could not be supplied was that the stores were still awaiting stock from Britain. Parsons, however, offered to solve this problem by purchasing sufficient brooms to satisfy the Umbilo camp's needs. As far as the waterproof sheets were concerned, a consignment from Britain was expected to arrive in Durban between 12 and 15 March 1902. These were to be forwarded immediately to the Umbilo camp. The stores could also only provide 240 soup cans, 10 short, but they made no alternative suggestion, as this shortfall was not considered of serious importance.

The major problem was still tents. The stores could provide only 48 hospital marquees, the requested 4 EP tents which were to be used strictly for hospital purposes, and 130 circular tents which were still at sea on the *Ingeli* and due in Durban only on 12 March 1902. Parsons deemed that CDL tents were not essential for the escort officers and declared that circular tents would probably be issued in their place.[73] Lieutenant Colonel Allatt responded swiftly to the above shortages and asked that 40 brooms-bas be purchased to start with, while the outstanding 100 could be delivered when the anticipated load from Britain arrived. The 240 soup cans were also considered to be sufficient if an additional 10 galvanised steel pails replaced the outstanding 10 soup-cans. Besides this, the Umbilo camp now required 130 6-foot tables and 260 forms, instead of the smaller number asked for. Regarding tents, Allatt stated that 130 circular tents, 48 marquees and 4 ESP tents, the latter for hospital purposes, would be sufficient. A further 6 double-lined or double-roofed tents of any sort were requested for the officers' quarters . To get the Umbilo camp up and running, Allatt asked that all these stores be delivered at the Umbilo Station between 21 and 24 March 1902.[74]

The logistical wheels of the British army were now turning, and Lieutenant Colonel Parsons ordered the brooms to be bought, the 10 galvanised steel pails to be provided, and the tables and forms to be added to the existing list. The list of tents was amended, with 12 CDL tents to be issued and the balance to be made up by the circular tents on board the *Ingeli*. All the items were to be despatched to Umbilo Station on 21 March 1902.[75] Most of the listed equipment was duly despatched. Eleven zinc basins and 55 soil buckets were not included – the manufactures, Masmo & Broadbent, delivered only 130 and were expected to complete their order by Saturday. The ordnance officer could also not supply $3\frac{1}{2}$ gallon zinc washing tubs, and as a substitute had to exhaust the stock of zinc basins. To solve this problem he undertook, as soon as tubs were received from the Cape Colony, to exchange them for the zinc basins.[76] The bulk of the requisitioned equipment was on its way, and the Umbilo camp could now be erected.

The equipment delivered fell into four broad categories. Firstly, there was the cleaning equipment such as basins, brooms and brushes of various kinds. Secondly, equipment for manual labour such as shovels, wheelbarrows and saws was ordered. Thirdly, the largest variation of equipment was associated with feeding the prisoners and included spoons, knives, forks, kettles and plates, and lastly, supplies for accommodation such as the tents, and furniture such as tables, arrived at the site. What was strikingly absent from this list were beds to match the 4 200 blankets. It is possible that some equipment such as beds and chairs were to be transferred from Tin Town to Umbilo, but if not, the Boer prisoners could anticipate sleeping on wet ground.

Once most of the equipment had been delivered, the Royal Engineers could continue with the erection of the Umbilo camp. The grounds were systematically drained, levelled and trenched[77] and the tents raised. To facilitate easier administration and management of the camp, it was laid out in streets. Names such as Victoria Road, Kruger Road, De la Rey Road and Kings Road seemed to integrate that which was familiar to the Boer prisoners with that which the new rulers wished to impose on those they held prisoner in the camp.[78] For official and administrative purposes the following buildings were erected: a guard room of approximately 12m X 6m X 3m with two cells and a veranda 2m wide all round; a commandant's office 14m X 5m X 3m with a 2m veranda all around. Shelters with forage stores at the end were also erected containing space for 20 mules. These were 3.6m X 3m X 2.4m in size. There was a latrine with three seats for the officers, and for the soldiers on duty a wash-house and latrine.[79]

Providing a cooking range for the soldiers was more problematic. Although the facility had been granted, the foreman of works for the Royal Engineers had to consult Lieutenant Colonel Allatt as to the number for whom the cooking range would be required before it could be built.[80] On receiving the figure, the engineers started erecting the cook's shelter. The camp commandant for the Umbilo camp, Captain HB Trevor, did not consider this to be sufficient for the escorts who were convalescents, and thus wrote to Allatt asking whether the cook's shelter could not be converted into a cookhouse with the full range of equipment.[81] Allatt took the camp commandant's suggestion a step further, and requested a cookhouse for the convalescent escort troops, arguing that the prisoners had a cookhouse and that if the prisoners had one, surely the troops should have one too.[82] The request had the full support of the commandant of Durban, and he forwarded the request to Colonel HF Rawson of the Royal Engineers.[83] The response of Rawson was curt: 'Cookhouses are not admissible. The fact that the men are convalescents does not give any grounds for the erection at Umbilo. Convalescent Camps are not even provided with Cooking shelters, and the latter were authorised by CRE Army in the case of Umbilo as an indulgence.'[84] This harsh telegram concluded the matter. To feed the POWs, the camp had a kitchen which was fitted out with 'every convenience'. The kitchen, or cookhouse as it was referred to, was 12m X 6m X 3m. The rations were kept at the quartermaster and ration store.[85] Wood required for cooking was supplied to the camp, but because there was a large supply of wood about the camp, only half the weight of wood allowed for the prisoners was drawn.[86] Roughly 450 kilograms of coal were also used on a monthly basis.[87]

The provision of the various other amenities, including the laying on of water and electricity from the main Durban supplies, was largely carried out by the public works department at a cost of £3 036 2s 2d. The fact that the construction took place at the same time as the carpenters' strike, which lasted from 24 February to 1 April 1902, caused a great deal of difficulty and delay.[89]

These services were not always provided without difficulty as exemplified by a power failure that occurred on 4 April 1902, owing to damage to the wires caused by an ox wagon driver's whip. Steps were duly taken to prohibit the use of long whips, and a notice to that effect was published in the *Natal Mercury*. Despite this action and promises that precautions would be taken to prevent another power failure, the electric lights around the prisoners' enclosure were out again for the whole night of 8 May 1902. This time, the power failure was due to the breakdown of a transformer. Although the second incident was difficult to prevent, Colonel Rawson, felt that he needed to provide an alternative supply of light in the form of oil lamps to ensure the safety of the

prisoners, and that therefore a reduction in the cost of the electric light would not be an unreasonable request. The town clerk, however, argued that, because of the fact that they had suddenly been called upon to supply a comparatively large amount of current a good distance away (nearly 10 kilometres) from their mains, and that within a very limited time, the suggestion by Rawson was unfair.[90]

To facilitate communication between Lieutenant Colonel Allatt and the commandant of Durban, the latter suggested that Allatt should have his office connected to the telephone system. To achieve this, the normal military procedure had to be followed and Allatt had to apply to the AAG, who referred the request to the Royal Engineers, Natal, for approval. The engineers had no hesitation in approving the telephone, which could then be installed by the Natal Telephone Company, with the cost being confirmed before being referred to the engineers for payment. This bureaucratic process was efficiently dealt with within eight days.[91]

The creation of the Umbilo camp was not always without problems, mostly due to military bureaucracy. When marquee tent bottoms arrived in the Durban harbour, the chief ordnance officer for Durban refused to supply some to the Umbilo camp because no application had been made for them.[92] Lieutenant Colonel Parsons informed Allatt that he had to submit a request for the tent bottoms. Only once this had been done, would they be delivered to Umbilo.[93] Once the tents had been erected and the necessary equipment set up, the Umbilo camp was fenced with barbwire to prevent prisoners from escaping. The strong wire fence, 1.83 metres wide with two rows of wire netting 1.83 metres high, left only one entrance into the camp, through the rough framed and braced gates, which were covered with barbwire and guarded by a khaki-clad sentry, armed with a rifle. In the words of Adjutant Charles Röcher, the gateway of the camp was fenced in so tightly with 35 wires that not even a cat could escape.[94]

Once the camp had been erected, the troops who were to act as escorts started to arrive. To save on manpower, the army decided to use only troops who were convalescents, such as Leigh Norris (No. 76402) and Dr Wicken (no. 5467) both from the convalescent depot at Howick.[95] Since the troops were recuperating, Lieutenant Colonel Allatt felt that he had to make special arrangements for them. To do this, he requested the following: two hospital marquees as a recreation tent and reading tent; one hospital marquee for officers who were convalescents; one hospital marquee for officers of the permanent staff; and one cooking range for the officers, to be placed in the available cooking shelter.[96] The DAAG had no problem with the order and the marquees were supplied.[97]

Equipment requested for the construction of the Boer POW camp at Umbilo

Items requested	Number	Number that could be supplied
Axes – Felling	2	2
Axes – Pick	2	2
Barrows – Wheel	2	2
Basins – Soup – Earthen	2 000	2 000
Basins – Zinc – Washing	180	169
Blankets – government supply	4 200	4 200
Blocks – Chopping	2	2
Brooms – Bas with handles	140	Nil. Only handles in store.
Brushes – Scrubbing – Hand	20	20
Brushes – Sweeping – Long handles	20	20
Boxes – Tool – Butchers	2	2
Balances – Spring – 80 lbs	1	1
Balances – Spring – 41 lbs	1	1
Cans – Soup	250	240
Chairs – Officers	12	12
Choppers – Meat – Mark III	2	2
Cleavers – Butchers	1	1
Dishes – Baking	20	20
Forks – Flesh	4	4
Forks – Dinner	2000	
Forms	40	40 – 6 ft (1.8 m)
Hooks – Butchers – 9 inch	12	12
Hooks – Bill	6	6
Knives – Cutting	4	4
Knives – Flaying – Large	4	4
Knives – Dinner	2 000	
Kettles – Camp	60	60
Plates – Dinner – Earthen	2 000	2 000
Pails – Galvanised steel	12	12
Saws – Cross-cut – 5 ft (1.5m)	1	1
Saws – Butchers	2	2
Shovels – Universal	12	12
Sheets – Ground – Waterproof	1 500	Nil available. On sea from Britain.
Spoons	2 000	
Steels – Butcher	4	4
Steelyard	1	1
Tents – circular	220	Nil available. 100 or 130 to be supplied as soon as consignment arrives from Britain.
Tents – CDL	40	Nil.
Tents – EP	4	4
Tents – Marquee – Large	4	8
Tents – Small	4	Nil available. Small and large marquee to be replaced by 48 hospital tents to make up the request.
Tables – 6 ft	40	40
Tubs – Zinc – Washing	40	40 – 3½ gallons (15.9 l)

The other camp: POW camp for African suspects

A second POW camp existed, from mid-1900 to early 1902, in Durban, during the Anglo-Boer War. This camp contained Africans labelled as 'suspects'. In reality these so-called suspects were Africans who were involved with the Boer forces in one way or another, either as scouts, herdsman or *agterryers*. Unlike their Boer counterparts, they were not deported but incarcerated on the Bluff and made to work on the harbour reclamation works. Generally it seems that they were badly treated by their African guards. In reaction to this treatment and the enforced labour, they would escape, pretend to be ill, or do as little work as possible. By early 1902, the extremely crowded conditions these prisoners of war lived in forced the authorities to parole them.[88]

Free State officers in the Umbilo camp, May 1902. Colonel Allatt is seated in the centre and Snymes, with the broom, in the front (WM).

An *agterryer* named Snymes at the Umbilo camp (WM).

POWs lazing around in Victoria Street, Umbilo camp. Note the African labourers to the right, a football being kicked around and a father holding his son's hand (WM).

The camp population

Those who resided in Umbilo were a motley crew of people, each with his own personal tale. By May 1902, there were 700 camp inhabitants.[98] Some, such as Frederick Jacobus Bezuidenhout who earned £50 000 p.a., were very rich. He complained that he was 'forced to join the Commandos with my stock by the Boer generals and never saw the proclamations issued by Lord Kitchener'.[99] Others felt that they had been sent to Umbilo unfairly. Gert Bosch had come from the concentration camp at Winburg where his tent mates had escaped, and in spite of his reporting the incident to the authorities he was sent to Umbilo as punishment. This was done solely because the orders were that should anyone escape from a tent, the others would be deported.[100] One Hendrik van der Merwe, aged 19, was arrested on 3 February for using foul and seditious language and intimidating witnesses. He was thus sent to Durban on 10 March 1902 by order of the general officer commanding, lines of communication, Johannesburg, and then on 19 March he was sent to Shahjahanpur in India. Van der Merwe had originally surrendered at Pretoria on 18 June 1900, and had taken the oath of neutrality. He did have one stroke of good fortune in that a JJ Stephenson of Fordsburg in Johannesburg had promised him employment as a painter when he was released from Umbilo.[101]

Others such as W Trotsmüller, Heinz Heine, Anton Ostendorp, F Kock, C Schlotfeldt, C Schmidt, V Freese, were 'foreigners', that is, men of German origin, who were naturalised in September 1899, but in July 1902 the provost marshal declared that although they had taken up burgher rights, they were not recognised as burghers, so were still to be regarded as foreigners. They were thus released under the same rules as other foreigners who wished to return to the Transvaal. Although no free passages were given to them to return to Germany, they were at liberty to do so.[102]

Amongst the POWs in Umbilo at the end of the war, were 11 penal servitude prisoners. Allatt, the SOP, was convinced that their continued presence in the camp would prevent the opening of the gates when all the other prisoners had signed the oath of allegiance. There were also two or three suspected Natal rebels and about twelve suspected Cape rebels in the camp, whom Allatt believed should have been handed over to the civil authorities. On 10 June 1902, there were 976 POWs in the camp.[103] In addition, there were those who were considered to be undesirables, and these included prisoners who had been sent from Johannesburg.[104]

The camp population was fairly mobile. Prisoners were given permission to be transferred to one of the concentration camps or even out of the country. JB Badenhorst, who was a resident in the Merebank concentration camp, asked the SOP for permission to have her 25-year-old son, George Diederick Badenhorst, who had been injured at *Talinne* on 26 September 1901 and was now an invalid, transferred from the Umbilo camp to the Merebank concentration camp.[105] In yet another case, the 35-year-old widow, Aletta van der Heever, also successfully requested that her 17-year-old son be transferred to Merebank to help her look after her younger children.[106] Seventeen-year-old Nicholas Postma of Rusten-

burg was granted permission by the general commander-in-chief to leave the Umbilo POW camp and proceed to Holland for educational purposes on the understanding that he did not return to South Africa until after the war had ended. On obtaining this permission, young Postma was first transferred to the Jacobs concentration camp until his father, the Reverend D Postma of Krugersdorp, could make the necessary arrangements for Nicholas's move to Holland.[107] Loyalty to the British by family members also allowed some POWs to be transferred from Umbilo. The feeble 69-year-old Andries Petrus Hendrik Gouws was allowed to join his son, who had done good service for the police in Johannesburg.[108]

Umbilo camp inhabitants were sometimes recommended for transfer to one of the Durban concentration camps on account of their age and infirmities. In such cases their medical certificates were attached to the applications sent to the army headquarters. Once these applications had been approved, arrangements were made with the superintendent of the specific concentration camp for the transfer of the men. These included Christoffel du Toit (66), Marthinus Prinsloo (65), Barend Jacobus Britz (67), Nicholas Jacobus Hauman (69), Michael Jan Marthinus Britz (64), Lourens Abraham Erasmus (78), Nicholas Petrus Prinsloo (63), Petrus Grobbler (62), John Edmund Maunsell Fanter (62), Cornelius Johannes van Staden (75), Wynand Johannes Pretorius (7), Wilhelmus Doyer (68), Herculas Petrus Nienaber (79), Johannes Gerhardus van Graan (72), Johannes Marthinus Vermaak (70), Edward William Walker (72), Hercules Petrus Nienaber (79) and Paul Bester Engelbrecht (71).[109]

Mere boys, the so-called *penkoppe* (young bulls), who were caught up in the war also ended up in Umbilo, initially for deportation. Along with the old burghers listed above they provide a glimpse of the peoples' army nature of the Boer commandos.

Penkoppe

Boys as young as 18 years of age actively participated in commando life. Although the very young *penkoppe* were too small to handle the 4 kilogram rifles, they served important functions such as herding the horses and cattle. Some of the *penkoppe*, aged between 12 and 19 years of age, such as Roland Schikkerling and Denys Reitz,[110] were amongst the most illustrious of the Boer fighters.

Profiles of some *penkoppe* (young bulls) deported from the Umbilo POW camp[111]

Sybrand Johannes Botha (9 years). Derdehoek, Wakkerstroom. Two brothers still fighting and two brothers-in-law already deported. To be deported with his father, a Boer leader.

Piet Wilhelm Pieterse (11 years). Verkyk, Wakkerstroom. Father died several years ago. Mother in Volksrust concentration camp with seven other children. To be deported with his brother listed below.

David Jacobus Pieterse (12 years). According to the British he looks older. To be deported with his brother.

Dan Joachim Jacobs (11 years). Roodepoort, Smithfield. Brother to the boy listed below. They are both to be deported to join their father and 14 year old brother.

William Jacobus Jacobs (12 years). Roodepoort, Smithfield. Their mother is in the Bethulie concentration camp with four other children.

Wiets Jacobus de Beer (11 years). Klerksdorp. Four brothers were captured at Paardeberg. To be deported with his father. Mother and three sisters in the Johannesburg concentration camp.

Johannes Jacobus van Wyk (14 years). Sabella, Kroonstad. To be deported to join his father. Mother in Kroonstad concentration camp with eight other children.

Pieter Ignatius Michel Lubbe (12 years). Welgelegen, Kroonstad. To be deported to join his father. His one brother is acting as a guide to British troops. Mother in Kroonstad concentration camp with five children.

Johannes Petrus Breytenbach (12 years). Brandwacht, Pretoria. To be deported to join his father and five brothers. Mother in the Balmoral concentration camp with three children.

Hendrik Joseph Combrink (10 years). Vaalbult, Carolina. To be deported with his father. Two brothers already deported and one still on commando. Mother and five children in a Natal concentration camp.

Daniel Jacobus Frederick Kruger (11 years). Mizpa, Bethal. To be deported with his father. Has a brother on commando and his mother and five children still reside on the farm.

Willem Johannes Lyon (12 years). Flensburg, Harrismith. Captured on the farm where his mother was residing. Elder brother a POW. To be deported with his brother. Died in the Durban harbour on 21.3.1902.

NJ de Lange (13 years). Waterval, Wakkerstroom. Father on Bermuda and one brother still on commando. Mother and six children in the Pietermaritzburg concentration Camp. Must be deported.

JMC Bekker (12 years). Rietvlei, Heidelberg. To be deported to join his father. One brother still on commando. Mother and four children in the Heidelberg concentration camp.

Lodewykus Willem Janse van Vuuren (10 years). Leeuwdrift, Waterberg. Father captured and held in Pretoria. Should be sent to join his father. Mother in the Nylstroom concentration camp with five children.

Gerhardus Joseph Fourie (11 years). Vlakfontein, Bethulie. Father and brother aged 14 still on commando. One brother aged 19 deported. Mother in the Bethulie concentration camp with two children. To be deported as a POW.

ML Bezuidenhout (8 years). Sent to the Heidelberg concentration camp.

BP Pieterse (9 years). Sent to the Standerton concentration camp.

SJ Smit (11 years). Sent to the Howick concentration camp.

Penkoppe (young bulls) in the Umbilo camp (WM).

Prisoners at the Umbilo camp aged between 64 and 84 years (WM).

Sanitary and health arrangements

Considering the checkered history of camps created by the British in the Anglo-Boer War, a supreme effort was made to keep the Umbilo POW camp clean and healthy. To achieve this it was necessary to involve the camp inhabitants, and they had the mundane task of sweeping their tents. The bulk of the sanitary duties, however, rested with the supervisor, Mr GE Danby and his 26 African contract workers. The Africans received a salary of £2 per month and Danby 10s per day. Together they were responsible for cleaning outside the tents and the remainder of the camp. They were assisted by six drivers, four of whom received a salary of £3 per month and two who received £2 per month, who had the duty of carting the rubbish away.[112] For the purposes of personal hygiene there were four wash-houses approximately 6m X 5m X 2m in size and three latrines with 26 seats each.[113]

Despite these facilities and the staff appointed to look after the sanitary conditions, the sanitary pits in the camp do not seem to have been in a clean and hygienic state. On 10 September 1902, Danby commented about the disgraceful condition of the sanitary pits. Urine and general refuse matter was lying in open pits despite an attempt to bury it. In the same locality and for a radius of about 200 yards (183 m), the ground was strewn with the general refuse of the camp. The stench arising from these pits permeated the camp.[114]

Notwithstanding the sanitary conditions as reported by Danby, the permanent prisoners and those who arrived from overseas camps generally enjoyed good health. There were very few patients, and those who were sick were predominantly those who had contracted the illness elsewhere. The only time illness was prevalent in the camp was when news reached the men that the next transport ship waiting to deport POWs had arrived in the harbour! The sick were admitted to the camp hospital, an A type hut 40m X 8m X 3m in size with its own ablution room of 5m X 3m X 2.5m and a cook house of 3m X 3m X 3m in size, and with 30 beds. Apart from the British medical staff, they were also attended to by Dr Krieger, a Boer.[115]

The daily bread

The distributors, Messrs Sparkes & Young Food Store, delivered bread, which had been baked by L Baumann & Co, Bakers, Confectioners and Biscuit Manufacturers, daily at 6:00 to Umbilo with the exception of days when new Boer prisoners arrived at the camp by train. On these days the bread was delivered directly to the camp. It was up to the DAAG to notify Baumann when he needed the bread to be delivered to the camp. On all other days the bread was collected from the store and brought to the camp.[118]

The daily routine

To make the administration and management of the camp more effective, a daily routine was established. The prisoners rose between 4:00 and 5:00. The cook then had to go and boil the kettle. Rations for breakfast were issued at 6:15 and the prisoners had until 8:00 to prepare and consume their meal. While awaiting breakfast, the prisoners would shower or merely hang around in the camp. At 13:00 the burghers would have dinner consisting of meat, potatoes and other dishes. For the rest of the day, the prisoners would attend to camp duties, laze around and await any news regarding their freedom. This monotonous routine was broken by frequent visits from the women and children from the three Durban concentration camps. These visitors were generally only allowed into the camp on specified days and were limited to 30 visitors over the age of 13. One day a week was allocated to each camp, with a Wednesday being assigned to the Wentworth concentration camp and a Friday to the Merebank concentration camp. Owing to the fact that the schoolteachers at Merebank were unable to comply with these arrangements because of their educational commitments, they were granted permission to visit the camp on a Saturday.[116] The visitors were allocated a tent immediately to the west of the library. Here they were supplied with tea or coffee and biscuits at 7:30, 12:00 and 16:00. During the visits, prisoners could enquire about the whereabouts of their families from visitors and other news was exchanged, but censors would listen to every conversation. For Adjutant Röcher, the visits did much to make the monotonous life bearable.[117]

Education and religious activities formed an integral part of the daily routine during the few short months of the Umbilo camp's existence. A school, where tuition was given in Dutch and English, was opened in the camp by JAS Faustman, an attorney, who had practised his profession in both the Orange Free State and the Transvaal prior to the outbreak of the war.[119] Religious meetings, generally conducted under the trees in the camp, were held by Ds JP Wolhuter from Piet Retief. He had surrendered on 1 March 1901, and was subsequently first sent to the Volksrust concentration camp, and then in October 1901, to Tin Town in Ladysmith. He was, however, earmarked for deportation because of his anti-British sentiments and for 'preaching in such a manner calculated to stir up disaffection against British rule'. Once in Durban, he requested permission to be able to help serve in the Jacobs concentration camp which had no religious minister of its own, and where his wife was employed as a schoolmistress. Because his services were required in the concentration camps, he was not deported.[120] Wolhuter was supported by visiting ministers, such as Ds WP Rousseau of Pietermaritzburg. For the rest, the men generally gathered every evening in their tents to conduct *huisgodsdiens* (evening devotion)[121] while the *Christelijke Jongelings Vereeniging* (Young Men's Christian Association) held their daily meetings in tent No. A10 at 18:30.[122] A package of religious books, donated by the relief committee in Cape Town, was distributed amongst the prisoners.[123]

Playing sport, as was the case in the overseas camps, formed an

Dirk Odendaal doing some *tolletjies brei* (crocheting) to pass the time. Koornhoof looks on (WM).

A customised postcard of TB van Niekerk. Photographs in the camp were taken by photographers such as Davy Benowitz (WM).

important part of the daily routine in Umbilo. Teams made up of prisoners from the Transvaal, the Orange Free State and members of the garrison, competed against one another. In quoits, a team of Transvalers, captained by Frank Duminy, beat the Free Staters, captained by VC de Villiers, by four to two. A series of ping-pong tournaments was also organised. Unfortunately the tennis courts at Umbilo were never completed, despite the fact that the required materials were purchased. The main reason for this was that the call for volunteers to complete the tennis courts evoked no response.[124] At one point a cricket match was played between a garrison team and a nondescript prisoners' eleven, resulting in a win for the Boers by 64 runs, with Bester top scoring with 45 runs. Some really bored Boers even took to playing marbles.[125]

But it was the more physical sports which the prisoners enjoyed most. A football match was played between the garrison and the Boers, the latter lovingly referred to as 'Our Boys' in *The Tick*. Unlike the cricket match which had not been well attended, the camp inhabitants flocked to the football game. This game was drawn. According to the editor of *The Tick*, the draw was because of the lamentably bad play of 'Our Boys'. The concept of combination was unknown to them and every player hogged the ball until it was taken from him or else he merely kicked in the direction in which his toe pointed. The few who could play kept up some semblance of expertise, but had to give up, as they received no support. The frequency of handling the ball and the number of opportunities to shoot at goal that were lost showed what was to be expected 'from those rough and ready practices where soccer is played with a bit of Rugby thrown in'.[126] A second match, won by the garrison, ended up in a fist fight. For those who found the football too delicate, boxing lessons were given by Jan Vermeulen, 'who was also willing to demonstrate the effects'.[127]

Some cultural activities were practised in the Umbilo camp such as singing and playing musical instruments like the harp, while singing lessons were given by Floris Coetzee.[128] A recreation tent in the camp with electric lights, a gramophone, and tables and chairs, allowed POWs to pass their time by playing cards, talking[129] or staging the odd concert.[130] The double marquees in the centre of the camp were used as a library and reading room, managed by a library committee, with General Cheere Emmett as the president. The committee was largely responsible for the selection of suitable reading material in Dutch and English.[131] In an attempt to provide the prisoners with what the camp authorities deemed as appropriate reading material, 119 copies of *The Transvaal from Within* by JP (Percy) Fitzpatrick, were despatched to the camp, to be issued to those POWs who wanted one.[132] On the fringes of the camp society, were those who attempted to deal with the monotony of camp life by indulging in a different form of recreation. F Berry received 96 hours imprisonment with hard labour in the guard room cells for being in possession of intoxicating liquor.[133]

A fair number of prisoners preferred to shun sport and culture in favour of economic endeavours. In the Umbilo camp there was a variety of shops. Philip Appelgrein opened a barber's shop where shaves and haircuts were given. A photographer took last-minute pictures before the

POWs departed, and Taylor's Cash Store promised its clientele that it would order what it did not have in stock. Taylor's also sold fresh fruit every day.[134] Others crafted ornaments such as wooden picture and photograph frames, wove ties, shawls and sashes in cotton, silk and cotton wool, made silver rings, or created souvenirs such as cards, which were embellished with the coat of arms of the two Boer republics. All these articles were sold at the post office tent.[135] Even the *penkoppe* got in on the commercial act by baking and selling *pannekoek* (pancakes).[136] Professionals, such as Attorney Faustmann, tried to revive their pre-war careers by offering to do any legal work with neatness, accuracy and efficiency, while others, such as Lukas Marthinus du Toit, an unlicenced auctioneer and appraiser, tried his hand at something new by announcing sales.[137] Apart from the shops and ventures belonging to the prisoners, an official camp store was situated quite close to the entrance into the camp. The rent paid by the proprietor was used for the amusement fund.[138] Alongside this formal economy an informal economy also existed. The 14 prisoners who shared a marquee with Röcher bought all they needed from an Italian, Dangero, a fellow POW who worked in the hospital. He was allowed more freedom than the other prisoners and he could thus visit places where he was able to purchase goods more cheaply than those available in the camp.[139] A possible source of supply would be someone like Ebrahim Suleman who was given permission by the Durban corporation to erect a fruit and vegetable stand close to the camp.[140]

The Tick

Some prisoners kept themselves occupied by producing a weekly publication, *The Tick*. This four-page publication, edited by BB van der Spuy, lasted for three editions during June 1902. It contained articles in both Dutch and English, and was passed by the censor before it was published by SR Allpass at the post office tent. The main aim of the publication was to expose its readers to material for the moral, social and intellectual development of the camp inhabitants. For this reason, *The Tick* covered those issues that were of local interest, while avoiding political and religious controversies. It generally contained humourous anecdotes of camp life and the war. Examples of this included an elaborate report on a snoring competition won by JW Treu. A typical humorous war story was the following: 'While a man was lying flat firing, a cannon ball from behind entered between his heels and ripped his body in two equal parts.' Says the other 'At Magersfontein a lyddite shell at a distance of 15 miles hit a man so full that the only trace left of him was the remnants of his boots.' The first of these newspapers was published on 5 June 1902, five days after peace, and contained a large variety of titbits, ranging from an editorial, and articles on issues such as the stock exchange, to advertisements, quotes, camp news and notices. Subsequent editions followed a similar pattern. One story tells of an old burgher from one of the inland camps who came to Umbilo to obtain papa's consent and at the same time parade his new fiancé, a young girl of 18. However, when strolling around the camp, the young lady saw and recognised a pre-war lover who was supposed to have fallen during the war. Love proved too strong and, forsaking her aged betrothed, she flew into the arms of her newly reunited lover, leaving poor Oom Jan to weep alone! It is often believed that the Boers had very little knowledge of or interest in economic affairs. This is however not the case. Instead the POWs in the Umbilo camp were actually advised to study the fluctuations of the stock exchange, and to follow commercial and financial markets, as well as to analyse the factors influencing markets and political developments.[141]

Various groups of prisoners photographed in the Umbilo camp. Those preparing for their meal (bottom right) are from left to right: H Durand, F Durand, AJ de la Rey, J Botes, S Schoeman, GJ Greeff, CG Röcher, JJ Bezuidenhout, JN Kritzinger, HA Kruger, A Graham. Seated in the front are M van der Walt and F Viljoen (WM).

A number of prisoners such as G Baumann, BR Kamann and JW Bullock found official employment in the Umbilo camp as intelligence officers, interpreters and censors.[142] Boer corporals were also used to act as room-corporals responsible for keeping the bittereinder and captured POWs separated from the surrendered burghers. They also had to see to it that the tents were neat, and had to report on the strength of the tents every morning. Seven POWs were employed at 2/6 per day to conduct parties of prisoners to railway stations.[143] Some of the prisoners even found employment outside the POW camp. Hendrik Bredenham, a boy of 13, was employed by Mr WW Barrett of Sydenham as a cowherd, at a rate of £1 per month, between 6 July 1902 and 5 December 1902. During his five months of employment, Hendrik withdrew 4/3, leaving a balance of £4 15s 9d due to him. On his discharge Barrett paid him only £3, leaving £1 15s 9d outstanding. When Bredenham asked Barrett for the amount owing, the latter refused to pay him as he held Bredenham responsible for the death of his dog. Barrett had at some earlier date given Bredenham some poison to kill stray cats, but unfortunately Barrett's dog had also eaten some of the poison and died as a result. Bredenham did not accept this and he took the matter to the police, who referred it to Mr WR Saunders, the Umlazi magistrate. The verdict of the magistrate was simple: Barrett had no right to reduce the boy's wages, and he was therefore instructed to pay Bredenham a further £1 10s, while being allowed a deduction of 5s as a punishment fine for 'perhaps slight carelessness' on behalf of the youngster.[144]

This was not the only time that WW Barrett had problems with a POW in his employment. On 18 September 1901 the case of Johannes Adendorff had appeared before Magistrate Saunders. Adendorff was employed by Barrett, but deserted after working a few days. As a result Barrett had him arrested under the Master and Servants Act.[145]

The various economic activities were not only initiated to alleviate boredom, but also used at times to support families residing elsewhere. Prisoners were known to send money and letters to their wives in other concentration camps. One such person was Mr F Eksteen, who sent £5 to his wife in the Merebank concentration camp.[146]

At least one POW who arrived at Umbilo on 2 June 1902, despite good security measures, managed to escape two weeks later. Antonie Francois Kock (de Kock?), aged 33, and a former judge in the Transvaal, escaped from the camp at 6:30 on Monday 16 June 1902, via the gate of the prisoners' enclosure, using a forged pass. Prior to his capture Kock had left the country and gone to Europe in 1900, only to return via Port Elizabeth under the name, it is believed, of Polensky, at which point he rejoined the Boer commandos. He was captured in December 1901, tried at Graaff Reinett and sentenced to penal servitude, but the sentence was commuted. Although a warrant of arrest was issued, explaining that Kock was '5'10" tall, had brown eyes, a slight beard and dark hair, with a rather large mouth and thick lip', he was not recaptured. At a court of enquiry held under the presidency of Captain HWM Down on 18 June 1902, it was found that Kock had escaped either on a forged pass, or because of the culpable negligence of the NCO on duty. The NCO was released from arrest without prejudice, to face a future trial in the event of sufficient evidence being found.[148]

Nominal Roll of Staff at Umbilo camp at 8 August 1902[147]

Rank	Name	Rank	Name
Capt	AA McHardy (SOP)	Private	Stone (Waiter, Officers' Mess)
Lieutenant	CC Bicknell (ASOP)	Interpreter	G Baumann
Sgt	EA Tagg	Interpreter	WA Bester
Sgt	Lees	Interpreter	C van Laun
Private	Keogh (Storeman)	Interpreter	JW Bullock
Private	Manion (Transport Orderly)	Civilian Clerk	GJ Wilson
Private	R Balshaw (Post Office Orderly)	Typist	BR Kamann
Private	J Slater (Telegraph Orderly)	Foreman Works	T Winn
Private	Bryan (Overseer African workers)	Boer Corporal	WD Wills
Private	Preston (Cook Officers Mess)		

Six African Sanitary Workers
Six African Transport Workers
British Force attached to Umbilo to act as escorts and fatigue parties

The above list excludes officers' servants

Transvaal officers in the Umbilo camp (WM).

Repatriation

When the war was over all POWs wanted to go home immediately. Some, such as JAS Faustmann, were even prepared to pay all the expenses if it would mean getting home earlier. This could in reality not happen and the repatriation process became a drawn-out and difficult affair. At Umbilo, the process could only commence once the surrendering of the commandos was completed and they had signed the oath of alligiance or an equivalent declaration.[149]

The commandant of the Umbilo POW camp, as was the case in all other POW camps, received instructions on how to deal with the men in his camp.[150] All men were expected to sign the oath of allegiance in triplicate before being allowed to go home. Each man also needed to be in possession of a signed and certified copy of the document.[151] Originally it was stipulated that if a POW was taking the oath in a town other than that of his permanent residence, the commissioner of the prisoner's residential district needed to be consulted first. Because it caused too much delay, this plan was abandoned.[152] Consequently, books containing oath forms were sent to the POW camp,[153] and Lieutenant Colonel Allatt[154] and Captain AA McHardy, then SOP at Umbilo, were permitted to oversee the process.[155]

Taking an oath of allegiance to Britain was not easy for many Boers, who remained suspicious of the undertaking. Therefore, on 2 July 1902, Generals Louis Botha, Christiaan de Wet and Koos de la Rey communicated the following message, in Dutch, to all POWs in South Africa and elsewhere:

> We wish to inform you all that Peace has been concluded on the 31st May 1902 under the terms and conditions as published and that all Burghers, then in the field, have laid down their arms under the terms of Peace and by doing so, have acknowledged to be British subjects. H.M. Government is willing, that each Burgher, who might object against the taking of the oath of allegiance shall be permitted to sign the following declaration: I (here to fill in name, place of residence, ward and district) adhere to the terms of the agreement signed at Pretoria on 31 May between my late government and the representatives of H.M. Government and I acknowledge myself to be a subject of King Edward VII and I promise to own true allegiance to him, his heirs and successor according to law.
>
> We advise you all, who have not already taken the oath of allegiance to sign this declaration, whereupon you will be sent back to your homelands as soon as arrangements can be made.[156]

The visit to Umbilo by General Schalk Burger, former vice-president of the Transvaal, did much to introduce some peace of mind amongst the prisoners in the camp, despite his being aggressively questioned by one Coetzee.[157]

The *Vyf Lekker Kêrels van Oom Koos de la Rey*. Seated: JN Kritzinger, AJ de la Rey, GJ Greeff. Standing: JJ Bezuidenhout, CG Röcher (Africana Museum).

General Schalk Burger informing the inhabitants of the Umbilo camp of the peace terms (WM).

Once the oath of allegiance was taken, arrangements had to be made with the districts to which the Umbilo POWs wished to proceed.[158] A process, which would be duplicated thousands of times, then took place. POWs were sent either to a concentration camp where their family was residing or to the one nearest to their homes. Here they would be treated as residents, and budgeted for in the ordinary monthly expenditure of the camp until such time as they left for their farms with their 30 days ration supply. Their supplies would be classified: 'Exceptional issues to Class-A'. If the POW was sent to the camp for reason other than the one stipulated above, any issue made to him, both while resident in the camp and on leaving the camp, would be categorised as 'Exceptional Issues to Class B'. The costs of the ration issues made to the men while resident in the concentration camps was judged at an average rate of 8d per day. These expenses were then entered into the concentration camp journal at the end of the month.[159] Between the end of June and 7 July 1902, nearly 900 POWs were released from Umbilo.[160]

Once the POWs who had resided in Umbilo had left, the camp did not close, but became a depot for all returning prisoners of war disembarking at Durban. Up to early 1903, with the arrival of the *Ionian* with 794 POWs and the *Lake Manitoba* with 956, the camp was continuously occupied by a stream of POWs passing through, and the work of classifying those men according to their districts and arranging for their despatch home was done by the staff in the camp, that is those who had gained some experience with the repatriation of the Umbilo inhabitants at the end of the war.[161]

To deal with the vast numbers of returning POWs, the following scheme was devised for the reception and subsequent distribution of the new British subjects. On the day of arrival in Durban, Commandant Bester and either Interpreter Bullock or Attenborough, or both, if possible, along with Corporal Wills, would visit the ship to answer the questions asked by POWs and the commanding officer on board ship.

Table showing number of ex-prisoners of war returning to South Africa, via Durban and Umbilo[162]

Date of Arrival	Ship	Port of Origin	No of POWs
19.07.1902	Tempelmore	Sri Lanka	400
11.08.1902	Golconda	India	500
18.08.1902	Safari	India	17
21.08.1902	Englishman	India & Sri Lanka	1 109
30.08.1902	Canada	St Helena	1 000 (450)*
07.09.1902	?	St Helena	1 000
10.09.1902	Malta	St Helena	1 000
21.09.1902	Ionian	India & Sri Lanka	1 000
22.10.1902	Oratava	St Helena	982
11.11.1902	Ionian	India	785
30.11.1902	Orotava	India	997
02.12.1902	Montrose	India	466+ 511*(999)
22.12.1902	Aurania		195
03.01.1903	Ionian		794
03.01.1903	Lake Manitoba		956

Abraham Bester

The rank of commandant, held by Abraham Bester, was not bestowed by his fellow Boers. He gained this rank as the unpaid commandant of the Tin Town POW camp. On the transferral of this camp to Umbilo, he accompanied the establishment. The 36-year-old Bester, originally from the Free State, and a qualified attorney, also served as a burgher agent and an intelligence officer from October 1901 onwards. His services were so highly regarded, that Lieutenant Colonel Allatt described him 'as a good man in any capacity' and recommended him for a reward.[164] To the *bittereinders* this would have been an example of someone regarded as a 'joiner'.[165]

Generally, no POWs were allowed to disembark, except those whose friends or family could vouch for them, whose wives were resident in the Durban concentration camps or who were well-known Boer officers. Those who were allowed ashore had to remain in Durban on passes which were issued by Commandant Bester, or an officer, and had to report to Umbilo the following morning.

Date	District (number of POWs in brackets)	No
	Districts to which Boer POWs returning via Durban and the Umbilo camp were deported.[163]	
16.08.1902	Vryheid	3
16.08.1902	Bethlehem (8); Bloemfontein (24); Boshof (6); Fauresmith (30); Ficksburg (22); Harrismith (8); Heilbron (2); Hoopstad (3); Jacobsdal(3); Kroonstad (16); Ladybrand (4); Rouxville (25); Smithfield (10); Vrede (2); Wepener (5); Winburg (8).	184
26.08.1902	Pietermaritzburg concentration camp (7); Merebank concentration camp (18); Wentworth concentration camp (9); Jacobs concentration camp(5); Howlck concentration camp (3); Ladysmith (4).	46
02.09.1902	Kroonstad (54); Bloemfontein (108); Kimberley (25); Bethulie (25); Springfontein (14); Brandfort (106); Winburg (64); Heilbron (13); Norvalspont (5); Harrismith (4); Aliwal North (12); Vredefort Road (7).	437
13.09.1902	Brandfort (99); Bloemfontein (80); Bethulie (100); Kroonstad (43); Winburg (48); Harrismith (20); Kimberley (34); Aliwal North (22); Springfontein (9); Heilbron (21); Norvalspont (1); Dordrecht (1).	478
29.09.1902	Kimberley (22); Heilbron (64); Winburg (40); Kroonstad (76); Aliwal North (24); Harrismith (75); Bethulie (27); Brandfort (23); Doornbult (25); Bloemfontein (59); Springfontein (48).	483
01.11.1902	Kroonstad (71); Rouxville (15); Phillippolis (16); Senekal (1); Ficksburg (3); Ladybrand (15); Harrismith (5); Hoopstad (6); Boshof (10); Bethelhem (29); Vredefort (1); Heilbron (74); Bethulie (15); Jacobsdal (2); Bloemhof (78); Winburg (44); Vrede (19); Brandfort (2); Wepener (11); Smithfield (13); Fauresmith (55); Edenburg (1).	486
15.11.1902	Piet Retief (18); Utrecht (4); Wakkerstroom (22); Jacobs concentration camp (1); Vryheid (9).	54
29.11.1902	Vryheid (2); Pietermaritzburg (1); Wakkerstroom (19); Utrecht (5).	27
01.12.1902	One ex-POW to Merebank to look after his sick wife, the other, a *penkop*, to join friends.	2
01.12.1902	Wakkerstroom	19
01.12.1902	Utrecht	5
04.12.1902	M.Cronje to join his parents in the Merebank concentration camp.	1
04.12.1902	J.J. Bezuidenhout to join his parents in the Jacobs concentration camp.	1
04.12.1902	Vryheid (1)	1
05.12.1902	Ex-POWs to Merebank to join family, one being J Breed.	6
05.12.1902	Volksrust concentration camp	10
23.12.1902	Vryheid (6); Pietermaritzburg (1), Utrecht (3); Wakkerstroom (19).	29
07.01.1903	Zeerust(7); Lichtenburg (18); Heidelberg (16); Wolmaranstad (6); Klerksdorp (6);Vryheid (4); Krugersdorp (142); Lydenburg (12); Zoutpansberg (48); Potchefstroom (22); Middelburg (48); Waterberg (16); Carolina (8); Wakkerstroom (9); Volksrust (1); Piet Retief (1).	364

Once disembarked, the POWs were transported the short distance to Umbilo by the NGR, as a rule ten to a carriage. Their baggage was loaded under the guidance of the military landing officer and either placed on the train or was sent later, in which case a Boer baggage guard kept watch over it. On arrival at the Umbilo Station, the interpreters and military supervised the detrainment of the Boers and conducted them to the camp. If it was early in the day, the baggage was taken to the camp, but if it was a late arrival, the baggage was left under an African guard of four boys and a headman until the following morning.

On arriving at the camp gate, Bester and Wills, who were waiting for the POWs, armed with the necessary number of the Umbilo camp ration chits, counted the men into batches of 16, filled in a chit, and then passed on the batch and chit to the nearest conductor, who led the prisoners to the specified tent. Sixteen men were placed in one marquee and eight in a bell tent. Once the conductor had shown the men their tent, he would hand over the chit to the 'most intelligent Boer', show him the ration stand, and direct him to draw some provisions immediately. The quarter-master would be there to see to his needs. The conductor would also explain that each tent required two cooks, and he would then return to the gate to receive the next batch of 16. Once the prisoners were settled in, Bester would have the orders for the following day typed out and placed on the noticeboard. The prisoners were allowed to leave the Umbilo camp, but were requested to return by 21:00, although special night passes could be issued.

On the first day after their arrival, the Boers were left to find out the whereabouts of their families, generally through information provided by the many women who visited Umbilo from other camps in Durban. Commandant Bester would also post up the orders for the parades the next day, with details of how the men were to be marshalled at the registration tent, which was marked by a red flag. The registration started as soon as possible, but only one person could enter the tent at a time. Bester used the nominal rolls received from the ship's captain as a basis, and proceeded to check each man's POW number, his initials, name, district, where he wished to go to and whether he could support himself or not. If the prisoner desired to proceed to a district other than his own, he had to furnish a reason for his choice. In cases where the POW numbers were not given on the nominal rolls, the complete name, age and full home address was registered. The quartermaster, assisted by Corporal Wills and any other available Boer officers, issued the prisoners with blankets and clothing which were charged to the repatriation department. With this process completed, the prisoners could start looking forward to returning home.

On the day of departure, all baggage had to be stacked outside the camp gates by 8:30. To facilitate packing on the railway carriages, signboards were erected in sequence, starting with the concentration camp furthest afield. Each prisoner was requested to place his kit opposite the signboard of his destination. Loading luggage of those headed for the furthest destination began first. The quartermaster had to ensure that four days' rations were allocated and placed in each carriage. The trucks and carriages had to be ready by 12:00. The burghers would then have lunch, before Commandant Bester and Corporal Wills would commence calling the rolls, counting each man, who was now at last really free, and directing him out at the gate according to whether he was bound for the Orange River Colony (ORC) or the Transvaal train. The quartermaster would also be at the gate, checking any illegal annexation of government stores. The men for the first train were lined up only after the 16:00 'Up mail' had passed, and the second group took their places soon afterwards.[166]

These well-laid repatriation plans soon came under serious strain. A telegram from the provost marshal in Pretoria to the SOP in Umbilo stated: 'It is reported from Standerton that the Boers who arrived there from Umbilo on Sunday July 27th had neither blankets nor food.' In order to prevent this from happening again, the provost marshal requested that an officer be placed in charge of any train containing more than 100 POWs and that an intelligent NCO be placed in charge of smaller groups. It was subsequently also decided that 2 000 blankets would be issued to Umbilo, and charged to the repatriation department, so that there would be enough blankets to hand out to all men, and not only to the old men.[167]

The port of Durban, as well as the military authorities, had difficulty coping with the large number of prisoners arriving, because of the limited rail transport. As a result, the governor of Natal, Sir HE McCallum, asked the secretary of state to ensure that no more ships were sent to Durban for a month after the docking of the *Ionian* on 21 September 1902. McCallum believed that by then they would once again be prepared to receive prisoners at a rate of 1 000 every ten days.[168] One of the reasons for the congestion of POWs and the insufficient rail transport was mentioned on 25 August 1902 by David Hunter, the managing director of the NGR. He complained that the arrangement of conveying returning Boer prisoners by rail from the Point to Umbilo, and then re-entraining them for the Transvaal or the ORC after a stay of 24 hours was very unsatisfactory, as this meant the loss of an engine for the greater part of the day on which the men were disembarked, and an entire day's loss of the rolling stock in which they were conveyed to Umbilo. According to Hunter, if the POWs were despatched directly from the Point to their destination, or some other central point in the Transvaal – if this was necessary for distribution purposes – there would be a considerable saving in engine power and rolling stock, and this would mean that Durban could manage the anticipated arrival of 1 000 POWs per week.[169] The provost marshal, however, considered his suggestion to be impractical.[170]

In their frenzied attempts to repatriate the POWs as soon as possible, the NGR assigned ten men to a compartment. In August 1902, Captain W Bonham criticised this, saying that the manner in which ex-POWs were being transferred back to the interior was unsatisfactory. He believed that no more than six men should be put into one compartment. Furthermore, he wished Boer officers and officials to be placed in first-class accommodation. He also complained that the train only stopped at Umbilo for ten minutes, which was not long enough to complete the task of loading the luggage.[171]

Hunter disputed the latter accusation, saying that the carriages were already left at Umbilo Station the day before departure to enable men to load their baggage. According to Hunter, the entraining that took place on the main line could be done with the greatest ease by having the ex-prisoners formed up in lots of ten. This method allowed 1 000 prisoners to be entrained and the train to be despatched in seven minutes. The suggestions put forward by Bonham were also frowned upon by Hunter. To allow the NGR to transport only six men per compartment would mean that the ordinary 'coloured' passengers would be inconvenienced as their carriages would be withdrawn to transport the Boer prisoners. Furthermore the NGR would have to run additional trains, which they could ill afford because of the limited haulage power available. There was already a large accumulation of goods traffic waiting to go to the Transvaal, making it virtually impossible to deal with the demands from the interior with any degree of satisfaction.[172]

A further problem which arose in the repatriation process revolved around the weight of the luggage of the Boer POWs. Each POW was allowed 50 lbs (22 kg) free.[173] The military authorities considered it extremely impractical to weigh the luggage of each man individually.

Instead, Captain McHardy requested that an official from the NGR be present in the Umbilo camp, with a weighing machine, from daybreak till 16:00 on the day of the departure of the prisoners, as he did not have enough staff to weigh the baggage. The rationale behind such a cumbersome process was to deal with the economics of rail freight. The NGR could not allow unlimited quantities of luggage and anything exceeding the weight limit had to be paid for.[174]

Despite these problems, special trains which left Umbilo on 26 August 1902, with 450 ex-POW Boers each, practically cleared the Umbilo camp.[175] This, along with the reduced rates given to those POWs returning home at their own expense,[176] such as Egbert, Edward and Willie van Bart who went home to their mother at Umkomaas,[177] and the free passes and second-class tickets issued to POWs returning home with their families from the Durban concentration camps,[178] greatly relieved the congestion. By all accounts few problems were experienced in the repatriation process from then on. A minor difficulty was that not all

POWs forwarded from Umbilo were welcome in the districts they wished to return to. The resident magistrate at Ermelo, for example, requested that William Robertson Keet not be sent back to Ermelo as 'his presence would be particularly undesirable'.[179]

The feelings about life in Umbilo are best summed up by Charles Röcher: Life was monotonous beyond belief. Time became the greatest enemy. Being a POW is the worst occupation in the world. We received news from the battlefield via the new POWs that arrived frequently, for example, Jan Botes who arrived wearing my best pair of pants which he had inherited after my capture. My thoughts never deviated from my brothers in the field and my longing for them made matters worse. I tried to study, but could not. The two months I spent in Umbilo were the worst I ever experienced in my life. No wonder that on my departure on 29 June 1902, for Potchefstroom and then for St Andrews College in Grahamstown and finally Paris, I was more ghost than man.[180]

For several former POWs the repatriation journey ended in Durban. Frederick Devensing, a prisoner of German descent, did not wish to return to Johannesburg, but preferred to take up employment offered him by John Nicol & Son, a firm of carpenters in Durban. He had been captured in March 1901, and deported to India. Devensing returned to South Africa on board the *Ionian*, on 24 September 1902, and was taken to the Umbilo POW Camp. To give him permission to remain in Durban, the authorities first had to establish whether or not Devensing was a rebel or an undesirable. As he was neither, but a carpenter by trade who had originally arrived in the republics as a child, he received permission to live and work in Durban.[181] Likewise, employment was offered in Durban to ex-prisoner Stefanus Johannes le Roux by Murdocks Store in Umbilo Road in January 1903. As with Devensing, Le Roux had to obtain permission to take up employment in Durban.[182]

By February 1903, the repatriation from Umbilo had been completed and the camp was deserted. The Durban corporation purchased the buildings from the military for £1 221 5s 6d.[183] The following year, the Durban corporation offered the Umbilo POW camp to the police who were guarding the Chinese workers residing at the old Jacobs concentration camp, subject to a charge of £10. The inspector of police, however, found that the site, which was nearly five kilometres from the site at Jacobs, unsuitable as a camping ground for the police.[184] The Indian Immigration Trust then moved their depot to the Umbilo camp grounds at a rental of £25 per month.[185]

POWs entraining at the Umbilo Station. These men returned home in open cattle trucks despite assurances that this would not happen (WM).

1. *Natal Mercury*, 27.10.1899.

2. PRO, CO 179/207: diary of events W Hely-Hutchinson, 27.10.1899.

3. PRO, CO 179/207: letters from Boer POWs handed to Commander FRW Morgan, 28.10.1899–3.11.1899.

4. NAR, SOP 5: army order regarding the position of POWs.

6. 12.1900.

5. Preller, GS, *Ons Parool. Dae uit die dagboek van 'n krygsgevangene*, pp.66–74; WM, 4502/21–28: *Oorlogsherinneringe van Jan Geldenhuys* (Ou Dad) pp.19–22; WM, 4141/2: *Gevangenis – Beschrywing van Cornelius Petrus van Zyl* – Augustus 1902, p.4.

6. NAR, SOP 22: orders for convoying POWs, 28.10.1901.

7. WM 4141/2: *Gevangenis – Beschrywing van Cornelius Petrus van Zyl* – Augustus 1902, p.5.

8. *Natal Mercury*, 19.4.1900.

9. *Natal Witness*, 21.6.1900.

10. *Natal Mercury*, 24.8.1900.

11. *Natal Mercury*, 15.8.1900; 17.8.1900.

12. *Natal Mercury*, 1.9.1900.

13. Swanepoel, I: notes from newspapers on prison ships, no page or date.

14. *Natal Witness*, 5.7.1900; 13.7.1900.

15. *Natal Mercury*, 22.9.1901.

16. *Natal Mercury*, 7.1.1902.

17. *Natal Mercury*, 4.3.1902.

18. *Natal Mercury*, 26.6.1902.

19. PAR, GH 559: intercepted letters of Natal rebels held on board the *Catalonia*, 23.5.1900.

20. Preller, pp.71–72.

21. WM, 4141/2: *Gevangenis – Beschrywing van Cornelius Petrus van Zyl* – Augustus 1902, pp. 6–7.

22. WM, 6324/1: concert programme on board *Aurania*, 28.9.1901.

23. PAR, GH 562: letter A O'Neill to L O'Neill, 22.5.1900.

24. WM, 6324/1: programme of a concert held on board *Aurania*, 28.9.1901.

25. PRO, CO 179/216: minute paper on gifts for Boer POWs in Durban, 18.7.1900.

26. *Natal Witness*, 17.5.1900.

27. Fischer, M, *Tant Miem Fischer se kampdagboek. Mei 1901 – Augustus 1902*, pp.81–82.

28. NAR, SOP 33: four letters Buchanan, Forsyth & Co. to MB Foster, 13.11.1901, 29.11.1901, 10.12.1901, 17.12.1901.

29. PAR, PM 18: letter BJ Badenhorst to commandant of Durban, 29.5.1900.

30. PAR, GH 1448: release documents of JFC Bosse, prisoner on board the *Yorkshire*, 6.11.1900.

31. *Natal Witness*, 30.7.1900.

32. See for example the *Natal Witness*, 25.8.1900, which contained eight names.

33. NAR, SOP 12: documents regarding POWs paroled from Tin Town POW Camp, 11.6.1901.

34. NAR, SOP 5: memorandum regarding parole conditions, 8.2.1901.

35. PRO, CO 179/211: despatch regarding detention of suspects on neutral vessels, 12.4.1900; parole documents of HAW Wickert and CH Kasier, 11.1.1900.

36. PRO, CO 179/208: documents pertaining to the arrest of CT Schmidt, 2.12.1899–7.12.1899.

37. PRO, CO 179/210 and 179/215: documents surrounding the arrest of PO Nissen, 2.1900–11.1900.

38. PAR, CO 179/209 and 179/216: documents related to the parole in Durban of E Harms, 2.2.1900, 8.10.1900.

39. PRO, CO 179/211: letter Commandant Morris to W Hely-Hutchinson, 4.4.1900.

40. PAR, GH 545 and 531: documents relating to 11 Boer political prisoners sent to Durban, 27.7.1900–2.8.1900.

41. NAR, MGP 5126: telegram commandant Durban – MGP, 22.10.1900.

42. NAR, PMO 52: documents relating to the November conspiracy, 21.1.1902–21.4.1902.

43. PAR, GH 533 and 545: documents related to the transferral of 14 Boers to Tin Town, 3.2.1901–5.2.1901.

44. NAR, SOP 12: correspondence relating to the Von Backstrom and Bosman families, 13.6.1901–19.7.1901.

45. NAR, SOP 16: correspondence and statements relating to J Dongoumoo, 24.7.1901–10.8.1901.

46. NAR, SOP 5: letter Commandant Morris to SOP Natal, 22.2.1901.

47. NAR, SOP 31: memorandum on undesirables deported from Vryburg to Durban, 11.4.1902.

48. NAR, MGP 154: correspondence relating to JHD Kruyshaar, 18.11.1901–22.11.1901.

49. NAR, SOP 5: documents relating to E Boshoff, 8.2.1901.

50. NAR, SOP 8: correspondence pertaining to the position of surrendered Boers in Durban, 21.3.1901–7.4.1901.

51. NAR, SOP 17: documents regarding AT Tolmay, 9.7.1901–18.9.1901.

52. NAR, SOP 11: letter SOP Cape Town to SOP Natal, 21.5.1901.

53. NAR, SOP 24: letter commandant Durban to APM, 19.11.1901.

54. NAR, SOP 25: orders relating to POWs from provost-marshall, 6.12.1901.

55. PAR, GH 793: letter TK Murray to Lord Kitchener, 20.1.1902.

56. PAR, GH 1574: minute paper HE McCallum to AH Hime, 17.5.1901.

57. NAR, SOP 11: letter SOP Major MB Forster to DAAG, Natal, 24.5.1901.

58. NAR, SOP 11: letter SOP Major MB Foster to DAAG, Natal, 10.9.1901.

59. NAR, SOP 34: memorandum DAAG Umbilo, Captain AA McHardy to chief paymaster Natal, 30.8.1902.

60. PAR, GH 1452: memorandum of land deal between the Durban municipality and the military, 13.11.1901.

61. *De Kerkbode* 19(19), 15.5.1902, p. 375

62. The *Natal Mercury* 26.6.1902.

63. Liebenberg, BJ, *Andries Pretorius in Natal*, pp.155–184.

64. *Natal Mercury*, 13.4.1916.

65. *The Tick* (2), June 1902, p.2.

66. *The Tick* (1), 5.6.1902, p.1.

67. *Natal Mercury*, 13.4.1916.

68. WM, photographs of Umbilo camp, unnumbered.

69. NAR, SOP 32: agreement general officer commanding Natal and the African Boating Co. Ltd., 14.1.1902.

70. PAR, GH 793: letter TK Murray to HE McCallum, 20.1.1902.

71. NAR, SOP 29: letter Lieutenant CC Brickhill to COD Natal, 5.3.1902.

72. NAR, SOP 29: letter Lieutenant Colonel HDE Parsons to ordnance officer, Pietermaritzburg, 6.3.1902.

73. NAR, SOP 29: letter Lieutenant Colonel HDE Parsons to SOP Umbilo, Lieutenant Colonel HTW Allatt, 9.3.1902.

74. NAR, SOP 29: letter Lieutenant Colonel HTW Allatt to Lieutenant Colonel HDE Parsons, 10.3.1902.

75. NAR, SOP 29: letter Lieutenant Colonel HDE Parsons to ordnance officer Pietermaritzburg, 12.3.1902.

76. NAR, SOP 29: letter ordnance officer Pietermaritzburg to Lieutenant Colonel HDE Parsons, 22.3.1902.

77. *Natal Mercury*, 26.6.1902.

78. *Natal Mercury*, 26.6.1902.

79. PRO, WO 108/296: report on the work of the Royal Engineers in Natal, 1899–1902.

80. NAR, SOP 29: telegram Captain HH Turner to Lieutenant Colonel HTW Allatt, 10.4.1902.

81. NAR, SOP 31: letter camp commandant Umbilo Captain HB Trevor to Lieutenant Colonel HTW Allatt, 6.4.1902.

82. NAR, SOP 31: letter Lieutenant Colonel HTW Allatt to commandant Durban, 7.4.1902.

83. NAR, SOP 31: telegram commandant Durban to Colonel HF Rawson, 7.4.1902.

84. NAR, SOP 31: telegram Colonel HF Rawson to commandant Durban, 9.4.1902.

85. PRO, WO 108/296: report on the work of the Royal Engineers in Natal, 1899–1902.

86. NAR, SOP 33: note Lieutenant Colonel HTW Allatt to officer commanding Army Service Corps, Durban, 4.6.1902.

87. NAR, SOP 35: memorandum from Captain AA McHardy to Army Service Corps, Durban, 14.10.1902.

88. PAR, NHD II/1/32: documents on the treatment of African suspects on the Bluff, 1900–1902.

89. PAR, NCP 8/2/2: coast district engineers report for 1902, pp.15–17.

90. DAR, 3/DBN 2/1/1/168: letter Colonel HF Rawson the town clerk Durban, 9.5.1902: 3/DBN 2/1/1/18: letter town clerk Durban to Sir ?, 13.5.1902.

91. NAR, SOP 29: correspondence regarding a telephone for Lieutenant Colonel HTW Allatt, 11.2.1902–18.2.1902.

92. NAR, SOP 31: telegram ordnance officer Durban to Lieutenant Colonel HDE Parsons, 12.4.1902.

93. NAR, SOP 31: telegram Lieutenant Colonel HDE Parsons to Lieutenant Colonel TW Allatt, 18.4.1902.

94. NAR, GS Preller collection A. 787, 62: diary of C Röcher, p.108.

95. NAR, SOP 31: nominal roll of non-commissioned officers and men, admitted into and discharged from the convalescent depot Howick, 24.3.1902.

96. NAR, SOP 31: telegram Lieutenant Colonel HTW Allatt to Colonel HM Lawson, 31.3.1902.

97. NAR, SOP 29: telegram Colonel HM Lawson to Lieutenant Colonel HDE Parsons, 8.4.1902.

98. *De Kerkbode* 19(19), 15.5.1902, p.375.

99. PAR, SOP 32: letter FJ Bezuidenhout to SOP, Durban, 8.3.1902.

100. NAR, SOP 32: letter G Bosch to Lieutenant Colonel HTW Allatt, 26.5.1902.

101. NAR, PMO 58: letter F de S Short to army headquarters, 14.6.1902; NAR, PMO, 58: copy of letter signed by JJ van der Merwe, 7.5.1902.

102. NAR, SOP 33: letter on German foreigners in the Umbilo camp to Lieutenant Colonel HTW Allatt, 16.7.1902; NAR, SOP 33: letter provost marshall to SOP, 19.7.1902.

103. PAR, SOP 33: letter SOP to DAAG, 10.6.1902.

104. PAR, SOP 32: letter SOP to paymaster, 10.3.1902.

105. NAR, SOP 29: letter JB Badenhort to SOP, 21.6.1902.

106. NAR, SOP 29: correspondence between SOP Natal and HM Bousefield, 14.2.1902 and 15.2.1902.

107. NAR, SOP 29: memorandum Lieutenant Colonel Poore to general officer commanding, Natal, 6.2.1902; NAR, SOP 29: memorandum superintendent Jacobs camp to commandant, Durban, 18.2.1902.

108. NAR, PMO 54: telegrams regarding the transferral of APH Gouws, 26.4.1902–27.5.1902.

109. PAR, PM 57: medical certificates Lieutenant Colonel HTW Allatt to prime minister, 1.6.1902; NAR, PMO 54: list of burghers not to be deported because of age, 6.2.1902–22.4.1902.

110. Marais, P, *Penkoppe van die Tweede Vryheidsoorlog 1899–1902*, pp.7–8.

111. NAR, PMO 3563: lists of *Penkoppe* that were to be deported, 5.1.1902.

112. PAR, PA 5389: *Umbilo Camp. General scheme for redistribution and subsequent distribution of ex-prisoners of war*, p.9; NAR, SOP 34: note Captain AA McHardy to Major HA Coddington, 15.9.1902.

113. PRO, WO 108/296: report of work of Royal Engineers in Natal, 1899–1902.

114. NAR, SOP 34: letter GE Dawby to DAAG, Umbilo, 10.9.1902.

115. PRO, WO 108/296: report of work of Royal Engineers in Natal, 1899–1902.

116. NAR, SOP 3: memorandum Lieutenant Colonel HTW Allatt to TK Murray, 9.4.1902 and 16.4.1902.

117. NAR, GS Preller collection, A. 787, 62: diary of C Röcher, pp.201–202.

118. NAR, SOP 35: letter officer in charge to DAAG, Umbilo, 8.12.1902.

119. *The Tick* (1), 5.6.1902, p.1

120. NAR, SOP 29: note Lieutenant Colonel HTW Allatt to WP Rousseau, 7.3.1902; NAR, SOP, 32: particulars on Wolhuter; *De Kerkbode* 19(22), 5.7.1902, p.413.

121. *De Kerkbode* 19(19), 15.5.1902, pp.375–376.

122. *The Tick* (2), 12.6.1902, p.2

123. NAR, SOP 32: letter CP Schulz to superintendent, Umbilo, 6.5.1902.

124. *The Tick* (2), 12.6.1902, p.3.

125. *The Tick* (3), 26.6.1902, p.1.

126. *The Tick* (3), 26.6.1902, p.1.

127. *The Tick* (1), 5.6.1902, p.1.

128. *The Tick* (1), 5.6.1902, p.1.

129. *The Tick* (2), 12.6.1902, p.3.

130. *The Tick* (3), 26.6.1902, p.4

131. PAR, P 5389: *Umbilo Camp. General Scheme for reception and subsequent distribution of ex-prisoners of war*, p.10.

132. NAR, SOP 33: letter war office to the general officer commanding, Natal, April, 1902.

133. NAR, SOP 32: note SOP Natal to camp commandant, Umbilo, 26.5.1902.

134. *The Tick* (1), 5.6.1902, p.1.

135. *The Tick* (1), 5.6.1902, p.1; *Natal Mercury*, 26.6.1902.

136. *The Tick* (2), 12.6.1902, p.3.

137. *The Tick* (1), 5.6.1902, p.1.

138. *Natal Mercury*, 26.6.1902.

139. NAR, GS Preller collection, A.787. 62: diary of C Röcher, p.109.

140. DAR, 3/DBN 8/1/111/3/2: letter granting E Suleman permission to erect a stand, 21.4.1902.

141. *The Tick*, (1), 5.6.1902; *The Tick*, (2), 14.6.1902; *The Tick*, (3), 26.6.1902.

142. NAR, CS 226: document on employment of men in the Umbilo camp, 14.1.1903.

143. NAR, SOP 34: note Colonel RM Ireland to HA Coddington, 5.9.1902; note HA Coddington to Colonel RM Ireland, 7.9.1902.

144. NAR, SOP 35: statement by Hendrik Bredenham 5.12.1902; NAR, SOP 35: note WR Saunders to Captain McHardy, 24,12,1902; NAR, SOP 35: letter Captain McHardy to the Natal police, Sydenham, 26.12.1902.

145. *Natal Mercury*, 19.9.1901.

146. NAR, SOP 29: memorandum SOP to HM Bousfield, 24.2.1902.

147. NAR, SOP 34: description of staff attached to the Umbilo camp, 8.8.1902.

148. NAR, SOP 33: note Lieutenant Colonel HTW Allatt to the press censor, Durban, 15.7.1902; NAR, SOP 33: particulars of a POW who slipped out from Umbilo camp on 16 June 1902.

149. NAR, SOP 33: letter W Dunn & Co. to the commandant Durban, 16.6.1902.

150. NAR, SOP 33: letter Lieutenant Colonel HTW Allatt to general officer commanding, Middelburg, 24.6.1902.

151. PAR, GH 545: telegram general officer commanding, Natal to HE McCallum, 12.6.1902; NAR, SOP 33: letter provost marshall to SOP Natal, 9.7.1902.

152. PAR, SOP 33: letter Lieutenant Colonel HTW Allatt to prime minister, 14.6.1902.

153. NAR, CS 100: letter colonial secretary to military secretary, 4.7.1902.

154. NAR, CS 95: letter private secretary to Lieutenant Colonel HTW Allatt, 13.1.1902; NAR, CS 95: telegram Lieutenant Colonel HTW Allatt to imperial chief commissioner office, 4.6.1902.

155. NAR, CS 148: letter military secretary to colonial secretary, 2.10.1902.

156. PAR, GH 707: translation of telegram sent to the Boers by the Boer generals, 2.7.1902; NAR, SOP 33: Dutch copy of the telegram, 4.7.1902.

157. PAR, SOP 33: letter SOP Natal, to DAAG. Natal, 10.6.1902.

158. PAR, GH 546: telegram general officer commanding, Natal to governor, 20.6.1902.

159. NAR, Ploeger collection, A 2030 51: circular, F. 20.

160. NAR, SOP 33: letter Lieutenant Colonel HTW Allatt to provost marshal, 7.7.1902.

161. PAR, GH 563: telegrams SOP to camp superintendents, 25.8.1902.

162. NAR, GH 563: telegrams DAAG to the governor, 19.8.1902, 13.09.1902, 22.10.1902; NAR, GH 563: list HE McCallum to Milner, 17.9.1902.

163. PAR, GH 563: telegrams SOP to governor 29.11.1902, 4.12.1902, 3.1.1903, 6.1.1903.

164. PRO, WO 108/155: final recommendations for civilians, 3.6.1902.

165. NAR, CS 226: documents regarding employment for POWs in the Umbilo camp, 14.1.1903.

166. PAR, PA 5389: *Umbilo Camp. General Scheme for redistribution and subsequent distribution of ex-prisoners of war, passim.*

167. NAR, SOP 34: telegram provost marshal, Pretoria to SOP, Umbilo, date unknown; telegram chief ordnance officer to SOP, Umbilo, 20.8.1902.

168. PAR, GH 564: letter HE McCallum to Milner, 17.9.1902.

169. NAR, SOP 34: letter general manager, NGR to assistant quartermaster general, Durban, 25.8.1902.

170. PAR, PM 32: letter acting general manager of the NGR to the secretary of the prime minister, 1.9.1902.

171. PAR, PM 32: memorandum W Bonham to HE McCallum, 26.8.1902.

172. PAR, PM 32: letter acting general manager of the NGR to the secretary of the prime minister, 1.9.1902.

173. NAR, SOP 35: memorandum station master Umbilo to DAAG, 14.11.1902.

174. NAR, SOP 35: letter Captain AA McHardy to Lieutenant Radford, 14.11.1902.

175. NAR, GH 563: telegram SOP to HE McCallum, 26.8.1902.

176. PAR PM 32: telegram DAAG to prime minister, 7.9.1902.

177. NAR, SOP 34: letter HA van Bart to SOP, Cape Town, 17.7.1902; NAR, SOP 34: letter SOP, Cape Town to SOP, Natal, 23.7.1902.

178. NAR, SOP 35: letter Major FA Tyler to the commandant Durban, 24.6.1902.

179. NAR, SOP 35: telegram Captain W Bonham to SOP 16.9.1902.

180. NAR, GS Preller collection, A. 787, 62: diary of C Röcher, p.201.

181. PAR, PM 33: letters Captain AA McHardy to attorney-general, 6.10.1902 and 15.10.1902; PAR, PM 33: note secretary of the prime minister to DAAG 31.10.1902.

182. PAR, PM 36: note secretary of the prime minister to SOP, 12.01.1903.

183. DAR, 3/DBN A 1/1/1: report Durban corporation town reports on liabilities, 1903.

184. PAR, MJPW 129: letter deputy mayor to minister of justice, Pietermaritzburg, 17.6.1902.

185. PAR, NCP 8/1/10/6/20: Indian immigration report, 1902/1903.

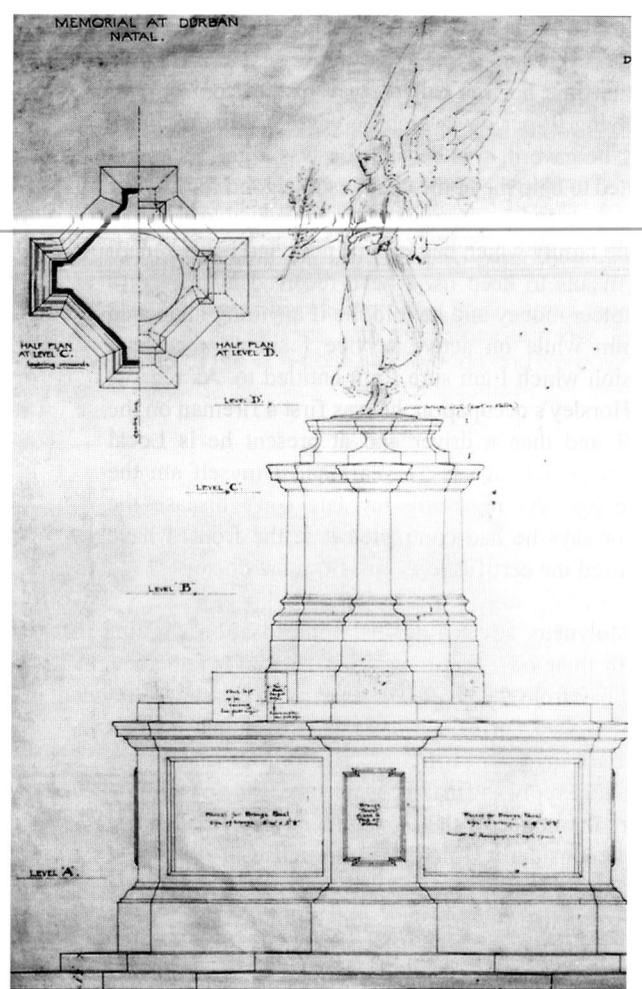

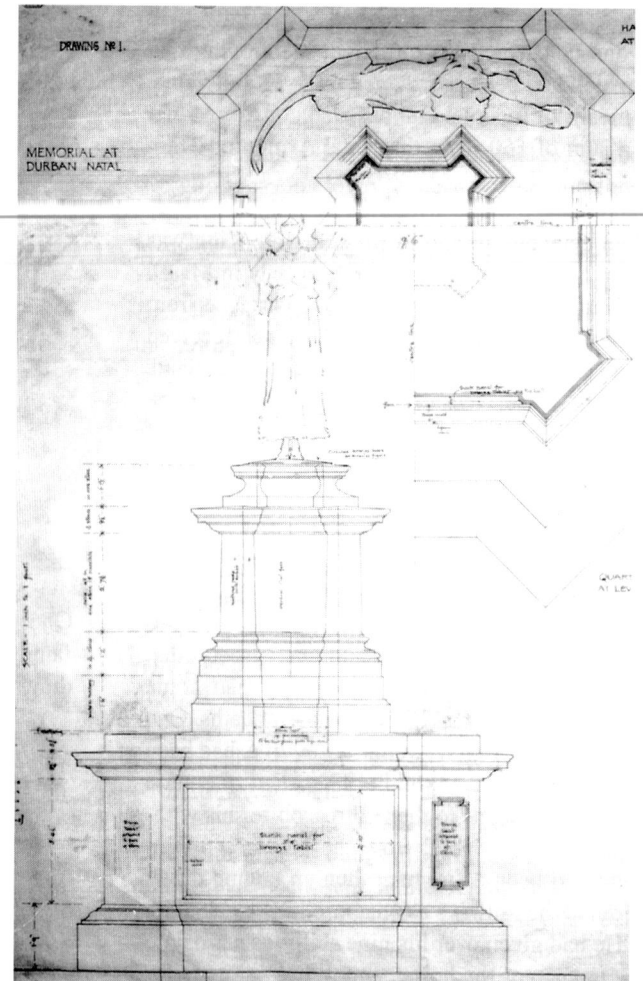

Design drawings for the Volunteer Memorial by Hymo Thorneycroft, 1904 (City Architect's archives).

Volunteer Memorial, town gardens (PAR).

Villiers arrived, as a prisoner, on board the *Ranee* on 10 June 1901, with acute pain and in a state of semi-collapse and was admitted to the ship's hospital at once. In the hospital, Dr AE Chambers diagnosed him with acute peritonitis with the following signs and symptoms: 'great pain and tenderness on pressure, lympanitis and disturbed abdomen, dullness in lower part of abdominal cavity, quick and feeble pulse, temperature 101. There was no vomiting tongue was dry and evaded: there was no history of enteric, dysentery, or appendicitis.' To treat these symptoms opium and small quantities of milk and brandy were administered. By the evening Chambers noticed a slight improvement. On the morning of 11 June 1901, De Villiers showed no sign of recovery despite having taken in some food. Just after 14:00 his condition deteriorated suddenly and his temperature shot up to 107°. Soon afterwards he passed away, according to the death certificate, as a result of pneumonia. A coffin was sent out to the *Ranee* at 16:30 by tug and the body was returned to Durban. The following day, 12 June 1901, De Villiers was buried at site 34, plot 12 in the West Street Cemetery, leaving a wife who was living with her father, D Blignaut, in the Heilbron district.[20] All that remains of the tombstone erected in honour of De Villiers is a broken-off splinter with the words 'on board'.[21]

En route to Bermuda from Durban, a second prisoner passed away on board the *Ranee*. John Daniel Kish aged 56, died of pneumonia on 21 June 1901. He was buried at sea.[22] Gert Johannes Swanepoel also died en route from Durban to Bermuda, on 10 September 1901, aboard the *Montrose*, and he too was buried at sea. He left two rings, a watch and chain and a bag of clothing to his family. The jewelry was forwarded to his wife, HJ Swanepoel. The bag of clothing was left in the possession of WH van Rensburg, a family friend, who wrote to Swanepoel's family informing them that the deceased had lent £4 10s to different burghers, which he would collect on their behalf.[23]

As land dwellers, Boers did not like to be buried at sea. The deaths of two POWs, WJ Potgieter, aged 28, of Welgevonden in the Pretoria-district on board the *Manilla*, on 12 February 1902, and WT v d B. Leibrandt, aged 21, of appendicitis on board the *Columbian* on 14 February 1902, prompted some prisoners of war, Field-Cornet George Lyons, PJC Marcs, JC Pretorius, JH Munnik, JJ Wessels, M Roberts and BG Oosthysen who, like Leibrandt, originated from the Harrismith district, to ask that Leibrandt be buried ashore as the *Columbian* was in the outer anchorage close to land. Their reasoning was that Leibrandt's relatives resided in Harrismith and if he was buried in Durban 'it would be great consolation to them to be able to see his last resting place if hostilities ceased'. The signatories of the letter were even prepared to carry any extra cost attached to the funeral. The death of Leibrandt at 17:00 was considered as being too late to change the arrangements and he was buried at sea. The assurance was, however, given that such a request would be considered in the future. True to his word the staff officer prisoners of war (SOP), Lieutenant Colonel Allatt, did look into the matter which was, in his words, based on sentiments and prejudice against burial at sea. He enquired about coffins and available tug transport in an attempt to assess the feasibility of complying with the request

The state of three Boer graves in the West Street Cemetery in 1999. Top: HJ Odendaal; centre: LM Engelbrecht; bottom: CJ de Villiers (Wassermann collection).

and recommended that the wishes of the POWs be honoured. Allatt's view was supported by the commandant of Durban. With the support of the commandant, Allott could inform the military landing officer, Lieutenant HR Radford, of the procedure to be followed if a Boer POW died in either the Durban port or harbour. On receiving the notification of the death of a POW, Radford had to contact the undertaker, JH Wade of 51 Queen Street Durban, on the telephone number 187 X 287. Wade would then send a coffin out by the first available tug, which would return with the corpse. The undertaker would then finalise the necessary arrangements.[24]

That these plans were not immediately implemented is borne out by the burial at sea of two Boer POWs who died in the Durban harbour at about this time. Marthinus Hendrik Britz of Doornkop, Kroonstad, who died on 25 February 1902, and Hendrik Oosterwald Uys of Schoongezicht, Wakkerstroom, who died on 1 March 1902. Thirteen-year-old Willem Johannes Lyons of Flensburg, Harrismith, died of enteric fever on board the *Columbian* on 21 March 1902, and was also buried at sea.[25] This happened despite the military landing officer asking SOP Allott to organise a bearer party to bring the body of Lyons from the tug to the hearse waiting at the jetty.[26] Matters did not improve, and JWW Steyn, who died on board the *Mohawk* in the Durban harbour, was likewise buried at sea.[27] The reason for continuing with the practice of burying Boer POWs at sea was probably owing to the inefficient service provided by the undertaker, J.H. Wade, and the sluggish reaction by the military. Although a contract was concluded with S Dove of 23, 1st Avenue for the burial of troops and POWs dying in Durban for a period of one year commencing on 23 May 1902, it came into effect [28] a day too late for JWW Steyn. Moreover, as this new contract was signed a week before the war ended, it failed to be in time for the Boer POWs dying in Durban harbour who wished to be buried on land.

For the Boer POWs incarcerated in the Umbilo camp, the matter of death and burial was less complicated, for they were all automatically buried in the West Street Cemetery. What did, however, remain a major problem was to return the possessions of deceased POWs to their relatives. W Leibrandt, a resident in the Ladysmith concentration camp, whose son, WT vd B Leibrandt, had died on board the *Columbian*, received £1 8s 10d and a silver watch. Leibrandt senior, however, also wanted his son's trunk of clothing and waterproof overcoat forwarded to him. The military immediately forwarded the trunk of clothing but could not account for the overcoat.[29] The possessions of PS Brits of Rust-en-Vrede, Rouxville, and LF Engelbrecht of Grootdam, Rouxville, both of whom had died in July 1902 in the Umbilo camp, were still lying in Durban by mid-October 1902. Unsure of what to do, Captain AA McHardy asked the Red Cross for advice. The Red Cross suggested that McHardy contact the resident magistrate of Rouxville, H Barry, as he would be willing to receive the belongings of the deceased and to return them to the respective families. This concluded the matter and the belongings were forwarded to Barry on 15 November 1902.[30]

In at least one case the family wanted not only the possessions of the deceased POW returned, but also the bodies. Thirty-one-year-old MA Heyns of Schoongezicht, Bethlehem, died in the Umbilo Hospital on 1 September 1902, of dysentery which he had contracted in Ceylon (Sri Lanka).[31] On hearing of the death of her husband the widow of Heyns, through the office of the magistrate of Bethlehem, asked that all goods belonging to the deceased be forwarded to the magistrate and 'also to have his name marked on his grave in order that his widow may recognise the grave when she proceeds thither at some future date'.

To adhere to the first request was no problem and the belongings of MA Heyns arrived in Bethlehem on 20 November 1902. The second request set a malfunctioning bureaucratic machine in motion. Captain McHardy informed the magistrate of Durban that Heyns was buried in the 'town cemetery'. This confused Magistrate Broome as he was unsure of which cemetery McHardy was referring to McHardy then had to elaborate by explaining to the public works department that Heyns was buried in the cemetery closest to the Umbilo camp. At the same time he wanted to know if the grave could be identified and what he should do to have the name of Heyns placed on his grave. The matter was now referred to P Burns, the general cemetery caretaker, for comment. Burns explained that Heyns was buried in site 34 block 3 and that he could point out the grave to anyone who wished to visit it. To have the name of Heyns displayed on the grave by any means, the site needed to be secured for perpetuity by paying the sum of twenty shillings On receiving this information McHardy referred the matter back to the magistrate of Bethlehem and the widow of Heyns, adding that 'I have no funds for the purpose I am sorry to say'. Widow Heyns indicated that she also did not, at the time, have the money to secure the grave site. She, however, enquired if the grave could be reopened to identify the corpse for life insurance purposes and also to have her husband's remains removed for burial on her farm. These requests were referred by McHardy to the mayor of Durban who, in turn, forwarded it to the inspector of nuisances, WC Daugherty. Daugherty, before forwarding the matter to the medical officer of Durban for comment, explained that positive identification was possible without opening the grave. To have the body removed for re-interment would only cause 'serious trouble and nuisance'. The medical officer concurred, and the matter was again forwarded to the magistrate of Bethlehem. Three days before Christmas, he informed the widow Heyns that, for insurance purposes, her husband could be identified by other means, but, that Michiel Arnoldus Heyns could not be reinterred on the farm near Bethlehem.[32] In the end no tombstone was erected for Heyns in Durban.

INVENTORY of the Effects of _Bethleham Deceased_ No. __4__

_N. S._ Regiment of _____ on his admission into the

Hospital at _Umbilo_ Date of Admission _9 3 . 8 . 0 2_

Date of Discharge, Transfer or Death _____ _7 . 9 . 0 2_

BAGS {	Clothes			Gauntlets	prs.	
	Kit			Girdle, Lancers		
	Stable			Gloves, Leather	prs.	
	Waterproof & Hook			Handkerchief, Cotton	*	
Belt, Woollen				Ditto Silk	*	
Blacking, Tin				Hat, Cocked		
Boot Laces, pairs				Haversack		
Box, Schoolmaster's			HEAD-DRESS, complete {	Bearskin Cap		
Braces, pair				Busby		
Brassard				Cap, Lance		
Brasses, Button				Cap, Sealskin		
Books		*	σ 2	Chaco		
BOOTS, pairs {	Ankle	*		Helmet	‡	
	Knee			Feather, Bonnet		
	Wellington			Helmet Cover, Khakee		
Breeches, pairs			1	Hold-all		
BRUSHES {	Brass			Hose-tops, Highland, prs.		
	Clothes			Housewife		
	Hair	*		JACKET { Full		H
	Lace			Undress		
	Shaving	*		Jersey		
SHOE {	Hard			Kilt, Highland		
	Blacking			Knife, Fork and Spoon	*	
	Polishing			Knife, Clasp		
Cap, Forage, Strap & Badge				Lanyard		
Cap, Night		*		Leggings	prs.	
Cap, Fur				Mitts, pairs { Worsted		
Cap, Field				Fur-lined		
Case, Plume				Pantaloons prs. ‡		
Cloak and Cape				Plaid, Highland		
Coat, Frock				Powder, Polishing Tin		
Coat, Great, and Cape				Puggarees		
Comb, Hair		*		Purse & Belt, Highland Corps		
Comforter				Putties, pairs		
DRAWERS, pairs {	Calico			Razor and Case	*	
	Cotton	*		Rubber, Horse		
	Flannel	*		Sash	‡	
Fez				Scarf, Highland		
Frock		‡		SHIRTS { Flannel	*	σ
Frock, Khakee drill		‡		Cotton		
Gaiters, Duck		prs.		SHOES { Highland prs.		
" Highland		"		Canvas "		
Garters		sets		Soap pieces		

SOCKS, pairs { Cotton	prs.	*	
Worsted	"		
Sponge			
Spurs	prs.		
Stockings	"		
Tin of Grease			
Tin, Mess, and Straps			
Covers for ditto			
Tassel for Fez			
Towels			
Trowsers, Cloth or Tweed } prs.			3
Trowsers or Trews, Serge or Tartan } "			
Trowsers, Khakee drill	"		
Tunic			
Turban, Cloth			
Turnkey and Worm			
Valise and Straps			
Vests, Flannel			
Waistcoat			2
Watch			
Cash			
Medals			
Rifle or Carbine { Complete	†		
Incomplete	†		
Revolvers	†		
Swords or Claymores	†		
Bayonets, Sword	†		
" Common	†		
Scabbards, Bayonet, Sword or Dirk	†		
Belts, Pouch	†		
" Waist	†		
Bottles, Water	†		
Ammunition, rounds			
picture frames			3
vests			2

* When any of these articles are issued for the Man's use in Hospital, a reference should be here made to the No. of the Cheque in Army Book, No. 42, shewing such issue. † Only when in the Field on Active Service. ‡ Insert description.

No. of Pack in Store_____

Issued from Store on _____

Received by me _____

J. E. S. Levenson
Pack Storekeeper.
Sgt:
_R. A. M. C_

A list of the belongings of MA Heyns (NAR).

Deaths: Umbilo POW camp

Surname	Name	Age	Date	Place of death	Place of burial	Cause of death	Residence
Brits	PS	52	28.7.1902	Umbilo	West Street site 32 block 20		Rust in Vrede Rouxville Free State
Britz	Marthinus Frederick	25	25.2.1902	Durban Harbour	At sea		Doornkop Kroonstad Free State
Cox	EF			Durban			
de Villiers	Carel Johannes	20	11.6.1901	On board SS Ranee	West Street site 34 block 12	Peritonitis Pneumonia	Eerstegeluk Hebron Free State
Engelbrecht	Barend Johannes	20	17.5.1902	Umbilo	West Street site 23 block 20		England Vryburg Cape Colony
Engelbrecht	Lourens Frederick Marthinus	52	30.7.1902	Umbilo	West Street site 29 block 34	Chronic Diarrhoea	Grootdam Rouxville Free State
Erasmus	JR			Durban			
Klassen	Pieter Willem	47	24.3.1902	Durban Harbour	At sea		Eandsfontein Bethlehem Free State
Kruger	Gert Daniel	20		Durban Harbour?			Retvlei Krugersdorp Transvaal
Heyns	Michiel Arnoldus	41	1.9.1902	Umbilo	West Street site 34 block 34	Dysentery	Bethlehem Free State
Leibrandt	Willem Theodorus van der Berg	21	14.2.1902	On board SS Columbian	At sea	Appendics	Harrismith Free State
Luus	AJ	34	2.6.1902	Umbilo	West Street site 16 block 38		Lotsgronde Soutpansberg Transvaal
Louw	JH	22	14.12.1902	Umbilo	West Street site 24 block 16		Herbert Cape Colony
Lyons	Willem Johannes	13	21.3.1902	On board SS Columbian	At sea	Enteric Fever	Vensburg Harrismith Free State
Odendaal	HJ	49	4.5.1901	Durban	West Street site 33 block 12		Bethlehem Free State
Potgieter	Willem Jacobus	28	12.2.1902	On board SS Manilla	At sea		Welgevonden Pretoria
Steyn	Johannes Willem Wessels	56	22.5.1902	On board SS Mohawk possibly Durban Harbour	At sea		Reinfontein Winburg Free State
Uys	DC	68	13.12.1902	Umbilo	West Street?		Vrede Free State
Uys	Hendrik Oosterwald	54	1.3.1902	Durban Harbour	At sea		Schoongezicht Wakkerstroom Transvaal
Venter	LJ	18	13.5.1902	Umbilo	West Street site 24 block 20		Heilbron Free State
Viljoen	JJ	51	5.1.1903	Umbilo	West Street site 6 block 32		Fauresmith Free State

The end of the war and returning home via Durban did not mean that POWs had escaped death. Cornelius Johannes Gerhardus Vermaak, aged 50, of Sweethome, Vryheid, died on board the *Ionian* on 9 September 1902, on his way back to Durban from Bombay (Mumbai).[33] Although most others at least made it past Durban, the 18-year-old Frans Albertus Botha of Boschkop, Ladybrand, while on his way home died in the Pietermaritzburg Military Hospital on 3 January 1903.[34] The last Boer POW to die in Durban was the 15-year-old JJ Viljoen of Fauresmith in the Orange River Colony, who died on 5 January 1903, in Umbilo. Viljoen was buried in the West Street Cemetery on site 6 block 32.[35]

Today some tombstones erected by the relatives of the POWs buried in the West Street Cemetery still survive. The graves of those POWs not marked by a tombstone are lost forever, just as surely as are the final resting places of those buried at sea in or near the Durban harbour. This is a sad indictment on past governments who had memorials erected to the Boer POWs who died in camps in, for example, India and Sri Lanka, but neglected those closest to home. In paying the ultimate price in the Anglo-Boer War, some Durban volunteers and Boer POWs were subjected to an ironic geographical twist. While the Boers were buried in Durban or in the harbour area, the volunteers were generally buried in the interior. Enemies became united in death, but the Great Divider removed these warriors even more firmly from their homes and loved ones.

1. PAR, NT 1291: Hall to Molyneux, 28.9.1899.

2. Robinson and Co, *Natal Volunteer Record*, p.53.

3. PAR, NCP 4/2/1/9: report of the select committee (No. 9, 1900) on compensation to widows and dependents of volunteers, 5.6.1900.

4. Volunteer Compensation Laws had been enacted in 1872, 1885, 1888 and 1895. Act 23 of 1895 was in force at the time of the outbreak of war.

5. PAR, NT 52: letter prime minister to colonial secretary, 18.7.1900.

6. PAR, NT 52: letter prime minister to colonial secretary, 6.6.1900.

7. PAR, NT 52: adjutant, DLI to paymaster, volunteers, 31.1.1900.

8. PAR, NT 52: letter Egeland to Lieutenant Owen, 5.2.1900.

9. PAR, NT 52: letter GK Espeland to Lieutenant Owen , 12.2.1900.

10. PAR, NT 52: letter secretary of state to prime minister, 13.5.1900.

11. PAR, CSO 1643: letter chairman volunteer and war relief Committee to colonial secretary, 3.5.1900.

12. PAR, NT 52: letter prime minister to commandant of volunteers, 3.7.1900

13. PAR, NT 52: letter prime minister to colonial secretary, 25.11.1900.

14. PAR, NT 52: letter Will Gordon Sprigg to treasury Natal, 1.9.1900.

15. PAR, NT 52: Captain Molyneux to Mrs Sturgeon, 11.7.1900.

16. PAR, CSO 1676: letter Major Molyneux to minister of lands and works, 13.5.1901.

17. PAR, CSO 1643: telegram General R Buller to prime minister, 3.4.1900.

18. PAR, CSO 1670: letter General Wolfe-Murray to colonial secretary, 7.6.1900.

19. Field visit to West Street Cemetery, 10.9.1999; West Street Burial register for 1901.

20. NAR, SOP 1190: memorandum regarding the death of CJ de Villiers, 12.6.1901.

21. Field visit to West Street Cemetery, 10.9.1999.

22. NAR, SOP 16: letter captain *Ranee* to chief staff officer lines of communication, 8.7.1901.

23. NAR, SOP 30: documents regarding the death of HJ Swanepoel, 29.11.1901–21.3.1902.

24. NAR, SOP 29: correspondence regarding the burial of Boer POWs on land, 12.2.1902–22.2.1902.

25. WM, list of Boer POWs who died in Natal, no date.

26. NAR, SOP 29: correspondence regarding their burial of Boer POWs on land, 12.2.1902–22.2.1902.

27. WM, list of Boer POWs who died in Natal, no date.

28. NAR, SOP 32: memorandum regarding the change of undertaker, 23.5.1902.

29. NAR, SOP 29: documents regarding the possessions of WT van der B Leibrandt, 27.2.1902–3.3.1902.

30. NAR, SOP 35: documents regarding the possessions of PS Britz and LFM Engelbrecht, 18.10.1902– 6.11.1902.

31. NAR, PMO 65: telegram about the death of MA Heyns, 2.9.1902.

32. NAR, SOP 35: documents on the death of MA Heyns, 13.9.1902–22.12.1902.

33. PAR, GH 563: minute paper reporting on the death of CJG Vermaak, 25.9.1902; NAR, SOP 35: memorandum on the death of CJG Vermaak, 24.12.1902.

34. NAR, SOP 35: memorandum on the death of FA Botha, 6.3.1903.

35. Field visit to West Street Cemetery, 10.9.1999; WM, list of Boer POWs who died in Natal, no date.

PART THREE

DURBAN:
A LOGISTICAL GATEWAY

Ships and railway at the Point (Edwards).

The earliest theoretical efforts to improve access for ships into the estuarine Bay of Natal were those of Lieutenant Gibb RE in 1846. Three years later, Hardy Wells and Pilkington, engineers from the Cape, had drawn up extensive proposals for the construction of groynes and piers. In 1849 John Milne commenced work on the North Pier as an extension of the sandy Point. Though incomplete, his work began to achieve results, but he was abruptly fired by the governor in 1857. Between 1859 and 1864 the Natal government spent an enormous amount of its budgets on an abortive scheme for the building of another pier designed by Captains Abernethy and Vetch of the Admiralty. After the Vetch pier, several proposals were presented by John Coode (1871 and 1877) and Peter Paterson, the colonial engineer.

Then came a period of progress (1881-1894) under a newly constituted Harbour Board with Harry Escombe as chairman. Edward Innes, as resident engineer, continued work on the incomplete Milne pier and began a southern equivalent. After Innes' untimely death in 1887, Cathcart Methven continued the two piers with some modifications and in addition began the necessary quay constructions in the inner harbour. A major political row between Methven and Escombe about the merits of the comparative lengths of the piers led to Methven's dismissal in 1894 and eventually contributed to the fall of Escombe's government in 1897.

The assistant engineer, Charles Crofts, then took over the work. But this also entailed further investigations and reports from eminent harbour engineers, Hartley and Barry (1897 and 1902), which supported most of Milne's, Innes's and Methven's ideas and work. Fifty years after Milne had commenced work, the piers began to facilitate tidal scour, but not without the assistance of a massive fleet of some 15 dredgers. [1]

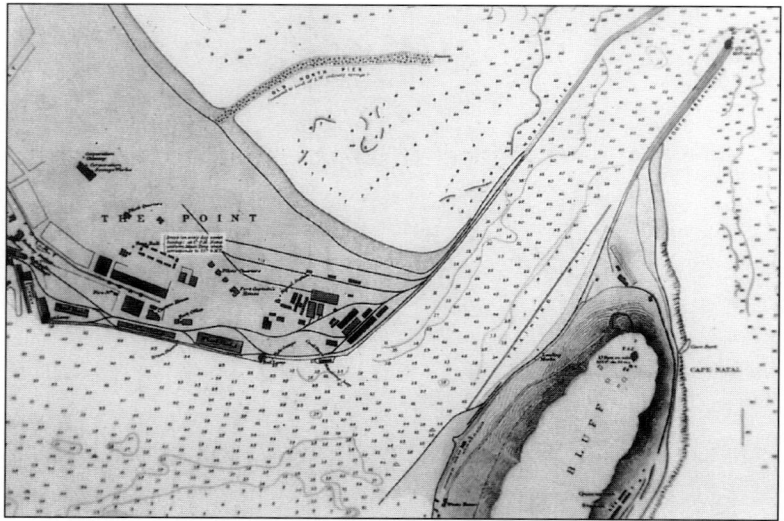

A synoptic chart showing the various engineering proposals for the harbour entrance between 1850 and 1889 (Hartley Barry report, 1897).

CHAPTER 9

THE PORT OF DURBAN
Brian Kearney

The port of Durban played a critical role as a gateway in the movement of men and goods from elsewhere in the world into the main theatres of the war. It also played a role in their return, and in the movement of thousands of Boer prisoners who were forced to leave their country for distant destinations. But only in the late 1890s had the development of the port and its facilities for the handling of ships, men and goods, reached a state which could be described as functional.

The development of the port

Over the 50 years prior to the Anglo-Boer War, an extraordinary saga of conflict between men and ships and waves and sand had unfolded; a saga of two piers and an ubiquitous sandbar which prevented easy entry of shipping into the safe haven of the Bay of Natal of unfinished engineering works; of long-ranging conflicts between politicians and engineers; of contests for control over harbour matters between a central colonial administration and an independent harbour board; and of rivalry between overseas experts and local know-how. This had been a controversial colonial affair which had drained the limited resources of the colony on more than one occasion and which had given the port of Durban a poor reputation in the shipping world. Durban was a port where the bulk of an increasing number of ships had not been able to reach the safe haven of the inner harbour and which were required to sit out in the outer anchorage, from where their passengers and goods had to be moved by smaller craft. One specific consequence of this was that during the period between 1840 and 1880 there had been no less than 60 shipwrecks off the town. [2]

By 1899, the north and south piers, which protected the entrance channel, reached lengths which afforded a safe shipping course for many vessels and, perhaps even more significant, the channel had been continuously dredged for over 15 years to provide a reasonable depth of water for shipping. However, the staccato pattern of construction work and the continuous changes of policy and directions in administering these engineering works led to a situation where the port was always behind time in some way. Thus finance and energy devoted to the very difficult work on the two piers deviated the necessary attentions and resources away from the facilities required inside a safe harbour in the form of quays and wharfs and all their related facilities. What was the point of facilitating the entry and departure of vessels across the sand-bar, if there was no way of servicing and handling their cargoes within the bay?

In 1900, Joseph Dunn, London correspondent for the *Central News*, described the changes which had taken place in the port since the Anglo-Zulu War of 1879 and the Anglo-Transvaal War of 1881 and, in particular, their economic consequences:

A factor of stupendous importance ... has been the advantage derived by the military from the great improvements effected at Durban harbour during the last decade. Had it not been for the highly satisfactory depths – unprecedented in the history of the Port of Natal – which have been secured by the execution of a great plan of harbour improvement ... it may be definitely asserted without possibility of contradiction that the conduct of the Natal section of the South African war would have been fraught with well-nigh insurmountable difficulties ...

... The average bar depth at Durban at the time of the Zulu war, 1879, was only 6ft 6in at low water. In June of that year it was 5ft 2in ... By the time of the Boer war of 1881 a slight improvement had taken place, the average bar depth for 1881 being 7ft 11in ... In connection with both of these campaigns the troops were landed with the greatest difficulty, and at an immense expenditure of time and money ... the soldiers had to be landed from the outer anchorage and brought over the bar battened down in lighters ... horses as well ... had to be landed in lighters ... Needless to say this operation entailed great inconvenience on the men and frequently resulted in damage to the horses ... the cost of landing men and horses at Durban was then enormous. It ranged from £2.10s to £7 per horse, and it is said as much as 10s per man was paid ...

Last year the average bar depth was 19ft 7in at low water, spring tices ... at the present time – 22 foot 6 inches (or 28 foot 6 inches at high water) ... From September 20th, the date when the first batch of the Indian Contingent arrived at Durban, to April 1, 1900, 10,778 horses were landed at the Point. These have cost 10s each to land. That means an expenditure of, say £5,400. At the time of the first Boer war this would have meant an expense of more nearly £ 70,000.[sic]

Dunn calculated that were all the 57 000 officers and men to have been landed by lighters during 1899 and 1900, this would have cost approximately £30 000. So there were considerable economic advantages in landing them directly at the quayside, '... as the transport vessels were able to come into the harbour and rope up at the wharves'.[3]

By 1899, the usefulness of the harbour had improved in a great

The Royal Scots regiment disembarking by basket at the outer anchorage during the Anglo-Zulu War, 1879 (Rosenthal).

The entrance channel and the north and south piers under construction, ca.1895. The sea breaking over the sandbar is clearly visible at the end of the piers (KCL).

Construction of quay walls and reclamation works at St Paul's wharf, ca. 1900 (LHM).

The end of the Bluff across the entrance channel (KCL).

The entrance channel and Point from the Bluff. The harbour workshops are clustered at the end of the Point. A large bucket dredger is working in the channel (KCL).

many ways, and yet, in many others, it had remained half-built and somewhat chaotic. The rudiments of a reasonable system were in place: some quays existed with others under construction; and there was some wharf space – about 300 m. This was not very much when compared, say, to the 156 m length of one ship, the *American* which arrived at the port on 18 November 1899. There were also a few closed sheds; a very unreliable hydraulic crane system and a limited railway network. But the biggest problem was that it all took place in a very small and congested space at the end of the Point, with a tenuous railway linkage to the hinterland which had to pass through the town of Durban.

Imagine arriving, as the British regiments did from India in September 1899: if one's ship was shallow enough in draft to cross the bar it could pass through the channel into the Bay of Natal, and one would then witness much going on which would have explained the complications of the distant and recent past of the developing port. Approaching the Bluff to the left, one would have observed a very large concrete block manufacturing plant on the seaward side, just beyond the quarantine station; here the blocks were being made for the enormous underwater construction of the southernmost pier or the Innes breakwater, named after its founder engineer. The breakwater itself would have been approximately 75% of its final length, having had the seal of approval of two eminent British harbour engineers, Hartley and Barry in 1897. This breakwater was intended to act as a bulwark against the seas from the south-east and stop the sand from drifting across the channel. At the end of the pier, timber staging jutted out of the water and along the top of the pier ran a railway for transporting blocks and stone. The railway also served the block yard, and brought stone and sand from quarries to the south of the town skirting the south-western shores of the bay.

The concrete block yard at the Point with goliath crane (KCL).

The Point and the wide reclaimed beaches towards Addington (KCL).

On one's right, behind the large dredgers sucking sand from the channel, one would have seen other civil engineering works, with another block yard, a goliath crane and the partially completed north pier; beyond the pier lay the wide flat beaches which had emerged as a reclamation caused by the construction of the piers. Projecting into the sea from this beach stretched the remains of Vetch's pier of the 1860s. Around the corner of the Point lay a group of harbour workshops and then a dense cluster of shipping, sometimes four abreast, hugging a short section of completely rebuilt quays, together with all the paraphernalia of the port which included a row of corrugated iron sheds, tall groups of hydraulic cranes served by a large hydraulic station and electricity-generating plant beyond. In amongst all this stood a customs house, a railway station, a crude passenger terminal, a small boat dock, and a slipway. Behind these appeared a streetscape of imposing Victorian facades, housing shipping and coaling companies and agencies, and in the background rose old sand dunes with salt-sprayed vegetation; above which loomed the time ball. A motley collection of compounds, housing and shacks extended into the distance. Beyond the dense cluster of shipping, and towards the town, one would have noticed further quays under construction, close to where the tall ships, which still came into port, were moored. The construction of these additional quays had been accelerated when it became obvious that the port was about to be strained to its limits.[4]

One example which will serve to illustrate the kind of bureaucratic inertia which impeded the physical development of the port was the provision of public toilets along the wharfs. In December 1896, the port captain had alerted the Port Advisory Board to the shortage of toilets at

Point Road, ca. 1902. The Vasco Da Gama clock stands at the entrance to Alexandra Square with the hydraulic and electricity power station beyond (KCL).

The Point from the Bluff showing workshops, quayside sheds, Point Road, old sand dunes and the time ball (LHM).

Hydraulic cranes at the Point quayside (LHM).

Constructing new quay walls using timber piles and staging with concrete block walls between (LHM).

the docks. In August 1897, the mayor of Durban, Benjamin Greenacre, reminded the government of the urgent need for 'public water closet latrine accommodation ... at different places at the harbour and along the wharfs ...'. However, a year later, in December 1898, the harbour engineer, Charles Crofts, and Prime Minister Albert Hime were still debating the costs and other aspects of the problem. Fortunately, for the relief of the British troops and others passing through, the amenities were provided by 1899.[5]

The port as a warrior's gateway

This was to be a warrior's gateway for the next three years. In between the comings and goings of hundreds of thousands of men and animals, and thousands of machines and guns, and mountains of goods, the harbour works would go on – day and night. And somehow, Natal's shipping trade, reduced though it was by war, was also expected to continue.

Despite these physical conditions, a fairly well-oiled administration existed, which had learnt to cope with many problems and constraints. In fact, the chaotic development of the port had provided the port administration with a preparation which would enable it to work well with the naval and military authorities, since it was used to dealing with almost any kind of extraordinary set of circumstances, including emergencies and crises. The administration of the port included the port captain, the shipping master and the harbour master, clerks and various supervisors, tug and boat crews, and engineers and pilots. Since the port was still considered a dangerous one, as it is today, a rigorous pilotage system had long been in existence to move ships in and out of the harbour. Other officials included the wharfmaster and his staff of wharfingers and tidewaiters; the customs officer and staff; signal men and, of course, the harbour engineer and his assistants. In addition there were many other assistants to help with berthing, loading and unloading and all the other requirements of a port.

Tasks requiring unskilled labour were carried out by a large contingent of workers: a great number of contract stevedores were drawn primarily from Mozambique and other East African countries; a fluctuating pool of *togt*, or periodic daily labourers, fulfilled the demands arising from the nature of the port; and numerous groups of specialised assistants, such as the *madrasees*, were employed in the port captain's department as boatmen.

The primary duty of the port during the war was to facilitate the efficient arrival, berthing, unloading and loading and the coaling and victualling of many military transports, cargo ships, cattleships and colliers. This involved the handling of men, guns, armaments, ammunition, horses, mules and donkeys, steam traction engines, food, clothing, forage, tents, building materials, firewood and hundreds of other commodities to supply the might of the British empire war machine.

It also required the handling of thousands of POWs and prison ships

with their guards and supplies. In addition it included the handling of sick and wounded soldiers and hospital ships. Above all the port officials had to work in close co-operation with the railways, since the port was essentially not a terminus, but a point of transfer from one mode of transport to another. With the onset of war, the administration would have to liase, firstly with the Army Service Corps, and then closely with the naval transport officer (NTO), also referred to as the divisional transport officer (DTO), and then later would fall under the jurisdiction of that officer.

The naval transport officers and the workings of the port

The smoothness of operation, especially in the first few weeks of the war with large numbers of ships, troops and animals arriving from India, was probably as a result of the fairly good relations that had come to exist between the port and railway authorities, and their newfound association with Captain van Koughnet, the NTO in Durban. Van Koughnet had commenced his duties on 6 November 1899. On that day he informed the governor of his appointment, having taken over from Sir Edward Chichester, who had taken up a post at Cape Town. On the transport officer's staff were a chief boatman, W Mahoney; a carpenter, WC Lacey and a chief engineer, WJ Richardson.

Captain GE Holland, a member of the Loyal Indian Marine, had come from Bombay, India, with the first of the Indian contingent, and succeeded Van Koughnet on the latter's retirement to England in October 1900. He clearly thought that Van Koughnet's retirement would also mean his own transfer so, before his anticipated departure, he expressed high praise for the port captain, Ballard, his deputy, Gordon, and the pilots of the port 'who have had a most trying time'.[7] Similar compliments were paid to David Hunter, the general manager of the NGR. Somehow, and it is not clear why, Holland stayed on as NTO until April 1901, which proved favourable for the co-operative work of the port, considering that the British military had become its chief customers. In February 1901, the director of Indian Marine requested that Holland move from Durban to Rangoon, Burma, where he was to be promoted to commander, and this development precipitated a shuffle of transport officers around the various ports of the country.[8] Once again Holland expressed his gratitude to the local officials, this time including Charles Crofts, the harbour engineer; Dr Fernandez, the port health officer; Black, the Point signalman; George Mayston, the collector of customs and Kennedy from the wharfmaster's office.[9]

Van Koughnet's and Holland's terms of office had not been without certain problems. Even as early as November 1899, commercial shipping companies were claiming refunds on port dues caused by delays arising from the preference given to arriving troopships and, by March 1900, the port captain was reporting severe strain on his staff resulting from the enormous increase in shipping. Sometimes this boiled over into friction, as occurred in March 1900, when Signalman Black complained of the abusive behaviour of a crew member, Newham, of HMS *Terrible*. An apology was duly received from the ship's master. By contrast Captain Morgan of HMS *Tartar* on his departure from Durban, went out of his way to mention the valuable assistance the same signalman had given the navy, saying that he could not 'speak too highly of his ability, zeal and great civility'.[10]

Unfortunately, Holland's place was taken by a very different kind of officer, Captain Herbert G King-Hall, who took over on 6 April 1901. Within three weeks conflicts had arisen over the coaling of the collier *Nyassa*. McConnachie, the goods' superintendent at the Point, informed Hunter, his manager, on 9 May 1901, that the naval authorities were now occupying all the berths alongside the wharves. A limited number of berths had previously been available to commercial shipping. The *Nyassa* found herself wedged between transports which were also coaling, thus reducing her coaling rate to a third of what it could have been. The *Nyassa's* former berth at St Paul's wharf had been occupied by transports, the *British Princess* and the *Victorian*. McConnachie noted that under Holland's control, the berth at St Paul's wharf had been reserved for intercolonial colliers and not for naval purposes and that, under the new NTO, the *Nyassa* had now been placed in the single berth available for general shipping. McConnachie went on to suggest that the NTO should have 'made himself conversant with the true state of affairs ...' and that there would have been no complaints if 'the Naval Authorities could only be induced to exercise their powers in a common sense and business like manner'.

In a memo to the minister of lands and works, the general manager of the NGR, Sir David Hunter, noted that the position was untenable as the situation had recently been changed (probably on King-Hall's appointment), and that the port captain had been made the subordinate of the NTO. Hunter went on to state: 'We have got on remarkably well with all Naval and Military Authorities, and I should be sorry to see anything like a cleavage; but there seems to be, from remarks made by the public to myself, a good deal of feeling upon the way in which the Naval Authorities are using the Port to the exclusion of General Colonial interests in the matter of trade etc.' Hime commented that the change in naval transport officers had not been conducive to the satisfactory working of the port.[11]

Another difficult situation arose in October 1901, when once again Captain King-Hall appeared to have made unreasonable demands on the port captain. On 9 October, King-Hall telegraphed the governor, requesting that 'my requirements must be complied with regarding government vessels being berthed in the harbour'. Evidently, King-Hall had 'instructed' Ballard to move a transport vessel, the *Wingfield*, into the berth occupied by a sailing ship at H shed. Ballard said that he could not accede to the demand as it would mean the complete stoppage of the work on two sailing ships. In any event the *Wingfield* was occupying a good working berth. Ballard told Prime Minister Hime that the imperial authorities had taken possession of the new H shed in addition to A and B sheds. They had also blocked the 'outlet' between H and I sheds. He

NOTICE.

ALL Boats when approaching after dark any of Her Majesty's Ships which are in Durban Harbour, with the object of coming alongside, are warned that they will be hailed, and they must be prepared to answer the hails in a satisfactory manner. After having answered the hail, the boat or boats must stop and keep at least 20 yards from the ship, and wait until permission is given for her to come alongside.

Should any boat after having been hailed three times fail to reply, she is liable to be fired upon.

All boats approaching any of Her Majesty's Ships after dark, but not intending to come alongside, should keep well clear of the vessels and not pass closer than 100 yards.

FRED. R. W. MORGAN,
Commander,
Senior Naval Officer Present.

H.M.S. "Tartar,"
At Durban, 20th October, 1899.   9515 lbcd

Shipping triple berthed at the steam shear legs, Point docks (KCL).

Goods stacked in the open at Alexandra Square, Point (KCL).

Shipping at the outer anchorage off Durban (LHM).

The point from the Bluff with a large number of ships, many triple berthed at the limited quay facilities (KCL).

Goods covered with tarpaulins as a result of a limited number of sheds (NSL).

stated that he was anxious to avoid any friction but '... Captain King-Hall is overstepping his authority in making arbitrary unreasonable demands ... if the Imperial traffic was all going forward I would look with a lenient eye to his anxiety to get his ships discharged but the fact is that the port is again getting blocked with Imperial stores'. King-Hall, in the meanwhile, had complained to the commandant of Durban, Colonel O'Neill, who requested Ballard to carry out King-Hall's instructions. Again the services of David Hunter were called on by the prime minister, who authorised him to 'use any amount of oil for troubled waters', and Hunter immediately went to see both parties to settle the dispute.[12]

In the light of this, it is interesting to ponder what may have been behind a query from King-Hall to the colonial secretary, regarding the status of the Admiralty reserve in Durban.[13] Did King-Hall wish to claim that the port fell within an Admiralty reserve which would thus provide the naval authorities and himself with absolute control? But in effect there was no such reserve! King-Hall also became embroiled in an argument with Captain Ballard about whether a cargo ship like the *Ashmore*, carrying coal, should be allowed port facilities—duty free like the regular transports. Ballard dismissed the claim, saying '... the steamer *Ashmore* brought a cargo of 3 783 tons of coal for the Imperial Service, and that voyage was of the nature of a Merchantman'.[14]

Problems in the port: congestion and delays

The significant increase in shipping and cargo in the port certainly resulted in serious congestion. In January 1900, the port captain complained of the state of the port with all the sheds and almost all of the wharf space having been commandeered by the military. Over and above normal shipping and troop transports, he also had to take care of four hospital ships.[15] Local trade and commercial shipping were the most affected. As early as October 1899, the military authorities had agreed to charter their own coaster, the SS *Putiala*, for moving men, animals and goods between the various South African ports, thereby shrewdly bypassing commercial shippers and adding another vessel to the transports and naval ships which would enjoy the privileges of war.[16]

By September 1900, the military had taken over 511 830 square feet, or 11¾ acres (47 550 sq. m) of the dock area. This included sheds A, B, E and F and many open spaces in and around the docks. Complaints were numerous throughout the war, relative to delays and expense incurred because ships required for the war were given absolute priority. In October 1899, the *Avondale Castle*, a regular mail liner, was kept outside the port for several days while five transports were allowed to berth.[17] In the same month, the *Annesley*, carrying 1 800 tons of general cargo, had arrived off Durban on the 6th and entered the port the next day, but was not given a berth until the 19th and it took until 3 November for the ship to be discharged, with it only leaving port nine days later.[18] To add to this, most wharfs were not available to commercial shipping, St Paul's wharf, for example, only being returned to civilian use in October 1901.

The congestion which resulted from the sudden dominance of military needs superimposed over ordinary shipping requirements became a subject of some enquiry at the end of the war. Colonel Morgan of the Army Service Corps blamed the lack of staff for the problem, notwithstanding 'large numbers of businessmen, clerks, shop assistants etc., refugees from the Orange River Colony and Transvaal, who came forward readily for employment with the Army Service Corps'.[20] There can also be no doubt that the massive reliance on rail transport and the lack of animal-drawn vehicles contributed greatly to blockages at the port as well as at places inland. Goods were arriving but not being despatched. The large number of British reinforcements which poured into Natal in the first few months of 1900 stretched systems to the limit and, by March 30, there was a large accumulation of goods at the Point docks.

Strangely, at the May 1900 sitting of the Natal parliament, there was no mention of any blockages, but rather a somewhat triumphant statement by Benjamin Greenacre which followed the governor's opening address and which included the comment: 'We are pleased to hear that the railway management has so successfully dealt with the heavy military traffic, and that the prompt and satisfactory discharge of Her Majesty's transports has been facilitated by the improved depth of water on the Bar, and by the efficient services of the Port authorities.'[21]

Rear-Admiral Sir Edward Chichester, who had earlier served in Durban, was appointed as principal transport officer for the British in South Africa for the first 13 months of the war. Giving evidence to the Royal Commission of Enquiry in 1903, he described the situation of the port of Durban from a logistical viewpoint:

> ... I commenced at Durban, where I was first, which is a capital port, the best of the lot. The ships came in there, and we even got as big a ship as the "*Majestic*" in at one time. They went in alongside the wharf, and we got men and horses wharved practically out of the ship alongside. The native labourers there are wonderfully good men – the Zulus: they would tear their fingers off for the English, and there was hardly ever a ship kept outside. Occasionally we had to keep a ship outside if there had been a gale of wind (there is a bar there which silts up sometimes) until they got the suckers ... (At Cape Town) we had the greatest delay there because ships coming out from England which were wanted for Durban and Port Elizabeth, had to coal at Cape Town ...[22]

Apparently, the military authorities had a great deal of organisational trouble in Cape Town because of the local harbour board, though Milner often overruled them to give Chichester his own way. Chichester also considered that certain members of the board may have been deliberately obstructive to the British cause: 'There were a lot of rebels, I know, wearing crowns in their caps down there.' Fortunately for the military in Natal, the Natal Harbour Board had been dissolved by Harry Escombe in 1894 and there seems to have been little or no interference from the Port

A pyramid of fodder at the Point (KCL).

Captain Chichester and staff at Simonstown (*War Pictures*).

Advisory Board which took its place. In reality, the board consisted of meetings of the port captain, Ballard, and David Hunter. The net effect of all this was that in Durban the military was always given preferential treatment, and this had commenced with the initial commandeering of most of the entire quay length and the taking over of all the port sheds. At least in Cape Town, the local agents and shipping companies had a board which attempted to protect their interests.

Surprisingly, Chichester also thought that despite the accumulations of stores at the port, there were fewer problems in Durban with respect to the blockages of supplies than anywhere else. This can probably be ascribed to the efficiency of the local harbour administration in Durban rather than to any superior facilities. It may be true that the kind of 'patriotic' co-operative arrangements between the commercial world and the military, which had been made in the early months of the war, had also contributed. These collaborations included the Union Steamship Company providing the use of their private tugs to assist with the berthing of troopships,[23] and the African Boating Company providing gangways.[24] Problems, however, did occur: the *Pandua* succeeded in pulling a large three ton hydraulic crane off the wharf into the water on 9 October 1899; and conflicts between ships requiring coaling and ships offloading generated high levels of irritation.

The application of quarantine

Given the international role of the port of Durban and especially the number of ships which arrived there from the ports of India and the east coast of Africa, a rigorous system of pratique and quarantine had been put in place to prevent the transmission of diseases such as smallpox, yellow fever, cholera and the plague. This required the chief medical officer of the port to board each arriving vessel for a thorough inspection before it would be permitted to enter. On any hint or suspicion of illness on board, the crew and passengers would immediately be placed in quarantine, either on the ship or at the quarantine station. It seems that from the beginning of the war, the strictness of the application of the quarantine regulations was overruled by the governor in abeyance to the urgency of the time. Thus soldiers arriving, and their animals, were all given pratique, though the crews on board their ships had to fulfil the quarantine stipulations.[25] However, it appears that some ships, upon arriving, tried to avail themselves of the concession. The *Lusitano*, a Portuguese liner, arrived from Lourenço Marques on 30 October 1899 without a pilot and without any pratique being granted. Ballard promptly turned the ship around and sent her back to Delagoa Bay.[26] When the *Braemer Castle* was taking on refugees at Lourenço Marques in November 1899, several 'natives and Indians' suffering from smallpox were turned back. In February 1900 a transport ship, the *Urlana* from India, was delayed for a week at the outer anchorage when smallpox was discovered on board.[27]

Coaling in the port

Another important function which the port fulfilled was that of supplying coal to visiting steamers and this also created difficulties during the war. The process of coaling had always been a problem in the port, especially since a vessel would have to shift from her discharging berth to another place where the coal was stored. An ingenious alternative was to use an old ship's hulk moored out in the bay as a coaling place. At the time of the Anglo-Boer War there was no mechanical facility, so most of the coal supplied was carried on board ships by African workers known as 'coalies', a derogatory term for the lowest rung of worker on the *togt* labour ladder.

The supply of Natal coal to Durban had, of course, been seriously interrupted by the war in Northern Natal, and this compounded the problems in October and November 1899. Ironically, the Natal government which had generously offered 12 000 tons of Natal coal to the British government before war commenced, now, on 18 October, telegraphed an urgent request for 10 000 tons of coal from Britain, as the daily output from the Natal mines had dropped to about 500 tons. They also requested coal from the naval stores in Cape Town and Delagoa Bay, adding that, in addition to the demands from shipping and the railways, the electricity-generating plants which lit Pietermaritzburg and Durban, as well as the Durban sewerage works, all needed coal.[28] Thus for the time being, Natal could not be relied upon to provide much coal for shipping and this, in turn, thrust an additional burden on Cape Town and meant that every ship coming to Natal had also to call in there for coal. Such a situation went on until June 1900, when the war shifted out of Northern Natal and into the Transvaal. In March of the same year, the Durban town council noted that there was also a serious shortage of coal in the town for domestic purposes.

By 1901, however, the production of coal from most of the Natal mines had once again reached a stage where coal was being exported from the port, but not without logistical problems. On the resumption of trade, strong representations had been made to Captain King-Hall to dedicate a berth at St Paul's wharf for the use of exporting colliers. In November 1901, he noted that the colliers were not loading continuously, and he explained how the collier 'comes alongside, and at present, remains there for days obtaining no coal and preventing other vessels using the berth, which is one of the best in the harbour'.[29] The port captain considered that the problem lay with the very high demand for bunkering

Stevedores lifting goods with block and tackle (NSL).

Workers coaling a steamer by basket at St Paul's wharf (KCL).

A small steamer taking on coal. Bamboo Square and the chimney of the municipal power station are visible in the distance (LHM).

coal which was taking precedence, but King-Hall thought that the higher price of bunkering coal, with the associated profits, was the actual cause. The following month, December 1901, King-Hall made a suggestion to overcome the situation through the erection of a small coaling jetty near the south end of the main wharf. Ballard strongly supported the proposal as this would also assist with the coaling of lighters and the hulk, *Dundee*. The harbour engineer, Charles Crofts, investigated the suggestion but dismissed it in terms of its high cost, and thought it to be a waste of money, since it was 'shortly to be proposed to construct [a] quay wall along this site'. He would also have had in mind a longer-term proposal for shifting the entire coaling operations of the port across the bay to the Bluff channel.[30]

The effects of the war on the port

In spite of all these factors, and the various new dimensions and difficulties which had been added to the port functions, the port captain could report that an extraordinary amount of work had been carried out by the port during the war years: 1899 showed a 33% increase over 1898 in tonnage of ships handled, with a total of 1,7 million tons. An indication of the stage of development of the harbour is reflected in that, at that time, one third of all shipping still had to be lightered to and from the outer anchorage. Surprisingly, the 'men-of-war' only represented an insignificant fraction of 3%. The total tonnage in 1899 increased by only 10% over 1898. However by 1900, the total tonnage of shipping arriving at the port had increased by 77%, and by 1902, increased by 82% over 1899 to 2,4 million tons.[31] The collector of customs, G Mayston, in his 1901 report, said that the increase in the value of the import trade in 1901 'was simply astounding', being 61.6% over that of 1900. Setting aside the needs of the government and the military, the increase in civilian trade was 60.2%.[32]

Reconstructing old timber wharfs at the 'shear legs' (KCL).

Ships Arrivals at Port Natal 1898 to 1902					
	1898	1899	1900	1901	1901
Number of ships	792	925	1 134	1 118	1 115
Total tonnage of vessels	1 321 852	1 763 370	2 339 991	2 360 172	2 443 030
Number at the outer anchorage	176	201	248	268	222

What had also changed quite significantly during the war years was the arrival at the port of a large number of non-British vessels and vessels of foreign and colonial origins. Whereas in 1899, ships from the UK had numbered 80 in comparison to a total of 84 foreign and colonial vessels, by 1902 the latter totalled 420 in comparison to 148 British craft.

A good deal of this increase had been as a result of trade with Australia. In his 1900 report the collector of customs noted: 'New South Wales has sent us £13 000 worth more, South Australia has sent £31 000 worth more, West Australia £11 000 worth more, and what is especially noticeable, Victoria has sent £76 000 worth more ...'

Thus the maritime 'machine' which fed the war effort was both an imperial and an international one, purchased with pounds sterling. There had also been a significant increase in coastal vessels – from 26 in 1899, to 385 in 1902. Many of these traded with Delagoa Bay. But since nearly all of these increases were ascribed to the war and to military purposes, their effect on the port would be temporary and of no real sustainable value to the town.

1.   PAR, NHD: Natal Harbour Board and harbour department records from 1879 to 1902.

2.   PAR, NHD 1/1/6: Natal Harbour Board, abstract of wrecks and casualties, 1886.

3.   *Natal Witness*, 10.9.1900.

4.   PAR, NHD III/3/2: harbour engineer's report, 28.9.1899.

5.   PAR, NHD II/1/8: documents relating to latrines at the Point, 16.12.1896 to 8.2.1899.

6.   PAR, GH 587: Van Koughnet to governor, 6.11.1899.

7.   PAR, CSO 1661: report on the port captain's department at Durban, 16.10.1900.

8.   PRO, MT 23/126: director of transports to first naval officer, 5.2.1901.

9.   PRO, CO 179/218: Commander Holland to governor, 6.4.1901.

10. PRO, CO 179/213: Commander Morgan to Rear-Admiral Harris, 18.7.1900.

11. PAR, MJPW 117: documents relating to port difficulties, 9 and 10.5.1901.

12. PAR, GH 588: governor to prime minister, 9.10.1901.

13. PAR, CSO 1676: Captain King-Hall to colonial secretary, 16.5.1901.

14. PAR, CSO 1678: port captain to colonial secretary, 22.6.1901.

15. PAR, NHD III/3/2: report of port captain, 24.1.1900.

16. PRO, CO 179/207: Hely-Hutchinson to Chamberlain, 28.10.1899.

17. PAR, NHD III/3/2: port captain correspondence, 9.10.1899.

18. PAR, NHD III/3/2: port captain correspondence, 18.11.1899.

19. KCL, newspaper cutting book: 1929–1945.

20. *Royal Commission on the War in South Africa*, p.110.

21. PAR, NPP 61: reply to governor's speech, 7.5.1900.

22. *Royal Commission on the War in South Africa*, p.419.

23. PAR, NHD III/3/2: port captain correspondence, 19.9.1899.

24. PAR, NHD III/3/2: port captain correspondence, 28.9.1899.

25. PAR, NHD III/3/3: port captain correspondence, 26.1.1900.

26. PAR, NHD III/3/2: port captain correspondence, 30.10.1899.

27. PAR, GH 588: NTO to governor, 11.2.1900.

28. PRO, CO 179/206: governor to admiral, 16.10.1899.

29. PAR, CSO 1691: NTO to colonial secretary, 23.11.1901.

30. PAR, NHD II/1/137: report, harbour engineer, 9.12.1901.

31. PAR, Blue Books for Natal, departmental reports, 1898–1902.

32. PAR, NHD II/5/17: report of the collector of customs, 31.12.1900, p.6.

33. PRO, WO 32/8119: telegrams concerning diversion of mail steamers from Cape Town, 16.9.1901, and 17.9.1901.

34. PRO, WO 32/8124: minute, extension of martial law to the Cape ports, 7.9.1901.

A type K&S 4-6-0 locomotive of the NGR near Boshoff's Station, outside Pietermaritzburg (KCL).

The first railway station at the Point with the engine and coaches of the Natal Railway Company (LHM).

CHAPTER 10

RAIL AND STEAM
Brian Kearney

The Natal main railway line

The nineteenth century was an age of steam and rail and, by 1899, railways were a worldwide phenomenon. It was not surprising, then, that the Natal railway system should have played such a pivotal role in the Anglo-Boer War. However, it is of interest to note that neither the British military nor the Boers had any real experience of a railway war. An American critic, A Stickney, compared the use of the railways in the American Civil War with their use in South Africa: 'The distances ... are such as to make the supply of any considerable armed force under existing circumstances impossible except by line of railway. The nature and difficulties of the problem of supply, for large bodies of men, is a matter which has apparently had no careful study at the hands of the English army officers.'[1]

The Natal railway main line system was approximately 300 miles (480 km) long, running between the Point and Charlestown on the Transvaal border, with branch lines up the coast to the Tugela River, and south as far as Umzinto, while northwards a line ran from Pietermaritzburg to Greytown. The chief characteristic of the main line was the steepness of the gradients and the sharpness of the curves. A train running from Durban to Ladysmith had to ascend a total of some 4 200 metres in stages, each of which was greater than 700 metres. No sooner was the height of a particular stage reached when it was almost all lost on a downward run before the next ascent began. Singleton described the effects of these stages: 'The matter of train loads is consequently a most difficult problem, and under ordinary conditions it is necessary, for practical and economical reasons, to alter the goods train load no fewer than thirteen times between the port and the border station ...'[2]

This was the line which carried the British military machine and all its paraphernalia into action and which brought back the wounded and ill, the prisoners of war, and the Boer women and children to the concentration camps. The first tenuous rail line had been commenced in June 1860 from the Point to Durban and this represented the first railway line in southern Africa, and the second on the continent. Initiated by a private company, it ran along the edge of the Bay of Natal and joined the fledgling town of Durban to the dockside village at the Point. By 1867, another arm stretched out northwards towards the Umgeni River and to the quarry, which supplied stone for the building of Vetch's doomed pier. After several years of typical Natal prevarication, the line was finally extended inland to the capital city, Pietermaritzburg, in 1880, and six years later, after spasmodic efforts, reached Ladysmith. From here, two lines wound through the difficult Drakensberg escarpment. By 1891 one was running to Charlestown on the Transvaal border, and by 1892, the other extended to Van Reenen on the border of the Orange Free State. In the late 1870s, work had also begun on the north coast line. In 1879, David Hunter took over as general manager of the newly formed Natal Government Railways.[3] By 1899, Natal could boast a total of 500 miles (800 km) of single-line rail of a 3ft 6in (1.06 m) gauge, though a short section of the railway from Durban Station to South Coast Junction (Rossburgh) had been doubled by March 1900.

At the time of the outbreak of war, the town of Durban had a T-shaped layout of railways circumscribing its suburbs and meeting in the centre of the town which also formed the junction for the Point line. A train from the docks would thus have to traverse the four kilometres into the central railway station, and then, either move northwards along the branch line to the Umgeni, or take the main line southwards towards the Umbilo River, from where it then swung west and inland towards Pinetown. Thus all the war traffic from the sea to the fronts had to pass through the centre of the town.

The Esplanade line was only opened as an alternative route to the south in 1932. This bypassed the town centre and effectively cut it off from the bay.

Railway administration

Durban was also the headquarters of the NGR, the chief administration being located in the main railway station building. Major GMcD Elliott R.E., left Cape Town on 9 November 1899 to act as assistant director of railways (in South Africa), with instructions to take over the NGR. He was also to report on making the same arrangements as had been made in the Cape, where the military had taken over command of the Cape Government Railways.

On 23 November, Lieutenant Colonel EPC Girouard, the director of railways, left Cape Town with General Buller and, on arriving in Durban, proceeded to Hunter's offices where he found that the general manager did not see any difficulty in dealing with military traffic himself and thus did not concur with the decision which the military had made. Girouard attempted to enforce his authority, but General Buller decided to accept Hunter's opinion and his wish to remain in control.

They thereupon drew up a working agreement, which included the appointment of Elliott as assistant director of railways in Natal. It would be his task to pass all accounts and convey all military requirements to the NGR. In addition, it was 'expressly laid down that the control of arrangements of the railway should remain in the hands of the civilian administration, and it would be no part of the railway staff officer's duty to interfere with the working of the railway or its civilian staff'.[4] Thus it came about that the Natal system of administration differed from that in the Cape and elsewhere in the country. As Girouard himself observed,

Sir David Hunter, general manager of the NGR from 1879 to 1906 (CAR).

Sir David Hunter

David Hunter can be said to have been the father figure of the Natal Government Railways and supervised its main period of growth in the last quarter of the nineteenth century. He had been born in 1841 at Broxburn, Lingowshire, in Scotland, and gained his early railway experience as a young boy with the Northern British Railways Company in Edinburgh where he served from 1853. He worked his way up through the stores, the accounting section, the traffic department and then became assistant to the general manager. He was a member of a large number of statutory boards and government committees. As a result of his contributions to the British war efforts, he was mentioned in despatches by Generals White and Buller and Lords Roberts and Kitchener. He retired from the NGR in 1906.

The Central Railway Station was designed by W Street Wilson and built in 1895. Two additional storeys were added in 1898 (LHM).

Lieutenant Colonel EPC Girouard, the military director of railways in South Africa (Amery).

Guns on NGR rail trucks at the Point (Pinetown Museum).

this worked out well since the railway 'fed General Buller's army with the greatest ease, and when the Transvaal was annexed it became one of the main sources of supply to the whole army'.[5] Writing in 1903, Girouard obviously decided to ignore the problems which arose towards the end of the war.

The Cape and Natal compared

An important component of the 1899 agreement between the military authorities and the NGR was an agreed schedule of costs, based on an earlier arrangement between the NGR and the war office of 1889. Buller recorded in October 1900 that: 'On my arrival in Natal in November 1899, I found that a Military agreement was in existence with the N.G.R. for the conveyance of troops and stores. Its conditions seemed high when compared to those of the Cape, but as it was in existence I reported the conditions to the War Office and they were, apparently, accepted.'[6] By October 1900, the military authorities were obviously beginning to back-track on this agreement and Hunter was forced to defend the NGR position and make comparisons with the Cape railways, which the military claimed were less expensive to operate. Hunter indicated how difficult it was to make such a comparison, since the Cape rates were based on the system of the 'short truck', while Natal used, according to universal practice, the actual weight to determine fees. Thus the charges per ton in the Cape depended on whether the wagons contained a larger or smaller tonnage. He also pointed out that wagons were not always filled to their capacity. Clearly there was a great deal of difference between the Cape and Natal lines, the latter being, in Hunter's words 'handicapped by physical conditions out of all proportion to the Railways of the Cape ...'. He continued: 'the facts are pretty well known by the Railway Officers of South Africa; but only my colleagues and myself who have been trying to solve the problem of the economical working of these lines for 20 years know how much is involved in them.' Hunter also indicated that the 1899 contract had been based on peacetime rates and fares, and had not been raised to meet the greatly increased expenses involved during the period of war, particularly additional costs which had been caused by the shortage of local coal.

Furthermore, Hunter took an offensive position in his argument raising, among other issues, the low landing expenses at the harbour in Durban, which were, in many ways, a result of the expenditure of large sums of 'colonial 'funds and the effort of many years of work. At Port Natal the military authorities also occupied 11 acres of 'what is undoubtedly the most valuable space in South Africa, absolutely without charge'[7] (and they had the use of all the harbour sheds). Hunter also pointed out that in Natal it was not necessary to apply a costing which would justify the return of empty trucks, as was the case in the Cape, but 'every wagon returning empty is loaded with coal and the probability is that during the time this traffic lasts, we shall have to run up empties to work down coal traffic'. His final thrust was to remind them that all military stores at the port were loaded without charge, and those from Durban itself were carted and loaded by the railway department at their own expense.

However, the minister of lands and works was dragged into the argument and, by November 1900, the NGR was forced into a compromise agreement with the military, to be effective from 1 January 1901, providing for a 25% reduction for the conveyance of officers and men, and a 50% reduction in the cost of goods transported. With respect to the transport of animals, Hunter must have convinced the military of his case by comparing the cost of conveying 18 horses from East London to Standerton over 745 miles, which cost £23.9.2, while moving animals from Durban to the same destination only cost £15.2.7. The authorities thus retained the prevailing cost of conveying animals.[8]

Troop trains

The wisdom of retaining an experienced staff and administration was, in fact, based on efficiency, proof of which had emerged even before the commencement of hostilities, when the first British troops were landed from the SS *Gaul* on 20 September 1899. Further evidence of railway competence again became apparent when volunteer regiments were hastily despatched from Durban after 29 September, and in October when large numbers of soldiers, animals and munitions began to arrive in Natal from India, and needed to reach the hinterland as speedily as possible.

From the time of the first five of these ships being berthed at the docks, the troops were all landed in Ladysmith – 300 km away – in less than 24 hours. At least something worked well in Natal. According to Singleton, the arrangements with the military had 'been cordially adhered to throughout the war, with admirable results, and a large and frequently emergent traffic ha[d] been conducted throughout the campaign'.[9]

The early efficiency of the NGR did not go unnoticed by the governor, who wrote to Chamberlain on 7 October that:

> ... four transports were berthed at the wharf on that day (5 October) – the first at 11.30 a.m. and the last at 4.55 p.m. They brought 70 officers, 1 793 Non-Commissioned Officers and men, 80 followers, 188 horses, 108 mules, 6 guns, 16 carriages, 1 Maxim, 118 tons of baggage, 700 boxes of ammunition and 1 520 tons of stores. The whole of the above was despatched in ten trains. The first train started at 5.15 p.m., the last at midnight. Three trains went 72 miles to Maritzburg – the other seven 191 miles to Ladysmith. The last train reached Ladysmith at 5.45 p.m. on 6th October ... on average, the troops for Maritzburg arrived there within less than twelve hours, and those for Ladysmith within less than 24 hours, from the time the respective transports were berthed at the wharf. The ordinary traffic of the railway was carried on as usual. This creditable

Troops despatched from Durban between 20 September 1899 and 1 April 1900				
Troops	**Officers**	**Men**	**Horses**	**Guns**
Indian Contingent	340	7 791	2 792	29
Imperial troops	1 480	42 266	5 446	73
Volunteers	43	1 320	760	6
Irregular troops	134	3 164	1 780	–
Total	1 997	54 721	10 778	108

An NGR goods train at the Point with a Dübs 'A' locomotive (LHM).

The interior of the main platform shed at the Central Durban Railway Station (KCL).

When the troops passed through the railway stations situated between Durban and Pietermaritzburg, they were often greeted by groups of well-wishing local residents who provided them with tea and other comforts. At Gillitts Station, the trains stopped to replenish water supplies and stayed for a few minutes, and 'Whenever a troop train was coming in, the station-master at Gillitts would send a message to the women of Hillcrest and we would all traipse down and make big fires on Gilletts Station, on which we would boil water and make paraffin tins full of tea for the soldiers who went through.'[11]

Hopefully, the troops who filled their water bottles from the four-gallon paraffin tins of tea were not later to suffer from stomach-related illnesses. However, it was recorded that at least 'the men dressed in khaki for the first time' and those who were usually crowded in open trucks and herded like animals, left Gillitts as 'cheery folk, full of enthusiasm, laughter and fun ...'[12]

At Pinetown Station a British 'Tommy' actually suffered a wound before he even met the enemy! A 'kind' Pinetown lady who wished to show her appreciation for the brave soldiers who were passing through directed a pineapple through an open window of a compartment as the train pulled out, and 'inflicted a grimy slash on Tom's cheek, which turned septic in the absence of medical treatment and left a permanent scar'.[13] Tom Pickup later went on to serve in wars at Gallipoli and then New Guinea, with his scar as evidence of a 'Pinetown' wound.[14]

The Point Railway Station which was also designed by W Street Wilson (NSL).

Local Gillitts residents greeting British soldiers passing through on open rail trucks (*The Highway Mail*).

Passengers wait to board a third-class coach at the Point Railway Station (KCL).

Escombe Railway Station (Pinetown Museum).

Northdene Railway Station (Pinetown Museum).

Sarnia (Pinetown Bridge) Railway Station (KCL).

Pinetown Railway Station (PAR).

Kloof Railway Station (Pinetown Museum).

Botha's Hill Railway Station (KCL).

performance illustrates the capacity for organisation of Mr David Hunter, C.M.G...[10]

There were so many similar accounts of railway successes at the time that it can only be concluded that the performance of the NGR during the earliest phase of the war was one which must have evoked a great deal of pride in civil servants who would have certainly been rather disillusioned at the early and disastrous reverses suffered by the British forces in Natal. At least this was one local endeavour which had proved to be extremely successful.

Sir David Hunter, reporting on the work of the NGR in 1900, said:

The Military traffic has had to be worked according to the necessities of the case, involving special trains at all times of the day, as well as on Sundays (the train men employed in working the latter receiving extra pay), also the movement from point to point of empty vehicles to fit in with the disposition of troops. The Military traffic has therefore, in the nature of the case, been more costly to work than a similar tonnage of ordinary traffic, and the remuneration has been considerable below the rates derivable from ordinary traffic. The Department has also had to face the expenditure of additional trains in working forward, from the Port to the various coaling stations, the necessary supplies to meet the wants of locomotives, a service which was economically performed in the past by down trains to a large extent using returned empty vehicles. The condition of things since the war began, however, has meant that the bulk of the traffic has been proceeding from the Coast inland, and the Department has had to arrange for the return of empty vehicles with only a very small percentage of them earning any Revenue. Under normal conditions, it need hardly be stated that the Department was generally able to provide a paying load for all wagons returning to the Coast.[15]

In addition to the contributions which the NGR made in the early phases of the war in terms of the enormous number of rail movements for British soldiers and local volunteers, Singleton, in *Battlefields Revisited*, noted that water supplies were also provided to troops along the line by erecting '... on the side of the line adjacent to the camps, cylindrical tanks of galvanized iron, which were filled from clusters of tanks fitted on railway wagons and brought by train from the railway pumping stations ...'.[16] Medical stores and provisions were distributed along the line with two purpose-fitted vans from the Durban base. In addition, the NGR staff provided electricity from accumulators fitted on trucks to at least four hospitals; they adapted special carriages for the 6-inch. guns; prepared six armoured trains; mounted searchlights on trucks and, finally, became involved in the massive programme of reconstruction of the railway lines, culverts and bridges which had been destroyed before the Boer retreat from Northern Natal.

In some ways, it is surprising that the Boer forces did not take greater and earlier advantage of the very tenuous nature of the Natal railway system – perhaps this resulted from their own inexperience of a 'railway war'. However, early in the war, a contingent of the Natal Police was sent to Inchanga to protect the tunnel there and the Botha's Hill cutting from possible Boer attack.[17] Hunter had also made arrangements for the protection and guarding of the lines and bridges on the main line, particularly in the hilly country between Hillcrest and Inchanga, and along the north coast line between Verulam and the Tugela. Subsequently Hunter was requested by the general officer commanding, lines of communication, to arrange for this defence system to be applied to the whole of the north coast line, commencing at Durban and running to the Tugela, and so guard duty was 'being done continuously by European Guards in addition to the patrolling of the Line during the night by Indians'.[18] This probably came about as a result of the fear of a Boer attack on Durban via Zululand. Bridge guards and Indian night patrols were withdrawn from the north coast line in March 1900.

Indian railway worker on the line near Drummond (PAR).

A bullet in a turban

The Indian railway workers were given the task of periodically checking the rail line between Hillcrest and Inchanga to prevent sabotage by the Boers. One night near Drummond while they were engaged in this work, a party of British soldiers who were guarding the line opened fire on them. Fortunately there were no casualties, though afterwards one of the workers, Jaggernath, removed a bullet from his turban.[19]

The railway workshops

Besides the NGR administration, Durban was also the technical centre of the system housing an extensive depot for wagons and carriages, and well-equipped workshops for carriage and locomotive repairs and manufacture. Durban was where the hospital trains were fitted out; trucks transformed to carry guns, armourments and searchlights. Rolling stock damaged in action in Northern Natal was sent to the locomotive workshops in the town for repair. An interesting and somewhat apologetic report was prepared by Instructor D. Horsley, on 15 November 1899, for his superintendent, Reid, on locomotive No. 53 damaged in the Chievely armoured train incident:

> Sorry to have to report the damage to Armour Clad Engine No 53 and damage to the tender also trucks that were attached to, near Frere. The armoured train left here this morning (Estcourt) with 2 wagons in front and 3 behind. After running to Chievly it was ordered to return to Estcourt, & when rounding the curve at the foot of the Irvine's Bank, the front wagons were derailed & the Boers fired shell at the Engine doing a great deal of damage to smoke box, side of fire box and framing in several places, other parts of the Engine suffering from its shelling effect, which will be seen when examined in Durban. It was so badly damaged, I could do nothing than send it to Durban. As things are so serious up here it will be advisable to have another in its place if one should be available. I went out with the Ambulance train to see what damage was done to the trucks and line but we were not allowed to go near to pick up the wounded so I could not tell to what extent the damage was. I sent off Fireman Stewart to work the Engine on to PMBurg, Driver C. Wagner being injured was sent to the hospital here. I have been informed that Driver Wagner and Fireman Stewart worked well under heavy fire to get Engine liberated, so as to save Engine as much as possible, their conduct being highly commended. I have everything ready to make a move on very short notice. I have had one wagon of coal brought from Highlands, leaving at Highlands something like 32 tons, 8 tons brought to Estcourt. [sic][21]

George Reid, the superintendent of locomotives, NGR (PAR).

The NGR locomotive maintenance shed, Durban (NSL).

A train derailment at Camperdown

On her way by rail from Estcourt to Durban Jessica Sykes experienced a derailment which may well have been an act of sabotage by the Boers. At the time her train was approaching Camperdown there were no fewer than 14 troop trains bound from Durban to the hinterland and the loosening of nuts on a bend of the railway may have been intended to interrupt their progress .

She described the events: 'About half an hour after we left Maritzburg, and just as we were approaching a station called Camperdown, our train received a violent jerk; we heard a low grating sound beneath us, the wheels seemed leaving the train, and we came to a sudden stop, which gave us a severe shaking. We heard a tremendous concussion, and our carriage, which was next but one to the engine, was filled with a stifling, blinding cloud of steam ... On looking out of our window we were able to see our locomotive lying prone on its side in front of the train, entirely blocking the six lines of railway ...

'The engine driver was very seriously hurt and his assistant had been carried away frightfully scalded ... the iron rails on the line where the engine had fallen were torn and twisted and broken like so many strands of straw, and the ground was ploughed up to a depth of 2 or 3 feet in front of the prostrate machine ...'

'The fact was, though we did not know it at the time, that this accident was no accident at all, and had been cunningly planned by some Boer spies or sympathisers, who must have spent some considerable time in carrying out their nefarious work. For later when the railway line was examined to investigate the cause of the mishap, it was discovered that the "nuts" had been removed which fastened down the railway line at a sharp turn in the road ... four of these (troop) trains, had they not been delayed by overloading in arriving at their appointed time, would have been waiting on the side lines at Camperdown Station, waiting for the mail train - i.e. the one in which we were seated - to dart between them; and had the engine been overturned in their midst, one can hardly bear to think of the horrible scene which would have ensued'.[20]

In addition to the two railway employees named in Horsley's report, there was evidence of another driver, Crowshaw, who appeared to have lost his nerve during actions near Colenso in December 1899, 'though he had shown great courage in driving trains under fire'.[22] A member of the DLI, Sergeant Borain, who was also a railwayman, drove an armoured engine 'through shot and shell' hauling armoured and unarmoured wagons to rescue Captain Molyneux and the 'A' Company of the DLI at the Langeverwachte Bridge.[23]

Seventeen weeks

Like most colonial departments of the time, the NGR kept meticulous records. Probably in response to the disagreements which had developed between his railway system and the military, Hunter had very detailed statements prepared regarding all truck movements in Natal between December 1901 and April 1902. Amongst other information, these tabulated reports included the details of all trucks despatched from the Point and Durban for each day of each month, listing the number carrying supplies, ordnance and animals, and making reference to the number of ambulance train movements and the number of special trains. It is assumed that the latter carried Boer prisoners and women and children, as their destinations included Umbilo, Merebank, Wentworth, Jacobs and the Point.

The totals provided were impressive. During these 17 weeks, a total number of 7 962 trucks were supplied for exclusive military use, which represented a weekly average of 468. (Col. Landon, the director of supplies, had requested 700 per week.) Of the total, 1 968 trucks carried supplies, and 1 805 carried 'remounts', which converted to some 75 735 animals altogether. In addition, there were 105 movements of ambulance trains and 179 special trains, and all this was carried on one single rail line besides the civilian traffic allowed.[24]

By August 1901, the impact of the military on the Natal railway system was being felt in a number of places in the colony. During the parliamentary session, at that time FS Tatham, the member for Ixopo, asked if the House had noticed an advertisement in the Government Gazette from HG Gordon, a Richmond timber merchant which had stated that he was compelled to close his retail store, owing to the impossibility of obtaining material from Durban by rail. He also asked whether it was true that traders in Pietermaritzburg and up-country towns had been seriously hampered by the inability of the railway department to carry their goods. The minister of lands and works responded by laying on the table a list of rolling stock on order and the dates at which such stock was expected to arrive. He noted that the total tonnage carried by the railways was double the amount for the same period in the previous year. Given the statistics provided for the 17 weeks, it is probable that the trading conditions in the smaller country towns only got worse during the last year of the war.[25]

Delays and blockages

The enormous strain on the single line of the NGR over the three years of war would also have produced logistical problems. As early as December 1899, minor conflicts broke out between the Natal harbour Department and the NGR over rail goods which were blocking the wharves at the Point.[26] It was inevitable that two transport systems which required such close co-operation and integrated planning should encounter conflict over goods disembarked but not despatched. Once again space at the extremely limited number of wharves at the Point was at a premium. This problem would arise again and again during the war, and the blockage was not always because of a bottleneck at the Point, but sometimes resulted from blockages at the other end of the line, for example, at the border with the Transvaal, which then caused a ripple effect back to the starting point. At other times delays occurred because of a severe limitation in the number of railway trucks.

But the worst of the blockages was to appear towards the end of the war when, for many reasons, vast quantities of goods and animals began pouring into the conquered territories. Early in 1902, the commanding officer of the Natal district office in Newcastle complained to the governor about such a problem. Stores and supplies were accumulating in great quantities at the Durban docks. During the previous December some 1 247 tons of goods were being railed daily through to the Transvaal border, although the assistant director of the railways, Major Livingstone, thought that this should be raised to not less than 1 500 tons per day. The solution, which both men argued for, was a substantial increase in rail trucks to be allocated to the military 'though it may involve a temporary inconvenience to some of the Civil Population of the Colony'.[27] Livingstone went on to explain that the director of supplies, Colonel Landon, who was obviously applying pressure down the ranks, had stipulated that if 100 short trucks were to be despatched from each of the South African ports every day 'he could feed the men of the army satisfactorily, and find half rations for the animals, and that any falling off from this minimum was a serious matter, as, although the men might still be fed, the horses and mules would become unfit owing to want of proper nourishment'.[28]

The critical nature of this supply situation certainly raises the question as to whether the 'scorched earth' policy of the British forces, which was reaching its zenith at this time, was not the main reason for the absolute necessity of importing massive quantities of rations and forage, for there would have been almost no local economy to be relied on in the hinterland. In addition, many rail trucks were now being used to move thousands of Boer prisoners of war to Durban, either to the Umbilo camp, or to ships for overseas exile, and they were also used to convey many more thousands of Boer women and children to concentration camps in Natal. A further use of rail trucks was to carry the building materials and other requirements for the scores of camps being established, both for Boers and Africans, in the interior. The inadequacy of the Natal line became clearly evident.

Major Livingstone went on to make an impassioned plea to David

Hunter citing the serious military impact of these blockages, and suggested measures to be implemented:

> ... if less than this be done the problem of constructing new railway lines, having both a Military and Civil value, of completing existing and starting new lines of blockhouses which play such an important part in clearing large areas of the enemy, and lastly of working the mines and feeding the ever increasing population of Johannesburg, will become impossible of solution. It seems clear that, apart from the actual fighting, the question as to whether Lord Kitchener's schemes can be prosecuted with vigour, or will take a long time to be carried into effect, depends almost entirely on what the Railways can do both with respect to tonnage despatched and expeditious transport ... at the present moment, there is a congestion of traffic between Durban and Maritzburg which not only has reduced the Military output from this Port but necessarily means that trucks previously despatched are being delayed.[29]

Livingstone put the blame on heavy despatches which had been for the trade of the colony. David Hunter explained that unless the demands for blockhouse materials and ordnance stores were to be restricted, there was nothing he could do. He did, however, mention that five new locomotives had recently been landed and would be running within ten days. They were to be followed by another ten and 'I have cut down Natal Civil requirements to bare requirements'.[30] So the shortage of rail trucks may have been only one dimension of the problem. In a later telegram to Livingstone he pointed out, with some justification, that on one day in October 1901, about 2 500 tons of traffic had been loaded at the Point, which represented more than the entire rail traffic to all parts of South Africa including that of the military. One solution to the blockage between the port and Pietermaritzburg was to march animals from the Point, through the various remount posts, to the capital city, from where they would be entrained for the hinterland.

After the declaration of peace, there were still problems with blockages, and again an apparent shortage of trucks, but this time it seems that the repatriation of Boers back to places close to their homes was only one reason. Hunter, writing to the prime minister in July 1902, commented that 'It is somewhat remarkable that the Military are clamouring for more truckage when at the same time there is an accumulation at the Border owing to the inability of the C.S.A. Railway Administration to remove same ... and since Monday I have discontinued acceptance of Military traffic for stations beyond Charlestown, and this will continue until a clearance is effected.'[31] He also noted the irony, that after peace had been signed, his railway was still carrying very large amounts of supplies to the Transvaal, some 1 250 tons from Durban and the Point daily, while simultaneously large quantities of military stores and forage were being sold at Elandsfontein at post-war sales. For example, in a

Returning prisoners of war

In respect of returning prisoners of war, Captain Binham, the provost marshall, who was responsible for the return of prisoners, wrote to the governor on 26 August 1902: 'The present state of accommodation is too low. Burghers have so many goods and chattels, it would be unfair to deprive them, that to put 10 men in a 3rd class carriage for a railway journey of 48 hours or more is overcrowding. A fair allowance is 6 men to a compartment.

'There are a considerable number of Boer officers and officials with each party, and they are entitled to first class accommodation. The percentage is usually 5 to 6 per cent of the prisoners ... The train that takes prisoners merely stops at Umbilo Station for 10 minutes as though taking up ordinary passengers. To entrain 1 000 Boers decently and in order much more time is necessary, and it is requested that some arrangement might be made by which the railway carriages provided could be sent to the station and left there for an hour or so to admit of orderly entrainment.' (sic)[32]

Most of the Boers were probably so keen to move out of Durban, however, that they would probably have entrained in two minutes although perhaps, without the captain's sense of order.

Rail trucks at the Point docks (PAR and LHM).

Horse and mule trolleys

Horse and mule-drawn trolleys were also used extensively in Durban and at the Point to move goods to and from the docks. The local system of trollies had developed specifically in the 1870s as a response to the very ineffectual working of the Point – Durban rail line. In addition, considerable numbers of horse, mule and ox-drawn wagons were used throughout Natal during the war to transport goods and equipment. For example, on 19 August 1900, 400 wagons left the army ordnance depot in Durban.[34] Wagons also had the advantage of being independent of a 'line'.

Mule trolleys outside the wharf sheds at the Point (LHM).

three-week period in July 1902, 18 964 tons of goods and 3 372 animals were despatched from Durban and the Point. It appears that at least one part of the mighty military machine was unable to stop!

Steam traction engines

One of the serious deficiencies of the military use of the railway transportation system was the way in which all activities were tied to the rail line. Traditionally, the British army, the Hussars, Lancers, Yeomen and even the artillery had come to rely heavily on horses. An interesting development in the latter part of the nineteenth century was the appearance of an alternative and independent form of road transport which used steam as the driving energy. By 1899, several British firms were producing steam traction engines and among these were Fowlers of Leeds, Burrells, McLarens and Avelings. Early in October 1899, the war office decided to send a number of these engines to South Africa.[33] Colonel Templar was appointed director of steam road transport and a new Royal Engineers Company (45th) was formed, with sappers and drivers drawn from a variety of other military units. After making military modifications and some unsuccessful trials, mainly owing to the wet weather conditions, 11 engines, 35 trucks, three vans and all the associated equipment were loaded on to the *Bulawayo* for transport to Cape Town on 11 November 1899. The ship docked there on 12 December 1899, and a 'comedy of errors' commenced.

In Cape Town, after numerous decisions and reversals, the company, under Captain GP Scholfield, was finally informed that it was to serve under the director of railways. The steam traction engines had to be removed from the ship in order to reach a separate consignment of 'buck waggons' which were intended for Cape Town. The railways department telegraphed the GOC in Natal to enquire whether he would like some engines, but no response was received. Then a decision was taken to send the unit on to Port Elizabeth, where it arrived on 19 December 1899. After offloading 17 trucks by lighter, an urgent telegram arrived, requesting the *Bulawayo* to proceed to Durban, where two traction engines were needed. The remainder were initially intended to return to Port Elizabeth.

As it turned out, no engines were required in Natal. On 22 December, McLaren, one of the civilians accompanying the engineers, informed the unit that five engines had been unloaded in Durban and then the following day informed Port Elizabeth that all the engines and the equipment were being offloaded. Men were then to be sent to Natal to assist with operating them there. It has never been clarified who ordered the engines for Natal. In the meanwhile Colonel Templar had been bringing another consignment of engines from Britain on the *Denton Grange*, which ran ashore at Las Palmas.

On 3 January 1900, the remainder of the company in Port Elizabeth was now ordered to proceed to Natal, where they arrived on the 10th. By 12 January 1900, they had reached Frere, where a variety of menial tasks were accomplished, such as carrying stores across the Blaawkrantz River.

A steam tractor being larded at the Point (Newnes).

A McLaren No. 603 steam tractor at Frere (REM).

Steam tractors at the Point (KCL).

McLaren No. 603 hauling stores at Frere (REM).

Unfortunately continuous heavy rain made conditions difficult for men and horses, let alone for steam traction engines. General Buller severely criticised the 'management of the engines'. The unit then remained idle for some weeks. When the weather cleared in February, an offer was made to take 100 tons of supplies daily to Springfield, but this was declined and 'it was now quite evident that traction engines were not required in Natal and ought never to have been sent there ...'[35]

At that juncture, Colonel Templar arrived in Frere. At Las Palmas they had transferred the engines and gear from the *Denton Grange* to the *Yoruba* and the *Siberian* for shipping to Cape Town. Templar arranged

with the general officer commanding, on 10 February, to remove the company from Natal and return to the Cape, and most of the engines were sent to Durban by train! A Burrell engine broke down at Howick and was eventually despatched to the Cape for repair, also by train. While waiting for four days at Durban for the arrival of the *Urniston Grange*, the trucks were repaired. On 25 February 1900 the entire outfit arrived back in Port Elizabeth. Scholfield noted that their reception there was 'a pleasant experience after Durban'.[36] Clearly the British army was still very much a horse-based organisation, and new-fangled devices such as traction engines were simply too modern.

An NGR train with a type K&S 4-6-0 locomotive at Berea Road Station (KCL).

1. Stickney, A., *The Strategic Role of Railways*, p.9.

2. Singleton, J, *The Battlefields of Natal Revisited*, p.50.

3. Heydenrych, H and Martin, B, *The Natal Main Line Story*.

4. PRO, WO 108/378, EPC Girouard, History of the Railways during the War in South Africa, 1903.

5. Ibid.

6. PRO, CO 179/218. Buller notes on the War, 24.6.1901.

7. PAR, GH 532, notes by general manager, NGR, 6.10.1900.

8. Ibid.

9. *The Natal Mercury*, Singleton, 27.10.1900.

10. PRO, CO 179/206, Hely-Hutchinson to Chamberlain, 7.10.1899.

11. *The Highway Mail*, 19.3.1971, pp.12–13.

12. Ibid.

13. Ibid.

14. Ibid.

15. PAR, NGR annual report, p.8.

16. Singleton J, *The Battlefields of Natal Revisited*, p.53.

17. *Natal – Descriptive Guide and Official Handbook*, p.106.

18. PAR, MJPW 116, Hunter to minister of lands and works, 13.2.1900.

19. Sykes, J, *Sidelights of the War*, 1900, pp.111–113.

20. PAR, MJPW 116, Driver Horsley to Loco. Superintendent Reid, 16.11.1899.

21. PRO, CO 179/207. Hunter to minister of lands and works, 9.12.1899.

22. Ibid.

23. PRO, WO 108/120, NGR trucks supplied to the military, 6.4.1902.

24. PAR, NCP 4/2/1/110, legislative assembly No.10, 1901.

25. PAR, NHD III/3/2, port captain correspondence 9.12.1899.

26. PAR, GH 535, Major H. Livingstone to general manager, NGR, 30.1.1902.

27. Ibid.

28. ap.cit., PAR, GH 535.

29. PAR, GH 535, general manager, NGR to Major H Livingstone, 30.1.1902.

30. PAR, GH 546, Hunter to prime minister, 30.7.1902.

31. PAR, GH 564, Captain Binham to governor, 26.8.1902.

32. PRO, WO 108/377, report on steam road transport in South Africa, 1903.

33. PRO WO 108/245, report from ordnance officers in South Africa on the working of the army ordnance department, 19.18.1900.

34. Report on steam road transport.

35. Ibid., p.8.

CHAPTER 11

HORSES, MULES AND DONKEYS OF WAR
Hazel England and Brian Kearney

At Port Elizabeth a horse memorial was erected in 1905. The sculpture was executed by Joseph Whitehead and paid for by public subscription in recognition of the services of innumerable horses which perished during the Anglo-Boer War. The commemorative statue bears the following inscription: 'The greatness of a nation consists not as much on the number of its people or the extent of its territory as in the extent and justice of its compassion'.[1]

The Anglo-Boer War was one of the last wars where the horse, the mule and the donkey played a major logistical role on the sides of both combatants. In other respects the war marked a technological turning point where these animals were used together with other forms of energy such as steam and electricity. The suffering and deaths of many animals were an important part, but only one dimension of the story. The dependence on animals for the mobility of the Boer commandos, and the British, colonial and volunteer forces during the war is often underestimated. An evaluation of the functions of the imperial government's remount department alongside the Boers' use of horses provides some insights into this dimension of the war, and explains the enormous numbers of animals which came through the port of Durban between 1899 and 1902.

A wounded war horse (*The Graphic,* 27 October 1900).

Boer horses and British remounts

Horses had been imported to the Cape from the East, and from Europe and Britain over a period of some 250 years. The resulting crossbreeds became adapted to the climate and evolved into the South African horse. This was also known as the Boer horse and was an agile breed able to cover vast distances in rough terrain and to survive in the open veld for most of the year. The Boer forces were mounted on dual purpose animals which had been broken in by their owners, but which were also trained for transport, traction and hunting. An intimate bond existed between a Boer and his horse.[2]

After the declaration of war in October 1899, some 15 000 armed Boer horsemen, supported by wagons with guns and supplies, invaded Northern Natal, with the objective of reaching the sea and the port of Durban. If they needed to replace their horses, the Boers were initially supplied with remounts from the republican government supplies, or they were given new mounts by sympathetic supporters or else they simply commandeered horses from isolated farms. Once the war reached the later guerilla phase, the Boers divided into small mounted units. Raiding parties of extremely mobile, armed horsemen were able to penetrate deep behind the British lines, where they sabotaged rail lines, attacked camps and burned convoys. Dubbed by the press as 'warrior farmers', they had to rely on captured British horses or wild horses for remounts.[3]

The Boers also faced extreme problems in feeding their animals and, even from the commencement of the war, there were difficulties in providing fodder in Natal as well as elsewhere in South Africa.[4] The situation became even more critical during the later phases of the war when the British 'scorched earth' policy effectively blocked the supply of food for animals from regions such as the eastern Free State which had been the main sources of supply.

By contrast, the British remount department, in peacetime, included a small but effective corps which consisted of an inspector general of remount, three assistant inspectors, two captains of staff and three veterinary officers. Experienced remount officers annually purchased 2 500 suitable horses of various breeds from established local and overseas sources. The commissioned cavalry officers provided their own large 'chargers' or 'troop horses', which were trained for jumping, charging and parade drill, but the other ranks in the cavalry and mounted units were provided with horses by the remount department.

Purchased horses required by the military included 'cobs' and 'hacks', which were smaller multi-purpose animals suitable for riding or traction.[5] After being tested for disease, horses were transported by contracted shipping companies to remount posts in England, and the 'soft' animals would be conditioned, groomed and exercised before transfer to cavalry and mounted infantry regiments for training. Supervised by a riding master, the troopers would be trained in equestrian and fighting skills thus producing experienced riders and disciplined animals. The British climate dictated that most horses would depend on supplies of fodder during the winter months.[6]

During the initial stages of the Anglo-Boer War, particularly in the

Cobs were 'short-legged or stout' horses. Hacks were 'half-bred horses or ordinary saddle horses for the road', the term being an abbreviation of Hackney. Chargers were horses ridden by officers in the field. Mules were either the off-spring of a 'he-ass' and a mare, or of a 'she-ass' and a stallion.

Preparing bales of fodder (War Pictures).

Tent pegging at Aldershot (Golding).

A fair number of horses were sold at good prices to the British military authorities by farmers from the East Griqualand district.[8] Between 1 October 1899 and 2 October 1900, 9 202 local horses had been purchased out of a total of 20 558. Colonel W Birbeck, the inspector general of remounts in South Africa, noted that Staff Captain Mackenzie had bought cobs and mules under a contract with Julius Weil & Co. A thousand mules had been delivered at Durban at £42 20s each. Excluding freight this amounted to £35 per mule and he observed that Weil's profit must have been large.[9]

set-piece battles, the imperial forces suffered heavy losses of horses and the situation required an increased number of fresh troops and remounts. Colonel Stevenson, the inspector of remounts in Natal, recorded that 25 558 horses arrived by steamer or were purchased in Natal between 1 October 1899 and 11 October 1900, for counter-offensive strategies. A large number of animals had also been brought to Natal by the Indian army units whose contribution included: '... 6 700 horses, 1 600 mules and ponies and hospitals for sick horses ... In addition 2 650 horses for the Mounted Infantry were given by the Indian Cavalry and Imperial Regiments and 1 200 horses [were] donated by the Indian Princes ...'[7]

The sources and transport of animals

The increased demand, owing to a high attrition rate and inadequate local purchases and in spite of the gifts from India, led to horses and mules being acquired from a great number of countries around the world. Principal among these were Australia, Argentina, Canada, Hungary, Italy, Spain and the United States. Of the total number of 206 063 remount horses shipped to South Africa between September 1899 and December 1901, the largest number, 76 131, came from the USA. Large numbers were also sent from Britain itself, as well as from Australia, Argentina and Austria. During the same period, the USA also contributed the greatest number of mules, that is, 67 624 of a total of 91 769. The losses at sea of horses was slightly higher: 3.49% of horses compared to 2.55 % for mules.[10] Donkeys were purchased from Italy and Spain.

In the *Times History of the War in South Africa*, Amery wrote: 'The transport of horses and mules by sea is no unimportant matter, as horses are far from good sailors, and even with every provision in the way of special fittings suffer severely ... Over 13 000 horses, as against 2 000 odd mules, died at sea, and many times that number perished because they were put into the field before they had properly recovered from the effects of the voyage.'[11] But it was also the way in which ships were

AN ACT OF MERCY. A LAST KINDNESS TO A TRUSTY FRIEND. THE GRAPHIC 30-12-1899 pg.881

'An act of mercy – a last kindness to a trusty friend'
(*The Graphic*, 30 December 1899).

Number of horses and mules shipped and lost between 1.9.1899 and 31.12.1901				
Horses			**Mules**	
From	**Total**	**Lost**	**Total**	**Lost**
United Kingdom	46 038	172		
India	3 050	60	500	1
Australia	19 730	625		
United States	76 131	2 448	67 624	1 813
Argentina	25 872	192		
Austria	23 938	497		
Canada	11 304	458		
Italy			5 102	28
Spain			8 543	504

charted for the transport of animals that contributed substantially to the losses, since the remount department's contracts with shipping companies specified that the ship's owner was responsible for all forage, fittings, water and attendants, and these provisions would have varied widely between companies. Between September 1899 and July 1902, over 520 voyages were made transporting animals to the war zone. Notwithstanding the way in which veterinary surgeons, dedicated military staff and civilian horse-keepers were sometimes used to ensure that the animals landed in good condition, the temporary arrangements made on board and the ordinary cattlemen used by the chartered companies often proved unsuitable. On board ship the horses were best housed in fitted stalls which allowed for some movement and for feeding, while mules were generally transported in large pens, each holding five animals, with each mule being haltered with a rope.

The cost and loss of animals

The Royal Commission of Enquiry into the War held in 1903 stated that altogether 518 794 horses and 150 781 mules and donkeys were supplied by the imperial authorities for the war and that 347 007 (67%) horses and 53 339 (35%) mules and donkeys had been 'expended' during the campaign. The total expenditure on horses, mules and donkeys, excluding the freight costs, was £15 339 142. The commission concluded that: '...the chief cause of the loss of horses in the War was that they were for the most part brought from distant countries, submitted to a long and deteriorating sea voyage, when landed sent into the field without time for recuperation, and there put to hard and continuous work on short rations.' In addition horses from the northern hemisphere arrived in the South African summer with heavy winter coats. Kitchener also thought that the large losses could be attributed to 'large numbers of improvised mounted men with little or no knowledge of horse-mastership'.[12]

Tales of horror

Many ships failed to provide even basic measures to safeguard the animals. On 19 June 1900, one of the chartered 'cattleships', the SS *Anerly*, arrived in Durban carrying a sorry tale of death and destruction. The ship had left Melbourne for Newcastle in New South Wales where it was scheduled to take on 283 bullocks. On returning to Melbourne, she encountered heavy seas and lost 224 cattle overboard. She was refitted there for transporting horses and left on 9 June 1900 with 250 on board. The ship ran into gales on 17 June, first from the north-west and then from the south:

> ... high seas began to flood the decks both fore and aft. The gale continued till the 21st on which day it veered to the west; the sea was mountainous, the ship labour-

ed and passage on the decks became impossible. The seas which broke over the side smashed down the stalls, tore the tarpaulins off the hatches and flooded the lower deck. The storm continued with more or less intensity till Sunday the 24th when the fittings on the foredeck were wrecked, and large quantities of water got below. Between the 21st and the 24th, scenes of horror were continually occurring. A heavy sea would sweep the decks breaking down the stalls and carrying the horses and debris with irresistible force before it, dashing them up against the sides of the ship or hurling them down the hatches in dozens at a time where they lay in heaps, kicking each other to death, some transfixed with broken spars, others struggling helplessly ... Nothing could be done to help the poor animals until death quieted their struggles, for every man on deck was in jeopardy from the heavy seas sweeping across the vessel ... On the 1st of July another gale was experienced, and this also wrecked a number of stalls that had been left intact from the former gale ... Again on Saturday the 14th July, another storm was encountered, and the vessel had to heave to ... Out of 250 horses shipped at Melbourne, the *Anerly* only landed 49 ...[13]

The *Natal Witness* report concluded with reference to local indignation at the disaster and questioned whether the ship had been 'properly fitted up to carry live stock through heavy weather'. Two months later, on 14 September 1900, the *Yarrowdale* berthed in Durban from Melbourne with an equally disastrous tale, but this time it was mainly cattle and

Riding on board ship (War Pictures).

Disembarking horses and mules with boxes from the *Douene Castle* at Cape Town for Natal (*The Illustrated London News,* 9 September 1899).

sheep which had suffered – some 493 sheep and 60 cattle being lost overboard. On this occasion the *Natal Witness* carried an article strongly recommending that the remedy against further disasters of the type was to prohibit all vessels from carrying livestock on exposed decks and to enforce the compulsory quartering of all animals in 'sheltered and substantially constructed stalls'.[14]

As a small measure of improvement, the military authorities increased the number of hands per animal from per 20, as it had been at the commencement of the war, to 1 per 15. Since some ships, like the *Rippingham Grange* (July 1900) and the *Norfolk* (15 July, 1900), each carried over 1 000 horses, this would mean a complement of about 70 cattlemen per vessel. Ironically, notwithstanding the precautions which were implemented, remount officers were quoted after the war as stating that 50% of the Australian horses, which had been acquired on Lord Roberts' recommendation, 'were unfit for any purpose whatever'.[15]

Disembarkation, railing and marching

While some horses had to be offloaded at the outer anchorage from transport vessels, onto the decks of lighters or tugs using slings or horseboxes, by far the majority were landed at the Point quays and either lowered in a horsebox, or walked directly down gangways onto terra firma. They would initially be received by a remount conductor, assisted by a party of African hands. From here they were either railed or marched directly to the war front, or sent to remount stations in the hinterland, such as Weston near Mooi River. A particular problem arose with respect to the narrow gauge of the Natal rail line. The narrow trucks meant that it was only possible to transport six horses in each truck, compared to eight or nine as had been the case in Britain, as the animals were best transported

Landing horses in horse boxes at the Point, February, 1900, (Richards).

Entraining horses (*The Graphic*, 21 October 1899).

standing parallel to the track, in two groups, facing each other, with a space between for forage and water. The larger English horses in particular created problems with the implementation of this method.

Since the main remount depot in Durban for the duration of the war was at Lords Ground, large numbers of animals were marched there, tied in groups of three or five. The new arrivals were 'soft' because they were in need of shoes and often unbroken to bridle and saddle. Early in 1902, an experiment was conducted which involved an attempt to drive horses in very large groups from the SS *Montezuma*. A certain Captain FG Hughes observed from the ship how the horses were propelled down the gangway and collected together in a ring formed by the hands. When between 100 to 140 had been thus collected, they were then led off by a mounted man, with two or three others following at 'a smart canter', to Lords Ground. Hughes was most concerned about the way the horses were routed along a macadamised road and reported the affair and the apparent 'ill treatment' of the horses to the secretary of state for war in London. An enquiry was instituted, which confirmed that the route was not macadamised but 'a sandy lane.' However, Kitchener reported to the war office that the experiment would not be repeated, 'owing to the difficulty of preventing the horses from straying along the road', and the previous method was reinstated.[16]

Glanders and quarantine

Before the outbreak of war in January 1899, the principal colonial veterinary surgeon, Watkins Pitchford, communicated with the Durban town council concerning the suppression of glanders in the borough. In particular, he wished them to establish a system of controlling horses coming into the area from outside. He considered that 'the difficulty of

Glanders was a horse disease which infected the respiratory system, the liver and spleen and other organs. The disease was easily spread, especially through stables, and the only effective measure in dealing with it at the time of the war was to destroy the animal and bury the carcass. Unfortunately there are no available records of the number of such cases brought in to Durban while martial law was in effect, but horses infected with glanders arrived from Australia in February 1900.[19]

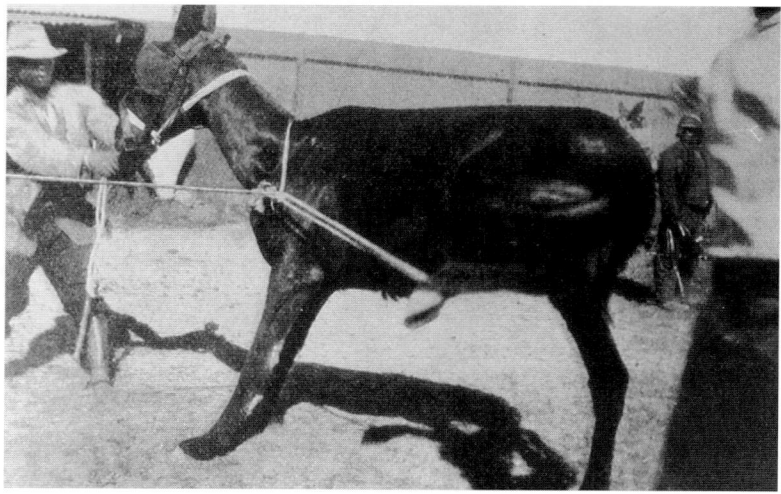

Branding mules with a broad arrow at the Lords Ground remount depot (*The Black and White Budget*).

Farriers at work at Aldershot (Golding).

eradicating the disease in Durban is great as Glanders has taken a firm hold upon the stables of the larger horse-owners and probably to a less extent upon private stables'.[17] Evidently 1898 had been a very bad year in Natal for horse sickness, lung sickness and glanders, and the situation in Durban threatened the entire stock of the colony.[18] Watkins Pitchford proposed building a small depot away from the town centre, where newly arrived horses could be quarantined for 24 hours and inspected by the district veterinary surgeon. The scheme, however, encountered problems over the difficult issue of compensation to horse owners until the Natal government clarified the situation by introducing Act No. 23 of 1899, whereby no compensation would be paid for glandered horses which had been introduced into the colony three months prior to their being tested.

The structures to control such sicknesses had not yet been put in place when war broke out, and the great irony was that Natal became literally invaded by tens of thousands of horses, most of which had completely escaped quarantine and regulations as a result of martial law. In these cases the responsibility for controlling the disease was passed directly to the army veterinary department and the surgeons attached to the remount depots.[20]

Local horses

Given the problems associated with the importation of horses from elsewhere in the world, it was not surprising that many military men regarded local horses as preferable. Colonel Thorneycroft, of Thorneycroft's Mounted Infantry, said:

> Towards the end of the campaign I had every variety of horse, but I impressed fully upon the men the necessity of looking after their South African ponies, as I knew that the supply, in all likelihood, with a protracted campaign, would not last, and I so warned them that they took the greatest interest and pride in looking after their Colonial South African ponies; so much so, that after two years of campaigning there were a large number of those original ponies which were issued to me at Pietermaritzburg still in the ranks of my regiment.[21]

He disliked the other horses provided as the 'Colonial-bred pony was ... better to start with, he had not come aboard ship and had his heels worn down by the long voyage from South America, North America, or Australia. He was accustomed to the climate and class of forage that he would get, and he was found to be more efficient than other horses that came out and were rapidly sent to the front ... without any rest at all'. Thorneycroft made a particular point of stressing how foreign horses had been shipped without shoes, and he preferred to have them shod beforehand since 'if they are not they wear their heels down so low that when they come off there is nothing on which to nail a shoe'.[22]

The remount depots: Lords Ground

Lords Ground, also known as the Durban Show Grounds, was a portion of the original ordnance land (owned by the war department) and, before the war, it had been leased to the agricultural society to be used for their annual show. It was situated about a mile (1.6 km) from the Point docks and close to the main railway line and the main road inland. There was also sufficient space for exercising horses and accommodating staff, so it had most of the attributes of a class A remount depot. It was suitable for handling 3 000 horses, though it was not as large as the depots at Port Elizabeth or Weston.

Besides the kraal, stables and paddocks for horses and other animals, a large remount depot required an enormous amount and range of equipment including water troughs; mangers for fodder; fodder stores covered with tarpaulins; corn crushers and chaff cutters; boilers for linseed oil; stocks, slings, and forges for shoeing horses; breaking saddles; clipping machines; 'dandy' brushes; road-sweeping devices and carts for the removal of manure. In addition, facilities were required for the disposal of the carcasses of dead animals,[24] and the checking of the hooves of the horses before the animals were branded with a broad arrow three inches (75 mm) above the hind leg. Remount depots were also very labour-intensive establishments which was to generate further problems before the end of the war. By May 1902 the staff at Lords Ground consisted of seven officers; three veterinary surgeons; 36 conductors; one clerk; seven non-commissioned officers, 648 hands, one *sowar* and six *syces*.

While the site of Lords Ground seemed eminently appropriate in some respects, especially in terms of access, it was to prove problematic with respect to drainage, the removal of carcasses and health in general. Probably as a direct result of the enormous number of animals passing through Durban in the early months of 1901 and the wet weather of the summer, the state of the depot became such as to attract the serious attention of WC Daugherty, the inspector of nuisances. On 9 March 1901, he inspected Lords Ground with the medical officer of health, Dr Sam Campbell, and found great accumulations of mud and manure in the stables, paddocks and yards. In August 1900, Daugherty himself had arranged for the railways to provide trucks for the removal of manure away from the depot, but this process had since been suspended. Complaints were being received from the surrounding residents about the offensive smells. Dr Campbell was especially concerned about the probable occurrence of bubonic plague in the town. They both agreed that nothing practical could be done to clean the site and the conditions of the site 'render[ed] it impossible to run such a large number of horses without giving rise to insanitary conditions'.[25] On their recommendation, the mayor, John Nicol wrote to the colonial secretary reporting on the 'grave menace' and asking 'that [he] would be good enough to assist [them] in obtaining the removal of the horses to some other site outside the Borough'.[26]

The colonial secretary immediately referred the problem to the general officer commanding for Natal, and Colonel Lawson responded

Colonel Thorneycroft (Wilson).

Sowar was the Anglo-Indian term for a 'native horseman or policeman'. A *syce* was a groom. The numbers of staff may have been higher before the establishment of the Gillitts Station in mid-1901.
The establishment of a class A Depot included 117 men and the following minimum staff: one major, two captains, one adjutant, two subalterns, one quartermaster, two veterinary officers, six trained dressers, one sergeant major, one orderly room sergeant, one quartermaster sergeant, three clerks (military or civilian), eight sergeants, two farrier sergeants, eight corporals, 30 shoeing smiths, 25 privates, ten batmen, one head conductor, one transport conductor, 12 saddlers and two general mechanics.[23]

Lords Ground from the Berea. The grandstand and stables are visible beyond the houses in the foreground (LHM).

on his behalf by indicating that everything was being done to improve the sanitary conditions of the site, as well as moving as many horses out of Durban as possible. In the meantime, John Nicol enlisted the support of Dr George Turner, who was the medical officer of health for the Transvaal and who, as a refugee, was temporarily resident in Durban. Dr Turner reported that he had inspected Lords Ground on 20 March 1901, together with Dr Campbell and A Douglas Cameron, the plague officer. While he found the site acceptable for use for agricultural shows, he was highly critical of the military authorities who had taken no steps to provide any form of surface drainage. 'The Military must have known that to confine a number of mules and horses, varying from one to two thousand animals, on such a limited area and during the rainy season must result in a nuisance'.[27] He strongly recommended that the depot be moved elsewhere. Turner's argument was also supported by Cameron, who reported: 'The place was in a filthy and water-logged condition, and the majority of the animals were standing knee deep in mud and slime, and the manure has not been removed for months. That such a place is allowed to exist in the centre of town – and close to one of our most thickly populated districts – is a grave danger to the health of the community ...'[28]

Once again, Nicol sought the government's assistance in having the depot moved out of town. On 27 March 1901, Prime Minister Hime suggested to the colonial secretary that the general officer commanding be informed of Dr Turner's report and of his previous experience and status. This report produced limited results and Colonel Lawson informed the colonial secretary on 26 April 1901 that a new paddock had been laid out; cinders were being used to raise the levels of the horse stalls; drains had been cut in the stables and kraals; a large quantity of manure had been removed and a new shed had been erected for the African hands. Quite clearly, the military authorities were not going to move the depot but 'they were doing their best to reduce the number of horses at Durban'.

However the mayor continued to exert pressure, this time based on the fear of bubonic plague. He called in the government's special plague advisor, Dr Ernest Hill, who reported on 21 May 1901 and concurred with the previous accounts. He observed swarms of flies, and commented on 'the danger at the present time in view of a possible invasion of plague ...' He went on to say that he thought 'it probable that a satisfactory site might be found in a less menacing situation'.[29] Colonel Lawson challenged Hill's report because of the remedial work which had been carried out and concluded: 'Under these circumstances I am sorry that it is not at present possible to consider the removal of the Depot to another site, a course which would be attended by many difficulties and which would seriously interfere with the arrangements for the supply of horses to the Troops now operating in the field.'[30]

On 10 August 1901, Dr Hill presented new arguments to the colonial secretary about the health of the neighbourhood where some 1 209 persons of various race groups lived within 250 yards of Lords Ground. He strongly supported the views of the medical officers and the inspector of nuisances, comparing their understanding of sanitation with that of the military authorities 'whose professional duties surely leave them little time to touch on even the outside fringe of the subject'.[32] But the pleadings and arguments had no effect. The municipality of Durban then tried an alternative course of action by offering a block of land at Congella to the military authorities in exchange for Lords Ground. The negotiations relating to this exchange were, however, to drag on for some time, probably because Lords Ground was owned by the war department.[33] It appears that the military eagerly accepted the alternative site at Congella, but for it to be used as a prisoner-of-war camp and not for the remount depot. Thus Lords Ground was to remain as a depot until the end of the war.

On 27 August 1901, Acutt, the mayor, wrote to Commandant O'Neill about a possible transfer of lands. He suggested that the use of Lords Ground by the military as a remount depot, from October 1899, had not only been a health menace, but had seriously inconvenienced the Durban and Coast Society of Agriculture and Industry and furthermore the Durban Amateur Athletic Association who sub-leased the land. The agricultural society had erected buildings to the value of £9 000 and the athletic association had also spent a considerable sum on tracks and cricket fields. In addition, the use of the site by thousands of horses from all over the world would mean that the grounds would no longer be able to be used for stock show purposes. Furthermore the ownership by a body such as the war department of a block of land close to the centre of the town could prevent the town from growing in that direction.

Thus he proposed that Lords Ground be sold to the corporation and that the corporation sell to the war department a block of land at Congella of the same area – 12.5 hectares. The corporation would provide railway sidings and fencing to the Congella site. This would mean that 'every facility available at the present Remount Depot will be afforded at Congella'. The net difference in value of the two portions of land – approximately £90 000 – would then be paid to the war department.[34] Since conditions in the town had returned to a state of reasonable normality by June 1901, the original lessee of Lords Ground, the agricultural society, now requested another site for their show. They were also offered a piece of land at Congella 'with railway sidings, electric light, close to the electric tram extension and the water main ...'.[35]

The Gillitts remount station

One consequence of the pressure exerted by the Durban town council and medical advisers was the establishment of a new remount station at Gillitts in about May 1901. Gillitts was a farming area, situated some 32 kilometres from Durban and, being 600 metres above sea level and on the main rail and road to Pietermaritzburg, its locality was much more suitable for a remount station and sick horse depot. Sixteen hectares of 'Dove' farm were leased from William Gillitt. The Royal Engineers, who were responsible for its establishment, described the layout as: 'built for 2 000 horses on the plan of the Johannesburg Depot, i.e. Kraals placed around an exercising track which itself encloses an area in which two Kraals are placed. The number of Kraals in all was sixteen ... they varied in size but the average size was about 100 yards by 75 yards'.[36] Post and pole fences were erected around the kraals, 14 of which were provided with stables of wood and corrugated iron, constructed over jarrah piles. Every two kraals shared a crush pen. About 180 metres away from the depot, two kraals were built for sick horses. The Royal Engineers also noted the suitability of the farm for drainage. The water supply was worked by a Worthington pump which raised water 68 metres to 24 reserve storage tanks of 4 600 litres each. A small dam had been constructed across a lower valley which could store about 18 million litres of water, and a road had been built from the main road and railway siding to the depot.

The Gillitts depot was staffed by an Indian remount unit which had arrived in Durban in February 1901 to bolster the understaffed English remount department at Lords Ground. By May 1902, the staff consisted of seven officers (four of whom were Indian), one veterinary surgeon, one clerk, seven conductors, three civilians, 17 non-commissioned officers, 137 African assistants, 28 farriers, 200 *sowars*, and 300 *syces*.[38] Only one death was recorded at the station. Syce Araija, a Hindu, is listed as having died of enteric fever on 4 May 1901.[39]

It was probable that the establishment of the Gillitts remount station did not lead to the closure of the facility at Lords Ground, since it was still necessary to have a remount depot as close as possible to the point of arrival of the animals. However, the creation of the Gillitts depot would have dramatically eased the pressure on Lords Ground and provided a convenient stopping place on the route to Pietermaritzburg and Weston, especially for horses, mules and donkeys which were marched

Mrs Halsted (born Gillitt) recalled stories told her by Mrs Gillitt senior about the depot and about Indian riders who practised cavalry charges with a sword, decapitating an animal which was then used for food.[37] The dam was sited at the present-day dip on Ashley Drive and has been increased in height by subsequent farmers such as Mr Halstead. Camp Road is another relic of the depot, having been the main access route from the railway and main road.

Indian remount staff at a tented camp (CAR).

Indian farriers at work (Edwards).

Thin, tired and battle-worn horses being driven through the Pinetown market square (Pinetown Museum).

A pack mule and his conductor (*The Black and White Budget*).

inland. By 1903 both Lords Ground and Gillitts were still in use as re-mount depots, the latter having been taken over by the South African Constabulary.[40]

The Royal Engineers also reported on a halting stage which was established at Westville 12 kilometres from Durban, about half way to Gillitts, to accommodate about 250 horses weakened by long sea voyages. Four and a half hectares of ground were enclosed by wire fencing and subdivided into three kraals. A barn was constructed for grain and forage, and water was supplied from a spring close by.[41]

According to oral tradition, a portion of Kirk's Farm at the foot of Field's Hill in Pinetown was also used as a staging post.

Mules and muleteers

Mules and donkeys were probably the unsung heroes of the war and not much was recorded about them. A refugee from Johannesburg, Billing-ton, who arrived in Durban in October 1899 immediately offered his services to the military as a conductor or muleteer. He had 'exceptional knowledge of these animals having been for some years on a mule ranch in Montana'.[42] When he went to Pietermaritzburg to apply to the director of transports he found that there were already 400 applications for a few conductor and sub-conductor posts and 'they never thought of offering the post of driver to any one but a Cape boy'. He was told that the Army Service Corps did not want white men as drivers, and recorded the fol-lowing:

We told him we were not aware that Cape boys had any monopoly of driving ... then they tried to scare us over the rations, saying only mealie meal would be given ... eventually our services were accepted ... everything, however was in fearful confusion, and not until forty-one hours had elapsed after joining could we draw anything to eat ... The next day our regular work began. We were allowed to pick our own teams, and I got a good one. They had to be watered and grazed, and at night had two feeds of grain ... meantime my duties were augmented by the conductors assigning to me the task of recording the number and description of every one of the one hundred and twelve mules in the lines, to which even the much-approved Cape boy was not equal.[43]

Horse, mules and donkeys used for transport (Pinetown Museum).

Emaciated horses in the field (Riall).

The mayor of Durban complained to the prime minister about the presence in Durban of such Cape boys in November 1899.[44]

The mule was essentially an animal with Spanish origins and much used in the New World, and the British seemed to have lacked the appropriate experience. Billington observed how the incorrect techniques which they used verged on cruelty. He made an important observation about the breast collar harness used on the mules, saying that he 'could only marvel that it has never received censure from the Royal Society for the Prevention of Cruelty to Animals'. Unless it was very carefully adjusted, it cut off the animal's breathing, and if it slipped too low the mule could not get a 'fair draught of its load'. He recommended to the colonial conductors that 'collar and harnes' should be used instead. Needless to say, such a recommendation was not taken seriously, though it may have lengthened or saved the lives of many mules.

The inconvenience of dead donkeys

A sad tale was related about several donkeys which died in 1903, near the Westville Hotel en route from the Point to Gilletts, and the story served as a reminder of the abuse of such animals during the war. The donkeys were left unburied for some time which 'caused a great nuisance to the public'. Dr Ernest Hill, as the first health officer for the colony, wrote to the colonial secretary to remind the general officer commanding that 'when any of the District Sanitary Inspectors or of the Natal Police (sic) notify to the Remount Department that dead animals belonging to them are lying by the road-side, or elsewhere, so as to be an inconvenience, (sic) that it is their duty immediately without delay to provide for their burial'.[45]

1. Port Elizabeth Tourism Bureau.

2. Van der Merwe, F, Perde in Suid-Afrika en Suid-Afrikaanse Perdetipes, in Thompson, N, *Die Wêreld van die perd.* p.32–33.

3. *With the Flag to Pretoria* Vol. 1, p.213.

4. Pretorius, F, *Life on Commando during the Anglo-Boer War 1899–1902*, pp.33–40.

5. Amery, LS, (ed), *The Times History of the War in South Africa 1899–1900*, Vol. VI, pp.411, 442.

6. *Encyclopaedia Britannica* Vol. XXVI, 9th Edition, 1903, pp.622–624.

7. *The Colonies in the War, The Transvaal War 1899–1900*, Illustrated London News, p.60.

8. KCM 2035: Dawes, H Edmund, 29.7.1939.

9. PRO, WO 32/8761: general report on remount operations in South Africa, 30.3.1903.

10. Amery, LS, (ed.), *The Times History of the War in South Africa*, Vol. IV, pp.650–658.

11. Ibid. p.428.

12. *Royal Commission of Enquiry into the War in South Africa*, pp.97–98.

13. *Natal Witness*, 20.7.1900.

14. *Natal Witness*, 15.9.1900.

15. *Royal Commission*, p.43.

16. PRO, WO 108/117: commander in chief, South Africa to quartermaster general, 10.5.1902.

17. PAR, PVS 2: Watkins Pitchford to minister of agriculture, 11.1.1899.

18. Rolando, SC, *Natal Veterinary Services 1874–1912*, p.140.

19. PAR, PVS 59: minute papers, 16.2.1900.

20. PAR, PVS 6: district veterinary surgeon to acting principal veterinary surgeon, 9.10.1900.

21. *Royal Commission on the War in South Africa*, p.19.

22. Ibid., p.19.

23. PRO, WO 32/8761: miscellaneous questions affecting remount depots, 31.5.1902.

24. Ibid.

25. PAR, CSO 1670: SG Campbell to town clerk, Durban, 10.3.1901.

26. PAR, CSO 1670: mayor of Durban to colonial secretary, 12.3.1901.

27. PAR, CSO 1670: Turner to colonial secretary, 22.3.1901.

28. PAR, CSO 1670: report of the plague officer, AD Cameron, 25.3.1901.

29. PAR, CSO 1670: Hill to colonial secretary, 21.5.1901.

30. PAR, CSO 1670: general officer commanding, Natal to prime minister, 5.7.1901.

31. Hill, E, *Report on the Plague in Natal*, passim.

32. PAR, CSO 1670: report by Dr E Hill, 29.4.1901.

33. DAR, 3/DBN 5/2/6/1/17: town council standing committees, 3.4.1902.

34. PRO, CO 179/220: documents concerning war department lands, 27.8.1901–27.11.1901.

35. DAR, 3/DBN 5/2/6/1/15: town council standing committee, 3.6.1901.

36. PRO, WO 108/296: report on the work of the Royal Engineers in Natal, 1899–1902.

37. Personal communication, Mrs Halsted.

38. PRO, WO 32/8761: remount depots in South Africa, 31.5.1902.

39. *The Register of War Graves in Natal*, 1904, p.211.

40. PAR, PVS 24: Dr ST Amos to principal veterinary surgeon, 28.4.1903.

41. PRO, WO 108/296: report on the work of the royal engineers in Natal, 24.6.1902.

42. Billington, HC, *A Mule-driver at the Front*, pp.2–5.

43. Ibid., p.5.

44. PAR, MJPW 72: mayor to prime minister, 22.11.1899.

45. PAR, CSO 1722: Dr E Hill to colonial secretary, 24.1.1903.

46. *Highway Mail*, 19.11.1999.

PART FOUR

DURBAN: MEDICAL SERVICES

Wounded being carried from the Princess Christian ambulance train
(*The Graphic* 2.12.1899).

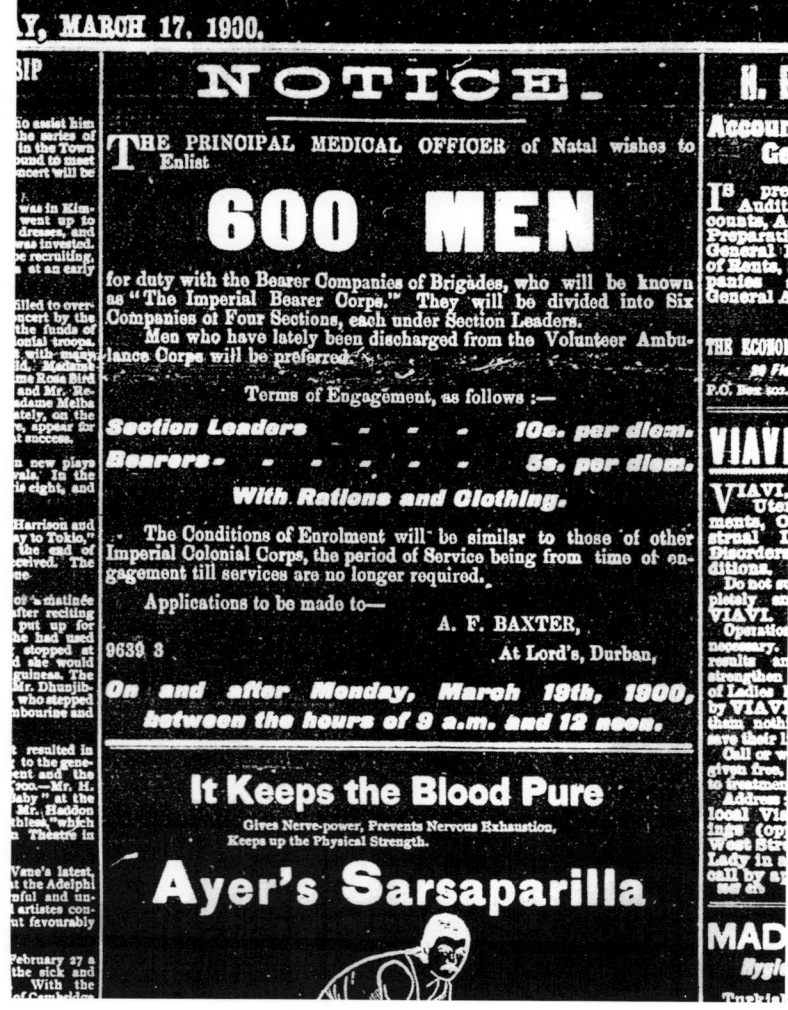

CHAPTER 12

MEDICAL SERVICES
Graeme Fuller

Introduction

The citizens of Durban were affected by the medical challenges of the Anglo-Boer War in several different ways. Local doctors, nurses and medical orderlies forming part of the volunteer force were mobilised and many of them were soon under siege in Ladysmith. Civilian hospital staff received extra patients from amongst the sick and wounded soldiers, and the refugees pouring into Durban from the Transvaal brought a new set of social problems and diseases, further stretching the facilities.

The newly formed Royal Army Medical Corps (RAMC) set about preparing for the campaign by establishing a base depot for medical stores in Durban and by arranging the conversion of trains and ships for the care and transport of the wounded. The excellent engineering skills available in Durban were put to good use by the military authorities. The Durban Women's Patriotic League assisted in the preparation of bandages, pads for splints and similar items.

The subjects of ambulance trains and hospital ships are covered in Chapter 14. These formed an integrated part of the system for evacuation and treatment of patients and contributed to the overall success of medical arrangements in Natal. The foresight and dedication of Lieutenant Colonel PW Johnston, senior medical officer in Natal during the preparation phase of the Natal Campaign, deserves special mention. He was generously assisted in all his endeavours by David Hunter, general manager of the NGR, and their efforts laid the foundations for the subsequent conclusion that: 'Of all the medical arrangements during the war, those during Sir Redvers Buller's campaign in Natal presented the most satisfactory features.' [1]

Many British and colonial troops with attached medical units passed through the city en route to the front, initially during the Natal campaign but also long after its conclusion. Durban remained the closest route for evacuation by sea to Cape Town and to Britain of sick and wounded from the Free State and the Transvaal.

A sponsored hospital, paid for by Alfred Moseley, a London businessman, was erected on land at Pinetown Bridge. The land and existing buildings were donated by Frank Stevens of Durban and the hospital was named after Princess Christian, daughter of Queen Victoria. The full story is told in Chapter 15. The Princess Christian Hospital was a major component of the evacuation chain, connected by three ambulance trains, one of which was also named after Princess Christian. The chain ended on board hospital ships in the port of Durban, which were used to accommodate as well as to transport casualties. The Princess Christian Hospital was later taken over by the RAMC and became the 13 Stationary Hospital. The officers' mess then functioned as the RAMC headquarters mess for Natal, serving as a residential and social facility for medical officers in transit to and from the front.

An important initiative was undertaken by a group of local Indians including Mohandas K Gandhi, then in legal practice in Durban. He offered the services of and subsequently organised a group of Indian volunteers into a corps of stretcher-bearers, known as the Indian Ambulance Corps. He was assisted in this venture by a medical missionary, Lancelot Parker Booth, the founder of St Aidan's Indian Mission, who trained the volunteers in their professional duties and accompanied them in the field. The story is dealt with in Chapter 13.

Another component of medical support to the fighting troops was the Natal Volunteer Ambulance Corps, raised mainly in Durban on the initiative of Colonel (later Sir) Thomas Gallwey, principal medical officer in Natal during Buller's campaign. This corps, commanded and trained by Major Wright, consisted largely of refugees from the Transvaal and eventually numbered 1800.[2] It rendered excellent service in the campaign leading up to the relief of Ladysmith and was disbanded thereafter.[3] A further unit, entitled the Imperial Bearer Corps, was raised in March 1900.

DLI Ambulance detachment, 1895 (DLI Collection).

Natal Volunteer Medical Corps

When responsible government was granted to the Colony of Natal in 1893, it was anticipated that imperial troops would be withdrawn over a period of five years, allowing the colonists sufficient time to make arrangements for their own defence. In pursuing this objective, the Volunteer Act (No. 23 of 1895, dated 8 August) reorganised the administration of the volunteer force in Natal.

Regulations under this act published in August 1895[4] and in July 1899[5] provided for the training of ambulance personnel by major units and the formation of a Natal Volunteer Medical Corps (NVMC). This was made up from the ambulance detachments of all volunteer units in the colony, under the overall control of a principal medical officer. The system was put into practice during the annual volunteer camp held at Richmond in 1898, and when the call came to mobilise for the outbreak of war the Volunteer Medical Corps was ready.

The medical officers

The medical officers already serving in the various Natal units were re-appointed into the Volunteer Medical Corps on 11 July 1899,[6] and medical support was then provided for each major unit during the early phases of the campaign. The principal medical officer was Major James Hyslop.

In 1899 there were 173 medical practitioners registered to practise

Major Hyslop, (later Lieutenant Colonel, D.S.O.) was the medical superintendent of the Natal Government Asylum in Pietermaritzburg, Surgeon to the Natal Carbineers and later president of the Natal Medical Council. Major Hyslop was born in Scotland and educated in Edinburgh, Berlin, Vienna and Munich. He was based in Ladysmith during the siege, in overall charge of volunteer hospitals and in control of medical support to Natal volunteer units. He was also involved at Laing's Nek in June 1900 and again in 1901. He commanded his unit in the Bambata Campaign (1906). The Distinguished Service Order was presented to him by the king on 29 October 1901. He was mentioned in Sir George White's and in Lord Roberts' despatches.

Archie McKenzie and Sam Campbell (Campbell, E).

Sam Campbell seems to have developed a taste for military activities because he remained active as a combatant officer in the DLI after the war and later distinguished himself in command of the DLI contingent in the Bambata Rebellion (1906). He apparently helped to attend to the wounded on both sides of the conflict after the end of the day's fighting. He played an enormous part in the medical, social, political and academic life of Durban in subsequent years and was instrumental in the establishment of both the Natal Technical College and Natal University College.

in Natal. Of these, 92 had known addresses in the colony, 23 were living elsewhere and there were 58 whose addresses were unknown.[7] At least 22 appear to have been active in the greater Durban area and five Durban doctors are known to have been mobilised for service with the local volunteer units at different stages of the war.

The medical officers accompanying the Durban Light Infantry were Lieutenant AW Hall, Lieutenant DJ McG Campbell and Honorary Lieutenant SG (Sam) Campbell. Dr Hall had been in practice in Durban since 1896 and was appointed additional surgeon to the DLI on 14 April 1897.[8] He was an active and enthusiastic member of the unit and his death from enteric fever on active service on 20 September 1900 was a great loss. He was the only NVMC officer to lose his life during the Anglo-Boer War.

Dr Archibald McKenzie had been appointed surgeon to the DLI on 18 February 1897, after the resignation of his predecessor, Surgeon Lieutenant Harrison, in May 1896. He was later to play a very prominent role in both military and civilian medical affairs in Natal. He was on leave overseas during the latter part of 1899, but appears to have entered into a private agreement with his lifelong friend and practice partner, Dr S.G (Sam) Campbell, to alternate their periods of military service.

The result was that Sam Campbell was appointed honorary lieutenant and went to war with the DLI, leaving McKenzie to run the practice. He expected to be relieved by McKenzie after two weeks, but instead became incarcerated in Ladysmith. He wrote a fascinating illustrated diary during the siege, giving graphic details of his experiences.[9] This has not been published in full but extracts appear in the story of his life,[10] originally a full-colour illustrated manuscript but later reproduced in red and black print and published privately, with appendices. The entry for Monday 27 November includes the following:

> How I long to be away from all this. McKenzie could
> come up and welcome if only we had rain connection
> but that seems a long way off. It was a dreadful over-
> sight to come away without a photograph of my dar-
> ling wife and children. I thought of course it was only
> to be 14 days and now it will soon be six weeks since
> I left ...[11]

Sam Campbell was tasked by Major Hyslop to assist at the volunteer hospital established outside Ladysmith at Ntombi. This hospital was under the control of Captain OJ Currie, formerly of the Natal Carbineers. Much more privation, distressing and frustrating work, malnutrition and ill health were to follow before Ladysmith was relieved. A total of 10 673 patients had been treated at Ntombi alone by 28 February 1900 and there were 583 deaths, 382 from typhoid and 109 from dysentery.[12]

Dr Archibald McKenzie, who had met Sam Campbell as a fellow Natalian at Edinburgh University, had subsequently shared digs with him in Edinburgh and then from 1889 had practised in partnership with him in Durban. McKenzie did not commence active service until 24 February 1900, by which time Ladysmith had been relieved and Sam Campbell was over the worst of his ordeal. At this time, McKenzie had realised the need for a residential facility to cope with volunteers convalescing after being released from the siege. A committee raised funds and found a suitable venue at Lancaster Lodge, Aliwal Street, Durban. This volunteer convalescent club remained in existence for eight months and provided free board and medical care for its occupants, the medical care being provided by Dr Sam Campbell when McKenzie left for the war. He rendered distinguished service in the Anglo-Boer War and was promoted to captain.

The fourth local doctor who served in the war was Dr David J McG Campbell, who also practised in Durban, and had assisted with training and medical support for the DLI during Dr McKenzie's absence in 1899. He was commissioned as a lieutenant in the NVMC on 7 September 1899. He was not in the siege but served in the relieving column and was involved in action at Frere.

Dr HE Fernandez was medical officer to the Natal Naval Volunteers,[14] ranking as surgeon lieutenant and was reappointed to the NVMC on 11 July 1899 with the relative rank of captain in the army. He was also incarcerated in Ladysmith and was attached to the component of the volunteer hospital which remained in the town. He was called upon to provide relief at Ntombi from time to time, due to illness of his colleagues, as recorded in Sam Campbell's diary. After the relief of Ladysmith he returned to his civilian duties but retained his maritime connection as chief medical officer for the port of Durban. He was much involved with the inspection of vessels for plague, which had reached epidemic proportions in Cape Town.

The other medical officers mobilised with the NVMC, with their parent units listed and showing ranks as at the end of the campaign, were as follows:

Captain OJ Currie (Natal Carbineers), from Pietermaritzburg, medical officer in charge of the Volunteer Hospital at Ntombi.

Captain HT Platt (Border Mounted Rifles) from Ixopo. He is famous for recommending the boot and spur as crest badge for the BMR. This is now the collar badge of the Natal Mounted Rifles, which absorbed the BMR in 1913.[15] He was praised for his coolness under heavy fire at Bester's Kop, when he assisted the wounded Captain Arnott whilst

Dr Sam Campbell as a major in the DLI, 1906 (Campbell, E).

Natal Naval Volunteers: Officers 1900. Surgeon Lieutenant Fernandez second from left, back row (Payne).

Dr McKenzie remained active in the Natal Medical Corps and later in the SAMC, rising to command the Durban company of the Natal Medical Corps as a major in 1906. He was a consultant to the Durban base hospital in World War 1 and was eventually honorary colonel of 1 Field Ambulance, Durban in 1937. His son, Dr (Lt Col) Duncan McKenzie, also commanded the Natal Field Ambulance from 1921. The McKenzie tartan was adopted in their honour in 1939 and continues to be worn by the present unit, now designated 1 Medical Battalion Group and still based in Durban. Dr McKenzie was a member of the Natal Medical Council and president of the local branch of the British Medical Association. He was chairman of the board of governors of his old school, Hilton College, from 1908 to 1934 and became a South African Party senator in 1929.[13]

awaiting a safe opportunity to bring up stretcher-bearers. He was twice mentioned in Sir George White's despatches. He was also involved in the Bambata Campaign.

Captain RA Buntine (Natal Royal Rifles – disbanded in 1913) from Australia, practised in Pietermaritzburg. He was the first member of entire Natal field force to earn a mention in despatches (by General Sir George White), after rescuing a wounded comrade under fire in the face of the enemy and bringing another wounded trooper to safety.[16] Later he was in charge of the volunteer hospitals in Ladysmith and in the Natal Legislative Assembly building in Pietermaritzburg.[17]

Captain CA Bowker (Border Mounted Rifles) from Port Shepstone served at Ntombi Volunteer Hospital.[18]

Lieutenant JE Briscoe (Natal Royal Rifles) remained outside Ladysmith.

Lieutenant William Black from Weenen: service unknown.

Lieutenant JE Neale and Lieutenant HB Currie from Johannesburg were in Ladysmith during the siege.[19]

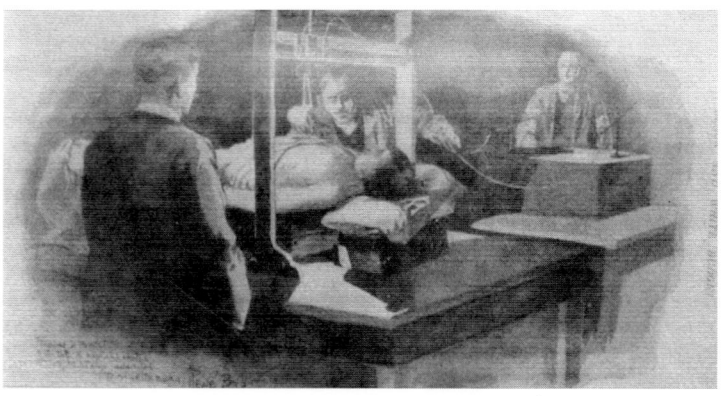

X-ray apparatus in use at the military hospital, Pietermaritzburg (*Black and White Budget*, Feb 1900).

Lieutenant RW Hornabrook (Natal Mounted Rifles) was sent from India to the Transvaal mines as a plague expert and volunteered for service with the NVMC. He rendered distinguished military service at Elandslaagte, where he captured 24 armed Boers single-handedly, and also during a Boer attack on Caesar's Hill camp, when although wounded himself, he rallied a party of Gordon Highlanders, whose own officers had been killed. He was mentioned in despatches.[20]

Civil Surgeons:[21]

Dr RP Mitchell, later medical officer to the Natal Volunteer Composite Regiment.

Dr A Wight, Dr Bride and Dr H Rochfort Brown (details of service unknown).

Mr A Allerston, radiographer, was in control of the NVMC X-ray machine.[22, 23]

A total of 18 nursing sisters served with the corps in the siege, six in Ladysmith town and 12 at Ntombi. Sister Lucy A Yeatman was in charge at Ntombi.[24] Constance Addison was the sister of a Durban doctor. The origins of the other nurses have not been traced. Their services were so much appreciated that they were each presented with commemorative silver shield brooches by the men of the Natal Mounted Rifles.[25] Eight Royal Red Cross nursing decorations were also awarded.

The following NVMC nursing sisters were mentioned in Sir George White's despatch of 2 December 1899: Lucy Yeatman, S. Otto, Ethel Early, Margaret Nicolson, Chrissie Thompson, Kate Driver, Kate Champion, R Davies, Santje Ruiter and Elaine Bromilow.[26]

Sergeant Major McLellan and 54 NCOs and men comprised the remaining members of the NVMC, drawn from each of the volunteer units. Troopers GWJ Thomas and S Harrop and Private J Waller lost their lives during the Natal Campaign.

Elements of the unit were officially credited with the following engagements: Klip Kraal, 18 October 1899; Elandslaagte, 21 October; Tinta Nyoni, 24 October; Lombard's Kop, 30 October; siege of Lady-

Natal volunteer hospital established in the Legislative Assembly building, Pietermaritzburg after the relief of Ladysmith (*Black and White Budget*, Feb 1900)

smith, End Hill, 3 November; Willow Grange, 23 November; sortie on Gun Hill, 7/8 December; Ladysmith, 6 January 1900; Acton Homes, 17 January; Vaal Krantz, Tugela actions and relief of Ladysmith, February 1900; Pepworth Hill, 2 March.

Apart from the volunteer hospitals established in Ladysmith and at Ntombi during the siege, the unit also staffed and ran the Assembly Hospital in Pietermaritzburg (50 beds) and a volunteer hospital in Dundee, active from June until at least September 1900.[27, 28] They were demobilised and returned home in October 1900.

Some members were called out again in 1901, including Major Hyslop. Hospital Sergant Major AC Wearner of the Composite Regiment of Natal Volunteers was mentioned in Lord Kitchener's despatches of 23 June 1902. He was also awarded the Distinguished Conduct Medal (D.C.M.).

Durban (Addington) Hospital and civilians engaged in Natal

In his evidence to the Royal Commission, Dr J Hamilton Balfe, medical superintendent of the Durban Hospital (Addington), stated that his hospital had not in general been used for the care of the sick and wounded in the war, but had assisted with care of several patients from 'the hospitals'. It did not receive any patients from the front.[29] It is noted elsewhere,[30, 31] however, that extra wards were installed at Addington during this and other wars. Statistical returns for the war period indicate that admissions almost doubled from 1 191 in 1898 to 1 973 in 1901. The ratio of males to females was 1 117 to 187 in 1901, which must indicate an abnormal situation brought about by wartime conditions.[32]

The disruption of civilian medical services and of society in general may be appreciated from Colonel Gallwey's figures for 'Numbers of Medical Practitioners (78), Nurses (145) and Subordinate Hospital Staff (European 700, Native 560) (Total = 1 483) engaged locally in Natal'.[33] These surprisingly high figures exclude persons in the volunteer units, those recruited in Britain and members of the Natal Volunteer Ambulance and Imperial Bearer Corps. Some medical practitioners were refugees from the Boer republics. Others came independently from Britain and elsewhere.

Royal Army Medical Corps

The Royal Army Medical Corps was in its infancy at the outbreak of the Anglo-Boer War. Its long and painful gestation had continued for over 40 years, with constant prodding from Florence Nightingale. The unsatisfactory conditions she had witnessed in the Crimean War had been due to a combination of scientific ineptitude, administrative chaos both in the army and the medical system and conservatism combined with indifference on the part of senior military authorities.

The NVMC was reorganised in 1903 and was mobilised again in 1906 for the Bambata Rebellion, under the title Natal Medical Corps (NMC). After the formation of the South African Medical Corps in 1913, the NMC was absorbed and Natal units were thereafter redesignated several times. Three Natal Field Ambulances (2 FA, 2 MBFA, 5 MBFA) were involved in the South West African Campaign and finally in 1935 the Durban Unit became 1 Field Ambulance. This was amalgamated with 17 FA in 1981 to form the current 1 Medical Battalion Group, SA Military Health Service (Reserve Force), which has proudly inherited the history of its parent units and is still based in Durban.

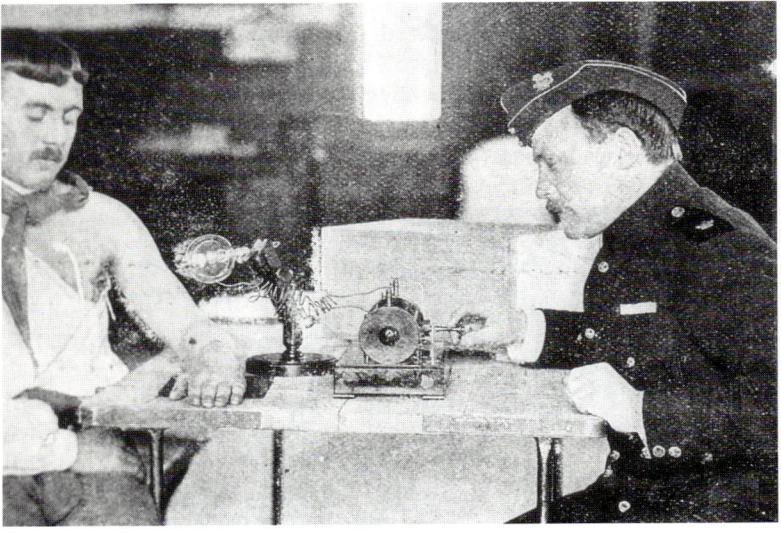

X-ray apparatus in use in Natal (Newnes).

Addington Hospital, ca. 1895 (Kearney collection).

Preparations in Britain

Meanwhile preparations were taking place in Britain and medical support units for an army corps, One Cavalry Division, and lines of communication were activated. The regular establishment of the RAMC did not possess sufficient personnel for this task and so various categories of reserves were also mobilised. Recruitment was begun and St John's Ambulance provided trained personnel for army service. It was soon recognised that civilian surgeons and other trained medical personnel would also be needed.

By the end of 1901 only 42% of medical officers in the field were RAMC regulars, 4% were volunteers and colonials and the remaining 54% were 'civil surgeons', most engaged by the war office.

Eight distinguished consultant surgeons were employed by the government at an impressive salary of £5 000 per annum. This somewhat controversial expense was justified on the grounds that the government could be seen to be providing the best possible care for the troops. It also meant that authoritative commentary was available at first hand from these respected surgeons. The best known amongst these was Mr (later Sir) Frederick Treves, who wrote an account of his work with the 4th Stationary Hospital in Natal.[42]

The full story of the work of the RAMC in Natal is beyond the scope of this book, but the development of the medical system in Natal is of some importance, since this system made use of Durban to accommodate and evacuate the sick and wounded.

Sir Frederick Treves (Fuller collection).

McCormack-Brook wheeled stretcher carriage

McCormack and Brook designed a 'wheeled stretcher carriage', complete with springs and rubber tyres and this design was adopted for use in Natal and elsewhere. It combined the virtues of mobility, strength and lightness and could be handled by one man on good roads or by two in rough country and added greatly to the comfort of the occupant in comparison to a stretcher.

Build-up in Natal

Troops already in Natal were formed into the 4th Division and they made use of the field hospitals, which had come from India. When General Buller arrived in South Africa on 31 October 1899, he divided his army corps and diverted the 2nd Division from the Cape to Natal, the 2nd and 4th Brigades having their medical units with them. The medical units of the 5th and 6th Brigades had rejoined by 12 December. The former field hospital for corps units was attached as a divisional hospital and the newly formed 9th Brigade received the divisional hospital of the 1st Division and the 3rd Brigade Bearer Company. During December, No. 4 General Hospital was also sent to Natal and was opened at Mooi River.

The 5th Division with its medical units complete, arrived in Natal at the end of December, followed by the 6th Division complete by 20 January 1900. By this stage the pool of available trained personnel of the RAMC had been used up and subsequent reinforcements were largely untrained.

No.1 Base Medical Stores & No.1 Advanced Depot

No. 1 Base Depot was established in Durban on 6 November 1899 to formalise control over medical stores. It was under the command of Major R McCormack, RAMC, assisted by Lieutenant Quartermaster Brook, two other RAMC staff and some civilians. A goods shed adjacent to the central station was made available by David Hunter, manager of the NGR. This was a convenient location for receiving supplies by train from the docks and for loading prior to movement inland by goods train.[44]

The McCormack-Brook wheeled stretcher carriage (Wilson).

smith, End Hill, 3 November; Willow Grange, 23 November; sortie on Gun Hill, 7/8 December; Ladysmith, 6 January 1900; Acton Homes, 17 January; Vaal Krantz, Tugela actions and relief of Ladysmith, February 1900; Pepworth Hill, 2 March.

Apart from the volunteer hospitals established in Ladysmith and at Ntombi during the siege, the unit also staffed and ran the Assembly Hospital in Pietermaritzburg (50 beds) and a volunteer hospital in Dundee, active from June until at least September 1900.[27, 28] They were demobilised and returned home in October 1900.

Some members were called out again in 1901, including Major Hyslop. Hospital Sergant Major AC Wearner of the Composite Regiment of Natal Volunteers was mentioned in Lord Kitchener's despatches of 23 June 1902. He was also awarded the Distinguished Conduct Medal (D.C.M.).

Durban (Addington) Hospital and civilians engaged in Natal

In his evidence to the Royal Commission, Dr J Hamilton Balfe, medical superintendent of the Durban Hospital (Addington), stated that his hospital had not in general been used for the care of the sick and wounded in the war, but had assisted with care of several patients from 'the hospitals'. It did not receive any patients from the front.[29] It is noted elsewhere,[30, 31] however, that extra wards were installed at Addington during this and other wars. Statistical returns for the war period indicate that admissions almost doubled from 1 191 in 1898 to 1 973 in 1901. The ratio of males to females was 1 117 to 187 in 1901, which must indicate an abnormal situation brought about by wartime conditions.[32]

The disruption of civilian medical services and of society in general may be appreciated from Colonel Gallwey's figures for 'Numbers of Medical Practitioners (78), Nurses (145) and Subordinate Hospital Staff (European 700, Native 550) (Total = 1 483) engaged locally in Natal'.[33] These surprisingly high figures exclude persons in the volunteer units, those recruited in Britain and members of the Natal Volunteer Ambulance and Imperial Bearer Corps. Some medical practitioners were refugees from the Boer republics. Others came independently from Britain and elsewhere.

Royal Army Medical Corps

The Royal Army Medical Corps was in its infancy at the outbreak of the Anglo-Boer War. Its long and painful gestation had continued for over 40 years, with constant prodding from Florence Nightingale. The unsatisfactory conditions she had witnessed in the Crimean War had been due to a combination of scientific ineptitude, administrative chaos both in the army and the medical system and conservatism combined with indifference on the part of senior military authorities.

The NVMC was reorganised in 1903 and was mobilised again in 1906 for the Bambata Rebellion, under the title Natal Medical Corps (NMC). After the formation of the South African Medical Corps in 1913, the NMC was absorbed and Natal units were thereafter redesignated several times. Three Natal Field Ambulances (2 FA, 2 MBFA, 5 MBFA) were involved in the South West African Campaign and finally in 1935 the Durban Unit became 1 Field Ambulance. This was amalgamated with 17 FA in 1981 to form the current 1 Medical Battalion Group, SA Military Health Service (Reserve Force), which has proudly inherited the history of its parent units and is still based in Durban.

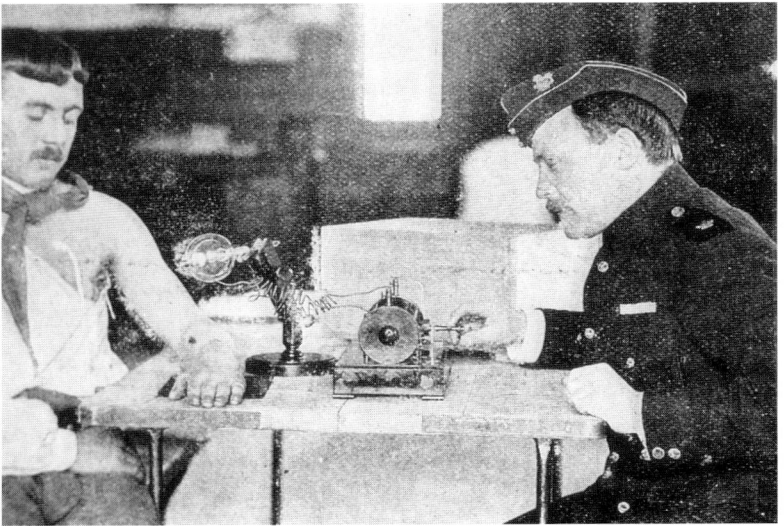

X-ray apparatus in use in Natal (Newnes).

Addington Hospital, ca. 1895 (Kearney collection).

Advances in medical science

There had been substantial advances in medical science in the latter half of the nineteenth century. The causes and methods of prevention of bacterial disease were well understood, although antibiotics took another half century to appear. Wound sepsis was often fatal but was less frequent under South African conditions than it was later under trench conditions in Europe. Effective remedies for many other diseases had been developed. Inoculation against typhoid, developed by Professor Almroth Wright at the Army Medical School, Netley, was proving to be beneficial, but its side effects were unpleasant and it was regarded with suspicion by the troops.

Simple common sense advice regarding purification of water and basic sanitary measures to protect the environment were made available to the troops and their officers, but was routinely disregarded and preventive measures were not effectively enforced.[4] The appalling toll of disease, particularly typhoid (also called enteric fever) and dysentery amongst the troops (including medical staff) and the victims of concentration camps, has been extensively documented elsewhere and is now well known. Although definitive antibiotic treatment had not yet been developed, such symptomatic and supportive measures as were available were rendered less effective by inadequate water supplies, persisting poor sanitation and ineffective measures to curb cross-infection under crowded conditions. Malnutrition brought about by siege conditions also made recovery from wounds or disease much less likely. The experiences of Campbell[35] give moving testimony to the suffering of all concerned and the impact of disease on the conduct of the war is apparent from various official reports. More recently De Villiers[36] has provided important insight and a modern scientific interpretation of the medical aspects of the war from both Boer and British perspectives.

Anaesthesia was routinely available, if not entirely safe, so that surgery had become less barbaric and more successful, but intravenous fluid administration for resuscitation and rehydration was still in the future. X-rays were already a reality and apparatus was made widely available with commendable speed in time for the war in South Africa.

The struggle for recognition

The army had failed to recognise the improved status in society now enjoyed by the medical profession. This had been earned by greater professionalism and sound scientific endeavour, but within the military system the doctor was tolerated with reluctance by the combatant officers and had no authority over troops. In 1854 each regiment had one or more surgeons, employed by the regiment and responsible to the officer commanding for the health of his troops. There was no co-ordination or supervision of medical officers and no opportunity for further training. A separate army medical department (AMD) existed and maintained control over garrison and camp hospitals, but did not interfere with regimental arrangements. This department had little influence in the higher

Inoculations on board ship (Cunliffe).

echelons of military administration and its director general was not even attached to the war office until 1869.[37]

A Royal Commission sat after the Crimean War and made recommendations, which brought about some improvements. These included a military hospital and an Army Medical School at Netley (Southampton), later moved to Millbank in London. An Army Hospital Corps (AHC) of orderlies and stretcher-bearers also came into being. Attempts were made to instil pride and professionalism instead of relegating these tasks to persons unfit for real soldiering.

In 1873 all regimental hospitals were abolished and replaced by properly constituted garrison hospitals, with laboratories, libraries and instruction facilities and all medical officers were brought under the control of the army medical department.

The AHC remained nevertheless a corps without officers and the AMD had no subordinates. This manifest absurdity, based primarily upon reluctance to give medical officers the authority to command troops, was allowed to persist until 1884, when AMD officers were put in command of AHC troops and the latter corps was redesignated as the Medical Staff Corps. Medical officers were still denied full military status and a set of cumbersome hybrid titles was devised for them. Their pay was less than that of other officers, in spite of better education and professional qualifications. Morale and recruitment in the army medical service was at an all-time low and many medical schools actively advised graduates against a military career.[38] Examinations for entry ceased and any applicant was accepted. Many of these were Irish graduates, who rendered distinguished service in later years. In spite of these limiting factors a great deal of good work was done by those remaining in the service and research of high quality was conducted.

The British Medical Association campaigned ceaselessly for improved conditions and standards and a special subcommittee reported in 1897 that:

> It is impossible ... to regard with equanimity the prospects of a great war. If such a calamity were to overtake us, it is difficult to see how we could avoid the utter collapse of the medical arrangements. A spectacle of misery and mortality, to equal which we must look back to the horrors of the Crimea, would not be a matter for astonishment.[39]

Under this sort of pressure the war office finally brought about sweeping changes and announced the birth of the new corps on 23 June 1898. The secretary for war, Lord Lansdowne, made a generous speech at a Guildhall dinner in which he referred to medical officers in the following terms:

> We are determined that there shall be no failure, either in theory or in practice, to treat them with the respect to which they are entitled. I insist on this point, because I have observed with very keen regret that there has existed for some time an estrangement between the Army and the profession.[40]

He also referred to the rank and status of medical staff and announced that:

> We propose a fresh start and to form, out of the Army Medical Staff and the Medical Staff Corps – a Corps, the officers of which will bear the same military titles as other officers of the Army, always on the clear understanding that these titles do not confer upon them any right of command outside it. We propose to give them these titles up to the rank of Colonel. Above that rank, we propose to retain that of Surgeon-General, with the rank and precedence of a general officer in the Army.
>
> Her Majesty, upon whose goodwill towards your profession I need not dwell, has been pleased to signify her intention of bestowing upon the newly formed Corps the title of Royal Army Medical Corps, a title which I am sure it will wear worthily.

Such was the background to the British army medical service at the start of the Anglo-Boer War. The motto adopted by the new corps, *In Arduis Fidelis*, was soon to be amply put to the test.

Arrangements in South Africa

In May 1899 there were 8 628 British troops in South Africa, of which 4 478 were in Natal. Colonel FJ Supple was the principal medical officer, based in Cape Town and responsible for the Cape and Natal. Lieutenant Colonel PH Johnston was senior medical officer in Natal, in charge of the Military Hospital in Pietermaritzburg. There were 28 RAMC doctors, three nursing sisters and 132 other RAMC troops in the country.[41]

In Pietermaritzburg a well-established 90-bed hospital existed in Fort Napier and there was a hutted hospital in the military camp in Ladysmith. A medical store existed in Cape Town and, when it appeared that hostilities might commence in Natal, stocks of medical and surgical equipment were gradually transferred to Durban and from there to Pietermaritzburg and to Ladysmith. With admirable foresight, Lieutenant Colonel Johnston made arrangements with the manager of the NGR to prepare a hospital train.

In October 1899 a large contingent arrived in Durban from India, bringing troops accompanied by three and a half British field hospitals and one so-called 'native' (i.e. Indian) field hospital.

Preparations in Britain

Meanwhile preparations were taking place in Britain and medical support units for an army corps, One Cavalry Division, and lines of communication were activated. The regular establishment of the RAMC did not possess sufficient personnel for this task and so various categories of reserves were also mobilised. Recruitment was begun and St John's Ambulance provided trained personnel for army service. It was soon recognised that civilian surgeons and other trained medical personnel would also be needed.

By the end of 1901 only 42% of medical officers in the field were RAMC regulars, 4% were volunteers and colonials and the remaining 54% were 'civil surgeons', most engaged by the war office.

Eight distinguished consultant surgeons were employed by the government at an impressive salary of £5 000 per annum. This somewhat controversial expense was justified on the grounds that the government could be seen to be providing the best possible care for the troops. It also meant that authoritative commentary was available at first hand from these respected surgeons. The best known amongst these was Mr (later Sir) Frederick Treves, who wrote an account of his work with the 4th Stationary Hospital in Natal.[42]

The full story of the work of the RAMC in Natal is beyond the scope of this book, but the development of the medical system in Natal is of some importance, since this system made use of Durban to accommodate and evacuate the sick and wounded.

Sir Frederick Treves (Fuller collection).

McCormack-Brook wheeled stretcher carriage

McCormack and Brook designed a 'wheeled stretcher carriage', complete with springs and rubber tyres and this design was adopted for use in Natal and elsewhere. It combined the virtues of mobility, strength and lightness and could be handled by one man on good roads or by two in rough country and added greatly to the comfort of the occupant in comparison to a stretcher.

Build-up in Natal

Troops already in Natal were formed into the 4th Division and they made use of the field hospitals, which had come from India. When General Buller arrived in South Africa on 31 October 1899, he divided his army corps and diverted the 2nd Division from the Cape to Natal, the 2nd and 4th Brigades having their medical units with them. The medical units of the 5th and 6th Brigades had rejoined by 12 December. The former field hospital for corps units was attached as a divisional hospital and the newly formed 9th Brigade received the divisional hospital of the 1st Division and the 3rd Brigade Bearer Company.[43] During December, No. 4 General Hospital was also sent to Natal and was opened at Mooi River.

The 5th Division with its medical units complete, arrived in Natal at the end of December, followed by the 6th Division complete by 20 January 1900. By this stage the pool of available trained personnel of the RAMC had been used up and subsequent reinforcements were largely untrained.

No.1 Base Medical Stores & No.1 Advanced Depot

No. 1 Base Depot was established in Durban on 6 November 1899 to formalise control over medical stores. It was under the command of Major R McCormack, RAMC, assisted by Lieutenant Quartermaster Brook, two other RAMC staff and some civilians. A goods shed adjacent to the central station was made available by David Hunter, manager of the NGR. This was a convenient location for receiving supplies by train from the docks and for loading prior to movement inland by goods train.[44]

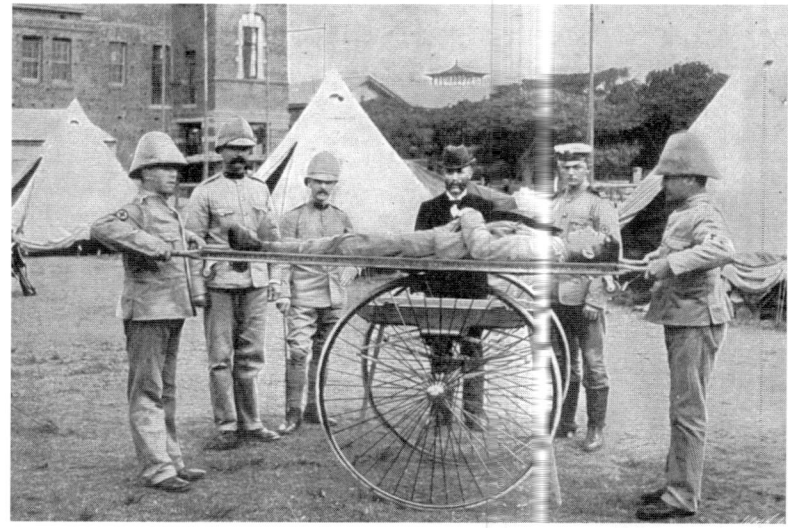

The McCormack-Brook wheeled stretcher carriage (Wilson).

Excellent communications were also provided, with a telephone manned around the clock.

Local sources for urgent replenishments were identified and discounts negotiated with the suppliers, including Lennon Ltd. The services of the ladies of Durban were also called upon to make bandages and splint pads.

An advanced medical depot was also established in three large covered railway vans under the charge of Lieutenant Quartermaster JB Short, which were sent forward to Colenso and replenished prior to the relief of Ladysmith.

Major McCormack also functioned as senior medical officer, Durban and medical disembarking officer. As such, he was much involved with the preparation and handling of hospital ships and trains.

Direction of medical services

Surgeon General WD (later Sir William) Wilson was originally sent out as principal medical officer (PMO) to the army corps under General Sir Redvers Buller. When the corps was split, as has been described, he remained in Cape Town as PMO in South Africa and the previous PMO, Colonel Supple, became PMO of the base and lines of communication in Cape Town. Wilson's capabilities were questioned by Lord Roberts, who described him to Lord Lansdowne as 'a poor creature and does not seem to have any idea of what is required'.[45] He was severely reprimanded for the inadequacy of arrangements at Kroonstad, but was kept in office, unlike his subordinate, Colonel Exham (qv). Other more sympathetic views are expressed in the *Times History*, which notes that:

> For nearly three years he had held the anxious and harassing position of Principal Medical Officer of the forces in the field. The many changes that took place during that time throughout South Africa, and the organising, splitting-up and reorganizing of medical units to meet them, under conditions of exceptional difficulty as regards medical personnel and transport, imposed an immense task upon which Surgeon-General Wilson brought to bear not only the requisite firmness and tact, but also an untiring devotion to duty.[46]

He received a knighthood for his services.

Lieutenant Colonel (later Colonel) R Exham arrived as PMO with Sir George White's forces in Natal and was then besieged in Ladysmith. Exham was severely criticised for his performance and was accused of cruel mismanagement, deceit and cronyism by Major Donegan, in charge of 18th Field Hospital in Ladysmith. He apparently diverted urgently needed 'medical comforts' towards his friends and deprived the patients needlessly.[47] Later he was dismissed as sanitary officer in Bloemfontein by Lord Roberts.[48] Colonel Exham provided a report on the medical arrangements he had made in Natal and in Ladysmith.[49]

Colonel (later Sir Thomas) Gallwey arrived in Natal as PMO of the 2nd Division on 15 November 1899 and took over from Colonel Exham, who was by then 'shut up in Ladysmith'. Gallwey was later praised for capacity and initiative, although it was also pointed out that he had the benefit of better trained medical troops and a more normal pattern of mobilisation compared to the other theatres of war. There were 'no exhausting marches, no short rations, nothing in fact to try the health of the men', but it was acknowledged that Gallwey and his staff made the best use of these advantages and introduced some new arrangements that proved of immense advantage.[50] These arrangements included the procurement and use of the hospital trains and ships, the recruitment of special contingents of stretcher-bearers and the development of a chain of evacuation hospitals along the railway line. Colonel Gallwey received the signal honour of a knighthood (rarely awarded to a colonel) for his services in this campaign. He returned to England late in 1900 and provided a report on his work in Natal.[51] His staff officer was Major W Baptie, later one of four RAMC doctors to be awarded a Victoria Cross in the Anglo-Boer War.

Colonel JA Clery, originally with 4th General Hospital, became PMO of the lines of communication in Natal and Lieutenant Colonel (later Colonel) WB Allin, PMO of 5th Division, became PMO of the field army in Natal.

Surgeon General Sir William Wilson, PMO, South Africa (Creswicke).

Colonel Sir Thomas Gallwey PMO Natal (Blake Knox).

Sir James and Lady Sivewright (*Black and White Budget*, 16.12.1899)

Development of lines of communication: hospitals in Natal[52]

The hospitals along the line of communication in Natal were developed as follows:

Improvised hospital established in Convent at Estcourt (Nov. 1899) expanded from 30 to 130 beds.

Existing hospital in Pietermaritzburg moved from Maritzburg College back to Fort Napier and increased from 250 to 1 020 beds.

No. 4 Stationary Hospital established at Frere in early December, then moved to Chieveley for battle of Colenso.

No. 4 General Hospital at Mooi River in January, increased to 920 beds by February.

No. 4 Stationary Hospital made up to 500 beds as a mobile general hospital on 10 January 1900 for Tugela army.

No. 1 Stationary Hospital opened at Frere and made up to 300 beds in January. After the relief of Ladysmith an improvised hospital of 1 000 beds was established in the barracks.

No. 7 General Hospital established at Estcourt in March 1900 with 920 beds.

No. 4 Stationary Hospital returned to Chieveley and received 400 bad cases from Ntombi.

A 1 000-bed hospital established at Howick at the end of May to replace Ladysmith Hospital.

Natal Volunteer Hospital established in Dundee in June for own forces there.

No. 14 General Hospital stationed at Newcastle in July.

Nos. 1 and 4 Stationary Hospitals became effectively General Hospitals at Charlestown and Standerton respectively.

In this way an efficient chain of establishments was created along the railway line to allow for patients to be treated and evacuated via Durban without undue delay. The need for additional stretcher-bearers to bring the wounded to these facilities for treatment was early appreciated and addressed by Colonel Gallwey. The offer of help from the Indian community made by MK Gandhi was accepted and put into effect.

The significant numbers of refugees and other persons without military training in Durban were also utilised in a Natal Volunteer Ambulance Corps. This corps was recruited largely by Major McCormack,[53] under instructions from Colonel Gallwey, and reached a total number of 1 800, arranged in four companies, under the overall command of Major Wright. Treves[54] describes their motley appearance and the improvement in their efficiency, whereby they earned the respect and gratitude of the soldiers. The following members of the NVAC were mentioned in General Buller's despatches: Privates J Domingo, F Clark, GH Howard and G Smith.[55]

After the disbandment of this unit in February 1900, many members re-enlisted in an Imperial Hospital Corps and an Imperial Bearer Corps, each 600 strong and also organised by Major McCormack.

Thanks to the efforts of all concerned, the medical arrangements in Natal were regarded as more satisfactory than those in other parts of the

Wounded British troops returning home (LHM).

country. In their final report[56] the Royal Commissioners referred to the difficulty of providing a sufficient supply of doctors and properly trained orderlies and commented that 'owing to a great extent to the energy displayed by the principal medical officers in Natal and the steps taken by them, the deficiencies were made up with commendable promptitude'.

The part played by the NGR was also substantial and received deserved recognition in the Royal Commission Report.[57] The citizens of Durban can be proud of the part their forebears played in this successful endeavour.

1. Amery LS, (ed.), *The Times History of the War in South Africa*, Vol. VI, p.516.
2. Ibid., p.518.
3. Treves, F, *The Tale of a Field Hospital*, pp.74–76.
4. *Natal Government Gazette*, 27.8.1895.
5. *Natal Government Gazette*, 4.7.1899.
6. *Commandant of Volunteers Report*, Natal Blue Book, 1900, Section F, p.4.
7. *Natal Almanac & Register*, 1899, pp.759–761.
8. English, GD, Extracts from Durban Light Infantry Regimental Records in Notes on History of Natal Volunteer Medical Corps, SAMC (unpublished, held by 1 Medical Battalion, Durban).
9. Campbell SG, *Diary of the Siege of Ladysmith*: manuscript in two volumes (Killie Campbell collection).
10. Campbell, E, *The Life of Sam Campbell, told in Verse and Letters by his Daughter* (original in Killie Campbell collection, also reproduced and published privately).
11. Ibid., Campbell, SG, entry for 27.11.1900.
12. Watt, SA, Intombi Military Hospital & Cemetery, *SA Military History Journal*, 5:6.
13. McKenzie, AG, '*Delayed Action': Life of Brig Gen Sir Duncan McKenzie*, pp.22–26.
14. Payne, SHC, *SAS Inkonkoni – 1885–1985*, p.16.
15. Goetzsche, E, *The Official Natal Mounted Rifles History*, pp.52, 79.
16. *Black and White Budget*, 24.2.1900, p.28.
17. Robinson & Co., *Natal Volunteer Record*, 1900, p.79.
18. Ibid., Campbell, SG, entry for 11.11.1899.
19. Ibid., Campbell, SG, entry for 31.10.1899.
20. Stirling, J, *The Colonials in South Africa: Natal Volunteers, Police & Guides*, pp.47–49.
21. Ibid., *Robinson & Co.*, p.79.
22. Ibid., Campbell, SG, entry for 25.11.1899.
23. Ibid., *Robinson & Co.*, p.79.
24. Ibid., Campbell, SG, entry for 3.11.1899.
25. Stratford, DO & Collins, HM, *Military Nursing in South Africa*, pp.5–7.
26. Ibid., Stirling, pp.47–49.
27. Gallwey, TJ, *Report on the Medical Arrangements in the South African War*, Appendix II, Medical Report on the Campaign in Natal, p.299.
28. Gallwey, TJ, *Daily Return Showing the Number of Deaths*, etc., Newcastle, 14.9.1900.
29. Hamilton Balfe, J, Minutes of Evidence taken before the Royal Commission upon the Care & Treatment of the Sick and Wounded during the SA Campaign, Paras. 14782–14790.
30. *Addington Hospital 1861–1961: Centenary Celebrations Brochure.*
31. O'Reagain, M, *The Hospital Services of Natal*, p.17.
32. Durban Hospital, Summary of Admissions, Diseases, etc., for 12 months ended 31st December 1901.
33. Ibid., Gallwey, TJ, Appendix to Minutes of Evidence ... , p.223.
34. Blake Knox, E, *Buller's Campaign with the Natal Field Force* 1900, Appendix 1, pp. 305–317.
35. Ibid., Campbell, SG, entry for 12.12.1899, et al.
36. De Villiers, JC, The Medical Aspects of the Anglo-Boer War, 1899–1902: Parts 1 & 2, *SA Military History Journal*, 6:2 and 6:3.
37. Lovegrove, P, *Not least in the Crusade: A short history of the RAMC*, p.16 et seq.
38. Whitehead, IR, *Doctors in the Great War*, pp.6–16.
39. McLaughlin, R, *The Royal Army Medical Corps*, p.18.
40. Ibid., Lovegrove, p.20.
41. *Report on Medical Arrangements in the SA War*, Part I: General Account, p.11.
42. Ibid., Treves, F.
43. *Report on Medical Arrangements in the SA War*, Part 1 General Account, p.16.
44. McCormack, R, in *Report of Medical Arrangements*, Durban, pp.314, 315.
45. Pakenham, T, *The Boer War*, p.383.
46. Ibid., Amery, p.529.
47. Ibid., Pakenham, pp.354–355.
48. Ibid., Pakenham, p.422.
49. Exham, R, *Report on the Medical Arrangements in the South African War*, Appendix 1, Report on Medical Arrangements of the Natal Field Force, pp. 283–288.
50. Ibid., Amery, pp.516–517.
51. Ibid., Gallwey, TJ, *Medical Report ...* pp.288–309.
52. Ibid., Gallwey, TJ, *Medical Report ...* pp.298–299.
53. Ibid., McCormack, p.315.
54. Ibid., Treves, pp.74–76.
55. Ibid., Stirling, p.48.
56. *Report on the Medical Arrangements in the South African War*, p.64.
57. Ibid.
58. *Black & White Budget*, 16.12.1899.
59. *Natal Witness*, 22.12.1899.
60. PRO, CO 179/209: letter Scott to Hely-Hutchinson, 31.1.1900.
61. PRO, CO 179/212: letter Hely-Hutchinson to commandant, 12.5.1900.
62. PRO, CO 179/212: letter Morris to Hely-Hutchinson, 13.5.1900.

CHAPTER 13

THE INDIAN AMBULANCE CORPS
Paul Tichmann

Until recently the Anglo-Boer War was portrayed as a 'white man's war', mainly because research and publications on the conflict paid little attention to the role and impact of the war on South Africa's black population.[1] From the beginning of the Anglo-Boer War the British government took a decision that, on principle, it would use only white soldiers against the Boers. Offers of combatants from various sources, including India, the government of the Federated Malay States; the Legislative Council of Lagos; Trinidad, the Canadian Indians, and the Maoris of New Zealand were turned down.[2] In the first year of the war 7 794 men and 6 671 horses were sent from India to assist in the defence of Natal. This included about 1 000 Indian 'followers' to serve as veterinary assistants, grooms and farriers. The remaining 7 000 Indian men included an Indian transport corps, hospital sweepers, orderlies, a corps of water carriers, a corps of grooms and another of *dhobies* (washermen). Each officer in the Indian army had an Indian cook as well as a groom to look after the horses. India also contributed generous gifts of remounts, hospital *tongas* (light ambulance carts) and other equipment as well as funds.[3] The 3rd Bengal Cavalry, a regiment composed of Sikhs, Rajputs, Jats and Moslems, subscribed a day's pay towards the Transvaal war fund.[4]

With the outbreak of the war, Natal's port town of Durban was in a state of great excitement. It was not only the European colonists and Afrikaners of Natal who were affected by the fervid preparations for battle, Indians in the Transvaal and in the northern areas of Natal had sought refuge in Durban. The Indian communities of Durban rallied to the support of the thousands of Indian refugees who entered the town. For some, refuge was found in a camp in Derby Street, while many found accommodation with family or friends. Indian merchants and traders in Durban also contributed to the Women's Patriotic League, formed for the purpose of providing assistance to wounded soldiers. Durban Indians also donated materials which Indian women used to make pillowcases and handkerchiefs for the Women's Patriotic League.[5]

The Anglo-Boer War engendered an interesting debate amongst South Africa's Indian communities. The Indian communities of Natal, comprising indentured labourers, 'free' Indians, merchants and traders, were, at this time, subjected to a range of discriminatory laws and practices. Conditions on some of the sugar estates were harsh.[6] Indian merchants and traders, whose ventures were perceived as a threat by European colonists, found their progress blocked by hostile laws and practices. How were Indians in South Africa to respond to the war between Britain and the Boer republics, given that their rights had been denied by both the British and the Boers?

In a letter to the *Natal Mercury* an Indian commentator called on the Indian community to forget their grievances against the British and argued that: 'Every Indian should bury the hatchet and reserve his resentment for the future, and come forward for the defence of the Colony.'[7] However, there were some who felt that they owed no loyalty to the British and that the Boer struggle was a just one.

Early Indian pro-war initiatives

Mohandas Karamchand Gandhi, the London-trained Indian barrister who was engaged in assisting Indian merchants and traders of Natal and the Transvaal in resisting the attack on their rights, was one of the leaders who argued that Indians should offer their service in the war. Gandhi had noticed that many of the English traders and lawyers had enrolled as volunteers with the outbreak of the war. He felt that the war provided Indians with an opportunity to disprove the charge that 'they went to South Africa only for money-grubbing and were merely a deadweight upon the British'.[9] Gandhi saw service in the war as a way of proving the loyalty of South African Indians to the British empire and in this way ensuring that their rights as British citizens in South Africa would be protected.

On 16 October 1899 about 100 Indians assembled at a meeting held under the auspices of the Natal Indian Congress at the congress hall in Durban, to decide on their response to the war. At this meeting Gandhi argued that Indians were in South Africa as British subjects and that: 'It would be unbecoming to our dignity as a nation to look on with folded hands at a time when ruin stared the British in the face as well as ourselves, simply because they ill-treated us here.'[10]

As a result the meeting took a decision to offer service to the British authorities, and on 19 October 1899 Gandhi sent a letter to the colonial secretary conveying the decision of the Indian leaders:

> About 100 English-speaking Indians of Durban met together at a few hours notice on the 17th inst. to consider the desirability of unreservedly and unconditionally offering their services to the Government or the Imperial authorities in connection with the hostilities now pending between the Imperial Government and the two Republics in South Africa.[11]

MK Gandhi attached to the letter a list of the names of a portion of the volunteers and indicated that they had been medically examined. He argued that although they did not know how to handle arms, 'there are other duties to be performed on the battlefield' and the Indian volunteers would be prepared to perform any tasks necessary, without pay. The motive for the offer, Gandhi explained, derived from a desire to prove that 'in common with other subjects of the Queen-Empress in South Africa the Indians were ready to do their duty on the battlefield'.[12]

Gandhi also approached Harry Escombe, the former premier of Natal, with the idea of an Indian volunteer corps. Like the Natal government, Escombe was also impressed, and supported the Indian offer of unconditional service.[3] The principal under-secretary informed Gandhi, in a reply dated 23 October 1899, that the Natal government was deeply impressed with the offer and indicated that it would be taken up should that prove necessary.[14]

Indian efforts to find a role in the war came to fruition when, in early December 1899, General Buller asked the Natal government to assist in raising an Indian Ambulance Corps which would not be required to work within the range of fire. The public works department was given the task of raising, administering and managing the corps and sent telegrams to the various estates requesting that they allow Indian indentured labourers to volunteer, and also enlisted the assistance of the protector of Indian immigrants.[15]

Dr LP Booth and Percy Clarence

In a further effort to secure the acceptance of the 'Indian offer', Gandhi met with the protector of Indian immigrants and also sent a telegram to the colonial secretary, pointing out that his group of Indian volunteers had been 'taking lessons in hospital work' under Dr LP Booth and that they were ready and eager to embark for the front. Booth, an Anglican missionary and medical doctor, and a friend of Gandhi, also wrote to the colonial secretary, informing him of the capabilities of the Indian volunteers, whom he had trained. In an effort to promote their cause, Gandhi travelled with Booth to Pietermaritzburg where they met with the colonial secretary and with the senior medical officer, Colonel Johnston, and the chief engineer of the public works department. As a result of this meeting the Indian volunteers were accepted as the leaders of the Indian Ambulance Corps. On 11 December 1899 Gandhi sent a telegram to Pragjee Bhimbhai, in Bellair, a suburb on the outskirts of Durban, requesting him to prepare the volunteers in anticipation of their being called to the battle front. Gandhi had asked Booth to accompany the corps. However, the Anglican bishop of Natal, Bishop Baynes, felt that Booth was needed for mission work and should not join the corps unless there was a real need for him. This was unacceptable to Gandhi who wrote to Bishop Baynes arguing that Dr Booth was 'indispensable for the Corps' and that without him 'a Corps of nearly 1 000 men would be without a medical adviser'.[16] Dr Booth was subsequently given permission to accompany the corps.

A letter from Percy F Clarence, who had been appointed superintendent of the Indian Ambulance Corps, to the chief engineer of the public works department provided an indication of the number of men sent from various sugar estates: 'Messrs Reynolds Bros. 104 men and 1 overseer; Mr Campbell 205 men and 1 sub-overseer; Shires Bros. 65 men and 2 sub-overseers; Mr Gandhi 34 men; the men engaged at Durban and PmBurg 45 men; Saville Bros 37 men; Sutton and Clarkson 15 men'.[18] In

An example of the oppressive laws aimed at Indians was the Natal Dealers Licences Act No. 18 of 1897 which gave municipalities the power to control the issuing of trading licences. Several municipalities in Natal, including Durban, used the act to restrict the granting of licences to Indian merchants and traders.

A dramatised view of Indian stretcher-bearers assisting a wounded British soldier (Wilson).

RK Khan, one of the leaders of the corps (*Who's Who in Natal*).

The leaders of the Indian Ambulance Corps with Dr Booth (Singh collection).

addition there were 67 men and 1 sub-overseer from the Elandslaagte collieries.

When the Boer forces occupied the districts north of Colenso nearly all the indentured Indians working in the Elandslaagte collieries fell into their hands. The Boer commandos tried to force the indentured Indians on the beleaguered garrison at Ladysmith. Sir George White, already short of rations, refused to receive them and they returned to the Boer side. The indentured labourers and their families, totalling 234, were found by a Reuter's special correspondent, wandering on the veld beyond Bulwana north-east of Ladysmith.[19] After making their way to the military camp at Frere they were sent to Durban as refugees, where they arrived on 11 December 1899. On arriving in Durban a large number of the indentured labourers volunteered to return to the front as stretcher-bearers.

Dr LP Booth

Dr Lancelot Parker Booth had trained as a medical practitioner in Durham, England and was appointed as the district surgeon and medical officer for Alexandra County in 1876. He was made a deacon in the Anglican Church in 1883 and ordained in 1885. Thereafter he established an Indian mission in Durban including St Aiden's church and school and a clinic. In June 1900 he was appointed as dean of St John's and rector of Umtata.[17]

Called to the front

Mohandas Gandhi and the other leaders of the Indian Ambulance Corps were called to the front on 13 December 1899. The leaders of the corps included Gandhi, RK Khan a barrister, and shopkeepers, clerks and artisans. On the day of their departure the Indian communities held a meeting at the congress hall in Durban to bid farewell to the corps and to Dr Booth who was subsequently appointed by Colonel Gallwey as its medical officer. Harry Escombe gave a reception at his residence, in honour of the leaders of the corps.[20] After the reception, Parsee Rustomji, Indian merchant, philanthropist and close friend of Gandhi, invited only the leaders to a dinner at his house.[21]

A telegram from the superintendent of the Indian Ambulance Corps, Clarence, to the chief engineer of the public works department on 14 December 1899 indicated that the leaders and 50 Indian men had left Durban at 2:10 on 14 December and arrived safely at Estcourt at 15:00, and that Gandhi was to arrive with some 40 more later that same day.[22] At Estcourt they were met by the superintendent of the corps, Percy Clarence. [23]

At this stage the corps was made up of more than 25 leaders and approximately 600 bearers. While the Natal government paid the Indian bearers 25 shillings per week (white orderlies were paid 35 shillings per week), the leaders served without pay.[24] Indian leaders had paid for the uniforms of the leaders and had also undertaken to support the families and dependants of the leaders where this was necessary. The traders also provided the Indian Ambulance Corps with extra amenities for their camp life and supplied large quantities of sweets, cigarettes, cigars, pipes, tobacco and other gifts.[25]

The Indian stretcher-bearers proceeded to Chieveley Station on the following day, where they were given their red cross badges and ordered to march to the field hospital, a distance of nine kilometres away. They were required to carry their rations and firewood as no wagons or water carts were available.[26] This was the day, 15 December 1899, on which General Buller had led the British forces in an attack on Colenso, in an attempt to break through to Ladysmith. However, the Boer counter-attack forced the British troops to withdraw, with 145 soldiers killed, 762 wounded and 220 missing or captured.[27]

Dusk was falling by the time the corps reached the place where they were to set up camp and the men were hungry, tired and thirsty. The battle of Colenso had just ended and the Indian bearers saw the wounded being transported by ambulance wagons and European stretcher-bearers from the base of operations to the field hospital, where their wounds were dressed. Before the Indian stretcher-bearers could set up camp or have something to eat or drink, Colonel Gallwey, the principal medical officer attached to General Buller's army, approached Booth and asked whether his men would be able to carry the more than 50 wounded to the hospital that had been set up at Chieveley Station. The corps agreed to march immediately to the field hospital to begin the task of transporting the wounded.[28] Three bearers were assigned to each stretcher and each leader took charge of three stretchers. The leaders had the task of directing the stretcher-bearer parties, interpreting instructions, administering first aid and medicines when necessary and attending to and feeding the wounded.[29]

Between 19:00 and 21:00 the Indian Ambulance Corps carried approximately 45 wounded officers and soldiers from the field hospital to the Chievely Station hospital, a distance of about nine kilometres, over rugged terrain. It was nearly midnight when most of the Indian stretcher-bearers were able to have a meal. While the leaders were provided with tents, the bearers slept in the open. The following morning they were on duty even before breakfast and between 6:00 and 11:00 had removed more than 125 wounded officers and soldiers to the Red Cross train near the field hospital and had again carried the more serious cases to Chieveley Station. While returning from their work the stretcher-bearers received orders to strike camp and march to Chieveley Station from where they were to take the train to Estcourt. General Buller had ordered a retreat.

The Indian Ambulance Corps arrived at the station at 15:00. The station master, however informed them that they would have to wait as he could not tell them when carriages would be available, which resulted in the stretcher-bearers spending the next 36 hours waiting at Chieveley Station. To aggravate matters they were informed that they would have to fend for themselves for the night. The only water available at the station was for hospital patients and station staff, which forced them to resort to using dirty water from a nearby pool to cook their food. Their sleep was disturbed that night by the movement of 15 000 of Buller's troops who

Indian stretcher-bearers carrying a patient in a *dhoolie* (Wilson).

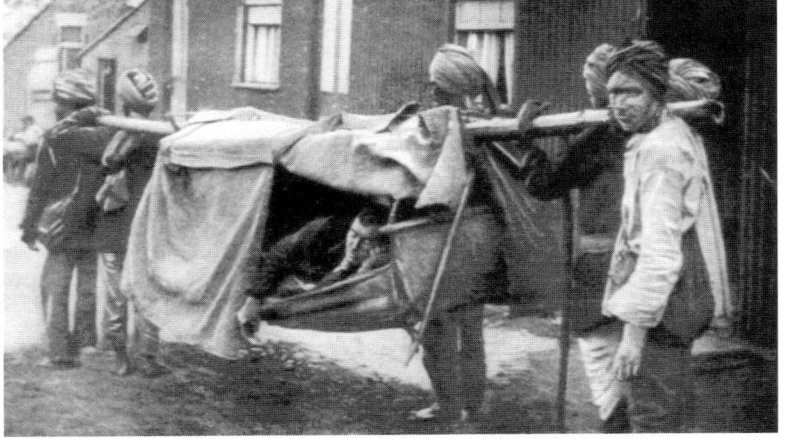

Indian stretcher-bearers with a *dhoolie* in the battlefield (KCL).

had broken camp and marched by with heavy artillery. The following day the stretcher-bearers were packed tightly into open trucks and, after a five hour's delay, proceeded to Estcourt. Here they camped in the open for two days, exposed to sun and rain. On 19 December, they received orders to disband temporarily. Before they were sent back to Durban, Colonel Gallwey personally thanked them for their service and informed them that they would probably be called on again.[30]

Improvements and reorganisation

By the 23 December 1899, the chief engineer of the public works department had communicated with Clarence, and thereupon corresponded with the principal medical officer concerning a number of improvements to the Indian Ambulance Corps. He suggested that the sugar estates be contacted to enable the speedy recruitment of volunteers and that the corps be provided with a wagon for the carrying of camp utensils, tents and food, a water cart, and tents. With regard to stretchers, he remarked: 'It should be seen to beforehand that the proper number of stretchers is in readiness on the arrival of the Indians. As to these, Mr. Clarence tells me, he had nothing like the proper proportion of stretchers, viz.: 1 to each 8 or 12 bearers, and, therefore the men were not so useful as they might have been.'[31] The letter went on to praise only Booth, Gandhi and 'the trained and educated Indians' for their services.

On 27 December 1899 the chief engineer of the public works department wrote to Dr. Booth, on behalf of General Wolfe-Murray, expressing the gratitude of the military to the Indian Ambulance Corps for their assistance and asking whether they could be counted on for similar assistance. The correspondence indicated that wagons, water-carts and tents would be made available for about 900 bearers and that all preliminary arrangements had been made so that the corps could be assembled on 1 January 1900 if this was necessary.[32] As a result Gandhi contacted all the leaders and members of the corps and asked them to keep themselves in readiness to set out at a moment's notice. In a telegram of the first week of January 1900 Gandhi informed Colonel Gallwey accordingly:

> 500 free Indians are ready to do ambulance work as before until the war is over and to follow the General. They have registered their names at my office and are ready to start on instant notice. Most of the former leaders are also ready. Doctor Booth has obtained leave and will act as medical officer as before and consents at our request to act as superintendent if called upon or in any other way you wish. So that our Durban Corps is now complete in itself and anxious to start work if there is any scope.[33]

The public works department and Clarence again approached the managers of the sugar estates and secured the services of a number of indentured labourers for the Indian Ambulance Corps. In less than three days a corps of about 1 100 Indian volunteers had been organised. About 300 of the volunteers were 'free' Indians and the rest indentured labourers released from the estates and collieries. The corps had 30 leaders, including Gandhi.[34] The Indian Ambulance Corps proceeded to Estcourt by train on 7 January 1900, where they had a two-week wait before being called for active duty at the front. Dr Booth used the two week period to train the bearers and their leaders. He taught them how to lift the wounded, place them on the stretchers and carry them, and also made the Indian volunteers perform long marches on extremely rugged ground.

After two weeks in Estcourt the corps received orders at 2:00 on 24 January 1900 to prepare themselves to entrain for Frere at 6:00.[35] General Buller had led a second attempt at relieving the siege of Ladysmith. The main focus of the engagement was the struggle for possession of Spioenkop, a hill overlooking the Tugela River, about 30 kilometres from Colenso.[36] The corps was to assist in removing the wounded in this engagement, which became known as the battle of Spioenkop. The British forces had succeeded in seizing Spioenkop, but were severely routed in a Boer counter-attack. In this, one of the bloodiest battles of the Anglo-Boer War, British casualties amounted to 350 dead, 1 000 wounded and 200 captured.[37] From Frere the stretcher-bearers had to march a distance of 40 kilometres in order to reach the British military headquarters at Spearman's Farm. About five kilometres from Spearman's Farm, in a bushy area below Spioenkop, tents had been pitched to form a field hospital. After having their wounds dressed, the wounded were to be removed from the field hospital to Spearman's Farm. A temporary pontoon bridge had been erected across the narrow stream that lay between the field hospital and Spearman's Farm.

On the morning after their arrival at the camp, Major Bapty, secretary to Colonel Gallwey, informed the Indian Ambulance Corps that there were many wounded soldiers to be removed from the field hospital. The possibility of the Boers dropping a shell or two on the pontoon bridge could not be ruled out, and Bapty warned the stretcher-bearers accordingly. He also informed them that they were not required to work within the line of fire and were therefore not under any obligation to take the risk. Bapty indicated that he would be glad to lead the stretcher-bearers if they were prepared to cross the bridge. The leaders and the bearers indicated that they were prepared to follow him and so crossed the pontoon bridge to remove the wounded from the field hospital.[38] By that evening almost all the wounded had been brought from the field hospital at Spioenkop to the stationary hospital at Spearman's Farm. The Indian Ambulance Corps spent three weeks moving the wounded from the field hospital to Spearman's Farm and from Spearman's Farm to Frere. Frere Station was being used as a base where the wounded had to be brought before being transported to the general hospital. It was claimed that on occasions they covered a distance of 40 kilometres three or four times in one day.

General Buller once again attempted to enter Ladysmith, this time by capturing the summit of a small hill, Vaal Kranz. Although the British managed to seize Vaal Kranz they were driven back by a Boer counter-attack and retreated across the Tugela River. While the stretcher-bearers were engaged in removing the wounded at Vaal Kranz, shells from the Boer guns fell a short distance in front of them. On 28 February General Buller's army succeeded in entering Ladysmith, breaking its 118-day siege. As a result of the siege the inhabitants were stricken by fever and the town was littered with debris. The authorities approached the Indian Stretcher Bearers Corps, which provided 200 men to clean the town and the surrounding area.[3]

The corps disbanded

Soon after the relief of Ladysmith the Indian Ambulance Corps was disbanded, as Red Cross units from Britain had arrived in South Africa.[40] Gandhi had kept meticulous record of all expenditures incurred and donations received. In February 1900 he wrote to the colonial secretary requesting that the 'Queen's Chocolate' for soldiers and volunteers be given to the leaders of the Indian Ambulance Corps as well. However, his request was turned down on the grounds that the gift was 'confined to enlisted Non-commissioned Officers and men'. In April 1900 Gandhi made an offer to the leaders of the Indian Ambulance Corps, who were not paid for their services, 'to take up without fee any legal work that I can do in Durban for you or your friends to the extent of five pounds during the course of a year from today, while I remain in South Africa'. Still searching for some form of recognition, Gandhi wrote to the chief engineer of the public works department in July 1900, requesting that the Indian bearers be given certificates of discharge and pointing out that 'Major Wright of the white Ambulance has given his bearers their discharge certificates'[41] The chief engineer was reluctant to accede to Gandhi's request on the grounds that the Indian bearers were 'highly paid' and that most of them were indentured Indians lent to the imperial government by managers or proprietors of sugar estates and others. He also expressed concern that should certificates be issued to all members of the Indian Ambulance Corps there would sooner or later be a similar application from members of the Native Labour Corps. He, however, expressed a willingness to provide certificates of discharge to 'Mr Gandhi and the educated Indians who in the capacity of Sirdars and otherwise volunteered and gave their services practically free'.

Rewards finally arrived. The work of the Indian Ambulance Corps was honourably mentioned in General Buller's despatches and the leaders of the corps were awarded war medals for their service. Sir John Robinson, the first prime minister of Natal, likewise praised the Indian Ambulance Corps for its role during the war and stated:

> Though you were debarred from actual service in the field, you were able to do excellent work in succouring the wounded. I cannot too warmly thank your able countryman, Mr Gandhi, upon his timely, unselfish

An ox-drawn water cart used by the ambulance corps (Wilson).

In the matter of the Law No. 4 of 1885, "To Establish a Register of Trade Marks in Natal."

NOTICE IS HEREBY GIVEN, that application has been made on behalf of BARCLAY & FRY, Limited (a British Joint Stock Company of limited liability duly incorporated under British Laws), of the Grove, Southward, London, England, Tin Box Manufacturers, for the registration of the following Trade Mark :—

Particulars may be obtained upon application at my office.

A. E. HARRINGTON,
Comptroller of Trade Marks, Natal.

Office of the Registrar of the Supreme Court, Pietermaritzburg, Natal, 17th March, 1900.   97

The queen's chocolates and the official registration application for the trademark for the tin (Richards).

Stretcher-bearers with *dhoolies* (PAR).

and most useful action in voluntarily organising a corps of bearers for ambulance work at the front at a moment when their labours were sorely needed in discharging arduous duties which experience showed to be by no means devoid of peril. All engaged in that service deserve the grateful recognition of the community'.[42]

A number of letters to the editors of various Natal newspapers also praised the action of the Indian stretcher-bearers. Gandhi, who had returned to India in 1901, in describing his experiences as part of the corps spoke of 'a perfect order, perfect stillness' in the British camps and described the existence of a 'spirit of brotherhood irrespective of colour or creed'.[43] He and other leaders within the Indian communities were hopeful that the loyalty displayed by Indians to the empire would result in Indian grievances being attended to. In a letter to British parliamentarian, WS Caine, regarding the treatment of Indians in South Africa, Gandhi, writing in March 1902, expressed the hope that 'the contributions of the local Indians in Natal to the present war may be taken into account in dealing with the question'.[44] However, their hopes were soon dashed as British victory in the war did not result in the removal of anti-Indian legislation. The Immigration Restriction Act and the Dealers Licenses Act continued to be thorns in the flesh, particularly for the Indian merchant and trading classes of Natal. The imposition of a £3 tax on ex-indentured labourers and their families placed a severe burden on them, forcing them to renew their indentures.

Stretcher-bearers and leaders at rest (Singh collection).

Although the participation of the Indians in the ambulance corps did not result in any amelioration in the conditions of Indians in Natal, they gained valuable experience. Gandhi later argued that, as a Hindu, he did not believe in war, 'but if anything can even partially reconcile me to it, it was the rich experience we gained at the front'.[45] The discipline and rigorous marches were to be useful in preparing Gandhi and other leaders for the passive resistance campaigns between 1907 and 1913. In all probability Gandhi's experiences in the war contributed to his later rejection of violence and his philosophy of non-violence and passive resistance.

1. Two of the few publications which deal with the role of black people in the war are: Warwick, P, *Black People and the South African War 1899–1902*, and Siwundhla, HT, *The Participation of Non-whites in the Anglo-Boer War, 1899–1902*.

2. Amery, LS, *Times History of the War in South Africa*, Vol. III, p.44.

3. Brain, JB, *Indians and the South African War of 1899–1902*, p.2.

4. Amery, p.45.

5. Gandhi, MK, *The Collected Works of Mahatma Gandhi*, Vol.3, p.147.

6. See for example: *Report of the Indian Immigrants Commission 1885–1887*.

7. *Natal Mercury*, 3.10.1899.

8. Pyarelal, *Mahatma Gandhi: The Discovery of Satyagraha – On the Threshold*, p.269.

9. Gandhi, MK, *Satyagraha in South Africa*, p.113.

10. Ibid. p.114.

11. Pyarelal, p.273

12. Gandhi, MK, *The Collected Works of Mahatma Gandhi*, Vol.3, p.114.

13. Ibid., p.127.

14. Meer, F (ed.), *The South African Gandhi: An Abstract of Speeches and Writings of M.K.Gandhi*, 1893–1914, p.747.

15. PAR, PWD 4964/99: chief engineer, public works department to protector of immigrants, 8.12.1899.

16. Gandhi, MK, *The Collected Works of Mahatma Gandhi*, Vol.3, p.127–128.

17. Brain, JB, *Christian Indians in Natal 1860–1911*, p.215–218.

18. PAR, PWD 4964/99: Clarence to chief engineer public works department, 12.12.1899.

19. Pyarelal, p.279.

20. *The Natal Advertiser*, 14 12.1899.

21. Gandhi, MK, *The Collected Works of Mahatma Gandhi*, Vol.3, p.129.

22. *The Natal Advertiser*, 14 12.1899.

23. Meer, F, p.760.

24. Pyarelal, p.179.

25. PAR, CSO 9585/1899: Gandhi to colonial secretary, 15.12.1899.

26. Pyarelal, p.283

27. Knight, I, *Colenso 1899: The Boer War In Natal*, p.55.

28. Pyarelal, p.283.

29. Pyarelal, p.279.

30. Pyarelal, p.281.

31. PAR, PWD 147/1900: chief engineer to principal medical officer, 23.12.1899.

32. Pyarelal, p.282.

33. Gandhi, MK, *The Collected Works of Mahatma Gandhi*, Vol.3, p.133.

34. Pyarelal, p.275.

35. Gandhi, MK, *The Collected Works of Mahatma Gandhi*, Vol.3, p.139.

36. Knight, p.78.

37. Pyarelal, p.288.

38. Ibid., p.290.

39. Warwick, p.133.

40. Gandhi, MK, *The Collected Works of Mahatma Gandhi*, Vol.3, p.134.

41. PAR, PWD 2458/00: chief engineer to general officer commanding lines of communication, 24.7.1900.

42. Gandhi, MK, *The Collected Works of Mahatma Gandhi*, Vol.3, p.160

43. Ibid., p.222.

44. Ibid., p.223.

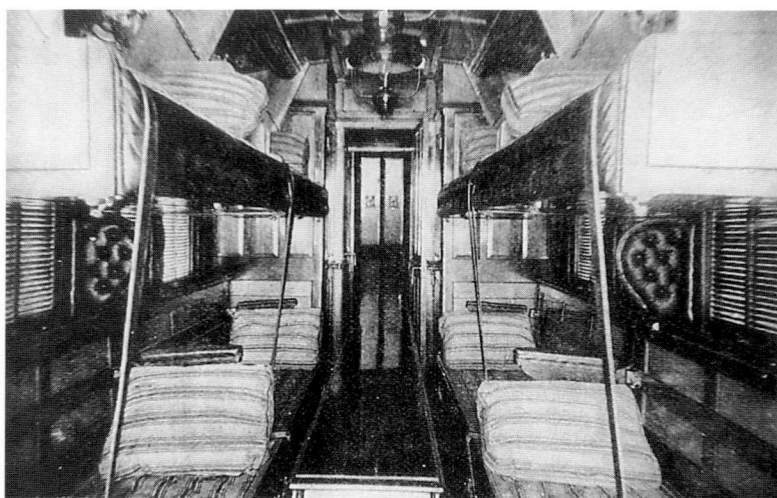

Interior of the No.1 hospital train. The seating on both sides of the corridor was converted to beds for patients (Newnes).

An ambulance train in the field collecting wounded men (Treves).

CHAPTER 14

AMBULANCE TRAINS AND HOSPITAL SHIPS
Brian Kearney

Ambulance trains

The Anglo-Boer War took place within a social and technological context which was characterised by the extensive use of machinery. Two components of Victorian technology which provided the British troops with some advantages were the use of ambulance trains and hospital ships. Trains had first been used as ambulances by the Germans during the Franco-Prussian War of 1870 and they could carry the wounded and sick with much greater comfort and speed than any other form of transport. Ships could easily be furnished with the necessary facilities of a fully equipped hospital and could also be used to convey men to larger medical facilities either in the Cape or in Britain. In addition both of these modes of transport provided far more comfortable conditions than field hospitals as well as being able to utilise the benefits of electricity for refrigeration, lighting, cooling and food preparation.

One characteristic of the development of Durban at the time of the war was that both the industrial and government infrastructure could respond to extraordinary demands for unusual productions. In the last months of 1899 and the early part of 1900, two urgent needs arose: the necessity for the adaptation of trains to ambulances and the conversion of ships into hospitals. In both cases the work was carried out with great speed and apparent success by the NGR workshops and private contracting companies.

The far-sighted David Hunter, manager of the NGR, had already anticipated the need for moving wounded soldiers from battlefields in Natal and, as early as the end of September 1899 he had made arrangements for a train to be converted into an ambulance. The alterations had been designed and specified by the principal medical officer in Pietermaritzburg, Lieutenant Colonel Johnston, while the actual work was completed by the carriage-building section of the NGR workshops in Durban.[1] Captain BHF Leumann who had been appointed medical officer in charge of this hospital train, 'in the event of hostilities', had already inspected it in Durban by 2 October 1899[2]

Hunter described this train as consisting of a kitchen van, four second-class corridor lavatory carriages, two first-class corridor lavatory carriages and a guard's van. Accommodation was provided for 72 patients. Hunter also arranged for the preparation of three covered vans containing medical supplies and stores.[3]

At the enquiry into South African hospitals conducted in Durban in September 1900, Professor Cunningham asked David Hunter about the position of the kitchen, which was located at one end of the train and queried whether or not its isolation was a source of major inconvenience. Hunter responded that the arrangements worked very well, and made the strange statement that it was very difficult to turn trains around, but Cunningham's criticism did seem valid.

By 9 December 1899, a second and identical train had been requisitioned by the military and prepared in the Durban NGR workshops. The second train was to be commanded by Major Surgeon Brazier Creagh. Both trains ultimately provided a much-needed service, operating between the war front and the various hospitals in Natal, together with the hospital ships in Durban harbour, for the subsequent 30 months. The ambulance trains brought men from the battles and from field hospitals to general hospitals in Estcourt, Mooi River, Howick, Pietermaritzburg and Pinetown Bridge (Sarnia). Of these, only Princess Christian Hospital at Pinetown Bridge had been sited close to the railway line. In other instances, men would still need to be transported some distance to the hospitals, probably in horse-drawn ambulances. It was, no doubt, for this reason that, during the first part of the war, the ambulance trains worked in tandem with hospital ships lying in the Durban harbour, since the trains could be brought right onto the wharf from whence injured men could be lifted onto the ship. This would also have explained why a hospital ship such as the *Lismore Castle* was initially used as a base hospital for some four months.

The Princess Christian ambulance train

Apparently Princess Christian herself originally suggested the idea of a Red Cross ambulance train which would be prepared in Britain to serve the war effort in South Africa. In October 1899, the British Red Cross Society communicated with David Hunter, through the secretary of state for war, enquiring as to whether they would be able to take over any train in Britain, in the process of construction for the NGR.[4] Through the crown agents for the colonies, the NGR had developed a good working arrangement with the Birmingham Railway Carriage Company at Smithwick for the complete manufacture of carriages and thus the idea of using a train, under construction at the time, would have simplified the process.

Hunter thought that it was quite unnecessary 'to interfere with the vans being built in England, and of which, for general purposes, we are in urgent want ...'. On 5 October 1899, the agent general in London telegraphed Hunter in Durban to inform him that the Red Cross committee, headed by Sir John Furley, had travelled to Birmingham to inspect the train and was awaiting his urgent reply. Hunter responded by informing them that a hospital train had just been completed in Natal and the NGR was willing to let the Red Cross take it over, but that the particular train in preparation in Birmingham could not be spared. Hunter must also have suggested to the Red Cross that their best option was to use the services of the Birmingham Railway Carriage Company to build a new train since

The Princess Christian ambulance train at the war front (KCL).

Loading wounded men onto the Princess Christian ambulance train (Richards).

The Princess Christian ambulance train reaches the docks at the Point (Ridpath and Ellis).

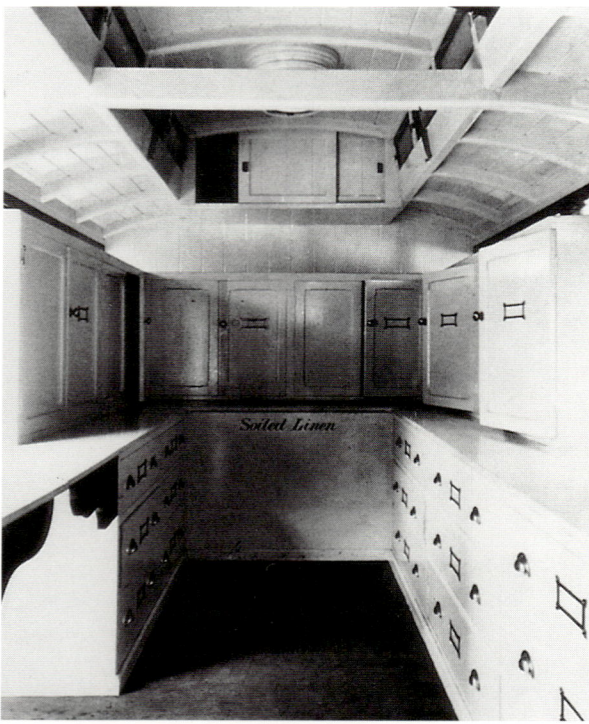

Interiors in the Princess Christian ambulance train (PAR).

that company was completely familiar with all the Natal requirements.

The company was contracted by the Military Equipment Company of Pall Mall on 18 October 1899 and commenced construction of the train under the direction of Furley. The contract period was to be for 12 weeks so that the train would be ready by January 1900. To achieve this 'Extra hours, night shifts, or helping one another individually were gladly faced, the men frankly saying that they knew the importance of time in the work in which they were engaged.'[5] The result was that the train was ready within ten weeks. Princess Christian and her daughter inspected it in Birmingham in December 1899.

The design of the train was based on the Natal specifications for carriages which could not exceed eight foot (2.43 m) in width to fit the narrow Natal gauge of three foot six inches (1.09 m). Seven bogie carriages included vacuum brakes and were each 36 ft (11 m) long and 8 ft (2.43 m) high. The Natal Witness provided a full description of the carriages and their uses:

> No.1 carriage contains three compartments. The first is fitted with linen cupboards, the extreme end being occupied by a zinc-lined ventilated chest for soiled linen. The adjoining apartment is for two invalid officers – the beds, a locker, and a couch by day. "Next door" beyond the curtain, is accommodation for two lady nurses, who add a dash of colour to the scene with their capes of scarlet. No. 2 carriage forms the doctor's quarters – bedroom, dining room (to hold half-a-dozen), and the surgery. In the last-named, along one side, runs the wide bench for dispensing with drawers underneath. Occupying about half the opposite side are shelves and racks for bottles and glasses; while there is also space for an operating table. Carriages 3,4,5 and 6 are hospital wards. Each contains 22 beds – 18 for invalids, 4 for attendants – ranged on either side in three tiers, with a passage 2 ft. 3 in. between. The bed consists of a light iron frame with netting of wire across, on which is placed a hair mattress – tightly sewn down in transverse rows of stitches, forming a series of rolls 4 in. wide – which allows for it being folded into a small space. The frames with the beds on them are laid on iron brackets, where they are easily secured. When wanted for use the bed is taken down and the invalid transferred to it from the ambulance; it is then lifted into the carriage, and raised by means of pulley blocks and adjusted on the brackets. No. 7 carriage contains a 4 ft. 6 in. cooking range, filters, refrigerators, cisterns, coal and wood bins, and all accessories for cooking for a hundred persons. Adjacent is the guard's compartment and beyond, the pantry and the cook's quarters. In addition to two doctors, two nurses, and the driver and guard, 15 orderlies are employed on the train, every carriage of which has a

Interiors in the Princess Christian ambulance train (PAR).

The exterior of the Princess Christian ambulance train (PAR).

The staff of the Princess Christian ambulance train
(*Natal Mercury* weekly, 7.10.1904).

lavatory and a closet, and a small stove with a kettle for heating water ... the general impression is one of airiness and brightness, the white colours of the interior adding to the light and cheerful appearance.[6]

The primary design problem was the way the accommodation had to be fitted into the width, which was restricted by the narrow rail gauge. In addition, it was expected that the train would have to travel over great distances and thus had to be self-contained. Even stoves were provided for cold nights through the Karoo, and hair whisks for flies in summer. On the exterior, the bold red cross against a white background stood out from the teak walls. David Hunter provided additional details concerning the running of such trains, including comments on driving:

> The smooth and careful working of the hospital trains is a matter to which great attention is desirable, as the result of many cases depends upon the comfort with which the patient is conveyed by railway. Drivers when working hospital trains should exercise their best skill to do so with smoothness, avoiding jerking and jolting, and taking every precaution likely to promote the comfort of those travelling in the train. There should also be great pains taken to prevent bustle or pressure when the patients are being taken in or taken from the trains; and the public should be respectfully restrained from coming to the station platforms when this work is going on.[7]

The train arrived in Durban in packages on board the *Raglan Castle* on 6 March 1900, and was assembled by the staff of the NGR workshops under GW Reid, the superintendent, and John Brown, the carriage foreman, and completed within a week. A festive and celebratory trial run took place the following day; the train was filled with local and military dignitaries and their wives, and it went as far as Pinetown Bridge, where refreshments were served and patriotic speeches were delivered. On the morning of 19 March, the train made its first hospital trip passing through Pietermaritzburg and going on to Northern Natal. It was the first train to cross the temporary trestle bridge over the Tugela, from whence it steamed into Ladysmith to take on wounded and sick for transfer home. The first surgeon in command was Lieutenant Colonel Forrester, who was subsequently succeeded by Surgeon Lowe.

By the 31 August 1900, 10 621 wounded men and invalids had already been carried in the No.1 train; 8 143 in the No. 2; 4 160 in the Princess Christian train and another 7 076 invalids had been moved in special trains. The Princess Christian ambulance train continued in service in Natal until 1902, at times venturing as far as the Transvaal.

The hospital ship *Orcana* leaving the port (Singleton).

Hospital ships

The great difficulty that has to be faced at present is the evacuation of the Intombi hospital with its nearly 2 000 sick. I am convinced myself that the cheapest and best way of clearing our hospitals is by the creation of good hospital ships, I have already had some made at Durban. To prepare a ship there, costs £3 000 – £4 500 and when prepared I am told they are better than the hospital ship *Maine* which cost £25 000. My advisers calculate that the last hospital ship we sent to England cost £3 000 to prepare and that the freight alone of the invalids she conveyed would have amounted to £12 000.[8]

Such were the words of General Buller in March 1900. One of the first ships to be converted for use as a hospital in Britain was the *Spartan*. The work was carried out under the direction of the Royal Army Medical Corps (RAMC), by Savory & Moore, in November 1899. In addition to the provision of three hospital wards and one fracture ward with a total of 62 cots, 50 patients could be accommodated on the main deck and 14 officers in cabins. The ship was equipped with an operating theatre, a dispensary, a drying room and laundry, messes, kitchen and pantries, and a mortuary. Electric lighting, refrigeration, electric fans and kettles were provided, as well as the 'Schimmelbusch' system of sterilising dressings. A steam-operated winch/lift hoisted the patients in their cots from the wharfside to the wards. The *Natal Witness* considered that 'the vessel was fully equipped with every modern appliance that a beneficent Government could furnish to any establishment for the alleviation of suffering, and the cure of the wounded'.[9] Of the nine hospital ships which were to work out of the port of Durban, only two, the *Spartan*, and the *Trojan*, had been fitted out in Britain, while the *Maine* had been partially completed in the USA. The remaining six were all converted in Durban.

Most of the work in fitting out these vessels as hospitals was carried out by a group of subcontractors who were experienced in building and shipping work. These included Hunt, Leuchars & Hepburn; James Brown; HA Chadwick and the McIntyre Brothers. The latter were sanitary engineers and plumbers, and they had fitted out the *Avoca*, *Orcana*, *Simla* and the *Dunera*. They had also worked on the *Nubia*, the *Lismore Castle*, the *Maine*, the *Spartan* and the *Trojan* and on the transports, *Assaye* and *Tagus*. The work on the *Dunera* was completed on 4 May 1900 and this included lining the floors of the mortuary and operating theatre with lead; providing baths and water closets to wards, and supplying lead-lined troughs and galvanised steel troughs for ice boxes.[10] On 5 May 1900, 221 patients were transferred to the *Dunera* from the general hospital in Ladysmith.[11]

In addition to the hospital ships, a large number of transports were either converted or used without any alterations being made for the conveyance of invalids (also referred to as convalescents or sick transports) to Cape Town or Britain. Some of these, such as the *Sumatra*, were

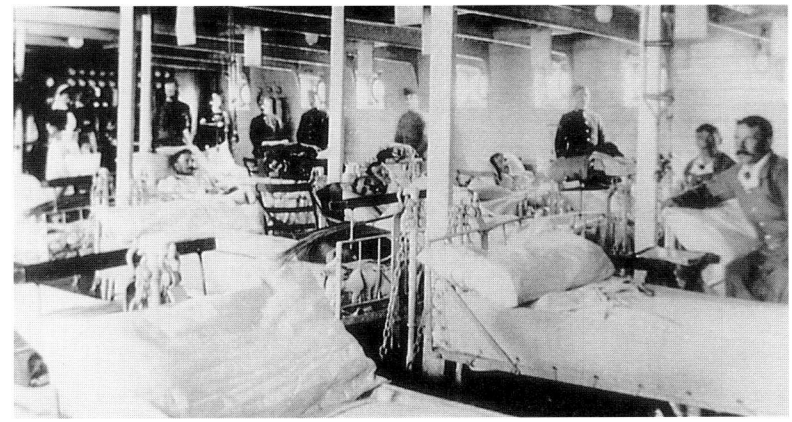

Wards on the hospital ship *Spartan* (Edwards).

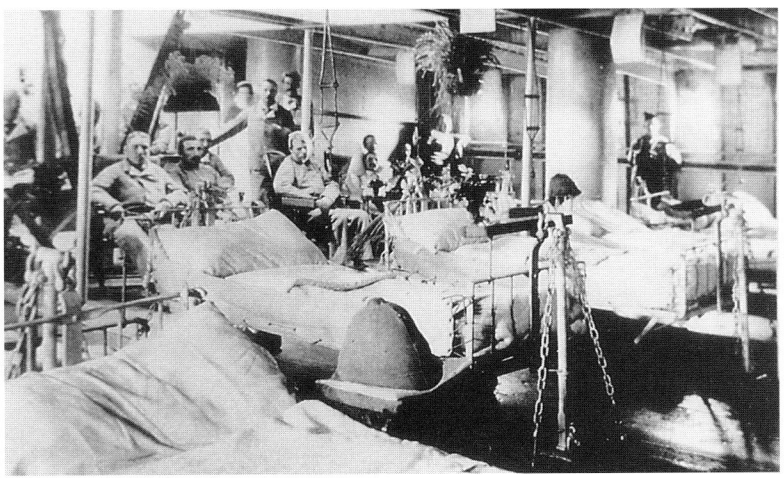

Men recuperating on the hospital ship *Trojan* (War Pictures).

Images of life on board a hospital ship
(*The Illustrated London News,* 10.3.1900).

contracted through the Pacific & Orient (P&O) line, while others, such as the *Roslin Castle*, were taken over from the Castle Mail Packets Co. By the second half of 1900, Major McCormack could report that a regular programme had been established whereby either a hospital ship or an invalid vessel would leave Durban every fortnight. By the end of August 1900, a total of 30 transport ships had been used to move convalescents and at least five of these were ships had been previously detained by the authorities for carrying suspected contraband. Colonel Gallwey provided statistics to show that, between the 6 October 1899 and 24 August 1900, these ships had carried 446 officers and 9 827 men. The largest number taken on any individual vessel was 724, on the *Assaye,* a convalescent ship, on 13 June 1900. The ships were staffed by officers and men of the RAMC, civil surgeons, nurses, men of the St John's Ambulance Brigade and the Imperial Hospital Corps. In July 1900 the medical staff on board all these ships totalled 311.

Hospital ships at Durban[12]								
Ships		**Staff**				**Beds available**		**Doctors in Charge**
Name	**Date of completion**	**Officers**	**Civil Surgeons**	**Nurses**	**Others**	**Officers**	**Men**	
Lismore Castle	4 December 1899	–	4	5	30	20	142	Surgeon Brodie
Nubia	6 January 1900	1	4	9	44	40	275	Major Lucas
Avoca	31 January 1900	1	5	6	46	33	269	Major Rose
Orcana	6 March 1900	1	4	6	32	21	182	Major Gerrard
Simla	9 April 1900	1	5	6	41	40	275	Major Deeble
Dunera	2 May 1900	1	2	5	40	27	284	Major Holt
Spartan	UK	1	2	3	20	21	118	Major Woodhouse
Trojan	UK	1	2	3	20	21	121	Major Burnside
TOTAL	**8**	**7**	**28**	**43**	**273**	**223**	**1666**	

The *Maine*

The most famous hospital ship to work out of Durban was the *Maine*. This converted cattleship from the north Atlantic trade had been organised by the Maine committee of ladies, including several prominent American women, among them Lady Randolph Churchill. The ship was contracted to the Royal Navy for fitting out in November 1899 and all costs were to be borne by the ladies' committee. Initially there were several queries concerning the conditions of the take over, the nationality of the officer to command her and the type of flag she would fly.[13] The *Maine* was to be modelled on the *Missouri*, which had seen service as a hospital ship in the Spanish-American War. Several alterations were needed, besides a thorough cleaning and painting. These were obviously not carried out satisfactorily for, on the arrival of the *Maine* in Durban in January 1900, several further alterations were required and were attended to by the naval carpenter, Lacy.

The hospital ship *Maine* (Newnes).

The Duke of Connaught hoisting the Union Jack on the *Maine* (Special number of *The Illustrated London News*).

The medical staff of the hospital ship *Maine* (*The Black and White Budget*).

Lady Churchill and her son John Strange on the *Maine*
(*The Graphic*, 5.5.1900).

The Churchills boarding the *Maine* at Durban (Newnes).

What resulted from the various phases of work was a transformed cattleship, complete with an operating theatre, and two new decks providing five hospital wards with 218 beds. The ship had X-ray apparatus in the theatre, electric lighting and fans, disinfecting sprays, India rubber flooring, electric kettles, stoves and laundry machines, a steam disinfector and electric refrigerators. All the wards were painted white and it was reported that, 'perhaps the most comfortable part of the ship [was] given over to Lady Randolph Churchill whose cabin [was] decorated in a manner suggestive of a lady's boudoir, rich in the luxuries of silken hangings and cushions'.[14]

Several of the staff had previously worked on the *Missouri*. Colonel Hensman was principal medical officer, and had three doctors under him: Eugene Dodge and Heth Hodman of New York and CH Webb of Philadelphia. The chief nursing sister was Miss ME Hubbard who had been head of the hospital staff at Savannah. There were four women nurses and 16 male nurses from the Mills Training School. Evidently most of them had resigned from good positions to offer their services.[15] However, after the first voyage to Durban, there were only four of the original crew left. The male nurses and orderlies had been engaged for five months at $30 per month to perform nursing duties, for which they were qualified, but after the ship first got to sea on 24 December 1899, they were ordered to scrub and clean down the wards, a task normally carried out by deckhands. Among many other complaints, the staff found that, even before reaching South Africa, the water had become almost undrinkable owing to rusty tanks. When they got to Durban they discovered that the *Maine* was to be used to convey convalescents home instead of fulfilling its original purpose of being a coastal hospital ship. All the staff agreed that the ship was not suitable for this task.

In the words of one of the nursing staff who left the ship, Lady Churchill 'played the great lady philanthropist with much fuss and feather'.[16] On 4 January 1900 she had every scrap of religious literature on the ship 'brought up on deck and the whole pitched overboard for the moral instruction of the fishes'. On her birthday on 10 January 1900, the *Maine* crossed the equator and a free fight ensued over the shaving of one of the American staff, all while Lady Churchill and a Miss Warrender took snapshots from the bridge. When the *Maine* reached Cape Town on 22 January:

(a) round of wild gaiety began, Sir Alfred Milner and other potentates came on board, and there was a big reception on shore with Americans absent. Durban was reached January 29 – brilliant breakfasts, receptions, luncheons, dinners and teas were the order of the day ... the time was passed in lounging drinking and smoking – by the ladies as well as the men.

When her funds ran short, Lady Churchill sold some of the ship's stores. More gaiety followed when the *Maine* returned to Cape Town in March and more stores were sold. When the ship reached Madeira with wounded men, such as Sergeant Grantham, who were very anxious to reach home, Lady Churchill went ashore to dine and delayed the departure of the ship. The sergeant died that night. Lady Churchill persuaded the captain to stay another day and then pleaded for another, but on the last occasion she was informed that the ship would sail without her if she was not back at a certain time. After leaving Madeira for London, she arranged for all the nurses' salaries to be raised.

The evidence of doctors, nurses, orderlies and masseurs

The Royal Commission appointed 'to consider and report upon the care and treatment of the sick and wounded during the South African campaign' visited Durban during September 1900 and interviewed a large number of witnesses.[17] Among these were several persons who had worked on the hospital ships as nurses, orderlies, doctors or hospital visitors and they provided valuable insights into the many dimensions of life on board ship. On 20 September 1900, a masseur from Johannesburg, JR Brinsley Sheridan, testified to problems experienced on the hospital ships, *Trojan, Maine, Simla, Orcana* and the *Lismore Castle*. Sheridan explained how his work took him to the various ships in the harbour or at the outer anchorage and he told of how, while massaging the men, he had many opportunities to talk to them. In his evidence he described how an Australian, Sister McNeill, had nursed 50 patients on her own on the *Orcana*. He also told of the shortage of food, especially vegetables, on the *Lismore Castle*, where Trooper Baines of the Imperial Light Horse, who was suffering from enteric and dysentery, was given only condensed milk. He also mentioned a certain Mrs Louch who, although not a qualified nurse, had been put in charge of a ward on the *Orcana* with 'a great many bad cases'. He explained that he had tried to assist in improving the circumstances by calling on Mrs Jonathan Peel of the Durban Women's Patriotic League, requesting that bread and brandy be provided to certain ships. His most damning statement concerned the way Dr Ernest Hill, who was later to become the first medical officer of health for Natal, treated a patient with a temperature of 105° and he stated:

> I remember one morning that I was attending a man for stiffness of the elbow joint. In the next bed there was a man who had been ill for several days, and the Sister told me that morning that his temperature was over 105. About 10 o'clock in the morning this man was asleep when the doctor of the ward on his rounds came in and caught hold of the pillow and jerked it from underneath the man, waking him up. He said "How dare you be asleep when the medical officer is going his rounds; you ought to be ready with your board." I felt it very much. There is a Sergeant Williamson, who is at present the steward of the Cheltenham Club at home, who can corroborate what I say. The doctor's name was Ernest Hill.[18]

Sheridan did distinguish 'good' hospital ships from others. Most complaints from the men apparently came from the *Lismore Castle*, and

REPORT

OF THE

ROYAL COMMISSION

APPOINTED TO CONSIDER AND REPORT UPON THE

CARE AND TREATMENT

OF THE

SICK AND WOUNDED

DURING THE

SOUTH AFRICAN CAMPAIGN

𝔓resented to both 𝔥ouses of 𝔓arliament by 𝔠ommand of 𝔥er 𝔐ajesty.

Men recuperating on the hospital ship *Nubia* (Newnes).

while the *Trojan* was the worst managed of all, the *Avoca* was the best. Conditions on the *Simla* were so poor that all the orderlies had apparently left.

Sheridan's evidence must have shocked the members of the Royal Commission, for their time thereafter was occupied in attempting to search out the truth. All the subsequent witnesses completely contradicted Sheridan's evidence. These included Surgeon L'Estrange and Major Gerard of the *Orcana*, who produced returns to show how food and vegetables had been purchased; an unnamed hospital orderly on the *Lismore Castle*; and a patient on the *Orcana*, Corporal Fraser of the mounted infantry. The latter did, however, praise Sheridan's skills, citing the way he had successfully treated a Corporal Boddye who had been 'crushed between two trucks at the Point', although Dr Hill had thought him to be a hopeless case. Mrs Benson of the Durban Women's Patriotic League explained to the commission that, as there was a shortage of fresh milk in Durban, the local population also had to make do with condensed milk. The following day Sister McNeill's testimony completely contradicted all Sheridan's evidence.

The hospital ship *Nubia* at the Point docks (KCL).

The hospital ship *Lismore Castle* moored at a partially built quay at the Point (KCL).

The testimony of Sister Roberts

It was likely that the closing of ranks of the social classes in the medical world of the time explained these extraordinary contradictions. Another case was to preoccupy the commission during their investigations in Durban. On Friday 21 September 1900, Nursing Sister Roberts was called and examined.[19] She explained that she had been the first nurse on the *Sumatra*, boarding about 4 November 1899. Roberts elaborated: 'We had nothing whatever to dress the men's wounds with when first they came down from the front, but Captain Holland went into the town and got necessaries just before we started, and all the men were attended to. I was alone until the Sunday at five o'clock, when we started for Cape Town. Then two more Sisters came on board. Dr Haigh was in charge.' She constantly spent her time dressing the wounds of about 300 men, mainly 'the Gordons and Leicesters from Eland's Laagte'. Her chief complaint was that the only food for patients on the *Sumatra*, a P&O ship, was dry bread and tea. Dr Haigh had told her that he could not order proper food because of red tape. She further explained that she herself had eaten very well in the saloon.

After reaching Cape Town on the *Sumatra*, she was appointed to the *Lismore Castle*, once again as the first sister on board. This time the problem was the other nursing staff whom she blamed for neglecting their patients. Thereafter she also had experience on other convalescent transports, the *Roslin Castle* and the *Assaye*. On the latter she found that Dr Stirling was not 'a fit man to attend to the number of patients that were on board. He absolutely refused to attend to them ...'. She went on to explain that she had looked after them as best she could and even 'tore my aprons and dresses up to make bandages to dress their wounds until we got to the Cape'. Officers on board had suggested to her that she expose the doctor's negligence and she did report him to the captain of the ship.

To support or refute her testimony, the commission called several more witnesses. The first of these was Dr van Niekerk of the *Lismore Castle*, who had been superintendent of the Johannesburg Hospital for seven years and in private practice for some four years. He disputed all Sister Robert's statements, saying that he had observed no grounds for complaint on the ship, though there had been a lack of order for the first few days. He concluded his evidence by saying that he had learnt that morning that Sister Roberts was not qualified. He was followed by witness after witness, including Captain van Koughnet, the chief naval transport officer, and Captain Holland, his assistant. Van Koughnet explained to the commission how the contracts had been arranged between the military authorities and the shipping companies and that it was the responsibility of the latter to provide 'victuals' and doctors. Holland thought that Sister Roberts's statement about the lack of food on the *Sumatra* could not possibly have been true and he had heard no complaints about any of the ships which he had fitted. He also clarified how the 'convalescents' took men back to Britain who were quite able to travel by ordinary transport, while the hospital ships were kept for the specially bad cases.

Another unnamed orderly on the *Assaye* told of considerable friction between the doctors and nurses on the ship, and of how Sister Roberts had been particularly unpopular with everyone. He did, however, corroborate her allegation that the lack of organisation was the fault of Dr Stirling. Useful information was provided by Lieutenant Brook, the quartermaster at the Durban Base Depot Medical Stores, and included details about the way medicines and stores were requisitioned and supplied to the various vessels. The only witness to support Sister Roberts's views was a schoolteacher called Haggar, who was also the secretary of the local Durban YMCA. He had 'missionary medical' experience in New York and Melbourne and had seen a great deal of the Franco-Prussian War. As YMCA secretary, he had regularly visited most of the hospital and convalescent ships and his evidence provided balanced information about the wide range of conditions. On visiting the *Sumatra*, he found that many men had no pillows, blankets or mattresses and were 'simply lying as one might have been picked up from the field'. He sent notes to the various Durban churches; the needs were announced the next day from the pulpits and he was later able to deliver loads of pillows to the ship. He confirmed the diet of bread and tea, noting that the men were simply ravenous for food. One example which he cited was of a member of the Gordon Highlanders,

> ... who had been shot through the lower jaw and could not open his mouth so as to get his little finger between his teeth. I saw him with a piece of dry bread and some tea. He simply looked at me first of all, and held the bread in one hand and the tea in another ... the man said "This is all I have had for 36 hours." At that moment a young lady handed him a little pot of jelly. "My God," he said, "this is a godsend![20]

Two pensive nursing sisters on a hospital ship (Newnes).

A nursing sister consulting with a doctor and orderly on the hospital ship *Nubia* (Newnes).

During some 20 to 30 visits to the *Lismore Castle* Haggar had observed serious dissatisfaction on the part of the orderlies who were threatening to resign, and witnessed disputes between doctors and nurses and between the nurses themselves: 'I think the nurses quarrelled with the orderlies, and one of the doctors sided very much with the nurses.' The last witness to be called in Durban was Dr Haig, a civil surgeon, who had been in charge of the *Sumatra*. His evidence was extremely brief and he said: 'Haggar represented himself as a doctor. He introduced me to Sister Roberts, and recommended her to me as a nurse. He was called "Dr" Haggar, and I took it for granted that he was a doctor practising medicine.'

A nurse attending a patient on the hospital ship *Lismore Castle* (*The Illustrated London News*, 10.2.1900).

Dr CH Haggar

According to the 1906 *Natal Who's Who*, Dr CH Haggar had been educated for the church with doctorates in philosophy and divinity. Haggar was born in East Anglia in 1854. After giving up the ministry, he had lived a varied life, having experienced the Franco-Prussian War and then spent some time in Townsville and Adelaide in Australia, as a professor of languages and chemistry. He had come to Durban shortly before the Anglo-Boer War and taken up the post of secretary of the YMCA. He entered local politics in 1906, winning a seat for the Durban borough for the Labour party. He was a declared state socialist.

1. Royal Commission of Enquiry into Hospitals, p.462.

2. PRO, CO 179/209: Captain Leumann to principal under-secretary, 2.10.1899.

3. PAR, MJPW 70: Hunter to minister of lands and works, 4.10.1899.

4. PAR, MJPW 70: prime minister to secretary of state, 7.10.1899.

5. *Natal Witness*, 24.1.1900.

6. *Natal Witness*, 20.3.1900.

7. Royal Commission of Enquiry into Hospitals, p.462.

8. PRO, WO 32/7896: General Buller to secretary of state, 8.3.1900.

9. *Natal Witness*, 15.11.1899.

10. *Industries*, 15.5.1900, p.153.

11. PRO, WO 32/7901: medical staff diary, 8.5.1900.

12. Royal Commission of Enquiry into Hospitals, p.316.

13. PRO, MT 23/114: principal transport officer, South Africa to director of transports, Admiralty, 10.2.1900.

14. *Natal Witness*, 26.1.1900.

15. *Natal Witness*, 8.6.1900.

16. *Natal Witness*, 20.11.1900.

17. Royal Commission of Enquiry into Hospitals, pp.460–479.

18. Ibid., p.463.

19. Ibid., p.470.

20. Ibid., p.477.

21. KCL, MS 90 Lamport Gillespie: correspondence Corp Rahilly, 23.1.1900.

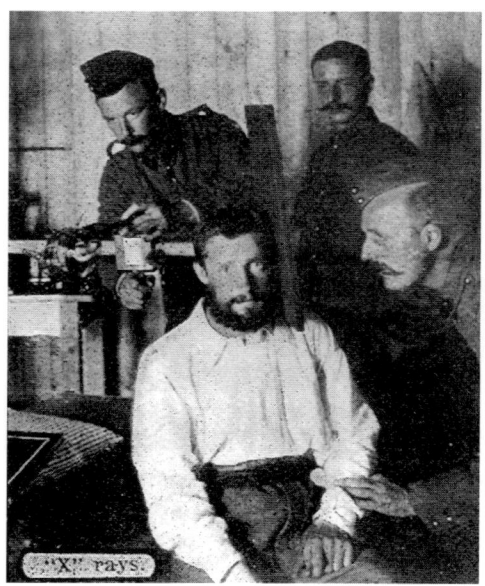

Using an X-ray machine at the hospital (Singleton).

strategically accommodated in different areas surrounding the pavilions and government wards. An orderlies' tented camp, later considered responsible for fever, was separated from the hospital by an open space, while the doctors and nurses resided in the Pinetown Bridge estate house.

The hospital staff

Major Mathias of the RAMC, the military representative, remained in charge of all the staff including the civilian surgeons, medical officers, dressers, attendants, nurses, orderlies, and kitchen and cleaning staff. The city of Bristol was well represented among the professional medical staff. Chief Surgeon Professor J Paul Bush had left his practice at the Bristol Infirmary and vacated a prestigious lecturing post at the University College of Bristol in order to serve his country during the war. Additional medical specialists included, amongst others, Dr George Worthington, a house surgeon from St Bartholomew's Hospital, London, who had formerly practised in South Canara, India, where he had acquired experience in tropical diseases. Dr Flemming of the Royal Bristol Infirmary had been appointed to oversee the new hospital X-ray room, with the objective of locating foreign objects imbedded in patients without having to use probes. Dressers included Dr A Crilland of the Bristol Eye Hospital and Dr Pierce, the casualty officer of the Bristol Infirmary. The presence of so many experienced surgeons at the hospital can only be explained by the anticipated influx of battle casualties associated with the

The medical staff of the hospital around Alfred Moseley (Pinetown Museum).

Dr CH Haggar

According to the 1906 *Natal Who's Who*, Dr CH Haggar had been educated for the church with doctorates in philosophy and divinity. Haggar was born in East Anglia in 1854. After giving up the ministry, he had lived a varied life, having experienced the Franco-Prussian War and then spent some time in Townsville and Adelaide in Australia, as a professor of languages and chemistry. He had come to Durban shortly before the Anglo-Boer War and taken up the post of secretary of the YMCA. He entered local politics in 1906, winning a seat for the Durban borough for the Labour party. He was a declared state socialist.

1. Royal Commission of Enquiry into Hospitals, p.462.

2. PRO, CO 179/209: Captain Leumann to principal under-secretary, 2.10.1899.

3. PAR, MJPW 70: Hunter to minister of lands and works, 4.10.1899.

4. PAR, MJPW 70: prime minister to secretary of state, 7.10.1899.

5. *Natal Witness*, 24.1.1900.

6. *Natal Witness*, 20.3.1900.

7. Royal Commission of Enquiry into Hospitals, p.462.

8. PRO, WO 32/7896: General Buller to secretary of state, 8.3.1900.

9. *Natal Witness*, 15.11.1899.

10. *Industries*, 15.5.1900, p.153.

11. PRO, WO 32/7901: medical staff diary, 8.5.1900.

12. Royal Commission of Enquiry into Hospitals, p.316.

13. PRO, MT 23/114: principal transport officer, South Africa to director of transports, Admiralty, 10.2.1900.

14. *Natal Witness*, 26.1.1900.

15. *Natal Witness*, 8.6.1900.

16. *Natal Witness*, 20.11.1900.

17. Royal Commission of Enquiry into Hospitals, pp.460–479.

18. Ibid., p.463.

19. Ibid., p.470.

20. Ibid., p.477.

21. KCL, MS 90 Lamport Gillespie: correspondence Corp Rahilly, 23.1.1900.

CHAPTER 15

THE PRINCESS CHRISTIAN HOSPITAL
Hazel England and Brian Kearney

From the battlefields the wounded would be taken to collecting stations, and thereafter treated in field hospitals, before being transported by train to stationary hospitals. Ultimately they would be sent to a base hospital, a hospital ship or convalescent vessel for repatriation to the United Kingdom. The hospital which was established at Pinetown Bridge in 1900 complemented the stationary hospitals in Natal and was initially called after the name of the railway station. It was thereafter named the Princess Christian Hospital.[1] Later it became known as the 13th Stationary hospital.

Stapleton Grove convalescent home: 1879

A small convalescent hospital had been established in Pinetown during the Anglo-Zulu War of 1879 in the home of Captain Harford, on the farm Stapleton Grove. This was situated close to the railway line running from Durban to Pietermaritzburg and near to the Pinetown Bridge railway halt, which was named after the railway bridge built in 1878 across the Umbilo River. At this halt steam trains stopped to draw water from the Umbilo River, deposited the postbags and then collected passengers and farm produce.

The halt was connected by a gravel farm road to the main road between Durban and Pietermaritzburg. At an altitude of 1 125 ft (343 m) above sea level and 17 miles (27 km) away from the coast, Pinetown had always attracted honeymoon couples and holidaymakers who wanted a healthy retreat, away from the oppressive Durban heat and humidity, and these conditions were considered equally favourable for nursing the sick and wounded.[2] The Stapleton Grove convalescent home met all the military transport requirements.

Proposals for a military hospital

Frank Stevens, a Durban businessman, owned a property south of the Pinetown Bridge halt and Stapleton Grove farm on which he was building a large brick and iron house with bay windows. On 23 October 1899, he wrote to the prime minister, offering the property and the buildings to the government 'for the use of the convalescent wounded'.[3]

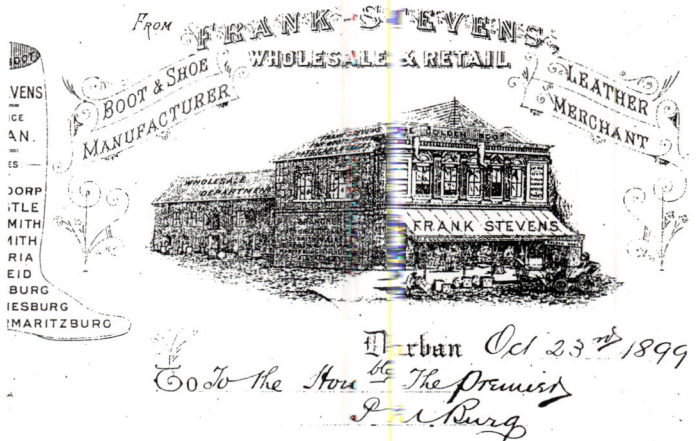

The hospital at Pinetown Bridge from the railway line. Visible are the various wood and iron structures and in the foreground the railway truck with an electrical accumulator (Pinetown Museum).

Stevens explained that he was intending the structures to become part of a hotel and private sanatorium, citing the fine climate and availability of water as important factors in his plans. He described the house as containing six large and six smaller bedrooms, and a large dining room of 40 ft by 20 ft (12m by 6m). There was also a smaller house on the property which had six bedrooms, a dining and sitting room and which he considered suitable for the accommodation of nurses and medical staff. Furthermore, he suggested to the prime minister that Doctors Campbell and McKenzie could confirm the suitability of the place.

Prime Minister Hime asked the governor to put 'the generous offer' to the military authorities. They, however, declined the offer, stating that the 'arrangements already made are sufficient to meet our requirements'.[4] Sometime thereafter, however, the offer must have come to the attention of Major McCormack, the senior medical officer in Durban, who accepted the proposal and commenced to set in motion plans for a hospital on a larger scale than Stevens had initially envisaged. Major HB Mathias of the Royal Army Medical Corps (RAMC) inspected the site at Pinetown Bridge and accepted the offer from Stevens 'as the site proved so good in every aspect'.[5]

Alfred Moseley of London, an old colonist with a 25-year connection to Natal, and who must have been well known to Stevens, now became involved and exercised 'great patriotism' by purchasing 600–700 tons (6 000–7 000 kg) of medical equipment and building materials in London, at his own expense, for the military hospital. The programme was supervised by Major Mathias and the consignment of equipment and materials left London on 28 February 1900 on the transport *Assaye* and arrived in Durban on 26 March1900.[6]

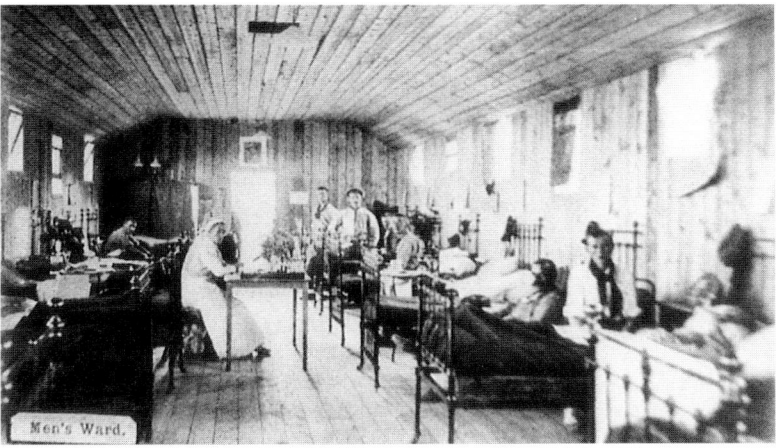
A ward in the Princess Christian Hospital (Pinetown Museum).

The layout and design of the hospital

The problem of transporting equipment from the port of Durban to Pinetown Bridge was resolved when David Hunter, the general manager of the NGR, offered his assistance, notwithstanding that it was a time when the railways were fully committed to moving troops and war material. The combination of civilian generosity and British medical expertise, supported by the Natal government, resulted in the rapid erection of a hospital of 100 beds. A further 100 beds were installed when the need arose at a later date.

The buildings included four pavilions, five government wards, an operating theatre, an X-ray room, a dark room and a dispensary. Each pavilion building was divided into two wards of 12 beds separated by a sisters' room and a hallway in the centre, with a linen room and pantry at one end and a bathroom and toilet at the other. The prefabricated pavilions were built of timber framing with corrugated iron walls. Internally the walls were lined with matchwood and green calico, and white calico lined the ceilings. Catering was provided in a kitchen containing a full baking unit manned by professional staff. Additional rooms included a laundry with large linen and supply stores. Medical personnel were

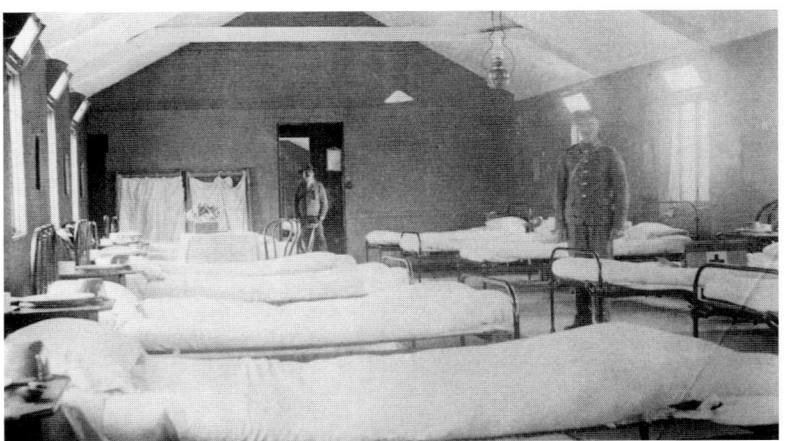
A ward in the Princess Christian Hospital (Pinetown Museum).

Using an X-ray machine at the hospital (Singleton).

strategically accommodated in different areas surrounding the pavilions and government wards. An orderlies' tented camp, later considered responsible for fever, was separated from the hospital by an open space, while the doctors and nurses resided in the Pinetown Bridge estate house.

The hospital staff

Major Mathias of the RAMC, the military representative, remained in charge of all the staff including the civilian surgeons, medical officers, dressers, attendants, nurses, orderlies, and kitchen and cleaning staff. The city of Bristol was well represented among the professional medical staff. Chief Surgeon Professor J Paul Bush had left his practice at the Bristol Infirmary and vacated a prestigious lecturing post at the University College of Bristol in order to serve his country during the war. Additional medical specialists included, amongst others, Dr George Worthington, a house surgeon from St Bartholomew's Hospital, London, who had formerly practised in South Canara, India where he had acquired experience in tropical diseases. Dr Flemming of the Royal Bristol Infirmary had been appointed to oversee the new hospital X-ray room, with the objective of locating foreign objects imbedded in patients without having to use probes. Dressers included Dr E Cridland of the Bristol Eye Hospital and Dr Pierce, the casualty officer of the Bristol Infirmary. The presence of so many experienced surgeons at the hospital can only be explained by the anticipated influx of battle casualties associated with the

The medical staff of the hospital around Alfred Moseley (Pinetown Museum).

war. Dr EA Nathan, the former house physician at St Mary's Hospital, London, was soon called upon to treat the debilitating effects of enteric fever and dysentery, which claimed increasing numbers of victims as the war progressed.[7] The doctors were assisted by five nurses under the supervision of Sister Lawrence, the sister-in-charge. Other staff included 30 St John's Ambulance attendants, six non-commissioned officers, 26 hospital orderlies and 40 Africans. Six weeks after the staff had arrived in Durban, the hospital had been erected, with the first patients being admitted on 8 April 1900.[8]

The hospital and the NGR

The support provided by Sir David Hunter and the NGR extended far beyond the transport of equipment and the material needed for the erection of the Princess Christian Hospital. The railways were also responsible for arranging for the supply of electricity for three Natal military hospitals, including the Princess Christian. The first electricity to be used in Pinetown took the form of an accumulator or battery which was charged at the Durban NGR workshops, and housed on a flat-bed railway truck which was kept at a siding at the Pinetown Bridge halt.[9]

The Princess Christian ambulance train transported medical cases and war wounded from the battlefields to the Pinetown Bridge halt, where they were placed on a metal stretcher rack, before being moved on Major McCormack's wheeled stretchers to the hospital. To accommodate the large stretcher rack, the platform surface near the hospital road was widened by railway workers. The resulting asymmetrical platforms remained for many years after the war as a reminder of the hospital trains.[10] Patients who required prolonged convalescence were transferred in the

A group of Irish nursing sisters (*The Black and White Budget*).

The officer's ward at the hospital (Pinetown Museum).

Princess Christian ambulance train from Pinetown Bridge to the hospital ships berthed in the harbour and then eventually repatriated to England.

Mail trains delivered post daily to stations along the main line and after the war confusion arose about letters meant for Pinetown, but delivered instead to Pinetown Bridge halt. Naming of stations was a railways responsibility and so the name of Pinetown Bridge halt was changed to Sarnia Station.[11] In addition to the normal transport of patients and medical supplies, Sir David Hunter also generously arranged for special trains to transfer guests from Durban to the Princess Christian Hospital for the official opening on 25 May 1900.[12]

Princess Christian of Schleswig-Holstein

Helena, (also known as Lechen), the fifth child, and third daughter of Queen Victoria, became Princess Christian of Schleswig-Holstein of Denmark after her marriage to the impecunious Prince Christian in 1866. A constant companion to her mother, she often translated German correspondence. Two of Princess Christian's older sisters had organised the nursing arrangements on the German side during the Franco-Prussian War. Princess Christian was an energetic member of the British Red Cross Society and, in addition to her keen interest in the Red Cross ambulance train, which was also named after her, she initiated the creation of the Army Nursing Reserve. This nursing unit had an initial enrolment of 200 nurses and she is reputed to have interviewed every candidate herself. Her son, Prince Christian Victor, a captain in the King's Royal Rifles, died of enteric fever in Pretoria on 31 October 1900. It was not until September 1904, however, that Princess Christian and her daughter, Princess Victoria, came to South Africa to visit his grave. Although the train that transported her to Durban passed the site of the Princess Christian Hospital, it did not stop, as the buildings had already been dismantled in 1902.[16]

The opening of the Princess Christian Hospital

Invitations were sent out by Alfred Moseley requesting the attendance of senior military figures and prominent citizens of Durban at the opening of the hospital. Named after Princess Christian of Schleswig Holstein, the daughter of Queen Victoria, who had always taken an interest in nursing, the Pinetown Bridge hospital was opened on her birthday on 25 May 1900.[13] After the bishop of Natal, the Rev D. Baynes had blessed the hospital, a speech was made by Colonel Morris, the commandant of Durban, in which he thanked Mosely, Frank Stevens, the medical staff and all the people who had made 'this ambitious humanitarian project' a reality. Reference was made to the first patients admitted on the 16 April 1900, who were victims of a railway accident in Pinetown, and the troops, suffering from enteric fever who were subsequently admitted, were also mentioned. General Wolfe-Murray, the officer commanding the lines of communication, was unable to attend the function, so the hospital was formally opened by Colonel Morris. Refreshments were served on the lawns to the elegantly dressed dignitaries before they returned to Durban by train.[14]

The opening of the hospital on 25 May 1900 (KZN Museum Service).

Illustrated address presented to Moseley on 20 July 1900 (Pinetown Museum).

In the South African War

BOVRIL

gave Vigor to the Fighter,

Strength to the Wounded,

and

Sustenance to the Enteric.

Bovril formed an important part of the Emergency Rations, and was one of the principal supplies of both Base and Field Hospitals throughout the Campaign.

The testimonials to the strengthening and sustaining power of Bovril would fill a book. They have been repeatedly included in the Official Reports of the Royal Army Medical Corps. They have formed part of the thrilling accounts of the newspaper correspondents. They have been embodied in the stories of eye-witnesses of scenes at the front and in the hospital tents. They have been part and parcel of the interesting letters written by the soldiers themselves to their relatives and friends at home. Doctors and nurses, officers and privates, soldiers and civilians, have pronounced the unanimous verdict that as a stimulating, nourishing, and sustaining food in the smallest compass, Bovril is without a peer.

Whether to the soldiers fighting at the front, or to the man at home battling against the inclemencies of the weather, weakness, and disease,

IS LIQUID LIFE.

(Special number of *The London Illustrated News*)

An interesting observer at this function was Sir John Furley, the director of the British Red Cross. Furley had been intensely involved in the design and construction of the Princess Christian (Red Cross) ambulance train in 1899. He had arrived in South Africa to inspect the work of the Red Cross in various places, and was attempting to make his way to Johannesburg. According to him: '... he had got no further than Pinetown where he arrived on the day that Mr Moseley's magnificently equipped hospital was handed over as a gift to the Natal Government.'[15]

On the 20 July 1900, Alfred Moseley was presented with an illustrated address in the Durban town council chambers, by the mayor, John Nicol, on behalf of the people of Durban, for his contribution to the war effort. Moseley left Durban and the Princess Christian Hospital was handed over to the military. New medical staff were appointed and the hospital's name was changed to the 13th Stationary Hospital.

The patients

Enteric fever among the troops had been encountered on many campaigns. Accurate medical knowledge regarding the causes of enteric, typhoid, dysentery, and camp fever had not been discovered at the turn of the century. An extract from a chapter on the medical services in *The Illustrated London News Transvaal War 1899–1900* presents an example of views of the time:

> Nevertheless a vast floating population of some 50,000 troops a large proportion of whom are mounted, scanty water supply, and consequent pollution of the soil and surroundings, account for the prevalence of enteric fever and dysentery. We need not attribute these diseases to the foul water that flowed from Cronje's last laager ... Whether the disease be enteric or typhus fever, whether again it is contagious, as seems probable, or is only contracted through the medium of food and water previously contaminated by flies or other insects, or whether it is conveyed in the dust are points not yet fully determined.

The patients in the Princess Christian Hospital did not escape this scourge. On 8 June 1900, patients comprised 19 officers and 117 other ranks, of which 38 had enteric and 17 were diagnosed with dysentery, without any fatalities recorded.[18] An analysis of hospital admissions from 16 April 1900 to 20 July 1900, provided by Dr Worthington, recorded a very different picture. Of the 327 patients treated 19 had died, 71 had returned to duty, 18 went to convalescent homes and 167 were sent home as invalids, while 52 remained in hospital. Enteric fever accounted for 165 cases or 50.5% of those admitted.[19]

During its existence, about 5 000 patients passed through the hospital's wards and only 47 deaths occurred. Cases of enteric fever accounted for 26 fatalities followed by seven deaths from dysentery and these included Lieutenant Colonel Waring and four privates of the RAMC, in addition to a private from the St John's Ambulance Brigade. Medical staff were given inoculations to prevent fever, but these only served to decrease the severity of the infection. Thirty-nine of the deceased were buried at St John's Anglican Church, where a sandstone memorial was erected by the Pinetown Guild of Loyal Women in 1922, replacing the damaged headstones. Roman Catholics who died were buried at the Mariannhill Mission Cemetrey.[20]

Boer patients

It was said that, on the battlefields during the first phase of the war and later amid the guerilla fighting, the British remained 'unfailingly humane' in nursing wounded Boers.[21] Petrus Pretorius, a POW from the Jacobsdal Commando, was treated at the Princess Christian Hospital for pleurisy, where he died on 2 July 1902. He was buried at St John's Church Cemetrey, and his name was included in the Boer War Memorial, (with the full honours accorded to British fatalities).[22] Several other Boer POWs were treated at the hospital. GF Muller was found to be unfit to 'travel by sea' and was admitted as a patient to the hospital in December 1900 where he remained until February 1901, before being sent under escort to Tin Town in Ladysmith.[23] Frans Johannes van Dyke, aged 37, of the Rustenburg Commando, who had been captured on 15 July 1901, and taken to Cape Town, fell ill with an 'inflammation of the liver' on the prison ship *Armenian* off Durban. He was initially transferred to the hospital ship *Simla* and then admitted to the 13th Stationary Hospital on 2 November of that year[24]

On the 31 May 1902, the hospital closed and the equipment was returned to England, together with the staff. In his report on the Princess Christian Hospital, Dr Worthington thanked David Hunter of the NGR for his support and expressed gratitude to the people of Pinetown for their gifts of fruit.[25] The medical care given by volunteers and members of the RAMC at the Pinetown hospital justified the motto of the corps: *In Arduis Fidelis*.

1. Record of the Transvaal-War 1899–1900, *The Illustrated London News* p.77–78.

2. Natal Women's Institute, *Annals of Pinetown*, pp.4–7 and 19.

3. PAR, MJPW 71: Stevens to prime minister, 23.10.1899.

4. PAR, MJPW 71: prime minister to Stevens, 28.10.1899.

5. *Natal Mercury*, 26.5.1900.

6. Worthington, G, The Princess Christian Hospital in South Africa, *British Medical Journal*, April 1901, p.919.

7. Pinetown Museum, untitled document on the Princess Christian Hospital.

8. *Natal Witness*, 3.4.1900.

9. Harrison, CW, *Natal Illustrated – Official Railways Guide and General Handbook*, p.290.

10. Interview: Mr and Mrs Gordon Munro and Mr and Mrs John Munro, April 1994.

11. O'Keefe, B, *Pioneers Progress*, p.43.

12. *Natal Mercury*, 26.5.1900.

13. *Natal Witness*, 3.4.1900.

14. *Natal Mercury*, 26.5.1900.

15. *Cape Times*, 31.7.1900.

16. *Natal Mercury*, 31.10.1900, 5.10.1904 and 6.10.1904.

17. Record of the Transvaal-War 1899–1900, *The Illustrated London News* p.77–78.

18. Worthington, G, The Princess Christian Hospital in South Africa, *British Medical Journal*, April 1901, p.919.

19. Ibid.

20. Pinetown Museum, correspondence: Trotter, EL, and Trotter, B.

21. Reitz, D, *Commando – A Boer Journal of the Boer War*, p.169.

22. Pinetown Museum: return of deaths at the No. 13 Stationary Hospital.

23. NAR, SOP 511: senior medical officer, 13th Stationary Hospital to commandant Durban, 22.2.1901.

24. PAR, SOP 511: senior medical officer, 13th Stationary Hospital to commandant, Durban, 3.11.1901.

25. Pinetown Museum, correspondence: Major Gen MacLennan of Royal Army Medical College to Mrs McCartan, 22.3.1977.

CIVILIAN VICTIMS OF THE WAR

Boers returning home from the Wentworth
concentration camp, July 1902 (LHM).

The exodus of Uitlanders from Johannesburg (Brown).

The Royal Hotel, Smith Street (LHM).

Refugees leaving Johannesburg (Wilson).

CHAPTER 16

'WE ARE NOT SKUNKS': REFUGEES AND UITLANDERS

Ian Swanepoel

With the shadow of impending war looming large over the Boer republics and the British empire, the people of Durban showed very little interest in the growing friction between aggressive imperialism and assertive republicanism. Although a Durban newspaper, the *Natal Mercury,* reported on the shooting of Tom Edgar by a South African Republic policeman (ZARP) and the subsequent protests by Uitlanders, the news did not really have an impact on Durbanites. Even reports on the petitions forwarded by the Uitlanders raised few eyebrows. It was only on 21 June 1899 that a regular column entitled the 'Transvaal Situation' started to appear in the *Natal Mercury.*

As the crisis worsened, so the awareness of the Durbanites rose, fuelled by newspaper articles and the sporadic arrival of people, especially from the Transvaal. On Saturday 1 July 1899, notices appeared announcing a public meeting to be held that evening at the queen's statue in the town gardens to express sympathy with the Uitlanders of the Transvaal. This was the first of many public gatherings at the statue. In spite of the short notice, over 3 000 people attended the meeting. There were five speakers and Mayor John Nicol opened the meeting. One of the speakers summed up the mood:

> 'This great meeting of the people of Durban could never have gathered as it had done at a few hours notice except under the influence of an overpowering feeling that the time had come when it was necessary for them to break the silence they had hitherto maintained with respect to the position of South African affairs and bring themselves into line with other towns in South Africa which had spoken or were about to speak on this great political question.'

After a number of fiery speeches, the following resolution was passed: 'The meeting of the citizens of Durban affirms the justice of the policy of Her Majesty's government as represented by the High Commissioner which claims equal political rights for all white inhabitants of the Transvaal as in other parts of South Africa, and declares its opinion that only by the grant of such rights will lasting peace be secured.' When the meeting ended, the crowd sang 'Rule Britannia' and concluded with loyal cheers of 'God Save the Queen'[1]. Durban was now firmly committed to the cause of the Uitlanders in the Transvaal.

The arrival of refugees in Durban

The first refugees sneaked into Durban almost unnoticed. What was known as the July season in Durban, when visitors would arrive from up-country, started unusually early in 1899. This was, at first, attributed to a sudden unseasonable cold spell in the Transvaal. It was not very long before it became obvious that political unrest, rather than the cold weather, had driven these pre-war refugees to Durban.[2] Perhaps they felt that the troubles in the Transvaal would be resolved and they could return to their homes at a later stage. After all President Paul Kruger of the Transvaal was making conciliatory statements repudiating the warnings of expected violence which appeared in the more sensational newspapers. He was even reported to have said: 'Who talks of war? We have no trouble with England.'[3] Besides, a room could be obtained in a good boarding house for £4 7s 6d a month, or, for the more affluent, there was the Royal Hotel.[4]

As tension between Britain and the Transvaal increased, and attempts at mediation failed, so more and more people from the Transvaal, the Orange Free State and Northern Natal started arriving in Durban. By September 1899, trains, crowded with passengers, had to be run. It became common to see crowds of people gathered at the station in the evenings to meet the train from the Transvaal.[5] In early October, the arrivals, now referred to as refugees, caught Durban by surprise and, as many of them were destitute, they slept in the town gardens.[6] The refugees continued to descend upon Durban, but by now, the Zuid-Africaansche Spoorweg Maatschappy was providing only coal and cattle trucks to convey them. The average number of passengers per truck was 53 men, women and children.[7] Not all of these early refugees remained in the city, and many were sent on to East London, Port Elizabeth and Cape Town. It soon became evident that some facilities had to be provided, so it was decided that 'destitute persons desirous of using the town baths would be admitted between 8.00 and 9.30 a.m. on payment of one penny and a note from the YMCA'.[8]

After the declaration of war, the flood of refugees increased dramatically as people tried to flee and avoid being caught up in the war, while others were expelled by the Transvaal authorities. As the route via Northern Natal was now closed, the refugees from the Transvaal now had to travel from Pretoria and Johannesburg to Lourenço Marques by train, and then on to Durban and other coastal towns by ship. Again the journey was undertaken in coal trucks and it took about 24 hours from Pretoria to Lourenço Marques. During the latter half of October 1899, Lourenço Marques was crowded with refugees of diverse nationalities, various social classes and many walks of life. The local hotels were charging about double the going rate and many refugees were sleeping in make-shift shelters, in sheds, under verandas or in the open. Those unable to pay the high prices charged for meals had to subsist on bread and coffee doled out by the British relief committee. The wife of the British consul, and other kind-hearted ladies did their best to assist the women.[9] When, at last, they were able to board a ship, the journey to Durban took 24 hours. In October, the *Tintagel Castle* embarked 1 800 passengers and the *Avondale Castle* 1 000, a large number of which disembarked at Dur-

Refugees leaving the Transvaal (Raoul-Duval).

The term 'Uitlander'

The term 'Uitlander', when directly translated means 'outlander' and was used as a derogatory term to describe foreigners who came to the Transvaal after the discovery of gold, and who did not became burghers of the republic. Although meant to be uncomplimentary, it soon became almost an honorary title and the only term available to collectively identify a multitude of nationalities on the Witwatersrand, who were non-burghers of the Transvaal.

Refugees waiting to embark at Lourenço Marques (Wilson).

ban.[10] This odyssey was to be repeated many times during the war by ships such as the *Entre Rios*, the *König* and the *Umbria*. To assist the British Indian refugees, a request by MK Gandhi was acceded to: immigration laws were relaxed and free visiting passes were issued to allow Transvaal Indians to enter the colony and to remain for three months.[11] This step pleased Abdul Caadir, a leading light in the Natal Indian Congress, to such an extent that, in a letter to the Natal government, he expressed his gratitude to the authorities 'for having graciously offered facilities to the British Indians from the Transvaal now in Delagoa Bay for coming to Natal and remaining in the Colony during the present crisis'.[12]

On board the *Tintagel Castle* bound for Durban

When I arrived on board the S.S. Tintagel Castle on Monday night, October 30, I found that there were over 1,800 refugees on board. The scene was one to be remembered, and to a keen observer afforded a striking object lesson as to the extent and magnitude and cosmopolitan nature of the British Empire. Europeans and Asiatics, and natives of Africa, as well as loyal Colonists from Canada, Australia and New Zealand, all mingled together in this unique crowd; all affected by a common misfortune and all claiming allegiance to a common flag. I use the word claim advisedly, for it was easy to discern in this crowd numbers of Russian Jews, Germans, Italians, as well as other foreigners who had recourse to Britain for that protective influence which their own nation could not or would not afford them. The *Tintagel Castle* sailed at 6 o'clock the following morning. Twenty four hours later she was at Durban, and after calling at East London, Port Elizabeth and Mossel Bay, at all of which places she discharged a portion of her human cargo, she arrived safely in Table Bay on Wednesday afternoon the 8th November.[13]

To deal with the mass migration caused by the war, the Durban port captain, Ballard, issued provisional instructions not to allow any more refugees from Lourenço Marques to land at Durban other than respectable British subjects. Apart from the port captain the British consul in Lourenço Marques, Carnegie Ross, later followed by Fritz Crowe, also had to assume the position of gatekeeper. They were required to provide a pass to refugees wanting to land in Durban, which meant that all refugees bound for Durban were screened to determine whether they were of suitable British stock, while refugees of other nationalities were generally denied a pass to proceed. The IRO, Harry Smith, was instructed to ensure that these regulations were strictly enforced.[14] The shipping companies were informed likewise, and told that any disregard of the order would be dealt with under the Immigration Restriction Act or under martial law.[15] The strict application of these laws was not only aimed at keeping undesirable refugees out, but also at ensuring that entry was denied to potential Boer spies.

The authorities in Durban deemed these restrictions necessary. The city was already bursting with destitute and unemployed Uitlanders of all classes. Some characters, on disembarking in Durban, disappeared into

Passengers landing by basket from ships at the outer anchorage (LHM).

the crowds adding to Durban's problems. Amongst these were a Mr and Mrs Moore, who were bound for East London, the former critically ill, and a Mrs Wilson and her child, whose husband had run away from home. Owing to the large number of unemployed refugees in the city who met the ships from Lourenço Marques looking for friends and relatives, it was relatively easy to slip ashore and mingle with the crowds.[16]

Once ashore, after having escaped from the Transvaal and Lourenço Marques, the real problems began for many of the refugees. CH Haggar of the YMCA, described events at his office on a Monday morning:

Case 1. Woman with two children, husband's whereabouts unknown, no money, not a change of clothing. Brings me a note from a gentleman who knows her to be respectable. My funds are exhausted, and all the clothing left was an old black skirt – that was better than nothing, and she took it.

Case 2. Woman with four children; husband supposed to be in Johannesburg; rent and relief stopped; could get work but who is to look after the children? Besides, what can a woman do with four children, and only £2 per month at the most?

Case 3. Very delicate woman; no shamming about her; has two children; her husband went to Ladysmith with a convoy before the siege; has heard nothing since; all relief stopped, and is in arrears for rent; needs a prolonged course of medical treatment. All I could do was to express sympathy and give her a little clothing for her boy. She had no money; neither had I, and the poor woman has to live on hope – a very cruel protector.

Case 4. Woman with two children, husband an invalid, does not want charity, does not want to be separated from her children. Wants work with decent pay attached to it, in order that she may buy bread for the little ones.

Case 5. A poor woman stood at the door of my room, unable to speak because of the lump in her throat. After some minutes, she said, "I have never asked for help before, and it will be too cruel for me to go and perhaps be told 'There is no money'. I have come to you because I come from Australia. My husband is dead. My name is ..." I would have given something for a dark corner where I could have had a good cry. [sic][17]

Tales of impoverishment and distress amongst civilians as a result of the war were by no means isolated incidents as the following two further cases suggest:

Lettie Bartlett appeared before the magistrate on a charge of vagrancy. Police Superintendent Alexander stated that the woman had come from Johannesburg a year before. She had obtained employment as a

Refugees departing for Cape Town (*War Pictures*).

A refugee woman and child on the *Tintagel Castle* (Dickson).

maid. For some time she had tried in vain to obtain news of her brother, whom she had left in Fordsburg. Her distress affected her mind, and as her mistress could not keep her, she was discharged. She refused to become a beggar and the Salvation Army had taken her in hand, but she had broken out of the barracks, and was arrested. The district surgeon certified that she was in poor health through lack of food. After two weeks in hospital, she was again brought before the court. Superintendent Alexander said he would send the unfortunate woman to his wife to see what could be done for her.[18]

Daniel Coleman and John William Brown, after spending some time in the prison in Lourenço Marques were viewed as vagrants because they were destitute. On their release they were expelled from the city by the Portuguese authorities. On 5 August 1900, the British consul, Fritz Crowe, had no choice but to send the two gentlemen to Durban.[19]

However, not all of the refugees arriving in Durban were in a state of economic or psychological depression. Many were people of means or position, such as Magistrate Jackson of Newcastle and the council of the town who arrived in Durban, via Lourenço Marques on board the *König*.[20]

Fortunately for the town of Durban, it managed to dispense with some of the refugees. On 1 January 1900, it was reported in Cape Town by the central relief committee that a transport steamer, the *Cheshire*, had been placed at the disposal of the Mansion House relief committee to convey refugees, who would be in a position of supporting themselves, to Britain.[21] Roughly two months later, a notice appeared in the *Natal Mercury*, which advertised another such journey:

> **Transport for Refugees,** *Canada.*
> Passengers are requested to be on board by 2.00 p.m. on Thursday 8 March 1900 at the wharf. The following regulations must be observed:
> (a) Women and children in all cases will have separate quarters from men.
> (b) Blankets will be provided, and will be issued at 6.00 p.m. and must be returned by 6.00 a.m. daily.
> (c) Bags must be provided for luggage, and must not be of a larger superficial capacity than 13 x 20 x 24 inches.
> (d) Knives and forks must be provided.
> (e) Refugees will be required to clean their quarters.
> (f) In the case of infants and small children, sufficient condensed milk must be provided to last the voyage.
> (g) Medical comforts will be provided from Cape Town.[22]

It seems that not all refugees were happy with the arrangements for their voyage home as can be gathered from the following letter signed by 'A disabled Nurse, Refugee from Johannesburg' which appeared in the *Natal Mercury* on 21 March 1900:

> I am sending a warning to refugees. You issue information that passage would be given free to England

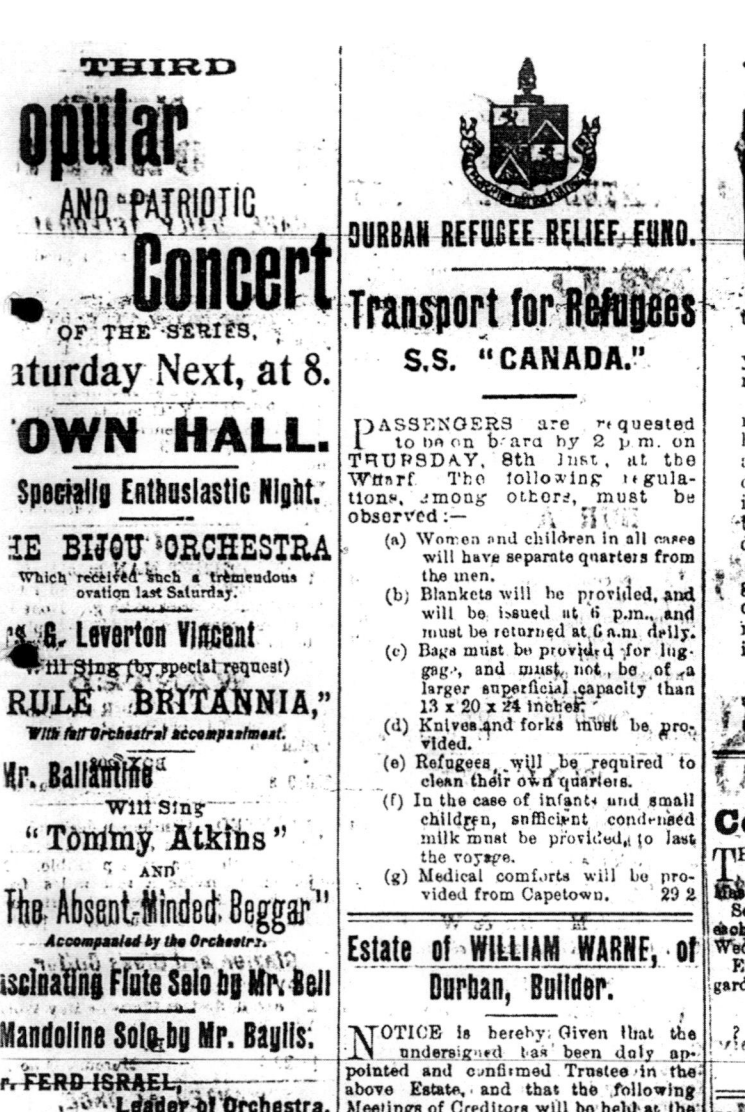

(*Natal Mercury*, 6 March 1900).

per transport steam-boats, chartered for that purpose by the Imperial Government, to refugees who might be desirous of getting to their friends. One of these left Cape Town in January or December, and ever since Christmas Durban has been agitating for the same supposed good thing. At last, after two months delay, the *Canada* is granted, and those who had been anxiously awaiting the boon are informed that most complete arrangements have been made for the comfort of the refugees, and they see she is a boat of noble dimensions – 10,000 tons. They complete their arrangements, never dreaming of more or less than second or third class accommodation (I am told that second class tickets were issued in Maritzburg.) Alas for our expectation. On going aboard we can find no quarters save first class (saloon) which are habitable to our ideas and usages. We are told to wait until visitors have left the ship, and our quarters will be assigned to us and our comforts assured. We wait and wait. and then all are consigned to the lower regions – bare rooms occupied by, and only fit to be occupied by troops, accustomed to warfare and rough living and usage, not fit certainly for frail women and tender babies to face the horrors of wind and wave, and the terrors of sea-sickness. Can it be that the Imperial Government care so little for those who have lost all and suffered so keenly, while Boers, the perpetrators of unheard-of outrages, Cronje and his staff, rough prisoners are overwhelmed with kindness and conveyed to Simonstown first class. Whose is the fault of mismanagement? Any who may in future ask free passage per transport must be prepared for the roughest usage and quarters. Why and how is it that when a ship is chartered by the Imperial Government, first class passengers can be taken, paying 6s.3d per day, getting the best of everything, while those who are not able to pay, having lost all, have to rough it in every way? Are you aware that we were, one and all, sick or well, old or young, single or married, children and babies, consigned to the troop decks, with bare tables, tin mugs, iron spoons, tin plates, soup served in tin boilers, (hard boiled beef), potatoes boiled in their skins, not even washed? For tea we had bread and margarine, tea served in boilers, all in the roughest style, just as the troops have it. The provisions supplied are certainly not equal to the steerage of the Cunard boats of the seventies. We have no beds at night, troop hammocks are hung for us. I would warn all who are in any way disabled by accident or illness not to accept free passage per Imperial transport.[23]

It is difficult to determine the number of refugees who arrived in Durban, as only fare-paying passengers were recorded and shipping companies and the railways brought refugees in gratis if they could not afford the fare. But Superintendent Alexander of the Durban borough police estimated that by March 1900, 20 000 refugees had arrived in Durban.[24]

Hilda Bowesa

During the early stages of the Anglo-Boer War, one Charles Guinnie brought Hilda Bowesa from Jagersfontein in the Orange Free Sate to Durban. For three years she worked for Mrs Guinnie until the latter moved to East London. After the war ended, she did not return to the Free State, but remained in Durban, losing all touch with her relatives in the Free State. During her stay in Durban, she gave birth to a child whose father, John Julis, a Griqua, worked in Johannesburg. In July 1910, 11 years after she had been brought to Durban, she was arrested for entering Natal without a pass. In court it came to light that she was 'a moral person' and she produced three testimonials from employers she had worked for after Mrs Guinnie. The position of Hilda was highly irregular and she was fined for entering Natal without a pass and granted an inward pass to provide her time to contact her family in Jagersfontein, as the authorities intended to deport her. Fearing deportation, Bowesa moved temporarily to the Polela division. On her return to Durban, she was again apprehended, but managed to have her inward pass renewed. The renewal and her application for permanent residence in Natal was approved on 26 July, 1911.[25]

After the fall of the capitals of the Boer republics, the initial waves of refugees subsided. These waves, however, did not dry up completely. Uitlanders who had remained on the Witwatersrand could only depart for Durban after the occupation of Johannesburg, while, for the duration of the war, the military continued to send undesirables, political prisoners and all kinds of unsavoury characters to Durban.

On 10 January 1901, the vice-consul of France wrote to Superintendent RC Alexander informing him that seven Russian men were coming to Durban at the expense of the British government. These men were without means, and the vice-consul would be most obliged if the superintendent would do all that was necessary to feed and lodge them until the day of their departure.[26] To Alexander this was an imposition on Durban, and the final straw. He, therefore, wrote to the mayor, explaining that he had, apart from the Russians, two families from Port Elizabeth who required food and lodgings until they were able to join their husbands in the Transvaal. Numerous undesirables were being sent to Durban in a similar manner to those mentioned, who should, in no way, as far as Alexander was concerned, be considered the responsibility of Durban or Natal.[27] The complaints of Alexander seem to have made little impact, for on 16 January 1901, a telegram from Hely-Hutchinson to Milner informed the police chief that the military authorities were sending down more indigent Uitlanders who were to remain in Durban pending their passage to Europe, or until their consuls were able to take charge of them.[28] The enclosed instructions made it clear to Alexander that the Natal government had undertaken, in the interests of humanity, to feed and house these refugees during their stay in Durban and he had to see the mayor at once and make the best provisions he could for the necessary food and shelter. Alexander was to report back as to the arrangements made.[29] These were only the first of a stream of refugees who were granted permits to leave Johannesburg for Durban. Many of them were indigent, which placed another burden on the already over-extended city of Durban.

The last refugees

The numbers of this new wave of refugees were swollen by others who were allowed to proceed from Europe to Durban, hoping to get back to the Transvaal, and by individuals still arriving from Lourenço Marques, such as Thomas Henry Fowler. Fowler arrived in Lourenço Marques from Barberton in early 1900. He had little money and decided to remain in Mozambique, hoping that he would be allowed to return to the Transvaal. A year later this had not materialised and, by now, he was broke, could not find employment and was ill. Fritz Crowe, therefore, took the opportunity of sending him to Durban.[30]

The military authorities also provided permits for refugees to move from the Cape Colony to Durban. In June 1900 alone, 80 people arrived from the Cape. Their ranks were swollen by between 200–300 time-expired men from the colonial forces. These were recruited from amongst the Uitlanders, who arrived in Durban almost penniless, and having served their time for the empire, were dumped in Durban – to the agitation of Mayor Nicol.[31]

The overcrowding in Durban in June 1901 was so serious that Superintendent Alexander was forced to bring the situation to the notice of the mayor. Refugees were having to sleep in outhouses, and boarding houses were allowing six people to sleep in a room which could barely hold six beds, while every hotel was crammed. Among the new arrivals were a large number of the vagabond type. Not only was the burden of feeding and looking after the destitute refugees becoming greater, but maintaining law and order was becoming more and more difficult as the numbers of refugees increased.[32] At the start of the war, the European refugees were housed in camps and buildings in the borough and special police were stationed at these sites to protect them and enforce law and order, and the African refugees were housed temporarily at a section of Lords Ground before being despatched to their homes. Now it was an entirely different situation, with white refugees living wherever they could find a place to sleep and the African refugees, totalling about 1 500, scattered throughout the backyards of Durban.

On 3 September 1901 seven Americans were allowed to disembark from the *Walmer Castle* for the purpose of transhipment to Lourenço Marques. However, instead of going to that port, they surreptitiously proceeded via Charlestown to Standerton without passes and under suspicious circumstances. The men were immediately deported to Durban, on the advice of the magistrate of Standerton, by the military authorities. Their arrival in Durban infuriated the IRO, Harry Smith, for according to him 'if their presence is not desirable in the Transvaal it is equally undesirable here. The Transvaal should, I submit, hit upon another method of dealing with persons whose presence in that Colony is objected to – say the shipment of such characters to the country of their birth'. With both the American consul, AH Rennie, and the Union-Castle Mail Steamship Co. Ltd., which had originally brought the men to Durban, refusing to take responsibility for them, they remained in the custody of the military authorities.[33]

How then did the town of Durban react, and manage to deal with the influx of thousands of people of all classes and various nationalities?

Managing the refugees in Durban

With Durban caught unawares and the city swamped by thousands of refugees, action needed to be taken. The first step was an urgent telegram on 24 October 1899 from Hely-Hutchinson to Joseph Chamberlain, quoting the mayor of Durban: 'Matters critical, 1 100 aliens landed yesterday, prisoners let loose, not five per cent British, understand 8 000 more of the same class still to come, absolutely imperative these must not land in Durban.'[34] The problem facing Durban was enormous. The town was overcrowded with mostly destitute and poverty-stricken refugees, while the Transvaal government had apparently emptied its jails of 'dead-beats, pickpockets and gaol birds' and sent them to the British colonies as refugees. This caused the exasperated mayor to refer to these refugees in his city as 'Rand Scum'.[35] The most sensible way to deal with the crisis was to employ the existing charity organisations and to create additional relief committees.

Durban charity and patriotic societies

Before the advent of the Anglo-Boer War, there were two main charities operating in Durban, the Durban Benevolent Society and the Durban Home for Men. The Durban Benevolent Society had been in existence since 1854 and was run by volunteers, relying on donations for their funding, such as for example £20 from Mr J Brown, a bequest from the late Mr S Butcher for £500, and £100 donated by the Durban Turf Club.[36] At the July 1899 meeting, 12 ladies were present and Mrs Hulston was elected president, Mrs Alexander secretary, and Mrs Cottam treasurer. Each member had a certain number of cases allocated to her to investigate and manage. Whilst the society gave cash under some circumstances, in other cases vouchers were to be redeemed at certain businesses for clothes, food, rent and medicines. Apart from giving assistance, the Durban Benevolent Society had a small home referred to as 'The Institute' with a matron in charge, to provide accommodation for old and frail people with no resources.[37]

The minutes of the Durban Benevolent Society contain many pathetic stories, intermingled with tales of generosity by individuals. For example, Mrs Manton applied for help to support her 90-year-old blind father. She was allocated ten shillings per month, and £1 was given to her to pay for his transport to Durban. Just prior to the war, in August 1899, a letter from a resident in Congella recommended that an old resident of Durban, who was destitute after the death of her husband, should be admitted into 'The Institute'. She was quite unable to earn anything towards her own keep and was duly admitted. A case in point of charity at work was the story of a German woman, Mrs Girbach, who, with her three small children, arrived from Johannesburg without any means of support. As a result, the society paid £2 10s for a week's stay at a boarding house for the family. Girbach had left her husband behind in Johannesburg and had found work for him in Durban, but he had no way of getting to the coast. When a Mrs Jamieson heard of their plight, she gave the society a cheque for £5 5s, which was forwarded to Mr Girbach, enabling him to travel to Durban to start his new job. A similar charitable contribution came from Mrs Nicholson of Richmond, who offered three bottles of milk per day, which were gratefully accepted for use at the 'The Institute'.[38]

As the Anglo-Boer War progressed, it became a status symbol to contribute lavishly to charities such as the Durban Benevolent Society. On 1 September 1900, Mrs Walmsley contributed £1 000 towards the maintenance of the home for girls and women, and a further £1 000 conditionally on the same amount being contributed in Natal. This attracted considerable attention in Durban, and as a result several of Walmsley's friends promised contributions.[39]

As the war progressed and the refugees started to pour into Durban, the demands on the Durban Benevolent Society increased enormously. Whereas during June 1899, 29 individuals received assistance, by January 1900, the number of cases had increased to 93. It was during this time that a new problem arose, that of husbands volunteering for the army and making no provision for their wives, as with the plight of Mrs Holt. She applied for assistance as her husband had gone to the front leaving her without means. An order for 4s 2d of groceries fortnightly, and a small loaf of bread daily was allocated to her. Similarly, Mrs Harper, with three children, asked for help, saying that her husband had given up a well-paid job to go to the front, leaving them penniless.[40] These were not isolated instances and several more women were forced to seek aid for similar reasons.

At times even parents would abandon their children. One such case was that of a Professor Jensen, his wife and daughter, who left three children, two boys and a girl, with a Mrs Armstrong with no money, owing her £11 in maintenance. As a result, Mrs Armstrong applied for assistance, and received 3s 6d for provisions and one large loaf of bread daily, for two weeks. The Armstrong boys were afterwards sent to the Trappist Monastery at Mariannhill, and the little girl to an orphanage.[41] If the orphanage was the St John Orphanage in Berea Road, she would have been with 21 other girls and the two sisters who were in charge. The

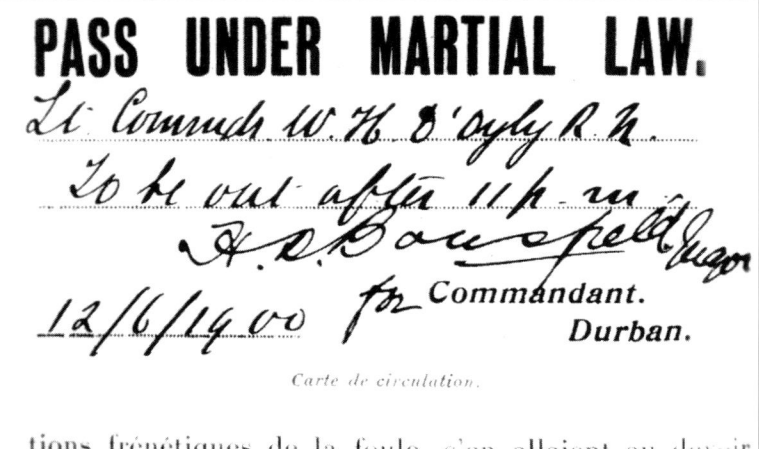

Martial law pass (Raoul-Duval).

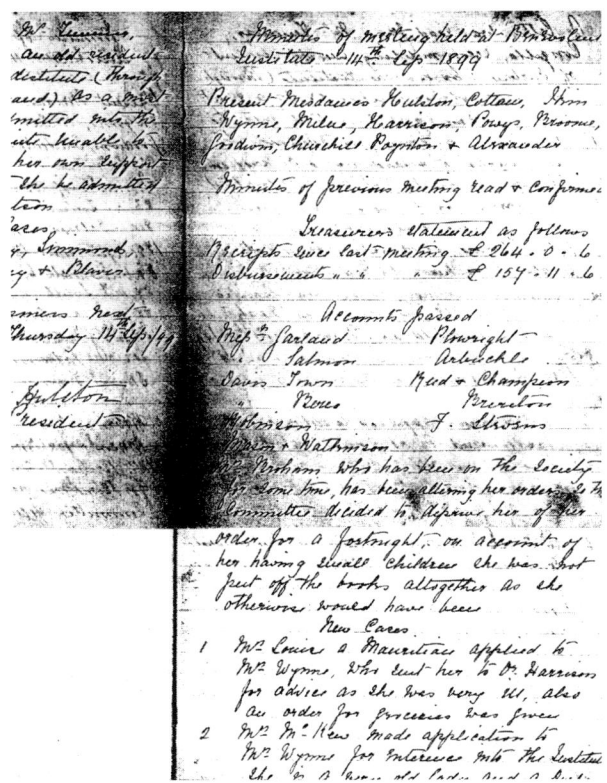

sisters trained the girls for domestic work and they were well versed in scrubbing, washing, cooking and plain dressmaking and, after being trained, positions were found for them.[42] An equally sad case was that of a Mrs Callahan, whose son had been diagnosed as being insane and liable to become violent. She requested the train fare to take him to the asylum in Pietermaritzburg.[43] With the increase in refugees, inevitably, some not entirely honest people would try to live off charity, as is borne out by the following cases minuted. A Mrs Broham, supported by the Benevolent Society for a period of time, surreptitiously made changes in her allocation, and, as a result, the committee decided to withhold provisions for a fortnight. On account of her having small children, she was not just discarded altogether, as would otherwise have been the case. In another instance, Mrs Larsen used her refugee status to procure aid from both the Durban Benevolent Society and the relief committee. When caught out, she was refused aid by both institutions.[44]

The chief objective of the Durban Home for Men was to look after 'those poor men who accept help only as a means of giving them the opportunity to help themselves'. The organisation kept extremely detailed records as the annual report of July 1900 shows. During this year the home admitted 1 305 men, of whom 647 were tradesmen, 217 clerks and 441 unskilled labourers. Of these men 936 were Protestant and 369 Roman Catholic. The cosmopolitan nature of the refugees is borne out by their nationalities: 615 were English, 104 Irish, 148 Scottish, 29 Welsh, 10 Dutch, 39 colonials, 25 Americans, 89 Germans, 32 Scandinavians, 132 French, and 81 came from other countries. Although the Durban Home for Men was a charitable organisation, it had certain rules: the use of alcohol was not allowed, and if the applicant was not ill or physically handicapped, he had to work and earn his keep. Those who could not find work were given the job of breaking stones at the quarry, receiving 2s 6d at the end of the day which entitled them to a bed and three meals. During 1900, 438 men worked at stone breaking earning an average of 2s 6d per day. The average number of days worked by the stone breakers was 11. Presumably the prospect of swinging a 14 lbs ($\pm$ 6 kg) hammer every day provided many with sufficient incentive to look for less arduous work. During 1900, the home served 43 376 meals of which only 6 099 were free, the rest being paid for. They sent 38 men to hospital, of whom one died, while 210 left after temporary assistance.[45]

Living at the Durban Home for Men might have been austere, but at Christmas time during the war, the inmates were given an excellent dinner, prepared by Mrs Peel and other ladies of the relief committee. One of the inhabitants recalls: 'We could hardly expect roast beef in abundance, and plum pudding in unlimited quantities, to say nothing about the sweets in great variety. Ripe fruits of the season were being consumed very rapidly, as we were all blessed with good appetites, and, with the aid of large quantities of soft drinks, anyone may imagine we had an excellent time of it, especially as we had free smokes in the bargain'. The tables were attractively set and the walls were hung with British flags and decorated with patriotic mottos. After dinner there was entertainment in the form of music, singers and recitations suitable for Christmas time.[46]

In addition to the Durban Benevolent Society and the Durban Home for Men, other patriotic and benevolence societies were also formed in Durban at the time of the war. They included the Loyal Ladies' Guild, the Jewish Girls' Patriotic League, Durban Jewish relief committee and, by far the most active, the Women's Patriotic League. The latter was founded on 18 October 1899, and disbanded exactly a year later. The president was Lady Robinson and the vice-president Mrs G Payne. The objective of the league was: 'To minister to the needs of the sick, wounded and suffering amongst the Imperial and Colonial troops of Her Majesty'. There were 25 work centres which made 3 505 shirts, 3 459 pairs of socks, 609 pyjama suits, 950 nightingales, 314 cardigan jackets, plus dressing gowns, pillows, cushions, and eiderdowns. Sir John Furley, chief commissioner of the British Red Cross, made a special request to the league to supply the Red Cross with fitted kitbags. To pay for this he made available a sum of £500, and he received 513 kitbags, each containing 1 shirt, 1 pair of pyjamas, cap, sponge, sponge bag, socks, handkerchief, brush and comb, toothbrush, soap and a towel.

The Women's Patriotic League otherwise collected money to finance their work and, during their existence, had £2 989 5s 5d donated to them by the public and businesses. On one occasion, 300 boys from Durban High School and the Durban Boys' Model School staged a 'Military Concert' and 'Assault at Arms' with physical drills and patriotic songs to raise money for the organisation. The advantages of making donations, ranging from clothes to foodstuffs, was that it was acknowledged in newspapers, like the *Natal Mercury* and the *Natal Witness*, which in turn provided good publicity for donors. For example, in an acknowledgment in the *Natal Witness* of 10 May 1900, amongst many other gifts were 104 pillowslips and 20 handkerchiefs, donated by Mohandas Gandhi.[47]

An organisation that worked closely with the Women's Patriotic League, and shared the same objectives, was the Absent-Minded Beggar Relief Corporation. Patriotic organisations such as these relied heavily on the generosity of the public and at times additional funds were created. This was the case when Boatswain Murphy of the *Lismore Castle* drowned while attempting to save a seaman who had fallen off a dredger. As a result of this accident, a fund was started to send some money to his widow and seven children. In a very short time £2 was collected.[48] Other organisations such as the YMCA, the Salvation Army, the Jewish Girls' Patriotic League and the Durban Jewish relief committee also contributed to alleviating the plight of refugees. The latter organisation was formed on 24 September 1899, under the chairmanship of P Wartski to meet and assist the Jewish refugees leaving the Transvaal. Whenever there were Jews amongst the refugees arriving from Lourenço Marques, Wartski would meet them at the harbour and direct them to Lords Ground or the drill hall. Other Jewish people were assisted to join their families in the Cape Colony. For those unable to find a home, the Jewish relief committee had rented a house in Prince Edward Street, with the female members of the committee attending to the needs of the families residing in the house. This house was relinquished on 5 July 1900. From the funds collected, the Durban Jewish relief committee paid a shilling a day to each applicant. By 28 May 1901 the Durban Jewish relief committee had received 429 applications for assistance and advice. In most cases employment was found for the refugees, thereby making monetary assistance unnecessary.[49]

The response of the Durban town council

To deal with this influx of refugees in an official and structured manner that would prevent the entire benevolence burden falling on charities, Mayor John Nicol decided to appointed a committee under the chairmanship of J Ellis-Brown. This committee consisted of four councillors and 12 men and women, including five ladies who also served on the committee of the Durban Benevolent Society. The new committee, called the Durban refugee relief committee, with WO Cook as the secretary, had the task of managing the most pressing needs, namely, accommodation, food and clothing.[50]

As a first step, notices were placed in the *Natal Mercury* by the Durban Benevolent Society asking for donations for the refugee relief fund. In the process, £4 029 5s 4d was collected for the refugees.[51] It soon became clear that the burden of caring for refugees was too much for Durban to carry alone. As a result, Nicol along with the Newcastle town council which was then living in exile in Durban, applied to the Mansion House fund for assistance. This fund, named after the official residence of the mayor of London, collected money to assist victims of wars and disasters. The appeal elicited a response and £170 000 was allocated to South Africa. This had to be distributed, under the chairmanship of Lord Milner, to refugee centres throughout South Africa. During the first 15 weeks of the war, £11 000 from the Mansion House fund was donated to the Durban refugee relief fund.

Accommodation

With finances secured and some donations received, accommodation had to be found for the thousands of up-country refugees. As a first step the police canvassed households to see who would be prepared to accommodate refugees. The Durban and Coast Agricultural Society offered their show grounds (Lords Ground) and marquee tents were erected to house men. By the beginning of November 1899, 1 100 men were living at Lords Ground, which would also be used as a military camp and a remount depot. The borough police had to recruit 16 special constables and one sergeant, whose task it was to maintain law and order in the encampment and to guard the remount depot.

The African Boating Company gave their newly completed barracks, intended for their African staff, as accommodation to house women and children. Soon these barracks provided for 400 women and children, guarded by one special constable. Under the auspices of the

The Absent-Minded Beggar
By Rudyard Kipling

When you've shouted "Rule Britannia" – when you've sung "God save the Queen" –
When you've finished killing Kruger with your mouth –
Will you kindly drop a shilling in my little tambourine
For a gentleman in Khaki ordered South.
He's an absent-minded beggar and his weaknesses are great –
But we and Paul must take him as we find him –
He is out on active service, wiping something off a slate,
And he's left a lot of little things behind him –
Duke's son, cook's son, son of a hundred Kings –
(Fifty thousand horse and foot going to Table Bay!)
Each of 'em doing his country's work (and who's to look after their things)
Pass the hat for your credit's sake and pay – pay – pay.

The African Boating Company barracks in Point Road (LHM).

Refugees cooking at Victoria Park (*The Black and White Budget*, 23 December 1899).

Bell tents at Victoria Park refugee camp (LHM).

refugee committee, a large encampment was laid out at Victoria Park.[52] Victoria Park, the area now bounded by Boscombe Terrace, Sea View Street, Brickhill Road and Gresham Place, contained 190 tents, many of which had been purchased at prices between £1 10s and £4 10s. Five special constables kept order and protected the 900 occupants. Streets of uniform width were laid out and the building lines were rigidly adhered to. Water was laid on, convenient stand pipes were placed throughout the camp and four electric lamps were erected. Sanitary arrangements were made and wash-houses of corrugated iron with cement floors were built for men and women. After a visit by Lord Milner and the sanitary committee, the sailcloth lean-to and the bell tents were replaced by square houses, still of canvas, but with a framework of timber with a pitched roof. For the good of all concerned, it was necessary that a few general rules be drawn up, such as: 'behave respectfully; don't quarrel with your neighbours; and keep the premises clean'.

This canvas town became a unique little village which gave refugee families the opportunity of living together. Most of the men in the Victoria Park camp worked and those who could not find work in town obtained employment in the Durban corporation relief works at 18s per week. Housewives were busy cooking, washing and mending clothes, and older children attended school, while younger ones played in the ample spaces of the park. One writer of the day describes the area as 'A cosy little suburb which nestles in the sea-splashed dunes'.[53]

Other accommodation was found at Messrs Butcher & Sons' warehouse, Messrs EL Acutt's premises in Smith Street extension, the Union Buildings, Payne's Buildings, and the DLI drill hall which was evacuated to be used by the refugees. Mariannhill Monastery sheltered 60 refugees, Verulam 55 and a further 50 found shelter on the outskirts of Durban.

Food

Along with accommodation, the most pressing need was food. To deal with this, the refugee relief committee set up kitchens which provided a breakfast of porridge, bread, coffee, sugar and milk; the midday meal was soup and bread and in the evening, bread and coffee were served.[54] Those with some money could obtain meals at Quinn's Restaurant which had a special menu for refugees, with breakfast costing 3d, dinner 6d, and supper 3d. In November 1899, Quinn's served 9 990 meals and, at that price, could still show a profit of £18 12s 6d.[55] For those with more resources, the Courthouse and New Pine Restaurants were offering refugee meals at 1s.[56] For those providing their own meals the Durban market prices in 1900 were apples 1s to 3s per 100, bananas 6d to 1s 3d per 100, cabbages 1s to 3s per dozen; ducks sold for 4s each, while fowls cost 1s 6d to 2s 9d each. Meat prices per pound were rump steak 9d, good sirloin 8d, prime ribs 7d, topside 7d, and salt beef 6d to 7d.

Food and shelter were not the only expenses incurred by the refugees and the Durban refugee relief committee. Travelling costs to friends and family, and medical and funeral expenses needed to be provided for.

With the monies donated by the Manson House fund and collected that locally running out fast, it was understandable that the central relief committee at Cape Town ruled that: 'All able-bodied men are expected to be off the relief lists by 31 March 1900.'[58]

Economic activities

One of the most important aspects of managing the refugees in Durban was to keep them from being idle or to exploit them as a readily available workforce. The departure of the volunteer regiments for the front at the beginning of October 1899 gave impetus to the campaign headed by Superintendent Alexander to recruit out-of-work men who had not originally joined up for the various irregular units of infantry and mounted troops. This recruitment drive, no doubt driven by both patriotic sentiments and the hope of having an opportunity to exact revenge for the predicament many refugees found themselves in, was so successful that 7 000 men joined up, of which 1 400 volunteered as stretcher-bearers, while others became hospital ship orderlies, and 300 joined the Railway Pioneer Corps.[59]

This did, however, not empty the streets of Durban of idle loafers. As a result, Mayor Nicol wrote to Prime Minister Albert Hime, on 16 February 1900, reminding him that some time back the government had suggested that a road, to be called Brickhill Road, be constructed to the Umgeni River, and he felt that this would be an ideal opportunity to provide work for the able-bodied refugees in Durban.[60] At the same time the Durban refugee relief Fund committee, in trying to obtain employment for the 600 to 700 men in Durban, appealed to the colonial undersecretary to approach the government for assistance in finding employment for them.[61] The minister of lands and works offered to employ the men in the Natal harbour department to clear the bush in the area bordered by Shepstone and Rutherford Streets and the reclaimed area at a wage of two shillings per day.

At first it appeared that none of the refugees were prepared to work for a wage of two shillings per day, but shortly afterwards between 60 or 70 men, the majority of whom were married, agreed to the proposal. Of these, only 55 eventually turned up for work, and eventually only three remained. The harbour engineer, Charles Crofts, who found it impossible to clear the bush with only three men, said he would rather try to draft the remaining trio into better paid jobs. The three men, B Johns, E Zeiss and John Taylor, were rewarded for their willingness and were employed elsewhere. Other Uitlanders also found work. Joseph Crampton for example was employed in his trade as a coppersmith, while others were employed by the Durban corporation. A hundred men assisted at the Umlaas waterworks and helped dig the foundations for the new electricity building at three shillings per day. Their labour was rewarded by a wage increase in October 1901. These men seem to have been the exception as the rest of the men refused the employment offered.[62]

As 31 March 1900, the critical date by which all able-bodied men

Square canvas houses at Victoria Park refugee camp (LHM).

The Indian market adjacent to the Grey Street mosque (LHM).

The Alice Street power station (LHM).

The clear water reservoir at the Umlaas waterworks (Henderson).

were to be removed from charity, drew near, the Durban refugee relief committee again appealed to the Natal government to employ refugees. The reply was short and to the point: 'As you may have seen from the newspapers, the refugees absolutely refuse to work for two shillings a day. The information contained in the newspapers has also been confirmed by a private letter which I received from Mr Crofts. I can do nothing for them.'[63] This problem was not confined to European refugees. Eighteen African refugees, ten of whom came from Lady Grey in the Cape Colony, six from Basutoland and two from Zululand, were given employment in the public works department, but when their demand for £4 per month was refused, all but one left. A further letter from Engineer Crofts summed up his view of the attitude of the refugees: 'I fear that there is a goodly number of our so-called refugees who, though quite willing to receive the aid and protection of the Government, object to doing anything in return.'[64]

To a certain extent Crofts had oversimplified matters. Most Uitlanders came from positions in which they had been well paid, compared to what they were being offered in Durban. Furthermore, many of these men filled positions as overseers of African labour, managers and numerous other professions and were not manual labourers or willing to be downgraded to a lower status. At the same time, the white worker militance sweeping Durban at the time, as exemplified by the strikes of the tram workers and carpenters and joiners, must have found favour amongst the Uitlanders. Viewing themselves as loyal British subjects who were in a predicament because of their allegiance must have convinced many that they had the right to charity. Bearing this in mind, Acutt, who was in charge of the arrangements for the relief of destitute men, made a suggestion to Prime Minister Hime. He proposed that the money earned by these men be handed over to the Durban refugee relief committee, who would in return feed the men at the rate of eight pence per day, and provide clothes and boots, while allowing them to occupy their present premises. The balance of their earnings would be handed to them when they left Durban. This recommendation must have filled the men with disgust and a feeling that they were being exploited. Despite the complexity of the situation, the colonial secretary agreed to Acutt's suggestion.[65]

The attitude of the Uitlanders did not endear them to many Durbanites. The journal *Industries* provided pragmatic advice to the 'helpless refugees' who spent their 'whole day idle, because no man hath hired them' in the town gardens, remarking that they should not refuse the work offered by the government or corporation.[66] The *Natal Mercury* of 30 March 1900 addressed some of the major issues

> The refusal of the refugees to accept the offer of the Government to provide work at 2s. per day can, to a certain extent, be understood in this country, but we are much afraid that if the Imperial Government are applied to for funds to keep the refugees as they are, they will promptly turn around and say that, if the able-bodied refugees will not accept such work, they can do nothing in the matter. It is absurd, as one of the objectors stated, to say that by accepting the Govern-

ment's offer the price of labour would be reduced in the Colony. The work suggested by the government is not work that there is any urgent necessity for doing, and if they get it done by other than refugees it will be by natives, and will cost half the amount now offered. Of course, it seems very hard that men accustomed, perhaps, to wages of 10s. to 20s. per day should be asked to do manual labour at 2s. per day, but the difficulty is there is no other suitable work that can be offered, that is, work at a higher figure. Emergency work of the kind proposed is quite out of the ordinary run of things, and neither degrades the man who does it, nor affects the man who is engaged in other work requiring more skill, and consequently paid for at a much higher rate. No man is ever degraded by earning his own living, and we think that those at Lord's who are able to work and decline to do it are making a mistake. Surely, if they get 12s. per week out of which they pay 5s. for their food, they would be better off and feel far more independent than they are at present; but, of course, it is entirely a matter for themselves.[67]

That such criticism did not alter the mindset of many of the refugees, either towards charity or towards work, can be gathered from their letters to the *Natal Mercury*. One gentleman stated that he could not possibly live on less than £25 per month. Another wrote that, while he was grateful for what was being done for them, what about giving them some meat and tobacco? Someone else wrote to the *Natal Mercury*, enquiring as to how he could live and maintain a decent appearance on one shilling a day. He went on to ask what the refugees had to do with the Durban Benevolent Society as: 'We are no paupers dependant on Durban charity, we are placed in our present position through our loyalty to the Empire, and this, evidently, the Society cannot understand.' He pointed out that there was plenty of money to their credit and challenged the society to ask for sufficient funds.[68]

Another refugee wrote, 'Many Johannesburg men are asking themselves whether this money so kindly subscribed for their aid is being rightly and properly disbursed?' He continued by stating that at 10:00 on a Friday morning he had observed a large crowd of respectably dressed men and women standing outside the Durban Benevolent Society's office waiting for the weekly dole: 'One by one they slunk away, ashamed of being seen, ashamed of being treated as paupers. Men, women, yea and ladies, broken-hearted, being made public exhibitions for over two hours on the pavement awaiting charity.' The author goes on to describe the paying of the allowances as a vile system of benevolence. In reaction, the *Natal Mercury* ran an editorial pointing out the inaccuracies in the letter, such as the fact that the Durban Benevolent Society did not pay the allowances but that this was done by the Durban refugee relief committee who had offices in the same building, and the huge task of trying to house and feed the large number of refugees.[69]

A view of the Point and the Bluff from the town centre. The bush which required clearing was located at Cato Creek in the middle distance (LHM).

The Point docks developed towards the town across the reclaimed land at Cato Creek (Harrison).

While employment for refugee men was plentiful, work for young ladies was scarce, possibly because of the attitude towards working women prevalent at that time. The remarks of Colonel Schermbrucker in the Cape Assembly demonstrated his opposition to women's rights: 'She had only one right, to contribute to the comfort of man. They should not go against the will of the Creator when he formed woman from the rib of man.'[70] Because of these prejudices, women could only find jobs as nurses, counter assistants in the ladies' section of department stores, and as typists, although men were also employed in this capacity as this advertisement shows: 'Wanted, thoroughly experienced bookkeeper, preference given to one who is an efficient shorthand writer and typist, a permanent situation to a suitable man.' Another sphere of work available to white women was as domestics in the wealthier households, as is evident from the following advertisements in the Durban newspapers at the end of 1899 and the beginning of 1900:

Wanted – Responsible white nurse girl about 16 for nurse to two children.
Wanted – white maid servant for general housework and plain cooking, Clark Road.
Wanted – white girl to mind infant and to assist with housework.
Wanted – Young girl will find comfortable home with small compensation with family on Berea in return for service as mother's help, one child.
Wanted – Governess to teach English, painting and music.[71]

Many hotels and boarding houses provided positions for housekeepers and maids, while retail businesses employed many young men and women. For those young Uitlander ladies requiring a new challenge, the Dainty Cigarette Company at 537 West Street was looking for white girls to learn cigarette making.[72] In the *Natal Mercury* 25 vacant situations were advertised. Two ladies, Mrs Carlisle and Miss Johnstone, offered to find positions for women and girls who were in distress. They offered to place them in employment as domestics, needlewomen and laundresses.[73] They seemed to be successful as their agency existed for several months.

The mechanics of the war itself also provided employment for Uitlander women. On 27 September 1901, the general superintendent of the burgher camps wrote to the Uitlander committee in Durban saying that, owing to the unsatisfactory manner in which the Boer women in the concentration camps performed their duties when appointed as assistants to the camp matron, it was decided, if possible, to obtain the services of young women of British parentage. They would be paid £4 per month with accommodation, rations and uniform. Six to ten assistants would be required in each camp, but it would not be possible for children to accompany these ladies. BW Brayshaw, the secretary of the Durban Uitlander committee, immediately submitted the names of the following women: Nurse Nettleton for the position of matron at the Balmoral concentration camp, and GF Esselen, who resided at the corner of Berea and Vause Roads, for the position of matron at the Irene concentration camp.[74] The general superintendent soon complained that the women who had been sent up as assistants by the Uitlander committee, as a rule, had proved most unsuitable for the work they had undertaken to do and many had to be returned to the coast. The ill-assorted set of women sent up had, in very few instances, shown few qualifications which suited them for the work of assistants to the camp matron. This did not prevent the authorities at the Merebank concentration camp from approaching the Uitlander committee, on 16 November 1901, to offer six positions for young women to act as probationers in the hospital. The rate of pay was now five shillings per day with rations and accommodation.[75]

Many refugees, instead of railing against fate, tried to make the best of a bad situation, and to provide for themselves and their families. They did this in various ways: some opened roadside stalls, or shanties, selling fruit and vegetables, others sold aerated water, some started boot-black stands. Still others formed themselves into street bands or organised pea and thimble. All these activities were strictly against the bye-laws, but the police turned a blind eye to the violations as the more people who could earn a living, and get off the list of those requiring relief, the better, for more and more refugees were arriving requiring assistance. Another enterprise that was tolerated, albeit reluctantly, was skittle alleys, a game of skill, whereby one could win money by knocking over skittles. Police Superintendent Alexander said he realised that the people running these were not very scrupulous or above taking advantage of the fools who patronised them, but it was a way for them to earn money and not be a burden on the relief committee.[76] Some refugees displayed even greater initiative and started businesses in Durban similar to those they had practised on the Witwatersrand. These entrepreneurs were unlikely to close these enterprises once the war ended and they returned to Johannesburg, thus providing a permanent benefit to Durban.

Charity continued

With refugees either without jobs or refusing to work, many were hard pressed to make ends meet on the allowance they were paid by the Durban refugee relief committee. Money for anything but food and a few essentials was hard to come by. With the Christmas of 1901 approaching, luxuries and toys for children were not likely to be forthcoming. To break the monotonous cycle, Mrs Pitt, the wife of the caretaker of the Victoria Park encampment, set to work to provide a little Christmas cheer for the children. She collected money from the ever-generous public and local merchants. Before long she had £37 and she then set to work. The DLI was approached and Bandmaster Grant not only promised the services of the band, but sent along a huge cake. A marquee was borrowed, and Messrs Hunt, Leuchars & Hepburn provided timber for a bandstand which Mr Pitt decorated with greenery. A Christmas tree stood in the centre of the tent and was laden with a wealth of toys and presents. Then the youngsters arrived, all 300 of them, all as well dressed as their mothers could manage. At 15:00, the band started playing and various

Young women and their soldier friends (LHM).

Durban Benevolent Society

REFUGEE RELIEF FUND,

WORKING with a Committee appointed by the Town Council, will be glad to receive Donations in aid of the work of Relieving Destitute Refugees.

Office: Colonial Mart, Smith Street.

Open every Monday, Wednesday, and Friday, from 10.30 a.m. to 12.30 p.m.

EDWARD W. EVANS,
Hon. Treasurer.

Box 307.   2511 tc

contests took place. There was a recitation competition and the *Natal Mercury* reporter and Mr Stewart were called upon to adjudicate. For the older girls there was a doll-dressing competition and for the younger ones a skipping contest, while the boys played a basket game.[77] For one day the children could forget the present and recall the happier times before they became refugees. Victoria Park was not the only place to give the children a Christmas treat.

The Reverend Hodges organised festivities at the West Street Wesleyan schoolroom. There were children of all ages up to 15 years and, in several cases, the mothers of the very young children came as well. They were given tea and cake and the reverend's helpers saw that everyone got their share. Mr Lewis entertained the children with his magic lantern and, at the end of the proceedings, Mr Abraham and Mr Polkinghorne handed the children either a book or toy as they filed out. Not only the children were entertained that Christmas. At the ABC barracks, on a Wednesday evening, when the schools had broken up for the holidays, the children of the barracks gave a concert. For the previous two months, Miss Dexter, a refugee herself, had daily instructed the younger children. The result was a concert with songs, glees, dialogues and recitations. The fathers, who were living at Lords Ground, were invited to join the families for the entertainment. A vote of thanks was proposed to Miss Dexter, and the proceedings were brought to a close with the children singing the national anthem.[78]

The Durban charity organisations and Uitlander views of the concentration camps

With the creation of the Merebank concentration camp in September 1901, Durban was exposed to the another side of the horrors experienced by civilians in time of war. The accusations aimed at the British of inhumane treatment of concentration camp inhabitants throughout South Africa were denied by the Guild of Loyal Women in a letter to *The Times*.[79] Mrs J Liege-Hullett, the wife of the speaker of the Natal house of assembly, adopted a more hands-on approach and visited several of the Natal concentration camps. Her verdict was simple: 'They (Boer women and children) are as well or better cared for than our own refugees. Look at the orders the Boer women place for clothes. The charity is misplaced. We take care of their women, and their men have no anxiety and carry on fighting.'[80] Liege-Hullett's visit was followed by that of a deputation of the Durban refugee relief committee, which included the chairman, J Ellis-Brown and the secretary, WO Cook, to the Merebank camp. Very little empathy existed in this group for the Boer women, children and elderly, and most of the observations were tainted by hostility. This caused them to comment on the three boys they found smoking and the Boer women whom they described as 'very helpless as a whole', and being 'too lazy to keep their centre washing trough free of refuse' and 'could not desist from their favourite pastime of stretching the truth'. Furthermore they considered the food dispensed to the inhabitants to be

better than that the Uitlanders were receiving. Their final verdict was that the British government did all they could for the Boer women and children.[81] A letter to the *Natal Mercury* probably summed up the general feeling of the Uitlanders and Durbanites towards the inhabitants of the Durban concentration camps: 'A number of Boer refugees were seen in Durban during the past days. If appearances are to be relied upon refugeeism at the expense of the British government is not altogether heart-breaking or flesh-reducing.'[82] Despite the negative images of the inhabitants of the Durban concentration camps the Durban Uitlander committee was not averse to dumping the children of British refugees at Merebank. When Mrs Penn, the mother of three young Uitlander children, Stephen (11), Claude (10) and Freddy (7) took so ill that she was admitted to hospital, nobody was prepared to take the three youngsters in. Instead on 16 June 1902, the Durban Uitlander committee sent them to Merebank.[83]

As their second winter approached, those destitute refugees who remained in Durban and Pietermaritzburg began to suffer from the cold, and an appeal was made to the colonial secretary for a grant to purchase blankets and warm clothing. Dr Scott, of the Uitlander committee, asked Henry Bale, the attorney-general, if any money was available from the funds with which he was connected. Unfortunately, there was none. The attorney-general immediately wrote to Prime Minister Hime outlining the problem and went on to say:

> It seems a monstrous thing that Boer refugees should be maintained at the cost of the Imperial Government at camps and elsewhere, (I am told that some are being maintained at the Central Hotel at comparatively enormous cost) and yet our own people are dependent upon charity, which has been almost exhausted. Do you not think the Government could make a grant of a few hundred pounds towards so worthy an object? It has been pointed out to me that we make a grant to Mauritius, and after that to the West Indian Fund.[84]

The argument about maintaining Boer women and children in concentration camps was often used when money was being asked for, everyone conveniently forgetting that it was Lord Roberts's policy of burning farms and destroying livestock and fodder that put the Boers in the camps in the first place. The ministers recommended that an amount of £250 be granted to purchase blankets and warm clothing. Mr Cook of the Durban Refugee Relief Fund lost no time in submitting an estimate of his requirements:

9 rolls of flannel 40 yards ea @ 14 1/4d per yard	£21 7s 6d
12 rolls flannelette 18 yard pieces @ 6s 3d per piece	£ 3 15s 0d
12 rolls flannelette 40 yard pieces @ 6d per yard	£12 0s 0d
200 rugs (coloured) 62 × 66 @ 4s 6d each	£45 0s 0d
50 suits (assorted sizes) for boys @ 6s 9d each about	£16 17s 6d
Boots assorted	£30 0s 0d
Ready-made underwear	£21 0s 0d
Total	**£150 0s 0d**

Cook's receipts, after buying from S Butcher & Son, N Anstey & Co., D McDonald and Mandelsoh & Co amounted to £149.18s.6d.[85]

During the two years and nine months of its existence, the Durban refugee relief committee was to spent a total of £63 946 5s 0d. In the process they dealt with 3 844 cases, organised 955 passages for people back to Britain and elsewhere due to illness or for other reasons, and found work for 2 496 persons.[86] This rightly could be regarded as a truly remarkable effort, not only on the part of the Durban refugee relief committee, but also by all other charities involved, as well as the local and colonial government, which somehow managed to feed, clothe, accommodate and employ the Uitlanders.

Deaths in Merebank Concentration Camp compared to those in Durban

Durban seems to have been a reasonably healthy town at the beginning of the 1900s. During 1901, 882 births and 502 deaths were registered amongst the European population in the town. This effectively meant an average birth rate of 31,5 per thousand and an average death rate of 16,5 per thousand. The death rate for the European population, however, decreased from 16,5 per thousand in 1901 to 15,6 per thousand in 1902. This could possibly have been owing to the fact that many of the Uitlanders who had lived in similar conditions as the Boers in the concentration camps, or in the accommodation supplied in the town by the various relief organisations, had left. The possibility, however, also exists that the medical help and conditions had improved in the town, as regular donations to the Epidemic Hospital and other medical institutions were received. This enabled the medical authorities to take proactive steps to prevent the spreading of diseases.

The diseases prevalent in Durban were very similar to those in the Durban concentration camps. In both areas, enteric fever, dysentery, gastro-enteritis/diarrhoea, pneumonia and influenza were common. The most notable difference was measles, a disease the Boer prisoners had brought with them from the interior and which subsequently spread like wildfire through the camp where they were living in crowded conditions. In both Durban, where the Uitlanders stayed, and in the concentration camps most deaths were caused by gastric and respiratory diseases as indicated in the table below.[87]

Order	Disease in Durban	Disease in Merebank camp
1	Diarrheal diseases (24.5%)	Diarrheal diseases (28.2%)
2	Respiratory diseases (8.1%)	Respiratory diseases (26%)
3	Enteric fever (7.6%)	Measles (13%)
4	TB and Phthisis (7.1%)	Enteric fever (11.5%)
5	Bright's disease (5.6%)	Meningitis and Convulsions (5.5%)
6	Heart disease (5.3%)	Whooping cough (2.2%)
7	Meningitis and Convulsions (4%)	Marasmus (2.2%)[88]

NOTICE.

UNTIL further order all PUBLIC CANTEENS MUST BE CLOSED AT 9 p.m. ANY PERSON ABROAD IN THE BOROUGH AFTER **11 p.m.,** will be liable to be stopped and questioned, and if unable to give a satisfactory account of himself, will be arrested and dealt with as a suspicious character.

EDWD. C. BETHUNE, Lieut.-Col.,
Commandant Durban.

24th October, 1899   9517

Superintendent Richard Alexander
(*Who's who in Natal*).

Crime and the refugees

By December 1899, the population of Durban had apparently increased by several thousands. Extra police were required to cope with the increased population and, as a result, one detective, 13 white and six African constables on full pay, three special sergeants at 5s per day, and 74 special constables at 3s 6d per day were employed.[89] During this time, the police station was also used as a recruiting office, and one of the problems that Superintendent Alexander faced was that several policemen had joined the volunteer units, which left him with a number of inexperienced replacements.[90] When the Boer capitals had fallen, he therefore asked 'if his twenty old hands and an inspector and sergeant could be released from the military as they could easily be replaced by the militia encamped round Durban'.[91] Six months later, the superintendent was still complaining of losing constables who took higher positions in other forces after serving the mandatory 12 months with the police.[92] Alexander also had to contend with other problems in the force. The policemen complained about their low pay while Alexander, as head of the borough police, and on whose shoulders fell the task of maintaining law and order in Durban and managing the refugees, held a rank equal to the youngest sub-inspector in the Natal Police. Despite these constraints, Alexander and his force seem to have done an admirable job.

The monthly report of the borough police in July 1899 described the crime in Durban as trifling. Then again only about 50 Europeans, plus those driven down from the goldfields through their own misconduct, were unemployed. The latter required a great deal of supervising and the citizens were warned to be careful whom they employed or assisted with alms. Begging was strictly prohibited, and those in need could obtain both food and shelter at the Durban Home for a reasonable day's work.[93] Despite the sudden increase in population, the crime figures in Durban remained low for the period up to June 1900, as may be ascertained from the table below. Of the 432 people arrested in Durban, only 36 were Europeans, despite this group forming the majority of the population. In contrast, 247 Indians and 149 Africans were arrested during this period, which indicates that crime prevention in Durban was focussed on the latter groups and not on the influx of Uitlanders

The imposition of martial law seems not to have had much effect on the average citizen of Durban as the public obeyed the regulations, and when respectable persons were arrested for being out after curfew, which started at 23:00, they were generally let off with a warning. Martial law must have contributed to the low crime rate as it made anyone out on the streets very conspicuous, while extra patrols were also on duty, both in town and in the suburbs. The advent of martial law was responsible for the criminals, who had come down with the genuine refugees, leaving Durban and moving to Cape Town where martial law had not yet been declared.

'That social evil'

One of the most annoying problems for the police was prostitution, referred to as 'That Social Evil'. In the beginning of 1899, there were a certain number of harlots in the town, as in every seaport, but not nearly as many as there were 18 months later. Driven out of the Transvaal and coming down from Delagoa Bay, they came as refugees and continued to ply their trade in Durban. Various euphemisms were used to spare the feeling of ladies who read the newspapers, and prostitutes were referred to as 'Continental women' or 'Unfortunate women'. One of the difficulties the police had was trying to get witnesses to come to court to give evidence. The arresting officer would give evidence that the woman had accosted men in the street, but without the corroborating testimony of a second party, all the woman had to do was deny it, and it was the policeman's word against the woman's and she got the benefit of the doubt. As more and more of these women arrived, letters began to appear in the newspapers accusing the police of not doing their duty, which provoked the superintendent to reply in his report: 'There is only one way to put a stop to this evil, and that is for those who are accosted, to give the offenders in charge and to appear in court against them, if not, to hold their tongues and not advertise their weakness.' The men who harboured these women and extracted high rents for the premises they occupied were equally difficult to convict. When one of these men was accused of living off the earnings of a prostitute, he would swear on oath that he was a man of means, and the woman was living with him, which the woman would corroborate. Between December 1899 and June 1900, of 91 women arrested for prostitution, only 23 were brought before the magistrate. Fourteen were fined and nine discharged. The police felt that the laws in the colony differed from those in England and, either the laws had to be changed, or the magistrate had to take a more common sense attitude to those incidents brought before the court.94 Another case that highlighted the inadequacy of the laws was that of an Indian who had let six houses on his block of ground to 16 of these women, from whom he obtained heavy rents, yet the police could not obtain a conviction.95 In one instance the constable saw a suspect stop and speak to six gentlemen in succession before he could reach her, but, because none of the witnesses would appear against the woman, and the constable was unable to state the words she had actually used, she was acquitted. A method the police used was to arrest the prostitute. She spent the night in jail and the next morning the police set bail at £4. If she did not appear in court and forfeited the bail, this was, in effect, a £4 fine.96

The Central Police Station, West Street (LHM).

As the war progressed it became more difficult for Alexander and his men to police Durban. By January 1901, the city was burdened with people described as 'the dregs of society, whose inclination and character would not permit them to volunteer for the ranks or to work as labourers in the interior'. In May 1901 the police reported that the borough was overrun with vagabonds from all parts of the world. Scarcely a ship arrived without the police receiving information that certain disreputable characters were on board.97 This new wave of refugees was steadily increasing, bringing fresh arrivals from all quarters, some with the hope of reaching Johannesburg at the earliest opportunity, and others who had

Durban borough policemen (Newnes).

Crime	Europeans	Africans	Indians	Total
Abduction		3	2	5
Adultery		4	9	13
Assault Common	5	22	8	35
Assault Indecent		2		2
Assault with Intent	1		7	8
Breach of the Peace		5	3	8
Cattle Stealing		1		1
Contempt of Court	2	16	2	20
Contravening Borough Laws				
Fisheries Law			16	16
Illegal Immigration Act			156	156
Liquor Act			1	1
Masters and Servants Act		41	16	57
Police Act – Desertion	1			1
Sunday Trading Act		1		1
Deserters	2			2
Vagrancy Laws		2	1	3
Debts	1			1
Murder			1	1
Witchcraft		7		7
Theft	7	15	17	39
Native Law		19		19
Fraud	3		2	5
Embezzlement	1	1		2
Seduction		4		4
Interfering with Police		2	1	3
Indecency	1			1
Contempt of Martial Law	5			5
Falsity			2	2
Faction Fighting		1		1
Obtaining money under false pretences	2	3	2	7
Possession of stolen property	1			1
Forgery			1	1
Fraud and Embezzlement	1			1
Theft and Fraud	1			1
Theft and Embezzelment	2			2
TOTALS	36	149	247	432

Summary of arrests in Durban for 12 months ending 30 June 1900[100]

been driven from the Witwatersrand by the military. As a result, the police were forced to appeal to Durbanites to help them keep this unsavoury element in proper order by becoming security conscious, something they had not previously had to do. It was explained that tramps or beggars should not be encouraged, as this was one of the methods adopted by thieves to gain access to properties.

The arrival of the above refugees and fortune seekers altered the notion of Durban being a relatively crime-free city. The table of arrests for the year ending in June 1900 shows how circumstances had changed. By July 1901, a year later, crime had increased dramatically and two burglaries, four cases of housebreaking and theft, 31 cases of theft, one case of rape, one unnatural offence, three cases of fraud, and 15 cases of assault had been reported. Furthermore, during this month there were 1 241 cases for contravention of the bye-laws, and the Liquor Act and of vagrancy. The borough police were under stress despite the fact that 32 persons had been arrested for the mentioned crimes. As the population increased, so did traffic, and 83 traffic violations were recorded for July 1901, prompting Superintendent Alexander to request that the 15th Borough bye-law be amended to include the words 'cycle and motor cars', otherwise he had no authority to interfere under the present law to reduce reckless driving.[99] Ricksha pullers were responsible for a further 94 offences, ranging from pulling a ricksha in a dangerous manner to not heeding the red poles. Besides the police having to deal with the refugee population, the members of the military also posed numerous problems for those responsible for maintaining law and order.

With the borough police straining under the workload of trying to manage an overcrowded Durban, while dealing with the new and different kind of refugee, some relief was experienced as Uitlanders gradually received permits to return to the Transvaal

A group of ricksha pullers in central Durban (LHM)

The Durban Uitlander Committee

With the various charity organisations caring for all the primary needs of the refugees, the latter found themselves in a position whereby no association existed that could address their political situation. On Saturday 24 March 1900, almost six months after war had broken out, 28 men gathered in a Mr Frost's office for a meeting of Transvaal Uitlanders. Mr FW Blood was voted into the chair. The opinion of this gathering was that a public meeting 'of the inhabitants of the ZAR commonly referred to as Uitlanders and who are at present residents in Natal should be convened to discuss questions of pressing importance affecting South Africa'. A steering committee consisting of FW Blood, R Hoskin, EJ Pakeman, FC Dumat and WTH Frost was appointed.[101] The next meeting was held in the Durban town hall on 2 April 1900, and was attended by 100 Uitlanders. At this meeting it was decided to arrange a general meeting as soon as possible to air the Uitlander views on the war and to elect a committee which would manage their affairs.[102]

On the evening of Tuesday 10 April 1900, the Transvaal Uitlanders and Natal politicians, men and women alike, filled the Durban town hall to capacity. It would be their privilege that evening to affirm their continued loyal support of that great statesman in South African affairs, Sir Alfred Milner. After several stirring and patriotic speeches, the following motion was carried:

> We British subjects, residents of the South African Republic, known as Uitlanders, at present living in Natal, desire to affirm our adherence to the support accorded at public meetings held at Johannesburg to His Excellency the High Commissioner, Sir Alfred Milner, in the negotiations carried on by him with the South African Republic and to record our complete satisfaction with his later attitude and policy and our profound appreciation of the great service he has rendered to the Empire. That it is desirable to constitute an Uitlander Committee in Durban to protect the general interests of Uitlanders and this resolution shall serve the purpose of a constitution and we now resolve and agree to adopt the following constitution:
>
> 1. That it is our desire, and we direct that the general welfare of South Africa shall be our chief aim, and that any action taken by us shall, so far as possible, be in consultation with, and in agreement with similar bodies elsewhere and generally with all Uitlanders.
> 2. That the committee shall consist of 30 members, any vacancies now left unfilled to be filled by the present elected members.
> 3. Such committees shall be vested with power to watch the interests of Uitlanders generally, in questions which may arise, and to convene public meetings whenever they may think fit; they may fill vacancies,

Uitlanders meeting around the queen's statue in the town gardens (PAR).

Milner visiting the concentration camp at Merebank (PAR).

Durban Uitlander Committee (PAR).

The Durban Club, Victoria Embankment (LHM).

appoint any executive committee and such officials as may be required, delegating to them such authority as they may deem advisable.

4. Funds shall be raised by voluntary subscriptions from Uitlanders.

The gathering then elected the following individuals to the Durban Uitlander committee: R Baumannn, FW Blood, W Parry-Brown, Dr Carrick, H Davis, Von Dessauer, FC Dumat, H Evans, AL Field, J Forrest, WTH Frost, Gabriel F Green, TR Haddon, AL Hands, JC Harris, M Heilbut, R Hoskin, Howes, M Mills, J Innes-Murray, EJ Pakeman, Poynton, J Sellar, R Shauks, J Horne Shaw, EL Tauffe, J Thompson, A Tucker and HA Warren, from which an executive committee of nine members was elected. A vote of appreciation was extended to the Durban mayor to which he replied under laughter: 'The Durban people sincerely sympathised with the Uitlanders in their troubles, and would do their best for them. They would, however, be as pleased to see them home again as they would themselves.'[103]

From then on the composition of the Durban Uitlander committee varied greatly. Between 23 July 1901 and its disbandment on 14 July 1902, 46 different people served on the committee at various times with only Green, Hands and Blood of the original committee keeping their positions throughout. During this time 50 meetings were held BW Brayshaw attended 47 of these, while members such a S Alexander and EW Bond did not attend a single meeting.[104]

On 20 April 1900, the Durban Uitlander committee faced its first crisis. An emergency meeting was called to see what steps could be taken regarding a report they had received of 116 Uitlanders on board the *Entre Rios*. The immigration authorities would only allow 26 of these passengers to disembark at Durban. The meeting agreed to send a telegram to the Uitlander committee, Pietermaritzburg, to place the matter before the governor, saying it was monstrous that British citizens were prevented from landing on British soil. Due to the fact that the authorities had been warned of the possibility of spies aboard the vessel, only those passengers who could satisfy the immigration officer that they belonged to, or had relatives in, Natal were allowed to land. For this reason only 45 men, women and children disembarked.[105] Ten days later a similar complaint was raised pertaining to the *Tintagel Castle* and the *Herzog*. Initially very little sympathy came from the authorities who did their best to keep the refugees they regarded as unwanted out. This they did by declaring that those intending to land either had to have friends in Natal or were to be former residents of the colony. The persistence of the Durban Uitlander committee, supported by the Durban refugee relief committee, however, paid off as the restrictions were later applied only to 'people against whom reasonable grounds of suspicion existed'.

The committee also raised the issue of compensation with the Natal governor, while a mass meeting, attended by 5 000 people was organised on 1 June 1900, at the queen's statue to congratulate Lord Roberts on the occupation of Johannesburg. In consultation with the Pietermaritzburg Uitlander committee the names of 30 men, commercial representatives of the refugees, were submitted for a tour of inspection to Johannesburg.[106]

With the return to the Transvaal being visualised, the Durban Uitlander committee started to register refugees who desired to go back to the Transvaal and, when Lord Roberts annexed the Transvaal on 1 September 1900, the lists were almost complete, and three weeks later, three copies of the register were sent to the governor, who forwarded one to the high commissioner. There were 4 489 European adult males, 2 218 women and 4 673 children, making a total of 11 400 Europeans applying to return to the Transvaal. While no such register existed for Africans, 1 086 Indian males, 451 women and 639 children, totalling 2 176, signed up to return after consultation between MK Gandhi and the Durban Uitlander committee. In total 13 763 refugees registered.[107] To accommodate refugees returning from Europe, and others who might have neglected to register, the Uitlander committee created a supplementary register which would be forwarded to the authorities from time to time.

The optimism that followed the occupation of the Transvaal was soon thwarted, and by the end of August 1900, the refugees were still awaiting permission to return to the Transvaal. In the meantime the Durban Uitlander committee dealt with a great number of matters: the registration of the refugees who wished to return home was completed; complaints were lodged because advertisements for employment on the imperial railways were only published in Cape Colony newspapers; dissatisfaction was expressed at the appointment of some individuals to the civil service in the Transvaal; the question of rents, mortgages, licenses and taxes on the Witwatersrand were raised with the military governor of Johannesburg; the possibility of job opportunities for Uitlanders in the 'new colonies' and conditions for the return of refugees to the Transvaal were negotiated with the NGR.[108] By the time the fourth report of the Durban Uitlander committee was published on 19 September 1900, very little had changed. The continued uncertainty regarding rail travel and the difficulty in keeping the army and civilian population in the Transvaal supplied with food meant that the Uitlanders remained in Durban.[109] As the Transvaal slowly came under complete British control, the Durban Uitlander committee had to ensure that merchants who remained in Johannesburg, and who were suspected of trading with the Boers, did not gain an unfair advantage. As a result provisions and general supplies forwarded to the Witwatersrand were distributed directly by the director of civil supplies.[110]

Apart from wanting to return home to resume their lives and to escape the constraints of refugee life, many wanted to secure their possessions. An item of news that caused consternation among the refugees was a notice in the *Pretoria Government Gazette* of 5 September 1900. that all goods stored at the government storage depot in Pretoria would be sold if not claimed within three months. The Durban Uitlander committee immediately wrote to Governor Hely-Hutchinson, pointing out that, if unclaimed goods or furniture were sold before residents could return, it would cause serious loss to the owners, who had no representative in the Transvaal. The committee, at the same time, enquired if some arrangement could be made to allow, after careful and proper

investigation, those in dire straits to sell and transfer land or property, or to raise money by means of a mortgage.[111] The military governor of Johannesburg reacted promptly to enquiries about the condition of houses and furniture or businesses, and the authorities were generally sympathetic to the Uitlanders, but they were an army of occupation, and were responsible for the maintenance of law and order and could not allow a sudden influx of returning residents, mostly without any income, and in some cases without homes.

The major task of the Durban Uitlander committee was, however, to assist in the organising of the return of refugees. As a first step in preparing for their eventual return, books of permits were issued to Uitlander committees, mayor's committees or resident magistrates. These authorities would retain the permits until the receipt of a telegram from the high commissioner authorising the issue of permits to certain persons on certain days. On production of the permit at a railway station, the station master would issue a ticket to the station named on the permit on payment of the difference between the single and return fare, or on production of a return ticket dated 1899, or on production of a certificate from a committee or resident magistrate, to the effect that the person was in straitened circumstances and required assistance.[112] The insecurity of the lines of communication, and the subsequent difficulty of keeping the army and civilian population already in the country supplied with food and other necessary items, precluded the committee from offering much hope of an early return for large numbers of Uitlanders. The military governor of Johannesburg did, however, envisage the return of some refugees from 15 October 1900 onwards. In the light of this news the secretary of the Durban Uitlander committee, AP Field, hastened to warn that the 'committee has nothing whatever to do with the selection of persons to return in the first and successive bunches. The selection will be made by the High Commissioner, and on receipt of his advices, due notices will be given to all parties concerned'.[113]

The hopes of returning were dashed again. The Durban Uitlander committee was instructed to arrange for the return of 300 refugees per week from 18 October 1900 onwards. Just prior to departure, the committee was informed by High Commissioner Milner, without giving any reason, that the trains which were to have transported the refugees had been indefinitely postponed. In the meantime, the Durban Uitlander committee continued to address matters relating to the return of the refugees. Daily registrations of refugees took place between 10:00 and 12:00, while the NGR refreshment contractor, CW Tomkins, agreed to supply tea and coffee at Inchanga, Pietermaritzburg, Volksrust and Standerton free of charge and meals at the reduced price of 1s 6d once the Uitlanders were allowed to return in mass. Representations were also made to Milner to allow refugees who had joined the Natal volunteers or any of the irregular forces, and who could produce a good conduct discharge and some evidence of finding employment on their return, to return free on any troop train to Johannesburg.[114]

The latest delay infuriated many Uitlanders. Matters were made worse when the *Natal Witness* published an article on the delays suffered by the refugees and their reactions, admitting that the refugees had had a trying time and that their disappointment at not being able to return to their homes was great, but the newspaper went on to castigate them for holding protest meetings instead of waiting patiently for the authorities to allow them back. As a result, a petition was signed and presented to the Durban Uitlander committee asking them to call a meeting to discuss the question of their return to the Transvaal. A gathering of the signatories of the petition was held near the queen's statue in order to elect five representatives who would meet with an equal number of the committee to draft resolutions which would be submitted to the appropriate authorities. Five representatives were elected, and before the meeting broke up a gentleman who gave his name as Joseph Jones harangued the crowd and read from an article in the *Natal Witness*. After he had read extracts, the paper was placed on the ground and burnt, with someone remarking that they were purifying the newspaper by fire. A respectably dressed individual suggested they do the same to the newspaper's offices. This was rejected with contempt, while one of the crowd shouted 'We are not skunks.' Shortly afterwards the meeting broke up.[115]

As a result of the unhappiness owing to the delay in their return to the Witwatersrand, the Durban Uitlander committee proposed a public meeting to discuss their position. At the request of Lord Milner the meeting was postponed for a fortnight. This the committee heeded.[116] In the meantime several special meetings were held by the Durban Uitlander committee. At the meeting held on 29 November 1900 several resolutions were adopted, including '... we refugees in public meeting assembled respectfully request that His Excellency the High Commissioner will make very urgent representations to the Imperial and Military Authorities to adopt such measures as will allow of our immediate return to our homes from which we have been exiled for more than 14 months'.[117] Milner responded with a statement in which he admitted the 'growing feeling of irritation, amongst the Uitlanders at the continued refusal of the military to allow their return, and it is impossible not to sympathise with the thousands of people kept in enforced idleness, who have borne hardships with extraordinary courage and patience, and many of whom are now in distress'. Milner also had to admit that false expectations had been created amongst the Uitlanders that they would be able to return home from October onwards. According to him the guerilla war made it unsafe to move large numbers of civilian people and the supplies needed for their survival and to kick-start the economy. As a solution he suggested the creation of an advisory body that represented all Uitlanders and which could render three services: to disseminate true information to fellow Uitlanders; receive suggestions and transmit these to the authorities and assist in carrying out any approved proposals.[118] Although Milner had bought some time, he could not delay the proposed public meeting by Durban Uitlanders indefinitely. On 3 December 1900 the town hall was packed to capacity. In a meeting punctuated by conflicting emotions and statements, the serious divisions in the refugee ranks and between the Durban Uitlander committee and some sections of the refugee population came to the fore. Those who had been present at the meeting on 1 November 1900, when a copy of the *Natal Witness* was burnt, emerged as a rival group. Airing the viewpoint of those Uitlanders

who felt that the systems in place had failed them was Newby Fraser, who described himself as 'not a member of the refugee committee; only a humble refugee'. Fraser's speech, as described by the *Natal Mercury* of 4 December 1900, was typical of the mood and of the clashing statements that evening:

What was the use of appealing to Sir A. Milner. (Hooting) In his last statement he simply told them they were just in the same position they were six months ago. He promised that the Military Governor was prepared to receive refugees two months ago at the rate of 3 000 a week. He asked if that was carried out? ("No") Would it ever be carried out? ("Never") They did not ignore Sir A. Milner – ("Oh," and cries of "Yes, you do") – but they must go direct to headquarters. They were grateful to the troops for what they had done, but there was no use of lauding them to the skies when there was absolutely no necessity for it. ("Oh") He suggested that a committee be formed of refugees in Durban to get passes and proceed to Johannesburg, where they could look after the interests of the others and endeavour to obtain employment for those left outside. The next suggestion he was to make was with regard to the position of the refugees in Durban and elsewhere. Fifteen months had taken a big slice out of a man's life-time. There were three classes of refugees: the moneyed class, the middle class and the artisan class. The moneyed class represents about ten percent of the refugees, and they did not care how long the war lasted. They could drive around in their carriages and pairs – (applause) – and live in luxury and keep servants. The second class had lost nearly their all, while the third class had to live in tents, in huts, or sleep on the Back Beach. What was to become of them ("Shift sand") – (Laughter) Again, this was no adjourned meeting. This was forced on Uitlander committee by the petition (Applause).[119]

Whilst disunity appeared in refugee ranks and anger towards Milner and the military increased, the Durban Uitlander committee, operating from the high-class Durban Club, persevered with its work. Issues such as permits from unknown sources which allowed certain Uitlanders to return to the Transvaal, the employment of non-refugees in the Transvaal civil service, complaints about the distribution of the Mansion House relief fund and the sentencing of discharged members of the irregular corps for trivial offences were raised with the appropriate authorities.[120] The committee also continued with the recruitment of men for forces such as the Utrecht Mounted Police and the Johannesburg Mounted Rifles.[121]

The new year, 1901, brought favourable conditions to many refugees in Durban. The process of repatriation finally gained momentum. The allocation of permits by HT Ommanney, the secretary of permits in

Johannesburg, after recommendations by the Durban Uitlander committee from the applications they received, soon became a contentious issue. In general the Uitlander committee seems to have recommended people of some standing in the community or with business interests. Examples of this were AA Marks, a British tobacconist of Pretoria; G Fox, an undertaker of Germiston;[122] J Aldridge, a restaurant keeper and property owner of Pretoria; FW Parkin, a builder and contractor of Johannesburg;[123] Mrs CE Wood, the wife of a member of the Durban Uitlander committee and WH Stone, a large sanitary contractor.[124] Others favoured by the permit system were men who had served in an irregular corps[125] and those who had to return to the highveld on medical advice such as John and Sarah Welch who resided in Victoria Park.[126] When refugees managed to obtain a permit to return to the Witwatersrand without their jurisdiction, the Durban Uitlander committee were quick to complain:

> Exception was taken by this Committee to the granting of facilities to Mr Martin, manager of Messrs Cuthbert & Co's business, in a wire addressed to His Excellency the High Commissioner dated 13 December last, on the ground that the firm had traded with the enemy throughout the War. A copy of which wire I enclose together with His Excellency's reply. Knowing the difficulty with which permits for women are obtained, my Committee cannot help expressing their surprise at Mrs Martin obtaining a permit to return. Mr & Mrs Martin remained in Johannesburg throughout the War, the latter obtaining permission to visit Durban within the last two months. We are now informed that she has not only obtained a permit for herself but also her mother. The comments and feelings of the refugee women who have suffered so much during the last two years, and who are still unable to return are exceedingly bitter, and are only natural when the circumstances are considered.[127]

Against this background many refugees anxious to return to the Reef, were using all sorts of ruses to get permits. For example, a man would apply for a permit for himself and his family, including several adults who obviously were not kin, or a husband and wife would claim to have seven or eight children, several of these 'children' would turn out to be adults, not related to them. The garrison adjutant was forced to rule that no male over the age of 16, or female over the age of 20, or a married person could be included in these permits.[128]

On 7 May 1901, the Chamber of Mines notified the Uitlander committee that Lord Kitchener had sanctioned the raising of 300 recruits from refugee ranks to be used as mine guards to replace men withdrawn for work on the mines, on condition that the pay did not exceed five shillings per day and rations. As a result, 100 permits were issued to each of the four mining companies. When refugees did, however, manage to return to the Transvaal, matters did not always work out for them. In

Durban celebrates the return of volunteers, October 1900 (LHM).

September, for example, 50 men were deported back to Durban to be refugees again, because they refused to continue working on the mines under the conditions stipulated by Kitchener.[129]

By 15 November 1901, Alfred Milner felt that he could rely on the safety of the railways, believing that the threat of the Boer commandos was less than before in areas through which the lines ran. As a result, Lord Kitchener was prepared to authorise an increase in the return of the Uitlander population by issuing more permits. By then 450 mine stamps were working and nearly 10 000 people had returned to their homes. The next few months saw a steady stream of returning refugees, and, by the beginning of 1902, they were returning at a rate of 6 000 a month. Before the war was officially over, 45 000 people had returned to the Witwatersrand.[130]

Throughout this time the Durban Uitlander committee endured, raising issues varying from the abolition of martial law in Durban to the apparent human rights abuses by Boer forces. The final meeting took place on 14 July 1902, almost 90 days after peace was agreed. Only three members, Ogilvie, Hands and Airey were present, and the meeting was concluded by the reading of a letter from the secretary of the high commissioner which approved the dissolving of the Durban Uitlander committee and expressed appreciation 'of the valuable work performed by the committee in Durban'.[131]

The final celebration

The last celebration in Durban was the signing of the peace treaty on 31 May 1902. The news was received in Durban on Sunday, 1 June 1902, and, by noon, a special edition of the *Natal Mercury* was on sale but, before the paper went on the streets, notes were sent to the churches in the vicinity informing them of the news. The next morning, the corporation placed a notice in the *Natal Mercury* informing the public that a thanksgiving service would be held that day at 11:00 in the town hall and asking businesses to close between 10:30 and 12:00 to enable staff to attend the service. A fireworks display took place that evening at the Royal Natal Yacht Club, the fireworks having been purchased by the corporation for the occasion. Although no public holiday was declared, the town hall was filled to capacity, and even the corridors were crowded with worshippers. Reverend GE Weeks conducted the service and the Reverend Abraham read from the scripture. The mayor, LE Acutt, and nine members of the town council, together with 20 ministers from various churches in the Durban area, attended the ceremony. The fireworks display that evening was well patronised. War was finally over and the refugees could all go home.[132]

1. *Natal Mercury*, 3.7.1899.

2. *Natal Mercury*, 1.5.1899.

3. *Natal Mercury*, 4.5.1899.

4. *Natal Mercury*, 21.1.1899.

5. *Natal Mercury*, 2.10.1899.

6. *Natal Mercury*, 14.10.1899.

7. Froes, T, *Expelled from the Randt*, p.12.

8. *Natal Mercury* 18.10.1899.

9. Froes, p.25.

10. Froes, p.30.

11. PRO, CO 179/216: letter from department of revenue and agriculture India to secretary of state India, no date.

12. PRO, CO 179/206: letter A Caadir to Natal government, 16.10.1899.

13. Froes, p.30.

14. PAR, IRD 694/1900: letter from commandant Durban to IRO, 1.10.1900.

15. PAR, IRD 695/1900: circular from IRO to all shipping companies, 2.10.1900.

16. PAR, IRD 627/1900: letters from British consul Lourenço Marques to commandant Durban, reply by IRO, 25.6.1900.

17. *Natal Mercury*, 10.7.1900.

18. *Natal Mercury*, 27.9.1900.

19. PAR, IRD 667/1900: letter from British consul Lourenço Marques to commandant Durban, 2.8.1900.

20. PAR, CSO 1633: telegram from British consul Lourenço Marques to commandant Durban, 5.1.1900.

21. PAR, A 1538 Durban Uitlander committee: letter from C Bird to Durban Uitlander committee, 24.6.1901.

22. *Natal Mercury*, 6.3.1900.

23. *Natal Mercury*, 21.3.1900.

24. DAR, 3DBN /5/2/5/3/6: borough police report, 4.1900.

25. PAR, SNA 2422: documents on Hilda Bowesa, 27.7.1910.

26. PRO, CO 179/217: letter from French vice-consul to RC Alexander, 10.1.1901.

27. PRO, CO 179/217: letter from RC Alexander to the mayor of Durban, 11.1.1901.

28. PRO, CO 179/217: telegram from the governor to the high commissioner, 16.1.1901.

29. PRO, CO 179/217: letter from AH Hime to governor, 16.1.1901.

30. PAR, GH 1044: letter FH Crowe to commandant of Durban, 22.1.1901.

31. PAR, GH 561: letter from the mayor of Durban to the governor, 1.7.1901.

32. PAR, GH 561: letter from the superintendent of police Durban to the mayor, 26.6.1901.

33. PAR, CSO 1711: documents relating to seven American undesirables, 30.8.1902–23.9.1902.

34. PRO, CO 179/207: telegram from W Hely-Hutchinson to J Chamberlain, 24.10.1899.

35. *Natal Mercury*, 27.10.1899.

36. LHM, Durban Benevolent Society: minutes 6.1901, 3. and 7.1902.

37. LHM, Durban Benevolent Society: minutes 7.1899.

38. LHM, Durban Benevolent Society: minutes 7. and 8 and 9.1899.

39. *Natal Mercury*, 1.9.1900.

40. LHM, Durban Benevolent Society: minutes 1.1900.

41. LHM, Durban Benevolent Society: minutes 5.1899.

42. *Natal Mercury*, 9.3.1900.

43. LHM, Durban Benevolent Society: minutes 5.1899.

44. LHM, Durban Benevolent Society: minutes 9.1901.

45. *Natal Mercury*, 27.7.1900.

46. *Natal Mercury*, 27.12.1900.

47. *Natal Witness*, 10.5.1900.

48. *Natal Mercury*, 20.3.1900.

49. Cohen, SG, *A history of the Jews of Durban 1825–1918*, pp.169–183.

50. *Natal Mercury*, 13.8.1900.

51. *Natal Mercury*, 23.1.1900.

52. *Natal Mercury*, 27.10.1899.

53. *Natal Mercury*, 7.8.1900.

54. *Natal Mercury*, 27.10.1899.

55. *Natal Mercury*, 9.12.1899.

56. *Natal Mercury*, 14.11.1899.

57. *Natal Mercury*, 21.7.1899. and 5.5.1899.

58. PAR, NHD 11/1/25: letter from secretary Durban refugee relief fund to colonial under-secretary, 29.3.1900.

59. DAR, 3/DBN 5/2/5/3/6: borough police report, 4.10.1900.

60. PAR, NHD 11/1/24: letter from mayor of Durban to prime minister, 16.2.1900.

61. PAR, NHD 11/1/25: letter from Durban refugee relief committee to the colonial under-secretary, 27.3.1900–8.5.1900.

62. PAR, NHD 11/1/25: letters to and from harbour engineer and secretary of Durban refugee relief committee, 27.3.1900–8.5.1900.

63. PAR, CSO 2271/1900: letter from minister of lands and works to colonial secretary, 29.3.1900.

64. PAR, PWD 54/1900: letter from chief engineer PWD to minister of lands and works, 12.3.1900.

65. PAR, CSO 2030/1900: letter from colonial secretary to prime minister, 16.3.1900.

66. *Industries*, 18.4.1900.

67. *Natal Mercury*, 30.3.1900.

68. *Natal Mercury*, 5.1.1900

69. *Natal Mercury*, 10.1.1900.

70. *Natal Mercury*, 12.8.1899.

71. *Natal Mercury*, 8.12.1899 and 18.12.1899.

72. *Natal Mercury*, 24.1.1900.

73. *Natal Mercury*, 28.3.1900.

74. PAR, A 1538 Durban Uitlander committee: telegrams from GW Bradshaw to general superintendent burgher camps, Pretoria, 1901.

75. PAR, A 1538 Durban Uitlander committee: letters to and from general superintendent of burgher camps and secretary of Uitlander committee,

76. DAR, 3/DBN 5/2/5/3/6: borough police report, 1.1900.

77. *Natal Mercury*, 25.12.1900.

78. *Natal Mercury*, 22.12.1900.

79. *Natal Mercury*, 21.9.1901.

80. *Natal Mercury*, 7.10.1901.

81. *Natal Mercury*, 22.11.1901.

82. *Natal Mercury*, 10.1.1902.

83. Wohlberg, AU, *The Merebank concentration camp in Durban*, 1901–1902, p.195.

84. PAR, CSO 1675: letter from attorney-general to the prime minister, 21.5.1901.

85. PAR, CSO 1676: letter from secretary of the Durban Refugee Relief Fund to attorney-general, 10.6.1901.

86. PAR, GH 1044: newspaper report, name and date unknown.

87. Wohlberg, pp.205–209.

88. Wohlberg, p.210.

89. DAR, 3/DBN 5.2.5.3.6: borough police report, 5.12.1899.

90. DAR, 3/DBN 5/2/5/3/6: borough police report, 4.1.1900.

91. DAR, 3/DBN 5/2/5/3/6: borough police report, 6.7.1900.

92. DAR, 3/DBN 5/2/5/3/6: borough police report, 5.8.1901.

93. DAR, 3/DBN 5/2/5/3/6: borough police report, 5.7.1899.

94. DAR, 3/DBN 5/2/5/3/6: borough police report, 6.7.19■■.

95. DAR, 3/DBN 5/2/5/3/6: borough police report, 4.10.1■■0.

96. DAR, 3/DBN 5/2/5/3/6: borough police report, 12 5.1■■0.

97. DAR, 3/DBN 5/2/5/3/6: borough police report, 6.■.19■ .

98. DAR, 3/DBN 5/2/5/3/6: borough police report, 2■ 1.1■■1.

99. DAR, 3/DBN 5/2/5/3/6: borough police reports, 4.7.1■ 1 and 5.11.1900.

100. PAR, CSO 1677: summary of arrests in Durban for ye■ ending 30.6.1900.

101. PAR, A 1538 Durban Uitlander committee: minutes c■ preliminary meeting, 24.3.1900.

102. PAR, A 1538 Durban Uitlander committee: minutes m■■ting, 2.4.1900.

103. *Natal Mercury*, 11.4.1900.

104. PAR, A 1538 Durban Uitlander committee: attendance egister, 23.7.1901–14.7.1902.

105. PAR, A 1538 Durban Uitlander committee: minutes o■ he executive committee of the Uitlander committee, 20.4.1900.

106. PAR, A 1538 Durban Uitlander committee: minutes o■ he meeting, 30.4.1900.

107. *Natal Witness*, 21.9.1900.

108. *Natal Mercury*, 22.8.1900.

109. *Natal Mercury*, 19.9.1900.

110. *Natal Mercury*, 11.10.1900.

111. *Natal Witness*, 21.9.1900.

112. PAR, CSO 1662: high commissioner's instructions for he return of registered refugees, 20.11.1900.

113. *Natal Mercury*, 11.10.1900.

114. *Natal Mercury*, 31.10.1900.

115. *Natal Witness*, 1.11.1900.

116. PAR, A 1538 Durban Uitlander committee: minutes o■ pecial meeting, 19.11.1900.

117. PAR, A 1538 Durban Uitlander committee: minutes o■ pecial meeting, 29.11.1900.

118. PAR, A 1538 Durban Uitlander committee: minutes o■ pecial meeting, 30.11.1900.

119. *Natal Mercury*, 4.12.1900.

120. *Natal Mercury*, 30.11.1900, 7.12.1900.

121. PAR, A 1538 Durban Uitlander committee: telegram t high commissioner, 5.12.1900.

122. PAR, A 1538 Durban Uitlander committee: letter from GH Bradshaw to HT Ommanney, 25.5.1901.

123. PAR, A 1538 Durban Uitlander committee: letter from GH Bradshaw to HT Ommanney, 5.56.1901.

124. PAR, A 1538 Durban Uitlander committee: letter from GH Bradshaw to HT Ommanney, 21.6.1901.

125. PAR, A 1538 Durban Uitlander committee: letter from HT Ommanney to general officer commanding, Natal, 22.1.1902.

126. PAR, A 1538 Durban Uitlander committee: telegram from GH Bradshaw to HT Ommanney, 26.9.1901.

127. PAR, A 1538 Durban Uitlander committee: letter from GH Bradshaw to HT Ommanney, 23.5.1901.

128. PAR, A 1538 Durban Uitlander committee: letter from the garrison adjutant to the secretary of the Uitlander committee, 31.10.1901.

129. PAR, A 1538 Durban Uitlander committee: letter from chamber of mines to A Mackie Niven, date unknown.

130. Amery, LS, *Times History of the War*, p.23.

131. PAR, A 1538 Durban Uitlander committee: minutes of meetings, 1.1900–14.7.1902.

132. *Natal Mercury*, 2.6.1902.

A typical scene in the Jacobs concentration camp. Women and children collecting their wood rations (NCHM).

CHAPTER 17

THE DURBAN CONCENTRATION CAMPS: MEREBANK, JACOBS AND WENTWORTH
Annette Wohlberg

Searching for a way to cut off the Boer fighters in the field from food and supplies, the British army under Lord Roberts had begun to burn the homes and crops of the burghers who were away on commando as early as February and May 1900, leaving the inhabitants without shelter and food. Simultaneously the British army had to provide protection for burghers who had surrendered under the various proclamations. This necessitated the erection of the first concentration camp at Mafeking. With the onset of the guerilla phase of the Anglo-Boer War, Lord Kitchener, the successor to Roberts, intensified the land clearance and scorched earth policy. This left many thousands of people, both black and white, destitute. The British military authorities now herded these civilians, who were accused of supplying food, shelter and information to the commandos, into hastily erected concentration camps in certain major towns with easy access to railroads. The aim of this military strategy was to provide accommodation for the homeless, but more importantly, to use the women and children as pawns on a military chessboard to force the Boers to surrender. Initially very little thought was given to where these camps were erected as long as they were set up in places that were administratively and logistically convenient and were secure from a military point of view. As a result, once the process got under way many serious problems and difficulties regarding accommodation, food, fuel, sanitation and general health conditions developed, and these were only addressed after they had become so apparent or so pressing they could no longer be overlooked. In the meantime thousands died in the disease-ridden, overcrowded camps with their inadequate accommodation, meagre rations and poor sanitary conditions. From March 1901, separate concentration camps were created for black people. Conditions in the camps for African people were, if anything, even worse than those established for Boers.

By the end of the war there were 44 concentration camps in the former Boer republics and the two British colonies, mostly for Boer women and children and accommodating more than 116 000 people. There were more than 60 camps for the black people accommodating more than 115 000 Africans. Approximately 28 000 people died in the Boer concentration camps, 22 000 of whom were children. Although little data exist on the number of black people who died in the concentration camps, more than 14 000 deaths were recorded, and more than 80% of these were among children.[1]

Why did the British military authorities go to the trouble and expense of erecting three new concentration camps south of Durban?

The reasons for erecting the Durban concentration camps

Initially, the concentration camps were administered by the military, on much the same basis as the male prisoner-of-war camps. Although conditions in the concentration camps varied greatly, the quality of life was determined by the personality and ability of the camp superintendent, the site of the camp, the planning involved and the facilities and supplies available.[2] In the early stages of the war, most camps were overcrowded, with inadequate accommodation, insufficient bedding and blankets, meagre rations and poor sanitary conditions. The exposure of these appalling conditions and consequent high death rates, by particularly Emily Hobhouse, led the British government to be subjected to great criticism. This in turn resulted in the secretary of state for war, St John Broderick, taking immediate steps to counteract the extremely high death rate.[3] For example, the Ladies' Commission, under the leadership of Millicent Fawcett, was appointed to investigate the conditions in the concentration camps. A further decision that was taken was to relieve the pressure on the overcrowded concentration camps in the Transvaal and the Free State by reducing the size and population of these camps. In order to accomplish this, a number of the inhabitants were transferred to camps set up south of Durban.

This humane element was, however, but one consideration for moving concentration camp inhabitants to the newly erected camps outside Durban. The Boer women were perceived by many in the British army to be the motivating force in the Boer determination to continue the fight, in spite of having had their capitals captured and the country laid waste. To break the resistance, a psychological war was embarked upon, whereby the women and families of those men still on commando were, as a punitive measure, removed to a foreign country, Natal. Others identified for such a move were those women whom the British authorities considered to be troublesome and undesirable.[4] This category included women who made themselves objectionable to the authorities by showing open contempt, hatred and disrespect or by merely being classed as 'morally undesirable females'.[5]

The third reason for erecting the three concentration camps south of Durban was an economic one. There were four railway lines connecting the harbour towns of Durban, East London, Port Elizabeth and Cape Town with the interior of South Africa. The rail link between Durban and the Witwatersrand provided the shortest and most cost-effective route which could be used by the British to convey supplies, remounts, equipment and soldiers, as well as the much-required rations for the concentration camps in the Transvaal and Orange Free State. This, together with the fact that hundreds of Uitlanders who were in Durban wished to return to the Witwatersrand to restart their economic activities, caused great congestion and delays on the railway lines. By moving some of the concentration camp inhabitants to Durban, the British authorities could relieve the railways of the necessity to supply the heavily populated up-country concentration camps with goods. In turn, this was bound to leave the railways free to transport the necessary stores, foodstuffs, and so on required by the British forces in the Transvaal and the Orange Free State. Lastly, such a move would also make space for the Uitlanders to return to the recently reopened gold mines on the Witwatersrand.[6]

Indian fruit and vegetable shop in the Jacobs concentration camp. Products such as these supplemented a diet lacking in nutrients (NCHM).

The site and location of the Durban concentration camps

At the turn of the twentieth century, the coast to the south of Durban was either sugar plantations or a wilderness of dense natural bush and forest, intersected at odd intervals by footpaths. This vegetation was home to a variety of buck, birds, snakes and monkeys.[7] Climatically the region experienced mild winters and hot, humid summers with rain throughout the summer months and thunderstorms frequently accompanied by strong winds. During the summer of 1901–1902, the winds were so strong that tents, including the school tent at Merebank, were blown down and the contents scattered all over. The camps were within walking distance of the beach, and consequently rather sandy.[8] It was in this physical environment that the three coastal concentration camps, Merebank, Jacobs and Wentworth, were erected.

The Merebank concentration camp was the first to be built in September 1901. It became the largest concentration camp to be erected during the war and it was situated at the then almost uninhabitable bayhead area, south of the railway line to Isipingo, near what is today the Clairwood Racecourse. This site was identified by the authorities for a number of reasons. Firstly, land was available and fairly level, thus facilitating the building of huts and the pitching of tents. Secondly, this site was outside the borough of Durban, on the south coast railway, still within easy reach of Durban and military supervision, but away from the main congested railway line to the interior. Furthermore the camp was to be erected next to the Merebank siding, from which a line had been extended to the Merebank Brick & Tile Company, to allow for the easy delivery of raw materials.[9] A further distinct advantage of building the Merebank concentration camp on this site was that it was close to the main pipeline supplying water to Durban from the Umlaas Waterworks, from which an unlimited supply was made available, by the Durban municipal authorities, to the general superintendent of burgher camps, Sir TK Murray, at 3 shillings per 1 000 gallons (4 561 litres).[10]

Despite these advantages, the location of the site faced one major problem. The camp was situated at the foot of a low hill from which water drained into the site. The flat, swampy ground on which the camp was pitched sloped slightly from both sides towards a central drain or little stream, into which all surface water from rain, wash-houses, and so on ran, and thereafter flowed slowly into a large mere from which there was no outlet. On the side that faced Durban there was a large morass which drained towards the camp.[11] Even today the area remains swampy, wet and unused.

This sandy, swampy and wet site, teeming with frogs, fleas and mosquitoes, was condemned by the Fawcett Commission during its visit to Merebank on 6 and 7 December 1901. The commission summarised their findings as follows: 'It is in a swamp, and unless it can be drained it will continue to be hopelessly waterlogged.'[12] For this reason they condemned the Merebank camp site and recommended that it should be moved to another site as soon as possible.[13]

In spite of the recommendation, the authorities failed to move the camp. Instead they appointed a medical board of enquiry which interviewed 16 witnesses, after which they sent their report to the governor of Natal, Sir Henry McCallum. In its report the board concluded that, although the terrain was not ideal, it was not necessary to abandon the site. Instead, they recommended that only the tents on the western end of the north side and the extreme western area of the south side were to be vacated as these positions were too damp, and they suggested that the inhabitants of these areas be transferred to the south side of the camp.[14] The rationale behind this decision soon became apparent. Merebank was part of a greater plan, whereby three camps were to exist in close proximity to one another, thus precluding any relocation of Merebank.

Despite the high commissioner, Lord Alfred Milner's, preference for a higher altitude, the next two sites were once again positioned on the coast south of Durban. The first area selected was in the vicinity of the Jacobs siding, approximately three kilometres north of the Merebank concentration camp.[15] As in the case of Merebank, the land was flat and supplied with water by the borough of Durban. A great financial advantage to this particular site was that the Durban Bay Lands Company had loaned their land at Jacobs to the war office without charging rent.[16] The third concentration camp, Wentworth, was to be erected on a piece of land north of Jacobs, situated along the Bluff railway line. Again the land was flat and had a reliable water supply. Even though the latter two camps were not constructed on swampy soil as had been the case with Merebank, they still faced many of the same problems, especially with fleas and mosquitoes, since they were located in the same geographical and climatic belt as Merebank.

The administration and organisation of the Durban concentration camps

When Lord Kitchener took over command from Lord Roberts, he transferred the responsibility of the concentration camps to the civil authorities.[17] Although the Transvaal and Orange Free State concentration camps were passed over to civil authorities during March 1901, the Natal concentration camps were only handed over to civil administration on 1 October 1901.[18] When this occurred, the Natal burgher camps department took over not only a large quantity of camp equipment, but also the administration and management. The administration of the Natal burgher camps was placed under the direction of the governor of Natal, Sir Henry McCallum, who had to report to the British high commissioner in South Africa, Lord Alfred Milner, who in turn reported to the colonial office.[19]

McCallum entrusted the administration and organisation of the camps in Natal to the Natal burgher camps department which had its head office in Timber Street, Pietermaritzburg. At the head of this department was the general superintendent of burgher camps (GSBC) for Natal, Thomas Keir Murray.[20] As part of his duties he had to select the staff to run each individual camp and, in the final instance, he had to answer for the construction of the camp, the sanitary arrangements, transport, hospitals, purchasing of all stores, and for the finances relating to those affairs.

To help him with this vast task, he appointed camp superintendents in each of the camps under his jurisdiction. The men initially selected were Hugh Moberley Bousfield at Merebank, Leonard Francis Drake at Jacobs and Frederick George Philip Peters at Wentworth. The task that lay before each of these superintendents was multifaceted and entailed an enormous amount of work and supervision, which included receiving train loads of mostly Boer women and children, and organising the food and other requirements needed to provide shelter and nutrition. They were also in charge of sanitation and transport and general duties including those usually assigned to magistrates, health officers, boards of management, municipal officers and commissioners of oath.

In each of the three Durban camps, the camp superintendent was assisted by a team of administrators including an assistant superintendent, as well as doctors, and a hospital matron and her staff. He was also aided by a camp matron and her staff, whose duties included seeing to the general well-being of the camp inhabitants, as well as administrative matters such as drawing up lists of medical supplies required by the camp inhabitants. She was responsible for distributing medicine, handing out articles to the destitute, and educating the Boer women on the British view of child rearing. His team also consisted of the head commissariat and his staff; the sanitary staff; camp police, teachers and many other officials.

The sanitary arrangements in all camps were carried out by the local sanitary contractors, under the supervision of the sanitary inspectors appointed by the Natal Burgher Camps Department. In all camps the dry earth pail method was adopted, and all sewage pails, slop pails and dust bins were cleaned on a daily basis. The latrines, which were made of corrugated iron, were reasonably clean and well looked after. This could be attributed to the fact that disinfectants were used freely on a daily basis and that all dry refuse was burned, which contributed greatly to maintaining the health and cleanliness of the camps.[21]

For any concentration camp, including the three Durban camps, to function properly, rules needed to be adhered to. The Natal concentration camps had their own sets of rules which were very similar to those in the Transvaal and Free State concentration camps. They were translated from English into Dutch/Afrikaans and posted up at the superintendent's office. Ideally, a copy was also to be placed on a board in the living quarters.[22] The administrative and management structure employed in the three Durban camps meant that they were governed along the lines of small towns under military rule. This enforced way of life and imposed administration was very foreign to the Boer people who generally still lived a pastoral lifestyle.

General Camp Regulations for the Natal Burgher Camps as published in Pietermaritzburg on 1 February 1902

1. All persons residing in these camps must do what camp duties are required of them, and carry out the instructions of the superintendents, who are responsible for the good order and cleanliness of the camps.
2. Heads of families are responsible for their tents or houses and surroundings, others must select one in each tent or house who will be responsible.
3. All persons in these camps should assist the authorities in every way to keep the camps clean, for the comfort of all, and to prevent sickness.
4. Any persons fouling the Latrines must be made to clean same; anyone noticing this should at once report the matter.
5. Every care should be taken to keep the Bath Houses clean. They must not be used for any other purpose. Water must not be wasted.
6. Wash Houses are provided, and no washing in the camp must be done elsewhere. No dishes or such things are to be washed in the Wash Houses.
7. Clothes must be dried on the places provided.
8. Anyone wilfully wasting water in turning on the taps to run to waste may be punished.
9. All lines must be cleared before 11 o'clock every morning. Tents rolled up and everything made tidy.
10. No refuse must be thrown about the camp, but placed carefully in the receptacles provided for same.
11. Water must be emptied into the tanks provided, and must not be thrown about the camp. The lids of these tanks must always be replaced.
12. Bathing, when possible, must only take place at such times as are decided by the Superintendent. No one is allowed to go near any Military camp, Rifle Range, Store, Railway line or station, without special permission.
13. No one must leave these camps without permission, and on no account can visits to the other camps be allowed without a pass from the Superintendent.
14. Everyone must be in the camp by sunset, and no one must leave before 9 a.m., without special permission.
15. All lights must be out by 10 p.m., except in cases of illness.
16. Any persons found outside their own lines after 10 p.m., may be punished. Single men must keep to their own quarters.
17. A representative from each house or tent must attend at the time and place appointed to draw rations.
18. No spirits must be brought into any camp except for sickness and with permission.
19. All letters must be properly stamped and posted unclosed at the camp Post Office.
20. Any cases of sickness or distress should be brought to the notice of the camp Matron.
21. All persons in these camps are reminded that everything is being done for their own benefit, and they must render what assistance they can. The Superintendent must see that the Regulations are properly carried out. Punishments may be imposed, if necessary under Martial Law.
22. All persons in these camps are reminded that everything is being done for their own benefit, and they must render what assistance they can. The Superintendent must see that the Regulations are properly carried out. Punishments may be imposed, if necessary under Martial Law.

The inhabitants of the Durban concentration camps

Once the decision had been made to send people to Merebank and later to Jacobs and Wentworth, the British authorities needed to identify possible candidates for these camps. The first group to be selected were those whom the British considered to be undesirable, for military reasons, which included exhibiting anti-British sentiments, harbouring burghers, having family members still on commando or for absconding, as was the case with Mrs WHJ van Rensburg of Strydpoort, Wolmaransstad; Mrs Christiaan Jacobus Theunissen from Goedgedacht, Lichtenburg; JM Nel of Witpoort, Wolmaransstad and widow MCP Meyer. Boer women were even being sent to Jacobs for being what was described as: 'undesirables writing to family on commando' or for 'using invisible ink'.[23] Included in this group were the wives and families of Boer leaders still on commando, who were often seen as troublemakers in the up-country camps, and thus sent to Durban. These included women such as Mrs AC and Miss Burger (the wife and daughter of the vice-president of the ZAR, Schalk Burger), Mrs J Smuts (the wife of General Tobias Smuts), Mrs SC Scheepers (the mother of Commandant Gideon Scheepers) and Mrs EW Hertzog (the wife of General JBM Hertzog) who were all sent to Merebank; Mrs Ben Viljoen (the wife of the Boer General Ben Viljoen), Mrs Beyers (the wife of General CF Beyers), Mrs Spruyt, Mrs Mostert and Mrs Frederick van Heerden who were sent to Jacobs.[24]

Amongst the group of 'undesirables and troublemakers' were those whom the British authorities considered to be 'of dubious character', or morally undesirable. This referred to those women who committed official offences, who swore and verbally abused the camp authorities or indulged in promiscuous sexual behaviour.[25] Accordingly 29 women of questionable character were sent to Merebank. One of these was Mrs Elizabeth Cornelia Pretorius who had been sent down from Pietersburg. She gave Camp Superintendent Bousfield considerable trouble, was prone to using filthy and abusive language if she did not get her way and, according to Bousfield, was a 'woman of not particularly bright morals'. On release from the camp after the war she, together with Mrs du Plooy, went to reside in the Umbilo ward. The exaggerated dress and appearance of these two women, whom Bousfield refers to as his 'Really show [sic] & fancy children', could be an indication that they had gone to do business as sex workers near the Umbilo POW camp.[26] Despite TK Murray's comment that the Natal concentration camps had become the dumping ground for all the bad characters from the Transvaal and Free State, this was not entirely true for, in actual fact, there were only a few women in the Durban camps who succumbed to and were guilty of immoral behaviour.

The second and smaller group of Boers sent to the Durban camps were those who volunteered to go, as they wished to be close to friends or family, or because they believed that it would be better, for example for health reasons, to live in the Durban camps.

Not all accepted the transfer to Durban without resistance, especially as at that time the move represented changing from one country to

The Slotter family photographed in front of their tent in the Merebank Concentration Camp. Household goods which can be identified include a sewing machine and a stove (WM).

Sarel Eekhout, the bearded gentleman in the centre, in all probability a hendsopper, and a group of inhabitants of the Merebank camp on their way to a picnic (WM).

Mrs SP Potgieter, seated in the centre of the photograph, of Potchefstroom and her family in Merebank (WM).

Mrs JE Lamprecht and her four children, from left to right: Henk, Anna, Christina and Roedolf Arnoldus photographed in front of their tent in Merebank. The boy seated in the front is Hendrik Jacobus Davidson is Lamprecht's adopted child (Africana Museum).

Tant Miem Fischer se **Kampdagboek**

Mei 1901 – Augustus 1902

Miem Fischer

Maria M Fisher, nee Smuts, was born near Bethal on 28 September 1867. On 14 March 1889 she married Willem F.J. Fisher. Their only son, Karel Jan was born on 21 January 1890. At the time when the Anglo-Boer War broke out in 1899, they were residing on their farm Bührmansvlei on the banks of the Vaal River. Her 80-year-old father, Adriaan Smuts, her husband and five brothers felt it their duty to take up arms against the British and continued to fight for the Boer cause after the fall of the capitals of the two Boer republics. By 29 May 1901 their farm had been attacked and plundered for the third time. On this day Miem Fisher started her diary which has subsequently been published. On 30 May 1901 she and her son were removed from their farm and taken to the Standerton concentration camp where they arrived on 6 June 1901. She was allowed to take two mattresses, pillows, blankets, a veldtafeljie, a bath, pot and kettle with her. She was one of the group of 500 who were informed on 10 September 1901 that they were to prepare to leave for Merebank. Three days later, they left Standerton on open coal trucks, but were transferred to third class railway carriages at Newcastle. After a 36-hour long journey they arrived at the Merebank Station at sunrise on 15 September 1901. Like other new camp inhabitants they were escorted to camp Superintendent Bousfield's office, almost as soon as they disembarked.

another. One such person was Mrs Christina Adriana Geldenhuis who had been interned in the Klerksdorp concentration camp together with her five children. Her husband, Evert, and son Hendrik were still on commando with General Koos de la Rey. Consequently she and her children were earmarked to be sent to Merebank. On the night before her intended departure she managed to escape.[27]

The thousands of men, women and children allocated for Merebank, and later for Jacobs and Wentworth, were sent down to Durban by train, normally in open cattle or coal trucks. Sometimes passengers were transferred from these open trucks to third-class carriages at certain points of their journey, most often at Charlestown or Newcastle. Most of the Boers found these journeys, which lasted anything up to five days in filthy, overcrowded trucks without toilets, very traumatic. Not only did they often experience humiliation, but also a variety of extreme weather conditions without any form of protection. It is thus not surprising that many camp inhabitants recalled vivid details of their trip to the concentration camps, and this remained foremost in their minds long after other aspects of camp life had faded.

The first concentration camp inhabitants to be sent to Durban were the 24 women and children who arrived at Merebank from Pretoria on 13 September 1901. Two days later, approximately 500 more inhabitants, some of whom were ill with measles, arrived from Standerton.[28] These people, and those that followed during the next couple of weeks, descended on the camp before proper sanitation and other arrangements had been completed. This, together with the fact that there was steady rain for 21 days almost immediately after their arrival, made settling into a camp still under construction difficult and awkward for staff and inhabitants alike. One of the first to be received at the Merebank concentration camp was Miem Fischer, renowned for her strong anti-British sentiments and author of the published diary, *Tant Miem Fischer se Kampdagboek, Mei 1901–Augustus 1902*. By the end of September, the number of inhabitants at Merebank had increased to 1 560 and by the end of 1901 to 5 327.[29]

The first camp inhabitants of the Jacobs concentration camp arrived on 17 February 1902. The first person to be registered was 17-year-old Nicolaas Postma, of Pretoria. He was transferred from Rustenburg and left the camp for the Netherlands on 5 May 1902. The first family at the camp was that of Andries Hendrik Steenkamp (4_) of Mooihoek, Piet Retief, who arrived together with his wife, Anna Francina (37), and their six children on 17 February 1902. The Steenkamp family was only to leave the camp for Volksrust on 12 November 1902. The last camp inhabitants to be received at Jacobs were POWs who were returning from the overseas POW camps.[30]

By March 1902 the Wentworth concentration camp was ready to receive the first of its camp inhabitants. The opening of the camp had been delayed by a carpenters' strike and consequent rise of militancy amongst the white workers in Durban, but by the end of March 1902, the camp had its first 33 inhabitants.[31] The first family to be registered was that of Johannes and Gertruida Malherbe of Potchefstroom with their five children between the ages of 18 and one. They had arrived in the camp on 25 March 1902, and left the camp on 6 August 1902. On the same day, the Otto family from Pretoria, and two African servants, Christina (aged 11) and Saris (aged 8), from Marico, also arrived.[32] Many of the inhabitants in the Harrismith concentration camp were transferred to Wentworth after the closure of the former camp in January 1902. In addition to these, in March 1902, inhabitants from the Howick and Pietermaritzburg concentration camps who gave trouble were sent to Wentworth.[33]

The majority of the Merebank inhabitants, as was the case with those in the Jacobs and Wentworth concentration camps, came from the Transvaal and were followed by those who came from the Orange Free State. A third group in the Merebank and Jacobs concentration camps were Natal rebels or families of Natal rebels who had supported the republican cause against their own government. The first of this latter group to be sent to Durban was Judith Rall and her five-year-old son, Adriaan Matthys, from Klippoort, Newcastle, who arrived at Merebank on 24 October 1901.[34]

The number of inhabitants in all of the Durban camps fluctuated from month to month. According to the census figures, the highest population count in the coastal concentration camps at any month's end during the war was registered at the end of February 1902 in Merebank, and at the end of March in the cases of Jacobs, Wentworth and Pinetown. The highest overall number of inhabitants at any month's end in each of these camps was, however, recorded after the end of the war on 30 June 1902, when men who had still been on commando, or who had been POWs in Umbilo, or one of the overseas POW camps, came to be reunited with their families before repatriation.

Sophia Scheepers

Sophia Scheepers, the mother of Captain Gideon Scheepers, executed as a Cape Rebel at Graaff-Reinet, was an inhabitant of Merebank at the time. The sisters of Scheepers worked as probationers in the Merebank camp hospital.

Table showing the month with the highest census in each camp during the war[35]

Camp	Date	Total
Merebank	February 1902	8 342
Jacobs	March 1902	3 080
Wentworth	March 1902	2 982

Table showing the census on 30 June 1902[37]

Camp	Men	Women	Children	Total
Merebank	1 633	3 445	3 808	8 886
Jacobs	559	1 299	1 373	3 271
Wentworth	644	1 287	1 285	3 216

Table showing the highest daily quota in each camp[36]

Camp	Date	Men	Women	Children	Total
Merebank	8.07.1902	1 682	3 441	3 801	8 924
Jacobs	27.06.1902	596	1 300	1 377	3 275
Wentworth	27.06.1902	637	1 294	1 287	3 218

A fair amount of flexibility existed in the population of the Durban camps as inhabitants were transferred between camps. This was normally done on request, when people wished to live in the same camps as friends or family, as this created a support system which was often lacking in an environment where they knew no one. Moves of this nature included people such as Mrs AM Craig and her seven children, who were transferred from Merebank to Jacobs; Magdalena Coetzer who went from Merebank to Jacobs; Francina Albertina Collien who was sent to the Pietermaritzburg concentration camp, and Mrs Ben Viljoen, who was transferred from Johannesburg to Jacobs, and then back to Johannesburg.[38] Although there were not a great many applications for permission to leave one of the coastal camps to reside with family or friends elsewhere, this policy was encouraged by TK Murray, as well as the individual camp superintendents. If individuals were to move out of the camp, the authorities would obviously save money and would be spared the responsibility of looking after the people concerned, as well as of transporting them back to their place of residence once the war ended. Permission was, however, only granted to live outside the camp if applicants were considered unlikely to cause trouble for the civil and military authorities. Within these parameters, Mrs J R Adshade and her two children were given permission to leave Merebank to go to Pretoria. On the basis of similar applications, people from the camps were given permission to reside with friends or family in Weenen, Noodsberg, Ladysmith, Helpmekaar, Greytown, Estcourt and even Bulawayo, to mention a few of the destinations.[39]

A small percentage of those living in the Durban camps were surrendered burghers or *hendsoppers*.[40] As a rule, Boers of such orientation were despised and frequent clashes occurred between the *hendsoppers* and the so-called *bittereinders*. Just how severe these clashes were, and how despised 'joiners' and *hendsoppers* were, can be deduced from descriptions of a number of incidents in the Merebank concentration camp. On one such occasion, on 18 December 1901, some Boer girls seized a *hendsopper* and struck off his hat when he threatened to take away their *Vierkleur* (Transvaal flag). In another, a *hendsopper* was forbidden to participate in the singing of Christmas carols, hymns and psalms after the church service on Christmas Eve.[41] *Hendsoppers* were continuously under verbal attack and very few of them escaped the sharp tongue of the Boer women who remained loyal to the Boer cause. It was not unusual to hear one of the women saying: "*Jou hendsopper; jy is te lafhartig en te sleg om vir jou land te veg – en nou lê jy hier en vrouens oppas.*" (You *hendsopper*, you are too cowardly to fight for your own country and now you are here looking after women.)[42] Such men who constituted a mere fraction of the Durban concentration camp population, found it virtually impossible to escape the wrath of the women and children who were hostile towards them.[43] Other men, who had taken a more active role in the history of the Boer people, were treated with much more dignity. One such man was Christoffel Lombaard, who was 80 years old and, who, according to his story published in the *Natal Mercury*, had left Somerset West at the age of 15 as a member of the Great Trek. Thereafter he had fought at the battle of Blood River (1838) and Congella (1842). In 1847 he had left Natal, but was brought back to reside in the Merebank concentration camp in 1901![44]

Escaping from Merebank

In March 1902, seven young men: JD Rossouw (18), FN van den Berg (18), JS de Kock (16), WJ Lowies (21), CGC Rocher (21), J Rocher (18) and JD Balt (15) were arrested on the charge that they wanted to escape from the camp to join the commandos. Due to the intervention of the fathers of the Rocher brothers and of Rossouw, Balt and van der Berg, the plan was thwarted. Superintendent Bousfield deemed it necessary to take action. He sent the seven young men to the Commandant of Durban who had them incarcerated on board a prison ship. In time only Lowies and Rossouw, the only two with war experience, were deported to India. The other five were allowed to return to Merebank.

Natal concentration camps

Apart from the three Durban camps and the Pinetown camp several other concentration camps existed in Natal. By the end of 1900 the first of these was the Pietermaritzburg camp, one of the oldest camps in the system, which opened in August 1900 close to the present day Botanical Gardens. This was followed by the opening of the Howick concentration camp in January 1901 and the small Eshowe camp which catered greatly for surrendered burghers from the Vryheid area. The last camp to be established in Natal was the Ladysmith concentration camp, which opened in February 1902 with the transferal of the Harrismith concentration camp to the Tin Town site previously used to house Boer prisoner's of war.

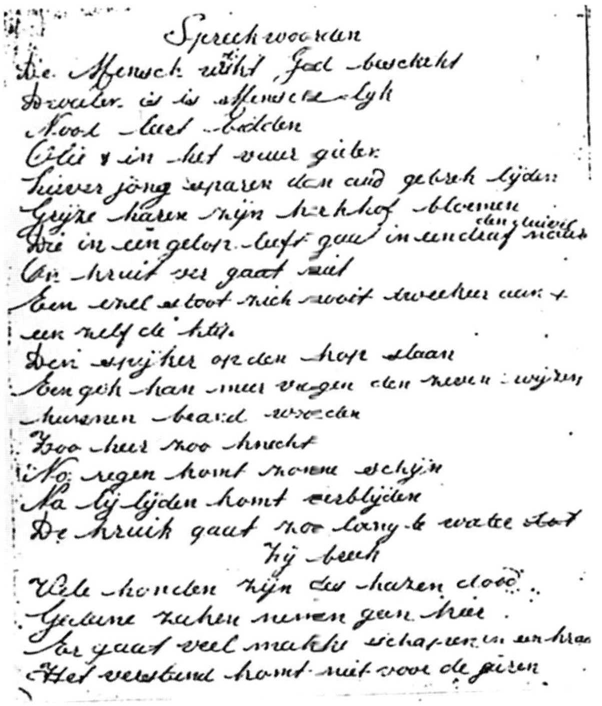
Spreekwoorden
De Mensch wikt, God beschikt
Dwalen is is menscheelyk
Nood leert bidden
Olie in het vuur gieten
Liever jong sparen dan oud gebrek lijden
Grijze haren zijn kerkhof bloemen
Die in een gelo[illegible] leeft gaat in een [illegible]
Onkruid vergaat niet
Een ezel stoot zich nooit tweekeer aan een zelf de steen.
Den spijker op den kop slaan
Een gek kan meer vragen dan zeven wijzen kunnen beantwoorden
Zoo heer zoo knecht
Na regen komt zonneschijn
Na lijden komt verblijden
De kruik gaat zoo lang te water tot hij breekt
Vele honden zijn der hazen dood
Gedane zaken nemen geen keer
Er gaat veel makke schapen in een hok
Het verstand komt niet voor de jaren

The diary of Hendrina Magaretha Scheffer

Sixteen-year-old Hendrina Scheffer started to keep a diary when she and her family were captured and removed from their farm, Kaffers-kraal near Ventersdorp, to the Potchefstroom concentration camp. The Scheffer family were later deported to Merebank. Throughout her stay in the above mentioned concentration camps she kept a diary, in the end filling fourteen books. What made her diaries special was that they contained very little information on the events in the camps but were filled with poems and prose on her dreams, fantasies, nature, her religious experiences and her romanticised admiration of the Boer leaders. The original diaries are housed in the Winterton Museum.

Hendrina Margaretha Scheffer 1905 (Carl Hollenbach private collection).

A chain braided by Scheffer from her hair in the Merebank camp. Her hair had to be shaven due to illness (Carl Hollenbach private collection).

The demographic make-up of Merebank was completed by African and coloured people who had accompanied Boer families into the camp as servants, playmates and, as in the unusual circumstance of the ten-year-old Gertruida Erasmus of Ventersdorp, as foster parents.[45] The African camp inhabitants may only have constituted 2% of the total population of the camps at most, but they experienced the same joys and sorrows as those Boer families they served. Unfortunately the Natal Burgher Camp Administration did not deem it necessary to keep records of the African inhabitants of the camps, as they were considered by the camp authorities, on instruction from the Burgher Camps department, to be non-people who were not budgeted for in any way. These African camp inhabitants received no rations or accommodation from the camp authorities, and were dependent on the Boer families they had come with for food and shelter. Proof that the camp authorities ignored the existence of the African camp inhabitants is evident in the lack of names to identify them. Instead they were merely entered to the roll as native, kaffir and black boy or girl. Only when they entered the hospital did their names appear.[46]

The clear economic and social divide which existed in the Afrikaner community prior to the outbreak of the war was ignored by the British authorities when they selected candidates for the three Durban concentration camps. As a result, the camp inhabitants came from all sections of the economic and cultural spectrum with rich and poor, the well-educated and the less educated all suffering the same humiliations, emotional traumas and hardships. This fact became an important binding power and driving force behind later Afrikaner nationalism.

Five Roomed House,

WITH PANTRY AND BATHROOM.

Design No. 148

Life in the Durban concentration camps

On arrival at either Merebank, Jacobs or Wentworth, the new camp inhabitants were taken from the train to the camp superintendent's office near the entrance to the camp. Here they were given tickets for their accommodation and all other requirements. They were then taken to their quarters by one of the officials. Thereafter the inhabitants had to live their daily lives within the limitations set by the authorities, regarding food, fuel, housing, medical facilities and education.

Accommodation and ablution facilities

On arrival in September 1901, the first Merebank concentration camp inhabitants were accommodated in bell tent marquees and canvas huts, but these soon wore out and needed repairing. After careful deliberation as to whether this was the best type of accommodation available, it was deemed advisable to construct wood and iron buildings to house the camp inhabitants, rather than replace the tents. This, it was believed, would not only be more comfortable, but also cheaper and better in the long run. Huts would need little repair, and could be sold or used for other purposes after the war. Eventually many of these buildings were sold to the Transvaal repatriation department, and some of the material from Merebank was even used to build the Laerskool Hartebeestfontein in the Western Transvaal.[47]

Once the decision had been taken to use wood and corrugated iron buildings, the tents in the Merebank concentration camp were replaced. These structures, together with the hospitals, schools, store rooms, staff quarters, ration houses, bathhouses, wash-houses and latrines were erected mainly by the Natal public works department. At times the construction was slow owing to the shortage of material and manpower.[48]

The corrugated iron and wood buildings erected at Merebank were about 30 metres long and were divided into six rooms, roughly 5m x 5m in size, with windows on the one side and an outside door on the other, to allow for a through draught of air. There was also a canvas screen in front of the door. A few metres separated two adjacent buildings and there were eight to ten such buildings in one row. Consecutive rows of buildings were separated by narrow streets. There were five or six such rows in one block, with each row and block being numbered. Unfortunately these buildings started leaking during April 1902.[49]

At Jacobs, the inhabitants resided in similar wood and iron houses. These houses were erected in blocks, alternating main streets and back streets. This arrangement was strongly recommended to prevent every street from becoming a slum. The main streets were kept spick and span, while the back streets were used for cooking, chopping wood, and so forth. An iron receptacle for refuse stood at every back door and was systematically emptied into a large brick-floored dustbin almost a square metre in size surrounded by a corrugated iron fence about 0,75 metres high. Next to each dustbin stood an iron two-handled slop tub. Each house consisted of one room with a floor of 5m x 5m and a height of 3 metres. The houses had lean-to roofs with a slope of about 18°. Each house had a front and back door, the front door being half glass. The houses constructed in Wentworth were very similar to those erected in Jacobs.[50]

In spite of constructing wood and iron huts, the authorities still faced a problem regarding the dampness of the soil floors as no wooden floorboards had been put into the huts. This caused many camp inhabitants, especially in the Merebank concentration camp, to have to wring out their bed linen every morning before hanging it out to dry![51] In an attempt to solve this problem, the authorities bought wool packs, distributing two per room. This seemed to eliminate the problem, because complaints about wet bedding ceased after this had been done.

One problem faced in all three concentration camps, by inhabitants and staff alike, was infestations of fleas, lice and mosquitoes. Fleas and lice covered the floor in the quarters of all camp inhabitants. The way in which the problem was approached underlined the great cultural divide which separated the camp inhabitants and staff in the camps. At Merebank, for example, the Boers got rid of the fleas by using ingenious methods such as cutting grass and then covering the floor with it. Once the fleas had crawled onto the grass, the grass was burnt and swept away and the problem was temporarily solved.[52] The staff members of the camp did not seem to have the same resourceful methods of getting rid of the bugs, for Kate French, one of the teachers stationed in Merebank wrote: 'All through the small hours [our companions] were a hunting. By the dim light of a candle, thro' the haze of my dreams, I heard, 1-2-3-4.'[53] This pest even encouraged the mother of Mrs DL Liversage, who resided in the Wentworth concentration camp, to write a poem on the flea infestation.[54]

The heat and humidity were to present another problem which all wood and iron hut dwellers had to contend with. The huts, which had no ceilings and were not well ventilated, were extremely hot, especially during the day. Furthermore, the walls were so thin that privacy was virtually non-existent, as one could hear was going on or being said in the room next door.[55] Where possible the total number of inhabitants in each room was restricted to six. This was, however, not always possible, as some families were larger than this, and generally preferred to live in one room rather than share a room with a stranger.[56] Despite these disadvantages, wood and iron huts were preferred by the camp inhabitants to the tents and marquees which most of them had experienced in the camps in the interior of South Africa.

With a few exceptions, furniture and bedding in these small rooms were in short supply. Many camp inhabitants had arrived with few clothes and generally no carpets, furniture or other essentials, as most of them had not been allowed to take many possessions when they were removed from their homes. It was therefore not uncommon to see milk or paraffin boxes acting as tables and chairs. Although the contents of the living quarters were generally scanty, they normally contained the following basic items which were supplied by the camp authorities to those who lacked them: a basin, kettle, bucket, broom, pillows, blankets and clothing.[57] In addition to these possessions, camp inhabitants were also encouraged to buy and sleep on cartels and stretchers made by the Boer men in the Merebank camp. Those with a little money also bought essential other items, either from the camp shops, such as the one in the photograph taken in the Jacobs concentration camp, or from shops in Durban.

Bathrooms and wash-houses were constructed to enable the camp inhabitants to take care of their personal hygiene. Each of the blocks within the Merebank concentration camp had its own bathrooms and wash-houses. They were made of corrugated iron and contained ten full-length baths for women, two for men and two for boys. The corrugated wash-houses were erected opposite the first row of accommodation quarters and were equipped with four taps each, two inside and two outside, as well as with tables and benches to enable inhabitants to do their laundry. Laundry had to be done during set times, but owing to a prob-

---

KENNIS GEVEN

Heer op Natals Grond, Spring zulke groote vloigen ront,
Ik glo die woord is neit tew grof,
Als ik zeg waar hulle spring, staan stof
Waar hulle met hulle bekken vat, byt hulle een eislijk gat,
Het is een zis pooteg deer,
Hulle is daar op uit om 'n mens te peer,
Probeer jy om hem te grijp, dan is hy al lank ont wijk,
Druk jy hom op die tafel stukken,
Dab meen dei Beuurt daar gebuur en ongeluk,
Want dei ontploffing is, maak en gedruis zoo dat het
klink en eider huis. Nou kort dei zant wert vlooyen, Die
kruyp in onsen kooyen. Dan zet hij op zijn prooi en loer,
tot dat nou kom leg dei Boer. Scheilyk word zy dan
Bespreng. Dei vlooi zoo en nare Deng,
Roip die Booire vrouwens dan weer,
hoor dei Bees Byt tog zoo zeer
Kryg zy hom Beet Nooit zal hy weer aan haar vreet,
Dan is het zy laste oogen blik
Wort gevryf en dood geknip
Dan vent dei ontploffing plaast
Eenegste geluyd en dat voor laast
Zoo wort heer mede kennis gegeven
zoo jy hom vang, laat hem neit meer leven
Maak kombarsen van zij vel
het is van Eropa zoo Bestel."

Aug. the 15th, 1902

The return of the lost son

According to the Afrikaner historian, Gustav Preller, relations between Boers and their African workers at times transcended time, distance and war. Preller's mother, a resident in Merebank, had, like most other women in the camp, very little or no contact with her husband and son who were still on commando. The news that both her son and husband had been captured reached her via Jan Inkosi (Nkosi), a Zulu who had worked for the Preller family on their farm near Paardekop in the present day Mpumalanga, before the war. When the Preller family moved away from Paardekop Nkosi returned to his family. Fifteen years later he arrived at Mrs Preller's quarters in the concentration camp with the news that her husband and son had been captured, and that the latter, Gustav, was about to be deported. After sharing some of her rations and coffee with him, Jan left. Acting on this information Mrs Preller send Gustav a Bible while he was on board the Manilla, in the port of Durban.

Wood rations being weighed and distributed in Merebank. Each adult received 12 kg of wood per week. A fair number of women complained about the size of the logs given to them, and had to rely on the goodwill of the African and Indian camp workers to transport these to their huts (NCHM).

lem with the water supply, women were often forced to do their laundry at night, or whenever else water was available.[58] Similar structures for bathing and laundry were also erected at Jacobs and Wentworth, with water being supplied by the Durban main water supply.

As is often the case when many people live together in close confinement, the Merebank ablution blocks were not always in good repair, and, on occasions, blocked drains were reported to the authorities. Drains were blocked either by sand, or because camp inhabitants used the bathhouses and wash-houses to do their dishes and laundry, despite the fact that camp regulations forbade them to do so. To keep the drains clean, and to prevent foul water from becoming stagnant and thus creating a breeding ground for mosquitoes, the drains needed to be brushed out on a regular basis. A team of Boer women were appointed to ensure that the toilets, bathhouses and wash-houses remained clean, and they were given permission to report those who did not keep the ablutions hygienic to the camp superintendent.[59]

Rations

Feeding the concentration camp inhabitants was a difficult and problematic task. The rations received by camp inhabitants when the concentration camp system was first implemented differed greatly from those received by the camp inhabitants in the greater Durban area, but even here the rations were never enough. The diet was restricted and especially lacking in the fresh fruit and vegetables, eggs and cheese, so necessary for the growth of children. To improve the nutritional value of the food supplied to the camp inhabitants, the camp officials received instructions not to accept damaged food or supplies of an inferior quality. In cases where there were numerous small children in a family, the superintendent of the camp could, on advice of the medical officer in charge, or on his own initiative, if it appeared necessary to him to do so, authorise that one or two of the older children receive the rations of adults; or if they were less than five years of age they might be given supplies of a 12-year old, for example.[60] The superintendent was also given discretionary power to issue extras such as fresh milk, meal, eggs, and the like to weak persons and children on the advice of his medical officer.

Rations such as meat, bread, potatoes, sugar, salt and coffee were received by queuing at one of the commissariat stores on a daily basis, where supplies were dispensed to the camp inhabitants in a block system. Fresh meat, one of the cornerstones of the diet, was bought from contractors in a frozen state and issued three times a week, while bread, either white or brown, depending on the order of the camp superintendent, was issued daily. This process implied that the collectors, many of them children, had to stand in long queues on a daily basis, generally for a considerable length of time in the hot tropical climate. The long delay on the ration queues often caused tempers to flare, and young children to start crying, but the wait sometimes also stimulated creativity in certain camp inhabitants, especially the children. For example, if the inhabitants had other important things to do in their quarters such as cleaning, cooking or looking after a sick person, they would merely place their dishes, basins or whatever container they had brought with them in the queue, and leave with the intention of coming back later, when they would once again take up their position in the queue where they had left the container.[61]

The rations issued at the ration stores were determined by the size and age of the family members. Not only were the rations rather meagre, but the diet was not a balanced one, and did not provide the necessary nutrients. Camp inhabitants tended to supplement their rations from one of the six stores which had opened in the camp, or from one of the Indian traders who came into the camp with fresh fruit and vegetables, or on one of their trips into Durban. Sometimes local residents also took pity on the camp inhabitants, and brought fruit and vegetables to the camp.[63] Firewood, too, was rationed and collected from the fuel depot, and then carried back to the living quarters.

As there were no communal ovens at Merebank or the other two concentration camps, inhabitants were forced to cook over open fires. Camp residents used bricks and corrugated iron and paraffin tins to construct their own fireplaces, which, in general, were 300–600 millimetres high, 300–600 millimetres long and about 300 millimetres wide. Two empty paraffin tins were then positioned, one at the back, and the other flat on the ground. The tins were cut open at the top and bottom and the fire was made inside these tins while the pots were placed on top of them. This method ensured that the fire was protected against the wind, and also helped to save fuel as well as keep sand out of the food.[64]

Ration scale in Natal concentration camps per week[62]					
Ration Scale No. 1 **Adults 12 years and older**		**Ration Scale No. 2** **Children 5 to 11 years**		**Ration Scale No. 3** **Children under 5 years**	
Meat	4 lbs (1,8 kg)	Meat	3 lbs (1,4 kg)	Milk	4 tins
Bread	7 lbs (3, 15 kg)	Bread	3¹/₂ lbs (1,6 kg)	Meal	3¹/₂ lbs (1,6 kg)
Potatoes or Potatoes	3¹/₂ lbs (1,6 kg) 1¹/₂ lbs (675 g)	Potatoes or Potatoes	3¹/₂ lbs (1,6 kg) 1¹/₂ lbs (675 g)		
Onions	1 lb (450 g)	Onions	1 lb (450 g)		
Rice	1 lb (450 g)	Rice	1 lb (450 g)		
Sugar	14 oz (400 g)	Sugar	14 oz (400 g)		
Coffee	7 oz (200 g)	Coffee	7 oz (200 g)		
Salt	3¹/₂ oz (100 g)	Salt	3¹/₂ oz (100 g)		
Wood	28 lbs (12,6 kg)	Wood	28 lbs (12,6 kg)	Wood	14 lbs (6,3 kg)
Candles	3¹/₂ per tent				
Soap	8 oz (230 g)	Soap	up to 8 oz (230 g)	Soap	up to 8 oz (230 g)

Education

Lord Alfred Milner and Sir TK Murray and the Fawcett Commission acknowledged the importance of the schooling of the Boer children, not only for educational and humanitarian reasons, but as the Fawcett Commission put it, to anglicise the children by 'instilling ideas of truth and discipline' into them.[65] To be able to achieve this, the British authorities could not rely on the Boer teachers in the camps. Instead they needed to bring in educators from England and other parts of the British empire, such as those who left Glasgow on 2 January 1902, and the 20 Canadian teachers who left Southampton on 3 May 1902, to take charge, with Boer teachers acting merely as assistants.

To introduce their political strategy in the guise of education, Alfred Milner had appointed EB Sargent as commissioner for education in the Transvaal and Orange Free State in November 1900.[66] He automatically also became the commissioner of education in Natal, when the Natal concentration camps were placed under the control of the Transvaal education department in October 1901. Sargent, in turn, appointed a number of school inspectors who visited the schools to ensure that the operation ran smoothly.[67]

In Merebank, Jacobs and Wentworth, the learners followed the same prescribed syllabi as those in other concentration camps. To achieve the ideal of imparting knowledge while indoctrinating the learners, it was necessary that English was the medium of instruction in all secular subjects such as reading, writing, arithmetic, history and geography, even for the young children. The language of instruction for religious education was the exception, and the mother tongue of the learners was used for this purpose.[68]

The school year was divided into four terms which were separated by school holidays. Each school day started at 8:00 and ended at 13:00. School attendance was compulsory, and therefore the employment of boys under the age of 14 for camp duties was considered undesirable.[69]

In the Merebank camp the children attended school under the supervision of the principal, Mr WH Hambly, an Australian by birth. He was assisted in his task by at least 25 teachers, including Mr DJH Viljoen, Mr Petrus van Straten, and Mesdammes E Meiring, A Schutte, S Prinsloo, M Erasmus, K French, C French, M MacAlister, E Smith, F Wellings, M Halliwell, A George and H Ladley.

By 12 March 1902, the newly established school in the Jacobs concentration camp had four teachers. Miss Ada Wallis and Miss Algar were appointed at Jacobs. Miss Wallis of 20 Roberts Road, Southampton, who was Miss Algar's companion on board ship on their journey to South Africa from England, died early in April 1902, and she was buried in the West Street Cemetery. Algar was so traumatised by the death of her friend that she obtained permission to live outside the camp until other teachers arrived two months later. Only then did she return to the Jacobs camp. For the extra expenses she had incurred in the process, she was refunded an amount of £5.[70]

In Wentworth the children attended school under the supervision of Mr William Nichols, who, as principal earned a salary of £240 a year, and was provided with a tent and rations. He too was assisted by teachers who came from other parts of the British empire. A few of these were soon to realise that, although they might have come to South Africa for adventure, or to further their careers or for patriotic reasons, their personal lives sometimes suffered. One of the schoolmasters, Mr C Gerlach, who lived in Row A, Block 1, Room 18, filed for divorce. His wife did not object, and pleaded guilty to some unspecified misdemeanour.[72]

To enable teachers to educate learners, school buildings, books and other equipment were required. With approximately 1 300 learners attending classes during the peak period of the Merebank camp's existence, more than one school building were required. As a result, a number of school buildings were erected. These ranged from marquee tents to corrugated iron and wood buildings with a veranda, capable of seating 200 children. Two large, well-ventilated huts with numerous windows, originally intended for police barracks, were also used.[73] Unfortunately, these schools were not very well-equipped – there were not enough desks for the learners to sit at, nor enough reading material and other books to go around, nor pens, nor even slates for the learners to write on.[74]

The number of children on the school roll varied considerably, but at its peak at the end of February 1902, the learner enrolment figure at Merebank was approximately 1 300.[75] The average enrolment figure at Merebank was 639 compared to an average attendance figure of 562. In comparison, the average enrolment at Jacobs was 415 compared to the average attendance of 344; Wentworth recorded figures of 181 and 149 respectively. This meant that an average of 83% of the enrolled learners at Merebank attended school regularly, at Jacobs 83% were in regular attendance and at Wentworth 82% went to school on a regular basis.[76]

Reacting against the educational problems, educational philosophy and the overtones of imperialism, some camp inhabitants decided to boycott the system by getting Boer ladies to teach their children privately in Dutch/Afrikaans. This was, however, soon prohibited by the authorities.[77] Despite the action taken by the authorities, it was evident that many children were influenced by the political thinking of their parents. This became clear at Merebank, when the learners boycotted classes after an article appeared in the *Natal Mercury* early in June 1902, depicting the Boers as an immoral nation who did not care about their country or their language.[78]

In spite of the facilities and politics that surrounded the education in the Durban camps, many children enjoyed going to school. One of the little girls who attended school in the Jacobs concentration camp, MJ de Beer (nee Coertze) was to recall many years later that she had cried when she heard that they were to depart from the camp and return home. She had not wanted to leave because she enjoyed going to school and was going to miss it. Even in her ripe old age she could still recite poems and verses she had learnt while in the camp![79] The reason for many children enjoying school was the fact that it enabled them to leave their living quarters and to play with other children while at the same time being educated.[80]

Education in the coastal camp was not restricted only to the children. In Merebank, for example, a class of 30 trained for the School Elementary Examination of the Cape University. Adults were encouraged

Top: The all girls Class 16 of the Merebank concentration camp school, with their teacher Petrus van Straten, photographed in March 1902. Boys of this age were either on commando or assisting their families with the daily camp chores (NCHM).

Right: The grave of Ada Wallis in the West Street Cemetery (Wassermann collection).

Bottom: Merebank camp inhabitants interrupting their task of collecting rations from the commissariat, Mr Hinnessy at store number 2 to pose for a photograph. Note the number of children, mostly boys, who are skipping school (NCHM).

to attend night school which provided classes in cooking, needlework, clay modelling, drawing, kindergarten work, science experiments and lessons on the science of entomology. In addition to these more formal classes, lantern lectures were also introduced with the sole purpose of enabling the camp inhabitants to learn something more about the British empire. At the lantern lectures, talks were delivered and slides shown on subjects such as London, Scotland, Canada, Clive in India and also on the Royal Navy.[81]

Religion

The majority of Boers were deeply religious people and Calvinism formed the basis of the social system. During the Anglo-Boer War, these religious principles were clung to more fiercely than ever before and, for many, the belief in God provided comfort and a source of strength in difficult times. For this reason, where possible, ministers of the various denominations to which the camp inhabitants belonged were appointed to the camp. The *dominee*, although not receiving a fixed salary from the British authorities, was provided with living quarters and officer rations. He also received an additional honorarium when leaving the camp if he had conducted himself satisfactorily and if good work had been done. For church purposes, school buildings and outdoor areas were used.[82]

At the Merebank concentration camp church services were held on a regular basis, mainly by one of the two resident *dominees*, Ds Johan Hendrik Enslin of the *Nederduitse Gereformeerde Kerk* (NG Church) congregation in Vrede and Jac van Belkum of the *Hervormde Kerk van de Transvaal* congregation in Rustenburg, or else the service was presided over by one of the visiting *dominees*, such as WP Rousseau of Pietermaritzburg.

It was an almost impossible task for the two resident ministers in Merebank to be able to visit or to minister to the spiritual needs of all the camp inhabitants. They were thus dependent on and supported by a number of fellow church *broers en susters*, who helped by visiting the sick, taking Sunday school, officiating at burials or even acting as lay preachers on a regular basis. In their endeavour to reach as many people as possible, regular church services were held by a *dominee* every week in each of the three sections at Merebank. On a Sunday, there were two services and, during the week, another service was held either on a Wednesday or a Thursday. These services took place in the school building, or in the open if the church building was too small to accommodate all the churchgoers and if the weather permitted. Attendance at the Sunday services was generally good, but the services during the week were poorly attended.[83]

At Jacobs, it was difficult to get a permanent *dominee*. Ds G Malan of Riversdal worked there for one and a half months until he was ordered to leave the camp because he had clashed with and refused to submit to the authorities. Thereafter a number of other *dominees*, such as Ds van Belkum of Merebank, Ds WP Rousseau of Pietermaritzburg and Ds AM

Nine of the 28 Sunday school teachers at Wentworth. Top left to right: Albertus Helm, surveyor and member of parliament for Wakkerstroom; Andrew Murray Hofmeyr, founder of the Hofmeyr Gedenk Skool. Seated in the centre: Mrs Frislich of Fordsburg, Johannesburg. Front: Nicolas James Devenish of Wakkerstroom (Africana Museum).

Hofmeyr visited the camp to conduct services. Later, Ds JP Wolhuter, from Piet Retief, who had been a prisoner of war in the Umbilo POW camp, ministered at Jacobs but unfortunately, owing to ill health, he was unable to do as much as he wished.[84] Wentworth too did not have its own resident *dominee*. Although some of the spiritual work at Wentworth was done by Ds Rousseau and Enslin and other visiting clergy, the bulk of the spiritual work fell on the shoulders of elders D Botha, J Bekker, AB Helm, Alleman and G Coetzee.[85]

The young people in all three Durban camps received special attention and, as it was impossible for the *dominees* to do all the work, they received assistance from the Sunday School teachers who discussed the coming Sunday's lessons with the *dominee* during the week. The team of 130 Sunday school teachers at Merebank, who taught the 2 650 children attending Sunday School, was led by Petrus van Straten. In Wentworth there were 35 Sunday school teachers who taught an average of 793 youngsters on a Sunday morning.[86] To accommodate the older children, confirmation classes were run under the direction of Ds Enslin and Ds van Belkum in all three coastal concentration camps. On 20 April 1902, van Belkum confirmed 42 or 43 of his congregational members at Merebank, while Enslin introduced 84 young church members to the Merebank congregation on the afternoon of 1 June 1902. During the existence of the Jacobs camp 83 youngsters were confirmed.[87]

It was also the task of the clergy to conduct the burials in the camp. During the first few months of the Merebank concentration camp's existence, funerals were virtually a daily occurrence, and in the absence of clergy, were conducted by one of the lay preachers, such as *Ouderling* (elder) van der Merwe who buried 31 inhabitants at Jacobs. Sometimes there were as many as three or four funerals a day and, on Tuesday 3 December 1901, eight burials were recorded in Merebank. These sad events even continued over the Christmas period when funerals were conducted on Christmas Day and on 26 December 1901 by Ds van Belkum and Ds Enslin respectively.[88] As the conditions in the camp improved, the number of burials decreased.

The funeral costs in the camps, normally borne either by the family or friends of the deceased, was fixed at between 15s to 25s per funeral. This was considerably less than the £4.10.0 to £6.10.0 which camp inhabitants had originally been charged. This massive drop in price was probably because the soapbox coffins for all the Durban camps were manufactured in Merebank by Mr RL Rothmann of Utrecht and his helpers.[89] The corpses were generally kept at a mortuary, a wood and iron building, which at Merebank was situated on the road to the station. From here they were taken to either the Merebank, Isipingo, Clairmont (Jacobs) or Wentworth cemeteries.

According to various camp inhabitants, as well as the Fawcett Ladies' Commission, mourners at the Merebank Cemetery were often confronted with graves which filled up with water and needed emptying before the burial.[90] Furthermore rumours existed that up to three corpses were buried in one grave. However, no evidence exists in official records or on the cemetery lists that this was the case. The only record of more than one person being buried in the same grave is that of the stillborn

Baby Hincliff and Marie Stell, the servant of Mrs van Rooyen of Dundee, who were buried in grave No. 381 in the Merebank Cemetery.[91]

The church and *dominees* also had other duties. Many Boer women and children had come to the camp virtually destitute, with little or no clothing. To help these destitute camp inhabitants, the camp authorities, relief committees in South Africa and Europe, the church, and a number of individuals provided money and clothes to alleviate the situation. Second-hand clothing and boots, linen, flannelette, chintz, sheet linen and other goods were sent from Switzerland, France, Germany and the Netherlands. The clothing given to Boer women and children was issued under the immediate supervision of the camp superintendent and camp matron, according to the needs of the applicants. The second-hand clothing from Germany and other countries was distributed by a specially appointed committee consisting of the Dutch Reformed minister, the camp matron and superintendent. This could, however, only occur after all items had been carefully searched, examined and fumigated by the steam disinfector at Merebank.[92]

Unfortunately not all gifts sent to the Boers by well-wishers reached their destination. One such case occurred in Jacobs. When Ds G Malan, the Dutch Reformed minister at Jacobs at the time, was called upon to sign the receipts, some of the consignments were not there. Furthermore, the number of items in the boxes did not agree with the invoices. Upon enquiring where the goods were, he was told that they had been given to inhabitants of the camp. Malan refused to sign the receipts as he had no proof that the goods had been distributed to the inhabitants. The next day he was told to leave the camp as he was regarded as a potential troublemaker, and so had to depart without further ceremony.[93]

Recreation

Daily life in the Durban camps did not only consist of chores, school, tending the sick and religious activities. The routine was broken by much needed recreational activities for all. To most of the concentration camp inhabitants, trips into Durban offered occasional relief from camp life. There they were able to shop, to spend time on the beach or to visit family or friends who were in one of the other concentration camps close by or the POW camp at Umbilo, or on one of the prison ships. According to Laurie Lloyd's memoirs, '... it was a daily sight to see the Boers [probably from Wentworth] going along to cave rock at the end of the Bluff for picnics, fishing, walking along the railway lines.'[94] These outings could only be undertaken once passes had been obtained.

The camp inhabitants also kept themselves occupied in a variety of ways, ranging from reading and writing letters, to making assorted objects which could be sold or given to friends as gifts. The clay at Merebank was good for pottery, and creative inhabitants used it to make clay pots, pans and ornaments. Some of the camp inhabitants even joined the choir or organised concerts, which were generally well attended.

In order to raise funds to help the less fortunate amongst them, some of the young female teachers at Merebank organised a successful bazaar in the camp. Camp authorities believed sport and exercise played an important role in everybody's lives, especially those of the children. For this reason, the Merebank camp superintendent, Bousfield, provided funds to buy equipment for sporting activities such as football, cricket and hockey. The camp authorities also organised sporting activities such as high jump, running, skipping and tug-o-war for the children.[95]

The children also found various ways of amusing themselves. Young boys entertained themselves by romping around, playing games, teasing girls and annoying African workers and they even played pranks on each other, such as throwing out the water someone had gone to collect for his mother. They played war, tops and marbles, got involved in fist fights and smoked, even though their mothers forbade them to do so. On one occasion the *hendsoppers* at Merebank organised a fight between 20 young English boys with pellet guns and 20 Boer boys with *kleilatte* (clay sticks) and *rekkers* (sling shots). The fight started and the Boer youngsters stormed, arms ready for the attack. They overwhelmed the English boys and took away their pellet guns. When the organisers wanted to take the guns back, the Boer youngsters refused, saying that the weapons were their spoils of war![96]

Sometimes children, especially the boys, were known to ignore camp regulations quite blatantly when playing. In one such incident at Merebank, on 6 April 1902, some of the boys went to amuse themselves on an empty railway truck standing somewhere along the railway line, despite regulations forbidding them to do so. When the truck started moving, another boy in the vicinity, the ten-year-old Stoffel van der Merwe, tried to stop the truck by applying the brakes. A policeman grabbed him and brought him to Camp Superintendent Bousfield. As punishment, Stoffel was sentenced to 15 lashes with a cane and 14 days hard labour, while the real culprits remained unpunished![97]

An unusual political and social experience for all Durban concentration camp inhabitants occurred after the signing of the peace accord on 31 May 1902. Festivities were organised for 26 and 27 June 1902 to celebrate the coronation of King Edward VI. To allow the new British subjects to share in the moment, and as a public relations exercise, a number of activities were organised. The Natal burgher camps department provided each adult camp inhabitant with what was termed a "coronation ration" consisting of one pound (450 g) of flour, half a pound (250 g) of sugar, a quarter pound (125 g) of raisins and one pound (450 g) of meat. All children over the age of two, but under the age of 12 got a tin of jam instead.[98]

Economic activities in the camp

A different way of dealing with the monotony of camp life was to find employment either inside or outside the camp and in this way earn some much needed money. Such initiatives ranged from working at the Merebank Brick & Tile Company adjacent to the concentration camp, to assisting at the Natal Brewery, making coffins, doing needlework, housekeeping for families in Durban or doing the laundry for the officers in the camp, or for fellow Boers. Children also earned money by raking the leaves, walking the horses of the British officers and other such chores. The money earned in this way enabled the camp inhabitants to supplement their food rations and to purchase other necessities at one of the shops in Durban or at one of the wood and iron camp shops.[99]

The shops erected in the various camps were generally well stocked, and sold a variety of goods including iron bedsteads, chairs, trunks, clothing, gramophones, calico, linen, flannel, cotton, needles, candles, matches, and foodstuffs such as tinned fish, bacon, butter, orange juice, tea, coffee, sugar, syrup, jams and other goods which may have been in demand. In fact they were allowed to sell anything except alcohol. The shops did, however, not stock fresh fruit and vegetables. These were sold relatively cheaply by Indian traders who came into the camp with supplies.[100] This gave those inhabitants with money the opportunity to buy food when rations were inadequate.

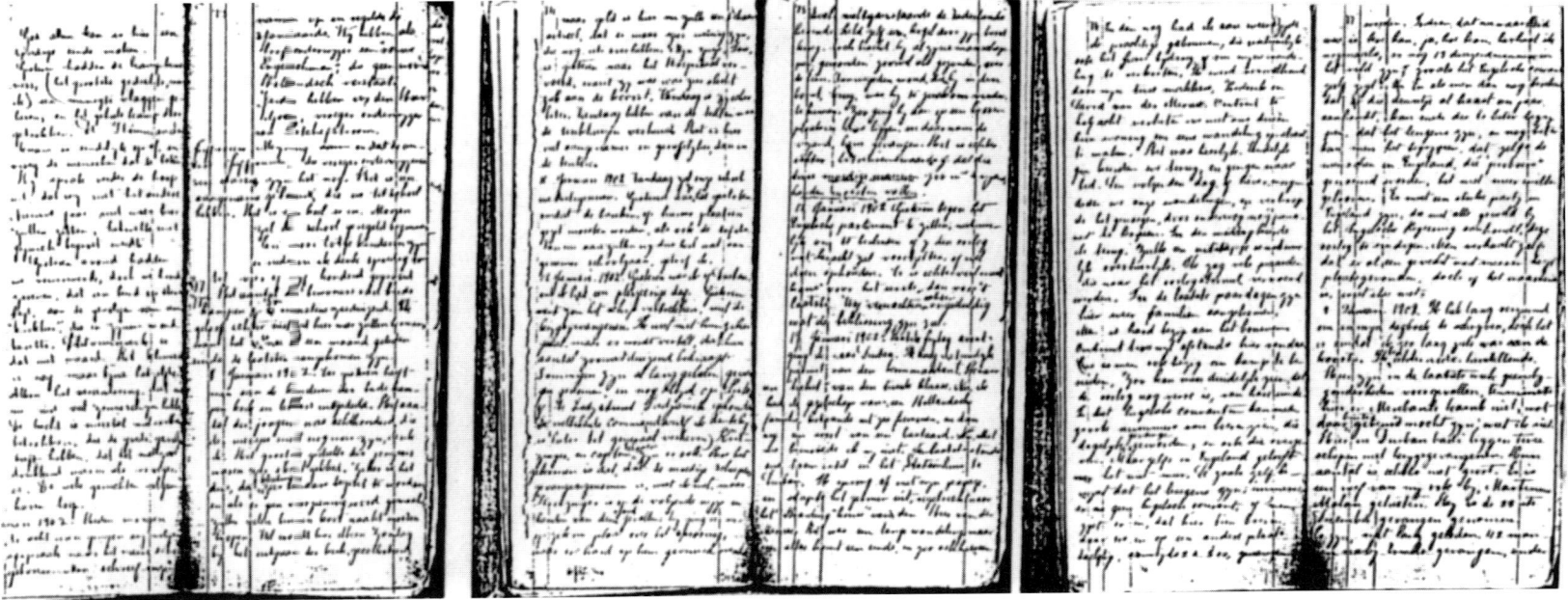

Top: Cohen's Store in Market Street in the Jacobs concentration camp. Note the chairs, chests and other household items for sale. Inhabitants purchased these to furnish their rooms (WM).

Bottom: Extracts from the diary of Petrus Jacobus Malan, referring to recreational activities in Merebank.

Health in the Durban concentration camps

In the light of the extremely high death rate in the Transvaal and Orange Free State concentration camps, one of the reasons why many women and children were transferred to the coast, special attention was paid to this aspect in the Durban camps.

The centre for health care in all the camps was the hospital and its staff, which were under the direct control of the camp superintendent. The hospitals and the medical and nursing staff in each camp were carefully monitored. Generally they were efficient and took great care in providing for and nursing the sick. In the endeavour by the Natal burgher camp department to promote healthy camps, TK Murray arranged for two railway compartments to convey convalescent children from the camps to the beach in Amanzimtoti on a daily basis.[101]

In Merebank the hospital was situated near the railway line and consisted of two well-lit wood and iron buildings which eventually housed four large wards accommodating 140 beds in total. Adjoining the hospital was a dispensary manned by the 56-year-old TR Morris, who was assisted by Arthur Greene.[102] Hospitals, with dimensions of 5m x 5m x 3,5m, were constructed using corrugated iron and wood at Jacobs and Wentworth.

The medical staff at an institution the size of Merebank needed to be comprehensive and, as a result, the hospital personnel totalled 45 by March 1902. Five of these were medical doctors, with Dr Leonard Hardy being appointed as senior medical officer. Two of the five doctors, Dr Hendrik Rademeyer and Dr James O'Reilly, were Boers, who thus gained more trust from the camp inhabitants than the British doctors, that is, Dr

Lyle and Dr WO Pou. In April, two further medical doctors, Dr Cole and Dr Spence, were appointed, bringing the total to seven. In September 1902, Dr Llewellyn-Jones replaced both Drs Rademeyer and O'Reilly who left the camp on 31 August and 3 September respectively. The rest of the staff consisted of the hospital matron Sister M Cochrane, her assistant and qualified as well as uncertified nurses and probationers.[103]

Jacobs and Wentworth, with their fewer inhabitants, required a smaller medical staff. Jacobs concentration camp hospital only had three doctors. They were Drs Philipson, Scholars and Field who, as in the case of Merebank, kept a careful record of the patients admitted into hospital. Sister WF White was one of the chief nursing sisters at the Jacobs Hospital.[104] At Wentworth, Drs Martin and Monckton were the medical practioners and Nurse Carr from Rietfontein was one of the probationers.

In order effectively to prevent the spreading of infectious diseases such as measles and enteric fever (today better known as typhoid), preventative measures were implemented. These included disinfecting the linen and utensils or equipment which had been used by patients who suffered from infectious diseases. The Merebank concentration camp even borrowed the Thresh steam disinfecto from the harbour department for this purpose.[105] Furthermore, each camp had a quarantine section, where those patients with infectious diseases such as measles were kept, in an attempt to prevent an epidemic.

During its existence, the Merebank concentration camp hospital admitted 759 patients, 91 of whom died. This represented 20% of all the deaths which occurred in the camp. The remaining 80% all died outside of the hospital. The first patients to be admitted into the hospital were received on 18 October 1901 with pneumonia, measles, tuberculosis,

Inside one of the wards of the Merebank Hospital. TK Murray claimed that it was one of the best hospitals in Africa (WM).

debility, bronchitis and nephritis. Of these seven patients, three died. The last patients to be discharged from hospital on the closure thereof, on 10 December 1902, were the 71-year-old Abram Bothma of Amsterdam, Transvaal and a 29-year-old teacher, Miss McCloud, who had been admitted with enteric fever[106]

Although patients were admitted into the Jacobs concentration camp hospital as soon as the camp opened, records were only kept from the week ending 27 March 1902. The first two patients whose names were entered in the hospital register, the 14-year-old Barend Kruger and the seven-year-old William de Beer, both died. The last patients to be admitted were Helena Landsberg (2) who was discharged on 23 January 1903, and Heila de Beer (14) who was admitted on 10 October 1902, but died in the hospital on 4 February 1903. The Jacobs Hospital failed to keep a record of the reasons for hospitalisation. Despite this it could be determined that 13 of the 49 deaths that occurred in the camp, or 27%, occurred in the hospital.[107]

The Wentworth concentration camp hospital opened its doors on 17 April 1902. The first patient to be admitted into the hospital was 20-year-old Annie van Rensburg of Womaranstad, with enteric fever. The last patient to be admitted into hospital at Wentworth was staff member HW Smith, on 9 September 1902, who had dysentery. The last patient to be discharged was 19-year-old Maria Bouwer of Heidelberg, who had been admitted on 4 September 1902 with pneumonia. In total 76 patients were admitted into the Wentworth Hospital before it closed its doors on 24 September 1902. Four of these patients died, one of heart disease, two of pneumonia and one of bronchitis and enteric fever.[108] This represented a mere 5,3% of the total number of people admitted to the hospital.

The hospitals were not only open to the European camp inhabitants and staff, but also to people of colour who worked or resided in the camp. The admittance of people of colour into the hospital did, however, not always occur without problems. As was the case in other hospitals in Natal at the beginning of the twentieth century, the majority of the white nurses felt it beneath their dignity to tend to Africans. This attitude was revealed at Merebank when a sick 19-year-old resident by the name of Klaas was admitted to the hospital with pneumonia on 6 April 1902, in spite of the efforts of two doctors who had attempted to intervene. The admission, although not the first instance of an African being admitted to the hospital, caused all Boer probationers, with the exception of three, to resign, since they did not want to nurse him. Five or six days later, the hospital and camp authorities were still struggling to replace the nurses.[109]

Notwithstanding the dedication of the medical staff and the pride they took in their work, they did not always succeed in convincing the concentration camp inhabitants of their commitment. Instead the inmates were suspicious and fearful of the camp hospital, as well as of the doctors and nurses, believing rumours that almost everyone who entered the hospital died there, that patients starved to death and that the nurses did not do their work properly. These rumours were encouraged by stories such as the one told by a certain Mrs Kesselaar, who maintained that the floor of the hospital was covered with sand and that she had poured out the medicine the nurses had given her rather than drink it.[110] Another

Merebank concentration camp memorial in the Garden of Remembrance, corner Sihlahla Street, Merewent (Wohlberg collection).

incident, where according to Miem Fischer a dying woman was left lying in front of a window naked, did just as much to foster distrust in culturally foreign British medical practices.[111]

All the precautions and care could not prevent hundreds of inhabitants from dying or suffering illness in the Durban camps. The most prevalent illnesses in the Merebank concentration camp, especially during the early months of its existence, were enteric fever, dysentery, gastroenteritis, diarrhoea, measles, bronchitis, pneumonia, broncho-pneumonia and whooping cough.[112] Measles was especially common during the first three months of Merebank's existence, when it was responsible for the majority of deaths in the camp. During October 1901 alone, 65% or 32 of the 49 deaths in the camp were as a result of measles and its complications. All the victims were children under the age of seven, except one, Petrus Harmse, who was 12 years old. By the end of 1901 the measles epidemic had subsided, and only isolated cases were thereafter diagnosed with measles.[113] During December 1901, the month in which the greatest mortality figure was registered at Merebank, the diseases previously mentioned were the cause of 45 of the deaths. Yet, during this time, only 15 patients were admitted to hospital with these diseases. Of these 15, one died in hospital during December 1901, and two more in January 1902.[114]

In spite of the occurrence of the various diseases, illnesses and injuries which occurred in the camp, the death rate in the Merebank concentration camp remained relatively low compared to camps in the Transvaal and Orange Free State. During its existence 453 persons, including people of colour, passed away in the camp, 104 of these dying during the month of December 1901. Of the 104 fatalities, 83 were children under the age of 12. In total, 104 adults died in the camp. The remaining 349 deaths were children. Gastro-intestinal diseases and respiratory complaints were responsible for more than 70% of the fatalities amongst the youngsters.[115]

Analysing the death list of the Jacobs camp shows that 49 inhabitants died in this camp. Of these, 20 died in hospital of stomach-related illnesses such as gastro-enteritis, enteric fever, diarrhoea and dysentery, with the next major cause being respiratory problems. Although this pattern was very similar to that in Merebank, there was one major difference – no one died of measles in the Jacobs concentration camp. However, the number of children who did not survive still far outnumbered the adults, making up a total of 69% of the deaths.

From the hospital and death register which was carefully kept at Wentworth, it is obvious that here too the majority of the 16 inhabitants who died in this camp suffered from either stomach-related illness or from respiratory problems. No patient was admitted into hospital or died of measles. As in the other two concentration camps, the greatest number of deaths in the camp were children, constituting 65% of the total.

Illness, disease and death spared no one, and inhabitants as well as staff needed to be admitted into hospital where some died. At times death even struck the same family more than once. Examples of such families in Merebank included the Wolmarans family of Driefontein, Standerton; the Hattinghs of Roodekranz, Bethal; the Van Dyks of Papkuilsfontein,

Sarah Johanna Jooste (28) from Heidelberg died on 16 December 1901 of enteric fever. She was buried in grave No. 114 in the Merebank Cemetery. Her 23-day-old unchristened daughter had died on 3 December 1901 of gastrointestinal catarrh and was buried in grave No. 62 (WM).

Standerton; the Du Plooys of Kooperfontein, Rustenburg; the Harmses of Zuiverfontein, Rustenburg, to name just a few. It was also not uncommon for a mother and her baby to die in short succession of each other. Amongst these were Ellie du Preez of Grootpan, Bethal and her one-month-old daughter; Johanna Cloete and her eight-month-old son; Sarah Jooste and her 23-day-old daughter and Elsie Schmahl and her 13-day-old son.[116]

The camp inhabitants who died in Merebank varied from the still-born to one-day-olds to the 87-year-old Gesina van Tonder of Vaalbank, Vryheid, who was the oldest camp inhabitant to pass away. The deceased were buried in one of three cemeteries. Twenty-two were buried in the Anglican Church Cemetery at Isipingo, 19 at the Clairmont (Jacobs) Cemetery and the rest at the Merebank concentration camp cemetery.

Similarly, those who died in Jacobs and Wentworth also varied in age, from the stillborn infant of WJ and MC van Rensburg in Wentworth and the ten-day-old Johannes Christoffel Steyn, son of JC and CW Steyn in the Jacobs concentration camp, to the 67-year-old Susanna Catrina Coetzee of Carolina in the Jacobs camp and the 61-year-old Frans Jaco-bus Visser of Lichtenburg in the Wentworth camp. These people were buried in the Jacobs and Wentworth Cemeteries.

Despite the good health care, and Murray's claim that the Merebank Hospital was the 'best hospital in Africa – of course not equal to larger hospitals but far better than anything else we have had',[117] all three concentration camps were viewed as detrimental to the health of the surrounding area. Even though the illnesses in the concentration camps correlated positively with those in Durban, the authorities continued to view the camps as threatening to the health in their vicinity. WR Saunders, the Umlazi magistrate, was even to write the following in his annual report: 'The general health of both white and black has been fairly good, excepting in the neighbourhood of Merebank Refugee Camp, where all suffer more or less from Dysentery, Diarrhoea, Fever and various other diseases, presumably caused by bad sanitation.'[118]

In presenting statistics such as those listed above, it is necessary to point out that the population in each of the camps consisted mainly of women and children who, for many months prior to admission into the camps, had suffered great privation on the veld and in the concentration camps from which they had been brought to Durban. The removal from the up-country concentration camps, and the terrible anxiety caused by war and the transfer had its consequences in the apparently excessive high death rate recorded during the first few months of habitation in the Durban camps, especially in Merebank. Once the population became more settled, the health of the people improved, and the death rates assumed more normal proportions.

To a certain extent the deaths in the Durban concentration camps were counterbalanced by births. During its existence, 51 births were registered in Merebank. This figure is, however, inaccurate, as not only does it fail to mention the births of the stillborn infants, but also, amongst others, the son of Johanna Magrita van der Merwe who was born on 1 October 1901, and Barend Havenga, born to Anna Magrita Havenga on 1 April 1902, who were omitted from the list.[122] The first entry in the birth register of the Merebank concentration camp was that recording the birth of the daughter of Jan and Catrina Krieg of Bethal, who was born on 14 October 1901. The last entry was made on 31 March 1902, recording the birth of the son of Hendrik and Elsie Schutte of Heidelberg. Unfortunately not all babies born in the camp were able to leave the camp at the end of the war. Fifteen of the babies listed in the birth register also died in the camp, mostly due to illnesses such as diarrhoea or gastro-enteritis.

Seventeen births were registered at the Jacobs concentration camp. Nine of the births were boys, and eight were girls. The first of these births to be recorded was the son of Thomas and Elizabeth Ferreira of Pietersburg on 17 March 1902. Seven of the babies were born before the signing of the peace agreement, while ten were born thereafter. The last child to be entered into the birth register was the son of Hendrik B and Catrina Helena Ferreira of Johannesburg on 9 December 1902, more than six months after the war had ended.[123]

An extract from the Jacobs camp hospital register. Note that no record was kept in this camp of the illnesses for which the inhabitants were submitted.

Deaths of Merebank concentration camp inhabitants[119]

Month	Total Pop	Men	Women	Children 5–12 years	Children 1–4 years	Children under 1	No. of deaths
Sept 1901	1 560	–	2	–	1	3	6
Oct 1901	3 570	1	4	7	27	10	49
Nov 1901	4 437	–	4	4	21	13	42
Dec 1901	5 327	2	19	12	42	29	104
Jan 1902	6 364	5	14	7	26	18	70
Feb 1902	8 342	1	13	4	12	7	37
Mar 1902	8 303	3	7	4	17	13	44
Apr 1902	8 259	2	5	–	8	9	24
May 1902	8 253	2	5	4	6	2	19
Jun 1902	8 886	2	1	–	6	6	15
Jul 1902	7 251	1	2	3	5	2	13
Aug 1902	4 620	–	4	–	5	3	12
Sept 1902	3 501	1	1	1	1	6	10
Oct 1902	2 245	–	2	–	–	2	4
Nov 1902	802	–	1	–	–	1	2
Dec 1902	?	–	–	–	2	–	2
TOTAL	–	20	84	46	179	124	453

The memorial erected at what is now the Anglican church in Isipingo for 22 Merebank camp inhabitants who died in the first months of the camp's existence. The first person to die in the Merebank camp, Martha Kaarlsen (67) of Ermelo is buried here. Strangely none of the graves of the 22 inhabitants are indicated on the map of the cemetery. Ironically the memorial is situated next to the grave of Dick King, whose epic ride in 1842, saved Natal from the Boers (Wohlberg collection).

Deaths in the Jacobs concentration camp[120]

Month	Men	Women	Children	Total deaths	Total population
Feb 1902		1		1	1 098
Mar 1902	1	1	10	12	2 587
Apr 1902	1	2	6	9	3 080
May 1902	0	1	5	6	3 074
Jun 1902	1	2	3	6	3 262
Jul 1902	(1)*0	1	2	3	2 300
Aug 1902	1	1	2	4	1 839
Sept 1902	1	0	0	1	
Oct 1902	0	0	3	3	1 535
Nov 1902			2	2	560
Dec 1902				0	
Jan 1903				0	
Feb 1903		1		1	
TOTAL	(6)* 5	10	33	(49)* 48	

* = Death of Abel Pienaar, a Merebank resident, in the Jacobs Hospital

Deaths in the Wentworth concentration camp[121]

Month	Men	Women	Children	Total deaths	Total population
Mar 1902	0			0	33
Apr 1902	0	1	4	5	2 962
May 1902	0		3	3	2 982
Jun 1902	0		2	2 (1)	3 218
Jul 1902	2	2	2	6	1 772
Aug 1902	0	1		1	1 286
Sept 1902	0			0	
Total	2	4	11	17	

The memorial erected in memory of the 19 Merebank camp and 49 Jacobs camp inhabitants who were buried in the Jacobs (Clairmont) cemetery. The memorial is to be found in Voortrekker Street in a stark industrial area (Johan Wassermann private collection).

PEACE AND BREAKING UP

Peace came with the Boers signing the terms of surrender on 31 May 1902. Many of the camp inhabitants in the Durban concentration camps were bitter and generally disgusted with the terms of surrender, believing that the Boer commandos should have continued to fight to the bitter end. Others again were pleased that the war had ended and that they could go home. But both groups had many unanswered questions which needed to be answered, preferably by one of their own leaders. This task fell on the shoulders of the former vice-president of the former South African Republic, General Schalk Burger. Burger visited the Natal concentration camps on an official information tour, and on the morning of 7 June 1902 he visited the Merebank concentration camp. Here he addressed the large crowd that had come to hear him from the platform of the veranda in front of Superintendent Bousfield's office. Burger's speech and the circumstances surrounding it were reported by the *Natal Mercury* as follows:

> The delivery of the address was undescribably pathetic. Old men, dull of hearing, held one hand open at the back of their ears to hear it all, while in the other they grasped strong sticks to support their bent feeble frames. From below broad, slouched crepe band hats gazed eyes that slowly filled with tears that were allowed to fall unchecked to the ground for neither hand could be spared to wipe them away. Among the thousands of women there was scarcely a dry eye. Bravely they tried to force down sobs.[124]

Later he also visited the Jacobs, Wentworth and Pinetown concentration camps. He used the same prepared speech, which had been approved by the Natal colonial authorities, at all the camps. He told his audience that peace had been declared, that the Boer leaders had tried every means to win the settlement they all desired, that is one ensuring independence, but that circumstances had compelled them to surrender to British terms. They should now be content that peace had been restored. He then gave the terms of surrender, and a long document drawn up by the burghers, giving reasons for the decision to lay down arms.[125]

After Burger's departure, camp inhabitants wanted to go home immediately. Matters were, however, not that simple, and they soon learned that the end of the war did not herald an immediate end to their misery in the concentration camps. For months after listening to Burger, they would still be going through the process of being repatriated.

Before the camp inhabitants could go home, all administrative structures had to be put into place. Furthermore all camp superintendents had to follow the prescribed instructions regarding the logistics and administrative arrangements for the repatriation process. These included matters such as taking the oath of allegiance, processing the applications by the camp inhabitants to return home, liaising with the newly formed repatriation committees, organising transport and determining which people could take care of themselves.[126]

All camp superintendents were instructed to receive written applications from heads of families for their return home, on the distinct understanding that they were in a position to support themselves and their families on arrival. This work required great care and supervision on the part of the superintendents, owing to the false declarations made by many of the burghers. Initially the process was very slow, but once instructions were better understood, the repatriation took place a little faster.[127]

At the end of the war, it had been decided that all concentration camps outside the Transvaal should be dismantled as soon as possible, and that the inhabitants of these concentration camps should be transferred to the Transvaal camps. To enable the authorities to transfer the Natal refugees back to the Transvaal or Orange River Colony as soon as possible, special trains had to be organised. For this purpose the acting general manager of the NGR made all facilities available, and also proposed to run special trains in quick succession to take the inhabitants to their homes. This time round they would travel mostly in carriages, as they were now British subjects, while their belongings were to be sent with them in open trucks.[128]

Arrangements were made that the Wentworth concentration camp was to be the first to be emptied. This camp closed its doors on 22 September 1902, when the last of its inhabitants were transferred to Jacobs. The majority of buildings were removed and sent to the Repatriation Commission in Pretoria. Twelve huts were also sent to the Transvaal department of education.[129]

The repatriation of the approximately 9 000 Merebank concentration camp inhabitants, which had started during July 1902, was completed by 10 December 1902, when the last 95 camp inhabitants left, before the Natal burgher camps department was taken over by the Transvaal burgher camp department on 31 December 1902. The two enteric patients in the Merebank camp hospital, Anna Bezuidenhout and HS Landsberg, and their families were transferred to the Jacobs concentration camp hospital, thus being partly responsible for this camp only finally closing in January 1903.[130]

Most of the equipment and materials from the three Durban concentration camps was either sold at a public auction, or forwarded to the Repatriation Commission in Pretoria. By the end of October 1902, most of the buildings in the Wentworth concentration camp had been taken down and forwarded to the Repatriation Commission in Pretoria. This included 12 sets of huts which were forwarded to the Transvaal public works department for the education department.[31]

With the repatriation completed, the sites of the Merebank, Jacobs and Wentworth concentration camps soon returned to their former state. Today all that exists in the place of the Merebank Cemetery is a Garden of Remembrance erected during the 1970s. The military-style barbwire guard fence and securely locked gates make this run-down garden inaccessible to the public. The sites of the other two concentration camps which exist in the present borough of Durban, are in a similar or worse predicament. All that remains of the Jacobs concentration camp cemetery is a small, unfenced, unkempt area, with a stone obelisk, recalling the names of those who were buried there, including the 19 Merebank camp

General Schalk Burger, former vice-president of the Transvaal, addressing the Merebank camp inhabitants and staff from the veranda of the hospital on 7 June 1902, informing them of the terms of surrender (WM).

In 1904 Renaud and Co. won a contract from the NGR to level land at the Bluff. To house their labourers they approached the Natal government for permission to lease the Jacobs concentration camp. Renaud and Co., were referred to the Durban Bay Land Company to which the property belonged. Their application failed as the Jacobs camp had been earmarked for the accommodation of the Chinese labourers imported to work on the gold mines.

Two POWs (Hans Steyn on the right) photographed by Davy Benowitz in Merebank prior to their repatriation to their home districts (Wassermann collection).

inhabitants. Lorry drivers stop and park their vehicles on the few remains of graves, which can be found when kicking and digging in the sand. A little further along the railway line, closer to central Durban, was the site of the Wentworth concentration camp. Today is graves are missing and no records exist of their location, as is the case with the graves of the Pinetown concentration camp.

Two POWs (Hans Steyn on the right) photographed by Davy Benowitz in Merebank prior to their repatriation to their home districts (Johan Wassermann private collection).

Wentworth camp inhabitants gathering in anticipation prior to their departure home. Wentworth was the first of the Durban concentration camps to close (LHM).

1. Pretorius, F, *The Anglo-Boer War 1899–1902*, pp.54–56.

2. Spies, SB, Women and the war in Warwick, P, (ed.), *The South African War: the Anglo-Boer War*, pp.169.

3. Otto, JC, *Die konsentrasiekampe*, p.139.

4. CD 853: p.109.

5. PAR, GH 554: monthly report Natal burgher camps, April 1902, 6.5.1902.

6. Wohlbergh, AU, *The Merebank concentration camp in Durban, 1901–1902*, pp.32–36.

7. Slayter, E, *Isipingo: village in the sun*, p.42.

8. Uys, I, *Heidelbergers of the Boer War*, p.204; RS Lawrence private collection (Australia): *South African diary of Kate French*, p.2.

9. PAR, MJPW 67: report of the NGR for the year 1898, p.10.

10. DAR, 3/DBN 1/1/3/23: Durban corporation rough minutes, p.165.

11. CD 893: p.33.

12. CD 893: p.12.

13. CD 893: pp.33–38.

14. CD 934: pp.41, 60–61.

15. CD 902: p.126.

16. PAR, GH 554: final report Natal burgher camps, 30.3.1903.

17. Spies, SB, *Methods of Barbarism. Roberts and Kitchener and civilians in the Boer Republics January 1900–May 1902*, p.193.

18. PAR, GH 553: monthly report Natal burgher camps, October 1901, 7.11.1901.

19. PAR, GH 793: letter Kitchener to McCallum, 30.9.190.

20. CD. 853: p.3.

21. PAR, GH 554: monthly reports Natal burgher camps, Oct 1901–Oct 1902; PAR, CSO 1732: report from E Noble to director of burgher camps, Transvaal, 30.6.1903.

22. PAR, GH 1452: general regulations for the Natal burgher camps, 1.2.1902.

23. NAR, A 2030 47: Ploeger collection, photocopies of reasons for being sent to the Jacobs camp.

24. NAR, PMO 49 and 52: correspondence regarding the transfer of people to the coast, 28.03.02. Fisher, MA, *Tant Miem Fisher se kampdagboek Mei 1901 – Augustus 1902*, pp.47.; Neethling, E, *Should we forget?*, p.114; Postma, MM, *Stemme uit die verlede: 'n versameling van beëdigde verklarings van vroue wat tydens die Tweede Vryheidsoorlog in konsentrasiekampe verkeer het*, pp.146–147.

25. PAR, GH 554: monthly report Natal burgher camps, May 1902, 11.6.1902; Rousseau, WP, *Notulen der conferentie van leeraren, arbeiders en arbeidsters in de burgerkampen in Natal gehouden in het burgerkamp te Merebank op den 24sten en 25sten Junie 1902*, pp.28–29.

26. PAR, GH 736: return of morally undesirables sent to Merebank as drawn up by RN Randall, 9.1.1901; NAR, SOP 35: memorandum from HM Bousfield to McHardy, 4.11.1902.

27. NAR, MGP 145: letter from refugee Klerksdorp to refugee Pretoria, 14.1.1902.

28. CD 893: p.33.

29. PAR, GH 554: monthly reports Natal burgher camps, 10.1902 –1.1903.

30. NAR, A 2030 77: Ploeger collection, photocopy of register of arrivals and departures.

31. PAR, GH 554: monthly reports Natal burgher camps, 3.1902 and 4.1902.

32. NAR, DBC 148: register of Wentworth camp residents.

33. NAR, GH 554: monthly report Natal burgher camps, 3.1902, 9.4.1902.

34. PAR, CSO 1732: reply by HM Bousfield to a request for the number of Natal refugees in his camp, 12.11.1901.

35. PAR, GH 554: monthly reports Natal burgher camps, 10.1901–7.1902.

36. PAR, CSO 1732: report E Noble to the director of burgher camps, Transvaal, 30.6.1903.

37. Ibid.

38. NAR, DBC 126: Merebank burgher camp register for residents A–L, pp.104 and 107.

39. NAR, DBC 130: nominal departure roll Merebank, passim; NAR, MGP 156: letters form P Carstens to J G Maxwell, 24.3.1902 and 11.4.1902.

40. Wassermann, JM, *The Eshowe Concentration and Surrendered Burghers Camp during the Anglo-Boer War (1899–1902)*, p.64.

41. Hobhouse, E, *War without glamour*, p. 37; Uys, pp.200–201.

42. WM, A 5890/90: Merebank-konsentrasiekamp ongepubliseerde herinneringe, 1, vir die boek *Kampkinders*.

43. Wohlberg, AU, *The Merebank concentration camp in Durban, 1901–1902*, p.92.

44. *Natal Mercury*, 20.11.1901.

45. NAR, DBC 126: Merebank burgher camp register of residents A–L, pp.217.

46. NAR, DBC 117, 126–133: registers of residents, nominal rolls and hospital registers, passim.

47. NAR, photo number 33212.

48. PAR, CSO 1732: report E Noble to the director of burgher camps Transvaal, 30.06.1902.

49. Photograph of the Merebank concentration camp, February 1902, in possession of the author.

50. NAR, A 2030 77: Ploeger collection, hand written notes by Ploeger.

51. Fischer, p.46.

52. Van Schoor, MCE, and Coetzee, CG, *Kampkinders 1900–1902: 'n gedenkboek*, p.47.

53. RS Lawrence private collection (Australia): *South African diary of Kate French*, p.2.

54. WM, A 5890/442: poem on fleas in Wentworth.

55. CD 893: p.34; Fisher, pp.77, 87, 108.

56. PAR, GH 212: memorandum Bousfield to Murray, 25.3.1902; CD 893: p.35.

57. Van Helsdingen, J, *Vrouwenleed: persoonlijke ondervindingen in den Boerenoorlog*, p.87.

58. PAR, GH 553: monthly report Natal burgher camps, 10.1901, 7.11.1901.

59. CD 893: p.34; PAR, GH 1452: general regulations for the Natal burgher camps, 1.2.1902; Fisher, p.54.

60. PAR, CSO 1732: report E Noble to director of burgher camps, Transvaal, 30.6.1902.

61. Neethling, p.128; WM, accession 5697: herinneringe van T Corbett.

62. PAR, CSO 1732: report E Noble to director of burgher camps, Transvaal, 30.6.1902.

63. Wohlberg, pp.111–120.

64. Neethling, pp.133–134.; Klem, MP, Die alledaagse lewe in die konsentrasiekamp, 1, *Tydskrif vir Volkskunde en Volkstaal* 2(32), April 1976, p.23

65. CD 893: p.207.

66. Spies, p.86.

67. PAR, CSO 1732: report E Noble to the director of burgher camps, Transvaal, 30.6.1903.

68. CD 819: p.204; PAR, GH 554: monthly reports Natal burgher camps, 9.1.1902 and 12.2.1902.

69. Wohlberg, pp.129–130.

70. NAR, CS 134: letter F Ware to the colonial secretary, 4.9.1902.

71. NAR, CS 97: letter assistant director of education for the Transvaal to the acting secretary to the Transvaal administration, Pretoria, 11.6.1902.

72. PAR, AGO 1/8/85: letter C Gerlach to attorney general, 10.07.1902.

73. PAR, GH 553: monthly report Natal burgher camps, October 1901, 7.11.1901.

74. Wohlberg, pp.130–131.

75. PAR, GH 554: monthly report Natal burgher camps, 2.1902, 12.3.1902.

76. NAR, *Transvaal Blue Book 1902–1903* (return of burgher camp schools).

77. Fischer, pp. 89, 115; *De Kerkbode* 18 (49), 12.12.1901, p.669.

78. A den Hartog private collection (Kroonstad): *Dagboek van Petrus Jacobus Malan*, pp.101–102.

79. Van Schoor and Coetzee, passim.

80. RS Lawrence private collection (Australia): *South African diary of Kate French*, p.2.

81. PAR, GH 554: monthly report Natal burgher camps, 4.1902, 6.5.1902.

82. PAR, GH 553: monthly report Natal burgher camps, October 1901, 7.11.1901; PAR, GH 737: despatch assistant secretary of the high commissioner to HE McCallum, 21.1.1902.

83. Wohlberg, pp.137–146.

84. Rousseau, pp.32–33.

85. Rousseau, pp. 15, 33.

86. NAR, A 173, Reverend & Mrs PF van Straten collection: testimonial by WH Hambly, 5.8.1902.

87. Fischer, p.109; Hobhouse, p.38.

88. Wohlberg, p.142.

89. PAR, GH 554: monthly report Natal burgher camps, November 1901, 10.12.1901; NAR, W 19/4 A: memoirs of I Kriegler, p.21.

90. WM, A 5890/91: N Coetzee collection, Merebank-konsentrasiekamp ongepubliseerde herinneringe, 2, vir die boek *Kampkinders*.

91. WM, A 5890/91: Merebank-konsentrasiekamp ongepubliseerde herinneringe, 2, vir die boek *Kampkinders*; NAR, DBC 132: Merebank refugee camp death register September 1901–December 1902; NAR, DBC 133: register of deaths.

92. PAR, CSO 1732: report E Noble to the director of burgher camps, Transvaal, 30.6.1903; PAR, GH 867: letter WP Rousseau to HM Bousfield, 14.5.1902; PAR, GH 867: memorandum TK Murray to all camp superintendents, 29.5.1902.

93. Neethling, pp.47–48.

94. KCL 4260: Bluff annals.

95. CD 893: p.37; *Natal Mercury*, 7.10.1901; PAR, GH 553: despatch Murray to Chamberlain, 21.1.1902.

96. Van Schoor en Coetzee, pp.34–35; Van Zyl, DH, *In die konsentrasiekamp: jeugherinneringe*, p.43.

97. Fischer, pp.105–106.

98. PAR, GH 1453: despatch HE McCallum to J Chamberlain, 23.7.1902.

99. Wohlberg, pp.154–158.

100. CD 893: pp.4, 35–36; PAR, GH 554: monthly report Natal burgher camps, November 1901, 10.12.1901.

101. PAR, GH 554: monthly report Natal burgher camps, 11.1901, 9.1.1902.

102. PAR, GH 631: assistant auditor general's report FH Hamilton to A Milner, 29.4.1902.; NAR, DBC 131: Merebank refugee camp hospital register, p.49.

103. PAR, GH 554: monthly report Natal burgher camps, 2.1902, 12.3.1902; NAR, DBC 131: Merebank refugee camp hospital register, p.1.

104. FAR, SRC A 21443: letter Sister White to the general superintendent, 13.11.1902.

105. PAR, GH 553: despatch TK Murray to J Chamberlain, 21.1.1902; PAR, DPH 6: despatch health officer to TK Murray, 13.1.1902; PAR, DPH 6: despatch HM Bousfield to the harbour engineer, 24.12.1901.

106. NAR, DBC 131: Merebank refugee camp hospital register, passim.

107. NAR, A 2030 77: Ploeger collection, hospital register.

108. NAR, A 2030 100: Ploeger collection, notes on health in the Durban camps.

109. A den Hartog private collection: *Dagboek van Petrus Jacobus Malan*, p.94; NAR, DBC 131: Merebank refugee camp hospital register.

110. WM: A 5890/91.

111. Fischer, p.93.

112. NAR, DBC, 131: Merebank refugee camp hospital register, passim.

113. Wohlberg, pp.185–193.

114. NAR, DBC 13: Merebank refugee camp hospital register, passim; NAR, DBC 132: Merebank refugee camp death register September 1901 – December 1902, pp.9–15.

115. Wohlberg, pp.193–196.

116. NAR, DBC 132: Merebank refugee camp death register September 1901 – December 1902, passim.

117. PAR, GH 553: letter from TK Murray to HE McCallum, 3.2.1902.

118. PAR, CSO 1944: annual report by the magistrate Umlazi for the year ending 31.12.1901.

119. NAR, DBC 9: weekly reports of deaths at Merebank; PAR, GH 554: monthly reports Natal burgher camps October 1901 – December 1902.

120. The total population represents the figure at the end of the given month, and does not necessarily represent the highest figure of the month.

121. The total population quoted is that registered at the end of the month, and does not necessarily represent the highest total of the month.

122. Wohlberg, pp.184–185.

123. NAR, DBC 121: Jacobs birth roll

124. *Natal Mercury*, 9.6.1902.

125. CD 1163: p.163.

126. PAR, GH 554: monthly report Natal burgher camps, July 1902, 6.8.1902.

127. NAR, CSO 1732: report by E Noble to the director of burgher camps, Transvaal, 30.6.1903.

128. PAR, PM 30: letter acting general manager of the NGR to AH Hime, 4.7.1902.

129. PAR, GH 554: monthly report Natal burgher camps, September and October 1902, 6.10.1902, 6.12.1902.

130. PAR, GH 554: monthly report Natal burgher camps, 12.1902, 6.1.1903; NAR, DBC 131: Merebank refugee camp hospital register, pp.48–49.

131. PAR, GH 554: monthly report Natal burgher camps, 10.1902, 6.11.1902.

CHAPTER 18

THE PINETOWN CONCENTRATION CAMP
Johan Wassermann

The establishment of the Pinetown concentration camp

In the early hours of 23 January 1902, General CF Beyers and 40 burghers charged the Pietersburg concentration camp. While holding Superintendent JE Tucker and other staff members captive, roughly 150 surrendered burghers were commandeered again. This daring attack caused the British great humiliation as they had been unable to protect Boer women and children in their care. Consequent punishment was not aimed at Beyers and his commando, but at the inhabitants of the Pietersburg concentration camp. On the advice of Major MBJ Jackson, Lord Kitchener instructed that the Pietersburg camp, including personnel, inhabitants and equipment was to be removed to Natal. The only viable site the Natal burgher camps department could offer was at Colenso, where the Pietersburg camp was established from 22 February to 11 April 1902.

From the outset, neither Lord Kitchener nor the Natal burgher camps department was very happy with Colenso as a site for a concentration camp. The Colenso camp was approximately 200 kilometres from Durban by rail. Transporting provisions, rations supplies and equipment from Durban to Colenso was a logistical burden that placed a strain on the NGR, as it took up time and rolling stock which were desperately needed for the war effort. The location of the Colenso camp also proved to be a problem for Sir TK Murray and his department. Administration and management of a camp geographically far removed from the main service centres of Durban and Pietermaritzburg, and distant from the other concentration camps, seemed to be counter productive. The only viable solution was to move the Colenso concentration camp.

Apart from the above factors, the authorities also wanted to move the Colenso concentration camp because of the security risk it posed. It was feared that General Louis Botha, who was active in the Vryheid area, might break through and attack the Colenso camp[1] to liberate the male inhabitants as Beyers had done. The possibility of an attack had also been voiced by Colenso camp inhabitants and the commandos. Thus it was decided that the camp would be moved to Pinetown.[2]

The idea of creating a concentration camp at Pinetown was not new. On 16 November 1901, Lord Milner had informed the secretary of state for colonies, Joseph Chamberlain, that another camp for 3 000 people had to be created close to the coast to accommodate an overflow from the overcrowded Transvaal camps with their high disease and death rates. Pinetown offered a suitable site for such a camp.[3] Shortly afterwards, the authorities decided that two more camps were needed in the coastal area to house 3 000 inhabitants each and Pinetown was mentioned again, this time more seriously when Sir HE McCallum suggested to Chamberlain that a hut camp be constructed there. However, such a step was subject to the approval of the terrain by the government health officer.[4]

The white bell tents of the Colenso concentration camp prior to their removal to Pinetown (WM).

Four days later, Pinetown was once again named as a possible site for a concentration camp in a telegram between Milner and Chamberlain.[5] The same proposal was put forward in a telegram from the high commissioner's office on 8 December 1901. The next day the Fawcett Commission, which had condemned the Merebank site as unfit for habitation, suggested Pinetown as a possibly healthier locale.[6] This idea was opposed later on the same day in another telegram, which stated that the major problem concerning a concentration camp in Pinetown was the shortage of water.[7] So, for the time being, plans for building a concentration camp in Pinetown were shelved. Jacobs and Wentworth were chosen as the locations for the two additional coastal camps, while the condemned site at Merebank was retained.

The fact that Pinetown had been dismissed as a possible concentration camp site was questioned by one of the old inhabitants, who recalled that during the Anglo-Zulu War, Pinetown, then a garrison town, had provided water for 1 000 troops and their horses. During that war the water of Pinetown had been highly thought of by Sir Baker Russell and the question arose as to whether the 'water was not sufficient for 3 000 people' or whether the problem was that 'the quality was not good enough'. Even Murray, who had rejected Pinetown as being suitable for a camp, could not escape the wrath of the old-timer when he was reminded that, having grown up in Pinetown, he should have recalled the rivers that ran deep and wide a few metres from his boyhood home. These rivers were still flowing strongly and served all the Pinetown residents.[8]

As a former Pinetown inhabitant with extensive experience of concentration camps, TK Murray probably knew the proposed area well enough to appreciate the inadequacies of the water as a permanent supply base, especially as 3 000 people, mostly women and children, would depend on it. It is to his credit that Murray did not allow his emotional attachment to Pinetown to influence his decision.

Thomas Keir Murray

Sir TK Murray (KCMG) was born and raised in Pinetown. By the time he had become the general superintendent of Natal burgher camps, he already had an impressive career behind him. He was a leading figure in sports administration; he had acted as prime minister in 1897 and was very prominent in the business field, which included being a director of the Natal Bank. At the outbreak of the war he raised two units, Murray's Horse and Murray's Scouts and served on General Redvers Buller's staff as an intelligence officer. Murray had extensive business links with the Transvaal and knew President Paul Kruger. He was knighted for his role in the completion of the Durban-Johannesburg railway line.

A forlorn girl with her doll in the Colenso concentration camp (PAR).

In the meantime, Murray and Dr TW Hime had inspected various places as alternatives to Colenso. When no viable sites could be found, Pinetown was once again considered because of its good railway and road links and healthy climate. This time it was decided, with the blessing of the governor, to overcome the lack of water by building a small dam on the Palmiet River, from which a steam pump could be used to pump water to the proposed campsite.[9] McCallum immediately obtained Lord Kitchener's approval of the plan,[10] and with the water problem taken care of, the process of dismantling the Colenso concentration camp began.

The next step was for the Natal burgher camps department to acquire the identified site, 1,6 kilometres north-east of the Pinetown station,[11] situated between Pinetown and New Germany on the northern bank of the Palmiet River. Thirty-one acres of level land was leased from the owner, Friederich Wilhelm Königkramer, at a monthly rental of £20 plus £140 compensation for the fruit and vegetables that could have been planted on the terrain. Although this arrangement seemed to be to the benefit of Königkramer, he apparently suffered financially, as the government only paid him in December 1902, four months after the camp had been closed down. Morever, the camp had ruined all grazing and no crops could be planted there because of the damage to the soil.[12]

The removal of the Colenso camp began only 50 days after it had been created.[13] This time the trip was only 200 kilometres. Although this journey was shorter than the one from Pietersburg, it was even more horrific in many ways. According to Ds AM Murray, a batch of inhabitants boarded the open trucks at Colenso on Saturday 29 March 1902. Shortly after boarding the train, two women apparently gave birth in front of the men and children on the train.[14]

The construction of the Pinetown concentration camp

The inhabitants of the yet-to-be-constructed Pinetown concentration camp started arriving from Colenso during March 1902. The first arrivals had no tents and spent eight days in houses formerly occupied by Indians. This accommodation was unsatisfactory and was described as dirty and damp.[15] Camp inhabitants arrived from Colenso over a period of several weeks up to 11 April 1902.[16] From the Pinetown Station, a private contractor moved the inhabitants, supplies and equipment to the campsite at 4s per ton.[17] As the camp inhabitants and equipment arrived, the camp started to take shape on a site which was perceived, at the time, as being the healthiest in the British empire.[18]

The camp terrain was surrounded by hills and lay between 340 and 400 metres above sea level. The site was fenced off from the surrounding farm and town land by barbwire.[19] The tents were erected, according to a military pattern, in long lines, far enough from one another for a fireplace to be built and for a vehicle to pass between them.[20] A total of 700 tents and canvas constructions was erected,[21] probably by the camp inhabitants themselves. Six-hundred of these were bell or round tents, 33 were medium-sized square marquees, 50 were large square marquees,

nine were 'EP' tents and eight were canvas constructions. These served as accommodation for housing, a school, a hospital and a church.

Besides the tents, there were also more substantial school buildings, teachers' quarters,[22] hutting and general housing constructed by the chief engineer on behalf of the imperial authorities at the cost of £491 11s.[23] The erection of good educational facilities in the Pinetown concentration camp was in line with Murray's policy that a good education for all camp inhabitants was of paramount importance. Before the erection of these buildings, the camp school had consisted of three large marquees, one medium marquee, three sail shelters and a bell tent that served as the office.[24] The Natal burgher camps department addressed the shortcomings of the school buildings and attended to the lack of furniture and equipment such as desks, chairs and blackboards.[25]

The biggest construction project in the Pinetown concentration camp was to supply sufficient water for the requirements of the camp. Although the operation, which took two months to complete, proved to be expensive, Murray justified it by stating that clean water reduced diseases and made life more comfortable.[26] During April 1902, a good water supply was reaching the camp[27] and, by May 1902, pipes had been laid to the pumping engine,[28] which consisted of a Worthington feed steam boiler and a six horse-power horizontal boiler. The water was pumped into 31 1 000 gallon (4 546 litre) tanks from which it was taken to all parts of the camp using gravity. All the construction was carried out under the auspices of Murray, an indication of how strongly he felt about the project.[29]

The good water supply was complemented by the effective latrine system. With 3 000 people in the camp, sanitation was a serious matter. Train loads of latrines were brought to Pinetown from Pietersburg via Colenso.[30] These latrines were made of wood and iron, with separate units allocated, and being identified for use of either boys/men or women/children.[31] As was the case with the Pietersburg latrines, these utilised the bucket system, and consisted of two sets of buckets cleaned twice a day, by two European and twelve African men under supervision of a Van Rensburg. The contents were removed by two sanitary wagons and dumped into a ditch dug daily for this purpose and filled in at the end of the day. The toilets were cleaned daily with carbolic powder and the buckets with hydrated lime.[32]

The camp inhabitants who were used to the wide open spaces of farms, struggled to adapt to the restricted toilet facilities. The situation was aggravated by the fact that up to 150 people had to share a single toilet. By the time the former Pietersburg camp inhabitants arrived in Pinetown, they had already experienced the concentration camp system for a year. The general rules for Natal burgher camps, in an attempt to impose order on those not yet used to the system, stipulated that: 'Any person fouling the Latrines must be made to clean same; anyone noticing this should at once report the matter.'[33] These regulations were enforced by toilet guards.

General refuse was placed in containers erected for the purpose amongst the tents and emptied on a daily basis. Tent inhabitants had to clean their tents as well as the surrounding area[34] while the children had to collect papers and tins scattered about the camp under the supervision of older boys.[35]

Although no direct evidence could be found of bathhouses in the Pinetown camp, the monthly reports state that all Natal concentration camps had such facilities. These bathhouses, presumably next to the Palmiet River, were supplemented by wash-houses for the exclusive purpose of doing laundry, which was dried only in allocated places. Cutlery, crockery, pots and pans were not washed in the wash-houses but at the tents, and the water was then emptied into the tanks provided. These tanks were then emptied by the sanitary personnel.[36]

Once the sanitary and water arrangements had been provided, a hospital was constructed in the camp. The hospital consisted of five 'EP' tents with six beds each, a marquee with two beds, and a bell tent which contained one bed serving as a maternity ward, providing a total of 33 beds for a camp with 3 000 inhabitants. This constituted a very high camp inhabitant to hospital bed ratio. The materials, staff, and the patients who had stayed behind until fit enough to travel were eventually moved from Pietersburg only when the hospital was completed. The hospital staff resided in an 'EP' tent and a bell tent, while food for the staff and patients was prepared in the hospital kitchen tent. The hospital linen was washed in two steam kettles and a burner was used to rid the hospital of excretions in the case of enteric fever,[37] to prevent the spread of diseases and make the hospital a much healthier place. However, the medical facilities were not considered to be very good by the Pinetown camp inhabitants.

The meat, rations and additional rations or supplies and comforts for the inhabitants were kept in wood and iron sheds and were dispensed to the inhabitants by a storeman between 8:00 and 19:00 daily.[38]

The camp facilities in the Pinetown concentration camp included a camp shop. This shop, under the direct administration of the Natal burgher camps department, sold a variety of items at fixed prices including furniture, foodstuffs such as vegetables, fruit, milk, and tinned food, clothes and even some luxury items. The shop was well supported by the camp inhabitants and served to supplement the dull diet as well as provide items necessary for day-to-day living.[39]

These camp facilities were a great improvement on those of Pietersburg. The Natal burgher camps department learned from the mistakes made in the concentration camps in the Transvaal and the Free State and attempted to remedy them. The inhabitants of all the Natal concentration camps, including those in the Pinetown camp, benefited from the improvements.

The Pinetown Railway Station at the time of the Anglo-Boer War – the point of arrival and departure of the Pinetown concentration camp inhabitants (Pinetown Museum).

The administration and organisation of the Pinetown concentration camp

The personnel of the Pinetown concentration camp consisted of the camp superintendent, JE Tucker; the medical doctor, D Henderson; the chemist, JH Williams; the hospital matron, Sister K Webb; her assistant, Pomeroy, and five apprentice nurses. The camp matron, Nurse Grafton, was supported by a relief matron, Pittendrigh, Nurses Keat and Phillips and 12 apprentice nurses, and three clerks, Messrs DM Stephen, J Gadd and C Korner, took care of administrative matters.[40] The camp also had 16 teachers from amongst the camp inhabitants[41] and from the soldiers who guarded the camp. These personnel served the Pinetown camp for most of its existence. After the war had ended, more qualified personnel were made available to Superintendent Tucker.

Superintendent Tucker, supported by his staff, controlled the Pinetown camp according to stipulated regulations, but in respect of matters such as housing, rations, water and sanitation, he used his own discretion. Tucker's task was not an easy one, as he was always on duty. He had to oversee the simplest of tasks, apply the rules and regulations, and administer supplies, equipment and his staff, whilst remaining impartial and patient. Tucker also had to have a knowledge of the Boer culture as well as being informed about food, sanitation, water, education, transportation and simple industries, such as gardening.

Tucker fared quite well in this almost impossible task. The Fawcett Commission thought he ran the Pietersburg camp efficiently and that his personnel were loyal and supportive of one another.[42] The British authorities shared this viewpoint,[43] and kept him on as superintendent during the removal from Pietersburg to Colenso and Pinetown and the subsequent transferral back to Pietersburg.[44] Miss Horton, a Pinetown resident during the time of the Anglo-Boer War, remembered him as '... very strict, and the Boers were made to clean the camp, and made to use the facilities provided for washing, etc.'.[45] Even JC Otto, renowned for his one-sided criticism of the concentration camp system, praised Tucker for his efforts to provide the Pietersburg camp inhabitants with quality meat.[46] This praise by Otto is disputed by CJ du Preez who recalled in 1981 that Tucker was tarred and feathered in the Pietersburg camp by the women, because they were angry about food and other matters.[47] This, however, was the only negative comment found and was relayed 80 years after the incident had occurred.

From the available evidence, it is difficult to evaluate Superintendent Tucker objectively. It must be remembered that a concentration camp was only as good as its superintendent, and the latter was only as good as the support he received from the appropriate camp authorities and his staff. Pinetown was easier to run than Pietersburg, as Tucker received good support for all aspects of his difficult task. Proof of the greater efficiency of the Pinetown camp is borne out by the fact that only 34 camp inhabitants died during the six months in Natal, while approximately 650 inhabitants died during the nine months in Pietersburg.

To manage the Pinetown camp successfully, Tucker needed the full support of his staff members.[48] Only one medical doctor was available, Dr Daniel Henderson, who had practised medicine for two years in Victoria-West prior to the war.[49] The first hour of Henderson's daily shift started at 9:00 in a section of the tent which he shared with the chemist. During this time he dealt with the sick, wrote prescriptions, and received reports from the nurses. From 10:00 onwards he visited the hospital first and the tents afterwards. The Fawcett Commission viewed Henderson as a very capable doctor who did a good job.[50] This view, however, was not shared by the Pinetown camp inhabitants. A number of inhabitants, including A de Jager, B Hofmeyr[51] and SJG Hofmeyr, accused Henderson of alcohol abuse,[52] while others accused him of negligence towards the sick[53] and in his prescriptions.[54] In his defence, it must be stated that Henderson worked under difficult conditions. For great lengths of time, he was the only medical doctor in the camp and had had to deal with 3 000 patients and hundreds of deaths in the Pietersburg concentration camp, which he probably considered could have been avoided under normal circumstances with proper support. JA Mollett, a camp inhabitant of Pietersburg, Colenso and Pinetown, describes the pressure under which Henderson had to work: 'One doctor for so many people was worth very little. It was difficult to locate him. We were always told he was busy with his rounds and that we should return the following day.'[55]

The next link in the medical support chain was the chemist, JH Williams, who dispensed the medicine prescribed by Henderson from the medium-sized marquee they shared.[56] Williams faced the same accusations as Henderson and was accused of alcohol abuse.[57] Apart from this, very little is known about him. The remaining medical personnel consisted of the hospital matron, Sister K Webb, a qualified nurse, formerly from Pretoria.[58] She managed the hospital and its staff, and all matters related to medical care. In this she was aided by Assistant-Matron Pomeroy, formerly from Cape Town, and five apprentice nurses. The hospital staff resided in one 'EP' tent and one bell tent. They all ate together, except for the apprentice Boer nurses who had to draw rations and reside with their families in the concentration camp.[59]

The job description of the camp matron included educating the Boer women on child rearing and aspects of hygiene. Nurse Grafton also had to select women from the camp who were younger than 20, as apprentice nurses and then train them to be neat, to take temperatures, dispense medicine and to prepare additional food as prescribed by the doctor. The apprentice nurses had to visit allocated tents between 8:00 and 9:00 and report to the camp matron on cleanliness as well as on the sick. Nurse Grafton then informed Superintendent Tucker of those who did not adhere to the personal hygiene regulations and reported the ill to the doctor. The camp matron had to accompany Dr Henderson on his daily rounds and take note of the seriously ill as well as those earmarked for additional food, and for later visits by the apprentice nurses.[60]

Nurse Grafton not only controlled the sick in the camp, but also had to determine, with the help of the apprentice nurses, the needs of the camp inhabitants regarding clothes, blankets and material. She personally visited each case before handing out clothes.[61] The people in the Pinetown camp badly needed clothes, blankets and material and £550 18s 4d was spent on this,[62] although they had already received such items in the Pietersburg camp.

The Pinetown camp as seen from Mount Moriah. The bell and marquee tents used to house the inhabitants are clearly visible (Bergtheil Museum).

A view of the Pinetown concentration camp towards the old Lutheran Church in New Germany. Note the military style rows in which the tents were pitched as well as the open tent flaps as per regulations (Pinetown Museum).

In general it seems that the small Pinetown concentration camp staff rendered a satisfactory job of managing and administering the camp and its diverse inhabitants.

The Pinetown concentration camp inhabitants

The people of the Pinetown concentration camp generally came from the Zoutpansberg, north of Pietersburg. Today this area forms part of Limpopo and its inhabitants are commonly referred to as 'Bosvelders' (people from the bushveld). They came from Buffelsberg, Haenertsburg, Houtbosch, Leydsdorp, Louis Trichardt, Low Country, Mara, Marabastad, Mapochsland, Moalitzisland, Pietersburg, Rhenosterpoort and Spelonken. Some individuals did come from other areas such as Krugersdorp, Pretoria and Johannesburg,[63] while a substantial number also arrived from Harrismith.[64]

The number of inhabitants in the Pinetown concentration camp fluctuated since Boer civilians captured in the Northern Transvaal were constantly being sent down to Pinetown. For example, 91 people captured during April 1902 by a column of Kitchener's Scouts under Colonel Johan Colenbrander arrived in Pinetown. They were sent via Pietersburg by AG Watt, the storeman, who had remained behind. Sending such captives down to Pinetown was not easy because of the lack of rail transport for this purpose.

Inhabitants were also constantly transferred between concentration camps in Natal and allowed to reside with friends and family outside the Pinetown camp. These circumstances, along with the fact that former POWs and burghers who had been on commando joined their families after the signing of peace on 31 May 1902, caused the number of inhabitants of the Pinetown camp to fluctuate. Generally, the number of inhabitants was marginally above 3 000, except during July 1902, when numbers dropped to 776 as many inhabitants were transferred back to Pietersburg. The highest number of inhabitants residing in the camp at a given time was the 3 148 inhabitants counted on 30 June 1902, consisting of 756 men, 1 148 women and 1 244 children.[65]

Financial expenditure on the Pinetown concentration camp

If the administration, management and facilities of the Pinetown concentration camp were to operate smoothly, certain expenses had to be met. During the existence of the Pinetown concentration camp running costs amounted to £2 161 15s 11d. The biggest expenditure was on stores, supplies and sundries for the approximately 3 000 inhabitants. This expenditure per inhabitant included food items such as meat, sugar and coffee at a weekly cost of 3/3d for adults, 2/6d for children over five years and 2/3d for children under five years of age. These expenses also included items such as soap and candles.[66]

The second highest expenditure was on salaries, and amounted to £4 080 14s 7d. This is higher than would normally be the case for the Natal burgher camps as the staff of the Pinetown camp were remunerated according to the Transvaal scale. The highest paid camp official was Superintendent Tucker, who probably earned more than the £40 per week paid to Natal burgher camp superintendents.[67] At the other end of the scale the hospital matron, Sister K Webb, earned £12 per month, free rations and a uniform allowance, while qualified nurses receive £10 per month, as well as the same advantages. The lowest paid personnel were the apprentice nurses from among the camp inhabitants. They received between 1/6d and 2/6d per day as well as extra rations.[68] Of the £1 817 11s 8d spent on housing, £1 572 went on the construction of the school and teachers' quarters.[69] The relatively small amount spent on housing and equipment can be explained by the fact that, when moving from Pietersburg, all equipment, including housing, was brought along. As regards the expenditure on fuel and water, £50 went into damming the Palmiet River and pumping the water to the Pinetown camp.[70]

The remaining payments were for clothing for those inhabitants identified by the camp matron and her staff as in need of help, and £412 19s 7d was allocated to medical supplies. Generally, the expenditure at the Pinetown concentration camp was low compared to other such camps in Natal. The reason for that was threefold. Firstly, very little equipment and construction was needed to set up the camp as it had all been brought down from Pietersburg; secondly, the Pinetown camp existed for only a short while before being transferred back to Pietersburg, and thirdly, the Natal burgher camps department was instructed not to make life overly comfortable for the former Pietersburg concentration camp inhabitants as they had been transferred to Natal as punishment for the attack by General Beyers.

Life in the Pinetown concentration camp

The contents of the ration scale and the amounts received by the Pinetown camp inhabitants were generally the same as that of the three Durban camps. It took the camp inhabitants some time to bridge the cultural divide and get used to food different from that which they were accustomed to. The bland diet, described as 'army rations' by FW Königkramer, was supplemented by fruit and vegetables from local farms, while fresh bread and meat were brought from Pinetown. According to Königkramer, 'the tinned meat or bully beef that replaced the fresh meat from time to time, was good and was sold by camp inhabitants to people outside the camp for 10 cents per tin',[71] probably to earn some sorely needed cash.

Local residents at times took pity on the concentration camp inhabitants and their predicament. According to Gibson Clendinning, his mother, Laura Clendenning, who was of Scottish descent, took fresh food from their farm, Ballingrohre at Sarnia, to the camp, and handed it to the camp inhabitants. This compassionate deed was apparently in response to the kindness of the Boers towards a family friend, Mrs Barett at Middelburg, during the Anglo-Transvaal War after her husband had been forced to flee to Natal.[72]

The least satisfactory aspect of the ration scale as far as the Pinetown camp inhabitants was concerned was the milk for children. The tinned condensed milk was diluted by ten parts of water to one part of milk to make it go further. This decreased the nutritional value and caused the milk to turn blue. To supplement this meagre supply, JSJ Jansen recalled her mother buying food and milk with money she kept in a belt around her waist. According to Jansen, the milk from Pinetown was a great improvement on that of Pietersburg, where many children had died because of the lack of nutrition in the milk and water mix.[73] The Pinetown camp inhabitants were also dissatisfied with the bread they received and requested Boer meal in order to bake their own bread, a request granted by TK Murray.[74]

The food rations, along with additional rations such as medical supplies, soap and candles, were kept in wood and iron sheds erected for the purpose. These rations were dispensed to the camp inhabitants between 8:00 and 19:00 daily. This process led to the collectors, many of them children, standing in long lines in the hot sun for hours, as the Pinetown camp did not employ the block system of issuing rations which had been recommended by the Fawcett Commission in Pietersburg. This resulted in bitter complaints by the camp inhabitants, but to no avail.[75]

For the preparation of the food, each adult and child over five years of age received 14 lbs (6.3 kg) of wood and each child under five years of age was given 7 lbs (3 kg) per week.[76] Pots and pans had been handed to the majority of the inhabitants on their arrival at the Pietersburg camp.[77] As there were no communal ovens, people used bricks, clay and galvanised iron to construct stoves and ovens outside the tents for communal use,[78] and the food was cooked on fires of wood and coal. The smoke from these fires hanging over the area must have resembled a modern-day informal settlement.

The Lubbe family photographed in the Pinetown concentration camp by HJW Pienaar (WM).

Johan Colenbrander

Colonel Johan Colenbrander was, himself, born and reared in Pinetown before embarking on a career in the Natal civil service and as a member of Kitchener's Fighting Scouts. Colenbrander Park in Pinetown has a plaque on the gate to commemorate him.

The Pinetown concentration camp on the farm of FW Königkramer, surrounded by rolling grasslands (WM).

A Boer woman and two boys pose awkwardly for a photograph (PAR).

Accommodation in the Pinetown concentration camp

The camp inhabitants resided in both the bell tents and the marquees. In general, no more than five people resided in a bell tent, 12 in a medium-sized marquee and 20 to 25 in a large marquee.[79] The only burgher who resided in an 'EP' tent was ex-Commandant HJC van Rensburg, the most senior surrendered Boer officer. The marquees were cooler in the day and warmer at night than the bell tents.[80] It would therefore have been perhaps more comfortable to live in a marquee, even with 12 to 25 other people, than in the relative privacy of a bell tent, which would be uncomfortably hot in the day and very cold at night. However, at least one former Pinetown camp inhabitant recalled the oppressive heat in a marquee, where it was so hot that blankets were tied to the outside of the marquees to create some shade for the children;[81] the situation in the bell tents would have been much worse. Gibson Clendenning summed up the situation with his comment: 'Can you imagine the heat in midsummer in a bell canvas tent? Life was not like the books tell it.'[82]

The tents acted as bedroom, dining room, lounge, kitchen and pantry all rolled into one. Within these tents the women tried to create a home with the few possessions they had and to re-establish dignity. Setting up home must have been difficult as most had arrived in the Pietersburg camp with little clothing and no bedding or furniture, and the camp authorities had to supply them with the basic necessities. By November 1901, 25% of the Pietersburg camp inhabitants still slept on the floor, as no beds were available.[83] It can therefore be assumed that this situation had changed very little by the time these same people arrived in Pinetown. Such tent towns were perfectly adequate for young, fit troops on the move, but were very trying for the elderly, and for the women and children they usually housed.

Although not overcrowded, it must have been uncomfortable to reside in the same tent, in a strange place, with the sick, and with people of different ages, of mixed genders and from different families.[84] What made matters worse was the fact that the Pinetown camp terrain had no shade, as most trees on this stretch of grasslands had been removed, presumably for security reasons.[85] This almost treeless, hot landscape was soon churned to dust by the thousands of feet endlessly wandering about the tents. When it rained, the dust quickly became mud, which made both walking and keeping the tents clean very difficult.

The most severe environmental hazard which tested the housing structures as well as the inhabitants was a terrible storm during the month of June 1902. Gale force winds and biting cold lasted the whole night, covering the camp in sand[86] after which a hailstorm broke. According to the official report, the storm destroyed numerous tents and completely ruined the school.[87] To the Pinetown camp inhabitants the storm was horrifying. Half the tents were blown down[88] and people had to flee from their collapsing tents into the darkness. Some took refuge in the washrooms while Missionary Hofmeyr wrapped his young son in a blanket and fled with his family to a nearby farm, Glenugie, occupied by Miss Eliza Scott. According to Mrs Betty Hofmeyr, the mother of the family involved, Scott received the family into her home 'with love as she was a

Christian who did a lot for the people in the camp'.[89] In 1981, 79 years after this incident, the young boy wrapped in the blanket, SJG Hofmeyr recalled Miss Scott's kindness, and especially the fact that she had fed him soft bananas while he felt ill and traumatised.[90] The Hofmeyr family was allowed to stay on at the Scott residence as the Natal burgher camps department rented temporary shelter in and around Pinetown while repairing the storm damage.[91]

This storm lashed most of Natal and destroyed tents in the Howick concentration camp and the Umbilo POW camp. According to Murray, greater destruction and injury was prevented because inhabitants of the other camps resided in huts.

Eliza Scott

Eliza Scott was the daughter of the Reverend Charles Scott. In front of the Pinetown Museum is a monument in her honour to commemorate the fact that she taught interdenominational Sunday School for 56 years in Pinetown. She also knew the Boers well as she had taught the children of Conrad Meyer of Inchanga. She died on 29 March 1913.

Health in the Pinetown concentration camp

Oral history sources in Pinetown maintain that no deaths occurred in the 'model' camp at Pinetown. It is difficult to trace the origins of this myth. It probably lies in the work of G Russell[92] who stated, without citing any sources, that the Pinetown concentration camp was the healthiest of all and that no deaths occurred. Also the *Annals of Pinetown*[93] carried the statement '... it is good to know that no deaths occurred in the Pinetown one', while an old Pinetonian, Miss Horton, remembered '... there were no epidemics amongst the Boers, nor did one man, woman or child die.'[94] The second reason for this myth may probably be accounted for in the fact that the site of the Pinetown camp was quickly overgrown and forgotten by a community who had no real emotional or any other attachment to it. In 1939, FA de Villiers, of Montclair, the *Ere-Sekretaris Eerons-helde-komitee*, wrote to Dr HS Pretorius, the head of the National Archives in Pretoria, stating that he had been given the task by the local Graves Commission of the *Nederduits Gereformeerde Kerk* synod to locate the cemetery of the Pinetown concentration camp. De Villiers visited the site just outside the boundary of the Pinetown borough. He found the area to be fenced in with a broken-down fence, and found no evidence of graves, only a few hollows which held no clues. This did not deter De Villiers and he requested Pretorius to supply him with a name list of the dead so that they could erect a monument.[95]

In response to this request, Pretorius supplied an incorrect list of names of people who had purportedly died in the Pinetown concentration camp, without grave numbers. Pretorius also erroneously stated that the camp had existed between 1901 and 1902.[96] De Villiers did not react to this incorrect information and it seems that his good intentions to erect a monument faded away. Whether this was owing to the Second World War, which was raging at the time, or because he could not locate the graves, or for any other reason, it is difficult to tell. What was at least established is that deaths did occur in the Pinetown camp. This information, it seems, was not shared with anyone outside the obscure committee which De Villiers chaired.

In the light of this episode, and with the site and all its accompanying relics completely lost within four decades, it is not surprising that a myth that no deaths occurred could take root. In reality, 20 people died in the Pinetown concentration camp, a figure far removed from the approximately 650 who died in Pietersburg. Pinetown seems to have lived up to its reputation of being the healthiest 'place' in the British empire.

The majority of the 20 people who died in the Pinetown camp, as was the case in other concentration camps, were children; 14 were under the age of five years . Only six of those who died were older than 12 years of age. Pneumonia, laryngitis, 'marasmus and debility' were the most common causes of death in the Pinetown camp. Apart from the climate, the low death rate and general healthy state of the Pinetown concentration camp could probably also be attributed to the good, clean water supply, the lack of epidemics such as measles, the fact that the weak and ill did not survive the Pietersburg camp and efficient administration by the Natal burgher camps department under Thomas Murray. An effective hospital probably did not contribute to the low death rate as the medical services offered were generally the same as those of Pietersburg. The result was that inhabitants remained very suspicious of the hospital which was culturally foreign to their accustomed health care. In the Pinetown camp a belief developed amongst inhabitants that people were actually poisoned in the Pietersburg camp hospital. A young man said that, as far as he knew, he was the only person to leave that hospital alive and that happened simply because his father forcibly removed him. The filth in the hospital was reputed to be incredible and the hospital remained locked overnight and was only opened the next morning.[97]

People did not only die in the Pinetown concentration camp, they were also born. The incomplete records show that during April 1902 five children, three boys and two girls, were born in the camp, while mention is also made of other births, some of these illegitimate.[98]

As with the Durban concentration camps, the Pinetown concentration camp was also viewed as a threat to the health of the surrounding area. A young woman from a farm near Inchanga had a mild attack of measles, as she had contracted the virus during a visit to the Pinetown camp.[99] This was immediately reported to the director of public health, as infectious diseases in the Natal burgher camps were to be reported weekly, in order to allow the health officer for Natal, E Hill, to take the necessary steps to protect the general public from 'adverse influences arising in connection with these camps'.[100] The health threat that the Pinetown concentration camp was perceived to pose to the general public did not end with the report of the case of measles. When Dr Jackson of Pinetown reported a case of diphtheria, Hill requested the district health officer for Upper Umlazi, Dr DM Campbell, to determine if the Pinetown camp water drained into the Umbilo River, the main source of water for Durban, or into any of its tributaries.[101] Campbell reported that the Pinetown camp water drained into the Palmiet River, which in turn flowed into the Umgeni River and he put their fears to rest.[102]

Religious activities in the Pinetown concentration camp

The religious services and pastoral work conducted at Colenso by *Dominees* WP Rousseau and AM Murray, with the approval and blessing of the Natal burgher camps department, were scheduled to continue in Pinetown. On their first visit, the *dominees* found the camp unprepared to receive them and they had to leave without accomplishing anything. A week later the camp was ready for visitors and Ds Rousseau returned. According to him, the spirit in the Pinetown camp differed from that of the other concentration camps in Natal, because the people seemed to be more devout. This he attributed to the numerous men in the camp, as they included church officials in their ranks. Amongst them was the missionary Stefanus Hofmeyr as well as several former members of the church councils, deacons and elders alike, from the various congregations and churches in the Zoutpansberg.

Organising the members of the three Afrikaans sister churches into a cohesive group proved to be very trying. After a meeting with all the men involved, Rousseau managed to arrange some form of co-operation between the *Hervormde Kerk* and the *Nederduits Gereformeerde Kerk*, but the *Gereformeerde Kerk* pledged only partial allegiance to the group. The main obstacle to full co-operation by the *Gereformeerdes* or *Doppers* was that they would be receiving sacraments from the other *dominees*. In order to overcome this problem they requested that Ds Jac van Belkum of Rustenburg, then in the Merebank concentration camp, should visit them for that purpose.

Despite this setback, Rousseau managed to conduct several services for both young and old and to hold catechism classes on the day of his visit. He also arranged for services to be held in the various wards of the camp, even when no *dominee* was present. This arrangement was not ideal, for Rousseau could only return a few weeks later for the confirmation service and to serve the *nagmaal* or holy communion.[103]

Fortunately for the Pinetown concentration camp inhabitants, Ds AM Murray of Weenen was able to reside in the camp during May of 1902. Murray, assisted by elders De Bruin and Badenhost, immediately put the numerous men to work and, using bamboo and a tarpaulin, they erected a 'tent der samekomst' which seated 900 people. In this church Ds Murray conducted two services every Sunday. According to him, the services were praised by the inhabitants[104] and so well attended that people could not always find a seat. To accommodate these extra people Ds Murray conducted a sermon every afternoon for three weeks. He also made an effort to visit the tents in the camp, an exercise he found time-consuming as well as spiritually and physically tiring, but which held great rewards. This pastoral work brought him into personal contact with the full range of people in the camp, including those who were sad and worried, those who opposed the Christian work done by him in the camp and those who had forsaken their Christian values, which was obviously true in some cases and confirmed by the illegitimate children in the camp. These visits proved very fruitful as many new people started to attend the church services.

The young people in the camp received special attention during Ds Murray's stay. The catechism classes started by Rousseau were continued and at a later stage Rousseau was able to confirm several young people, thereby receiving them as fully-fledged members of the church. However, it was in the Sunday school that the greatest effort was made. Forty teachers conducted Sunday school classes for 800 children in nine marquee tents. The initial composition of the Sunday school staff did not please Ds Murray and he made it clear to the teachers that to fill such a position they had to have accepted Christ as their personal Saviour. The result was that a number of teachers resigned in favour of those who had accepted Christ. Alongside the Sunday school, *De christelijke strevers vereniging* was also active amongst the youth of the camp. Although consisting of only 77 members, they were a united group and a strong bond formed between them as they worked side by side, and resisted the many distractions in the camp which they regarded as sinful.

The most rewarding period for Ds Murray in the Pinetown camp were the days between Ascension Day and Pentecost. Every afternoon from Sunday 11 May until Sunday 18 May 1902 he spoke to the camp inhabitants about the work of the Holy Spirit and they prayed for the blessing and grace of the Lord. On the morning of 18 May the Last Supper was celebrated and many people were touched. These Pentecostal revival meetings and services did not have the blessing of all the camp inhabitants, especially those who were more conservative Christians. Many apparently ridiculed the practices of evangelism and attended the meetings in order to mock the procedures. According to Ds Murray, many of these sceptics became touched by the Holy Spirit and were brought into the fold, although many other conservative camp inhabitants remained unmoved. This saddened Murray because dissenters included church-goers who claimed to know the Bible and who insisted that they were saved. These traditionalists embarked on a campaign to convince people that immediate salvation, as experienced during the meetings and services conducted by Murray, did not exist. The campaign did not deter Murray, who believed even more firmly that spontaneous conversion was a fact.[105]

Opposition to his revival meetings was not the only problem Murray encountered during his stay in the Pinetown camp. After conducting several marriages in the Colenso camp, he became unsure of the legality of the ceremonies. He contacted the attorney-general of Natal in order to enquire which law applied to marriages conducted in Natal burgher camps, and asked whether he should follow the Transvaal law, as the inhabitants were from the Transvaal, or whether he should conduct the service according to Natal marriage law.[106] The response was simple: 'No marriage can be validly contracted in Natal except by strict compliance with the laws of the colony.'[107] Murray subsequently complied and went on to conduct several, now legitimate weddings in the Pinetown camp.[108] These weddings must have been rather dull ceremonies considering the circumstances and the surroundings. After Murray had returned to Weenen, alternative arrangements had to be made for marriages. As a result, at least two such marriages were conducted by the local pastors in the Lutheran Church in New Germany. On 22 July 1902, Hendrik Barend Jospehus Strydom, aged 45, a widower, married Magdalena Gertruida Roux, nee du Preez, aged 26, with the consent of the orphan master in Pretoria. This was followed on 10 September 1902. by the marriage between Carl August Klatt, a missionary of Pietersburg who resided in the Pinetown camp, and a New Germany inhabitant, Auguste Louise Helene Auerbach, aged 29.[109]

The religious work conducted by *Dominees* Murray and Rousseau was greatly appreciated by the camp inhabitants. Before their arrival, members of the various church councils had conducted services and organised funerals and Sunday school meetings. At least during May 1902, the month when Ds Murray resided in the camp, those who died were given respectable burials, the children born could be baptised, and co-habiting couples could be legally married.

Education in the Pinetown concentration camp

Education in the Pinetown camp was conducted either by teachers formerly employed in the Transvaal, or by unqualified camp inhabitants acting as teachers. This differed from the other Natal concentration camps where a number of teachers had been imported from New Zealand, Britain and Canada as part of the attempted anglicisation process.[110] In Pinetown, therefore, the grand ideals of British imperialism could be said to have failed. Only two of the teachers working in the camp were viewed by Superintendent Tucker as being suitable for the post, as they adhered to imperialist ideals.[111] Parents, despite the poor quality of teachers and the overtones of imperialism, generally wanted their children to attend school, since it was the first formal education many would receive and it also decreased bad behaviour, bred by idleness.[112]

In Pinetown, as in many other concentration camps, schooling seems to have failed owing to a variety of reasons, one being that English was the medium of instruction. Death and illness had seriously disrupted some families, and children then had to fill the role of adults. They also had to perform work such as cleaning in and around the tents and collecting rations. Moreover parents harboured suspicions relating to the camp authorities and the teachers, many of whom were *hendsoppers*.[113]

Recreation in the Pinetown camp

One of the most difficult aspects of the monotonous routine of concentration camp life must surely have been finding ways to occupy the long hours of each day constructively. As in other camps, the inmates of the Pinetown camp regularly organised concerts and dances, with a certain Miss Snyman regarded as the belle of the ball. These functions were popular not only with the young people of Pinetown and New Germany, [114] but they attracted people from as far away as Inchanga. [115] Camp inhabitants did not carry passes as was the case in Pietersburg, where they had to have a pass to proceed more than 200 metres from their tents, and they were granted permission, on occasions, to attend functions outside the camp, on condition that they returned before sunset. [116]

The children must have enjoyed life in the camp as they had many friends. However, the impact of the war was felt by them as well, as demonstrated by a well-organised game which culminated in an attack on the Pinetown camp by a large group of boys, mimicking the attack by Beyers which had occurred in Pietersburg. The boys secretly constructed rifles out of wood and pieces of scrap metal from a nearby jam factory, and made bandoliers from banana peels and leaves. Early one morning, during a well-chosen moment, the guards at the gate were charged by a group armed with the shining toy rifles and emitting an exuberant war cry. This charge was backed up by several other boys who, under the leadership of a certain Hofmeyr, rolled empty water barrels, used for filling the steam trains with water at the Palmiet halt, down the stoney hill. There was great consternation and panic as the guards fled into the tents. The chaos lasted for quite a while before the guards and camp staff realised it was merely a prank. Although the boys could have been shot, the officer in charge managed to see the humorous side of the event and he persuaded the youngsters to pose for a photograph with their toy rifles and bandoliers!

> According to De Villiers and Kriel, this incident took place in the Merebank concentration camp, but several factors point to Pinetown as the real locale. For example the halt close to the camp and the stony hills: these features are present at the Pinetown camp, but not at Merebank. [117]

The boys who attacked the Pinetown concentration camp posing with their weapons (DeVilliers and Kriel).

Economic life in the camp

One way of passing the time and dealing with the humdrum of concentration camp life was to find employment, either in or outside the camp area. The idea of the inmates working appealed to Lord Kitchener, who supported the notion of using such a large labour force, as long as the camp inhabitants did not compete with loyalists or other deserving classes for positions.[118] Working kept the camp inhabitants busy and out of trouble. Apart from being good for their self-image, employment earned them some money so that they did not become totally reliant on the incarceration system.

Their skills lay predominantly in the field of agriculture, as the majority came from a farming background. As a result, a number were employed by farmers in the area.[119] This must have pleased farmers and camp inhabitants alike, as the former now had skilled employees, while the inhabitants of the camp partially enjoyed the freedom of the life they had been used to. Others relied on their entrepreneurial skills to earn some sorely needed money. A certain Mr Terblanche operated a taxi service, using a horse and carriage, between the concentration camp and Pinetown and he apparently earned a good income.[120] Others earned a living as shoemakers or by building stoves from corrugated iron. The more artistic and creative carved odds and ends out of wood, bone and horn.[121]

The most fortunate inhabitants of the Pinetown concentration camp, as far as work was concerned, were those who were employed by the camp authorities. Unfortunately they were few in number and consisted only of Van Rensburg and his assistant in charge of sanitation, 17 apprentice nurses, 16 teachers, and some toilet guards, while occasionally inhabitants were hired at 2s 6d a day to assist with administrative and organisational matters. The rest of the approximately 3 000 inmates were not employed and they relied totally on the camp authorities. Such folk had to carry on with their lives as best they could by performing routine tasks they were not paid for, such as cleaning, washing and preparing food.

Political activities in the Pinetown concentration camp

All concentration camps were politically divided. There were those siding openly with the British such as National Scouts, the so-called 'joiners', and those who had no fight left in them and had surrendered, the *hendsoppers*. Alternatively there were those who remained loyal to the republican cause to the last, the *bittereinders*. Pinetown was different from any other concentration camp, as men in the camp numbered 650 out of a total of 3 000, making up 20% of the population. These men, with the odd exception were *hendsoppers* and 'joiners'. To the *bittereinders* the difference between *hendsoppers* and 'joiners' was marginal as both had committed the ultimate crime against the Boer cause, that is they had forsaken the war effort.

Hendsoppers and 'Joiners'

'*Verrader, monster, vloek der aarde Vernederde skepsel der natuur Godswraak die u tot hede spaarde Verdelge u deur donder en helse vuur.*' These words, aimed at 'joiners', reflect only partially the hatred felt by bittereinders towards those who had forsaken the Boer cause by fighting on the British sides in units such as the National Scouts and the Orange River Colony Volunteers. For many years after the Anglo-Boer War had ended, Afrikaners who had fought on the British side were ostracised by Afrikaner society, including the church. *Hendsoppers*, or those who had laid down arms before peace was signed, but did not join the British, were treated with marginally more respect.

An indication of the strength of the 'joiner' movement in the feeder area of the Pietersburg and later the Pinetown camp is the fact that the National Scout movement under Commandant JG Celliers and Field-Cornet AZA Briel totalled 118.[122] There were great advantages in being a scout: scouts and their families were allowed to reside in Pietersburg. They received good rations and were paid. During December 1901, accommodation arrangements were altered and a separate camp was created for National Scouts and their families. By April 1902 the camp had a population of 517, consisting of 71 men, 223 women and 223 children. An added advantage was that the camp remained in Pietersburg when the transferral to Natal took place.[123]

However, some National Scout families were transferred from Pietersburg to Pinetown where they were intensely hated by the *bittereinders* and fights often broke out between these two factions, with the latter spitting on the 'joiners' and calling them lice and British 'arse-kissers'. The tensions became so extreme and the families of the National Scouts were harassed to such an extent that they had to receive their rations at a different time from the *bittereinders*.[124] This situation was very disturbing to both the National Scouts and the British authorities and, in an attempt to deal with this conflict, it was decreed that the families of National Scouts were not to be sent to Natal without the consent of head-quarters. Even if the families of the National Scouts behaved so badly that they had to be sent to Natal, a common punitive measure, the head-quarters of the army was still to be contacted in writing first.[125]

In spite of these orders, numerous families or individuals with 'joiner' ties still arrived in the Pinetown camp, such as 29-year-old Annie Terblanche, wife of J Terblanche, who was in 'government service'. She arrived in Pinetown on 20 May 1902 from the Zoutpansberg to work as a teacher.[126] To complicate matters, not only 'joiners', but also numerous *hendsoppers* ended up in the Pinetown concentration camp. The arrival of JJ van Aswegen and 23 other surrendered burghers, all but two from the Zoutpansberg area, is another case in point.[127]

The concentration camp authorities were obliged to protect both the *hendsoppers* and 'joiners' as they had obeyed the different proclamations to surrender and were now either neutral or loyal to Britain. In a concentration camp such as Pinetown, where there was a history of communication between Boer forces and camp inhabitants, extreme measures had to be taken by the military authorities to protect those who were neutral or loyal. Lord Kitchener thus decreed that an intelligence agent was to be placed in each concentration camp. These agents were to report directly to the director of military intelligence on what was happening in the camp, and were not to be under the authority of the camp personnel.[128] The outcome of this was that every word spoken by the *bittereinder* women was noted thereby adding anxiety and tension to an already overwrought situation.[129]

The situation became unbearable to the *bittereinder* women in the Pinetown camp. They were defenceless against the large number of 'joiners' who were trying to prove their loyalty to their new masters by spying on or by intimidating *bittereinders* to persuade them to cross the divide to the British side. In a desperate attempt to protect themselves, Superintendent JE Tucker was petitioned on 6 May 1902 by the women who asked for protection.[130] This was a rather hopeless measure by the *bittereinder* women who found themselves ostracised and under pressure from the growing number of 'joiner' men and their families as well as from the British military, so much so that they pleaded with the superintendent for some form of intervention. Any *bittereinders* accused of being troublemakers would often be removed from their families and transferred to Merebank, Jacobs or Wentworth concentration camps.[131] The women therefore had no choice in the matter, except to turn to Tucker, although they knew he had only limited power.[132]

Whether the women received the protection they requested remains unknown, but at least their petition brought their plight to the attention of Superintendent Tucker and possibly even to the Natal burgher camps department.

Peace and the repatriation back to Pietersburg

The peace treaty which was signed by the British and Boer forces on 31 May 1902 at Vereeniging meant the end of the war and the end of the two Boer republics. Before repatriation could take place, the inhabitants had to be informed of the terms of the peace treaty and of what awaited them. General Schalk Burger visited all the camps in Natal during this official tour and his final stop, on 11 June 1902, was to be at the Pinetown concentration camp. He was accompanied from the Merebank concentration camp by his wife and youngest daughter, whom he had last seen 17 months previously, and HE Povall, the buyer for Natal burgher camps. The group made the short but slow journey from Durban to Pinetown by train.

After their arrival in Pinetown, the party, along with Superintendent JE Tucker, went to the Imperial Hotel for breakfast. After breakfast Burger wasted no time in proceeding to the Pinetown camp. The camp, according to a reporter of the *Natal Mercury*, was set on a green slope surrounded by hills and valleys and it looked very picturesque, with the white tents, washed by the early morning rain, forming a contrast to the green surroundings. Despite the pouring rain, a large number of men, women and children gathered in front of Tucker's office. Schalk Burger enjoyed a dignified reception, while his wife was cordially welcomed by Mrs Tucker and the English ladies of the camp staff.[133]

While these formalities were taking place, a platform was built. Once Burger had ascended the platform, HJC van Rensburg, ex-commandant of Zoutpansberg and the most senior surrendered officer or *hendsopper* in the camp, joined him, and presented a carefully prepared address from some of the burghers 'to his honour SW Burger the Acting President of the ZAR on his coming to the Pinetown Burgher Camp'. In his rather sad address he thanked Burger for coming to inform them in person of what was going to happen to them. Van Rensburg continued that not all present could come to Burger 'with an open heart', as many had not done their duty to the South African Republic as they should have, but he trusted that right and justice would be shown to them as well. Those such as himself who had surrendered, although unable to render physical assistance, had never failed to pray for the success of their comrades. The ex-commandant then continued, somewhat contradictorily, by declaring that they still had the fullest confidence that their leaders would regain liberty and independence for all their people.[134]

The apologetic note of Van Rensburg, speaking on behalf of the numerous surrendered burghers in the Pinetown camp, did not impress Burger, and he told those assembled before him, in a bitter tone, that they had surrendered early and left the war to their fellow countrymen. There was no response to his rebuke.[135] Burger then informed the crowd, in a carefully prepared speech repeated at every camp gathering, of the terms of the peace treaty and the repatriation process which was to follow. Afterwards he answered questions from the crowd, mostly about when they would be able to return to their farms. When Burger had answered all the questions to their satisfaction, he received three cheers. He then conversed with members of the audience. At precisely 13:00, the Burgers left for Howick.[136]

After Burger's visit, all the burghers in the Pinetown camp immediately wanted to go home. Matters were not that simple, as Articles 1 and 11 of the peace treaty made provision for the repatriation of all inhabitants of the former Boer republics only on certain conditions. The first condition was that the burghers had to recognise the British sovereign as their sole leader, by signing an oath of allegiance.[137] As soon as they had complied with this, the second condition required that all burghers, including those in the Pinetown camp, were to be provided with transport home and with the necessary provisions to restart their lives. This process was not a simple one, for the British authorities had to arrange for the repatriation of the tens of thousands of POWs and concentration camp inmates, while at the same time ensuring that the former camp inhabitants would manage to fend for themselves.[138]

In the Pinetown concentration camp, Superintendent JE Tucker was central to the process of repatriation.[139] He acted as commissioner of oaths for burghers to sign the oath of allegiance to the king. What made Tucker's work even more difficult was the decision taken during June 1902 to repeat the earlier process, this time in reverse, namely to transfer the Pinetown camp, including inhabitants, personnel and equipment, back to Pietersburg.[140] This major exercise made both logistical and financial sense as the great majority of the inhabitants came from the Zoutpansberg area and total repatriation was therefore possible.

Once the decision had been made, the repatriation from Pinetown could start. The plan was for the inhabitants, equipment and personnel to be back in Pietersburg by the end of July 1902.[141] Special transport trains had to be arranged to accomplish this in batches. For this process to flow smoothly, the general manager, NGR, had to be informed of the exact number of Pinetown camp inhabitants involved on the Friday before each departure to allow him to arrange the trains, whilst at the same time considering the requirements of the military and civilians.[142]

The repatriation of the approximately 3 000 inhabitants and staff started on 2 July 1902 and was completed, without serious mishap, by 10 August 1902. This process took slightly longer than had originally been anticipated, but in view of the logistical and administrative scale of the repatriation, it required a tremendous effort. The camp was once again pitched south-west of Pietersburg on a gentle slope between the railway line and the Zand River. The inhabitants who had left Pietersburg as burghers of the South African Republic, now returned from Pinetown as 'loyal' members of the British empire, having lost not only their country and all their possessions, but also diminished in number by the lives lost in the camps. Amongst those returning from Pinetown were not only camp inhabitants, but also burghers who had surrendered after the peace had been signed and who had then joined their families in Pinetown as well as POWs from India[143] and the Umbilo camp. Here they met *bitter-einders* who had not been sent to Pinetown when it became clear that the camp would be repatriated to Pietersburg and also the joiners who had fought as members of the National Scouts on the British side.[144] This added a bitter dimension to the already battered Boer society which subsequently took decades to heal.

Not all former inhabitants of the Pinetown concentration camp returned to Pietersburg. Betty Hofmeyr was given a pass to join her family in the Cape Colony,[145] while Carl August Klatt who married a local lady remained in Pinetown.[146] However, few were this lucky and the vast majority did return to Pietersburg and its ruined countryside.[147]

In Pinetown all that remained was to dispose of the site and the equipment. The water pump and engine were taken over by the Royal Engineers, while the remaining buildings were sold off at a public auction at fair price.[148] The land rented for the site of the Pinetown camp was returned to Königkramer and life in Pinetown returned to normal.

1. PRO, CO 417/439: telegram HE McCallum to H Kitchener, 27.2.1902.

2. Neethling, E, *Should we forget?*, pp.216–217.

3. CD 853: telegram A Milner to J Chamberlain, 1.12.1901.

4. CD 934: telegram HE McCallum to J Chamberlain, 27.11.1902.

5. CD 853: telegram A Milner to J Chamberlain, 1.12.1901.

6. CD 902: telegram assistant secretary to the high commissioner to TK Murray, 8.12.1901.

7. CD 902: telegram assistant secretary to the high commissioner to TK Murray, 8.12.1901.

8. *Natal Mercury*, 18.2.1902.

9. PAR, GH 554: monthly report Natal burgher camps, 3.1902, 9.4.1902.

10. PRO, CO 417/439: telegram headquarters to HE McCallum, 28.2.1902.

11. PAR, GH 554: monthly report Natal burgher camps, 3.1902, 9.4.1902.

12. Bergtheil Museum: memoirs of MS Wolfaard daughter of FW Königkramer as conveyed to I Schwegmann, 29.12.1970.

13. Van Schoor, MCE and Coetzee, GC, *Kampkinders 1900–1902: 'n gedenkboek*, p.75.

14. PAR, A 72: diary of HF Schoon, p.793.

15. Postma, MM, *Stemme uit die verlede: 'n versameling beëdigde verklarings van vroue wat tydens die Tweede Vryheidsoorlog in konsentrasiekampe verkeer het*, p.50.

16. PAR, GH 554: monthly report Natal burgher camps, 4.1902, 6.5.1902.

17. PAR, GH 554: monthly report Natal burgher camps, 3.1902, 9.4.1902.

18. Chisholm, GG and Liebman, JS, *Longman's Geography for South Africa*, p.116.

19. Kriel, C and De Villiers, J, *Rondom die Anglo-Boereoorlog 1899–1902, 'n keur uit die fotoversameling van wyle Christofer Kriel*, p.60.

20. Bergtheil Museum: photograph of the Pinetown concentration camp, 1902.

21. NAR, DBC 11: register Pinetown

22. PAR, GH 554: monthly report Natal burgher camps, 5.1902, 11.6.1902.

23. PAR, PWD: Natal colonial papers, report of the chief engineer, 1901–1904.

24. CD 893, p.206.

25. NAR, DBC 13: register Pinetown.

26. PAR, GH 554: annual report Natal burgher camps, 14.10.1902.

27. PAR, GH 554: monthly report Natal burgher camps, 4.1902, 6.5.1902.

28. PAR, GH 554: monthly report Natal burgher camps, 5.1902, 11.6.1902.

29. PAR, PWD: Natal colonial papers, report of the chief engineer 1901–1904.

30. PAR, GH 553: letter from TK Murray to HE McCallum, 10.2.1902.

31. CD 893: p.203.

32. CD 819: pp.219, 261.

33. PAR, GH 1452: general regulations Natal burgher camps, 1.2.1902.

34. CD 893: p.203.

35. WM: Rapportryers collection, memoirs of JF Haar, 18.1.1981.

36. PAR, GH 1452: general regulations Natal burgher camps, 1.2.1902.

37. NAR, DBC 11: register Pinetown.

38. Bergtheil Museum: memoirs of MS Wolfaard daughter of FW Königkramer as conveyed to I Schwegmann, 29.12.1970.

39. CD 893: p.204.

40. CD 902: p.95.

41. PAR, GH 554: monthly report Natal burgher camps, 2.1902, 12.3.1902.

42. CD 893: p.207.

43. CD 893: p.218.

44. NAR, DBC 14: register Pinetown.

45. Pinetown Museum: 24/1602.

46. Otto, JC, *Die konsentrasiekampe*, p.95.

47. Van Schoor, MCE en Coetzee, GC, p.38.

48. Krugell, JE, *Die Pietersburg Konsentrasiekamp*, p.118.

49. CD 819, p.217.

50. CD 893, pp.205–206.

51. Neethling, E, pp.216–217.

52. Van Schoor, MCE en Coetzee, GC, pp.75.

53. Neethling, E, pp.216–217.

54. Van Schoor, MCE en Coetzee, GC, p.75.

55. Postma, MM, p.25.

56. Krugell, JE, *Die Pietersburg Konsentrasiekamp*, p.115.

57. Neethling, E, pp.216–217.

58. CD 819, p.217.

59. CD 902: p.95, and CD 893: p.206.

60. NAR, DBC 11: register Pinetown.

61. CD 819: p.375.

62. NAR, DBC 11: register Pinetown.

63. CF Beijers, *Korte geschiedenis van het konsentrasiekamp te Pietersburg, Zoutpansberg en naamlijst van der 650 vrouwen en kinderen aldaar gestorven 11 Mei 1901 – 30 Januari 1902*, pp.5–15.

64. NAR, A 2030 100: Jan Ploeger collection, handwritten notes.

65. NAR, A 2030 100: Jan Ploeger collection, handwritten notes.

66. PAR, GH 554: monthly report Natal burgher camps, 11.1901, 10.12.1901.

67. Wassermann, JM, *The Eshowe concentration and surrendered burghers camp during the Anglo-Boer War (1899–1902)*, p.38.

68. CD 934: p.55.

69. PAR, GH 554: monthly report Natal burgher camps, 5.1902, 11.6.1902.

70. PAR, GH 554: monthly report Natal burgher camps, 4.1902, 6.5.1902.

71. Bergtheil Museum: memoirs of MS Wolfaard daughter of FW Königkramer as conveyed to I Schwegmann, 29.12.1970.

72. Interview with H England, curatrix of the Pinetown Museum, 9.10.1998.

73. WM: Rapportryers collection, memoirs of JSJ Jansen, 18.1.1981.

74. PAR, GH 554: monthly report for Natal burgher camps, 4.1902, 6.5.1902.

75. CD 893: p.204.

76. PAR, GH 554: monthly report for Natal burgher camps, 11.1901, 10.12.1901.

77. Krugell, JE, *Die Pietersburg Konsentrasiekamp*, pp.70–80.

78. PAR: photographs on Colenso concentration camp.

79. NAR, DBC 11: register Pinetown.

80. CD 893: p.204.

81. WM: Rapportryers collection, memoirs of JF Haar, 18.1.1981.

82. Pinetown Museum: 24/1602.

83. CD 819: p.204.

84. Van Schoor, MCE en Coetzee, GC, p.38.

85. Kriel, C en De Villiers, J, p.60.

86. Van Schoor, MCE en Coetzee, GC, p.38.

87. PAR, GH vol. 554, monthly report Natal burgher camps, June 1902, 7.7.1902.

88. Postma, MM, p.50.

89. Neethling, E, p.216–217.

90. WM: Rapportryers collection, memoirs of SJG Hofmeyr, 18.1.1981.

91. PAR, GH 554: monthly report Natal burgher camps, 6.1902, 7.7.1902.

92. Russell, G, *Anglo-Boer War concentration camps in Natal, August 1900–1903*, p.36.

93. Pinetown Women's Institute, *Annals of Pinetown*, p.22.

94. Pinetown Museum: 24/1602.

95. NAR, 14/14/16: letter FA de Villiers to HS Pretorius, 2.10.1939.

96. NAR, 14/14/16: letter assistant-hoofargivaris HS Pretorius to FA de Villiers, 9.10.39.

97. Neethling, E, pp.111–112.

98. NAR, A 2030 100: Jan Ploeger collection, handwritten notes.

99. PAR, DPH 8: telegram from the district surgeon Camperdown, no date.

100. PAR, DPH 7: letter from E Hill to colonial secretary, 3.4.1902.

101. PAR, DPH 7: letter from E Hill to Dr DM Campbell, health officer Upper Umlazi, 4.1902.

102. PAR, DPH 7: letter from health officer Upper Umlazi Dr DM Campbell to E Hill, 24.4.1902.

103. *De Kerkbode*, no. 19, Deel xix, 1902, p.376.

104. Postma, MM, p.222–223.

105. Rousseau, WP, *Notulen der conferentie van leeraren, arbeiders en arbeidsters in de burgerkampen in Natal, gehouden te Merebank op den 24sten en 25sten Junie 1902*, p.25.

106. PAR, AGO 1/8/84: letter from AM Murray to AGO, 13.5.1902.

107. PAR, CSO 2401: letter from principal under-secretary to AM Murray, 11.4.1902.

108. NAR, DBC 149: register Pinetown.

109. German Evangelical Lutheran Church: New Germany, marriage register 1884–1907.

110. NAR, DBC 12: register Pinetown.

111. CD 819: p.146.

112. Symington, FC, *Die konsentrasiekampskole in die Transvaal en die Oranje-Vrystaat*, p.9.

113. Ibid., pp.28–34.

114. Bergtheil Museum: memoirs of MS Wolfaard daughter of FW Königkramer as conveyed to I Schwegmann, 29.12.1970.

115. PAR, DPH 8: telegram from the district surgeon, Camperdown, unknown date.

116. Postma, MM, p.92.

117. Kriel, C en De Villiers, J, pp.60–61.

118. PAR, GH 497: Telegram H Kitchener to HE McCallum, 25.5. 1902.

119. Pinetown Women's Institute, *Annals of Pinetown*, p.25.

120. Bergtheil Museum: memoirs of MS Wolfaard daughter of FW Königkramer as conveyed to I Schwegmann, 29.12.1970.

121. CD 853: p.89.

122. Grundlingh, AM, *Die "Hendsoppers" en "Joiners": Die rasionaal van verraad*, pp.198 and 206.

123. Krugell, JE, *Die Pietersburg Konsentrasiekamp*, p.170.

124. NAR, DBC 13: register Pinetown.

125. NAR, FK 619, CO 417/351: circular 137 of 11.4.1902.

126. NAR, DBC 107: register Pinetown.

127. NAR, MGP 3115/02: list of surrendered burghers to be send to Colenso, 22.2.1902.

128. NAR, A 2030 46: Jan Ploeger collection, handwritten notes on surrendered burghers.

129. Stockenstrom, E, *Die vrou in die geskiedenis van die Hollands-Afrikaanse volk*, p.176.

130. CAR, A 921 JE Tucker collection: petition to JE Tucker superintendent Pinetown concentration camp by Lettie Page and 126 others, 6.5.1902.

131. PAR, GH 1453: coronation instructions from TK Murray, no date.

132. CAR, A 921 JE Tucker collection: petition to JE Tucker superintendent Pinetown concentration camp by Lettie Page and 126 others, 6.5.1902.

133. *Natal Mercury*, 12.6.1902.

134. *Natal Mercury*, 12.6.1902.

135. PAR, GH 1453: letter HE Povall to TK Murray, 12.6.1902.

136. The *Natal Mercury*, 12.6.1902.

137. Hattingh, JL, *Die Irene Konsentrasiekamp*, p.229.

138. Krüger, DW, *Geskiedenis van Suid-Afrika*, p.442.

139. PAR, GH 554: monthly report Natal burgher camps, 7.1902, 6.8.1902.

140. Krugell, JE, *Die Pietersburg Konsentrasiekamp*, pp.155–160.

141. PAR, GH 554: monthly report Natal burgher camps, 6.1902, 7.7.1902.

142. PAR, PM 30: telegram general manager NGR to acting prime minister, no date.

143. Neethling, E, pp.222–223.

144. NAR, DBC 11: register Pinetown.

145. Neethling, E, pp.216–217.

146. German Evangelical Lutheran Church: New Germany, Marriage Register, 1884–1907.

147. Postma, MM, p.50.

148. PAR, GH 554: monthly report Natal burgher camps, October 1902, 6.11.1902.

Militia Infan
Yeomanry Ca
Volunteers—A
Inf
or

C—IN

Ind

Infantry—130 Batt
Cavalry—37 Regime
Artillery—6 Batter
Engineers and misc

Two West Indian R
Royal Malta Fencib
Lascars, Hong-Kong

D.—COLONIAL
RE

th American Co
Indies ...
Tian Colonies ...
Possessions ...
Tian Colonies

C—INDIAN AND COLONIAL FORCES

Indian Native Army.

	Men.	Horses.	Guns.
Infantry—130 Battalions ...	101,134	13,587	36
Cavalry—37 Regiments ...	18,575	673	
Artillery—6 Batteries ...	896		
Engineers and miscellaneous ...	4,385	14,210	86
	127,419		

	Men.
Two West Indian Regiments ...	1,822
Royal Malta Fencibles ...	373
Lascars, Hong-Kong and Ceylon ...	264
	2,459

D.—COLONIAL MILITIA, VOLUNTEER, AND RESERVE FORCES.

	Men.	Horses.	Guns.
		2,081	48
		610	24
North American Confederation...	58,414	1,143	19
West Indies ...	8,952	120	6
African Colonies ...	4,343	1,703	43
Asia Possessions ...	2,116		140
Australian Colonies ...	19,065	5,657	
	81,880		

GRAND TOTAL.

	Men.	Horses.	Guns.
	183,248	26,359	674
British Regular Army (British) ...	346,661		86
Reserve and Auxiliary ...	127,419	14,210	
Indian	2,459		
Black (other than Indian)	81,880	5,657	140
Colonial Militia, Volunteer and Reserve Forces... Canadian Irregular Militia	600,000		850
Total	1,341,687	46,225	

MOBILISATION OF THE BURGHERS.

It is reported in Johannesburg that the
Transvaal War Department has completed arrangements with the Netherlands Railway
Company for the mobilisation of the burghers
at any given centre on the shortest notice possible. Large numbers of empty trucks have
been stationed at various points along the railway lines, and have been placed at the service
of Field-cornets, for the despatch of men, arms,
and ammunition to the scene of general muster
in case of emergency.

TENOUR OF THE REPLY.

The secret session commenced at 7 o'clock,
and was not concluded until a quarter past 10.
For the President to be up at that time of night
is a most extraordinary occurrence, and quite
alone (remarks the Leader correspondent), and
but the most grave matters have been in
point of view—must have been up
of his Honour's attention to the
The answer to the
aud forwarded to be
be found to be
the Govern-

Liverpool

S.S.
ops,
on-
Lord

and

American Co
Indies
John
Con
law

PART SIX

THE INTELLIGENCE WAR

CHAPTER 19

INTELLIGENCE AND COUNTER-INTELLIGENCE

Johan Wassermann

The gathering of information, and the prevention of the enemy from gaining access to reliable disclosures has always been central to gaining an advantage in any war, and the Anglo-Boer War was no different. Durban, as a seaport, overflowing with refugees, made it easy for covert actions of whatever nature to occur. Fearing that valuable intelligence on troop strengths and other military data could reach the Boer forces, any person suspected of undercover manoeuvres was detained under martial law, while countless refugees were debriefed. At the same time extensive censorship was applied to newspapers, letters and cables and telegrams. Not all information obtained was helpful, as much of it was contradictory, fabricated or simply misleading.

Flashing lights over Durban

With the Boer forces commanding the upper hand during the early stages of the war, reports of mysterious lights flashing were received from all over Durban, sending both the police and the military on wild goose chases. The first sightings of strange lights were reported by the stationmaster of South Coast Junction, who said that the beams had emanated from the house of a certain Wallis in Seaview as well as the Bluff. Policemen, following up on the information, saw the same flashing lights on several nights and, as a result, Sergeant EN Brooke, who headed the investigation, decided to search the house of Wallis. Despite nothing suspicious being found, Wallis and his brother-in-law were hauled before the commandant, only to be released when further investigation verified their assurance that the only lights were those of their house. The following night, with the assistance of Captain Morgan and a naval party of the *Tartar*, the suspicious flashing lights originating from the Bluff were investigated. This time the embarrassment was even worse. The intermittent light was caused by a man who used a lantern to visit the outhouse from time to time.

Despite having two nonsensical experiences behind them, Brooke and Morgan dealt with the next report of unusual lights flashing at Northdene with the same dedication. They surveyed the area pointed out as the source of the light: a hill near Northdene. As no suspicious lights were seen they concluded that the Indians and Africans residing on the hill had possibly caused the illumination. This, however, did not settle the matter of flashing lights allegedly coming from Northdene and Cowies Hill. On

8 December 1899, a local policemen, L Corryngham, and four African constables were appointed to investigate the area. Despite keeping a strict watch at night and making numerous enquiries, no flashing lights or signalling was seen again in the area. The only information they could gain was that, prior to General Redvers Buller's arrival, lights flashed every evening between 20:00 and 22:00, and that they were no longer seen when he departed for Pietermaritzburg. Matters did not end here and the police and navy chased after numerous other flashing lights at places like Bellair, Pinetown and, once again, the Bluff. The latter incident, reported by a Mr Jameson of Bellair, even convinced the naval personnel who investigated it that signalling of some sort was going on, but Sergeant Brooke was by that stage convinced that none of the lights reported were of a sinister nature. Had the lights been those of Transvaal agents, their signals should have also been seen in the outlying areas and nothing was reported. Speaking, by now, from experience, Brooke concluded that sending out parties to investigate was of little use, as their approach would be known beforehand. To make doubly sure that his own assessment of the situation was warranted he suggested that 'a number of natives be placed on different hills, with instructions to keep place from where a light should come, would be more likely to be successful. They would have to be looked after by some white or whites who knew the district thoroughly'. [*sic*][1]

Suspected Boer spies in Durban

When it came to physically identifying spies, the populace and authorities in Durban hoped for better luck. Thanks to the *Strand Magazine*, *Graham's Magazine*, and the various *Penny Dreadful* publications, everyone knew, or thought they knew, what a spy looked like: he had a black beard, moved furtively, and was always behind walls, trees and other places of concealment, and spoke in a foreign accent.[2] Durbanites had seen many suitable candidates in the past. It was nothing new for suspicious, dubious and questionable characters to make their way from the Transvaal. Frans Ludwig von Veltheim, alias Karel Braun, Kurt, Baron von Veltheim or Kurtze, a 39-year-old, six-foot two-inches tall German or Austro-Hungarian, with the tips of three fingers of his left hand missing, was such a character. Described as a 'menace to the Transvaal', 'murderer of Woolf Joel' and a 'blackmailer', he was expelled to Lourenço Marques by the Transvaal government, who feared that he might disembark from the *Garth Castle* at Durban and work his way back to the Transvaal. To prevent this from happening, the Natal government was successfully petitioned by its Transvaal counterpart to prevent Von Veltheim from landing.[3] The Transvaal wanted others returned, like Josef Muhlbauer, who was accused of embezzlement. Thus they requested the Natal Police to arrest him when he arrived in Durban, so that he could be extradited to the Transvaal to stand trial.[4]

This co-operation ended with the outbreak of the Anglo-Boer War. Suspicious characters were, however, still making their way to Durban, only now they were no longer viewed as criminals, but as spies or agents working for the republics. Within two weeks of the commencement of the war, the authorities in Natal thought they had discovered a spy ring, led by the chief suspect, Nathan Marks and, believing it to be funded by the Durban branch of the National Bank, consequently stormed the bank on 23 October 1899 to procure the necessary evidence. Such evidence was not to be found,[5] as Nathan Marks was not a spy, but merely a secret detective sent to Durban long before the war broke out. The payments he received from the National Bank were his salary. The fact that he was languishing in prison was not appreciated by the Transvaal government and they requested that Marks be allowed to return unmolested to the Transvaal. Furthermore, the state secretary of the Transvaal, FW Reitz, apparently indicated they would take revenge and execute six British officers currently in their hands if the death sentence was passed on Marks.[6] Marks was kept in prison for a year before he was released on the orders of General Buller after which he boarded a ship, ironically bound for England.[7]

In terms of the question of the actual spies themselves, the most suspicious of characters were considered to be those who arrived from Lourenço Marques, with the intention of returning. One of a number of such suspects was GT Schmidt who was employed by Wilcken & Ackermann in Lourenço Marques, a company which had extensive trading links with the Transvaal. On completion of his business in Durban, Schmidt wanted to return to Lourenço Marques, but Commandant Scott would not allow him for, with an attack on Durban during December 1899 being a real possibility, Schmidt would be able to supply the fullest details of what he had heard and seen in Durban. Scott's decision had the full support of the governor who felt that: 'Persons who choose to pay a visit to a country which is being invaded by the enemy must be necessarily prepared to submit to restrictions and inconveniences which might be regarded in ordinary times as vexatious or unreasonable.'[8]

The closest scrutiny was reserved for those who arrived from Lourenço Marques and elsewhere with the intention of staying in Durban. It could have been very easy for a Boer spy to blend in with the thousands of refugees from the Transvaal whose numbers included numerous vagrants and scoundrels, such as Arthur Long, real name Alec Love, an ex-convict and burglar who arrived in Durban on board the *Induna*.[9] Other undesirable characters bordered on the ludicrous. One such person was the self-proclaimed British secret agent, a French citizen, Henry de Gunzburg, otherwise known as the 'The only Mr. Henry'. He came to Durban during the early stages of the war and stated that he was employed by the field intelligence department. 'The only Mr. Henry' soon became a nuisance, and his conduct led him to be arrested as a spy. As not sufficient evidence existed to have him court martialled, Captain Percy

Captain Percy Scott interrogating secret Transvaal detective, Nathan Marks (*The Illustrated London News*, 17 February 1900).

Scott suggested that De Gunzburg be detained as a source of danger. Within four days of his release the mayor of Durban complained that De Gunzburg was causing agitation amongst the refugees which might lead to rioting. During his four days of freedom, he pestered the newly appointed Commandant Morris claiming that he had extraordinary documents and letters pertaining to his endeavours as an agent for the field intelligence department, a fact the department in question denied strongly. As a result, De Gunzburg again ended up in jail.[10]

Not even women escaped attention, for example, the case of Fanny Scheff, a Russian woman. Scheff was described as 'short, stout, modest, full faced, dark, foreign accent, pasty complexion, with a Russian passport' duly endorsed by the consul in Lourenço Marques. She arrived in Durban on board the *Gironde* and was reported to have carried an important official despatch signed by President Paul Kruger, with the envelope marked 'M.K.M.K'. Subsequently, on the directions of the British consul, Scheff, who was illiterate, was followed by Detective Albert G Bryan to Durban. Here she was interrogated, harassed and had her luggage searched several times, without any evidence being found prior to her departure for Cape Town.[11]

Of those regarded as suspicious, Germans especially felt that they were targeted and not allowed to land in Durban. Complaints about restrictions placed on respectable Germans were forwarded to the governor of Natal, HE McCallum. The governor's response was biting: '... whilst anxious to do all in my power to meet your wishes at any time, it will be more convenient, if you would kindly avoid any abstract and indefinite generalities whenever possibly and refer me to something definite upon which I can cause the necessary enquiries to be made.' His request was soon granted. Two German passengers, Gustav Friederich, and Gustav Krueger arrived from Southampton on board the *Gascon*. They were not allowed to land, while others, such as Danes, Russians and Jews with very little money or possessions, were permitted to disembark. On asking why they were prevented from leaving the ship, the answer was that it was because of instructions they had been given. They were only given permission to land two days later on condition that they reported to the commandant of Durban.[12]

The cases of Waterton and Sundt — individuals suspected of espionage caught in the web of the intelligence war

Guy Waterton

More serious cases, such as the example of the Australian, Guy Waterton, also occurred. An adventurer of note, Waterton claimed to have been involved as an inspector of police in the Burma War, as assistant transport officer in the Anglo-Zulu War of 1879; as a lieutenant in the Tambookie uprising in the Transkei/Basotho Wars; and he allegedly served under Colonel Plumer in the Matabele War in 1896. His next adventure took him to Johannesburg where he met a certain Captain Patterson and a Lieutenant Hooper, who claimed that they were raising a force to fight the Boers. Their endeavours turned out to be linked to the Jameson Raid. Waterton stated that he needed little convincing to join the raiders, but that he soon discovered that 'these men were only canteen loafers and had not a penny piece to bless themselves with' although they said they were instructed by the British Government. When police in the Transvaal revealed the conspiracy, the ringleaders and the foot soldiers were apprehended. As a result, Waterton needed to go to Pretoria to provide an affidavit of the events that had occurred, for which he claimed he had received no money. The men were acquitted and they made Waterton the scapegoat, blaming him for their arrest.

With the Transvaal becoming too small for him, Waterton claimed to have brought down a consignment of 170 mules from Johannesburg to Pietermaritzburg for Chas and Edy Parker of Johannesburg. He received no money or food for this task, despite the intervention of Captain Murray and David Hunter, the general manager of the NGR. As a result Waterton made his way down to the Point in Durban and found work as a 'tall clerk' with Parker, Wood & Company. On 14 November 1899, the aforementioned company appointed him to go to Chinde in Mozambique. Waterton was, however, prevented by Captain Percy Scott from taking up this position, and he subsequently lost his job, whereupon he claimed that Scott had 'thus prevented me from earning a living'.

Waterton maintained that events took an even worse turn when, while sitting in the Bencorum Bar, Point Road, he mentioned that he had brought down mules for the imperial government without receiving payment. Soon afterwards he was arrested by a German-speaking detective for using seditious language and hauled before Scott, only to be released with a caution. Waterton then became ill and was admitted to hospital. Once discharged he heard that scouts were needed for the front and he promptly joined, but only made it as far as Pietermaritzburg before he was called out and told that the central investigation department (CID) in Durban had forwarded a wire declaring him unfit to go to the front. The same night when he went to fetch his bag from the showgrounds, he was arrested for vagrancy and brought before the magistrate in Pietermaritzburg, who fined him 10s or seven days in prison. After paying the fine he was re-arrested by the police at the Pietermaritzburg Station for leaving Durban without a permit, and jailed until he was brought back to Durban by a detective on the night mail train of 23 December 1899. Again Waterton had to face Percy Scott, and his sole retort was that he had not been informed that he was not allowed to leave Durban. His brief up-country sojourn brought him 14 days in prison, and afterwards he had to report to the police twice a week as part of his parole He complied with these instructions until one day he travelled to Bellair, outside the boundaries of Durban. Consequently he was once again arrested and dragged before Colonel AW Morris. This time he was jailed for three weeks. On his release he obeyed his parole orders, almost starving in the process until he finally escaped by joining the crew of the *Ormosia* to Melbourne.

Guy Waterton felt he had been unfairly treated and therefore took his case to Joseph Chamberlain and the lords of the Admiralty, demanding compensation of £50 000 for false imprisonment in Durban, for losing his appointment at Chinde, and for loss of time and expenses primarily caused by 'the cruel and disgraceful way I have been treated by Capt. Percy Scott during the time he was in office in Durban'.

A full-blown investigation followed the claims of Guy Waterton, revealing a totally different tale. On 14 November 1899, Waterton was charged for using seditious language but, due to a lack of evidence, he was discharged. Two days later, he wrote to Captain Scott asking permission from him to proceed to Chinde to take up an appointment in the services of Parker, Wood & Company. Permission was refused. In fact Waterton had never had an appointment with Parker, Wood & Company, and was merely applying for a position with the company in Chinde. He was refused the position owing to the character sketch Commandant Scott and the police had provided. On 18 November 1899, Waterton broke martial law and proceeded to Bellair without a permit, only to be brought back to Durban. Waterton then took to serious letter writing in an effort to improve his lot. He wrote to Scott asking to be tried by a board of officers, stating that he intended to bring his case before the governor of Natal. A second letter was written to Sir Redvers Buller, a copy of which was forwarded to Scott. In this he complained of the treatment meted out to him by Scott. By 28 December 1899, Waterton had a change of heart, probably realising that he was making no progress. As a result he forwarded a letter of apology to Captain Scott, asking to be forgiven for proceeding to Bellair without permission, and for writing a letter to Buller, complaining about Scott. For a while Waterton did manage to find employment with the African Boating Company as a tally clerk, but it was not long before he was dismissed for either dishonesty or drunkenness, the manager could not recall which. In the meantime, Waterton, despite his proclaimed military record, could not secure a position in any of the irregular forces which continuously advertised their services in the *Natal Mercury*. The reason was that he was believed to have worked for the Transvaal government as a spy during the time of the Jameson Raid, while his impressive war record was viewed as a fabrication. While drifting along in Durban he was accused of being constantly drunk and, in July 1900, he was sentenced to two months in prison with hard labour for the theft of a purse containing about 20 shillings and two gold studs.

The case of the 'thoroughly undesirable character' first reached the new governor of Natal, HE McCallum, during November 1901. His investigators into the case concluded that Waterton was a spy for the Transvaal government prior to the war. Waterton's tale was probably nothing more than that of a drifter and petty criminal attempting to gain some compensation, based on lies and fabrications.[13]

Johan Sundt

A similar case that crossed four continents and which also dragged Captain Percy Scott into the fray involved Johan Sundt, a Norwegian by birth, but American by nationality. When Johan Sundt was arrested as a suspicious character, the original notes on the enquiry held by Scott recorded that 'he is a spy'. This statement was, however, deleted and replaced with the word 'suspicious'. Early in November, he was brought before Scott. Sundt's statement was simple: he maintained that on 1 November 1899, the Cape government had deposited £826 into his Standard Bank account for carbons he had supplied. He immediately withdrew £100 and deposited the remaining money in his Bank of Africa account. The next day he withdrew £100 and purchased a diamond engagement ring. (The ring was valued in Durban at £50.) Later in the day he withdrew £10, and the next day, 3 November 1899, he withdrew £40 to pay for his passage to Lourenço Marques. On his way to Mozambique he was arrested in Durban. His sole reason for travelling to Lourenço Marques was to fetch his fiancé, Annie Campbell, so that they could leave for Europe.

This romantic tale did not impress Scott, and Sundt was remanded to stay in Durban while his statement was verified. On 13 November 1900 the American consul informed Scott that Sundt's intention was to return to London. The following day a statement was received from Sergeant Webber of Bethune's Mounted Infantry stationed in Umbilo, implicating Sundt in espionage:

> Friday the 11th Novb I was present in the "Globe Bar" where I was abthrust by private " Woldich" he pointed out to me that hee hat gott information from a certain "Ward" living in Durban, about a man by name "Sunt" as been a Transvaal "Spi" the said man turned out to be an old Detectiv from the Transvaal one of Dr "Leyds" special Amicary for buying T.D.B Gold. Concequently I was wondering wass such a man wass doing in Durban, and as said "Sunt" is a Scandanavian that became a easy matter for me for follow up his conversacion with his Friends, and also for me to abruths them in their native tongue. "Sundt" told mee that he wass surprised to see me wearing the Queens Uniform as hees sympaties wheere all on the other Side. I warned him not to use any expercions which could bring him into trouble, hee then became condidencial and told me that hee wass just arrived from Capetown, and intended to go trouh Lourenço Maarques for the Transvaal, he also made out that he hat informations for the "Transvaal Government" of the strenght of the British Seapoorts, for witch hee would receiwe tousana of Pounds. Nown him as a man willing to do anny dirty work for Money and also as a man ther always hhas been more or lees conected with shatty Transactions in the Transvaal, I made up my

Ulundi Court, the Royal Hotel, Smith Street, was a favourite haunt for locals and visitors to Durban (LHM).

mind to arrest him as a person been dangerous for the British Goverment. [*sic*]

This proclamation by Sundt's newly found friend led to his arrest. He appeared before Captain Percy Scott the following day at 15:00, where he was confronted with even more evidence. A stockbroker from Johannesburg, Frederick William Blood, stated at the hearing that he had known Sundt for roughly two years and that Sundt owed him a substantial amount of money. As a result he had Sundt brought before court on a regular basis, the last time towards the end of September 1899. Sundt even ended up in prison as a result of his bad debt to Blood. To settle the matter amicably, Sundt and his solicitor came to Blood's office and, one of the two, Blood remained unsure who, stated that Sundt was in the Transvaal secret service and would shortly have enough money to pay. Blood would not agree to this arrangement, and Sundt was taken back to prison, only to be released the next day. Blood never saw Sundt again until the fateful night of 11 November 1899, when he saw him entering the Royal Hotel in Durban.

Sundt admitted to Blood's accusations. He had indeed been sent to prison for owing Blood £205. He was released on condition that he pay Blood £2 per month. Up to November 1899, he had repaid Blood £50. The receipts for these payments were in Johannesburg. Blood denied this was true. Following this repudiation, Sundt once again claimed that he had received a payment from the Cape government for dealing in carbons, but for the first time he admitted that not all the money was his, but that some of it was for Peter Johnstone of the Hariot Gold Mining Company. He also admitted that he had only withdrawn £80 for the ring, now in the possession of the American consul. For the first time, he also revealed that on 11 October 1899, he had fled to Cape Town as he did not want to be enlisted in the Johannesburg police force to serve as a town guard.

On 21 November 1899, the interrogation of Sundt was resumed in Scott's office. Sundt was again questioned about the money paid to him. Sundt now acknowledged that he had transferred £650 to the Bank of Africa in Lourenço Marques. On being questioned by Scott as to why he stopped in Durban when planning to go to Lourenço Marques, Sundt answered that he had hoped to board a ship that would travel up the east coast of Africa via Lourenço Marques to Europe. The investigation into whether Sundt was a spy was now taken a step further. Sergeant EN Brooke sent a telegram to the police in Cape Town, enquiring whether any money had been paid to Sundt by the Cape government. The reply delivered a devastating blow in the case against Sundt: 'Johan Sundt statement perfectly correct but cannot send original draft.'

This was of no use to Scott. The damning evidence, as far as he was concerned, was provided by Webber and Blood, namely that Sundt was a Transvaal secret agent, a fact Sundt never denied nor confirmed. Furthermore, Sundt could not provide a satisfactory answer regarding his own dealings at Lourenço Marques, nor an address for his fiancé, Annie Campbell. Scott felt that Sundt was not the kind of person to be at large in Durban and he, therefore, with the consent of the governor, had Sundt detained, at first in the Durban goal and then on the *Columbia*. He was imprisoned on 3 December 1899.

On 14 August 1900, matters started to stir again. General J Wolfe-Murray, officer commanding, lines of communication, pointed out to Governor Hely-Hutchinson that Sundt had been imprisoned on his orders since 3 December 1899, and he felt that Sundt should be released. In his own continued search for new evidence to prove his innocence, Sundt had requested to have access to a lawyer to defend him. Wolfe-Murray granted him permission. Sundt declared his intentions to his lawyer, Harry Filmer, operating from 13 Acutt's Arcade. He would not sign any papers presented to him by the military to indemnify them from prosecution. Filmer advised him otherwise and, because Sundt would not take his advice, Filmer 'dropped' him. For Sundt, who had by now been imprisoned for almost nine months, the matter was simple: he could not indemnify the military for the treatment he had had to endure. He was adamant he would sue the British military for an amount of £ 25 000 for damages inflicted. The only way the military could solve the problem was to follow the suggestion of Wolf-Murray and deport Sundt to Europe. The governor could not offer any opinion on this issue as it was outside his jurisdiction. Wolf-Murray, therefore, on 29 September 1900, made a decision, 'There being no military reasons to prolong this man's detention, he may be released, but cannot be permitted to remain in Durban and he should be placed on board ship and sent out of the country.' On his release on 23 October 1900, Johan Sundt received his personal belongings which included a statement regarding his first wife and two children, and receipts and banking documents. He accepted £12 compensation for the deposit slip for £800 and his Bank of Africa cheque book the military could not produce.

Commandant Morris believed Sundt was 'one of the most troublesome and most dangerous prisoners we have at present' and he called on Wolfe-Murray to assist him in ensuring that Sundt would sail for London without touching South African soil again. His hopes were realised as the *Duke of Norfolk* travelled directly to London. In his attempt to get away as soon as possible, Sundt did not ask for a passage, but paid his own. In a cruel twist, the *Duke of Norfolk* was delayed for a day owing to bad weather and only left for London on 26 October 1900.

On his arrival in London, Sundt immediately put his intentions into effect. He employed the law firm of Tyrell, Lewis & Broadbent of Albany Court Yards, Piccadilly, to claim compensation from the imperial government for his unprovoked arrest as a Boer spy. The key witness produced by Sundt's lawyers was Peter Johnstone, the cowboy to whom half the £832, which had been paid into the account of Sundt in Cape Town, belonged. Johnstone was traced to 107 Fourth Avenue, New York, and brought to Britain to make a statement. In his statement, Johnstone declared that he had arrived in South Africa in 1897 and that he had been employed by Sundt working on railway contracts. On hearing about his knowledge of cattle and horses, they agreed that importing horses to South Africa from South America could be a profitable business. With war clouds gathering, and a large demand for horses anticipated, they decided in June 1899 that the time was ripe to start their importation business. As he could speak Spanish, Johnstone agreed to leave for South America to purchase horses. His salary would be £50 per month, paid by Sundt, as well as 10% of the commission on the sale of the horses. For the execution of their plan, Johnstone contributed £200 and Sundt £152. With Johnstone gone, Sundt promised to follow as soon as he had made arrangements. Upon his arrival in Argentina, Johnstone started buying up horses, but could only afford deposits, and he therefore wrote to Sundt at an address provided in Cape Town that he should proceed to Argentina as soon as possible, and bring the money to complete their transactions. Sundt responded in a letter that reached Buenos Aires at the beginning of December 1899, stating that he would travel to Argentina via England. When Sundt did not make good on his promise, Johnstone wrote several letters, both to Cape Town and Johannesburg, but received no reply. By August 1900 Johnstone was without money, and the transaction had folded. Being broke, and believing that Sundt had deserted him, he managed to obtain $100 to make his way to New York. Johnstone again forwarded several letters to Sundt in South Africa, but received no reply. Only in November 1900 did Johnstone receive a reply from Sundt. In a letter he wrote from Durban, forwarded to Johnstone via Buenos Aires, Sundt explained that he had been detained as a Boer spy in Durban. Several further letters from Sundt served to unfold to Johnstone the full tragedy of Sundt's tale. Having had their business venture ruined by the detention of Sundt, Johnstone had no hesitation in taking a steamer from New York to Liverpool and then on to London to make a statement on behalf of Sundt who, according to Johnstone, was never involved in political matters.

On these grounds the solicitors, acting on the behalf of Sundt, approached the British government for compensation. This was the start of a lengthy investigation, hampered by the technological constraints of the time. Communications with Captain Percy Scott, then in China on board the *Terrible*, took four months to complete. As the War Office had no documents on the detention of Sundt, they had to be obtained from the governor of Natal. By August 1901, with all the evidence gathered, the case could be concluded, and the following verdict of the law officers of the war office could be forwarded to the secretary for colonies, Joseph Chamberlain, and the lawyers of Johan Sundt:

> Although the evidence against Sundt that he was a spy (the charge on which he was arrested and detained) was unsatisfactory, we think, in view of the state of affairs in Natal and the matters subsequently referred to, that there was ground for his detention in the public interest as a prisoner under Martial Law. During Sundt's imprisonment he drew up for the Authorities information with regard to the Transvaal Secret Service, which, whether accurate or not, goes far to justify the suspicions of the Durban authorities; and his antecedents do not appear to be such as to make him deserving of particular sympathy. While we think the imprisonment seems to have been unduly prolonged, we are of the opinion, having regard to all the

JP de la Court Schröder, a member of the ZAR *Geheime Dienst* who was active in Natal during 1898 (G Kamffer).

De la Court Schröder's map of Natal indicating the battle order of the British forces in Natal (G Kamffer).

circumstances and also to the Natal Indemnity Act, that Sundt cannot maintain any claim in law, either upon His Majesty's Government, or the Local Authorities in Natal.[14]

This brought the curtain down on the personal tragedy suffered by an individual caught up in the web of war. It is to be doubted if Sundt was a spy. He was more likely an opportunistic businessman whose love for a woman took him to the wrong place at the wrong time.

In reality it was to be doubted if Durban was a hotbed for Boer spies during the Anglo-Boer War, as neither the names of Nathan Marks, Guy Waterton nor that of Johan Sundt appear in the registers of the *Geheime Dienst* (secret service) of the Transvaal.[15] Despite the lack of evidence, the fear that secret Boer agents could cause damage remained foremost in the minds of the Durban authorities. Prior to and during the royal visit of the Duke and Duchess of Cornwall in 1901 a strict watch was kept on the identified anti-British characters. Nothing, however, happened because '... the strong show of loyalty by the inhabitants, has had a most pronounced beneficial effect on the Boer mind, and will undoubtedly serve to counteract the many evil influences at work owing to the efforts of pro-Boers and secret agents of the enemy'.[16]

Unbeknown to the British, a member of the ZAR *Geheime Dienst*, JP de la Court Schröder, had been active in Durban and Natal during 1898, and then again from the end of June 1899 onwards. Schröder was a man with a military background, and with knowledge and experience of police work as well as experience as a journalist made thorough observations of the cargo ships docking in the Durban harbour and the kinds of goods they transported prior to the war. He supplemented his reports with relevant newspaper cuttings, detailed maps and sketches and even included photographs in his report. Information such as this could be used in a proactive manner for strategic planning. Opposed to that, and against which the authorities in Durban guarded, intelligence gathered during the war was of less value.[17]

Gathering intelligence from Uitlanders and other refugees

The thousands of Uitlanders and other refugees who defected to Durban prior to and especially during the conventional phase of the Anglo-Boer War were viewed and treated as potentially important sources of information. This is to be understood as they formed a hybrid group ranging from 'wannabe' military agents to political defectors, many of whom could provide information from the heart of the Transvaal in particular. They were of special value, since in-depth information concerning speciality fields such as mining, in which some had been involved, was not readily available by any other means. Although their input was not necessarily in the form of hard facts, what they revealed did paint a picture of the feelings and emotions prevailing in the republics, and they were able to provide sketchy impressions of the methods employed by the Boers, as well as the events and planning taking place, which could help the British to predict future intentions, and give their offensive momentum. Such information, gained from Uitlanders and refugees, remained important up to the fall of Pretoria on 5 June 1900, when the stream of refugees dried up and when the British military could revert to more traditional means of gathering intelligence.

For refugees from the Transvaal and the neighbouring areas to proceed to Durban via Lourenço Marques, they first needed to be cleared by the British consul, Carnegie Ross, who had his own elaborate intelligence system. This network consisted of refugees who came from Johannesburg and provided a limited input; secret agents who, despite a lack of organisation did furnish some details; Africans who infiltrated the Transvaal up to Barberton and Lydenburg to provide the consul with reliable intelligence; and lastly; information on suspicious persons would be obtained by the consul through the employment of agents in Lourenço Marques who, as part of their duties, had to monitor and spy on those who arrived in the city from the Transvaal and elsewhere.[18] In the light of the intelligence he had collected, refugees were cleared, and thereafter Ross would inform the authorities in Durban of the departure of the refugees, stating the number of people concerned, the date of departure as well as the name of the vessel assigned to transport them. Besides this, he would also inform the Durban authorities of the names of suspicious characters or of refugees that could provide helpful knowledge about circumstances in the Transvaal. On arrival at the dockside in Durban, those under suspicion would be questioned and searched, and the remaining refugees debriefed by the CID presided over by Sergeant EN Brooke. Once Brooke had gathered and analysed the information it was passed on to the commandant of Durban, who would act on it. It was then his responsibility to convey the information, to the governor and government of Natal, and to the officer commanding, lines of communication, as well as to the intelligence division of the British army.

The advantages and drawbacks of this system are best illustrated by the experiences endured by the refugees on board the *Umbria*, sent by the Natal government to Lourenço Marques for their evacuation. Fritz Crowe, the new British consul in Lourenço Marques, as Consul Ross was on board the *Umbria*, informed Commandant AW Morris of Durban on 17 May 1900 that all 250 passengers on board the *Umbria*[19] who intended to disembark in Durban were suspected of having ties with the enemy, and therefore needed to be searched and interviewed on arrival. Special attention was to be paid to the following passengers: A Rousseau and his wife, C Mckuskie and his family, C Ollendorf and M Ferreira who were believed to be Boer spies, and A Parker who was believed to be a secret agent. Numerous others, especially the passengers in Class 1, men and women alike, were also regarded as suspects. The two detectives on board the *Umbria*, Fred and Nathan, and a secret agent named Brodrick, compiled profiles on these suspects and presented the list to the military and the police upon arrival in Durban.

When the *Umbria* steamed into Durban harbour, Detective Fred informed Commandant Morris that all the passengers on board, and their luggage, were to be searched, as they were all part of a 'big scheme to interfere with the telegraphs, and to arrange for the escape of prisoners'. As these machinations were to take place not only in Natal, but all along the coast line, Fred wanted the 1 250 refugees bound for East London, Port Elizabeth and Cape Town to be searched as well. Apart from this general statement, Fred provided no hard evidence for his outrageous request. As a result Commandant Morris had the IRO, Harry Smith, Acting Port Health Officer Dr Ralph, Sergeant Brooke, and Fred go on board again, with the task of providing him with a thorough report. The investigation revealed that most of the suspects on the list forwarded by the consul either were not on board or had no intention of landing in Durban. Consequently, Morris allowed the bulk of the refugee-passengers to land in two groups, excluding those named by the consul, those heading for ports further afield, and those that were regarded as suspicious, including a Mrs Daniels. Refugees who remained on board were to be thoroughly searched the following day. Detective Fred was not happy with this arrangement, especially when local businessman, Ruben Beningfield, was allowed to land. As a result, he co-operated very half-heartedly with Sergeant Brooke and withheld the list of names of suspects provided by the consul. Detective Nathan on his part also provided no information.

Commandant Morris believed that reporting all the refugees on board a ship as suspicious persons, as Fred had done, was absurd. He therefore contacted Fritz Crowe, enquiring why he wanted a wholesale search of all passengers. At the same time he complained that Nathan and Fred had provided no information at all. Crowe replied that if a wholesale search was suggested by Fred, the latter had not done his work properly. Instead, Crowe suggested that only those he mentioned in his telegram as potential spies or troublemakers were to be searched, specifically for letters, and questioned, as some of them had not been screened before. Some of the suspects listed carried 'inordinate quantity and weight of luggage, which I advise examined for Johannesburg loot'. These instructions did not find favour with the commandant, as passengers bound for the Cape and their luggage would have to be brought in by tug from the outer anchorage where the *Umbria* was lying, and that on the basis of non-existent evidence. He therefore contacted Governor Walter Hely-Hutchinson for his opinion. Hely-Hutchinson suggested that an on-board search should be conducted while awaiting further detail from Lourenço Marques. His response was not received favourably as Commandant Morris, the IRO and Sergeant Brooke deemed it impractical because of the overcrowded conditions on the *Umbria*. In the process described above, on 19 May 1900 alone, ten telegrams were despatched between Durban and Lourenço Marques.

The volume of correspondence did not bring the commandant closer to resolving the crisis. In an attempt to solve the matter, he interviewed Fred and Nathan again. Only then did the truth start to emerge. The two detectives had quarrelled seriously during the journey and, as a result, Nathan did not want to proceed with the *Umbria* to Cape Town, but wanted to remain in Durban to return to Lourenço Marques. Neither of the detectives knew Broderick, the secret agent that was supposed to be on board. Further interrogation by Morris revealed that during the journey Nathan had provided Fred with written reports on suspicious passengers. Fred only admitted to receiving such reports, which were nothing more than rough notes, under duress. Only some of the Durban-bound passengers mentioned in these rough notes correlated with the consul's list of suspects. Of these, two, Mrs Daniels who had resided in Lourenço Marques for the past 18 months, and Mr Chauncey had already been allowed to land. This mistake was blamed by Morris on the negligence of the CID and IRD officers. Matters were, however, not out of hand, and a close watch was kept on Daniels and Chauncey, who were informed that they should advise the commandant of any change in address. The pair's baggage, when searched by customs, revealed nothing. A third suspect, Mr D Woolf, was also cleared, as he proved to have been very helpful to British subjects in Lourenço Marques. Hardly any information of value emerged about the other suspects except details such that Allendorf had supplied the Boers with goods and that Ferreira and Platnauer were members of the *Standard and Diggers News* staff. Others, such as EM Roberts, for no particular reason; Hamman, because he had acted as a town guard; Bowers alias Steele, who had allegedly been a cook to General PJ Joubert; S Levine alias JS Dudgeon; F Budge alias Bernard Franco; Brooke-Howard and his wife and their nurse, who were believed to be burghers who worked in Bremersdorp, and IM Hendon, a miner from Johannesburg who wanted to land in Durban to see a girl, were all regarded as suspicious.

In the light of the lack of real evidence and the overcrowded conditions on board, Commandant Morris felt that all Durban-bound refugees still on the ship should be allowed to land, and the *Umbria* should be cleared to proceed to the Cape. A clearly irritated Governor Hely-Hutchinson informed Consul Crowe, Commandant Morris and High Commissioner Alfred Milner accordingly. To ensure that none of these suspects slipped through the net, Hely-Hutchinson suggested that these passengers be thoroughly searched on arrival in the Cape ports, which would have been difficult since no martial law existed in the Cape Colony at the time. What the governor found most worrying was that he felt that the British consulate was being misled by its agents.[20]

RW Beningfield, a renowned businessmen and foremost Durbanite, who resided at 30 St Andrews Street, took exception that 'a low bred Peruvian' such as Detective Fred had suggested he was in possession of treasonable material, and he made it clear that he was annoyed that his loyalty had been disputed. He considered Fred to be a spy who had travelled up to Lourenço Marques on a French steamer, and he suggested to Commandant Morris that: 'When the authorities employ people for their Intelligence Department they should be compelled to select men who can be depended upon, and not people who give information which causes a loyal subject to be insulted.' Morris went to great lengths to soothe the bruised ego of Beningfield, and secretly agreed with the view of Fred's character. Fred, alias Levy, was a Jew appointed by Captain Percy Scott, and proved to be unreliable and was even suspected of being a double agent. It seems that it was difficult at the time to find reliable detectives to investigate and monitor the refugees heading for Durban, as

Morris reported that he had dismissed another for being drunk.[21]

Other ships ferrying refugees from Lourenço Marques, such as the *König, Tintagel Castle, Herzog, Matabele Incuna,* and *Gironde,* did not pose the same problems as the *Umbria.* All, however, arrived in Durban, crowded with possible informants ready to render data and, in so doing, feeling that they had performed a personal patriotic duty and had contributed to the imperial war effort. Numerous accounts on what was happening in the Transvaal are to be found in various archival collections, some of which are discussed in the section which follows. The intelligence, mostly gathered by Sergeant EN Brooke and his colleagues, may be divided into military, economic, political and social issues.

Important facts relating to military matters, including data on such aspects as strengths, movements, morale and armaments of the Boer forces, and the treatment of British POWs, were gained from arriving refugees. Especially valuable was information emanating from first-hand experiences, such as that supplied by a certain Mr Irvine who was arrested in Johannesburg and imprisoned at the racecourse in Pretoria. According to him, the prisoners were fed with food the Boers had captured at Dundee and they were housed in sheds. The officers were removed to the Staats Model School in Pretoria, where they could order their meals from the local hotels. Irvine also reported that Colonel Moller, captured near Dundee during the battle of Talana, was well.[23] Not all first-hand accounts could, however, be taken at face value. An Afrikaner like Reverend AJL (Adriaan) Hofmeyr who arrived on board the *Umbria,* claiming to be a distant relative of Jan Smuts, and who was likewise imprisoned by the Boers, had his own axe to grind with his kin as can be gathered from his accounts of mal treatment of POWs at the Staats Model School.[24] Nonetheless, such sources provided valuable information for the British military who could compare the circumstances with those described on 22 May 1900, almost six months later, which stated that the British POWs kept at Waterfall badly needed clothing and that their rations were inadequate. Furthermore, it was suggested that medicines needed to treat those suffering from typhoid and other diseases was limited, with the result that eight prisoners had died during the first week of May. Donations of food, clothes and money from British subjects who had remained in Johannesburg was not enough to make a difference.[25]

Eyewitness reports, such as that of Mr Lefeber, that 2 000 Boers from the Natal front had left Park Station in Johannesburg for Klerksdorp, gave a good indication of how the Boer forces were being redeployed.[26] Even more valuable information was provided by careless Boers themselves. Clarence H Eaton, who arrived on board the *Induna* on 11 April 1900, informed Major HR Bousfield that Commandant Grobler, who resided near him in Jeppestown, had told him that he would be leaving for Kroonstad to join his commando of 2 000 men, including the remainder of the Johannesburg Police who had been withdrawn from Ladysmith. The conversation with Grobler provided Eaton with information on apparent Boer tactics: 'He also told me that he ordered his men to take off their hats when firing and put them in front of them on the trench, and then fire from first one side and then the other of their hats'. Grobler's son elaborated on his father's tales, telling Eaton that General Louis Botha and 2 000 men, including the 2nd Irish, were also leaving for Kroonstad on 4 April 1900.[27] The problem regarding much of the input relating to military matters was that it was gathered from secondhand sources. For example, William M Rodgers supplied information which he, in turn, had gathered from a Russian guarding the civilian POWs at the racecourse in Pretoria. According to Rodgers '... Pretoria was completely surrounded with mines, containing 'Melanite' and electric communications with the Forts ... beyond the mines numerous man traps were constructed, covered in lightly, after the fashion of traps to snare rhinoceros or other big game'. Rodgers continued that 'shortly after his telling this, he (the Russian) was arrested and disappeared'. They had been told 'that he was suspected of telling secrets and had been sent away and told if he was seen in Pretoria, he would be shot; but no doubt he was shot'. Rodgers even attached a map which he believed depicted the defence plan graphically.[28]

Two similar questionable accounts, based on hearsay, were provided to Sergeant Brooke by John Fagan, a clergymen of the Church of England, who had left the Transvaal on 6 April 1900. In early March 1900, he had heard that 43 guns had come into the Transvaal and he mentioned this matter to Landdrost Munnik of Boksburg, who did not comment. Fagan's impression from the talk with the Landdrost was that they had been landed somewhere along the coast, probably near Inhambane but not at Delagoa Bay itself. The second story reported by Fagan relating to guns was told to him by his friend, Charles Brenton, namely '... that he had seen six large new guns pass Elandsfontein Junction'.[29]

More important than information on military matters, since it did not deal with hard facts, was news on socio-economic and political developments, providing the British with an insight into the inner feelings, thoughts and morale of those in the republics. Foodstuffs, except for coffee and sugar, were supposedly plentiful, while clothing, especially boots, blankets and hats, were scarce. The mining industry was said to be in disarray, houses in Johannesburg were being looted and occupied by burghers, and apparently, large numbers of Boers and foreigners were disheartened and refused to fight, hoping that the war would end soon, and that the government of the Transvaal was contemplating moving to Lydenburg.[30]

The case of the *Entre Rios*

A ship which left Lourenço Marques for Durban and encountered treatment similar to that of the *Umbria* was the French steamer, the *Entre Rios*. The British consul in Lourenço Marques reported to the authorities in Durban that several refugees on board were Boer spies who had obtained permits by false statements and under assumed names. The only names forwarded were those of Roe, alias Webb, and Beale. On arrival in Durban, the secret agent on board, Levy, delivered his report. As a result, several British refugees were refused permission to disembark in Durban.[22]

The available documents on Africans being used as spies and scouts by the British state that none came from Durban. These men were, however, in the hearts, minds and songs of the Durban Africans. In his report on the Durban magistracy for 1901, the local magistrate, JJ Stuart, described how he on two occasions during the year attended a concert given by a number of African men and women in aid of fallen scouts. The first was in a hall on the Berea, and the second in the town hall. [32]

Fortunately for the British military, such second or third-hand accounts, fabrications, and misleading or contradictory information, were balanced by reports that would have been a credit to any secret service. An example of such a laudable document was the report submitted by W Gregorowski, a former resident of Johannesburg, who arrived on the *Umbria*. The opening comment of his statement attests to a person who was able to blend into his environment, while at the same time distinguishing between fact and fabrication. He writes: 'To a Resident of Johannesburg, not engaged in trade, and not desirous of attracting attention, sources of information, were few. Many rumours were in time found to be unreliable.' In the light of his sober introduction, comments by Gregorowski that Johannesburg was fairly quiet and that no signs of fortifications were visible, and that reports of Boer victories were spread to boost Boer morale tend to be plausible. Gregorowski was also quick to realise that 'reliable rumours' had become scarce since the Boer security surrounding telegrams had been stepped up, and the *Standard and Diggers News* was withholding reports. Gregorowski accordingly chose the language used in his report carefully in an attempt to provide an unbiased view. He wrote of : 'Rumours that Burghers had fallen back on Boshof and that Mafeking was free on Wednesday last'. He mentions another piece of gossip: 'Rumour that there today was a strong party in favour of destroying the mines and Johannesburg'. [sic] Only when confident of the truth would Gregorowski relate what he felt to be an undisputed fact: 'A large number of Dutch families is to be found in various parts of Johannesburg specifically in Braamfontein and Fordsburg, Doornfontein ... some of these are from the Free State and some from Colesburg' and 'Commandeering of burghers has for some time past been almost continuous, still there are generally a considerable number of able-bodied men on leave, evidently indisposed to rejoin the Commandoes.'[sic] Quite clearly realising the importance of information and its manipulation, Gregorowski, concluded by commenting that 'The spirit of the people (Boers) is being kept up by false reports, suppression of news and other means.'[31]

It is to be doubted if the intelligence gathered in Durban, from suspected Boer spies such as Johan Sundt and Nathan Marks, or the Uitlanders, contributed much of strategic value to the British war effort. Most likely the efforts by Sergeant EN Brooke, the various commandants of Durban and their agents operating in Lourenço Marques and Durban merely served to discourage the gathering of intelligence on behalf of the Boers.

1. PAR, MJPW 116: documents on mysterious lights flashing at Northdene, Cowie's Hill and other areas, 29.11.1899–19.12.1899.

2. Thanks to Ian Swanepoel for this image.

3. PAR, IRD 3: request for in transit passenger Von Veltheim to land, 8.1899; PAR, CSO 1617: documents on Von Veltheim, 28.6.1899.

4. PAR, CSO 1636: documents on the extradition of Joseph Muhlbauer, 5.9.1899.

5. PRO, CO 179/207: minute paper on spies paid through the National Bank, 23.10.1899.

6. PRO, CO 179/207: minute paper on Nathan Marks 11.1899.

7. *Natal Mercury*, 21.12.1900.

8. PRO, CO 179/208: letter W Hely-Hutchinson to J Chamberlain, 13.12.1899.

9. PAR, IRD 3: memo on Arthur Long who had left Lourenço Marques for Durban, 8.7.1900.

10. PAR, GH 558: letter AW Morris to W Hely-Hutchinson, 7.4.1900.

11. PAR, GH 836: documents regarding Fanny Scheff, 26.10.1900.

12. PRO, CO 179/217: statements by G Friederich and G Krueger, 28.8.1901.

13. PRO, CO 179/227: documents regarding Guy Waterton, 1899–1902.

14. PAR, GH 555: documents on the detention of Johan Sundt, 10.1899–8.1900; PRO, CO 179/221: documents surrounding the case of Johan Sundt, 4.1.1902; PRO, CO 129/222: documents surrounding the case of Johan Sundt, 14.8.1902.

15. Kamfer, G, *The role of the secret service of the ZAR (De Geheime Dienst) before and during the first months of the Anglo-Boer War*, Paper presented at University of the Orange Free State, 12–15.10.1999.

16. PRO, CO 179/219: CID report on spies, 27.8.1901.

17. Kamfer, *The role ..., passim*.

18. PAR, GH 832: record of work of the intelligence department of the consul in Lourenço Marques, 5–10.1900.

19. *Natal Mercury*, 21.5.1900.

20. PAR, GH 563: minute paper on searching passengers on board *Umbria*, 17.5.1900–21.5.1900.

21. PAR, GH 559: letter RM Beningfield to AW Morris, 22.5.1900; letter AW Morris to W Hely-Hutchinson, 23.5.1900.

22. PAR, GH 831: documents regarding the *Entre Rios*, 17–19.4.1900.

23. PRO, CO 179/207: letter P Scott to W Hely-Hutchinson, 16.11.1899.

24. PAR, GH 559: statements by AJL Hofmeyr, 28.5.1900.

24. PAR, GH 559: letter AB Chauncey to AW Morris, 22.5.1900.

26. PAR, GH 559: report by EN Brooke on affairs in the Transvaal up to May, 1900, 10.5.1900.

27. PRO, CO 179/211: statement by CH Eaton before HR Bousfield, 19.4.1900.

28. PRO, CO 179/212: statement by WM Rodgers, 21.5.1900.

29. PAR, GH 559: statement by J Fagan, 14.4.1900.

30. PRO, CO 179/212: report on the state of affairs in the Transvaal up to 25.5.1900 as gathered from the passengers on board the *Gironde*, 1.6.1900; PAR, GH 559: letter DL Woolf to commandant Durban, 26.5.1900.

31. PAR, GH 559: report by W Gregorowski, 10.5.1900.

32. PAR, NCP 8/1/13/2/9: blue book on native affairs, report magistrate Durban, J. Stuart, 27.1.1902.

CHAPTER 20

CONTROLLING INTELLIGENCE BY MEANS OF CENSORSHIP

Johan Wassermann

To complement the intelligence work done in Durban, extensive censorship regimes were introduced under martial law, whereby the military had the right to control and access information by censoring both letters and articles to be published by the local publications. This process was not without its problems, which ranged from the lack of availability of suitably skilled manpower and the appropriate equipment to resistance to the censoring of correspondence, especially consular.

Logistical and staff problems faced by the censorship office in Durban

The censorship office in Durban was opened on 14 October 1899, with the arrival of TO Fraser, an experienced civil servant who had previously worked at the colonial office in Pretoria and the foreign office in Lourenço Marques. His instructions from the general lines of communications were clear: 'Prevent any information reaching the enemy which might be of use to him, stop anything passing along the wires which might reveal military operations, especially as to the movements of troops, report at once anything which might be of service to the Intelligence Department, and refer to the General of Communications any matter on which advice is required. Also to inform the local press at Durban that nothing referring to military matters is to be published without reference to the Censor.' The free rein given to him suited Fraser well and he appreciated the fact that he was not hampered by rules quite inappropriate to the circumstances. His task was nevertheless a daunting one, for not only did he have to oversee the control of cables and telegrams, but also monitor information in newspapers and letters.

It seems that the military did not place a high priority on this work as the censorship office in Durban had severe limitations. Until he was replaced in October 1901, Fraser had to complete his task with only a handful of assistants. The seven assistants for cables and telegrams he had to work with were generally lieutenants – convalescents discharged from the hospital who were relieved of their censorship duties as soon as they became fit to return to the front. At no time did the military, according to Fraser, pay any attention to the skills or abilities required to be a censor. As a result Fraser had to train and oversee each new convalescent assistant, while carrying most of the workload in the process. This resulted in the task of censoring roughly 200 cables per day, revolved around the routine of reading and passing messages, with very little investigation into some of the suspicious ones.[1] Finding staff to censor letters was

Commandant Captain Percy Scott and his naval staff with Major Bousfield at Scott's left, and seated, Brooke, Alexander and Fraser (Newnes).

equally problematic. In January 1900 when only six people were employed, serious clashes arose with the Cape Colony regarding the delay of letters. The problem was that the staff employed in the Durban post office for censoring could not cope with the workload of 11 000 letters on hand and seven bags of Dutch letters for the Transvaal. The staff anticipated that it would take five weeks to deal with the volume mentioned. To address the backlog, an inspection by the military was called for. As a result of this inspection Major Bird appointed more personnel. There was an improvement in the service although the appointed staff did not always meet the high criteria required for censoring letters.[2] One of the censors, Mr JR Dunn, former editor of the *Natal Advertiser*, complained to Attorney-General Henry Bale that some of the censors were not suitable for the work. According to him, Hese and Halle were, before their appointments, connected to a 'scurrilous Johannesburg newspaper' which spied on other peoples lives, while they also had commercial connections which could benefit from the knowledge they would gain by reading the letters they censored. In short, the men referred to were not the kind 'such a delicate and responsible duty should have been entrusted to'.[3] One can only assume that they were dismissed. They were not the only undesirable ones. Post office clerk H Waring was arrested for divulging information from the post office. He was detained in prison for three weeks pending a decision on what was to be done. According to Captain Scott, the incarceration, along with Waring's dismissal from the service, was adequate punishment for the offence committed.[4]

Eventually the 16 people employed proved sufficient, but Fraser thought that more attention should have been given to specially train people, appointed on a permanent basis, to work as letter censors. The selected members preferably needed to know how business practices functioned and be au fait with foreign languages. A further aggravating circumstance for the censor's office in Durban lay in the fact that the structure of command was chaotic. The office of the censor in Durban was not centralised, and although TO Fraser was told that he was under the control of the chief censor for Natal in Pietermaritzburg, he also received instructions from the chief censor in Cape Town, the censor in Pretoria and the officer commanding lines of communication and his staff. This invariably meant contradictory instructions. Working conditions were also poor. The original room inside the government telegraph operating room, in which the censoring of cables and telegrams took place, was so small that the Eastern Telegraph Company, out of sympathy, provided Fraser with a suitable room. His team was not allowed to use the government code and cypher machine, as they were not supplied with code books, but in mitigation they seldom found it necessary to communicate in code. The only dictionaries available in foreign languages were those borrowed from the Eastern Telegraph Company, while directories of addresses were not supplied by the military, but had to be borrowed.[5] TO Fraser was replaced, in October 1901, by a military man, Major Gardiner, formerly of the Royal Scots and the army audit department.[6]

Military information on a page in the *Natal Mercury*, 9 October 1899.

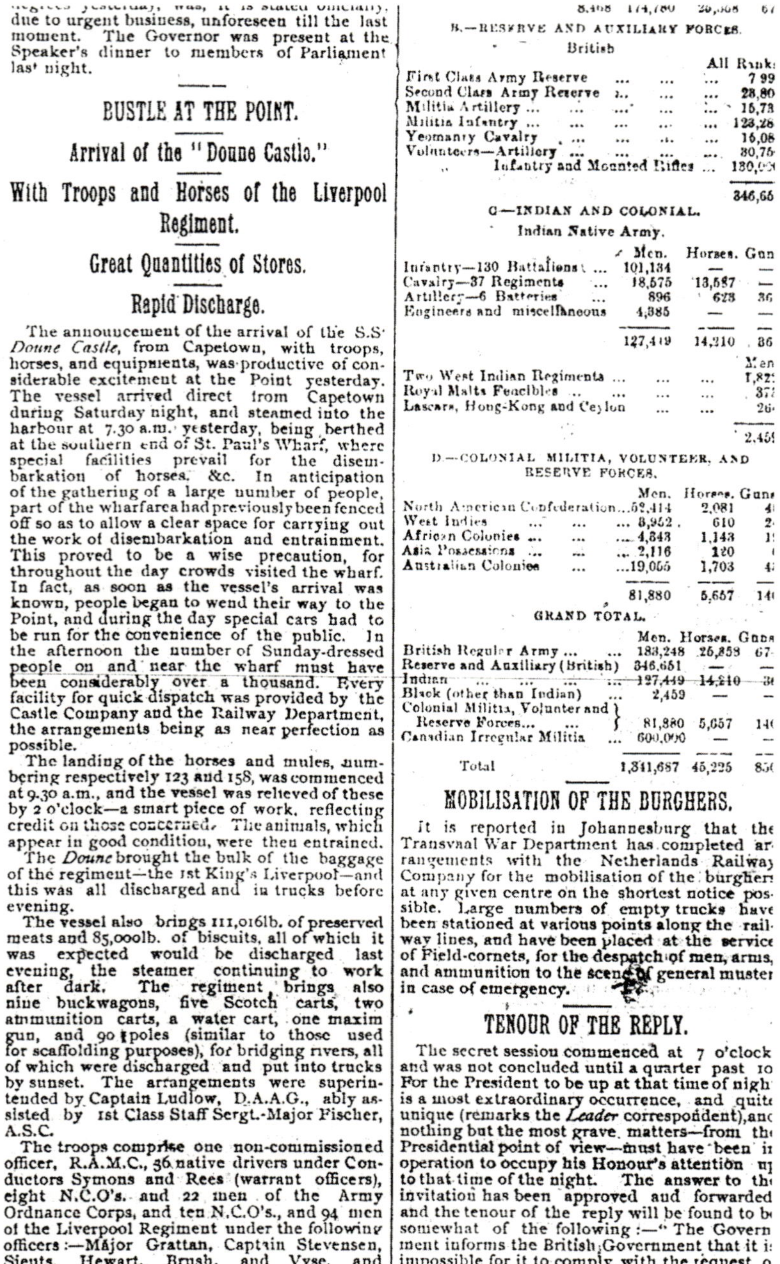

In the intelligence and information chain that exists during wartime, newspapers not only provide factual information such as the arrival of troops, but also provide insight into thought processes and political and economic issues that could influence a war. Often newspapers can provide information which is more up to date and accurate than intelligence reports. Open-minded journalist generally function free of any constraints and their news analysis, if printed as recorded, may enable one to predict future events. In this way newspapers could be an important source of information to the enemy and need to be controlled. As a result, instructions for newspapers and rules for press censors in Natal were made available on 27 November 1899.

The directions given to newspapers were clear. Any article relating to the war which the newspaper wished to publish needed to be submitted to TO Fraser, the press censor in Durban. The press censor would then either detain or alter the article if he deemed it injurious to the military. Once passed, each page of the submitted article should bear the press censor's signature. The article was now ready for publication. Once published, each newspaper was to send a copy of the publication to the press censor so that he could examine the contents to determine if the modifications had been implemented. Articles forwarded by accredited journalists in the field, which had already been passed by the press censor on the spot, were exempted from this process. At times it was necessary for Fraser to delete some part of these messages received from the battle front. The recipient and reporter were unaware of these changes as the adjusted message was sent overseas. Some of the accounts submitted to the local press had to be stopped even though they had been passed at the source, either because the censor at the front was unaware of the restrictions being imposed or was not in a position to know what impact the information sent would have locally. Although fears existed that information could be extracted from press cables in the process of transmission and utilised by others not entitled to them, TO Fraser doubted if this was possible.[8]

Very little fear existed in Durban that the press rules would not be adhered to, as both the morning and afternoon newspapers, the *Natal Mercury* and the *Natal Advertiser*, respectively, in true jingoistic and imperialistic style, provided full support for the war effort. The exception was *The Review and Critic*, which printed an article on the battle of Spioenkop in its issue of 3 February 1900, which was found to be offensive by Commandant Percy Scott. The sections he regarded as unsuitable he either underlined, or highlighted by drawing vertical lines between the columns. From Scott's viewpoint, derogatory comments were directed, by and large, at the British officers, as the following quotations indicate. References were made to behaviour reflecting '... discreditably on those in supreme command, on whom the responsibility for the untoward issue clearly rests. It is a repetition of the case of the Duke of York who marched his men up a hill and down again'. The article continued '... it was bad generalship not to know the topography of the locality and it was equally bad generalship not to have attended to the water question.' The

---

[Newspaper clipping reproduced on the page:]

...grees yesterday, was, it is stated officially, due to urgent business, unforeseen till the last moment. The Governor was present at the Speaker's dinner to members of Parliament last night.

BUSTLE AT THE POINT.

Arrival of the "Doune Castle."

With Troops and Horses of the Liverpool Regiment.

Great Quantities of Stores.

Rapid Discharge.

The announcement of the arrival of the S.S Doune Castle, from Capetown, with troops, horses, and equipments, was productive of considerable excitement at the Point yesterday. The vessel arrived direct from Capetown during Saturday night, and steamed into the harbour at 7.30 a.m. yesterday, being berthed at the southern end of St. Paul's Wharf, where special facilities prevail for the disembarkation of horses, &c. In anticipation of the gathering of a large number of people, part of the wharf area had previously been fenced off so as to allow a clear space for carrying out the work of disembarkation and entrainment. This proved to be a wise precaution, for throughout the day crowds visited the wharf. In fact, as soon as the vessel's arrival was known, people began to wend their way to the Point, and during the day special cars had to be run for the convenience of the public. In the afternoon the number of Sunday-dressed people on and near the wharf must have been considerably over a thousand. Every facility for quick dispatch was provided by the Castle Company and the Railway Department, the arrangements being as near perfection as possible.

The landing of the horses and mules, numbering respectively 123 and 158, was commenced at 9.30 a.m., and the vessel was relieved of these by 2 o'clock—a smart piece of work, reflecting credit on those concerned. The animals, which appear in good condition, were then entrained.

The Doune brought the bulk of the baggage of the regiment—the 1st King's Liverpool—and this was all discharged and in trucks before evening.

The vessel also brings 111,016lb. of preserved meats and 85,000lb. of biscuits, all of which it was expected would be discharged last evening, the steamer continuing to work after dark. The regiment brings also nine buckwagons, five Scotch carts, two ammunition carts, a water cart, one maxim gun, and 90 tpoles (similar to those used for scaffolding purposes), for bridging rivers, all of which were discharged and put into trucks by sunset. The arrangements were superintended by Captain Ludlow, D.A.A.G., ably assisted by 1st Class Staff Sergt.-Major Fischer, A.S.C.

The troops comprise one non-commissioned officer, R.A.M.C., 56 native drivers under Conductors Symons and Rees (warrant officers), eight N.C.O's, and 22 men of the Army Ordnance Corps, and ten N.C.O's, and 94 men of the Liverpool Regiment under the following officers:—Major Grattan, Captain Stevensen, Sieuts. Hewart, Brush, and Vyse, and Veterinary Surgeon Williams. A special train with 4 officers, 50 men and baggage, left at 6.15 p.m., followed at 6.45 by another

8,408 174,780 29,308 67

B.—RESERVE AND AUXILIARY FORCES.

British

	All Ranks
First Class Army Reserve	7 99
Second Class Army Reserve	28,80
Militia Artillery	15,73
Militia Infantry	123,26
Yeomanry Cavalry	16,08
Volunteers—Artillery	80,76
Infantry and Mounted Rifles	130,0
	346,66

C—INDIAN AND COLONIAL.

Indian Native Army.

	Men.	Horses.	Gun
Infantry—130 Battalions	101,134		
Cavalry—37 Regiments	18,575	13,687	—
Artillery—6 Batteries	896	623	36
Engineers and miscellaneous	4,385		
	127,419	14,210	36

	Men
Two West Indian Regiments	1,82
Royal Malta Fencibles	37
Lascars, Hong-Kong and Ceylon	26
	2,45

D—COLONIAL MILITIA, VOLUNTEER, AND RESERVE FORCES.

	Men.	Horses.	Guns
North American Confederation	52,414	2,081	4
West Indies	8,952	610	2
African Colonies	4,843	1,143	1
Asia Possessions	2,116	120	
Australian Colonies	19,055	1,703	4
	81,880	5,657	14

GRAND TOTAL.

	Men.	Horses.	Guns
British Regular Army	183,248	25,853	67
Reserve and Auxiliary (British)	346,661		
Indian	127,449	14,210	3
Black (other than Indian)	2,459		
Colonial Militia, Volunteer and Reserve Forces }	81,880	5,657	14
Canadian Irregular Militia }	600,000		
Total	1,341,687	45,225	85

MOBILISATION OF THE BURGHERS.

It is reported in Johannesburg that the Transvaal War Department has completed arrangements with the Netherlands Railway Company for the mobilisation of the burghers at any given centre on the shortest notice possible. Large numbers of empty trucks have been stationed at various points along the railway lines, and have been placed at the service of Field-cornets, for the despatch of men, arms, and ammunition to the scene of general muster in case of emergency.

TENOUR OF THE REPLY.

The secret session commenced at 7 o'clock and was not concluded until a quarter past 10 For the President to be up at that time of night is a most extraordinary occurrence, and quite unique (remarks the *Leader* correspondent), and nothing but the most grave matters—from the Presidential point of view—must have been in operation to occupy his Honour's attention up to that time of the night. The answer to the invitation has been approved and forwarded and the tenour of the reply will be found to be somewhat of the following:—" The Government informs the British Government that it is impossible for it to comply with the request of the Secretary of State for the Colonies to send delegates to a joint inquiry concerning the franchise question, for the reason chiefly that

Military information on a page in the *Natal Mercury*, 14 August 1899.

intelligence forces did not escape the barrage either: 'One may not, one cannot, suspect treachery, and therefore this failure on the part of the Intelligence Department to furnish necessary details must be set down to incompetence' and 'Spion Kop has shown us that the British Army is still as virile and plucky, as vigorous in its fighting quality as it ever was, but its commanders, whose bravery and self-sacrifice nobody can deny, are still as obstinate and disinclined to learn as ever they were.'[9]

Approving this critical article fell within the jurisdiction of the Durban press censor, TO Fraser. Point No. 7 of the 'Rules for press censors in the colony of Natal' stated that nothing should appear in newspapers that could be of service to the enemy, 'But information which cannot give assistance to the enemy, such as accounts of past operations (where these do not disclose details of organisation or numbers) and criticism respecting them may be passed.' As a non-military man, Fraser, not realising that officers should not be censured, decided the article did not contravene the censorship laws.[10] Although approved by Fraser, Commandant Scott regarded the hard-hitting and honest appraisal of some of the reasons for the British defeat as improper and, under martial law, he had all the copies of *The Review and Critic* seized, ordering that the office be locked up and that 'shut' be written on the door.[11]

A letter addressed to Mark Radebe, the editor of the first African newspaper founded in Natal, *Ipepa lo Hlanga*, from John H Gama from Swaziland, did not make it beyond the censor. Although the letter dealt mostly with tribal matters and the hardship caused by the war, the problems arose with the translation. Firstly a person had to be found that could translate the letter from *isiZulu* into English. The first two translations did not satisfy the governor and it needed a third translator to unravel the message to his satisfaction. By then 40 days had elapsed.[12]

Shutting up the offices of *The Review and Critic* (*The Illustrated London News*, 10 March 1900).

Although shut down after the appearance of only four of its issues in 1900, it was still expected that the publishers of *The Review and Critic* would pay the annual license fee of £5.[13] With the newspaper closed and with little prospect of it being published again during the war that dragged on, the owner, GP Cato, sold it to a local journalist, James Harcourt Stuart, in October 1901.[14] There was, however, always room for new newspapers that had no intention of reviewing the war too critically. One such paper that was to be published in July 1900 was *The public opinion of South Africa and Durban Weekly*.[15] If the *Times of Natal* were to be believed, *The public opinion of South Africa and Durban Weekly* as a Durban publication would do well as it would experience less interference from the censor than other Natal newspapers. In the words of the *Times of Natal* '... the Durban papers seem to be free from the censorship (while) the Maritzburg journalists are its victims; what the city censor considers the correct way of interpreting his instructions the Durban censor believes to be the wrong way.'[16]

The assumption by the *Times of Natal*, that Durban-based newspapers were less enthusiastically censored, was in all probability false. Proof of this lies in articles dealing with the dilemma surrounding the arrival of the *Umbria* in Durban. While the *Natal Mercury* carried no articles on the arrival of the *Umbria*, the *Natal Witness* not only reported extensively on its arrival, but under the heading, 'The "Umbria's" Exiles. What They Say Of The Transvaal', published a complete name list of all the passengers that arrived on board as well as their comments on what was happening in the Transvaal.[17] And this, while Sergeant EN Brooke was debriefing the passengers for exactly the same information.

What all Natal newspapers shared was the burden of censorship. What had initially been implemented to deny the republics information and to keep them in the dark regarding military movements by the British, had now turned on the people it was supposed to protect. In criticism of the censorship, the *Times of Natal* claimed: '... censorship was a mighty failure, for it became a weapon wherewith to injure the loyal, and had no effect on keeping information from the enemy. Morever, when it suppressed truth, lies were circulated, and when it suppressed lies it did not take the trouble to circulate the truth.'[18]

The censorship of diplomatic mail

The privilege granted by nations to one another's diplomatic delegations, by which the premises they occupied become part of their own country's 'territory', made these missions a natural centre for looking after the interests of their subjects. Safeguarding the interests of a country's subjects in times of war could also cause embarrassment to the host country and consular service alike, as proved to be the case in Durban. The first incident occurred when a clerk in charge at the Durban post office, by oversight, opened ten letters addressed to the German consuls in the Transvaal. The clerk in question was removed and the letters were forwarded to the German consul in Lourenço Marques, along with an apology.[19]

To prevent the repetition of such an embarrassing incident, improved censorship regulations relating to mail intended for Natal were implemented on 4 December 1899. The new rules made provision for the examination of all letters in sealed bags and, if deemed necessary, would be extended 'to letters passing between friendly foreign governments and their consular representatives, whether in the enemy's country or in the Cape or Natal'. A specific emphasis was placed on checking letters from Lourenço Marques. Diplomatic letters, if and when examined, were to be looked at by experts and afterwards forwarded 'with as little indication as possible of their having been treated', that is without the stamp of the censor being applied. The censorship net for consular mail was cast even wider to include the inspection of letters from consuls to consuls, from private individuals to consuls and consuls to private individuals. The exceptions to this rule were letters addressed to or coming from the United States consuls, which were not to be opened.[20]

In reality, these regulations hardly altered the status quo, and diplomatic mail, with the exception of letters meant for the USA consuls, was still to be subjected to scrutiny, causing the German consul, JA Rechsburg, to once again complain to the colonial secretary on 3 and 4 January 1900. What infuriated him was that he had complained earlier without response. One of the letters he had just received was dated 13 December 1899 and was mailed in Durban. A clearly unhappy Rechsburg asked for an explanation to the causes of the delay of delivery, while at the same time informing the Natal government that he would report the matter to the German government. This complaint and threat had the Natal government in a quandary and therefore the post master general, WG Hamilton, approached the military censor for an explanation. In his explanation the military censor, who 'worked under the General Officer Commanding Lines of Communication', stated that they had to examine the letters under martial law and according to the regulations implemented during early December 1899. Unfortunately the letters mailed to the German consul had been delayed over the festive season. In relaying the procedure to Prime Minister Hime, all the post master general could suggest was that the date stamping, indicating when letters to consuls were mailed and forwarded for censoring to Pietermaritzburg, should be suspended. The public and consuls would then be unaware of how long letters were kept. These explanations and suggestions did not provide an answer to the query of the German consul. When the response of the Natal government finally reached the German consul, the blame for the delay was firmly placed on the shoulders of the military: ' I have the honour to inform you that the Censorship of letters is in the hands of the military censors who are working under the directions of the General Officer Commanding Lines of Communications, and that the Colonial Government has no power to interfere in the matter, the Colony being under Martial Law.'[21]

The German consul was not the only one to complain at this point. The acting consul for Austria-Hungary also complained that a parcel of letters from their consul in Cape Town had been delayed and opened in the process. The response he received was exactly the same as that forwarded to his German counterpart.[22] Soon afterwards the Netherlands consul in Durban also complained that 'The flaps of the envelopes show most distinctly that they had been opened by a steaming process, and subsequently reclosed. Although I fully understand, that under the existing circumstances, the public has to bear inconveniences, I must certainly complain of letters being opened and closed again, except in any other manner, as is generally adopted by administrations of civilised countries.' Adding to these hard-hitting words the consul added that as 'a neutral country, which lives in peace and friendship with Great Britain, I might expect my official letters would be kept unviolated, but in the state same lately arrive – as above described – I think I am entitled to ask you to kindly make strong investigations, and let me know the result.' The answer forwarded to him was by now the standard one.[23]

Why then the continued examination of consular mail? The answer is simply that some consuls knew of foreign volunteers who were joining the republican forces via Lourenço Marques. Proof of this can be gathered in the following extract taken from the letter of one German consul to another: 'The *Herzog* carried men for the Transvaal forces. Also, Portuguese, French, and Italians came by the *Campana* for the same purpose.' Such knowledge of the movements of volunteers by consuls was important information to the British military.[24] This, however, did not mean that the practice of censoring consular mail would be accepted.

The ongoing clandestine opening of diplomatic mail addressed to or emanating from the consuls in Durban by the censors soon came under scrutiny from very high authority, the director of posts and telegraphs for the Netherlands, Mr Hamlany. Hamlany first complained on 13 January 1900 that letters addressed to the Netherlands consul, JHA Balwe, in Durban, from various other consuls, were opened at the Durban post office. The second time round the complaint was of a much graver nature. Two letters, one from the Netherlands minister of foreign affairs and the other from the Netherlands vessel of war, *Friesland*, addressed to Consul Balwe in Durban were opened. The request from Hamlany was simple, but loaded with serious diplomatic and political consequences: '... institute a very serious enquiry on this new and very grave attempt on the inviolable secrecy of correspondence and ... you will know how to put an end at once to such proceedings. You will oblige me a reply as early as possible ...' By now the examination of consular mail was a political matter rather than a military one and the Natal government could no longer protect the military by merely blaming them; they had to be confronted. The reply of the general officer commanding lines of communication, General J Wolfe-Murray, took very little cognisance of the grave diplomatic situation. The letters in question were opened by the CID in Durban on behalf of the military, and his suggested reply therefore was that 'It is regretted that at the time the letters in question passed through the Durban Post Office, a good deal of irregularities occurred, and the instructions issued on the subject of censorship of letters were imperfectly adhered to. As these irregularities happened some months ago, the Government of Natal took steps to deal with the matter; and on the behalf of the Natal Government I am to express my sympathy for the misadventure.' This response did not appeal to Post Master General Hamilton, since it shifted the blame to the post office. He

referred the Natal government to the regulations of 5 December 1899, which allowed the military censors access to all diplomatic mail with the exception of that to and from the USA. As far as censorship was concerned, the post office therefore had nothing to do with it. Whether the Natal government was happy that the military had spoken on their behalf, could not be ascertained.[25]

The complaint from the Netherlands was followed by one from the German ambassador to Britain, Count Metternich. The reply of the Natal government to this was to forward a similar reply to the one suggested by Wolf-Murray. Escaping responsibility in this manner was possible since the dates of the letters complained about fitted into the period when tampering with all consular mail could be blamed upon 'errors committed owing to the inexperience of officers and other employers which led to certain of the incidents to which the German government have called attention'.[26]

The results of the constant complaints by consuls and related parties about the examination of letters gave rise to a new set of regulations pertaining to diplomatic correspondence, which differed very little from the previous regulations. The military authorities in Natal could examine, at their discretion, all consular correspondence, except letters from or to the USA consuls, and correspondence between foreign governments and their consuls. All other consular mail deemed necessary to be investigated needed to be forwarded to Pietermaritzburg, where it would be censored by experts with as little indication as possible of anything having been opened. Such correspondence would then be forwarded, returned to senders or suppressed. To both the Natal government and consuls this was a great improvement of the system, as the Natal government was now relieved of the responsibility of carrying the burden on behalf of the military, while consuls could expect that at least inter-consular correspondence would not be censored.[27]

The Netherlands cruiser, *Friesland*, visited Durban during the week of 13 November 1899. The purpose of the visit was to make known officially the neutrality of the Netherlands. The Dutch consul in Durban, JHA Balwe, with the assistance of Governor Walter Hely-Hutchinson and Commandant Percy Scott facilitated the visit.

Kaiserlich
Deutsches Konsulat
für Natal.

65/00

D'Urban, 3ᵈ Jany 1900

Sir,

I have the honour to bring to your knowledge that already in November last year letters addressed to this Consulate had been opened by the Censor, and on my complaint made through my lawyer Mr G A de R. Labistour I received the enclosed letter written by the Postmaster of this town.

Today I have again to complain about a letter from the German Line which had been opened by the Censor and therefore I kindly request you to give such instructions that our letters for this Consulate will in future not be opened and no delay caused to their delivery.

I shall be obliged for the return of the enclosures.

I have the honor to be,
Sir,
Your obedient Servant
F.A. Hülsberg
Actg. Imperial German Consul

To the Honourable
the Colonial Secretary
P. M. Burg

The lifting of control of mail between consuls did not apply to cablegrams and, consequently, the complaints continued to come in. Acting German Consul V Mandelsloh complained to Governor Hely-Hutchinson that a cablegram that had arrived for him from the German consul in Lourenço Marques at 18:40 on 19 March had only been delivered during the morning of 21 March. He requested the governor '... to instruct the postal authorities to avoid such delay in future'. Hely-Hutchinson seemed more worried about the 'somewhat curt tone' of the letter and he noted '... that it is not to be expected that letters from Acting Consul should be framed with that reward for courtesy which is usual in ordinary diplomatic correspondence'. Whether the lack of courtesy could be ascribed to the position of Mandelsloh or his disgust at the treatment of their correspondence is hard to tell, but Hely-Hutchinson also complained of the curt tone adopted towards him by the acting consul for Austro-Hungary, Mr Auerswald.[28]

The recriminations from the various consuls and mounting pressure from white countries on the opening of the mail to and from their Durban consulate started to have repercussions. Governor Hely-Hutchinson felt 'that the inconvenience and friction caused by the practice are greater than any other advantage derived therefrom'. In this he had the support of General Wolfe-Murray who, likewise, regarded it as 'not worth the candle'. As a result the military reduced the censorship of consular mail to the barest minimum, which explained the lack of complaints after April 1900. The military could, however, not discontinue censorship of the indicated consular correspondence as the orders came from Britain, and the imperial government alone could adjust the ruling. With this support, Hely-Hutchinson approached the imperial government to have the censorship of any consular mail terminated. The Natal governor, at that point, suggested an underhand tactic. The various governments concerned should not be informed about the discontinuing of the practice of examining consular letters. His rationale was that the fear that consular letters could still be opened would prevent them from using such letters as 'a safe channel of communication with the enemy'.[29] Such callous disregard for international diplomacy did not find favour with the imperial government and the realistic features of the governor's recommendation were adopted so that the practice of opening consular correspondence was terminated.[30] Thereafter, complaints of tampering with consular mail virtually ceased. A single event did, however, flare up in September 1901. A letter addressed by CF Butz, a resident of the Eshowe concentration camp, to the German consul in Durban was partially opened, in ignorance, by the camp superintendent. Although a minor incident committed in innocence, Butz and the German consuls in Durban and Cape Town exploited the incident to their full moral advantage.[31]

In the process of censoring diplomatic mail, one loophole existed: correspondence addressed to the USA consulate in Lourenço Marques was not to be touched. When this became public knowledge, private individuals and especially banks, with the apparent co-operation of the American consul in Lourenço Marques, found it easy to escape censorship when forwarding correspondence to the Transvaal.[32]

The censorship of private mail

The censorship rules for private correspondence were divided into three categories: those pertaining to foreign countries, those relating to the Transvaal, the Orange Free State and Lourenço Marques, and correspondence within Natal. All the letters to and from foreign countries were to be examined by experts. After examination, these letters were carefully closed, and traces of any interference was, as far as possible, removed before forwarding them to the addressee or returning them to the sender. It was deemed very undesirable either to forward to addressee or return to sender letters labelled 'opened under martial law'. All letters to the Transvaal and the Free State were to be examined, and only those which appeared harmless, or which were bank drafts, were allowed to pass. Those not allowed to pass were either returned to sender, or suppressed or retained, depending on the advice of the censor. As far as local correspondence between British colonies and areas, and Natal was concerned, letters were only to be examined in the case of their being sent by certain individuals and, before that could be done, the permission of the officer commanding lines of communication needed to be obtained and kept on file.[33]

Monitoring the letters bound for overseas did bear some fruit regarding contraband trading. H van der Kuip, in a letter to his brother in the Netherlands, explained that he had already been in Durban for 18 days, after the ship he had worked on, the *Banque Cambria* was sold, having discharged its contraband cargo intended for the Transvaal one night. He clearly did not like Durban, as he described it as no place for strangers, especially if they spoke Dutch, as police were everywhere.[34]

The monitoring of other overseas-bound correspondence seems merely to have caused inconvenience to the addressee, rather than providing information on military matters. In a letter to the attorney-general of Natal, Jules D'Hotman complained that none of the letters, photographs, newspapers and Christmas cards he had mailed to Belgium between 15 December 1899 and 19 February 1900 had reached their destination. To ensure that his latest letter reached his youngest sister, 'the wife of Emile Vermeulen, a retired Belgian Banker, residing at one of her own private residences, the Palace Constantin, Nice, France' he called on the attorney-general for assistance.[35]

The greatest emphasis in censoring private correspondence was placed on mail moving to and from the Transvaal, Free State and Lourenço Marques. The bulk of these letters were of a personal nature and contained no information of any use to the British. Some valuable information was, however, gained such as the names and movements of foreigners who travelled via Lourenço Marques to join the Boer forces. Henry Dubreuil, in a letter to Mrs Dubreuil residing at 121 Princess Street, Durban, pointed out that seven French officers were on board a French steamer bound for Lourenço Marques. There were also 15 other foreigners: Italians, Greeks, Dutch and Germans, all heading for the Transvaal. They passed a British man-of-war and Dubreuil gloated: 'How enraged they must have been on board the British war vessel to see the greetings that were exchanged between the French steamer and the Dutch

Commandant, Durban, to Governor.

Commandant's Office, Durban,
29th January, 1900.

warded to His Excellency the Governor for information
the High Commissioner.

letter points out that German Steamers and French
amers are carrying men for the Transvaal Forces.

(Sd) Percy Scott,
Captain R.N. Commandant, Durban.

nslation received from Press Censor.

Extract from one German Consul's letter to another.

"The Herzog carried men for the Transvaal Forces.
lso Portuguese, French and Italians came by the
ampana for the same purpose".

man-of-war and that all those on board the French boat were enemies going to fight against them in the Transvaal while they were powerless to arrest them for we were in Portuguese waters.'[36] Letters with a similar content were from then on intercepted with regularity. Some of the information gathered included the following: Wilhelm Rantenberg travelled on a French steamer to Lourenço Marques to enlist with the Boers;[37] Captain F Stockl of the Austro-Hungarian army offered his services to the Transvaal;[38] Melchior M Velbrey of Alton, Sioux County, USA was on his way to enlist at Komatipoort.[39] A letter from Fried Krupp, from Essen in Germany, mentioned the supply of guns to the Transvaal.[40] Others from the republics invariably dealt with personal matters relating to the war. An example is the letter from Kate of Doornfontein, Johannesburg, to her cousin, LN McDonald of Airfield House, Pinetown, in which she noted that Eddie, along with all her brothers, was at the front on the Boer side.[41]

That the censorship of private letters, especially those bound for Lourenço Marques, was not well received is true. This dissatisfaction caused an agent of a steam ship company in Port Elizabeth to want to 'avoid the censoring of French letters by procuring the Post Bag before it goes to the Post Office'.[42] Although the censors could prevent such an event, they could not prevent the easiest way of circumventing the censorship process, that is taking letters by hand to Lourenço Marques.

Censorship of POW correspondence

The rules for censorship of letters from Boer POWs in Durban stipulated that they were to be sent to the censor in Durban, who would examine the contents and then stamp the letters, charging 2½ pence per ½ oz. The mail would thereafter be forwarded in the usual manner via Lourenço Marques.[43] The POW letters censored generally divulged personal emotions and intimate details, such as the letter from A O'Neill, a POW on board the *Catalonia*, in a letter to his mother and sister at Cookhouse in the Cape Colony, congratulating the former on her birthday and informing them that he had surrendered to the British at Ladysmith. In the process he provided information for which he had been promised some reward which he was yet to receive.[44] Letters with much more serious repercussions were those written by Natal Afrikaners imprisoned on board the *Catalonia* as POWs. In their letters they all wrote how much they missed their families, and asked for simple household things, stating their belief that all was in the hands of God, but in the process they revealed themselves, and others to be rebels, as can be gathered from the table below.

All the replies to the letters from the prisoners were to be addressed to the commandant of Durban. Although no important information was revealed in the POW letters, the authors did provide a glimpse of life on board the prison ship, their needs, their health and their emotions.[45]

Letters from POWs during the more advanced stages of the conflict provided more information, particularly regarding the participation of individuals in the war.[46] Particularly useful to the British military in oppressing the rebellion amongst Afrikaners in the Cape Colony were the letters written by prisoners on board the *Manilla* to family members and friends. Although aware by now that all letters were censored and that incriminating evidence could be used against the author or people they corresponded with, it still happened that incriminating evidence was revealed. Jacobus Theunissen, in a letter to Martha Human of Langverwacht, Riviersonderend, near Caledon declared that he was a British subject who originated from New Hantam, Naauwpoort in the Cape Colony. Such an admission was a giveaway and meant that he could be tried as a rebel, facing either the death penalty or stiff jail sentence.[47] The information gained from censoring the letters from POWs did not only provide useful information on rebellious British subjects in Natal and the Cape Colony, but even helped in casting the net wider, to Britain itself. Charles Dunlop, a member of the Irish Brigade until its disbandment, departed for London via Lourenço Marques. In the process he also left a letter addressed to his father, Frank Dunlop, a POW in Ceylon (Sri Lanka). In his letter, Dunlop Junior provided the addresses of the people he would be residing with in Britain, and a sure beaten track to the doorsteps of Mrs Allen, 21 Highgate Hill, London and Mrs Ruston, Inglenest, Horuchurch, Essex.[48]

Summary of the contents of the letters of Natal rebels and the sentences passed on them

NAME	SUMMARY OF CONTENTS OF LETTER	SENTENCE PASSED
JD de Klerk	To his wife, c/o Mrs Dewar, Navigation Collieries, Hattingspruit. Asks that clothes and money be sent. Complains about the food and being ill.	Deemed not to be Natal rebel.
JC Buys	To his father and mother, Kliprug, Dannhauser. Asks for £10 from his box at home. He, Piet and Izak would share the money.	8 months in prison and a fine of £100 or a further 3 months imprisonment.
A Eicker	To his wife, Angora Hill, Dannhauser. In his letter he provided the names of all the Natal rebels on board, stating that all were seasick.	5 months in prison.
HAI Davel	To his mother and sisters, Kliprug, Dannhauser. Asked for £8 to be sent. Mentioned being well treated. Suit, vest, socks and velvet trousers to be forwarded, plus a shirt for Jan.	9 months in prison and a fine of £100 or a further 6 months.
BJ Badenhorst	To his wife, Kempenveldt, Dundee. Asked for a box of clothes and £8. Warned her not to write about the war.	£100 or 3 months in prison.
HH Laatz	To his mother, Beith, Dundee. Asked to be sent some money if possible. Seasickness.	6 months in prison.
SL Strydom	To his wife, Dundee. Asked for clothes, biscuits. Warned her not to write on war matters. Sent 10 kisses to his daughter Tyra.	2 years in prison.
CJ Laas	To his wife, Angora Hill, Dannhauser. Sea-sick. News that Barend was still in hospital.	10 months in prison.
CJ Labuschagne	To his mother, J.Laas, Angora Hill, Dannhauser. Asked her to send the six of them £1 each. Requested biscuits and two rolls of tobacco for brother Andries. Asked that they do not let the farming deteriorate.	10 months in prison.
JC Buys	To his uncle, JC Buys, Vrischgewaag, Weenen. Mentioned that Groot Izak, Piet, H. Davel and his son are on board.	
JC Buys	To his brother-in-law, JP Lotter, Bergvliet, Middelrus. Seasick.	
JJM Buys	To his wife, Kliprug, Dannhauser. Seasick.	8 months in prison and a fine of £100 or a further 3 months.
JP Buys	To his wife, Kliprug, Dannhauser. Seasick. Asked for £3, clothes, tobacco, a comb, needle and cotton.	

The censorship of cables and telegrams

The rules for cables and telegrams, whether they were private or for the press, were that all communications should be shown to the press censor. Only after he had passed the item with the code word 'Passdurl' written on it, could it be despatched to other stations. The press censor could stop delivery of and retain all private telegrams. In such a case, the sender was notified as soon as possible. During the early part of the war, members of the public were allowed to use codes. This did not meet the approval of Fraser, who believed that codes could be used to convey secret messages or be altered to serve a subversive purpose. He thought the use of codes by civilians should be prohibited during wartime except in the case of banks. For the same reasons, the military halted the use of all codes during the early part of 1900, including their use by banks. The result was disastrous for financial institutions, and they came to a standstill. Fearing economic chaos, an exception was made for banks from 20 April 1900 onwards, on condition that they provided a translation of the codes they used to the censor and that the codes only be used to indicate the sum of money, the office of origin, and the authenticity of documents. The codes were only to be used between England and colonial banks and not between banks themselves. From the same date, the Reuters correspondents were allowed to use their 'indicator' words, which registered telegraphic names for the sender and addressee combined, to bring the news of the war to Britain.[49]

Mercantile houses were not permitted to send coded or cypher messages. This frustrated and hampered businesses immensely. On 28 August 1900, the secretary of the Durban chamber of commerce, W Burton, informed the Natal government 'that my committee are of opinion that the time has now arrived when some relaxation of the present restrictions over cypher telegraph messages might be allowed, so that individual firms may be permitted to telegraph in cypher especially between Natal and London.' Via the governor and high commissioner the military agreed to this. With censorship relaxed, and in an attempt to speed up the process of implementation, the offer by the Durban chamber of commerce to place at the disposal of the censor in Durban copies of the code books that might be used was accepted. In the end eight different codes were used by mercantile houses.[50]

The daunting task of censoring the cables and telegrams was carried out by TO Fraser and his staff. In May 1901 alone, 7 000 cable messages were censored. Of these 3 600 were coming into the country, while 3 400 were despatched. This equated to 84 000 per year or 200 per day. This excluded inland telegrams. Many of these messages, especially the press messages, were not short. During this time, other routine work had to be handled, while the censor office remained open to anyone for enquiries or to provide favours. When messages were thought to be undesirable, the senders were not informed, as that would place them on guard and prevent the military or police from taking action. In practice such action hardly ever took place.[51]

The result of censorship was that it deterred the public from attempting to send useless messages, especially by cable, while it also prevented Boer informants from trying to get undesirable messages out of Durban. Generally, people did not want to reveal private matters to a stranger and, therefore, would not communicate in written format. Others communicated as if the censor did not exist at all, and useful information was gathered such as that pertaining to the arrival of foreigners who wanted to join the Boer commandos in Lourenço Marques, while British merchants who traded with the enemy were also exposed. Such information was immediately forwarded to the chief of intelligence, or the officer commanding lines of communication, or the civil administration and more specifically, the commandant of Durban. Whether any benefit was ever derived from their work was not revealed to the censors.

1. PRO, WO 33/198: report on the work of censors in Durban, 19.7.1901.

2. PAR, PMG 83: letter postmaster Durban to postmaster general, 12.1.1900.

3. PAR, AGO I/III/75: minute paper on censorship of private letters passing through Durban post office, 13.9.1900.

4. PAR, PMG 83: documents surrounding post office clerk H Waring, 11.1899.

5. PRO, WO 33/198: report on the work of censors in Durban, 19.7.1901.

6. PAR, CSO 1689: appointment notice of a new press censor, 24.6.1901.

7. PRO, WO 33/198: rules for press censors in Natal, 12.4.1900.

8. PRO, WO 33/198: memorandum on the subject of ocean cablegrams during war at Durban, 25.6.1901.

9. *The Review and Critic*, 3.2.1900.

10. PRO, WO 33/198: rules for press censors in Natal, 12.4.1900.

11. PAR, GH 556: letter P Scott to W Hely-Hutchinson, 3.2.1900.

12. PAR, GH 562: intercepted letter addressed to MS Radebe, 28.6.1900.

13. PAR, CSO 1640: renewal of annual license of *The Review and Critic*, 6.2.1900.

14. PAR, CSO 1689: document on GP Cato ceasing to be the proprietor of *The Review and Critic*, 14.10.1901.

15. PAR, CSO 1652: declaration and bond for new newspaper, 11.7.1900.

16. *Times of Natal*, 3.12.1900.

17. *Natal Witness*, 21.5.1900; 22.5.1900.

18. *Times of Natal*, 3.12.1900.

19. PRO, CO 179/207: telegram W Hely-Hutchinson to J Chamberlain, 24.11.1899.

20. PAR, GH 531: report on military censors in Natal and the Cape Colony, 4.12.1899.

21. PAR, CSO 1637: letter in which the German consul complains about the opening of his letters, 3.1.1900.

22. PAR, CSO 1637: letter in which the Austro-Hungary consul complains about the delay in his mail, 4.1.1900.

23. PAR, CSO 1638: letter in which the Netherlands consul complains about the opening of his mail, 17.1.1900.

24. PRO, CO 179/209: extract from the letter from the German consul, 19.1.1900.

25. PAR, PMG 83: complaint Netherlands director of posts and telegraphs regarding the opening of mail, 13.2.1900.

26. PRO, CO 179/213: complaint by German ambassador to Britain regarding the opening of mail in Natal, 20.6.1900.

27. PRO, CO 179/210: rules for censorship of correspondence in Natal, 1.3.1900.

28. PRO, CO 179/211: memo on censors detained consular telegram, 23.3.1900.

29. PRO, CO 179/213: memo's on censorship of consular letters, 30.6.1900–20.6.1900.

30. PRO, CO 179/216: complaint by German ambassador to Britain about the opening of mail, 5.10.1900.

31. PAR, GH 867: letter from acting German consul complaining about the partial opening of a letter, 20.9.1901.

32. PAR, GH 531: minute paper on correspondence for the Transvaal is forwarded through the American consul at Lourenço Marques, 26.2.1900.

33. PAR, GH 531: instructions to censors, 14.3.1900.

34. PAR, GH 559: letter H van der Kuip to CA van der Kuip, 16.6.1900.

35. PRO, CO 179/210: letter of complaint by JD Hotman, 13.3.1900.

36. PRO, CO 179/209: letter H Dubreuil to R Dubreuil, 26.1.1900.

37. PAR, GH 531: letter P Scott to W Hely-Hutchinson, 20.2.1900.

38. PRO, CO 179/210: letter W Hely-Hutchinson to J Chamberlain, 10.3.1900.

39. PAR, GH 560: letter MM Velbrey to *The Alton Democrat*, 25.6.1900.

40. PAR, GH 560: letter commandant Durban to W Hely-Hutchinson, 28.8.1900.

41. PAR, GH 562: minute paper regarding intercepted letters connected with the Cape Colony, 18.10.1900.

42. PRO, CO 170/209: letter TO Fraser to commandant Durban, 9.1.1900.

43. PAR, GH 531: rules for censorship of correspondence in Natal, 1.3.1900.

44. PAR, GH 562: intercepted letters of Boer POWs on board the *Catalonia*, 23.5.1900.

45. PAR, GH 559: intercepted letters of Natal rebels on board the *Catalonia*, 23.5.1900.

46. PAR, GH 562: intercepted letters connected with the Cape Colony, 17.10.1900.

47. PAR, GH 561: list of letters from prisoners of war on board the *Manilla* to relatives in the Cape Colony, 10.5.1901.

48. PAR, GH 562: letter on the involvement of the Dunlop's in the war, 21.2.1901.

49. PRO, CO 179/210: rules for guidance of press censorship, 27.11.1899.

50. PAR, CSO 1657: Durban chamber of commerce asks for the relaxing of restrictions on cable messages in code, 3.9.1900.

51. PRO, WO 33/198: report on the work of censors in Durban, 19.7.1901.

PART SEVEN

THE WAR WITHIN THE WAR

Alexandra Square at the Point (PAR).

CHAPTER 21

TRADING WITH THE ENEMY: THE PRIZE COURT

Brian Kearney and Josh McCracken

'There cannot be a war of arms and a peace of commerce'.[1]
Durban was able to fulfil a gateway role in many ways by providing a place for the comings and goings of warriors, goods and animals, and was thus not necessarily the final destination of those movements. However, it could also perform the role of a gateway for a myriad of clandestine goods. So Durban was also involved in an aspect of the Anglo-Boer War which has attracted little attention from historians of the conflict, the British assault on the enemy's commerce. In many respects this became 'a war within a war'.

The nature of the port town in terms of economics and trade had, by the end of the nineteenth century, come to be largely characterised as a transit place, particularly for the export and import of goods to and from the hinterland and especially for the two Boer republics which had now become the enemy. Since it was the nearest British port to the initial battlefields, and was also the traditional sea link with the outside world for the Boer republics, Durban inevitably became a focal point of illicit trading activities and was chosen as the site of a British prize court. It was not a role from which the Natalians concerned derived much satisfaction.

By 1894, a completed railway line linked the Transvaal to Delagoa Bay in Mozambique, and this offered an alternative transit port to Durban. Lourenço Marques, being under the neutral Portuguese, was to become an easier option for the illegal movement of goods and people.

Leading Durban firms which had branches in the Orange Free State, the Transvaal or Lourenço Marques, were supplied and controlled from head offices in Natal. British firms trading with the Boer republics had previously used the port of Durban, but the war put an end to the legitimacy of such arrangements. Transit trade, however, was not easy to stop, and thus for the first part of the war many consignments of goods arrived in Durban where they were prevented from reaching their intended destinations in the hinterland. Neutral French, Dutch and German firms were entitled under international law to trade with the neutral Portuguese port at Delagoa Bay, except in contraband, but their pro-Boer sympathies reinforced the resentment aroused by British surveillance and interference.

The *Avondale Castle*

In the early hours of the morning of Wednesday 18 October 1899, the *Avondale Castle*, a passenger liner of the Castle Mail Packets Company, was approaching Lourenço Marques in Delagoa Bay. It had voyaged overnight from Durban on an urgent mission to go to the relief of at least 1 000 refugees in that town. The British consul in Lourenço Marques, Carnegie Ross, had requested assistance for these refugees from Governor Hely-Hutchinson who, in turn, had asked the Durban port captain whether a suitable ship was available. About 25 miles (40 km) off Cape Inyaca, a Royal naval vessel, HMS *Partridge* bore down on the *Avondale Castle* and forced her to stop. Commander Hunt of the *Partridge* boarded the ship and demanded her papers. He informed Captain Brown that she was being seized as she had some £25 000 of gold specie on board which belonged to the government of the ZAR, and he then ordered her to return to Durban under escort. A guard of four bluejackets and an officer were placed on board.[2] This was the first ship seizure of the war and was inevitably marked by contradiction and controversy.

What had transpired on Tuesday, the day before the seizure, was that the ship's owners had been requested by the National Bank of the ZAR in Durban to carry the gold to Lourenço Marques. Through the collector of customs in Durban, they had questioned the Natal government as to whether or not this gold was to be considered contraband. The governor and his advisors requested time to consider the question. The advice which the governor received from the attorney-general, Bale, was that it would be illegal to seize the gold specie. The ship had been due to sail at 11:00 that morning, but the governor, in attempting to clarify the issue, requested a slight delay in her departure until the afternoon. Having already promised the governor to proceed to Delagoa Bay with all haste to relieve the stranded refugees, the ship's owners informed the collector that they would detain the *Avondale Castle* only until 15:00 that afternoon, which was the latest time at which the ship could safely leave the harbour. A few minutes before 15:00 when Captain Brown and the agent of the Union-Castle Line, Wisely, were interviewing the collector, Mayston, about the specie, a telegram was received from Hely-Hutchinson authorising the ship to proceed to sea. When Hely-Hutchinson changed his mind a short while later, after receiving a telegram from High Commissioner Milner, the ship had already left.

On arrival back in Durban on 19 October 1899, at about 2:30 in the early morning, the vessel was boarded by the naval authorities, who removed the specie to HMS *Tartar* and ordered the *Avondale Castle* to return to Lourenço Marques to collect the refugees, which it duly did. Captain Morgan of the *Tartar* explained to the secretary of the Admiralty:

> Acting on your instructions conveyed to me by your telegram No. 231 of 18 October, I proceeded immediately on board the *Avondale Castle*, and found that the specie of the value of £24 197 was in the ship ... I took charge of the specie and had it embarked on board the tug under a guard of Marines, and after

having given a receipt to Mr S.C.Brown the master of the *Avondale Castle* I proceeded into harbour where the specie was transferred to HMS *Tartar*.[3]

Joseph Chamberlain at the colonial office, aware of the important role which shipping could play in subverting military efforts, had sent telegrams on 11 October 1899 to the Cape and Natal with instructions to 'search all British ships on the high seas and in British waters for contraband of war or any goods whatever being the property of the enemy's government'. On the 13th however, he contradicted this instruction saying 'that no ships were to be searched, and that enemy's goods were only to be searched on land'. The Admiralty was asked to give similar instructions to the naval authorities. On the same day, however, the foreign office, in ignorance of these instructions and counter instructions, wrote to the admiralty 'suggesting that if goods in the nature of contraband of war are carried in a neutral vessel and there are reasonable grounds for the belief that their real destination is the enemy or the agent of an enemy in a neutral port the searching vessel would be justified in bringing the ship carrying these goods into port for adjudication'. This instruction was sent out by the Admiralty on 14 October 1899 and thus the admiral in Simonstown had received a very different instruction from the governors of the Cape and Natal.[4] However, given the subsequent way in which the navy aggressively seized ships and cargo, it appears that they were enthusiastic about following this instruction, perhaps in an attempt to justify their existence in a war which had no maritime dimension. Needless to say, however, the owners of the *Avondale Castle* were extremely disturbed by these events and the case was to become an important one in the records of the prize court of Natal.

The authorisation of the Natal prize court

Under the Colonial Courts of Admiralty Act of 1890, both the supreme courts of the Cape and Natal had unlimited civil jurisdiction over the respective colonies and thus became colonial courts of admiralty. Section 2(3) of the act effectively endowed the colonial courts with the same jurisdiction as was enjoyed by the high court in England. A proviso in the act also conferred prize jurisdiction on such colonial courts of the Admiralty, but they could not execute this 'unless for the time being duly authorised'. Thus the Natal supreme court apparently required a specific commission or warrant to exercise this jurisdiction and to act as a prize court.[5]

The very unusual circumstances of the authorisation of the prize court explains much about the state of confusion which surrounded it. The procurator-general, Henry Bale, sought advice from his fellow attorney-general in the Cape about a host of issues; David Calder, the solicitor in prize, searched for published works which could assist with practice and procedure; Hely-Hutchinson, the governor and Hime, the prime minister, bombarded Milner with questions and problems. Milner, in turn referred these to Chamberlain, the secretary of state for the colo-

Joseph Chamberlain, secretary of state for the colonies (Wilson).

HMS *Tartar* anchored in the Bluff channel (KCL).

Alfred Milner, high commissioner of South Africa (Wilson).

Captain Percy Scott (Burne).

Sir Michael Gallwey (Kearney collection).

PROCLAMATION.

WHEREAS a Warrant bearing date the twenty-third day of October, One thousand eight hundred and ninety-nine, given under the hands of two of the Commissioners for executing the office of Lord High Admiral of the United Kingdom of Great Britain and Ireland and the Dominions thereunto belonging, and under the Seal of the Office of Admiralty, was, by authority of Her Majesty's Letters Patent, addressed to the Supreme Court of this Colony, requiring it, upon any Proclamation being made by the Vice- Admiral for the time being of Natal that war has broken out between Her Majesty and any Foreign State, <u>and not otherwise</u>, to take cognizance of, and judicially to proceed in, Prize Matters as indicated in the said Warrant.

NOW, THEREFORE, for the purposes aforesaid, I, by the authority vested in me as Vice-Admiral for the time being of Natal, do hereby make known and proclaim that war has broken out between Her Majesty's Government and the Government of the South African Republic and also between Her Majesty's Government and the Government of the Orange Free State.

Walter Hely Hutchinson.

24 th November, 1899.

Vice-Admiral for the time being of Natal.

nies. Chamberlain's staff were called in to provide responses. Sometimes the matters were taken to Lord Salisbury, the British prime minister, who in turn sought the advice of the law officers to the crown. Some issues were even referred to his cabinet for clarification.

Ultimately, the extraordinary paradox which characterised the work of the Natal prize court was that its deliberations were very often entirely overruled by the cabinet, or Salisbury, or more frequently, by Chamberlain himself. In many cases, no sooner had Bale and Calder begun to set the wheels of the court going, than an instruction would be received from 'on-high' to release a ship and its cargo. Apparently the major reason for such interference in the work of the court was the unexpected fear of international repercussions which followed the seizure of foreign ships in international waters. What then was the point of a colonial court of prize?

The prize court constituted

Prize was property captured from an enemy at sea in times of war and prize courts were courts specially constituted to decide on disputes arising from such seizures, according to international law.[6] Charles Smythe could have had the prize court in mind when he complained that the imperial authorities ignored the colonists except when there was some disagreeable task to be performed. The establishment and conduct of the prize court was one such task imposed on the supreme court of Natal. A judge of the supreme court presided at its sittings, the attorney-general of the colony became its procurator-general and the sheriff of Natal the marshal of the court. The vigour with which the commandants of Durban, especially Captain Percy Scott, pursued suspects created tension between the military and civilian authorities. It also led to unease for the procurator-general over legal niceties and incurred the indignation of foreign consuls on political grounds. Above all, it stirred resentment in commercial circles at genuine or alleged high-handedness.

The Natal prize court was commissioned by proclamation on 25 November 1899, as the first and only such court to exist in Natal. The lord's commissioner of the Admiralty had decreed that such a court could not be established under the normal warrant within the Prize Courts Act of 1894, but that the queen's proctor would issue the supreme court of Natal with a warrant to establish such a court at Durban 'with all possible despatch'.[7] Before Hely-Hutchinson issued a proclamation, the papers were referred to the chief justice, Sir Michael Gallwey, who approved the warrant. He requested copies of the rules to be furnished to the judge's library and to Durban, where sittings would be held in the circuit court building for the trial of prize cases. During the months when the circuit courts were held in Durban, the judge, to whom the circuit court of the district of Durban was assigned, would preside over the prize court. During the other months this would be the judge to whom chamber work was assigned.[8] Interestingly, it was only for the purposes of this commissioning of the court that the governor for the first time issued a proclamation that Natal was at war with the Orange Free State and the South African Republic.

The attorney-general of Natal, Henry Bale, was appointed as procurator-general of the prize court. Under him a young, Durban attorney, David Calder of the firm of Calder & Calder, was appointed as solicitor-in-prize to handle the preparation of the cases, much as a prosecutor would. Actual seizures of contraband were to be carried out by the deputy marshall, though he was not always available for the task, and was missing when both the *Herzog* and the *Bundesrath* were seized.[8] Initially confusion as to the actual seizures resulted when the Admiralty in Simonstown, which was unaware of the role of marshal and deputy marshal in the Natal supreme court, ordered the navy to hand ships and goods over to the collector of customs, as was the Cape procedure. This confusion was to lead to Mayston adopting a fairly active role in the entire process of the seizure of contraband.

But much confusion also arose, largely from the unfamiliarity of the situation. It had been a long time since Britain had been involved in a war against whites, armed with similar weapons, pursuing a comparable lifestyle and participating in international trade. The last occasion on which it had been necessary to operate British prize courts had been during the Crimean War, 40 odd years before. Prize courts had, however, been used during the American Civil War in 1863, which at times impacted on British shipping. The case of the seizure of the *Springbok*, a British barque, was cited in the correspondence concerning the Royal Navy's seizure of the *Bundesrath* and the *General*.[9]

Consequently, even the lawyers were unfamiliar with prize court procedure and there was a dearth of information on the subject. From the outset, Bale raised a series of important questions of legal principles concerning the nature of shipping neutrality, neutral destinations, trading with the enemy and contraband cargo. He quoted English and American authorities on these subjects, which provided contradictory advice. On these grounds, he requested the governor to seek clarification from either Milner or Chamberlain. He had also been issued with a set of Admiralty instructions which decreed that: 'All merchant ships (wishing?) to go to South African ports may be searched for contraband of war, wherever found, and of whatever nationality they may be; if it is found in ship and there are reasonable grounds for suspicion that it is intended for the

Sir Henry Bale

Sir Henry Bale, KCMG, KC was born in Pietermaritzburg in 1854. He had been educated at Pietermaritzburg College and Exeter Grammar School. Bale was admitted as an attorney to the Natal supreme court in 1875 and as an advocate in 1878. After serving on a number of statutory boards and councils, he was appointed a nominee member of the Natal legislative council in 1890 and, from 1893, was elected as a member of the legislative assembly for the city of Pietermaritzburg until 1901. He assumed the position of attorney-general and (unusually) minister of education in 1897. In 1901 he became the chief justice of the colony. During the absence of Governor McCullum, he acted as deputy governor from 1 December 1901.

DATE OF SEIZURE	NAME OF SHIP	GOODS SEIZED	MARKS	REASONS FOR SEIZURE
19.10.1899	GUELPH	303 Boxes bullets 75 cases empty cartridges 10 cases wads	ZAF	Property of the ZAR. Now in Queen's Warehouse, Point
	UMBILO	100 Boxes bullets 55 Boxes cartridge cases I case machinery 1 case cartridge cases and wadding 9 Cases uniforms	ZAF Govt SAR	Property of the ZAR. Now in Queen's Warehouse, Point ZAR. Queen's Warehouse, Point
	ROLLS	11 600 Railway sleepers	OVSR	Property of the Orange Free State Govt. Now in Railway Station at Durban but possibly taken by the Military Authorities
	GAUL	1 case Post Office boxes	SACA 3567	ZAR property. In Queen's Warehouse, Point
	KANYLER	4 cases twine	De Waal & Co.	ZAR property. In Queen's Warehouse, Point
26.10.1899	UMTALI	250 Boxes bullets 150 cases empty cartridges 14 cases safety cartridges 12 cases wads 1 case jute wads 1 case empty cartridges 1 box lamp reflectors	ZAF Baviaanspoort 4336/Barbeton NZASM	ZAR property. In Queen's Warehouse, Point Seized as Munitions of war Presumably the property of the Netherlands Railway. In Queen's Warehouse
	COUNTY OF FLINT	1 322 rails		Property of the Orange Free State Govt. Now on wharf in Durban
	KANYLER	95 cases telegraphic material	Vryheid Vootpandrift Railway	Seized as being ZAR property. Now in Queen's warehouse
	GUELPH	2 cases carbolic powder	Pretoria Government	Property of ZAR. Now in Queen's warehouse
	ARAB	50 cases potatoes	JWB & Co.Ltd.	Consigned to JWBeckett & Co. who is a Transvaal agent. Potatoes sold and proceeds deposited in bank
	NORMAN	1 case stationery	Klerk kantoor SAR	ZAR. property. Now in Queen's Warehouse
2.11.1899	ANNA AGNETE	590 casks cement	OVSS Railway	Property of Orange Free State Govt. Now in charge of Railway or possibly delivered to Military
	INYATI	21 cases uniforms (Bandoliers) 23 cases telegraphic material 11 cases uniforms	Commandant Generaal, Pretoria Dept. Telegraphs SAR, Pretoria Gouvernement, SAR	Property of ZAR. Delivered to Commandant of Durban for Military purposes ZAR property. Now in Queen's Warehouse Transvaal Govt. property. Now in Queen's Warehouse
2.11.1899	TINTAGEL CASTLE	50 cases syrup 4 cases custard powder 100 cases cheese 200 cases milk	TWB & Co Pretoria	Consigned to J W Beckett & Co. ZAR Contractors and Agents. The syrup and custard powder are in the Queen's Warehouse and the cheese and milk have been delivered to the military, who will, in due course, pay for same
	UMTALI	26 cases uniforms	Gouvernement, SAR	ZAR property. Now in Queen's Warehouse

DATE OF SEIZURE	NAME OF SHIP	GOODS SEIZED	MARKS	REASONS FOR SEIZURE
9.11.1899	MARIA	84 cases picks 20 cases handles 999 cases lubricating oil	NZASM	Property of Netherlands Railway and consequently of ZAR. Now in Queen's warehouse
	UMGENI	374 Boxes bullets 5 cases safety cartridges 86 casks empty cartridge cases 25 cases wax wads 4 cases jute wads 12 cases uniforms	ZAF Baviaanspoort Gouvernement SAR	Property of ZAR. Now in Queen's warehouse
	GAIKA	349 rolls copper wire 1 case pens 5 cases instruments	Telegraph Dept. SAR	Property of ZAR. Now in Queen's warehouse
	BRAEMAR CASTLE	177 cases milk 2 cases oatmeal 1 case seeds 1 case smoked hams 3 casks soda 1 case oil 2 cases sauce 32 cases shot	Various ZAF Baviaanspoort	Destined for the Netherlands Railway and therefore the property of the ZAR.
16.11. 1899	GAIKA	6 cases bookbinding requisites	State Printers Office SHRLP	ZAR. Now in Queen's warehouse
	KIRKDALE	486 rails 239 bundles of fishplates		Property of the Orange Free State Government Railway. Now in Queen's warehouse
	ILLOVO	3 cases bandoliers 12 cases uniforms	Commandant Generaal, Pretoria	Property of the ZAR. Now in Queen's warehouse
	DUNOTTAR CASTLE	2 cases chemicals 2 cases bandages 2 cases chemicals 2 cases oil 2 cases soap 1 case cocoa 1 case chicory 8 cases butter 2 cases salad oil 1 case apples 15 bags peas and beans 25 cases candles 5 bags coffee 60 bags rice 1 case provisions	ZAAA	Destined for the Netherlands Railway and therefore the property of the ZAR. Now in Queen's warehouse
23. 11.1899	KAISER	16 cases printing material and stationery	NF	Destined for State Printing Office, Pretoria. Govt. property. Now in Queen's warehouse
	ABANA	2 cases apparently machinery	NZASM	Property of Netherlands Railway. Now in Queen's warehouse
21.12.1899	GARTH CASTLE	3 cases paper 1 case books 1 case clothes		Destined for the Netherlands Railway. Now in Queen's warehouse
	GERMAN	1 case machinery	PPSM	For the Pretoria Pietersburg Railway, property of the ZARt. Now in Queen's warehouse
	CASPIAN	1 case telegraph instruments	PPSM	For the Pretoria Pietersburg Railway, property of the ZAR. Now in Queen's warehouse

enemy the ship (will be?) adjudicated upon in proper form.' Bale doubted whether the Natal prize court would recognise these instructions unless they were supported by law.

He also grew somewhat irritated when it became known that the collector of customs and the commandant were receiving direct information from the secretary of state and Milner concerning seizures and contraband issues. Bale complained: 'If I am not supplied with copies of such communications it will be impossible for me to advise satisfactorily. The employment of the Collector of Customs in prize matters is, I think, somewhat irregular.' This type of bureaucratic debacle was to colour the proceedings, not only of the prize court, but of the seizure of goods generally. On the one hand, the collector and the commandant, together with the naval authorities, constituted an energetic team of investigative and eager contraband police, while on the other hand, the chief legal and civil authorities, who would have to bear all the legal consequences, constituted reasoned voices of moderation and caution. This was specially the case when it involved possible international repercussions which could develop from the cases of intervention in foreign ships and goods. As Bale wrote to the commandant in January 1900, 'I trust that the greatest possible care will be taken in dealing with foreign ships so as to avoid international complications.'[10] Unfortunately, his advice was not heeded, and this seems all the more unusual, given that Scott had Bousfield, an experienced advocate, as an assistant.

During January 1900, when the court began to proceed with its business, Bale noted that there needed to be a distinction between goods seized from ships at sea, which would then become cases before the prize court, and goods seized on land, say at the dockside. The latter he believed should rightly come under the control of the military authorities. He also sought clarification regarding 'goods absolutely contraband' and 'goods conditionally contraband'; the issue of goods which had been seized before the prize court had been established and the ultimate disposal of goods seized. In response to Bale's queries the under-secretary of state in the foreign office, Francis Bertie, stated that the prize court had no jurisdiction to deal with articles seized on land. Contraband was not defined absolutely or conditionally but was confiscated 'because they are enemy's goods'.[12]

One of the first cases to come before the court concerned the detention in December 1899, at Durban, of foodstuffs and other supplies sent from Europe to Lourenço Marques for the Netherlands South African Railway Company. These had been shipped by the Dutch agents, Bisschop Masdag & Co and JH de Bussy, on three Castle liners – the *Braemer*, the *Dunottar* and the *Garth*. The Transvaal consul in Lourenço

George Mayston

Mayston had been born in Portsmouth, England in 1856 and had served for 21 years in the British customs and excise service. He arrived in Natal in 1898 to take up the position of collector of customs.

The customs house at the Point (Kearney collection).

Marques, G Pott, argued that these goods were not the property of the railway company but of the consignees, and thus should be released. Chamberlain advised that since the Netherlands Railway Company had been taken over by the Transvaal government, all such merchandise sent to them would be condemned as contraband, and he had already warned the Dutch government of this possibility. Mayston and Commandant Scott agreed to take the matter to the prize court for adjudication.[13]

During the eight weeks between 19 October 1899 and 21 December 1899, property was seized from no less than 24 ships of varying origins and ownerships. Most of the items were described as the property of the Transvaal government, but there were also goods intended for the Orange Free State. Included were munitions, machinery, railway supplies, telegraph materials, cement, food, picks, oil, copper wire, instruments, bookbinding materials, paper, uniforms and cloth. Of course, most of these had been ordered well before war commenced. David Calder recorded that by 16 January 1900, three major cases of seizure were pending in the court – these related to the *Avondale Castle*, the *Bundesrath* and the *Regina*.[14]

The confusion which attended the seizure of the *Avondale Castle* persisted after the establishment of the prize court, generating further friction between the military and the civilian authorities. Early in 1900, when the court had been in existence for over a month, the governor informed the chief justice that he had received a telegram at midnight from the senior naval officer at Durban complaining that the *Herzog* had not been handed over to the prize court because the deputy marshal could not be found when the ship had been brought in. The same difficulty had arisen with the *Bundesrath* shortly before. The governor would 'take it as a favour if instructions could be issued to ensure the accessibility of the deputy marshal'.[15] In correspondence with the commandant, Captain Scott, Calder explained that the elusive court marshal, RC Visick, and his deputy were appointed by the judges, and he was powerless other than to make representations.

After the *Avondale Castle* had successfully returned from Lourenço Marques to Durban with its refugee passengers, Sir Donald Currie formally laid a complaint with the Admiralty in London. In January 1900, Shepstone, Wylie & Binns, acting on behalf of the owners, claimed damages in the prize court on the basis of the facts of the case. These included the offer to assist the government with the conveyance of refugees from Mozambique; the unconcealed shipment of the gold specie; the open enquiries made to the government about the legitimacy of the cargo and the instruction via the collector of customs from the governor allowing the ship to proceed to Lourenço Marques. The claim amounted to £2 750 for delay and extra costs, including coaling. Calder noted that the *praecipe* had been issued on 12 January and the monition was served on 15 January 1900. In his report of October 1901 as procurator-general, Bale recorded that the agent of the National Bank of the ZAR had managed to persuade the Admiralty to release the specie on the condition that the money would not be sent to the Transvaal, and that the bank would pay all the crown costs including solicitors, and counsel's fees and even a 1% commission to HMS *Tartar* for storing the money! Apparently

the bank had been advised that they had a reasonable claim against the shipping company for not notifying them that 'exception was being taken to the money going forward'. The specie was released on 5 February 1900.[16]

The *Bundesrath*

It may have been an unfortunate coincidence for the future of white naval relationships that at the very time at which the German Reichstag was debating a considerable enlargement of the German fleet, with many members reluctantly dragging their heels over the issue, the imperial German mail steamer, the *Bundesrath,* was seized off Xavier Point, 200 miles (326 km) north of Delagoa Bay, by HMS *Magicienne*. The Royal naval vessel brought her into Durban as prize on 29 December 1899 and, inevitably, handed the ship over, not to the deputy marshal of the court, but to the collector of customs. Scott did, however, inform the governor that the ship's papers were handed over to the deputy marshal. By 4 January 1900 the ship was handed over to the marshal of the court.

The German consul in Durban, Rechburg, strongly objected that very day in a telegram to the governor, who immediately forwarded it to Milner and Chamberlain.[17] Also on that day, Admiral Harris informed the governor of the reasons for the seizure, stating that there had been a suspicious rearrangement of the ship's cargo while it was being pursued by HMS *Magicienne*. He also said that the German passengers on board had openly declared their intention of going to the Transvaal, and it was believed that a search would reveal arms in their baggage and contraband on board.[18] Bale, who was only appointed procurator-general of the prize court on 5 January 1900, recorded that he had advised the government that, 'in the exercise of the powers of visit, search and detention, great discretion will be required ... care must be taken not to subject to any vexatious interference the commerce ... of any nation not engaged in the war.'[19] On the same day, a judge of the prize court ordered the release of all the passengers except four and of the crew and the mails.

On 11 January 1900, Scott confirmed that four young German passengers had been detained as prisoners of war. The four were from the Transvaal and they had all been studying at the Hermannsburg Missionary Institute in Germany. In his interrogation, Scott determined that they had decided to return to the Transvaal at the behest of Dr Leyds. At least one of them, Friedrich Prigge, wished to serve the Boers as a chaplain. They requested Scott for permission to go on to Lourenço Marques, which he refused. A letter found on one of them aroused Scott's suspicions by revealing that two of them were hoping to get through to the Transvaal 'as missionaries' and 'thus escape the British authorities in Natal'.

The four passengers were Friedrich Prigge from Piet Retief; August Wenhold and Hermann Wickert from the Rustenburg area; and Carl Keiser from Hebron. Apparently they were all sons of Lutheran missionaries. During their detention in Durban, the prime minister received a visit from a Fritz Reiche of New Hanover, who informed him that 'a young German lady' from Noordsberg, who was engaged to Prigge, had received a letter from Prigge on the *Bundesrath* which confirmed their intentions of proceeding to the Transvaal. Reiche did not wish to be named 'in connection with the matter'.[20]

On 2 January 1900, Milner forwarded a strong request to the governor from Admiral Harris for the ship to be searched. Hely-Hutchinson agreed to have this done on the admiral's authority and responsibility, noting that it would be necessary to unload and then reload the entire cargo. Bale carefully noted that all proceedings in the case were being taken 'in the name of the crown' and thus were not the responsibility of the colonial government. The judge in prize thereupon authorised the unloading of the *Bundesrath*, which commenced on Sunday 7 January and was completed by Monday 15 January. No contraband was found, only cases of spirits, electric lighting gear, distillery machinery consigned to Johannesburg, and sugar, flour and rice consigned to traders in Lourenço Marques. On 18 January Bale received instructions from Chamberlain for the release of the ship, the cargo and the four young German prisoners. The order was applied for and granted by Justice Finnemore.

Bale, who had earlier maintained that the prize court had no jurisdiction over persons such as passengers, and had thus expressed his doubts over their detention, now expressed a similar doubt about the validity of the prize court's release of the four prisoners 'as the liability of the prize court only attaches to ships and not to the passengers'.[21]

While all of this was proceeding in Natal, a major international row had erupted between Germany and Britain over the seizure, not only of the *Bundesrath*, but also of a sister ship, the *General*, at Aden on 3 January 1900. On 4 January, Hatzfeldt, the German ambassador to Britain, protested strongly about the seizures, arguing in legal terms that proceedings before a prize court were not justified, and emphasising the neutrality of the ships and their ports of call. The following day, Hatzfeldt again wrote to Salisbury, stating that he was 'further instructed to request [Salisbury] to cause explicit instructions to be sent to the Commanders of British ships in African waters to respect the rules of International Law, and to place no further impediments in the way of trade between neutrals'.[22] Salisbury had referred the entire matter of the seizures to the law officers of the crown and, on 8 January 1900, two of the officers, Richard Webster and Robert Finlay, advised him to order the immediate release of the ship. In what seemed a full condemnation of the Royal Navy's actions, they stated that the instructions which had been given to search 'with the utmost vigour' had been misunderstood. They also advised that, 'the greatest caution should be exercised in stopping and taking in mail steamers owing to the serious public interests involved, and the risk of heavy claims should the capture turn out to be without justification.'[23]

But the damage had been done – a half-hearted debate in the Reichstag had turned into full-blown fury against the British actions, and the detention of the *Bundesrath* and other German ships was used to great effect by Count von Bulow to argue for massive increases in the German fleet.[24]

Before the *Bundesrath* was released, David Calder of the prize court expressed some confusion about how to proceed with the case, stating that the presence of enemy military on the ship was probably good enough grounds for its seizure, but that he needed 'a book on international law'. This was not surprising, given Bale's contention that not even Hely-Hutchinson had received any instructions about the prize court.

By 21 January, the Bundesrath had been reloaded and returned to Lourenço Marques. She then set sail early in February for Hamburg in Germany, but not before taking on 160 bales of wool on the instructions of Alex Uebel, a local agent acting for Durban agents Monhaupt & Co. On 13 February 1900, Scott advised Hely-Hutchinson that the acting imperial consul general of Germany, Rechburg of Monhaupt & Co, was trading with the enemy. He recommended that Rechburg be prosecuted and that the foreign office be asked to request his government to suspend him. Scott had enquired of the firm where they were obtaining wool and was informed that it had been bought locally in Lourenço Marques. In the meantime, the Bank of Natal had returned a bankdraft for £309 to Uebel for the wool, saying that it could not act in matters connected with wool dealings from Lourenço Marques. Scott went on relentlessly: 'Will you please let me know the name of the firm at Delagoa Bay from whom the wool was bought'. Monhaupt & Co. named three companies. Harrison, the government inspector of the National Bank of the ZAR then wired the Lourenço Marques branch of the bank for information. The response indicated that the wool came from the Transvaal and the Orange Free State through merchants, Kaufmann & Little in Ermelo. Harrison then suggested to Scott that the bond draft should be presented to Monhaupt & Co. to trap them, and thus prove that they were parties to the transaction. But Rechburg of Monhaupt & Co had already enquired about the bill and the bank had informed him that they had returned it to Lourenço Marques.

Given all these circumstances, Hely-Hutchinson enquired of the attorney-general if a prosecution would be likely to succeed and Bale advised against this course as it would be difficult to obtain the necessary oral evidence. He went on to remind the governor that, 'the subjects of a foreign state, especially of a consular rank must be treated as if incapable of an offence against the law of nations as far as possible, although the privileges of extraterritoriality which attach to an ambassador do not attach to a Consul.'[25] On 6 March 1900, the British government received a claim from the German East Africa Line, via the German ambassador, for damages in connection with the seizures of the *Bundesrath*, the *General* and the *Herzog* to the extent of 808 737 marks.[26]

Other prizes for an eager navy

Each one of the Royal naval vessels which comprised the fleet operating off Natal and Mozambique succeeded in capturing a 'prize'. On 16 December 1899, it was the turn of HMS *Forte*, which arrested the Norwegian sailing ship the *Regina* ten miles off Cape Inyaca and brought it into Durban. This was a 850 ton vessel under Captain O Evensen from Laurvik which had been commissioned in Amsterdam in June 1899 to sail to Java to collect cargos for the *Ermelo Spoorwig Maatschappij* and the Netherlands ZAR Railways. At Samarang, the *Regina* had started loading 26 907 railway sleepers, 200 bundles of rattan, packages of bamboos and boxes of ambulance goods on 25 September 1899, and it eventually sailed on 30 October for Delagoa Bay.[27] Some six weeks after its arrest, Henry Bale asked Hely-Hutchinson if he wished the prize court to proceed with the case. The ambulance goods had been released, but the ship and the remainder of her cargo were still in detention. Captain Evensen was demanding £992 9s 5d for freight charges from Java to Durban. The governor noted that once again the 'prize' had incorrectly been taken over by the over-eager collector of customs and thus could be deemed to have been seized on land and not at sea, and so should not be a case for the prize court. Scott, however, advised that the goods had definitely been seized at sea. Hely-Hutchinson then requested the case to proceed. After making arrangements through Labistour, the solicitor representing the ship's owners, for the sale of the sleepers to the Cape Railways, Captain Evensen continued to demand to be paid freight. Unfortunately there are no records to show whether the captain was satisfied but, on Chamberlain's instructions, the ship was released on 15 February 1900 and sailed to Port Elizabeth with the cargo of sleepers.[28]

HMS *Thetis* also had her opportunity on 6 January 1900, capturing the *Herzog* which was found to be carrying a German and Dutch ambulance corps and their equipment. The governor of Mozambique and some eight officers were also on board. Scott urgently requested Hely-Hutchinson to delay the judge of the prize court from returning to Pietermaritzburg so that he could consider the case in Durban. However, the governor informed Scott that if the ship had not yet been handed over to the prize court, the Portuguese governor and the officers should immediately be released. On the orders of the Admiralty, the ship itself was released on 8 January without reasons for its detention being given. In this particular case, David Calder was highly suspicious of the ship carrying a large amount of contraband and queried why members of an ambulance corps should carry revolvers.[29]

On 19 January 1900, HMS *Pelorus* joined her eager fellows when her crew arrested a German barque, the *Marie*, off Cape Inyaca. But the *Pelorus* also had bad luck for when the *Marie* was brought into Durban with a cargo of flour consigned to Arthur May & Co. of Lourenço Marques, no proceedings were taken and the ship was released. May & Co.'s representative in Durban apparently convinced Scott that the flour was not destined for the enemy.[30]

David Calder noted that, perhaps, the clearest case of 'prize' which came before the court concerned the seizure of the *Birkdale*. This was a

Rear Admiral Robert Harris, commanding Cape squadron, and staff, Simonstown (Newnes).

The British prime minister, the Marquess of Salisbury (Wilson).

A sailing ship moored at St Paul's wharf (KCL).

Stevedores loading flour at the Point docks (KCL).

general cargo ship which called in at Durban on its way to Lourenço Marques and was arrested on 8 February 1900 by an officer of HMS *Terrible*. The basis for Calder's sense of certainty about the case was the fact that the ship had only started on her voyage from Liverpool about 1 December 1899, well after the outbreak of the war. What became complex about the issue, however, was that there were no less than six interested parties. Some were concerned with steel plates and bundles of iron bars; some with boxes of soap; the Robinson Gold Mining Company and others with 2 500 boxes of candles; and others with cases of bottled stout. On condition that the consignees, Allen Wack & Co. of Lourenço Marques, agreed to sell the cargo in Natal, the ship was released in April 1900.[31] The court then released what it described as innocent cargo and the remainder, having been intended for the Transvaal, was detained in Natal until the end of the war. In his closing report on the prize court, the procurator-general, Henry Bale, also listed the *Galeka* which had been seized with butter and cheese. The goods were detained in the Queen's warehouse, probably not for long! Goods from the *Clan Macnab* and the *Matabele* were also detained by the court.

A chaotic port scene, Alexandra Square at the Point (KCL).

1. *Natal Mercury*, 25.1.1900.

2. PRO, CO 179/206: Hely-Hutchinson to Chamberlain, 19.10.1899.

3. PRO, CO 179/208: Commander Morgan to secretary of the Admiralty, 25.11.1899.

4. PAR, AGO 1/7/50: Chamberlain to governor, 11.10.1899.

5. Personal correspondence, L Pistorius, 17.10.2001.

6. Byrne, WJ, *Dictionary of English Law*, p.702; Oppie, AS, *Wharton's Law Lexicon*, p.803; Burke, J, *Jowitt's Dictionary of English Law*, p.434.

7. PRO, CO 179/208: Admiralty to secretary of state for the colonies, 25.10.1899.

8. PAR, CSO 1631: correspondence concerning warrant for the prize court, 24.11.1899.

9. PAR, AGO 1/7/50: Bale to prime minister, 9.1.1900.

10. PAR, AGO 1/7/50: the Marquess of Salisbury to Sir F Lascelles, 10.1.1900.

11. PAR, AGO 1/7/50: procurator-general to commandant, 9.1.1900.

12. PAR, AGO 1/7/50: minutes of prize court, 21.12.1900.

13. PRO, CO 179/216: Francis Bertie to colonial office, 29.1.1900.

14. PAR, AGO 1/7/50: minutes of prize court, 15.12.1899.

15. PAR, AGO 1/7/50: Calder to Bale, 16.1.1900.

16. PAR, CO 179/209: Hely-Hutchinson to Gallwey, 7.1.1900.

17. PRO, CO 179/220: report of procurator-general on the prize court, 30/10/1901.

18. PAR, CO 179/208: telegram Hely-Hutchinson to Chamberlain, 29.12.1899.

19. PAR, AGO 1/7/50: telegram Admiral Harris to governor, 31.12.1899.

20. PAR, AGO 1/7/49: report of the procurator-general on the *Bundesrath*, 2.2.1900.

21. CO 179/209: prime minister to governor, 6.1.1900.

22. PAR, AGO 1/7/49: report of the procurator-general on the *Bundesrath*, 2.2.1900.

23. PAR, AGO 1/7/50: Hatzfeldt to the Marquess of Salisbury, 5.1.1900.

24. PAR, AGO 1/7/50: law officers of the crown to the Marquess of Salisbury, 8.1.1900.

25. Amery LS, *The Times History of the War in South Africa*, Vol. III, p.63.

26. PRO, CO 179/210: attorney general to governor, 14.2.1900.

27. PAR, AGO 1/7/49: Count Metternich to the Marquess of Salisbury, 3.3.1900.

28. PAR, AGO 1/7/49: procurator-general to secretary of state, 27.1.1900.

29. PRO, CO 179/213: return of the prize court, 11.8.1900.

30. PAR, AGO 1/7/50: Calder to Bale, 8.1.1900.

31. PRO, CO 179/209: telegram Hely-Hutchinson to Chamberlain, 21.1.1900.

32. PAR, AGO 1/7/47: Calder to Bale, 3.4.1900.

Two views of Gardiner Street, at the centre of the town, where the merchants and banks occupied prestigious locations (LHM).

CHAPTER 22

TRADING WITH THE ENEMY: CONTRABAND
Brian Kearney

Merchants versus authorities

In addition to the almost farcical work of the prize court, a great amount of effort was expended by the British and colonial authorities in Durban in an attempt to stem the flow of contraband goods to the two republics. While the prize court dealt with possible contraband seized at sea, the bulk of suspect goods was handled in the customary manner of freight landed at the port of Durban. There was as little clarity regarding the dockside procedure as there had been in matters relating to the prize court and, once again, there were two opposing factions in this 'war within a war'. On the one side were the merchants of Durban who were keen to continue trade at all costs. This was a trade which was based on the use of Durban as a trans-shipment centre, with goods being ordered from elsewhere in the world and sent on to the traditional markets in the interior of the country. But now these markets were cut off by the war.

On the other side were the British military authorities like the commandants of Durban, particularly Captain Percy Scott, whose foremost duty was to apply martial law and prevent the trade in contraband. They were very ably supported by the collector of customs, George Mayston, who acted on information supplied by the censor, or by the British consul in Lourenço Marques, applying extraordinary almost jingoistic zeal, in the detention of any goods with the slightest hint or suspicion of irregularity. The colonial administration, including the governor, the prime minister and the attorney-general, inevitably had to support these pro-British actions, but they would also be faced with the task of smoothing the many ruffled feathers of local merchants, international traders and agents, shipping companies and white consuls. Sitting in judgement over all these complex interrelationships were the distant administrators of the colonial office such as Joseph Chamberlain and his colleagues in the foreign office. They often ruled on the legitimacy of the seizures, sometimes under pressure from foreign governments.

Confusion was at its height in the early months of the war with all these diverse and conflicting interests either adapting to, exploiting, evading or enforcing the wartime regulations. Certainly contraband did exist on a fairly wide scale and most of it passed through Durban and its twin transit port, Lourenço Marques.

Goods ordered before the war

As early as November 1899, 50 post office boxes were detained by the customs. They had been ordered by the Transvaal post office through the South African Contracting Association. The incident involved all the major combatants: the collector of customs and the commandant who had ordered their confiscation as goods intended for the enemy and the local German consul and the consul for Germany in Cape Town, who appealed on behalf of the consignees. The governor appeared to be confused about the appeal, and thought 'that it would be a convenience ... if I could be supplied with a set of instructions ...'; but the attorney-general was quite clear in advising that, as the goods had been in transit at the declaration of war, they could not be considered as contraband, and therefore advised their release.[1]

In January 1900, the prime minister also began to express nervous reservations about the far-reaching consequences of such seizures, stating that 'no liability attaches to the Natal Government in connection with the capture ... of goods'.[2]

Further episodes followed. Reflectors for railway lamps which had been imported for the Netherlands South Africa Railway Co. were detained.[3] Import agent Milne was happy for them to be passed to the NGR by the collector. On 20 October 1899, Scott stated that he was convinced that meal imported on the *Maria* by JT Rennie & Sons was going straight to the enemy. The company thereupon refused to carry the cargo to Delagoa Bay on another vessel, the *Matebele*, and promptly had it all offloaded.[4] The *Maria* was then emptied of virtually her entire cargo. Mealie meal from New York was confiscated by the collector and more railway goods were taken by the NGR.

Goods ordered after the outbreak of war

By early 1900, the war was sufficiently advanced to assume that most goods coming into Durban in transit either for the republics or Lourenço Marques had been ordered subsequent to the declaration of war and, in the words of Collins, the assistant manager of the Natal Bank:

> There is every reason to believe that since the commencement of the war, firms both in South Africa and in the United Kingdom have, in some cases knowingly, and in other cases, unknowingly, been selling goods to the Government agents or subjects of the hostile belligerents ... they should be specially warned that not only is such trading illegal, but exposes those engaged in it to heavy penalties ... There are mercantile firms, in the Transvaal especially, that are really branches of big London houses, and obtain nearly all their supplies from these houses ... We hardly imagine there is much likelihood of direct infringement, but it is necessary they should be specially careful as regards any orders coming from Delagoa Bay ...

He appended these comments to a copy of a proclamation which had been published both in London and Lourenço Marques in January 1900 which read:

> We do hereby warn all our subjects not to enlist or engage themselves in the Military service of the Government of either the South African or Orange Free State Republics, or in any way to aid, abet or assist either of the said Republics in the prosecution of hostilities; and not to carry on any trade or supply any goods, wares or merchandise to any person resident therein, or to supply any goods, wares or merchandise to any person for transmission to either of the said Republics ...[5]

During the first phases of the war, many goods entered the Transvaal directly through the port of Lourenço Marques, without passing through Durban. These were sent via the Suez Canal, and then down the east coast by white business houses, and were carried on German or French ships. It was impossible for the British authorities to prevent these shipments unless they made 'prize' arrests on the high seas. This was probably one reason why the Royal naval vessels lurked some miles off Cape Inyaca at the entrance to Delagoa Bay, where they could arrest shipping in international waters.

However, the main patterns of delivery which had developed from British firms involved the ships first calling at Durban to offload goods for Natal, before going on with the remainder of the cargo to Delagoa Bay, as a last port of call. It was this process which engaged the close scrutiny of the commandant and the collector of customs. Sometimes the white merchants used the facilities of British ships, but their goods destined for Lourenço Marques and the Transvaal became contraband in the port of Natal. This happened to soap from Holland imported by Gundelfingers in May 1900. The law officers of the crown overruled the commandant who had the soap confiscated and they ordered that it be delivered to Gundelfingers for sale in Durban. Hely-Hutchinson thought that this decision undermined the entire process.[6] The firm opted to place the goods in bond until the end of the war to appease the authorities.

At times British goods were also shipped on white ships. A consignment of stationery for Pretoria, shipped via Holland in May 1900, was detained in Durban. Sometimes only a portion of a cargo would be detained if it looked suspicious. Thus 20 kegs of sulphur shipped on the *Inchanga* were held back, while 35 packages of medicines continued on to Lourenço Marques.[7] All goods which had been consigned for the various railway companies in the two republics and detained in Durban were eagerly appropriated by the NGR, no doubt being viewed as a 'godsend', since they would have been useful for the major repairs necessary after the damages which the Boers had caused. These transactions were efficiently arranged through the military director of railways, and earmarked for the account of the military.

Shipping to Delagoa Bay

Mayston, obviously familiar with the prevailing patterns of the dual transit trade and the possibilities for trading with the enemy using the route through Durban and Lourenço Marques, issued a circular to all shippers on 19 October 1899. He specifically requested to be able to 'ascertain the Consignees and actual destinations of goods carried by your vessels to Delagoa Bay', and stipulated that '... before any goods are laden on your vessels there must be inserted on the Entry outwards particulars of the goods to be shipped for Delagoa Bay ... failing satisfactory replies relative to cargo for Delagoa Bay the Ships clearance will be withheld and the vessel cannot proceed'. The reaction of some members of the shipping world was to go to any lengths to be seen to be clean. At the end of October, the Castle Company elected to have all the goods carried by the *Tintagel Castle* examined by the collector. In doing this they incurred the wrath of the Portuguese consul when certain goods were detained.[8] Milner had suspected that the ship was carrying goods of military value for the enemy when an inspection of the cargo revealed charcoal, bullets and cartridge cases.[9]

The collector was particularly suspicious that large amounts of corned beef might be making their way to the Transvaal through Delagoa Bay and, by December 1899, the governor informed him that the British government had determined that all tinned goods and portable rations were to be treated as contraband. This had overturned an earlier ruling of November, in which the British cabinet had decided not to treat foodstuffs as contraband.[10] Hely-Hutchinson found this decision puzzling since the Boers would normally have easy access to fresh meat in the field and would therefore not need tinned goods and portable rations. They were, however, probably running short of other foodstuffs such as coffee, sugar and flour.[11] Chamberlain's response to the governor's observations was to point out that no specific instructions on contraband were possible and that each case and its effects would have to be individually evaluated, with the final decision being taken by the prize court![12] So the issue remained extremely cloudy: not all cases would go to the prize court in any event and if the prize court were to eventually decide, probably long after a seizure, how would the Royal Navy and the collector of customs know, in the meantime, what did and what did not constitute contraband?

Bale and Calder, together with Hely-Hutchinson, appeared to have relied quite heavily for principles and applications on an 1888 publication by Thomas Holland, *A Manual of Naval Prize Law*. However, Chamberlain warned them that Holland's book merely presented very general principles for the benefit of naval officers and should not be used to resolve all issues. Holland obviously took an interest in the shipping cases relating to Lourenço Marques and published a letter to the editor of the *Times* on 3 January 1900 in which he expressed his opinion that consignments destined for the Transvaal through Lourenço Marques fell within the category of 'cases liable to seizure'.[13]

Commandant Scott suggested that a system of deposit should be instituted whereby all shippers should guarantee their bona fides by de-positing a sum of 20 times the value of goods despatched to Lourenço Marques and if it were to be found that the goods left the town, they would forfeit their deposit. The colonial treasurer did not consider that exporters would agree to the idea.[14]

In his annual report for 1900, Mayston recorded that: 'Large quantities of goods consigned for the Transvaal and Orange Free State governments were seized, and in many cases the goods were made use of by the military during the war. Among the goods seized were 1 500 000 Martini-Henry bullets, 200 000 Mauser safety cartridges, and empty cartridge cases, wads and small shot. These have all been destroyed.'[15]

Three suspected merchants:
Balwe of De Waal & Co.

Several Durban merchants came to be suspected of considerable involvement in the contraband business with the Transvaal through Lourenço Marques, and at least three were regularly questioned. JHA Balwe of De Waal & Co. had served as the consul for the ZAR in Natal until October 1899 when he informed the governor that he had ceased representation.[16] He did however continue to act as consul for the Netherlands. Like Rechburg of Monhaupt & Co., who served as the German consul in Durban, he probably saw his consular position as providing him with a distinct advantage in terms of trading through Mozambique and also providing him with a level of immunity from prosecution. Furthermore, like many Durban houses there was also a branch of De Waal & Co. in Delagoa Bay where they carried freight with their own tug and three dinghies, three lighters and ten punts.

Balwe first came to the notice of the military authorities when Commandant Bethune went on board the *Tintagel Castle* late in the evening of 28 October 1899 to inspect the luggage of five Dutch passengers. Captain Harris told Bethune that six more passengers had booked under suspicious circumstances to travel to Delagoa Bay. Amongst these was Balwe. Bethune slept on board the ship that night and before she sailed early the next morning he interviewed all the suspect passengers. He advised the five Dutchmen to return to Europe 'as three of them were ex-Hollander officers'. He then interviewed Balwe and asked if he could search his luggage. 'While I was doing this he made the remark "I am astonished, as I made it all right with Colonel Bethune last night". I then said "May I introduce myself, I am Colonel Bethune ..." I had never met the gentleman before this morning.' Bethune explained to Hely-Hutchinson that he had a very short time to make up his mind and then decided to ask Balwe not to sail.[17] Strangely, Bethune later apologised to Balwe for this instruction.

In January 1900, the Durban censors translated a letter in which, Pott, the Transvaal consul in Lourenço Marques, had referred a Dutch-owned company, Turkstra & Co., to Balwe to assist with forwarding ten cases of goods including 'St Nicholas articles' to the Transvaal.[18] R Turkstra & Co. was a well-established bakery in Pretoria which had supplied the Boer forces in Natal with bread and rusks, though often mouldy on delivery.[19] Clearly the ten cases of goods had missed the Christmas celebrations of 1899. During the same month Scott noted that Balwe was using his consular status to convey letters from 'enemy's agents to people here', citing the example of a letter sent from Lourenço Marques to Balwe as the consul, but which the censor found to have contained instructions from Pott, the Transvaal consul there, to a certain Dutchman, Cousyn, as to how to reach the Transvaal from Delagoa Bay. Scott thereupon submitted to the governor that all Balwe's post be opened and that his conduct be reported to his government.[20]

After Scott's departure, Commandant Morris continued to keep De Waal & Co. under observation, noting that a new dimension had appeared in the way persons were able to reach the Transvaal – by obtaining tickets to Beira and other ports north of Lourenço Marques and then leaving the vessel at that port.[21] In May 1900 Morris told the governor that Balwe had applied to him for a permit to travel to Lourenço Marques for business purposes and that ' personally I have had nothing to do with him, but my predecessor, Captain Scott, specially warned me that he was a dangerous and suspicious man who had given him a lot of trouble ...' In a curious twist, typical of military affairs, Balwe had also informed Morris that De Waal & Co. had been appointed agents in Durban for the Army and Navy Co-operative Society to supply goods for the officers' messes. As many of the messes dealt with the society it was conceivable that the Durban firm might obtain information on the movements of regiments and other intelligence. Besides, here was lucrative business going to a firm whose branch in Lourenço Marques was believed to have close relations with the ZAR. Hely-Hutchinson was somewhat outraged by this proposition and asked Chamberlain to hint to the directors of the co-operative in London about the problem. Morris declined a permit for Balwe's intended visit.[22]

The mechanisms which De Waal & Co. used for moving contraband through Durban to the Transvaal must also have come to the notice of other trading companies and agents. Gundelfingers tried to use them to break a blockade on a consignment of soap, but on receiving information about this devious transaction, the commandant and the governor agreed to keep the goods till the end of the war.[23] Over and above the movement of men and everyday goods, De Waal & Co. also shipped some £19 000 worth of gold between Durban and Lourenço Marques between February and June 1900.[24]

De Waal & Co.'s premises at Point Road, Addington (LHM).

Wilcken & Ackermann

'Don't attempt to buy any more goods from here or at the Cape or you will get us into gaol. I shall make a final effort tomorrow to get permission to ship the flour and also to get a pass, but have no hope.' Gustav Ackermann wrote this from Durban to his partner in Lourenço Marques in January 1900 and the letter duly fell into Scott's hands. Scott, who described him as a well-known enemy's agent, also stated that Ackermann's application to get to Delagoa Bay would not succeed. Wilcken and Ackermann carried out their main business from Lourenço Marques and they too had their own punts and dinghies. Ackermann happened to be away in Cape Town at the outbreak of the war for medical treatment. He had returned on the *Dunvegan Castle* and stopped off in Durban for business purposes on 9 December 1899. In vain he had called on the assistance of Focke, the consul general for Germany in Cape Town. But Scott refused his application.[26]

Further correspondence from the firm to a Cape Town insurance company in May 1900 revealed that Wilcken & Ackermann had also been shipping gold from the Transvaal through Lourenço Marques – some £50 000 worth going via the *Herzog* to Rotterdam. Commandant Morris recommended the issue be handled by Milner in Cape Town since the insurance company was domiciled there.[27] During March 1901 Crowe, the new consul general in Lourenço Marques, informed the governor of Natal that the company had requested permission to export £108 000 worth of gold bar. At the same time a complex case arose concerning a very large consignment of Hungarian flour (some 13 000 bags) which was apparently destined for the Transvaal government through Wilcken & Ackermann, but had been detained in Durban where it was eventually sold. In addition to all the suspected contraband dealings, the company was also storing large quantities of goods such as candles consigned by British firms, like Niven & Mitchell of Robertson, Cape, who had decided to remain above board.

May & Co. premises in Point Road opposite Alexandra Square (KCL).

Arthur May & Co.

A key member of the information chain which had been established in the attempts to control trading with the enemy was the British consul general in Lourenço Marques. During the first phase of the war this office was held by Carnegie Ross. He was followed by Fritz Crowe and both communicated regularly with the Natal governor and the Durban commandant. In February 1900 the commandant had received two reports from Ross on the dealings of a Point Road company – Arthur May & Co. – which had been suspected of trading with the enemy for some time. The books of the Lourenço Marques Railway Company revealed that very large quantities of goods, including butter, flour, sugar and soap had been shipped by May & Co. through the port and then taken by rail to 'Incomati' Station. Ross noted that this was a small village with a population of three people and '... there is a good wagon road thence to the SAR border. It is not unreasonable to assume that these goods were intended for a better market than would be afforded by the tiny wayside station'. Scott advised a prosecution to make an example of the firm but cautioned that one difficulty would be obtaining evidence. He also intended refusing a travel permit to Arthur May.[28] The second report followed soon afterwards: 'The cargo of the sailing ship (American) *Sea Witch* consisting mainly of flour, all belonging to Messrs Arthur May & Sons is being sent up to the Transvaal as fast as it can be discharged ... any proceedings against the firm would have a most wholesome effect on doubtful persons and would encourage those who are endeavouring to obey loyally the provisions of proclamations.'

When further evidence of May's dealings in contraband became available, the governor referred the matter to Attorney-General Bale, who thought that the papers afforded a strong suspicion of guilt but raised several issues about jurisdiction. Nevertheless he was prepared to prosecute May '... if witnesses can be got from Delagoa Bay ...'. Hely-Hutchinson then requested Ross to obtain depositions from witnesses in Lourenço Marques. Ross considered that this would best be through the agency of a practised detective and that it would be a lengthy and difficult process. On these grounds and on the probability that witnesses would not come to Natal, Bale declined to prosecute.[29]

May also seems to have found a method of evading the strict permit system which Captain Scott had established for travel along the east coast. In March 1900, Consul Ross observed that the permit regulations were being easily and constantly evaded. He cited May, who made his bookings from Beira, as a case in point. Again he pleaded for prosecutions against Arthur May & Co. as well as De Vaal & Co. Clearly he was also under pressure from apparently loyal, local firms such as Weedon & Co. and Allen Wack & Co. '... who have given up their connection with the Transvaal, and thus deprived themselves of a livelihood ...'. However by May 1900, the collector of customs recorded that shipments by May & Co. had practically stopped – perhaps the constant investigations had brought results. In any event, on 22 June 1900, Crowe asked the governor if he could return guarantee moneys deposited by a Mr Zingel, the local representative of Arthur May & Co. in Lourenço Marques, but by August he had changed his mind and decided to retain the deposit. In September he asked the governor '... not to allow Arthur May & Co. to ship any foodstuffs ...'.[30]

The Lourenço Marques route

While it appeared that these three firms were dealing extensively with the Transvaal, numerous Durban companies which also had branches in Johannesburg and Lourenço Marques, and evidently complied with the martial law regulations, had started complaining to the authorities in December 1899 about the inequity of the situation. Findlay of McIntosh, Findlay & Co. threatened that his company would start using French or German steamers '... to the detriment of ourselves in many ways, and to the English shipowner in general'.[31]

At the same time reactions in the Durban shipping world began to reach a state of alarm. Rolfes, Nobel & Co. enquired urgently of the colonial secretary whether they would be able to continue to supply foodstuffs to Mozambique: '... we have every reason to believe that English & Continental Houses are shipping largely by French & German steamers to Delagoa Bay ... merchants here, who are already suffering very heartily thro' the war deserve to have the liberal consideration of your Government ...' Prime Minister Albert Hime responded 'that the shipment of foodstuffs by Natal merchants to Delagoa Bay is absolutely prohibited'.[32]

An apparent shortage of goods in Lourenço Marques during the same month led the local merchants there to plead their case with the governor of Natal through Consul Ross and to request him to allow goods lying in the docks at Durban to be forwarded to them. The collector of customs made the observation that the 'shortage of goods' was being caused by the speed at which goods were being sold to the Transvaal. He went on to explain how he had found a way of manipulating the processes. When agents and trading companies requested permits to ship goods to Delagoa Bay he would not refuse these requests, but often would withhold his signature from the entries and the shipowners would then decline to risk the shipments without his signature.[33]

Naturally these kinds of games played by an official had serious consequences, one of these being a war within the trading and shipping fraternity who were already in competition with each other for trade. W Chalmers Barker of the Lourenço Marques branch of McIntosh, Findlay & Co. accused Consul Ross of favouritism. He pointed out that Allen Wack & Co., one of the firms which the consul considered loyally above board, and who were responsible for the Royal Navy's coal and flour, were actually pressing wool in De Waal's wool press.[34] Matters did not improve when the collector detained goods marked BF & Co. presuming them to be for Buchanan, Forsyth & Co., a Transvaal firm, while they were actually intended for Blanck, Fontana & Co. of Lourenço Marques. The United States consul there, Stanley Hollis, also became embroiled in the consequences of the collector's and commandant's detentions of

goods shipped by an American company, Bendahan, Abejdid & Co.[35]

But contraband continued to flow, apparently unabated, to the Transvaal via this route. Commandant Scott was instructed to have all telegraphic orders for supplies from Lourenço Marques monitored and to be especially vigilant about orders for tinned meats and portable rations.[36] In December 1899, Hely-Hutchinson informed Milner that the present arrangements were not effectual in stopping contraband and that the real reason was that the Portuguese were not performing their duties as a neutral power. One consequence of this warning was that the British strengthened their consular legation staff from January 1900 to provide much more surveillance over imports and trade through the port of Lourenço Marques. By March detailed intelligence reports were being received of provisions for the Transvaal including the role of the Transvaal consul, Pott, in many of these transactions, and the exporting of gold from the ZAR by sea to Holland. A good deal of the contraband was also being purchased in Madagascar, Reunion and Mauritius.[37]

Sometimes no detective work needed to be undertaken at all. A passenger from Delagoa Bay who arrived in Durban on 11 April 1900 handed over a letter to Commandant Morris which revealed that the Transvaal government had ordered goods from McLaren & Sons of Glasgow.[38] The collector and Consul Ross were asked to keep a look out. Numerous other cases of suspected contraband were handled by the colonial authorities, most of them with some connection to Lourenço Marques. In March 1900, Bale dealt with a case of Transvaal gold coinage which appeared in Durban.[39] Gundelfinger applied to the commandant in June 1900 to visit Lourenço Marques and make arrangements to reship goods which had been blocked there.[40] The under-secretary of state in the colonial office adjudicated in an interesting case which involved alcohol, lemonade and rice from Germany and which clearly had international consequences, and in which the strict rules laid down by Captain Scott came to the colonial office's attention. As late as 1901 he was consulted in a situation involving detained goods removed from the SS *German*, intended for Lourenço Marques.[41] A Mr Pavey, newly arrived from that port, expressed his suspicions to the commandant about Cuthbert & Co. trading with the enemy. One of the last cases which the censor picked up concerned a letter from a London firm of tea and coffee merchants which declined an order from Johannesburg because too careful a watch was being exercised on goods passing through Lourenço Marques.[42]

Shipping in Delagoa Bay, from the fort at Lourenço Marques (KCL).

Improved surveillance at Lourenço Marques: Sir Roger Casement, Major Young and Fritz Crowe

Carnegie Ross, the consul in Lourenço Marques (until the end of April 1900), continued to express his concern about the 'unsatisfactory and inefficient nature of the arrangements for checking communication ...' between the two port towns.[43] Considerable efforts by the British government had been taken to address this contraband conduit, for in January 1900 they had brought Roger Casement to the consulate to set up an intelligence unit to provide information on contraband, specially arms. Casement was no stranger to Lourenço Marques having been posted there as consul general on 27 June 1895. It appears that his first posting was to eventually to exceed an ordinary consular one, since after the Jameson Raid of December that year, Casement was expected to report on the possibility of Germany supplying armaments to the Boers through the port.[44]

The intelligence department of the consulate had been formed in two sections: contraband and military. To obtain information they used unemployed men, both white and African, though Crowe reported that the former '... proved most erratic and unreliable ... they were contemptible people, willing to serve whomever paid them best'.[45] The contraband unit itself was split up into three sections: 'Customs, Railway and the Town'. The major objectives of their work were to ascertain if munitions were really passing to the Transvaal; to stop the passage of contraband goods; and to add to the existing list of contraband items. Casement stayed in this work until July 1900 by which time Fritz Crowe had taken over. Casement had obviously found the task tedious and frustrating and the chaotic conditions of the port extremely inefficient. This was not very different from his experiences some four years before when he advised anyone shipping through Delagoa Bay to claim loss of his cargo as soon as it was landed! After only one month at the task and having satisfied himself that no munitions were passing through the town, he already appeared bored with what appeared to be an impossible task and developed an alternative strategy which he put to Hely-Hutchinson:

> It is my conviction that the best course for Her Majesty's Government to ensure stoppage of this route to contraband of war for the S.A.R., is for the Military Authorities in Natal to send an expedition through British territory and Swaziland, to seize and hold, or else destroy, the Netherlands Railway. I am prepared to give personal assistance, and to bring several useful helpers from Lourenço Marques.[46]

The Natal governor in turn addressed this suggested course of action to both Milner and to the foreign office. Casement asked permission to go to Cape Town to lay his scheme before the military authorities. He left on HMS *Racoon* on 28 February 1900 to make his case for 'the easiest as well as the manliest line of behaviour'. Milner clearly liked the idea and with the approval of Roberts and Kitchener in April, Strathcona's Horse – some 540 men – embarked from Cape Town in May, one contingent bound for Durban and the other for Kosi Bay under Captain Steele accompanied by Casement himself. But the expedition ended ingloriously, when Milner, for reasons unknown, recalled the corps before they had reached their destination.[47] Casement stayed on in Lourenço Marques until July and then joined the military intelligence section in Cape Town.

It is possible that Carnegie Ross had been removed from the office of consul general and replaced by Crowe because he had been ineffective in stopping the flow of goods. It may also have been a result of Captain Scott's suspicions about Carnegie Ross. A letter from Ross to a correspondent had fallen into Scott's hands which suggested that Ross would see that post to Johannesburg was sent on if letters were to be sent with Cape stamps enclosed. An irate Scott had asked the governor 'Is this to be a recognised way of communicating with the enemy?'[48]

Clearly the foreign office viewed Lourenço Marques as a very weak link in the Transvaal contraband chain. Why did they send Casement back to the port? And why some few weeks afterwards, did Ross move out for the arrival of a new consul with a Royal Navy background?

Smuggling

At the time that Carnegie Ross left his consular post he received a report from Major HP Young, who had been appointed as the consular intelligence officer about three months before, at the time of Casement's arrival. The lengthy and detailed report provided fascinating evidence of the extensive smuggling network which had been established in the area by 1900.[49]

Young had come to the clear conclusion that there was 'much humbug going on at Delagoa Bay' and that it was fairly easy for the Transvaal government to receive contraband via the railway; that large amounts of smuggled goods were being taken by rivers and country roads; that the Portuguese government, and foreign firms and ships were hostile to British interests; and that everyone in government employ was making money while they could, in the belief that the Boers would win the war'.

Rifles and ammunition, he maintained, were being sent to Pretoria in iron pipes and drain pipes or disguised as cases of milk, or even in piano cases. Sometimes ammunition got through in passenger luggage. The customs house in Lourenço Marques was notoriously slack and little examination of goods took place. At times when 300 cases of goods were trans-shipped onto trains, only three would be inspected. Young also observed that recruits for the Boer cause were arriving disguised as Red Cross workers, having been recruited by Dr Leyds at 5s per day. On reaching Waterval Onder, they would 'tear off their badges and put on their uniforms'.

But the major portion of Young's report was filled with intriguing details about the river smuggling which he and his paid observers noted day and night. Various small tugs, lighters and even coalers would approach steam vessels, often at the Netherlands pier under cover of dark, mysterious lights would flash, and then goods were spirited away. So, by a complicated series of movements and transfers to other small boats, the contraband would reach the southern shores of Delagoa Bay close to the

Lourenço Marques from the fort (Newnes).

The customs house at Lourenço Marques (Raoul-Duval).

A fashionable street in Lourenço Marques (Raoul-Duval).

A back street in Lourenço Marques (KCL).

A country house near Delagoa Bay (Raoul-Duval).

mouths of the Tembe and Umbelusi Rivers. These were navigable by small craft for long distances across the flats of Maputoland. From the rivers, teams of African porters, of which there were no shortage, would then carry the goods over the Lebombo mountains into Swaziland or the Eastern Transvaal. A porter could carry a load of 60 lbs (27 kg) over 20 to 25 miles (35–40km) per day.

The southern smuggling network was apparently run by a gang which included Powell, Dupont, Major, West Shreder, Brash and Texas Wilson. Young had found that Major was a somewhat pliable character and ready to provide information at a price. The same gang, and others, were also returning with gold and wool from the Transvaal for export to Europe. In between the contraband and gold running they also indulged in smuggling cattle, often from Natal, into Mozambique with the aid of local African chiefs. And between all of these activities, they would spend their earnings on hard liquor in the local bars, the effects of which loosened their tongues. Major Young's spies were quick to note the detailed exaggerations of their tales of adventure.

Young provided further interesting information about the *Bundesrath* and the other steamers of the German East Africa Line. What seems to have been transacted to avoid the surveillance of the Royal Navy was that clandestine goods were exchanged between the ships of the line. Thus the *Bundesrath* had chlorine on board, useful in gold mining, but transferred it to the *Herzog* when the latter had already been inspected. After the *General* had been searched at Aden, she was released and continued on her voyage to Mozambique where she picked up contraband cargo at Beira, left there by the *Herzog*. Of course, the *General* was not searched again by the navy.[50]

By 15 May 1900, Crowe had been in the consulate for a few months and could already report on various contraband issues. He included details about Fritz Pincus, the local Reuters agent and a buyer for the Transvaal who openly boasted about his trading. Several large shiploads of goods had arrived in the previous weeks from Amsterdam, Lisbon and Havre bearing a variety of goods for the Transvaal. With a little pressure on the half-hearted Portuguese governor some of these goods were delayed. He also noted that an 'Indignation Meeting' had been called of all the local merchants, which had been arranged by Pott, the Transvaal consul, who remained in the background. Apart from protesting at the authorities' actions in stopping goods, the meeting also censured Crowe 'for having exceeded his duties'. He added an appendix to his report to the effect that the Portuguese authorities had received instructions from their home government to stop the large quantities of corned beef being shipped inland altogether.

Further reports from the consulate intelligence department dealt with numerous contraband issues and information concerning shipping companies, agencies and trading houses and their shareholders, their local transport and the types of goods they conveyed.

In October 1900, Crowe detailed the different contraband techniques used and the methods his agents had used to obtain information via the local customs and railway offices; the extensive bribery amongst officials and finally how he had successfully convinced the Portuguese governor that extensive smuggling of explosives was taking place in private luggage. The results were far-reaching: 'Whether the governor was sincere or false, he was obliged now to take action ... Director of Customs, and other officials were removed ... [and] a semi-military regime followed ...'[51]

Prominent Durban merchants

Over and above the major contraband route through Delagoa Bay, the authorities in Durban also had to deal with other cases of apparent 'trading with the enemy'. Some of these included prominent Durban and Natal merchants such as Parker Wood & Co. whose principal, AM Campbell, was a member of parliament. They had branches in Frankfort and Vrede in the Free State who had purchased goods through Lourenço Marques and requested the head office in Durban to pay. Attorney-General Bale did not consider this to be illegal since they were dealing with themselves, but he suggested to the prime minister that Campbell be warned of the risks he would be running if he were to export goods to the Free State.[52] Others, like Greenacre & Co., seemed to have gone out of their way to remain within the law, requesting the commandant for permission to cash ZAR bank notes from branches of the firm in the Transvaal.[53]

Towards the end of the war strong rumours appeared (probably from Lourenço Marques) that ammunition from Italy was being smuggled in butter tins. The collector of customs in Durban and the commandant had a busy time checking every consignment of butter especially that from Naples on board the *Köniz*. Having found that this was genuine butter, Commandant O'Neill assured McCallum, the governor, that he would keep a sharp lookout for butter brought in other ships from Italian ports.[54]

A tug and a small motor steamer leaving the port of Durban (Brown).

Durban: an open port?

There were a number of specific effects of the war on the exercise of trade in Durban. One of these was the enormous growth of goods retained in bond – in 1901 for example, of the total amount of £8 587 931 worth of civilian goods imported, some £3 627 077 were placed in bond awaiting the termination of the war.[55] This also necessitated an increase from 60 bonded warehouses in 1897 to 140 warehouses in 1902. Another effect was for the collector finally to give in to the complaints which merchants had been making since the mid-1870s about the inconvenient location of the customs house at the Point. In November 1901 a branch office was opened in the town of Durban itself. This probably also suited the collector's increased level of surveillance over contraband.

But much of this surveillance appeared to have been an exercise in futility, since prosecutions in law were apparently impossible to achieve. It is also likely that most of that initial energy demonstrated by other

Boats at the small boat dock, Point (LHM).

officials in Durban, who were charged with the administration of martial law, had been dissipated by the period before the declaration of peace. In March 1902, CHW Pollard an overenthusiastic military intelligence officer, produced a report which was highly critical of the port of Durban particularly with respect to contraband and the comings and goings of passengers and others. He maintained that permits were seldom examined; passengers 'luggage was not inspected; well-known persons were allowed through the port without any scrutiny of their baggage; ships' manifests were accepted as correct without question; landing goods into 'bond' was easily abused; smaller steamers left the port unwatched and anyone could have boarded them without any official observation; and

> ... the Customs is useless, the C.I.D. is useless, or worse, for detecting anything out of the ordinary police case ... my assertion is that Durban is an open port; open that is to the enemy. It may have been allowed to remain so under the idea that Natal is loyal, a pleasing theory but vitiated by its ignoring the large number of foreigners in Durban and elsewhere whose number is increasing and who are for the most part hostile to us. Durban is full of spies and Boer agents.[56]

Indian *madrasees* and their boats close to the steam shears and the customs house (LHM).

Somehow this all sounded familiar.

By 1902 the patterns of trade were already beginning to return to those which had existed before the war when Durban fulfilled the role of a transit port principally for the Transvaal. The collector noted in his report of that year that of the total of £11 843 261 worth of goods imported into Natal through Durban, an amount of £4 933 624 worth went to the Transvaal. Over and above profiteering through contraband, it seems that there were some merchants who certainly did well out of the war. In the same report Mayston commented:

> This Boer War has, undoubtedly, brought into the pockets of the people much increased wealth, and this increased wealth is followed by an increase of expenditure ...

and furthermore:

> The articles ... that form this classification are not necessities of life in the sense that foodstuffs are. They are very largely such as conduce to the comfort of living, but many of them might, at the push, be done without. We find increases in elaborate furniture, and in those articles which are manufactured to suit the higher tastes.[57]

1. PRO, CO 179/209: Hely-Hutchinson to Chamberlain, 3.11.1899
2. PRO, CO 179/208: Hime to Chamberlain, 8.1.1900.
3. PRO, CO 179/209: stores superintendent NGR to Milne, 8.11.1899.
4. PRO, CO 179/207: JT Rennie & Sons to governor, 20.11.1899.
5. *Natal Mercury*, 25.1.1900.
6. PRO, CO 179/216: correspondence concerning detention of soap, 3.5.1900.
7. PRO, CO 179/212: telegram Hely-Hutchinson to Chamberlain, 14.5.1900.
8. PRO, CO 179/207: governor to Portuguese consul, 2.11.1899.
9. PAR, AGO 1/7/50: Milner to Hely-Hutchinson, 18.10.1899.
10. PAR, AGO 1/7/50: Chamberlain to Milner to Hely-Hutchinson, 3.11.1899.
11. PAR, AGO 1/7/50: Hely-Hutchinson to Milner, 21.12.1899.
12. PAR, AGO 1/7/50: Chamberlain to Milner to Hely-Hutchinson, 26.12.1899.
13. PAR, AGO 1/7/50: Chamberlain to Hely Hutchinson, 8.1.1900.
14. PRO, CO 179/208: correspondence concerning guarantors and deposits, 15.12.1899.
15. PAR, NHD II/5/17: annual report of collector of customs, p.3.
16. PRO, CO 179/207: governor to colonial office, 25.10.1899.
17. PRO, CO 179/210: Bethune to governor, 29.10.1899.
18. PRO, CO 179/210: Turkstra & Co. to Balwe, 27.1.1900.
19. Pretorius, F: *Life on Commando during the Anglo-Boer War*, p.44.
20. PRO, CO 179/210: Commandant Scott to governor, 27.1.1900.
21. PRO, CO 179/211; Commandant Morris to governor, 10.4.1900.
22. PRO, CO 179/211: Hely-Hutchinson to Chamberlain, 4.5.1900.
23. PRO, CO 179/211: Hely-Hutchinson to Chamberlain, 22.4.1900.
24. PRO, CO 179/213: censor to commandant, 16.8.1900.
25. *Natal Who's Who*, p.19.
26. PRO, CO 179/209: Hely-Hutchinson to Chamberlain, 9.1.1900.
27. PRO, CO 179/212: commandant to governor, 16.5.1900.
28. PRO, CO 179/214: British consul, Lourenço Marques to commandant, 22.2.1900.
29. PRO, CO 179/212: commandant to governor, 25.2.1900.
30. PAR, GH 832: Crowe to governor, 6.8.1900.
31. PAR, CSO 1632: correspondence concerning shipments to Delagoa Bay, 5.12.1899.
32. PAR, CSO 1632: Hime to colonial treasurer, 5.11.1899.
33. PRO, CO 179/209:collector of customs to commandant, 11.12.1899.
34. PAR, GH 559: W Chalmers Barker to J McIntosh, 3.5.1900.
35. PAR, GH 831: W Stanley Hollis to Carnegie Ross, 18.11.1899.
36. PAR, AG 1/7/50: Buller to Scott, 13.12.1899.
37. PAR, GH 526: intelligence report by Paulson Nors, 31.3.1900.
38. PRO, CO 179/211: correspondence concerning McLaren & Sons,12.4.1900.
39. PAR, GH 557: Bale to Hely-Hutchinson, 1.3.1900.
40. PAR, GH 559: correspondence concerning Gundelfingers application, 18.6.1900.
41. PRO, CO 179/221: correspondence concerning German goods detained, 25.6.1901.
42. PRO, CO 179/213: press censor to commandant, 11.8.1900.
43. PRO, CO 179/211: Hely-Hutchinson to Chamberlain,11.4.1900.
44. Singleton-Gates, P, and Girodias, M, *The Black Diaries*, p.78.
45. PAR, GH 832: record of work in the intelligence department of the consulate-general at Lourenço Marques, May to October 1900.
46. PAR, GH 833: telegram Casement to Hely-Hutchinson, 5.2.1900.
47. Reid, BL, *The Lives of Roger Casement*, p.26–27.
48. PRO, CO 179/209:Scott to governor, 25.12.1899.
49. F&CO, Conf. 7316: Young to foreign office, 21.3.1900 and Young to Consul Ross, 3.3.1900.
50. Ibid.
51. PAR, GH 832:, record of work in the intelligence department of the consulate general at Lourenço Marques, May to October 1900.
52. PRO, CO 179/209: attorney-general to governor, 30.12.1899.
53. PAR, GH 559: minute paper commandant, 21.6.1900.
54. PRO, CO 179/219: McCullum to Chamberlain, 28.6.1901.
55. PAR, NHD II/5/16: report of the collector of customs, p.3.
56. PRO. WO 108/117: Pollard to director, military intelligence, South Africa, 17.3.1902.
57. PAR, NHD II/5/19: annual report of collector of customs, 1902, p.9.

The neighbourhood of Sea View Street where General Piet Joubert owned property at the outbreak of the war (LHM).

Pine Street with the municipal market on the right and Castle Buildings on the left (LHM).

CHAPTER 23

ATTEMPTS TO STRIP THE ASSETS OF THE TRANSVAAL

Johan Wassermann

One of the aspects that needed to be addressed by both the military commanders and the Natal colonial authorities was how to deal with the property of the republics and republicans in Durban. The first asset that came under scrutiny was that of the commandant-general of the Transvaal, General PJ (Piet) Joubert. Joubert had a property very close to the Durban beachfront, situated at 19 Sea View Street, subdivision A, erf number 12, block Z. The property was valued at £340 and was occupied by a tenant, W Brown. Thinking that he was acting for the benefit of the Durban public, RJ Staines brought this to the attention of Commandant Percy Scott, who informed Governor Walter Hely-Hutchinson,[1] who in turn approached Attorney-General Henry Bale for advice. Bale's recommendation was simple: 'I can find no authority for the confiscation under <u>jus gentium</u> of the immovable property of an alien enemy acquired before the commencement of hostilities. The rents and profits may, however, be sequestrated in order to prevent them from being remitted to the enemy, and Joubert may not deal with his immovable property while war is in progress.'[2] It was, however, not only the property of prominent individuals that was under threat in Durban owing to the war, but also any in which the Transvaal government had a stake.

The Durban branch of the National Bank of the ZAR

With the shadow of war looming large over South Africa, the Natal government decided that, as long as the National Bank of the ZAR did business in Durban and received coin at face value, the other banks in Natal had to follow suit.[3] This economic process did not last long and two weeks later, with the war in full swing, the National Bank informed the Natal harbour department that they were no longer accepting the Transvaal paper money.[4] Matters soon became even more complicated for the National Bank branch in Durban. On Tuesday 17 October 1899, the owners of the *Avondale Castle* were requested by the bank to take £20 317 in gold coins and £3 880 in silver, loaded into 12 boxes, to their branch in Lourenço Marques. Through the collector of customs, George Mayston, the Natal governor, Walter Hely-Hutchinson was asked whether the money would be regarded as contraband. After consultation with the Natal government and the attorney-general, Hely-Hutchinson decided that the currency could not be regarded as contraband and the *Avondale Castle* was allowed to proceed with its valuable cargo. The ship did not, however, reach Lourenço Marques as it was seized by the *Tartar* before reaching its destination and brought back to Durban.[5]

The reason for the reversal in position was that the amount of money involved left both the military and Natal government suspicious of the role that the Durban branch of the National Bank was playing in the war. The turning point came when Governor Hely-Hutchinson was informed that all republican spies in Durban were paid by the bank. He therefore forwarded the following telegram to the commandant of Durban, Lieutenant Colonel E Bethune:

> I learnt that Durban branch National Bank of S.A.R. is the medium through which all spies are paid. They are paid by cheque in the bank. Inspection of books would enable us to lay our hands on all spies and to answer certain questions which High Commissioner has asked me about doings of the bank. I have decided for the above and other reasons to make martial law general. My intentions will be kept secret and at 2.45 p.m. today bank will be entered and books examined: proclamation being issued at the same moment. Ministers concur and state that there will be no difficulty whatever in obtaining indemnity from the Legislature.[6]

These orders were executed like clockwork on Monday 23 October 1899. Minutes after martial law was declared, a party of marines and bluejackets from the *Tartar* halted outside the bank, which was situated in the Castle Buildings, West Street. The bluejackets marched via Pine Street to the back of the buildings, while the marines took up position on the pavement, with fixed bayonets. Soon a crowd gathered and watched as Bethune and Mayor J Nicol, Magistrate W Broome, Auditor-General WE Goldby and Town Clerk W Cooley entered the building. Three hours later, the armed force left the premises and returned to the Point.[7] What then had transpired inside the bank?

Once inside the bank, Goldby and the manager of the bank, JMC Leighton, sealed the safes in the presence of the magistrate. Goldby then examined the books and found that £15 2s 9d was paid to one Nathan Marks on instruction of the state secretary of the Transvaal. This information was immediately relayed to Bethune, and by the evening, Marks and two other suspects were under arrest. The only other Transvalers on the payroll were the Transvaal customs officials. An inspection of their books revealed nothing out of the ordinary. What Goldby could confirm was that the shipment on the *Avondale Castle* had been intended for Pretoria. The manager of the bank gave his full assistance to the investigation and the future running of the bank by declaring in writing: That no gold specie or paper money shall be transferred from any Branch of the Bank outside the S.A.R. or by the agents of the Bank in England to the S.A.R., O.F.S. and Delagoa Bay, during the war.'[8] Manager Leighton, did, however, request that the money taken from the *Avondale Castle* and transferred to the *Tartar* was to be returned as it was the property of the bank, and that he had no knowledge that the money was to be placed in the hands of the Transvaal government. Hely-Hutchinson agreed, although conscious that Leighton must have been well aware that the money was bound to be used by the Transvaal government.[9] Leighton kept his word and was lauded for his co-operation when he was later transferred to Cape Town.[10]

RT Harrison, an experienced banker, was appointed to inspect the future transactions and accounts of the National Bank. In fulfilling this task, Harrison had to monitor carefully all transactions between the various branches of the bank, inspect the books daily to ensure that no funds of the bank were applied to any purpose in the republics, that no drafts of the republican governments or their agents were honoured, that no coin, bullion or paper money was removed from the strong room except for legitimate purposes and that no payments were made to persons in the employment of the republics. If any irregularities were discovered the governor was to be informed.[11] These instructions were followed implicitly by Harrison and he diligently submitted his reports. With the full assistance of the nine staff members of the bank, all British subjects who spoke no Dutch, no irregularities occurred.[12] So efficient was Harrison, that Percy Scott, when he vacated his post as commandant of Durban, made special mention of his excellent work.[13]

Although the inspection of the National Bank revealed no traces of payment towards espionage, it did serve to deter the use of the Durban branch of the National Bank from initiating covert operations from behind the doors of a financial institution. For the rest of the war, the bank abided by the rules as can be gathered from the dealings of the Transvaalsche Koelkamers Beperk, later known as the Transvaal Cold Storage Company, with the financial institution under discussion.

The Transvaalsche Koelkamers Beperk

On 10 April 1899, despite the deteriorating relations with the Transvaal, AH Hime, the Natal prime minister, who also held the portfolio of minister of lands and works, signed a 25-point contract with S Gillingham, the managing director of the Transvaalsche Koelkamers Beperk. According to the contract, the Natal government would lease for 21 years a piece of land, '1 acre 3 roods 38 perches more or less', at the head of St Pauls channel, in the vicinity of Cato Creek at Addington, to the Transvaalsche Koelkamers Beperk.[14] In this venture the Transvaal government had by far the largest monetary interest of between £80 000–£85 000, mostly due to the need to satisfy the ever-growing number of consumers on the Witwatersrand, by importing meat, as the local cattle herds were decimated by lung sickness and the rinderpest. This capital was put to good use, and construction on the cold storage facilities, which started in July 1899, progressed well, until plans were interrupted by the outbreak of war.

With martial law in existence in Durban and the collector of customs trying his utmost to prevent any material that could assist the war effort of the republics from passing through the city, the construction of the cold storage facilities came to a halt. As a result, the manager of the National Bank of the ZAR, who had to deal with the finances for the construction of the facilities, wrote a letter to Commandant Scott concerning the delivery of ironware and machinery. This material was of great importance in the construction of the building, but was also viewed by customs as materials which could enhance the republican war effort. To prevent the cold storage facilities from being viewed as a forwarding centre for republican war material, Leighton suggested to Scott that the goods be stored, on order of the bank, in an ordinary warehouse, rather than as a seizure, in the Queen's warehouse, and released by permission of the commandant only. This would save the Transvaalsche Koelkamers Beperk a large sum of money and allow the military to control the use of the material.[15]

Via the governor and prime minister, the request was forwarded to the collector of customs for comment. According to Mayston, he could by law seize any goods destined for the Transvaalsche Koelkamers Beperk, as the Transvaal government held the largest monetary interest. He did suggest, however, that as the goods in question were intended for construction only, the company should be treated as a private company, with the proviso that the Natal government, in view of the contract with the company, have a lien upon the premises. In the light of this, Mayston treated the Transvaalsche Koelkamers Beperk as a private concern and did not seize the goods bound for the company but deposited them in a private warehouse, that of Mann & Stainbank. They would be kept there until required and then delivered under customs supervision, but this clearance did not relieve the goods from the possibility of seizure, subsequent to their release, because of the financial interest of the Transvaal government. Both the governor and the prime minister agreed to the arrangement.[16]

The *Transvaalsche Koelkamers* was built at Cato Creek close to the extended harbour wharfs (LHM).

The securing of access to the ironware and machinery did not solve the problem of accruing payments to the consulting architect, CW Methven, as well as to the contractors, or for the money owed for equipment and for the rent of the site, payable to the secretary of the harbour board. These payments were hampered by the difficulty in communicating between Pretoria and Durban, and the reluctance of Manager Leighton of the National Bank to consent to payments, despite sufficient funds to the tune of £12 000 being available.[17] With finances not forthcoming, the construction of the cold storage facilities again ground to a halt and the contractors faced financial ruin. To resolve the crisis, CW Methven contacted Commandant Scott and explained to him that the money needed to honour the obligations was in the bank, but that the bank manager was only prepared to release it with the permission of the commandant. The bank also held the documents required by customs for the release of all the cold storage machinery but required authorisation from Pretoria before any action could be taken. Methven therefore requested Scott to allow payments, and to give permission for a telegram to be sent to Pretoria, so that construction of the building could resume.[18]

Scott reacted immediately, but not in the manner Methven had hoped for. He suggested to the governor that the collector of customs should be consulted, but as far as he was concerned the money must be impounded 'as it is evidently money belonging to the enemy's agents'.[19] Hely-Hutchinson was more circumspect and suggested that payments be allowed. He did, however, think that since the development had links with the Transvaal government, their Natal counterparts 'might take possession of the whole thing either now or later on'. As a result, but also because the construction provided employment for a considerable number of British subjects, the governor allowed the credit in the bank to be used as payment, while the bank was also instructed to surrender the documents which enabled the machinery and iron works stored to be used in the construction.[20]

Permission to continue with the construction did not signal the end of the financial problems besetting the Transvaalsche Koelkamers Beperk. New instructions to banks doing business outside of the republics, issued by Lord Alfred Milner and Governor Hely-Hutchinson in early February 1900, resulted in the Durban branch of the National Bank of the ZAR again refusing to honour cheques drawn by the company against its credit. As a result, the inspector of the National Bank, RT Harrison, had to intervene by asking Scott to use his authority to allow payment for the following reason: 'The works when completed will certainly be of greater value to the Imperial Government than they are at present in the incomplete state; that is, in the event of the Imperial Government deciding upon confiscation of the property on account of the Monetary interests in the Company of the Transvaal Government.'[21] To this request Hely-Hutchinson assented, subject to the construction being under the close supervision of Harrison, who could halt operations and had to report immediately to the commandant if he had reason to believe that the building might in any way be used to the military advantage of the republics. To Hely-Hutchinson this was a departure from the letter of the regulations but not the spirit. He deemed this move necessary as the

Cathcart Methven

Methven, who practised in Durban as both an engineer and an architect, had come to the town in 1888 from Scotland to take up the position of harbour engineer. He continued to develop and build the entrance works started by his predecessor, Innes, and especially the construction of the two piers. In addition he commenced a 'training wall' inside the bay to assist the scouring action of the ebb tide. Amongst many innovations, he used models of the harbour works to develop and test his marine engineering ideas. He was also instrumental in the design of several dredgers which were specifically built for work on the harbour. Unfortunately his views were diametrically at odds with those of Harry Escombe and their disagreements blew up into a major political row in the early 1890s. Methven was dismissed as harbour engineer, though a later enquiry in 1895 cleared him of all the charges brought against him. His designs were also fully affirmed by later engineering consultants. In later life he worked as a reputable architect and an artist, while consulting widely on harbour engineering around the coast of South Africa and delivering addresses to numerous professional bodies on the subject.

Transvaalsche Koelkamers Beperk held no benefit to the republics, but, by preventing completion of the storage facilities injury would be inflicted on Natal and on a considerable number of loyal British subjects in Durban.[22]

As with his work at the National Bank, Harrison did his job well and could report that no covert actions had taken place. Notwithstanding, by 3 April 1900, he noted that the company was running out of funds and that the building would take another two months to complete. Manager Leighton made it clear that he would not allow any credit and the company had to secure assistance from an external source.[23] The Transvaalsche Koelkamers Beperk did this, and Dr Fehrsen, a temporary resident of Cape Town, advanced £1 000 in early June 1900, but the money turned out to be from a dubious source, as Fehrsen was arrested in Durban because of his anti-British sentiments while in transit from Lourenço Marques.[24] The construction process nonetheless went ahead, and cold storage became available during late June 1900, even before the construction was completed, although under unusual circumstances. The *Hindoustan* arrived in Durban from Buenos Aires with 400 head of cattle. As they had come from an infected port, the animals needed to be slaughtered before landing. Neither the Durban Cold Storage Company nor the Point Cold Storage Works could accommodate this consignment, leaving only the Transvaalsche Koelkamers Beperk. Despite these exceptional circumstances, the fear existed that such a step would be construed as dealing with the enemy.[25] This posed a dilemma, and Commandant Morris consulted the governor who in turn consulted the attorney-general. In the end, the verdict was that the meat importers involved, Niven, Mitchell & Cotts, could store their meat with the Transvaalsche Koelkamers Beperk, and that such a step would not be seen as trading with the enemy. Possibly feeling that certain principles were being broken, Morris, on receiving the green light from the governor, informed him that 'Messrs Niven, Mitchell and Cotts do not propose to sell their meat to this Company, but only store it with them for a short time'.[26] With this step the Transvaalsche Koelkamers Beperk made a dramatic entrance on the frozen meat scene in Durban, as it was the only company with the capacity to deal with such a vast number of carcasses. The corporation of Durban, which had at first refused to supply the company with water, now had to allow a connection to the mains.

With the facilities completed and in operation, the possibility of seizure by the Natal government still existed. To clarify its position, the company took the best legal opinion available from both England and South Africa. The legal advice given was that the Transvaalsche Koelkamers Beperk should, in the event of annexation of the Transvaal, stand towards her majesty's government in the same relation as that in which it stood to the government of the ZAR. If the Natal government should, despite this change in allegiance, decide to seize the company and thus not adhere to the contract, the directors could repudiate the repayment of the loan. The *Transvaalsche Koelkamers Beperk*, clearly, now had the upper hand.[27] The reminder by Inspector Harrison on 16 July 1900 that the *Transvaalsche Koelkamers Beperk* facilities were completed and in operation and that 'the works were liable to seizure by the Imperial Government' therefore did not make any impact.[28] The Transvaalsche Koelkamers Beperk could move ahead towards full operation and appoint EG Palmer of Sydney, Australia, as director in charge of the facility.[29]

From then on it seems that the tide had turned completely in favour of the Transvaalsche Koelkamers Beperk and the company went into full commercial operation. This lasted until the appointment of Henry McCallum as governor of Natal. He again took up the crusade against the Transvaalsche Koelkamers Beperk, raising two points with Lord Kitchener: had the Transvaalsche Koelkamers Beperk adhered to its contract by appointing three directors and what was the nature of the relationship between the Transvaalsche Koelkamers Beperk and the Combrink Meat Ring? McCallum had no doubt that the Transvaalsche Koelkamers Beperk, which by now had a contract with the director of supplies in Pretoria and rented storage facilities to the rival Durban Cold Storage Company, was controlled by the Combrink Meat Ring which, as a syndicate, contravened section 22 of the lease, and the lease itself was therefore liable to cancellation under clause 15. As a result, McCallum called on Kitchener to assist him in protecting the meat trade from 'tyranny and monopoly'.[30] It is doubtful if McCallum's drive had any effect. The ability of the Transvaalsche Koelkamers Beperk to supply meat at a cheaper rate than its rivals was what counted most to the military, who had to keep a constant eye on the escalating costs related to the war effort. As a result the meat contract of the Merebank concentration camp, which amounted to 5 000 kilograms in November 1901, was awarded to the Transvaalsche Koelkamers Beperk. Sparks & Young Limited, who had lost the contract, complained bitterly to Kitchener, but to no avail.[31] What had started out as a Transvaal company under threat of being seized on completion, turned out to be a business concern which profited from the war.

1. PRO, CO 179/207: correspondence regarding the property of PJ Joubert in Durban, 10.11.1899.

2. PAR, GH 555: minute paper regarding the property in Durban owned by PJ Joubert, 13.11.1899.

3. PAR, NT 68: letter from C Bird, treasurer, 5.10.1899.

4. PAR, NHD II/1/22: memo that Natal Bank no was longer accepting notes of the National Bank of ZAR, 18.10.1899.

5. PRO, CO 179/207: report from manager JMC Leighton, 25.10.1899.

6. PRO, CO 179/207: telegram Hely-Hutchinson to Bethune, 23.10.1899.

7. *Natal Mercury*, 24.10.1899.

8. PRO, CO 179/207: report by Auditor-General WE Goldby, 2.5.1899.

9. PAR, GH 556: letter Leighton to Hely-Hutchinson, 25.10.1899.

10. PAR, GH 560: letter RT Harrison to Commandant AW Morris, 16.7.1900.

11. PRO, CO 179/207: appointment of and instructions to RT Harrison, 26.10.1899.

12. PRO, CO 179/207: inspection report for the National Bank, 16.11.1899.

13. PAR, AG 6: extract of report by Captain Percy Scott referring to RT Harrison, 14.3.1900.

14. PRO, CO 179/214: Colony of Natal, legislative assembly, third session, second parliament, 1899, LA No.14, 1899.

15. PRO, CO 179/210: letter Leighton to Scott, 10.11.1899.

16. PAR, GH 558: letter Mayston to treasurer, 14.11.1899.

17. PRO, CO 179/210: letter BW Swemmer, secretary Transvaalsche Koelkamers Beperk to CW Methven, 18.11.1899.

18. PRO, CO 179/210: letter Methven to Scott, 29.11.1899.

19 PRO, CO 179/210: telegram Scott to Hely-Hutchinson, 29.11.1899.

20. PRO, CO 179/210: telegram Hely-Hutchinson to Hime, 30.11.1899.

21. PRO, CO 179/210: letter Harrison to Scott, 2.2.1900.

22. PRO, CO 179/210: letter Hely-Hutchinson to High Commissioner A Milner, 15.2.1900.

23. PAR, GH 559: letter Harrison to Morris, 3.4.1900.

24. PAR, GH 559: letter Morris to Hely-Hutchinson, 5.5.1900.

25. PAR, GH 560: letter Niven, Mitchell & Cotts. to Morris, 23.6.1900.

26. PRO, CO 179/212: various telegrams regarding the application to store meat with the Transvaalsche Koelkamers Beperk, 23.6.1900–28.6.1900.

27. PRO, CO 179/213: letter Hely-Hutchinson to Milner, 2.7.1900.

28. PRO, CO 179/213: letter Harrison to Morris forwarded to the governor for comment, 16.7.1900.

29. PRO, CO 179/214: contract between the Transvaalsche Koelkamers Beperk and EG Palmer, 12.7.1900.

30. PRO, CO 179/218: letter HE McCallum to Kitchener, 13.6.1901.

31. Wohlberg, AU, *The Merebank Concentration Camp in Durban, 1901–1902*, pp.215–216.

AFRICAN LABOUR
Johan Wassermann

JS Marwick

Marwick, despite the march, was not universally loved. In 1916 he became the first professional manager of the Municipal native affairs department in Durban. His participation in the creation of urban apartheid in Natal gave an ironic twist to his nickname of *Muhle*. During the centenary commemorations of the war, and notwithstanding the fact that the museum is named after Marwick, the Kwa Muhle Museum refused to have a plaque erected in his honour on their premises thus underlining his loss in popularity.

The arrival of African refugees in Durban

The looming Anglo-Boer War in 1899 prompted not only Uitlanders and other Europeans, but also Africans, to flee the Witwatersrand goldfields for port cities such as Durban. By the beginning of October 1899, less than two weeks before war broke out, this process gained new momentum as tens of thousands of African workers departed for destinations outside the borders of the Transvaal. The most remarkable of these migrations was the march under *Muhle*, or the 'kind one', better known as JS Marwick, the Natal native agent in Johannesburg. Part of his duty was to ensure that Zulu workers were monitored and that wages were safely and regularly remitted to the colony for tax purposes, specifically hut tax. Marwick was approached by thousands of Zulu workers who were afraid that the impending war would cause their earnings to be confiscated by the Transvaal authorities. They, therefore, expressed their desire to leave for Natal, but were unable to do so as trains to the colony had been suspended. Marwick felt he had to take action. Disturbed by the breakdown of law and order on the Witwatersrand, the Transvaal officials gave him permission to assist the Zulu workers in reaching Natal. Marching 30 abreast to the tune of traditional Zulu songs, and followed by stragglers, the 7 000 to 8 000 workers (their ranks obscuring petty criminals, thieves and other vagabonds) reached the Transvaal–Natal border on 13 October 1899. Two days later the seven-day, 356-kilometre march ended in Dundee. Tired, and anxious to get home, most marchers were easily convinced to pay out £1, or two weeks' wages, for a train ticket home, which for some was Durban.[1]

The consternation amongst Africans caused by the outbreak of war is immortalised in the story of Katie Makanya, as told to Margaret McCord. After arriving in Durban, via one of the last trains to leave Johannesburg, Katie had to wait for her companions, Ndeya and Mbambo, who, having missed the train, came down with the *Muhle* march. Mbambo and Ndeya finally arrived in Durban by train from Dundee, the former seriously ill because of the physically demanding nature of the march. In an attempt to earn some sorely needed money for the survival of the family group, Ndeya, when rested, set out to look for work. One of the few places in Durban with employment opportunities was the army barracks, presumably at Lords Ground. When Ndeya asked at the barracks if there were any saddles to repair, he was coaxed into the army as a muleteer, a position he filled for the duration of the war. Katie only received word of this development months later. To survive, Katie, with the aid of the Reverend William Makanya, found work in Essenwood Road. Her main task was to do laundry for a salary of 10 shillings a month and a room above the stable, with rations being included. She did this for the duration of the war and lost a child who died during that time.[2]

Makanya represented many others who had similar experiences. According to police reports, 1 500 African refugees were scattered through the backyards of Durban. Others were temporarily housed at a section of Lords Ground, which also accommodated large numbers of European refugees. In due course the Africans were despatched to the rural areas of Natal.[3] Many who had culturally dislocated themselves from traditional African society remained in Durban. Pimps, prostitutes, illicit liquor sellers and criminals, who were by now unable and unwilling to adjust to pre-capitalist tribal life, found a cosmopolitan destination such as Durban more congenial. Here they could render their services to their old clients, and also establish new ones, in a city changed forever by war.

The economic position of Africans in wartime Durban

The booming wartime economy in Durban attracted and benefited both Europeans and Africans. The radical growth in population, both military and civilian, African and Europeans alike, and the accompanying increase in demand for foodstuffs, provided new opportunities for the homestead economy and for independent African food producers. At the same time, the surge of activity in the Durban harbour led to a demand for unskilled labour, which was needed to load and unload ships and trains carrying supplies required to fight a war. Simultaneously, new economic opportunities were created for ricksha pullers, washermen and other workers. As a result, thousands of African workers joined the refugees and congregated in Durban, leading to a growth in the African communities in and around the city.[4]

According to Magistrate JJ Stuart, in his annual report for 1901 on Africans in Durban, three main classes of African workers existed in the city: ricksha pullers, domestic servants and *togt* workers. Although mentioned in his report, informal economic activities such as prostitution, and trade and barter, were not viewed by Stuart as being of significance amongst Africans.

Magistrate Stuart reported that little trade and barter was taking place, expressing the opinion that Africans did not 'understand business principles sufficiently to conduct large and remunerative concerns'. He, however, seems to have been mistaken. In his own report he referred to informal capitalist ventures such as beer-drinking establishments and refreshment rooms aimed at the African market which were doing increasing business, and he also mentioned how Africans from the rural areas were bringing curios, such as assagais, to sell to the large refugee and military population of Durban. The number of traditional healers operating in Durban also increased as the growing African population meant a greater demand for their services.[5] Superintendent RC Alexander, the head of the borough police, alluded to another important aspect

African workers gather in Johannesburg before marching to the Natal border (KCL).

Katie Makanya (McCord).

JJ Stuart

James Stuart was educated in both London and Cape Town. He entered the Natal civil service in 1888 and filled various positions, including that of acting assistant magistrate for Durban. In due course he established himself as an author and expert on Zulu affairs.

African stevedores at the Point docks (LHM).

African *togt* workers at the concrete block yard at the Point (LHM).

Although the magistrates were generally happy with the service provided by the rickshas, there were undercurrents. The pullers often tended to charge customers more than the regulated fee, but on the other hand, they were frequently cheated by Europeans. With little control over them at their barracks, they became involved in criminal activities, such as acting as pimps, by ferrying customers and prostitutes to and fro.

The most important group of African workers in the formal economy were the *togt* workers. They were positioned around the economic hub of Durban, the harbour and the Point area. Here they worked as stevedores, or were employed in transport or warehousing. To work as a *togt* labourer in Durban, a license was required from the Durban corporation which was available at 5 shillings per annum. In 1901, 48 530 such licences were issued. The advantages and disadvantages of *togt* labour were that the workers often did not abide by the regulations, and most were hired and paid on a daily or monthly basis. In 1901, they demanded 2s 6d per day, while at times they could earn as much as 4 shillings per day. Such wages, which were much higher than the prescribed amount, were paid by employers, while the *togt* labourers also demanded food and lodgings, a benefit they had not received prior to the war.[17] Magistrate Stuart blamed these circumstances on the whites who employed no co-ordinated strategies regarding payments of the high wages, thus opening themselves up for exploitation by the workers. SO Samuelson, the Natal under-secretary for native affairs, likewise condemned the 'excessive wages' paid to the workers as 'demoralizing' to Africans, as these high wages created a knock-on effect and newcomers to the labour market, rather than entering domestic service, opted to become *togt* workers.

The conditions surrounding the *togt* labour were unsatisfactory, and a cause of concern for the local authorities, especially because the increase in the African population in Durban placed enormous stress on the rudimentary infrastructure. Their apprehension can be deduced from statements made by Magistrate Stuart and Chief Superintendent Alexander. Stuart regarded the legislation then in place as inadequate for controlling and managing the Africans, especially the *togt* labourers. He described *togt* workers as a very independent and do-as-you-like class, 'sleeping in many instances, anywhere and everywhere'. Their nocturnal habits were largely due to inadequate housing, which the Durban corporation needed to supply 'in a free and liberal manner', to sustain the growing demand for and increase in the numbers of *togt* workers.[18]

It was thought that it would be ineffective merely to provide housing if measures were not taken to control the workers by means of general police supervision. To supervise and control the 15 000 African men and 500 women, Superintendent Alexander envisaged a compromise between social engineering, introducing new legislation to provide the police with more powers, and reviewing the administration of Africans. To prevent the African men employed in Durban from walking the streets at night, he wanted 'a proper compound or location ... erected at once, no matter at what cost', and he intended to make these men occupy it and pay rent. In addition to improved housing facilities, Alexander demanded that 'a proper pass system' be introduced, and that the number of African police-

that they, having no where else to go, return to their kraals'. Although he deemed it difficult to combat the panic, King-Hall suggested, in order to reverse the situation, that a camp consisting of tents should be rented to Africans to provide them with accommodation, while supervising their sanitary ways. The port advisory board immediately accepted the recommendation of King-Hall, and with the assistance of the mayor and various Admiralty contractors, the African workers were informed that they could reside at the Point area, in the tents erected, free of charge.[24] The improved living conditions did, however, not solve the problem of the shortage and subsequent high cost of labour in Durban. By the end of 1901, matters became even worse when the mines and industries on the Witwatersrand again came into production, luring even more economically active labourers away from Natal and Durban.

The labour crisis prompted the governor of Natal, HE McCallum, to convene a conference on 29 January 1902, at Newcastle, to deal with 'the abnormal rate of wages at present given to Natal natives both by the Civil and Military Authorities, and the steps to be taken to bring about a remedy'. The conference was attended by FR Moor, and representatives from the all the major stakeholders, namely the military, mining, agriculture, householders and forwarding agents at the Point.

According to McCallum, the military and especially the South African Constabulary (SAC) played a major role in contributing to ever-increasing wages for Africans. They paid Natal Africans as much as £4 10s per month, while also providing the rations and clothing given to Europeans. The situation was aggravated by the fact that the SAC was not a military department in the true sense of the word but, to all intents and purposes, functioned under the auspices of High Commissioner Milner. As a result the SAC acted in a high-handed manner, sending European touts to Natal to acquire labour without a government pass. The actions of the SAC, and also that of other military departments, as well as the NGR, who all employed thousands of Africans, placed the Natal government in a predicament, as African workers were never paid less than £2 per month. These varying, but high wages caused problems for the Natal government in their attempts to meet the military demands for labour. To the Natal government there was but one solution: the rate of pay for African workers had to be reduced drastically by all employers before a given date.

Mr Currie, who represented the landing and forwarding agents at the Point in Durban, expressed his reservations about cutting the wages of African labour. He maintained that African workers at the Point received 35–40 shillings per month, saying that they were housed and given food but not meat. Trained Africans, such as 'head boys', could receive up to 90 shillings a month. In exchange, these workers had to work whenever required, night or day. Their wages were clear profit as no portion went to touts. Their current wages constituted five shillings more than before the war, but the work had been less then. Although togt labour had become more expensive, Currie still favoured it as he believed the Africans worked well and were 'more economical than ordinary raw kaffirs on monthly wages'. In early 1902, the Point required a labour force of 7 000 African workers, but owing to the war economy, only 4 000 to 5 000 were available, resulting in a severe shortage, and thus preventing a cut in wages.

Although all present at the Newcastle conference agreed that wages for African workers, especially unskilled ones, had increased sharply owing to the war, few present, including the military, were prepared to cut the wages out of fear of a strike. What all parties accepted was that the wage for an African worker should be 30 shillings a month and five or ten shillings more for extra or dangerous work. This could, however, only be implemented once the supply outstripped the demand. FR Moor and the representative of the mining industry, J Livingstone, believed that this could only be achieved by flooding and saturating the market with workers from Mozambique who would undermine any strike and alter the supply and demand ratio.[25] On this note, the conference ended with no real commitment from any employer present to challenge the position of African labour in Durban and Natal.

By mid-February 1902, the shortage of African labour reached critical proportions in Natal and Durban. The military suffered most, especially in the labour-intensive remount and veterinary service departments of which a number were situated in and around Durban at Lords Ground and Gillitts. With the capitalist system of supply and demand

The village of Bamboo Square where marginalised groups of people found a home close to the docks. Many lived in small wood and iron houses and *togt* workers occupied the tiny shacks in between (LHM).

Another view of Bamboo Square immediately before the buildings were demolished. The two-storied barracks were built by the municipality. The sea and the north pier can be seen in the distance (LHM).

having failed to address the shortage of African labour, the assistance of the governor of Natal was solicited. In his capacity as supreme chief, McCallum managed to impound 1 000 African labourers. These workers were employed in various military departments in Natal, but mainly in the remount and veterinary departments. This supply did, however, not satisfy the demand, as the Royal Engineers needed an additional 600 workers, the remount department a further 500, and the Army Service Corps requested more than 600 extra workers. These enumerated requirements were over and above the numbers needed merely to replace those workers whose contracts had expired.

As a result, the governor was again approached, this time with a request to secure labour from Mozambique, as earlier suggested by FR Moor. Unfortunately for the military the news was disappointing. The governor-general of Mozambique did not consider it possible to allow the migration of Mozambican workers to Natal at that time, but hoped to be able to co-operate in the near future. This complicated matters for McCallum for, if at least 5 000 workers could not be imported to relieve the Natal Africans and to address the shortages, the Natal government would be unable to continue to comply with outstanding and further military requisitions for labour. This in turn would impact negatively on the economic heart of the colony, Durban. According to the governor, the enormous demands for labour by the railways, roads, mines and military had depleted the available labour sources in Natal. As a result, the kraals were practically depleted and he, as the supreme chief, had called out nearly every available man from the locations to supply compulsory labour.[26]

Part of the problem in obtaining labour from Mozambique was that in 1901 Lord Milner had concluded an agreement with the Portuguese government whereby, in exchange for labourers supplied to the Transvaal, a percentage of the goods imported to the Transvaal was to pass through Lourenço Marques. Milner had, at the same time, negotiated a deal on behalf of Natal, permitting the recruitment of labour from Mozambique. This was, however, not destined to take place as Natal was informed by the governor-general of Mozambique that the Transvaal had preference in terms of their labour.[27] With the possibility of obtaining labour from Mozambique thwarted, the military in Natal, by now in dire straits, enquired whether workers could be obtained from either the Transvaal, Free State, Cape Colony, Swaziland or Basutoland (Lesotho), or from Mozambique by any other means.[28]

South African Constabulary (SAC)

This force was formed in October 1900 under the orders of Lord Roberts, when it was thought the war was virtually concluded, and the SAC would be required to police the defeated republics. Major-General RS Baden-Powell was elected to command the corps and he recruited members in Britain, Canada, Natal, Australia, New Zealand and the Cape Colony. They had to serve in the field until the end of hostilities. By the end of January 1902, the SAC had 10 000 members. After peace was signed, the SAC was relieved of normal military duties and functioned as both a police force and an army of occupation.

How many Natal Africans were employed by the military in Natal to contribute to creating such a severe labour shortage in Durban and to drive up wages by 5 shillings a day? The military in Natal employed approximately 8 600 Africans, of which 1 200 were attached to the remount department, 600 to the sick horse depots, 1 100 to military supplies and 1 000 to the Royal Engineers. Agencies recruiting labour for the British army in the Transvaal and the Free State had, however, recruited 7 000 Africans from Natal. In total, 15 600 African workers from Natal were, by 15 March 1902, employed by the military. Despite the huge number of workers contracted to the military and the estimated 15 000 residing in Durban, the general officer commanding for Natal, Lieutenant General NG Lyttleton, did not believe McCallum's statement that the potential labour sources in Natal were depleted. He insisted that numerous unemployed Natal Africans were sitting at their kraals as they did not wish to work, and that no regulation existed to force them to make themselves available. As far as he was concerned, they preferred to sit idle and spend 'considerable sums of money at the present high rates of wages' that they had earned when working for the military and other enterprises. He believed that, once the money had been spent, the African workers would return, as a number had already done, and no labour shortages would exist.[29]

Before the accuracy of Lyttleton's viewpoint could be tested, peace was declared, bringing with it a serious change in the economic position of the African worker in Natal in general, and in Durban specifically, as the position of one of the key role-players in the labour market, in the form of the military, had been reduced. This meant that the wage benefits gained by African workers in Durban during the Anglo-Boer War were soon eroded, as the *togt* workers at the Point discovered. Their attempt to use their wartime position created by the shortage of labour to improve their working conditions and to negotiate increased wages failed. Their strike in June 1902, for an increase of 6d per day, was rejected. On the recommendation of Superintendent Alexander, all the strikers were dismissed. This had the desired effect and most of the workers returned to work under the existing dispensation.[30] The fact that the strike was not merely an attempt to gain better wages, but that it had multi-levelled undertones linked to the political, social and economic conditions experienced by Africans during the war is borne out by the report of Magistrate Broome. He attributed the strike to diverse causes: the fears of bubonic plague, the mistaken idea of the requirements of the Identification Act, and the higher demands placed by certain chiefs on their people. As a result, there was a considerable exodus of African workers from Durban who were not replaced by any new arrivals. Domestic servants also lost the privileged position they had held during the war, and Broome complained that in court masters and servants took up the time of the bench 'to a considerable and increasing extent',[31] presumably with economic grievances which had been overlooked when labour was in short supply.

Although the end of the war meant the termination of the high wages paid to African workers, they had been exposed to lasting impressions as a result of their experiences during the almost three-year war. They had been subjected to the militancy of the white workers in

Durban, specifically to that of the carpenters and joiners,[32] as well as the tram workers.[33] Simultaneously, they encountered ideas from Britain and other parts of the empire, brought in by soldiers and sailors. When nothing came of the promised assurances that their political and economic position would improve once the republics were defeated, dissatisfaction with their lot grew. The embryonic economic and political discontent, which existed as a result of the unkept promises and the change in their economic circumstances, was expressed in the first African newspaper in Natal, *Ipepa lo Hlanga* and the Natal Native Congress established in 1900. Although the call of the *Ipepa lo Hlanga, "Vukani Bantu!"* (Rise up you people) fell on deaf ears at first, as the newspaper was read only by those who were literate and who could afford it, the seeds of liberation had been sown.[34] The discontent at economic and social conditions that existed in Durban paved the way for the next struggle and the real South African War, which was fought to liberate Africans both politically and economically. In the words of MW Swanson: 'The Anglo-Boer War, with its aftermath of crowding, labour shortages and unrest among all groups, intensified the social forces that had shaped the issues in the past and brought to maturity Durban's great debate on the Native question.'[35]

The disenchantment of Africans with post-war conditions, which posed a threat to civic order, was sensed by at least one Durbanite, Major HR Bousfield, the assistant to Durban commandants like Percy Scott, who informed FR Moor, on Boxing Day, 1902 that '... the natives in town openly say that there will be a big native war within two years and that they the natives will drive out the white men from the country'. Such talk had apparently being going on for several months '... and the feelings amongst the natives down here makes me think it right to inform you ...'. Moor took little notice of the warning as he had received similar reports prior to this. Instead he considered them to be rumours associated with the aftermath of the Anglo-Boer War and of little importance.[36] How wrong he was, for the Bambatha Rebellion erupted in 1906!

1. Warwick, P, *Black people and the South African War 1899–1902*, pp.127–128.

2. McCord, M, *The calling of Katie Makanya*, pp.142–145.

3. DAR, 3/DBN 5/2/5/3/6: borough police report, 28.1.1901.

4. Duminy, A and Guest, B, The Anglo-Boer War and its economic aftermath, 1899–1910. p.534, in Duminy, A and Guest, B, *Natal and Zululand from earliest times to 1910. A new history.*

5. PAR, NCP 8/1/13/2/2/29: Natal blue book for native affairs, report of the Durban magistrate, JJ Stuart, 27.1 1902.

6. *Natal Mercury*, 21.5.1901

7. For a comprehensive analysis of the rise of African prostitution in Durban at the time of the Anglo-Boer War, see S Ramsay, Eve Noire: "Folk Devil" and "Guardian of Virtue". A study of the emergence of African prostitution in Durban at the turn of the century, in *Journal of Natal and Zulu History*, vol. XIV, 1992. pp.75–111.

8. PAR, NCP 8/1/13/2/29: Natal blue book for native affairs, report of the Durban magistrate, JJ Stuart, 27.1.1902.

9. Ramsay, passim.

10. PAR, NCP 8/1/13/2/10: Natal blue book for native affairs, report from the Durban magistrate, W Broom, 29.1.1903.

11. PAR, NCP 8/1/13/2/29: Natal blue book for native affairs, report of the Durban magistrate, JJ Stuart, 27.1.1902.

12. DAR, 3/DBN 5/2/5/3/6: borough police report, 28.1.1901.

13. DAR, 3/DBN 5/2/5/3/6: borough police report, 28.1.1901.

14. Swanson, MW, "The Durban System": Roots of Urban Apartheid in Colonial Natal, in *African Studies*, 35. 3–4, 76, p.162.

15. *Natal Mercury*, 21.5.1901.

16. PAR, NCP 8/1/13/2/10: Natal blue book for native affairs, report from the Durban magistrate, W Broom, 29.1.1903.

17. DAR, 3/DBN 5/2/5/3/6: borough police report, 28.1.1901.

18. PAR, NCP 8/1/13/2/29: Natal blue book for native affairs, report of the Durban magistrate, JJ Stuart, 27.1.1902.

19. *Natal Mercury*, 21.5.1901.

20. For a comprehensive study on aspects such as the control and management of Africans in Durban at the turn of the previous century see MW Swanson, "The Durban System": Roots of Urban Apartheid in Colonial Natal, *African Studies*, 35. 3–4. pp.161–176.

21. Swanson, pp.164–165.

22. Warwick, pp.132–133.

23. *Natal Mercury*, 30.1.1902.

24. PAR, CSO 1674: memorandum on the shortage of labour in the Durban harbour, 16.4.1901.

25. PRO, WO 108/116: despatch by McCallum on conference on wages for Africans, 23.1.1902.

26. PAR, GH 535: report on shortage of labour in the remount and veterinary departments, 15.2.1902.

27. Dhupelia, U, African labour in Natal: Attempts at coercion and control 1893–1903, in *Journal of Natal and Zulu History*, vol. V, 1982, pp. 36–48.

28. PAR, GH 535: letter Lyttleton to McCallum, 15.2.1902

29. PAR, GH 536: letter Lyttleton to chief of staff, 15.3.1902.

30. Warwick, pp.143–144.

31. PAR, NCP 8/1/13/2/10: Natal blue book for native affairs, report of the Durban magistrate, W Broome, 29.1.1903.

32. *Natal Mercury*, 21.2.1901.

33. Van der Tang, DB, White worker militancy in Durban: a study of tramway workers 1900–1939, M.A. thesis, University of Natal, passim.

34. Odenaal, A, *Vukani Bantu! The beginnings of black protest politics in South Africa to 1912*, pp.59–61.

35. Swanson, p.166.

36. PAR, SNA 1/1/298: reports by HR Bousfield re a threat of a 'native' uprising within two years, 26.12.1902.

CHAPTER 25

THE ECONOMIC IMPACT OF THE ANGLO-BOER WAR ON DURBAN: THE STRUGGLE FOR A FAIR DEAL

Johan Wassermann

Robert Jameson

Jameson was born in Kilmarnock, Scotland in 1832, and spent his youth with his father's regiment, the 79th Highlanders, in Canada and Gibraltar. He decided against a military career and ended up in Durban in 1856. Here he started a very successful business of manufacturing preserves and condiments. Jameson was associated with the Durban town council for more than 30 years, acting as mayor from 1895–1897. During this time he worked strenuously to improve sanitary and environmental conditions in the city, chairing the sanitary committee for many years. From 1895 he was a member of the legislative council for Durban County.

The traditional perspective of the economic impact of the war on Durban

The traditional historical view is that Durban and Natal experienced unprecedented economic prosperity during the Anglo-Boer War. The evidence for this point of view is legion. Durban harbour handled unprecedented volumes of traffic and the warehouses which the military had not commandeered were bulging with consumer goods. The NGR, with its headquarters in Durban, carried vast amounts of military traffic inland which partially compensated for the loss of railway earnings resulting from the termination of trade with the republics, even though trucks that returned to Durban brought soldiers, POWs and concentration camp inhabitants rather than goods for sale or export. Purchases of provisions by traders in Durban for the day-to-day running of the British army in the hinterland increased the demand for imported goods via Durban, which also compensated for the loss of revenue on goods bound for the interior. The large number of refugees in Durban, 20% of the population in 1901, became a potent economic force and spent an estimated amount of £74 419 in the first year of the new century. The informal economic sector was booming with houses of ill repute and bottle stores flourished. Heavy engineering and other manufacturing enterprises rose to the challenge that confronted them, such as the modification of the hospital ships. On the downside the war led to an increase in the cost of living, but this negative effect was counterbalanced by higher wages and more employment opportunities, so much so that the economy of Durban during the Anglo-Boer War was characterised by a constant shortage of both skilled and unskilled labour. The repatriation after the war of soldiers, POWs, refugees and concentration camp inhabitants also contributed to the economic prosperity of Durban. At the same time Durban, as the economic hub of Natal, experienced an influx of capital and immigrants.[1]

The evidence of economic prosperity referred to above is backed-up by impressive statistics provided by the collector of customs, George Mayston. From 1899 to 1900, the imports via the Durban harbour increased from 514 504 to 794 741 tons. Greatest import increases were in wheat and other grains, as well as in railway materials to repair the lines destroyed by the Boers. The demand for a variety of goods associated with the military such as food, alcohol and tobacco also showed a sharp increase. The most significant decline in imports for this period was in the form of timber, which was primarily used in the mining industry. The greatest trade via Durban was from Australasia and the Cape Colony.[2]

As far as exports via Durban were concerned, a downturn occurred from 1899 to 1900. Wattle bark dropped by 32 000 bales, coal by 78 000 tons, hides dropped by more than 50% from 13 006 bales to 6 546 bales, skins from 5 208 bales to 957 bales and wool, one of the important lifelines of the Durban economy, from 54 823 bales to 6 201 bales. Other products boomed as far as exports for this period were concerned. The demand for fish rose from 895 lbs (406 kg) to 15 271 lbs (6 926 kg), for grain from 593 tons to 6 669 tons, for preserves from 4 804 lbs (2 179 kg) to 274 651 lbs (124 581 kg) and for tobacco from 2 486 lbs (1 127 kg) to 704 944 lbs (319 762 kg). The main difference was that most of the export products that rose so spectacularly in the first year of the war, £5 911 518 in value compared to £522 290 in 1899, did not originate from Durban or its hinterland, but were products which ended up in Durban as a break of freight to be exported elsewhere.[3] Overland exports, mainly to the Boer republics, fell from £522 031 for the first quarter of 1899 to nil for the comparative period in 1900.[4]

By 1901, this situation had improved and the volume of imports was described by the collector of customs as 'simply astounding' while he recorded that 'shipowners reaped a rich harvest'. In percentage terms, imports rose by 61% from 1900. In tonnage this meant that 203 626 extra tons of goods were imported. More goods arrived than could be carried away by the trolleys and the railways, leading to congestion and theft in the harbour. Stocks to the value of £4 000 000 were held in bonded warehouses by both the Durban and Overberg companies. The export market also boomed, generating a sum of £1 147 453. Coal contributed £269 976 to this figure. In the words of Mayston: 'This Boer war has, undoubtedly, brought into the pockets of the people much increased wealth, and this increase in wealth is followed by an increase of expenditure, and on this expenditure Customs Duties have necessarily been paid, with the result that an increase in Customs receipts flowed.' Mayston, however, hastened to warn: 'I think, all things considered, Ministers must, as soon as we are quit of the Refugees and Military, be prepared for a set back in the Revenue.'[5] These words proved to be prophetic as in 1902 the export aggregate of all goods declined from a high of 186 963 tons in 1901 to 135 391 tons.[6] Soon afterwards the Natal economy went into a recession that lasted from 1903 to 1909. This was partially due to the decline of wartime expenditure in Natal which dried up when the military and the refugees left. Durban now had to rely on the traditional sources of trade, such as agricultural products from the Transvaal and what was now known as the Orange River Colony. This branch of the economy, however, took many years to recover owing to the scorched earth policy employed by the British army.

The struggle for a fair economic dispensation for Durban

Behind the economic success outlined above, forces were at work, requiring the concerted effort of the Durban commercial community led by the Durban chamber of commerce, in an attempt to ensure that the city would receive a fair slice of the profits to be made from the war. The first drawback was a predictable one, many skilled and economically active young men left Durban as members of the various volunteer regiments. What was more problematic in the early stages of the war was the loss of revenue from customs and the railways arising from the cessation of trade with the Transvaal and Orange Free State. To make matters worse, the military requested a remission of custom duties on all articles imported by or for the British army. The Natal government was not in favour of a total remission, fearing it would be resented by the local traders, while the duties which the colony stood to lose would be enormous. At the same time, the remission of duties could be exploited by importing goods under the guise of military supplies, with the intention of selling them on the open market. In the end, the Natal government yielded to the pressure and revoked duties as part of their contribution to the war effort.[7]

The fears expressed by the Natal government that an easing on the payment of custom duties would be exploited and leave some merchants unhappy soon proved warranted. The Durban chamber of commerce complained bitterly that imports which had been passed free of customs duties for the use by the British army had found their way into the general market. The Natal government promised to take steps to prevent similar occurrences.[8] The allegations by the Durban chamber of commerce that the scale of such fraud was enormous did not convince the collector of customs, G Mayston, who insisted that the number of 'leakages' was not great, as would be proved by any investigation.[9]

A case in point of a Durban businessman who abused the system by importing goods to be sold to the military as rations and then sold them on the open market was Robert Jameson. He claimed £4 695 11s in duties to be refunded to him for 528 bags of mealie meal he had imported from America on the *Bechuana*. A large portion of the mealie meal was found in the store of A Beckett, who was selling it to the public.[10] To complicate matters further, Jameson had apparently signed certificates, on entry, to place a hold on the mealie meal in case of fraudulent activities. This did not conform with regulations stipulating that a senior military officer of the Army Service Corps had to sign certificates to confirm that the goods were indeed for military use. Sidestepping this order, Jameson made 'special arrangements' to store the mealie meal for the military. In the process, Jameson failed to monitor the situation and the military received substitutes instead of the cleared goods. Because it was difficult to attach blame to him, Jameson was found to be innocent and a certain WH Edmonds had to pay the duty and a fine of £50. Whether the incident reflected an innocent mistake or an elaborate scam, the Natal government nonetheless immediately took action, informing the military that goods imported to be sold in canteens would no longer be exempt from duties.[11]

Fraud involving duties also had a negative impact in terms of gifts

Timber arriving from Scandanavia at Cato Creek (KCL).

African workers piling fodder at the Point docks (KCL).

Bales of wool awaiting export at the Point (LHM).

sent to soldiers. For example, James Nobel & Company received a box of 'Nestor Gianaclis' cigarettes sent to them from England for free distribution amongst the troops in Natal. The company applied for the consignment to be admitted duty free. Although the request was finally granted, the words of the collector of customs, Marston, on the matter give an indication of the scale of the problem which the customs faced in respect of unscrupulous business transactions:

> I have no doubt of the bona fides of Messrs J. Noble and Co., but it is not businesslike to allow merchants the privilege of free import for proposed distribution among the sick and wounded, especially where large quantities are concerned. The distribution should take place under the authority of and through recognized military channels. The motives of the givers are good, but, to save ourselves from others, who may be unscrupulous, we must guard the distribution.[12]

The abundance of goods imported via Durban which left the harbour crowded and cluttered provided the opportunity for other crimes, such as theft of military goods. Larceny in the Durban harbour ranged from the appropriation of 461 bottles of Perrier Jouet Campagne by employees of the Army Service Corps,[13] to pilfering of forage on a massive scale. On 23 December 1901, GA Mann and RH Stainbank, landing and shipping agents, along with two of their employees, T Williams and C Kershaw, as well as J Raubenheimer, a trolley proprietor, and one of his employees J Campbell, plus their 11 Indian and African workers, were arrested under martial law for the theft of forage. The military allowed the case to slumber for a month before handing the 17 suspects over to the civil authorities, who after a preliminary examination arrested several members of the military as accomplices. The investigation revealed that huge supplies of forage had been removed over a period of time, along with the tarpaulins used to cover the provisions.[14]

Dissatisfaction was also rife amongst the members of the Durban chamber of commerce regarding the practice in Natal of having certain agents purchase military stores by private arrangement. According to the chamber, in the interest of all concerned such purchases should have been made by public tender.[15] The military only responded to this complaint, which was lodged in May 1900, in September 1900, and then only after several letters from the Durban chamber of commerce and on the prompting of the Natal government. The reply from the officer commanding the Natal army was that he saw no reason to make any alteration in the method adopted for procuring supplies.[16] Clearly the concerns of the Durban chamber of commerce that the process was unfair to business did not concern the military, who did not mind paying more than they would if competition were introduced in the form of public tender.

Suffering from the economic restraints caused by the war, especially in trade with the republics, the Durban chamber of commerce asked their government in July 1900 when Natal merchants would be allowed to forward foodstuffs and clothing to towns in the Transvaal.[17] The fear of losing their established markets was real, as the government of the Cape

Colony had, on 28 July 1900, passed regulations which permitted goods to be moved from the Cape to sections of the Transvaal under British control.[18] At the same time in Durban the military used up to 500 railway trucks for transporting supplies to the Transvaal, with local businessmen only being allocated 5 tons worth of the available space.[19] By August 1900, with the conventional phase of the war on its last legs, a new concern arose for the Durban chamber of commerce, namely that the Lourenço Marques railway line to the interior of the Transvaal would be reopened before the lines from Durban and the Cape ports. This fear was fuelled by newspaper reports that foreign companies were stockpiling goods at Lourenço Marques, hoping to gain first access to the Transvaal market. The Durban chamber of commerce alerted the military to the fact that British trade would be seriously hampered and the 'mercantile and general interest' of Natal would suffer if the line from Lourenço Marques was to be opened before the Durban line.[20]

Not only were Durban businessmen struggling to maintain their old markets, especially in the Transvaal, but commercial traffic from the republics also came to a halt and all products from the republics were barred from being exported to Natal and the Cape Colony. This irked the Durban chamber of commerce who wanted one key product, wool, which formed an important segment of commercial activities in the city, to be brought from the republics. Much of the wool had, by now, been sitting in the republics since the outbreak of war and most of it belonged to British merchant houses. In an attempt to have the regulations altered, the Durban chamber of commerce contacted the foreign office in London. Lord Salisbury, on behalf of the British government, indicated that they would raise no objections to wool being exported from the Orange Free State or the Transvaal, as long as no parts of the proceeds were to go directly or indirectly to the republics. On this basis, the Durban chamber of commerce deemed it possible that wool could be brought down by the empty trucks that came from the hinterland, as it was in the commercial interest of the British public and merchants. The reaction from the Natal government when confronted with Salisbury's reply was evasive in nature: 'This matter is one entirely for the consideration of the Military Authorities, to whom your letter will be forwarded by his Excellency the Governor.'[21]

By now, the company of Reinhold alone had 4 000 wool bales sitting at Volksrust, ready for transport to Durban. The NGR, however, refused to allow any movement of the commodity until the Natal government had given the green light and they would not even provide storage facilities at Charlestown. The submissive attitude of the Natal government angered the Durban wool merchants and especially Reinhold, who commented that: 'The surprising feature of the matter to us is that the Imperial Authorities, who might reasonably be thought masters of the situation, entirely ignore the proclamation and are quite willing to facilitate things for us, whilst Natal still insists that the proclamation be observed and actually appears to place difficulties in our way.'[22]

As the Natal government and the military together prevented wool from being exported via Durban, businessmen found their own routes, and wool was exported via Delagoa Bay, Port Elizabeth and East London.

When this news broke, the Natal government was again confronted by the Durban wool merchants and urged to bring Durban onto the same footing and to allow for the restrictions to be lifted. Not only was the lack of wool sales a loss to the Durban economy, but the NGR was also deprived of lucrative transport contracts. At the same time, the potential damage to wool stored in various localities in the republics was a real prospect as the rainy season approached.

These petitions and protestations hardly moved the Natal government and the reply from Prime Minister Albert Hime was much the same as before: 'The question of the export of wool from the Transvaal and Orange River Colony to Natal is not one which the government of Natal can deal with. The matter has been fully represented by me to the Governor, and I am directed to inform you that His Excellency is in communication with Lord Roberts on the subject.' In the communication with Roberts the full implication of the restriction of wool exported via Durban was sketched: 'This wool will pay off indebtedness of Transvaal farmers to storekeepers and will enable storekeepers to pay off Durban Merchants and I understand that no money will pass to the Transvaal on account of it.' It seems that Roberts did not bother responding and the Natal government did not follow up on the matter thus allowing the broken cycle of credit to escalate. As a result, the Durban chamber of commerce, a month later, again alerted the Natal government that large quantities of wool were passing through Port Elizabeth and East London in an unrestricted manner, including all the stocks that would have traditionally passed through Durban. At the same time, the Durban chamber of commerce asked to be informed of the outcome of the representation to Lord Roberts.[23] The Natal government could not provide an answer as it had not received a reply from Roberts. What should have been clear to the Durban chamber of commerce and the Durban businessmen by now was that their government was both unwilling and unable to stand up to the military on economic matters. As a result, sectors of the Durban economy suffered much in 1900.

Although economic matters for Durban improved from early 1901 onwards and impressive economic figures could be quoted for the city and Natal, it never reached its full commercial potential during the war. One of the most important commercial setbacks for Durban is highlighted in a report from Major OC Armstrong of the Army Financial Services to Lord Kitchener dated 22 December 1901. Natal and Durban, according to Armstrong, were 'hardly worthy of serious consideration' as a base for supplying the army in the field with the necessary items as the businessmen were not financially strong enough to do this as well as to maintain their ordinary business. As far as Armstrong was concerned, the capacity did not exist to sustain large quantities of stock being held ready for immediate disposal, nor to keep the prices within the limits of those prevailing on the open market. To him the Durban market was 'absolutely inadequate to meet the large and sudden demands which might be put forward' and, from enquiries made, Armstrong 'did not think that the necessary capacity for expansion existed'. What also counted against Durban, according to Armstrong, was that 'even within the comparatively small amount of local purchases made at present, cases have

The interior of wharf shed No. 3 at the Point (KCL).

A quayside scene at the Point with stevedores, rail lines, wharf sheds, steam shear legs and the Bluff in the background (NSL).

occurred where our needs have been used to inflate prices. This risk would be greatly enhanced were the amount of local purchases seriously increased'. Armstrong's view was presented at length, on several occasions to Maydon, a member of the Natal legislative assembly who, in turn, informed the Natal government. Maydon expressed his entire concurrence with the opinion of Armstrong, agreeing that it was neither wise, nor advisable, for the British army in South Africa to rely on the Natal market for any large proportion of its supplies, and that it was better to keep importing what was required. With the agreement of the Natal government not to consider Natal, and specifically its economic hub, Durban, as a market for the provisions of military supplies, commercial activities in the city were dealt a further blow.[24]

The stance adopted by the Natal government had serious consequences, and played into the hands of the military where the idea existed that it would be cheaper to use a port such as East London for the importation of military supplies, and allow the Cape Railways to move these supplies to the Transvaal, rather than to focus on Durban and the NGR. According to the military assistant director of railways, a short truck that carried 7 tons of supplies would cost £23 4s 11d to transport goods from Durban to Standerton, a distance of 489 kilometres. A similar truckload from East London to Standerton, covering a distance of 1 198 kilometres, could be commissioned for £21 4s 7d. With the possibility of great savings to the military, but a substantial loss to Natal and Durban, David Hunter, the general manager of the NGR, had to act or lose the lucrative military business. As a result, he proposed some substantial reductions for the return of troops, baggage, ammunitions, guns and so forth from the front. Hunter also pointed out that to compare the Natal and Cape railways would be difficult, as the Cape used short or four-wheeled wagons, irrespective of the weight or character of the contents. According to Hunter, this provided a false picture as 'the actual charge per ton depends entirely upon whether the wagons contain a larger or smaller tonnage. In our experience the carrying capacity of a wagon and its actual performance varies largely; and especially in the case of hay and lucerne, of which a large volume of traffic has been conveyed, our experience is, that the actual load varies from three to eight tons, below the carrying capacity of our wagon stock'. David Hunter, furthermore, pointed out that it would be easier to compare the Natal and Cape systems as far as livestock transportation was concerned, and that to transport horses via Natal, over a distance of 489 kilometres, would mean a saving of £6 5s. The military were also reminded by Hunter that all military stores in the Durban harbour were loaded by the railway department free of charge and carried to the station at the expense of the NGR. He also deemed it necessary to refer to the fact that troops and military supplies passed more quickly through Durban, owing to the large sums of money spent on the harbour improvements. The convenience and speed that resulted from these improvements in itself lessened the expense. During the war, the military were also allowed to use 11 acres of harbour space, free of charge. Similarly, the harbour sheds at Durban had been all but wholly devoted to the use of the military without charge. These facts Hunter mentioned for the information of the military authorities who, he was sure, would 'see that Natal has done everything in its power to serve the Army at the least possible expense'.[25]

Hunter's argument played into the hands of the military and convinced them that Durban was the most viable port for handling imported military supplies. As a result, large consignments of goods passed through Durban to the advantage of the military, but to the detriment of private industry which would, from then on, find it even more difficult to secure truck space or to sell anything to the military.[26] This decision by the military to favour Durban as a port for military supplies, but not as a market, had dire economic effects, especially when the director of civil supplies in Johannesburg, CH Hamilton, in a circular dated 6 January 1902, restricted permits that allowed for the direct importation of goods to Johannesburg via Durban. This step served to cut off all Johannesburg merchants from their Durban suppliers and agents, and had serious consequences, especially as permits to Cape ports remained virtually unlimited. The Durban chamber of commerce immediately petitioned the Natal government who, well knowing that they had contributed to the situation by the economic policy they had adopted, made representations to Kitchener via the governor and the high commissioner. As 1902 progressed, the lack of availability of railway trucks for commercial use became worse, and it became virtually impossible for importers in the Transvaal and Orange Free State to have their goods forwarded from Durban. In an attempt to resolve the situation on many occasions 'ex-haustive reports upon the whole question' were forwarded to 'His Excellency the Governor, the High Commissioner and the Commander-in-Chief respectively' by Prime Minister Hime.

An example of the ongoing tussle was the complaint by the landing, shipping, forwarding and commission agents, HW Weedon & Company. They wrote to Hime on 11 February 1902 complaining that the position in the port of Durban in respect of handling traffic bound for the Transvaal was worse than ever. Because of the preference for military traffic, an almost total interruption of trade with the Transvaal had occurred. As was the practice, permits were obtained from the director of civil supplies for goods to be forwarded to the Transvaal. Weedon & Company had by then accumulated permits for 450 tons of goods dating back to December 1901 that needed to be forwarded. As a result, the clients in the Transvaal, who had initially ordered the goods, were angry at the non-delivery and were threatening never to use Durban as a port again. The Transvaal clients now either shipped their goods through East London or had them forwarded to Lourenço Marques, where goods seemed to pass with no hindrance. The only conclusion the company could come to was: 'Our friends in the Transvaal especially have for some time now been regarding Durban as a port in the most kindly manner but we regret to find that this feeling is rapidly disappearing under the disappointing experiences they have been treated to lately ... there is little doubt that our Port is suffering and that our neighbours at the

Merchants' row on Point Road included shipping companies, chandlers, and agents like Miller, Weedon & Co (LHM).

Cape ports are benefiting thereby.' Hime passed Weedon's letter on to Governor McCallum who for the umpteenth time wrote to Lord Kitchener highlighting the problems Durban was experiencing, compared to the Cape. Kitchener was asked to take the necessary steps to rectify and adjust the imbalance.[27]

The reply to the enquiries by the Natal government came from the military governor of Pretoria, Major General JG Maxwell and the director of civil supplies, CH Hamilton. Maxwell blamed the dilemma in which the Durban businessmen found themselves on the NGR who according to him needed 'rousing'. As the NGR could not accommodate the permits already issued to Durban merchants, it was decided not to issue new permits until those already issued had been worked off. As 75% of all the foodstuffs for the population of the Witwatersrand were generally imported via Durban, the impact was enormous in terms of customs revenue for the Natal government as well as for the Durban businessmen, who depended largely on the Transvaal for the sale of their goods. Driving home the impact of the decision by the NGR to lure military traffic away from the Cape Colony, CH Hamilton notified the Natal government: 'I would point out to you that from Cape Town, Port Elizabeth and East London we are getting a very rapid despatch of goods at present; in fact, we have to depend entirely on these ports now for our supplies.'[28]

As a result of the lack of truckage and the permit system, Durban companies, such as Clark & Thiselton, received instructions from their Transvaal clients 'to ship to no less than three Southern African Ports, i.e. East London, Port Elizabeth and Delagoa Bay'. This they duly did, 'shipping no fewer than 60 tons of goods for Messrs Reid Bros: per *Annerley* the bulk of which have been in our Bonds for over 2 years'. Clark &

Complaints by Johannesburg merchants to Clark and Thiselton

1. B Owen Jones & Co, Boksburg and Standerton: Would close down unless the stock held for them was forwarded.
2. Chandler & Co, Brewers Johannesburg: Wanted all shipments coming for them to be landed at East London or forwarded to Lourenço Marques.
3. VLL de Waegenaere, Portuguese consul in Pretoria: Wanted 500 cases of liquor to be forwarded to Lourenço Marques.
4. Reid Bros Ltd Johannesburg: Always entirely traded through Durban and all their stocks were held by Clark & Thiselton; wanted a portion of their stock forwarded to East London.
5. WM Cuthbert & Co, Johannesburg: Cape firm that always shipped via Durban; were struggling as 43 tons of boots and shoes needed to be forwarded.
6. CA Williams & Co. Johannesburg: Oil agents – would have to close down if their stock which had been in Durban for 2½ years was not forwarded soon.
7. Gordon Mitchell & Co, Cape company – would seriously consider diverting their shipments to Cape ports if matters were not speeded up.

Thiselton were adamant that their inability to forward goods by rail from Durban would affect the welfare of Durban and Natal, not only in the present, but also in future, and that the lack of service would reflect on the trade of the colony as contacts were being lost and contracts broken.

With businessmen not being informed of the real reason for their predicament, the secretary of the Durban chamber of commerce, G Burgess, on 17 February 1902 again took up his pen. In his first letter, he requested the Natal government to make the necessary representations to the authorities in the Transvaal for a more equitable distribution of permits in future, also asking that a larger proportion of civilian traffic be apportioned to Natal. In his second letter he requested the Natal government to acquire from Milner the statistics showing the tonnage of military and civilian traffic carried from each of the southern African ports into the Transvaal and the Orange Free State between November 1901 and February 1902. The Natal government responded aggressively, replying via the prime minister that with regard to the restriction on the importation of goods from Durban to the Transvaal the honour to inform Burgess that the statement of traffic to which he referred had already been asked for, and that the government would not relax its efforts to bring about a satisfactory solution to the present difficulties. Of the devastating accusation by the military that the NGR was to blame for the predicament of the Durban businessmen, not a word was mentioned.

The extent to which these restrictions impacted on Durban and thus Natal, which depended on the economy of its chief city, may be gleaned from the statement by JH Hullett of Kearsney Tea Estates: 'No goods are allowed henceforth to be sent forward to Johannesburg, hence all Natal produce, tea, sugar etc. are entirely shut out. We were just commencing to send tea forward after two years of exclusion during the war and now that the door is closed again it will be a most serious loss of business.'[29]

Although Durban might have gained economically from the war, the numerous factors outlined indicate how the economic community was hampered from taking full advantage of the commercial opportunities which the conflict brought. The most important contributing factor to this was the authoritarian manner in which the military dealt with the Natal government who did not have the ability or determination, despite the numerous petitions by commerce, especially the Durban chamber of commerce, to stand up on behalf of its Durban subjects. As a result, the Cape Colony, with its three ports, and Lourenço Marques must have made economic advances at the cost of Durban, with the latter becoming very much a military gateway. This economic situation was predominantly the fault of the Natal government, who opted not to support Natal markets and businesses as potential suppliers of military goods, but rather opted for short-term gains such as making the NGR almost exclusively available to the military, which relegated Durban to a mere forwarding point for military stocks. In making this decision, the Natal government gave substance to the fear expressed by the Durban chamber of commerce in its annual report of 1901, where it was noted that, since responsible government had been obtained in 1893 the towns in the colony had 'seen a serious decline in their political influence and a correlative increase in the political influence of the country and Agricultural Associations'.[30]

1. Guest, B and Duminy, A The Anglo-Boer War and its economic aftermath, in *Natal and Zululand from earliest times to 1910. A new history*, pp.345–372.

2. *Natal Mercury*, 6.3.1901.

3. PAR, NHD II/5/17: annual report – comparative port statistics for 1899 and 1900.

4. *Natal Witness*, 11.5.1900.

5. PAR, NHD II/5/17: report collector of customs for the year 1901, 26.2.1902.

6. PAR, NHD II/5/19: annual report by the port captain for 1902.

7. PRO, CO 179/213: documents dealing with remission of duties for the military, 21.12.1899.

8. *Natal Witness*, 29.5.1900.

9. PAR, NT 1/6/50: documents on duty-free goods for the military, 1.6.1900.

10 PAR, NT 1/6/55: request by Jameson for a refund of duties upon goods supplied to the military, 20.1.1900.

11. PAR, NT 1/6/50: documents on duty-free goods for the military, 1.6.1900

12. PAR, NT 1/6/55: minute paper on James Noble and Company asking for cigarettes to be admitted duty free, 6.1.1900.

13. *Natal Mercury*, 3.6.1902; 7.6.1902.

14. *Natal Mercury*, 25.1.1902 and 30.1.1902

15. *Natal Witness*, 29.5.1900.

16. PAR, CSO 1648: resolution by the Durban chamber of commerce that military stores should be purchased by public tender, 29.5.1900–3.9.1900.

17. PAR, CSO 1653: enquiry by Durban chamber of commerce of when trade in food and clothes with the Transvaal will resume, 26.7.1900.

18. PAR, CSO 1655: letter secretary Durban chamber of commerce to colonial secretary, 8.8.1900.

19 *Natal Witness*, 7.7.1900.

20. PAR, PM 19: letter secretary Durban chamber of commerce to colonial secretary, 15.8.1900.

21. PAR, CSO 1657: Durban chamber of commerce calling for a relaxation of trade restrictions from the republics regarding wool, 28.8.1900.

22. PAR, GH 531: letter B Reinhold to W Dunn and Co, 15.9.1900.

23. PAR, CSO 1658: Durban chamber of commerce regarding the relaxation of restrictions upon removal of wool from the republics to Durban, 12.9.1900; 15.10.1900.

24. PRO, WO 108/116: memorandum financial advisor's office to general officer commanding, 22.12.1901.

25. PRO, CO 179/214: rates of military traffic over South African railway lines, 8.12.1900.

26. DAL, annual report Durban chamber of commerce for 1901, 13.3.1902.

27. PAR, PM 27: documents regarding the restrictions of importation of goods from Durban into the Transvaal, 1.1902–4.1902.

28. PAR, GH 630: report from the military governor Pretoria and the director of civil supplies why the issuing of permits to Durban was stopped, 3.2.1902.

29. PAR, PM 27: documents regarding the restrictions on importation of goods from Durban into the Transvaal, 1.1902–4.1902.

30. DAL, annual report Durban chamber of commerce for 1900, 5.3.1901.

BIBLIOGRAPHY

In conducting the research for this urban history of Durban during the period of the Anglo-Boer War, the trails of the story were followed, with slight detours at times, from the Durban Archive Repository (DAR) and the Don Africana (DAL) and Killie Campbell (KCL) libraries to the Pietermaritzburg Archive Repository (PAR) and then via the National Archive Repository (NAR) in Pretoria to the Public Record Office (PRO) in London. At these institutions the collections listed below were meticulously combed to find documents from the public and non-public domains, ranging from official publications to eyewitness accounts to tell the story of a gateway to a war. During this process numerous librarians and archivists rendered exemplary service, without which this work would not have been possible.

Throughout this research journey the authors were confronted with the bugbear faced by numerous researchers in history: the reclassification of documents over time which leads to fragmentation of material, documents, maps and photographs alike, making it difficult or impossible to track down important material. An example of this experience was the removal of the plates from the Royal Engineers Report of their work in Natal during the war (PRO, WO 108/296). Despite all efforts these plates that could have provided valuable information on, for example, the Umbilo POW camp and the remount depots, could not be located. Equally frustrating is the fact that the constant reorganisation of some collections in the past, which resulted in different accession numbers, made it virtually impossible to provide comprehensive references, as these would not reflect the historical processes the collections were subjected to. As a result the following simple approach to citing was adopted which attempts to provide sufficient information for future researchers to track down the sources used: the name of the repository, the collection, including the volume numbers which were consulted, the nature of the source used and the applicable dates. This, along with the computerised search facilities available, will hopefully serve subsequent researchers well.

Frequently used abbreviations

AG	Auditor General
AGO	Attorney-General's Office
CD	British Blue Books
CO	Colonial Office
CSO	Colonial Secretary's Office
CS	Colonial Secretary
DAL	Don Africana Library

DAR	Durban Archive Repository
DBC	Director Burgher Camps
DBS	Durban Benevolent Society
DPH	Department of Public Health
GH	Government House
IRD	Immigration Restriction Department
KCL	Killie Campbell Library
LHM	Local History Museum
MGP	Military Governor Pretoria
MJPW	Minister of Justice and Public Works
NAR	National Archive Repository
NCP	Natal Colonial Publications
NCHM	National Cultural History Museum
NDR	Natal Defence Records
NGR	Natal Government Railways
NHD	Natal Harbour Department
NT	Natal Treasury
PAR	Pietermaritzburg Archive Repository
PM	Prime Minister
PMG	Post Master General
PMO	Provost Marshal's Office
PRO	Public Record Office
PVS	Principal Veterinary Surgeon
PWD	Public Works Department
SNA	Secretary of Native Affairs
SOP	Staff Officer Prisoners of War, Natal
WM	War Museum
WO	War Office

PRIMARY SOURCES
UNPUBLISHED ARCHIVAL MATERIAL

Africana Library – Johannesburg
Various photographs as acknowledged
The Tick

Bergtheil Museum – Westville
Photographs as acknowledged
Memoirs of Ms Wolfaard

Cape Archive Repository (CAR) – Cape Town
Photographs as acknowledged
A 921 – JE Tucker collection

Don Africana Library – Durban (DAL)
Durban chamber of commerce reports
Photographs as acknowledged

Durban Archive Repository (DAR)
Town Council Minutes (3/DBN)
Town Council Standing Committees (3/DBN)
Police Reports (3/DBN)

Durban Light Infantry (DLI) Archive
English, GD, Typewritten notes on history of Natal Volunteer
Medical Corps
Various photographs as acknowledged

Free State Archive Repository – Bloemfontein (FAR)
SRC A 21443

German Evangelical Lutheran Church – New Germany
Marriage register (1884–1907)

Killie Campbell Library – Durban (KCL)
Bluff Annals
Campbell, SG, Handwritten and illustrated diary of the Siege of
Ladysmith
Dawes, Edmund – KCM 2035
Elliot, Edward – Manuscript KCM 89/29/1/1
Lamport – Gillespie Papers MS 90
Marwick Papers – File 39 Book 2
Various photographs as acknowledged

Local History Museum, Durban (LHM)
Durban Benevolent Society, Minute Books
Photographs as acknowledged

Natal Society Library – Pietermaritzburg (NSL)
Various photographs as acknowledged

National Archive Repository – Pretoria (NAR)
Colonial Secretary (CS)
Director Burgher Camps (DBC)
GS Preller collection, (A.787)
Military Governor Pretoria (MGP)
Reverend and Mrs van Straten collection
Ploeger collection (A.2030)
Provost Marshall's Office (PMO)
Staff Officer Prisoners of War – Natal (SOP)
W 19/4 A: Memoirs of I Kriegler

National Cultural History Museum – Pretoria (NCHM)
Various photographs as acknowledged

Pietermaritzburg Archive Repository (PAR)
A 113
Auditor General (AG)
A72 – HF Schoon collection
A1538 – Durban Uitlander Committee
Attorney-General's Office (AGO)
Colonial Secretary's Office (CSO)
Director Public Health (DPH)
Government House (GH)
Immigration Restriction Department (IRD)
Melmoth Magistrate (1/Melmoth)
Minister for Justice and Public Works (MJPW)
Natal Colonial Papers (NCP)
Natal Colonial Publications (NCP)
Natal Defence Records (NDR)
Natal Government Railways (NGR)
Natal Harbour Department (NHD)
Natal Treasury (NT)
Prime Minister (PM)
Post Master General (PMG)
Principal Veterinary Services (PVS)
Public Works Department (PWD)
Secretary of Native Affairs (SNA)
Various photographs as acknowledged

Pinetown Museum
Correspondence: Trotter, EL, and Trotter, B
Correspondence: Mrs McCartan to Major General A MacLennan
Interviews: Mr & Mrs G Munro and Mr & Mrs J Munro
Various photographs as acknowledged
Return of deaths at No. 13th Stationary Hospital, Pinetown Bridge
Source unknown

Private Collections
Den Hartog, A collection (Kroonstad)
Hollenbach, C collection (Winterton Museum)
Kearney, BT collection
Lawrence, RS collection (Australia)
Matthews, D collection
Wassermann, JM collection
Watt, S collection
Wohlberg, AU collection

Public Record Office – Kew (PRO)
Cabinet Records (CAB)
Colonial Office (CO)
Merchant Transport (MT)
War Office (WO)

Regimental Museums – Britain
Light Infantry Office, Somerset, Stanton, E, *Diary*
Museum of the Royal Inniskilling Fusiliers, Enniskillen,
Regimental History
Royal Engineers Museum, Photographs of traction engines.
Royal Welch Fusiliers Museum, Kyrke HW, *Letters from the front*

South African Library – Cape Town (SAL)
Photograph as acknowledged

War Museum of the Boer Republics – Bloemfontein (WM)
Concert programme *Aurania*
Gevangenis beschrywing CP van Zyl
Herinneringe van J Geldenhuys
Herinneringe van T Corbett
Ongepubliseerde herinneringe vir boek oor kampkinders
Poem on fleas
Various photographs as acknowledged

West Street Cemetery
Burial registers 1900–1902

PUBLISHED ARCHIVAL MATERIAL

CD 819: Reports, etc., on the working of the refugee camps in the Transvaal, Orange River Colony, Cape Colony and Natal, London, 1901.
CD 853: Further papers relating to the working of the refugee camps in the Transvaal, Orange River Colony, Cape Colony and Natal, London, 1901.
CD 893: Reports on the working of the refugee camps in the Transvaal, Orange River Colony and Natal, London, 1901.
CD 902: Further papers relating to the working of refugee camps in South Africa, London, 1901.
CD 934: Further papers relating to affairs in South Africa, London, 1901.
Committee on Sales and Refunds to Contractors in South Africa, *Report*, War Office, London, 1905.
Debates of the Natal legislative assembly.
Debates of the Natal legislative council.
Good Hope Society, *Report of the Good Hope Society for Aid to Sick and Wounded in the South African War 1899–1902*, Cape Town, 1902.
Royal Commission of the War in South Africa, Minutes of Evidence, London, 1903.
Stratford, DO and Collins, HM, *Military nursing in South Africa, 1914–1994*, South African Defence Force, Pretoria, 1994.
Transvaal Blue Books 1902–1903.

SECONDARY SOURCES

Books
Amery, A, *Life of Joseph Chamberlain, V*, London, 1951.
Amery, LS, (ed.), *The Times history of the war in South Africa 1899–1902*, (seven volumes) London, 1900–1909.
Beijers, CF, *Korte geschiedenis van het konsentrasiekamp te Pietersburg, Zoutpansberg en naamlijst van der 650 vrouwen en kinderen aldaar gestorven 11 Mei 1901 – 30 Januarie 1902*, Pretoria, 1908.
Bhana, S, *Gandhi's Legacy, The Natal Indian Congress, 1894–1994*, Pietermaritzburg, 1997.
Billington, RC, *A Mule Driver at the Front*, London, 1901.
Bird, C, *Annals of Natal, 1945–1845* (two volumes), Pietermaritzburg, 1888.
Blake-Knox, E, *Buller's campaign: With the Natal Field force 1900*, London, 1902.
Boscawen-Wright, C, *With the Imperial Light Infantry Through Natal*, London, 1903.
Bridgeland, T, *Fieldgun Jack versus the Boers: The Royal Navy in South Africa*, Barnsley, 1988.
Brookes EH, and Webb, C de B, *A History of Natal*, Pietermaritzburg, 1965.
Brooks, R, *The long arm of the Empire: Naval brigades from the Crimea to the Boxer Rebellion*, London, 1999.
Brown, H, *War with the Boers*, Virtue, London, 1900.
Burleigh, B, *The Natal Campaign*, London, 1900.
Burne, CRN, *With the Naval Brigade in Natal*, London, 1902.
Campbell, E, *The life of Sam Campbell told in verse and letters by his daughter (A story of Natal)*, Durban, 1933.
Cassel & Co, *Cassell's History of the Boer War, 1899–1902*, London, 1903.
Churchill, WS, *London to Ladysmith via Pretoria*, London, 1900.
Chisholm, GG, and Liebman, JS, *Longman's Geography for South Africa*, London, 1900.
Creswicke, L, *South Africa and The Transvaal War*, (six volumes), London, 1903.
Cunliffe, FHE, *The History of the Boer War*, London, 1901.
Dick, J, *Historical Record of the Durban Volunteer Infantry Corps*, Durban, 1905.
Dickson, WK, *The Biograph in Battle*, London, 1901.
Duminy, A, and Guest, B, (ed.), *Natal and Zululand, From Earliest Times to 1910*, Pietermaritzburg, 1989.
Edwards, D, and Co, *The Anglo Boer War 1899–1900*, Cape Town, 1900.
Fischer, M, *Tant Miem Fischer se kampdagboek: Mei 1901–Augustus 1902*, Kaapstad, 1964 & Pretoria, 2000.

Froes, T, *Expelled from the Rcndt*, Cape Town, 1899.

Gandhi, MK, *Satyagraha in South Africa*, Madras, 1928.

Gandhi, MK, *The Collected Works of Mahatma Gandhi*, Vol. 3, Ahmedabad, 1960.

Grundlingh, AM, *Die "Hendsoppers" en "Joiners": Die rasionaal van verraad*, Pretoria, 1979.

Goetzsche, E, *The official Natal Mounted Rifles History*, Durban, 1971.

Golding, H, *Between two fires*, London, 190?.

Greenwood, TJ, *Fighting the Boers*, Bloemfontein, 1900.

Guest, B, and Sellers, JM, (ed.), *Enterprise and Exploitation in a Victorian Colony*, Pietermaritzburg, 1985.

Hall, D, et al., *The Hall Handbook of the Anglo-Boer War 1899–1902*, Pietermaritzburg, 1999.

Hall, R, *The South African Campaign*, Aberdeen, 1901.

Hannah Watson, J, *A Trooper's Sketchbook of the Boer War*, Glasgow, und.

Harding, W, *War in South Africa and the dark continent*, New Haven, 1900.

Harris, JC, *Refugees and Relief*, Westminster, 1901.

Harrison, CW, *Natal Illustrated Official Railways Guide and General Handbook*, London, 1903.

Headlam, C, *The Milner papers*, London, 1933.

Henderson, WPM, *Durban, Fifty Years Municipal History*, Durban, und.

Henning, CG, *The Indentured Indians in Natal, 1860–1917*, Durban, 1993.

Heydenrych, H and Martin, B, *The Natal Main Line Story*, Pretoria, 1992.

Hill, E, *Report on the plague in Natal, 1902–1903*, London, 1904.

Hobhouse, E, *War without glamour*, Bloemfontein, 1924.

Hurst, GT, *History of the NMR*, Durban, 1935.

Isaacs, N, *Travels and Adventures in Eastern Africa*, London, 1836.

Jeans, TT, *Naval Brigades in the South African War 1899–1900*, London, 1901.

Kaplan, H, *Historic Buildings of Pinetown*, Pinetown, und.

Kriel, C and De Villiers, J, *Rondom die Anglo-Boereoorlog 1899–1902: 'n keur uit die fotoversameling van wyle Christofer Kriel*, Johannesburg, 1979.

Knight, I, *Colenso 1899: The Boer War in Natal*, Durban, 1995.

Kearney, B, *A Revised listing of Important Places and Buildings in Durban*, Durban, 1984.

Knox, EB, *Buller's Campaign with the Natal Field Force of 1900*, London, 1902.

Kruger, DW, *Geskiedenis van Suid-Afrika*, Kaapstad, 1974.

Liebenberg, BJ, *Andries Pretorius in Natal*, Kaapstad, 1977.

Lovegrove, P, *Not least in the crusade: A short history of the Royal Army Medical Corps*, Aldershot, 1951.

Marais, JS, *The fall of Kruger's Republic*, Oxford, 1961.

Marais, P, *Penkoppe van die Tweede Vryheidsoorlog 1899–1902*, Pretoria, 1999.

Marix Evans, MF, *Encyclopedia of the Boer War 1899–1902*, Oxford, 2000.

Maurice, F, and Grant MH, *History of the War in South Africa, 1899–1902*, (four volumes) London, 1906.

Mckenzie, AG, *Delayed action, (Life of Brigadier General Sir Duncan Mckenzie)*, date and place unknown.

McCord, M, *The calling of Katie Makanya: a memoir of South Africa*, Cape Town, 1974.

M'Caw, R, *With the Ayrshire Volunteers in South Africa*, Kilmarnock, 1901.

McLaughlin, R, *The Royal Army Medical Corps*, London, 1972.

Meer, F, *The South African Gandhi: An Abstract of Speeches and Writings of M.K. Gandhi 1893–1914*, Durban, 1995.

Pinetown Women' Institute, *Annals of Pinetown*, Pinetown, 1970.

Natal – Descriptive Guide and Official Handbook, Durban, 1911.

Neethling, E, *Should we Forget?*, Cape Town, 1902.

Otto, JC, *Die konsentrasiekampe*, Kaapstad, 1954.

Odendaal, A, *Vukani Bantu! The beginnings of black protest politics in South Africa to 1912*, Cape Town, 1984.

O'Keefe, B, *Pioneers Progress*, Hilltop Publishers, Hillcrest, 1988.

O'Mahoney, CJ, *A Peep over the Barleycorn – Jack the Sniper*, Dublin, 1901.

Pachai, B, (ed.), *South Africa's Indians: The Evolution of a Minority*,

Pakenham, T, *The Boer War*, London, 1982.

Payne, SHC, *SAS Inkonkoni 1885–1895*, Simonstown, 1990.

Postma, MM, *Stemme uit die verlede: 'n versameling beëdigde verklarings van vroue wat tydens die Tweede Vryheidsoorlog in konsentrasiekampe verkeer het*, Johannesburg, 1939.

Preller, GS, *Ons Parool: Dae uit die dagboek van 'n krygsgevangene*, Kaapstad, 1938.

Pretorius, F, *Life on commando during the Anglo-Boer War 1899–1902*, Cape Town, 1999.

Pretorius, F, *The Anglo-Boer War 1899–1902*, Pretoria, 1998.

Pyarelal, *Mahatma Gandhi: The Discovery of Satyagraha – On the Threshold*, Ahmedabad, 1965.

Raoul-Duval, R, *Au Transvaal et Dans le Sud-Africain*, Paris, 1902.

Reid, BL, *The Lives of Roger Casement*, New Haven, 1976.

Reitz, D, *Commando – A Boer Journal of the Boer War*, London, 1930.

Riall, N, (ed.), *Boer War, the letters, diaries and photographs of Malcolm Riall from the war in South Africa 1899–1902*, London, 2000.

Richards, WA, and Sons, *The Anglo Boer War 1899–1900*, Cape Town, 1900.

Ridpath, JR, and Ellis, ES, *The Story of South Africa*, Sydney, 1899.

Robinson, CN, (ed.), *A Pictorial History of South Africa and the Transvaal*, London, 1899.

Robinson, and Co, *Natal Volunteer Record*, Durban, 1900.

Rosenthal, E, (complier), *Southern African dictionary of national biography*, London, 1966.

Rousseau, WP, *Notulen der conferentie van leeraren, arbeiders en arbeidsters in de burgerkampen in Natal gehouden in het burgerkamp te Merebank op den 24sten en 25 sten Junie, 1902*, Kaapstad, 1902.

Russel, R, *Natal, the Land and it's story*, Maritzburg, 1891.

Russell, G, *The Anglo-Boer War concentration camps in Natal, August, 1900–1903*, Durban, 1988.

(Salt, GES), *Letters and Diary of Lieut. G.E.S. Salt during the War in South Africa 1899–1900*, London, 1902.

Slayter, E, *Isipingo: village in the sun*, Durban, 1961.

Spies, SB, *Methods of Barbarism. Roberts and Kitchener and civilians in the Boer Republics January 1900–May 1902*, Cape Town, 1977.

Sandys, C, *Churchill wanted: dead or alive*, London, 1999.

Sawyer, R, *Casement: The Flawed Hero*, London, 1984.

Sevin-Desplaces, *Les Vaillants Boers*, Paris, 1903.

Singleton, J, *The Battlefields of Natal Re-visited*, Durban, 1900.

Singleton-Gates, P, and Girodias, M, *The Black Diaries*, London, 1959.

Stickney, A, *The Transvaal Outlook*, New York, 1900.

Stirling, J, *The Colonials in South Africa*, Edinburgh, 1907.

Stockenström, E, *Die vrou in die geskiedenis van die Hollands-Afrikaanse volk*, Stellenbosch, 1921.

Sykes, CAJ, *Sidelights of the war*, London, 1900.

Swan, M, *Gandhi, the South African experience*, Johannesburg, 1985.

The Graphic History of the War in South Africa 1899–1900, Wentworth, 1900.

The Natal Who's Who, Durban, 1906.

Tower, C, *Harry Escombe and Natal*, Durban, 1990.

Treves, F, *The Tale of a Field Hospital*, London, 1900.

Uys, I, *Heidelbergers of the Boer War*, Heidelberg, 1981.

Van Helsdingen, J, *Vrouwenleed: persoonlijke ondervindingen in den Boerenoorlog*, Kaapstad, 1903.

Van Schoor, MCE, and Coetzee, CG, *Kampkinders 1900–1902: 'n gedenkboek*, Pretoria, 1982.

Van Zyl DH, *In die konsentrasiekamp: jeugherinneringe*, Bloemfontein, 1944.

War Pictures, London, 1900.

Warwick, P, (ed.), *The South African War*, London, 1980.

Warwick, P, *Black people and the South African War 1899–1902*, Cambridge, 1983.

Whitehead, IR, *Doctors in the Great War*, London, 1999.

Wilson, HW, *With the flag to Pretoria*, (two volumes), London, 1900.

Witton, G, *Scapegoats of the Empire, the true story of Breaker Morant's Bushveldt Carbineers*, London, 1907.

Who's Who In Natal, Knox, Durban, 1933.

Wassermann, JM, *The Eshowe Concentration and Surrendered Burghers Camp during the Anglo-Boer War (1899–1902)*, Durban, 1999.

Journals

Bennett, DR, Strange Bedfellows: The Anglo-Boer War and the Mummy at the Museum, *The Palmnut Post*, 3 (1), March 2000.

Buchner, P, The Royal tour of 1901, the construction of an imperial identity in South Africa, *South African Historical Journal*, 41, 1999.

Dhupelia, U, African labour in Natal: Attempts at coercion and control 1893–1903, *Journal of Natal and Zulu History*, V, 1982.

Gray, E, Sir Percy Scott – The man who taught the navy to hit the target, *Military History*, August 1983.

Hall, DD, The Naval Guns in Natal 1899–1900, *South African Military History Journal*, June 1978.

Kamfer, G, *The role of the secret service of the ZAR (Geheime Dienst) before and during the first months of the Anglo-Boer War*. Paper presented at the University of the Free State, 12–15.10.1999.

Klem, MP, Die alledaagse lewe in die konsentrasiekampe, 1, *Tydskrif vir Volkskunde en Volkstaal*, 2(32), April 1976.

Lambert, J, White dominance and control of the Kholwa petty bourgeois elite with regard to the franchise and authority in late colonial Natal, *Kleio*, XXVII, 1995.

McCracken, JL, Irishmen in Southern African colonial parliaments, *Southern African-Irish Studies*, 1, 1991.

Meshtrie, U, White dominance and control in Natal, 1893–1903, *Journal of Natal and Zulu History*, VII, 1988.

O'Reagain, M, The hospital services of Natal, *Natal Regional Survey*, Vol. 8, UND, 1970.

Pearson, CA, *War Pictures*, Vol.1, No.1 – Vol.1, No.16, London, 1900.

Ramsay, S, Eve Noir: "Folk Devil" and "Guardian of Virtue". A study of the emergence of African prostitution in Durban at the turn of the century, *Journal of Natal and Zulu History*, XIV, 1992.

Swanson, MW, "The Durban System": Roots of Urban Apartheid in Colonial Natal, *African Studies*, 35, 3–4.

St Quentin, TA, The Remount Department from Within, *Empire Review*, April, 1902.

Worthington, G, The Princess Christian Hospital in South Africa, *British Medical Journal*, April 1901.

Newspapers/Magazines/Pamphlets

Centenary brochure, *The Natal Field Artillery.*

De Kerkbode, 1899–1902.

Industries, Durban Vol. I – III, 1900–1902.

Natal Advertiser.

Natal Government Gazette.

Natal Mercury.

Natal Mercury Pictorial, 1912.

Natal Mercury Volunteer Souvenir, Durban, 8.10.1900.

Natal Witness.

Newnes, G, *Under the Union Jack*, (Weekly), London, 1899–1900.

PA 5389 Arrival of POWs.

Review of Reviews.

The Black and White Budget.

The Cape Times.

The Graphic.

The Highway Mail.

The Illustrated London News.

The Illustrated London News, *The Record of the Transvaal 1899–1900*, London, 1900.

The Review and Critic.

The Standard.

The Tick.

Times of Natal.

THESES

Cohen, SG, *A History of the Jews in Durban 1825–1918*, MA, University of Natal.

Hattingh, JL, *Die Irene Konsentrasiekamp*, MA, Universiteit Pretoria, 1967.

Krugell, JE, *Die Pietersburgse Konsentrasiekamp*, MA, PU vir CHO, 1988.

Maphalala, SJ, *Participation of the Zulus in the Anglo-Boer War 1899–1902*, MA, University of Zululand, 1979.

Ronaldo, SC, *Natal Veterinary Services 1874–1912*, MA, University of Natal.

Siwundhla, HT, *The Participation of Non-whites in the Anglo-Boer War 1899–1902*, Michigan, 1977.

Symington, FC, *Die konsentrasiekampskole in die Transvaal en die Oranje-Vrystaat*, MA, Universiteit Pretoria, 1943.

Van der Tang, DB, *White worker militancy in Durban: a study of tramway workers 1900–1939*, MA, University of Natal, 1996.

Wohlberg, AU, *The Merebank Concentration Camp in Durban, 1901–1902*, MA, University of the Free State, 2000.

Personal communication

Brian Kearney correspondence with Foreign and Commonwealth Office.

Brian Kearney correspondence with David Pistorius, Garlicke and Bousfield.

Brian Kearney correspondence with Ralph Sharp, Railway Historical Society.

George Chadwick correspondence with Colonel IH McClausland, 11.3.1899.

George Chadwick correspondence with Lieutenant Colonel EJ Downham, 17.3.1999.

George Chadwick correspondence with Lieutenant Colonel RJM Sinnett, 1.12.1999.

Hazel England interview with Mrs Halsted.

Hazel England interviews with Mr and Mrs Gordon Munro and Mr and Mrs John Munro.

SABC Radio interview, Mrs Brandt, 17.3.1936.

Roll of Honour

Durban Volunteer Regiments

Ashdown	EWD	Bugler	DLI	24.10.1900
Barrett	HC	Pte	DLI	15.7.1900
Berry	CF	Pte	DLI	2.4.1901
Booth	JW	Pte	DLI	2.10.1900
Brown	D	Corp	DLI	22.12.1899
Copeland	F	Pte	DLI	15.11.1899
Cleghorn	GG	Pte	DLI	18.5.1900
Crosby	J	Sgt Instr	DLI	24.8.1900
Currie	C	Sgt	DLI	12.2.1901
Donne	AE	Sgt	DLI	12.10.1901
Espeland	E	Pte	DLI	16.11.1899
Francis	G	Pte	DLI	25.5.1900
Hall	AW	Surgeon Lieut	DLI	20.3.1900
Horsley	W	Pte	DLI	7.6.1900
McKay	E	Pte	DLI	17.5.1900
Moir	DQ	Sgt	DLI	14.4.1900
Oglesby	TD	Lieut	DLI	8.5.1900
Paton	F	Pte	DLI	23.4.1901
Plowman	CS	Pte	DLI	31.5.1900
Shoesmith	T	Pte	DLI	21.9.1900
Smith	E	Pte	DLI	23.4.1900
Sturgeon	AR	Pte	DLI	6.7.1900
Waller	J	Pte	DLI	8.11.1900
Walker	N	Pte	DLI	11.8.1900
Welch	R	Pte	DLI	16.4.1900
Will	AW	Corp	DLI	21.1.1902
Wilson	JTP	Pte	DLI	15.1.1900
Ash	VG	Tpr	NMR	
Clapham	WJ	Lieut	NMR	
Crickmore	JR	Tpr	NMR	
Grice	GV	Tpr	NMR	5.1900
Harrop	S	Tpr	NMR	
Inman	PE	Tpr	NMR	
Parkhill	J	Corp	NMR	27.4.1900
Schram	G	Tpr	NMR	
Thomas	G	Tpr	NMR	
Smith	J	Driver	NFA	
York		Sgt	NFA	8.1900
Adrain	A	PO	NNV	3.1900
Bennett	JS	Gnr	NNV	
Deeves	D	PO	NNV	11.4.1900
Hamilton	CJ	Gnr	NNV	
Harford	S	Gnr	NNV	16.10.1900
Jones	J	Gnr	NNV	
Stehn	A	Gnr	NNV	
Turnley	VSF	Gnr	NNV	

Imperial Troops

Andrews	H	Pte	ES (Vols)	4.5.1900
Ashmore	G	Pte	1st Bn Durham LI	17.5.1900
Babbington		Pte	KRR	12.4.1900
Barker	G	Cdtr	ASC	19.6.1900
Barnett	B	Sgt	3 Bn KRR	16.2.1900
Barrett		Tpr	TMI	3.5.1900
Benckwood	W	Pte	5th Lancers	2.4.1900
Brock	T	Gnr	8th DCo RGA	19.11.1900
Brodest	G	A/B	HMS Forte	9.6.1900
Browning		Pte	1st R Dragoons	12.5.1900
Cotterill	CH	Tpr	Strathcona's Horse	26.6.1900
Cox	J	Pte	1st Bn Durham LI	27.3.1900
Cox	T	Pte	2nd Bn Rifle Brigade	28.3.1900
Dickson	C	Pte	MMSC	15.1.1901
Dickson	E	Pte	1st Bn Durham LI	30.5.1901
Dickson	F	Gnr	RHA	29.1.1900
Dunlop	F	Dmr	2nd Bn Devon R	31.12.1899
Ellis	H	Sgt	1st RD ublin Fus	14.5.1900
Farmer		Pte	York & Lanc R	21.9.1900
Fingler	R	CPO	HMS Terrible	4.4.1900
Finnigan	J	Pte	Devon Regt	11.10.1899
Fitchener	W	Pte	2nd Bn KRR	23.5.1900
Fox	TJ	Pte	RFus	14.3.1902
Glasgow	G	Pte	1st Bn Black Watch	24.12.190
Graney	P	Fmn	HMS Philomel	20.11.1899
Hannack		Tpr	SALH	29.5.1900
Hardy	E	L/S	HMS Thetis	23.4.1900
Harrison	W	Pte	RMLI	7.3.1900
Haynes	A	A/B	HMS Terrible	27.1.1900
Hench	R	Pte	IHC	26.6.1900
Hicks	B	Pte	19th Hussars	11.6.1900
Hill	F	Pte	2nd Bn KRR	30.3.1900
Hooper	C	Pte	1st Glouc R	5.4.1900

Hopkins	J	Snlr	HMS *Terrible*	25.2.1900
Jones	E	Tpr	3rd Hussars	11.1.1902
Kidd	W	L/Cpl	2nd Bn Gordon Hldrs	22.5.1900
Ladkin	F	L/Cpl	1st Bn Manc R	11.4.1900
Lawless	J	CPO	HMS *Partridge*	1.8.1900
Lee	P	Pte	1st Bn KRR	29.3.1900
Leech	GW	Sgt	2nd Bn KRR	17.5.1900
Lockwood	H	Lieut	Scottish Rifles	25.2.1900
Mc. Nally	A	Pte	60th IY	19.7.1900
Manders	F	Pte	1st Glouc R	3.5.1900
Mattison	R	Pte	61st IY	31.5.1901
Milne	W	Pte	R Fusiliers	26.1.1900
Morris	C	Pte	Durham LI	28.3.1900
Neill	GD	Tpr	Driscoll's Scouts	8.8.1901
Pinder	A	Pte	5th Dragoon Guards	26.3.1900
Prest	JW	Pte	2nd W Yorks R	12.5.1900
Prosser	HE	Tpr	S Australian Contingent	12.6.1900
Rose	M	Nurse	Army Nursing Staff	3.1.1900
Rothwell	J	Pte	2nd Bn R Lanc R	2.5.1900
Ryder	CH	Pte	2nd Bn W Yorks R	15.4.1900
Scott		Cons	Tvl Constabulary	26.3.1901
Screech	A	Lieut	HMS Doris	17.3.1900
Senior	W	Gnr	31st Batt RFA	23.10.1902
Simons	J	Tpr	18th Hussars	4.2.1902
Simpkin	H	Fireman	HMS *Philomel*	3.11.1899
Smith	F	A/B	HMS *Terrible*	31.3.1900
Smith	WP	Pte	AOC	10.3.1900
Smith		Pte	2nd Mdx R	31.5.1900
Stewart	A	Tpr	9th Lancers	11.12.1899
Stubberfield	W	Pte	2nd Bn RW Surrey R	19.12.1899
Tauber	H	Tpr	8th Aust Comm Horse	24.6.1901
Thompson	G	A/B	HMS *Philomel*	10.1.1901
Thurston	A	Pte	2nd Bn Norfolk R	7.4.1902
Tindal-Atkinson	PW	Lieut	HMS *Partridge*	1.8.1900
Trundle	A	Pte	2nd Bn Rifle Brigade	8.5.1900
Twigg	J	Pte	KRR	2.12.1899
Vanbeck	M	Pte	5th Bn Lancers	1.4.1900
Waddingham		Pte	R Dublin Fus	23.2.1901
Walker	G	Pte	Liverpool R	6.4.1900
Whittle	RJ	Tpr	ILH	10.4.1900
Wood	J	Pte	Somerset LI	18.3.1900
Veare	H	Pte	2nd Dragoon Guards	14.11.1902

Roll of Honour

A total of 537 deaths were recorded in the Jacobs, Merebank, Pinetown and Wentworth concentration camps.

Panoramic view of Merebank concentration camp – February 1902

1. Camp superintendent's office
2. Merebank station and railroad to Durban
3. Hospital
4. Commissariat
5. Road to Durban
6. School
7. Camp shops
8. Wood depot
9. Camp C
10. Mortuary
11. Black staff accommodation
12. Camp B
13. Wash- and bath-houses
14. Coffin factory
15. Railroad to brick and tile factory
16. Steam disinfector and special laundry
17. Merebank Brick & Tile Co.
18. Offices of Merebank Brick & Tile Co.
19. Camp A

Insert: *A Warrior's Gateway – Durban and the Anglo-Boer War 1899–1902*,
Johan Wassermann & Brian Kearney (editors), 2002. ISBN 1-919825-85-1

Published by **PROTEA BOOK HOUSE**, PO Box 35110, Menlopark, 0102. © Protea Book House and the editors

JACOBS CONCENTRATION CAMP (47 recorded deaths)

Surname	Name	Cause	Date
Basson	Maria Magdalena	Enteritis colitis	28.04.1902
Bezuidenhout	Anna Maria Jacoba	Enteritis	03.03.1902
Bosman	Susanna Maria	Meningitis	29.03.1902
Bronkhorst	Johanna Lourencina	Dysentery	17.04.1902
Coetzee	Susanna Catrina	Asthma and colitis	03.07.1902
Coetzee/Coetzer	Adriana Susanna	Measles and pneumonia	17.03.1902
Coetzee/Coetzer	Johanna Margrita	Chronic diarrhoea	11.06.1902
Coetzee/Coetzer	Roelof Johannes	Measles and pneumonia	23.03.1902
Combrink	Johannes Jacobus	Diphtheria	18.06.1902
Davis	Jacoba Margritha	Chronic enteritis	27.06.1902
De Beer	Heila	Enteric fever	04.02.1903
De Beer	Hester Petronella	Bronchitis	19.06.1902
De Beer	Willem Abram	Measles	28.03.1902
De Jager	Johannes Marthinus	Enteritis	29.04.1902
Du Plessis	Heyla Lavina	Acute endocarditis	27.03.1902
Geldenhuis	Maria Francina	Convulsions	06.10.1902
Grobbelaar	Douw Gerbrandt J	Endocarditis	26.03.1902
Holtshausen	Lukas Johannes	Acute endocarditis	08.07.1902
Jooste	Johanna Carolina	Heart disease	14.05.1902
Joubert	Christina Petronella J	Dysentery	08.05.1902
Kruger	Barend Johannes	Dysentery	02.04.1902
Lewis	Johannes Felde	Catarrhal pneumonia	02.04.1902
Liebenberg	Sophia Charlotte	Gastroenteritis	12.03.1902
Lombard	Jan Petrus Le Grange	Bronchitis	27.04.1902
Luus	Susanna	Marasmus	26.07.1902
Manning	Eliza	Tubercular enteritis	02.10.1902
Marias	Catharina Elizabetta	Typhoid and pneumonia	03.04.1902
Meyer	Helena Elizabeth F	Chronic dysentery	02.04.1902
Nel	Johanna M	Pertussis convulsions	16.03.1902
Pieterse	Wilhelm Barholomew	Chronic dysentery	12.06.1902
Potgieter	Petronella Anna S	Gastroenteritis	03.11.1902
Potgieter	Willem Walter	Tubercular enteritis	05.11.1902
Prinsloo	Henrieetta	Peritonitis	11.08.1902
Roets	Johannes Michel	Enteritis and meningitis	01.05.1902
Schmaal	Hester Wilhelmina	Bronchitis	07.06.1902
Steenkamp	Andries Hendrick	Abscess lung and heart failure	19.08.1902
Steenkamp	Gertruida Susanna	Enteric fever	28.02.1902

Steenkamp	Lucas Cornelius	Catarrhal laryngitis	06.05.1902
Steyn	Johannes Christofel	Infantile convulsions	26.10.1902
Steyn	Sara Aletta Petronella	Cardiac failure and debility	31.08.1902
Strydom	Susanna Jacoba	Enteritis and asthma	11.08.1902
Van der Merwe	Hester Hendrina Aletta	Umbilicus	04.05.1902
Van der Venter	Christoffel	Morbus cordia	19.09.1902
Viljoen	Johannes Christiaan	Tabes mesenteric	09.03.1902
Viviers	Johanna Cornelia	Enteric	01.05.1902
Wallis	Ada A	Dysentery	05.04.1902
Yssel	Sarel Gerhardus	Pertussis and bronchitis	27.03.1902

MEREBANK CONCENTRATION CAMP (454 recorded deaths)

Surname	Name	Cause	Date
Alberts	Nicholaas Francois	Enteritis	22.12.1901
Badenhorst	Hendrik	Bronchopneumonia	02.12.1901
Badenhorst	Martha Jacoba	Bronchopneumonia	16.08.1902
Barnard	Hendrik	Measles	06.10.1901
Barnard	Ragel Magrita	Measles	30.09.1901
Bedford	Petronella Josephia	Pneumonia	14.03.1902
Beis	Amoo Rhee	Spasmodic croup	13.08.1902
Beukes	(unchristened)	Measles	30.09.1901
Beukes	Sarah Maria	Bronchopneumonia	26.11.1901
Beukman	Martinus Petrus	Diarrhoea	02.01.1902
Bezuidenhout	Andries Martinus	Measles	09.10.1901
Bezuidenhout	Anna	Measles followed by acute pneumonia	09.12.1901
Bezuidenhout	Casper Nicholaas	Catarrhal enteritis	06.12.1901
Bezuidenhout	Jacobus Daniel	Diarrhoea	10.03.1902
Bezuidenhout	Maria	Measles	19.10.1901
Bezuidenhout	Pieter Lodewikus	Chronic dysentery	02.09.1902
Bierman	(unchristened)	Dysentery	31.10.1901
Bierman	Francina Elizabeth	Enteric fever	18.12.1901
Bijl	Johanna Elizabeth	Marasmus	09.09.1902
(Black servant)	Kakejan	Enteric fever	30.12.1901
(Black servant)	Klaas	Pneumonia	10.04.1902
(Black servant)	Kleinbooi	Enteric fever	09.01.1902
(Black servant)	Nip	?	28.02.1902
Bodes	Petrus Stephanus	Infantile convulsions and pneumonia	01.01.1902
Bonthuisen	Anna Helena	Pneumonia	05.03.1902

Booysen	Hester Dorothea Paulina	Enteric fever	21.12.1901
Booysen	Marthinus Jacobus	Bronchopneumonia	09.03.1902
Borman (Bredenham?)	Johannes Christian	Enteric fever	09.03.1902
Botes	Magdalena	Pneumonia	13.01.1902
Botha	Gerhardus Johannes	Enteric fever	18.01.1902
Botha	Hendrina Cucilia	Measles and nephritis	25.10.1901
Botha	Hendrina Maria Magdalena	Diarrhoea	23.04.1902
Botha	Jacoba Catrina	Bronchitis	13.02.1902
Botha	Johannes Petrus	Marasmus and diarrhoea	13.05.1902
Botha	Maria Catrina	Goitre hemoptysis and cardiac failure	07.12.1901
Botha	Martha Elizabeth	Bronchopneumonia	07.12.1901
Botha	Matthys David	Bronchopneumonia	29.01.1902
Botha	Petrus Christiaan	Bronchopneumonia	26.12.1901
Botha	Willem Jacobus	Infantile convulsions	08.03.1902
Breedt	Anna Francina	Convulsions	09.04.1902
Breedt	Joseph Erasmus	Measles and nephritis	20.10.1901
Breedt	Louiza Jacoba Willemina Johanna	Burns and bronchopneumonia	24.06.1902
Brink	Daniel Johannes	Meningitis	08.02.1902
Brink	Gertruida Anna Susanna	Bronchitis	03.12.1901
Brits	Hester Magdalena	Enteric fever	11.03.1902
Brits	Maria Salmina	Peritonitis	15.08.1902
Britz	Martha Magdalena	Convulsions	20.06.1902
Broderick	Catrina Elizabeth	Enteritis	10.12.1901
Broekman	Susanna Johanna	Enteritis	09.12.1901
Buys	(unchristened)	Marasmus	09.11.1901
Buys	Johanna Elizabeth Catrina	Bronchitis	20.11.1901
Cloete	Johanna Cristina	Pneumonia	09.12.1901
Cloete	Johannes Christiaan	Bronchopneumonia	11.12.1901
Coetzee	Dirk Jacobus	Pneumonia	24.06.1902
Coetzee	Gertruida Magdalena	Gastroenteritis	21.12.1901
Coetzee	Johan Christian Lambrig	Dysentery	07.02.1902
Coetzee	Johannes Christian Lambrecht	Dysentery	28.03.1902
Coetzee	Maria Cornelia	Diarrhoea	01.12.1901
Coetzee	Martha Johanna Wilhelmina	Diarrhoea	01.01.1902
Coetzer	Susanna	Bronchitis	17.10.1901
Coetzer	Susara Susanna	Measles	26.10.1902
Combrink	Christoffel Jacobus	Bronchopneumonia	10.12.1901
Combrink	Gerhardus Jacobus Hermanus	Bronchopneumonia	26.03.1902
Combrink	Hendrik Josephus	Diarrhoea	10.03.1902
Combrink	Susanna Elizabeth	Bronchopneumonia	14.03.1902

4

Crafford	Johanna Willemina	Bronchopneumonia	01.07.1902
Crafford	Johannes Marcus	Enteric fever	05.07.1902
Croeser	Eleanor Georgina Frances Josephine	Measles and laryngitis	19.09.1902
Cronjé	Catrina	Ulcerating colitis	27.09.1902
Cronjé	Jacomina Hendrina	Measles	12.10.1901
Cronjé	Maria Margritha	Diarrhoea and marasmus	27.06.1902
Cronjé	Susanna Carolina	Bronchopneumonia	25.12.1901
Davids	Marthinus Steyn	Bronchopneumonia	12.03.1902
De Beer	David Johannes	Acute gastroenteritis	12.07.1902
De Beer	Hermanus	Marasmus	27.09.1902
De Beer	Johanna Catrina	Measles	15.01.1902
De Beer	Johanna Hendrina Alida	Bronchitis and pneumonia after measles	30.01.1902
De Beer	Johanna Maria	Bronchitis	17.04.1902
De Beer	Renier Jacobus	Bronchopneumonia	17.01.1902
De Beer	Wilhelmina	Diarrhoea, bronchitis and pneumonia	31.01.1902
De Bruyn	Nicholas Joachim	Bronchopneumonia and measles	16.11.1901
De Jager	Cornelia Elizabeth	Enteric fever	18.12.1901
De Jager	Maria Elizabeth Hendrina	Apoplexy	26.07.1902
De Lange	Johanna Margritha Elizabeth	Bronchopneumonia	25.05.1902
De Meyer	Jacobus William Johannes	Bronchopneumonia	08.02.1902
De Waal	Daniel Pieter Jacobus	Enteric fever	27.12.1901
De Waal	Frans Nicholaas	Bronchopneumonia	15.12.1901
De Waal	Magdalena	Bronchopneumonia	01.01.1902
Delport	Maria	Diarrhoea	13.06.1902
Dirks	Phillipina Christina	Bronchopneumonia	07.08.1902
Du Plessis	Catharina Magdalena	Measles and convulsions	06.02.1902
Du Plessis	Catrina Magdalena	Asthma	16.05.1902
Du Plessis	Johanna Sophia	Measles – died on journey from Pietermaritzburg	18.10.1901
Du Plessis	John Gabriel Stephanus	Enteric fever	01.02.1902
Du Plooy	Anna Elizabeth	Measles and bronchopneumonia	16.12.1901
Du Plooy	Johanna Magdalena	Measles and bronchopneumonia	14.12.1901
Du Plooy	Johannes Gerhardus Josias	Enteric fever	02.12.1901
Du Plooy	Oelof Abram	Diarrhoea	12.12.1901
Du Preez	(unchristened)	Debility	21.10.1901
Du Preez	Ellie	Tubercle of lung	24.10.1901
Du Preez	Margrita Maria	Bronchopneumonia	11.12.1901
Du Preez	Maria Catrina	Chronic enteritis	18.10.1902
Du Preez	Stephanus Francois	Dysentery and bronchopneumonia	24.12.1901
Duyts	Christian Joel Andries	Acute laryngitis	24.06.1902
Eksteen	Frederick Benjamin Ardendolph	Marasmus	18.05.1902

Els	Nicholaas Jacobus	Malaria	17.03.1902
Emmenis	Pieter Stephanus	Bronchopneumonia and diarrhoea	23.01.1902
Engelbrecht	Gertruida Johanna	Gastro-internal atrophy and exhaustion	08.12.1902
Erasmus	Catrina Gertruida	Cardiac and valvular disease	08.04.1902
Erasmus	Hendrik Jacob	Bronchopneumonia	27.03.1902
Erasmus	Hermanus Antonis	Gastroenteritis	27.06.1902
Erasmus	Johannes Isaak	Bronchitis	23.04.1902
Erasmus	Margaretha Petronella	Intestinal obstruction	26.02.1902
Erasmus	Maria Magrita	Acute heart failure	07.08.1902
Erasmus	Susarah Carolina	Pneumonia	18.12.1901
Esterhuizen	Johanna Wilhelmina	Bronchopneumonia	25.11.1901
Esterhuizen	Willem Mark	Measles and pneumonia	04.10.1901
Fick	Aletta Magrita	Diarrhoea	29.12.1901
Fleetwood	Catrina Maria	Meningitis	31.10.1901
Fourie	Hendrina Cecilia	Gastroenteritis	16.01.1902
Fourie	Hester Catrina Louisa	Gastroenteritis	03.01.1902
Fourie	Johan Lowies	Diarrhoea	11.03.1902
Fourie	Johanna Elizabeth	Chronic Bright's disease	12.05.1902
Fourie	Johannes Michiel	Gastroenteritis	09.01.1902
Freyer	Christina Magdalena	Enteric fever	29.11.1901
Geldenhuis	Hester Martha Alletha	Pneumonia, pleurisy and heart failure	20.02.1902
Geldenhuys	Jan Andries	Enteric fever	15.01.1902
Geldenhuys	Maria Elizabeth	Malaria	06.02.1902
Gouws	Petronella Katrina Aletta	Dysentery	13.12.1901
Greef	Susanna Maria Elizabeth	Gastroenteritis	23.12.1901
Grobbelaar	Geziza Maria	Pneumonia and mitral disease	30.12.1901
Groblaar	Martha Elizabeth	Diarrhoea	09.03.1902
Grobler	Elizabeth Hermina	Catarrhal enteritis	02.07.1902
Grobler	Maria Magel	Whooping cough	02.01.1902
Grobler	Nicholaas Johannes	Dysentery	06.01.1902
Grobler	Susarah Johanna Carolina	Diarrhoea	13.12.1901
Groenewald	Maria Elizabeth	Bronchopneumonia	27.04.1902
Gyser	Hendrik Josephus	Diphtheria	01.07.1902
Harmse	Catrina Maria	Diphtheria	14.12.1901
Harmse	Daniel Cornelius	Enteric fever	24.01.1902
Harmse	David Gerhardus	Gastroenteritis	31.01.1902
Harmse	Gertruida	Measles	21.10.1901
Harmse	Hendrina Johanna	Marasmus after enteric fever	15.01.1902
Harmse	Hester Louise C	Enteric fever	21.12.1901
Harmse	Jacoba Catrina	Dysentery	30.11.1901

Harmse	Magdalena Judith	Malaria and heart failure	08.03.1902
Harmse	Maria Jacoba	Bronchopneumonia	25.11.1901
Harmse	Petrus	Measles and pneumonia	28.10.1901
Harmse	Stillborn	Stillborn	06.04.1902
Harmse	Theunica Christina	Malaria	14.02.1902
Harmse	Willem Johannes	Enteric fever	28.05.1902
Hattingh	Aletta Fredrika	Measles	02.10.1901
Hattingh	Catrina Johanna	Measles	09.10.1901
Hattingh	Catrina Susanna	Measles and bronchopneumonia	14.09.1902
Hattingh	Clara Isabella	Measles	21.10.1901
Havenga	Barend Petrus	Diarrhoea	13.04.1902
Havenga	Elizabeth Magrita	Bronchopneumonia	09.01.1902
Helliks	Gertruida Maria Magdalena	Bronchopneumonia	06.12.1901
Henning	Willem Hendrik	Meningitis and enteric fever	18.03.1902
Heuser	Frederick Johannes	Measles	03.12.1901
Hewitt	Berkeley Trevor (child of Sister Hewitt)	Bronchopneumonia	28.03.1902
Hincliff	Thomas	Stillborn	10.08.1902
Horn	Hendrik Andries Jacobus	Intestinal obstruction	26.04.1902
Horn	Sarel du Toit	Bronchitis	18.07.1902
Jacobse	Johannes Lodewikus	Convulsions	02.11.1901
Janse van Rensburg	Francina Carolina	Measles and pneumonia	26.09.1901
Janse van Rensburg	Jacobus Hendrik	Diarrhoea	26.12.1901
Janse van Rensburg	Petronella	Measles	02.11.1901
Janse van Rensburg	Catrina Susanna	Asthma	04.02.1902
Janse van Rensburg	Francina Wilhelmina	Meningitis	13.03.1902
Jooste	(unchristened)	Gastrointestinal catarrh	03.12.1901
Jooste	Abraham Johannes	Diarrhoea	28.03.1902
Jooste	Sarah Johanna	Enteric fever	16.12.1901
Jordaan	Johanna Louisa	Enteric fever	04.01.1902
Jordaan	Martha Maria Catrina	Bronchopneumonia	24.12.1901
Joubert	Anna Elizabeth Johanna	Cerebral haemorrhage	22.06.1902
Joubert	Dorothea Johanna	Convulsions	15.03.1902
Joubert	Elsabe Cornelia	Bronchopneumonia and cardiac failure	14.12.1901
Joubert	Petrus Jacobus	Bronchopneumonia	13.12.1901
Kaarlsen	Martha	Debility and old age	22.09.1901
Kleinhans	Frederik	Malarial fever and bronchitis	15.10.1901
Kleinhans	Martha Magdalena	Pneumonia	07.02.1902
Kloppers	Anna Elizabeth	Enteric fever	09.02.1902
Kloppers	Christina	Bronchopneumonia	28.02.1902
Kock	Elzie Petronella	Croup	05.05.1902

Koen	Ignaas Michael	Died en route from Standerton, between Colenso and Estcourt – taken from the train at Mooi River by doctor	14.09.1901
Kok	Elizabeth Rebecca	Catarrhal enteritis and convulsions	07.11.1901
Kok	Martina Johanna Margritha	Diarrhoea	20.02.1902
Kriek	Hester Catrina	Enteritis	13.11.1901
Kriel	Magdalena Jacomina	Gastric ulcer and pernicious anaemia	23.04.1902
Kritzinger	(unchristened)	Marasmus	14.06.1902
Kruger	Anna Jacoba	Enteric fever	13.12.1901
Kruger	Johanna Louisa	Enteric fever	20.01.1902
Kruger	Alida Maria	Whooping cough	23.11.1901
Kruger	Alletha Margritha	Convulsions	01.04.1902
Kruger	Anna Catrina	Convulsions	06.04.1902
Kruger	Elizabeth	Diarrhoea	31.01.1902
Kruger	Emerenza Jacoba	Dysentery	04.12.1901
Kruger	Maria P	Central inflammation	10.01.1902
Kruger	Pieter Frans	Diarrhoea	08.04.1902
Kruger	Sophia ML	Measles and nephritis	24.10.1901
Labuschagne	(unchristened)	Diarrhoea	19.11.1901
Labuschagne	Anna Elizabeth Magdalena	Cerebral haemorrhage	03.10.1902
Labuschagne	Catrina Johanna	Dysentery	08.12.1901
Labuschagne	Cornelia	Diarrhoea	20.03.1902
Labuschagne	Heyla	Asthenia after enteric fever	13.01.1902
Labuschagne	Jan Hendrik	Diarrhoea	22.12.1901
Labuschagne	Wilhelmina Cecilia	Burns on arm and head, and acute bronchopneumonia	04.12.1902
Le Roux	Catrina Jacoba	Enteritis	24.12.1901
Le Roux	Cornelia Johanna Katrina	Enteric fever	24.12.1901
Le Roux	Johan Adam Beukes	Enteric fever	20.05.1902
Le Roux	Martha Francina Christina	Enteric fever	20.11.1901
Lombaard	Daniel Benjamin	Angina pectoris and enteric fever	20.01.1902
Lombaard	Josiah Renier	Bronchopneumonia	01.12.1901
Lombaard	Judith Dorothea	Bronchopneumonia	02.01.1902
Lombaard	Maria Catrina	Chronic tubercular ulceration of bowel	06.12.1901
Louw	Jan Adriaan	Measles, bronchopneumonia, rodent ulcer face	17.12.1901
Louw	Margrita D	Died in Durban and buried at Merebank – pneumonia and whooping cough	19.12.1901
Malan	Zachria Maria Magrita	Peritonitis and cardiac failure	14.08.1902
Mare	Maria Jacoba	Diarrhoea	16.12.1901
Mare	Martha Jacoba	Influenza, acute gastroenteritis and cardiac failure	10.12.1901
Marks	Anna Catrina	Malaria	05.03.1902
Marks	Christina Johanna Maria	Diarrhoea	17.03.1902

Matthyssen	Alida Cornelia	Measles and bronchopneumonia	14.11.1901
Meane	(unchristened)	Icterus neonatorum and debility	21.11.1901
Meyer	Cornelia Johanna Magrita	Gastroenteritis	26.12.1901
Meyer	Engela	Measles	29.10.1901
Meyer	Heyla Lefina	Diarrhoea	29.10.1901
Meyer	Johannes Petrus Stephanus	Enteritis	23.12.1901
Meyer	Susarra Johanna	Diarrhoea	08.12.1901
Minnaar	Johanna Catrina	Diarrhoea	08.05.1902
Minnaar	Sophia Magdalena	Enteric fever and malaria	14.05.1902
Moolman	Anna Helena	Gastrointestinal catarrh	18.01.1902
Moolman	Catrina Elizabeth	Bronchopneumonia	10.03.1902
Moolman	Jacob Jacobus	Bronchitis	16.09.1902
Moolman	Petrus Lafras	Whooping cough and convulsions	04.11.1901
Mostert	Susanna Josina	Debility after measles and bronchopneumonia	16.03.1902
Mulder	Magdalena Petronella	Bronchopneumonia	03.01.1902
Mulder	Susanna Elizabeth	Gastritis	13.12.1901
Muller	Susanna Aletta	Enteric fever	12.01.1902
Naude	(unchristened)	Convulsions	19.10.1901
Naude	Johannes Jurgens	Bronchopneumonia and diarrhea	18.12.1901
Naude	Petrus	Measles	29.10.1901
Nel	John Alfred	Bronchopneumonia	19.01.1902
Nel	Maria Catrina	Diarrhoea	25.10.1901
Nel	Maria Jacoba	Bronchitis	15.11.1901
Noortman	Johanna Wilhelmina	Diarrhoea	19.12.1901
Oberholzer	Daniel Cornelius	Measles	28.10.1901
Opperman	Catrina Wilhelmina	Enteric and bronchopneumonia	18.02.1902
Otto	Magrita Maria	Measles	29.10.1901
Paskin	Hendrina Johanna Catrina	Bronchopneumonia	18.05.1902
Pelzer	Maria Magdalena	Measles	30.10.1901
Piek	Judith Dorothea	Noma	10.10.1901
Piek	Willem Hendrik	Diarrhoea and syphilis (sic)	13.10.1901
Pienaar	Abel Jacobus	Accident – died in Jacobs Camp Hospital – abdominal internal injuries	20.07.1902
Pieterse	David Jacobus	Bronchopneumonia	10.03.1902
Pieterse	Jacobus Christoffel	Bronchopneumonia	02.07.1902
Pieterse	Jan Johannes	Diarrhoea	27.11.1901
Pieterse	Willem Jacobus	Cardiac failure	05.07.1902
Pietersen	Susanna Johanna	Enteric fever	17.03.1902
Potgieter	Elizabeth Catrina Adriana	Dysentery	06.01.1902
Potgieter	Geresina Magrita	Pneumonia	09.08.1902

Potgieter	Gert Johannes	Catarrhal enteritis	13.03.1902
Potgieter	Hendrik Johannes Abram	Diarrhoea	03.01.1902
Potgieter	Johannes	Bronchopneumonia	27.06.1902
Potgieter	Petrus Jacobus	Bronchopneumonia	03.12.1901
Potgieter	Stephanus Petrus	Gastroenteritis	26.12.1901
Potgieter	Willem Frederick	Bronchopneumonia	19.11.1901
Potgieter	William Thomson	Marasmus	19.03.1902
Prak	Johanna Susanna	Bronchopneumonia	02.12.1901
Pretorius	Ellie Magdalena	Enteric fever	03.12.1901
Pretorius	Gertruida Magdalena	Diarrhoea	24.01.1902
Pretorius	Jacoba Nicholina	Enteric fever	06.01.1902
Pretorius	Jan Adrian	Convulsions	24.03.1902
Pretorius	Maria Petronella Margaretha	Acute peritonitis	23.04.1902
Prinsloo	Elizabeth Maria Cecilia	Diarrhoea	18.12.1901
Prinsloo	Magrita Johanna	Dysentery	17.10.1901
Putter	Hermina Hendrika	Diarrhoea	11.12.1901
Putter	Paul Daniel	Diarrhoea	14.12.1901
Rensburg	Gezina	Bronchopneumonia	03.03.1902
Richter	Stephanus Paulus	Premature birth	30.12.1901
Robertse	Daniel Jacobus	Enteric fever, perforation of gut and peritonitis	19.07.1902
Robertse	Edward Hendrik	Convulsions	01.11.1901
Robertse	Jacobus Frederick	Diarrhoea and convulsions	10.06.1902
Robinson	Cecelia Johanna	Perinephritic abscess	21.11.1902
Roets	Jan Bastiaan	Measles and diarrhoea	05.11.1901
Roets	Maria	Lobular pneumonia	06.11.1901
Roos	Sarel Jacobus	Measles	25.10.1901
Roos	Walter	Enteric fever	08.01.1902
Roux	Carolina Petronella	Diarrhoea	02.04.1902
Roux	Esther Magrita	Enteric fever	18.01.1902
Sandilands	Frans Johannes	Bronchopneumonia	14.12.1901
Schabbort	Isabella	Pneumonia	13.01.1902
Scheepers	Hester Maria	Meningitis	29.12.1901
Scheepers	Hester Susanna	Bronchitis	03.01.1902
Schmahl	(unchristened)	Enteric fever	27.12.1901
Schmahl	Elsie	Apoplexy	23.12.1901
Schoeman	Christiana	Dysentery	11.08.1902
Schoeman	Elizabeth Catrina	Catarrhal enteritis	13.12.1901
Schoeman	Stephanus Johannes	Diarrhoea	18.01.1902
Schoeman	Wilhelmina Lodewika	Bronchopneumonia	10.12.1901
Schutte	Martinus Jacobus	Diarrhoea	01.01.1902

Slabbert	Jacob Johannes	Marasmus	02.11.1902
Slaberts	Johanna Jacoba Wilhelmina	Diarrhoea	24.03.1902
Smit	(unchristened)	Congenital debility	27.04.1902
Smit	Willem Cornelius	Pneumonia	11.10.1901
Smith	Alberta Johanna	Measles	20.11.1901
Smith	Anna Margrita Catrina	Bronchopneumonia	02.02.1902
Smith	Christian Josephus Cornelius	Diarrhoea	08.06.1902
Smith	Ellie Maria	Convulsions	22.04.1902
Smith	Engela Elizabeth	Cerebral congestion	30.07.1902
Smith	Johanna Jacoba	Gastroenteritis	09.01.1902
Smith	Maria Johanna Susanna Magdalena	Bronchitis and pneumonia	27.01.1902
Snyman	Catrina Helena	Enteric fever	28.02.1902
Snyman	Johanna Elizabeth	Whooping cough and bronchitis	21.01.1902
Snyman	Johannes Jacobus	Bronchopneumonia	04.05.1902
Snyman	Martha Catrina	Diarrhoea	02.12.1901
Snyman	Willem Petrus	Bronchopneumonia	06.12.1901
Spies	Helena Christina Jacoba	Enteric fever	07.02.1902
Spies	Johanna Jacoba	Gastroenteritis	16.02.1902
Spies	Willem Francois	Bronchopneumonia	21.12.1901
Stander	Adriaan	Convulsions	17.01.1902
Starck	Magdalena Jozina	Diarrhoea	18.01.1902
Steenkamp	Diedrik Johannes	Meningitis	22.02.1902
Steenkamp	Hester Catrina	Enteric fever	01.01.1902
Steenkamp	Johannes Paulus	Whooping cough	06.01.1902
Stein	Lukas Cornelius	Measles and pneumonia	29.09.1901
Stein	Susannah	Measles	19.10.1901
Stell	Marie	Bronchitis	10.08.1902
Steyn	Magdalena Elizabeth Susanna	Croup	10.06.1902
Steyn	Martha Helena	Bronchopneumonia	06.12.1901
Steyn	Petrus Jacobus	Measles	18.10.1901
Stols	Johanna Maria	Measles	03.10.1901
Stoop	Albertus Abraham	Croup	06.04.1902
Strydom	Barend Hendrik	Diarrhoea	23.11.1901
Strydom	Gert Roelof	Bronchopneumonia	18.01.1902
Swanepoel	Martha Aletta	Dysentery	01.11.1901
Swart	Martha Dorothea	Heart failure	10.01.1902
Swart	Martha Dorothea	Whooping cough	02.11.1901
Swarts	Gertruida Jacomina	Gastroenteritis and heart failure	29.12.1901
Swartz	Christian Frederic	Bronchopneumonia	28.11.1901
Swartz	Emerenza Adriana	Enteric fever	29.12.1901

Swartz	Hester Paulina	Bronchitis	31.01.1902
Swartz	Johanna Margrita	Gastroenteritis	04.02.1902
Swartz	Louis	Bronchitis	25.10.1901
(Tamil Indian)	–	Stillborn	28.05.1902
Taute	Samuel Jacobus	Bronchopneumonia	18.11.1901
Theunissen	Nicholas Jacobus	Carcinoma of liver	14.06.1902
Thompson	Thomas	Gastrointestinal atrophy	14.10.1902
Trytsman	Elizabeth Johanna	Enteritis	22.12.1901
Trytsman	Hendrik Johannes	Bronchopneumonia	21.09.1902
Trytsman	Martha Elizabeth	Asthma bronchitis	06.02.1902
Van Dyk	Jacobus Hendrik	Bronchitis	12.04.1902
Van Aswegen	Gerhardus Petrus	Diarrhoea	10.12.1901
Van Aswegen	Johanna Lodewika	Bronchopneumonia	15.12.1901
Van Aswegen	Pieter Jacobus	Bronchopneumonia and pertussis	01.01.1902
Van Dam	Hendrik Andries	Diarrhoea	21.12.1901
Van den Berg	Christian	Chronic dysentery	14.01.1902
Van den Berg	Christina Johanna Sophia	Diarrhoea	28.02.1902
Van den Berg	(unchristened)	Diarrhoea	28.05.1902
Van den Berg	Anna Elizabeth	Diarrhoea	01.11.1901
Van den Berg	Daniel Johannes	Marasmus	13.04.1902
Van den Berg	Johanna Christina	Bronchopneumonia	29.11.1901
Van den Berg	Susarrah Petronella	Enteric fever	27.12.1901
Van der Berg	Michael Daniel Bester	Measles	08.10.1901
Van der Merwe	Adriana Augusta	Enteric fever	15.04.1902
Van der Merwe	Agata Gertruida	Enteric fever	02.04.1902
Van der Merwe	Catharine Johanna	Enteric fever	08.11.1901
Van der Merwe	Catrina Elizabeth	Measles and bronchopneumonia	25.07.1902
Van der Merwe	Cornelius Johannes	Diarrhoea	06.01.1902
Van der Merwe	Daniel Jacobus	Diarrhoea	27.05.1902
Van der Merwe	Georgina Francina	Enteric fever	30.12.1901
Van der Merwe	Gertruida Sophia	Meningitis	27.02.1902
Van der Merwe	Hans Jacobus	Measles, pneumonia and convulsions	07.11.1901
Van der Merwe	Johanna Adriasina	Diarrhoea	06.12.1901
Van der Merwe	Maria Magdalena	Whooping cough and bronchopneumonia	10.01.1902
Van der Merwe	Petronella Catrina	Gastroenteritis	15.01.1902
Van der Merwe	Schalk Willem Albertus	Diarrhoea	18.12.1901
Van der Merwe	Susilia Gertruida	Bronchitis and debility	28.01.1902
Van der Nest	Elizabeth Susanna	Croup	12.05.1902
Van der Sandt	Engela Carolina	Bronchopneumonia	03.01.1902
Van der Walt	Anna Catrina	Enteric fever	09.02.1902

Van der Westhuizen	Jasper Cornelius	Diarrhoea	18.06.1902
Van de Venter	Stephanus Lukas	Enteric fever	24.12.1901
Van Dyk	Anna ME	Measles	06.10.1901
Van Dyk	Frans Johannes	Dysentery	03.03.1902
Van Dyk	Johannes Arnoldus	Dengue	03.03.1902
Van Dyk	Joseph Andries	Measles and dysentery	09.10.1901
Van Dyk	Theunis Louis	Tubercle of peritoneum	26.09.1901
Van Lelifelt	Malena	Asthma and bronchopneumonia	12.02.1902
Van Loggerenberg	Aletta Susanna	Catarrhal enteritis and convulsions	08.11.1901
Van Niekerk	(unchristened)	Enteritis	12.12.1901
Van Niekerk	Eva Catrina	Tuberculosis	12.12.1901
Van Niekerk	Gerhardus Albertus	Measles and bronchopneumonia	07.11.1901
Van Niekerk	Jan Albert	Diarrhoea	16.12.1901
Van Rensburg	Abraham Andries	Convulsions	14.07.1902
Van Rensburg	Hester Margritha	Enteric fever and diarrhoea	10.03.1902
Van Rensburg	Jacoba Johanna	Measles	05.10.1901
Van Rensburg	Johanna Sophia	Malaria	27.03.1902
Van Rensburg	Salina Francina Petronella	Diarrhoea	29.01.1902
Van Rooyen	(unchristened)	Heart failure	13.08.1902
Van Rooyen	Aletta HS	Enteric fever	08.01.1902
Van Rooyen	Anna Elizabeth	Enteric fever	20.01.1902
Van Rooyen	Bernard Gerhardus	Diarrhoea	25.06.1902
Van Rooyen	Christina Lodovina	Enteric fever	22.02.1902
Van Rooyen	Susanna Catrina	Peritonitis	27.08.1902
Van Rooyen	Willem Jacobus	Bronchopneumonia	24.03.1902
Van Schoor	Willem Adriaan	Pneumonia	20.01.1902
Van Staden	Elizabeth Hermina	Diarrhoea	14.12.1901
Van Staden	Isabella Elizabeth	Measles	04.03.1902
Van Staden	Jacobus F	Measles	10.02.1902
Van Staden	Martinus Johannes	Whooping cough and pneumonia	15.01.1902
Van Staden	Renier Jacobus	Dysentery	23.02.1902
Van Tonder	Gesina	Debility and old age	10.10.1901
Van Tonder	Hendrina Haminna	Diarrhoea	13.02.1902
Van Tonder	Roedolph Jacobus Petrus	Diarrhoea and bronchopneumonia	07.03.1902
Van Vuuren	Andries Johannes S	Bronchopneumonia	16.11.1901
Van Wyk	Albert Johannes	Measles	17.10.1901
Van Wyk	Christina Maria	Whooping cough	25.11.1901
Van Wyk	Engela Susanna	Croup	07.09.1902
Van Zyl	Anna Catharina	Bronchopneumonia	29.12.1901
Van Zyl	Jacob	Diarrhoea	30.11.1901

Veltman	Benjamin	Croup	12.02.1902
Veltsman	Cornelia Fredrikka	Asthma	21.02.1902
Venter	Hendrina Maria Magdalena	Measles	07.10.1901
Venter	Jacobus Daniel	Meningitis	11.01.1902
Vermaak	Engela Maria	Bronchopneumonia	07.03.1902
Vermaak	Jacobus Phillipus	Meningitis	30.01.1902
Vermaak	Salomon Cornelius Johannes	Enteric fever	06.12.1901
Viljoen	Elizabeth Freda	Bronchopneumonia	09.09.1902
Viljoen	Hendrina Wilhelmina Elizabeth	Pneumonia and enteric fever	01.05.1902
Viljoen	Johannes Matthys	Diarrhoea	29.11.1901
Viljoen	Karl Johannes	Convulsions	03.11.1901
Viljoen	Maria Hendrina	Acute lobar pneumonia	26.05.1902
Viljoen	Martinus Johannes	Dysentery	15.01.1902
Viljoen	Willem Christian	Diarrhoea	05.05.1902
Visagie	Alleta Susanna	Diarrhoea	24.02.1902
Vogel	Magdalena Jacoba	Diarrhoea	02.02.1902
Volschenk	Catrina Magdalena Elizabeth Johanna	Bronchopneumonia	01.03.1902
Volschenk	Gert Johannes	Diarrhoea	17.02.1902
Volschenk	Petrus	Bronchopneumonia	30.03.1902
Vorster	Barend Johannes	Diarrhoea	18.12.1901
Voster	Gertruida Johanna	Diarrhoea	17.12.1901
Voster	Josias	Measles	02.12.1901
Wentzel	Johanna Henrietta	Diarrhoea	16.11.1901
Wessels	(unchristened)	Marasmus	23.04.1902
Wiechers	Sybrandt Gerhardus	Enteritis	10.12.1901
Wilden	Hendrik Diedriks	Measles	08.10.1901
Wolmarans	Catrina Jacoba	Measles	04.10.1901
Wolmarans	Catrina Maria	Convulsions	08.10.1901
Wolmarans	Catrina Maria	Measles	17.10.1901
Wolmarans	Johanna Elizabeth	Influenza, bronchopneumonia and cardiac failure	14.12.1901
Wolmarans	Petrus Johannes	Diarrhoea and convulsions	24.12.1901
Wolmarans	Susanna	Pneumonia	02.10.1901

PINETOWN CONCENTRATION CAMP (20 recorded deaths)

Surname	Name	Cause	Date
Bisschoff	Marthinus Nicholas	Congenital debility	14.4.1902
De Jager	Johannes Jurgens	Haemophilia	22.6.1902
Janse Van Rensburg	Sarah Jacoba	Pneumonia	13.6.1902

nsen	Maria Magdalena	Pneumonia	25.06.1902
ius	Jacobus Christian	Inanition from birth	03.08.1902
iarais	Gesina Josina	Laryngitis	22.05.1902
Moulder	Theunis Johannes	Convulsions	12.04.1902
Neethling	James Edward	Acute enteritis	13.05.1902
Nel	Jan Hendrik	Marasmus	06.06.1902
Nel	Johannes Stephanus	Croup	11.05.1902
Olivier	Izaak Jacobus	Pneumonia	28.05.1902
Potgieter	Hendrik Jacobus	Chronic pneumonia	05.08.1902
Prinsloo	Elizabeth Johanna	Pneumonia	22.06.1902
Raaths	Wilhelmina Jacoba	Malaria, abortion and collapse	14.07.1902
Smith	Sarah	Laryngitis	28.05.1902
Snyder	Sussarah Magdalena	Congenital debility	29.04.1902
Van Staden	Johannes Jurie	Laryngitis	12.06.1902
Van Staden	Johannes Jurie	Marasmus	19.04.1902
Van Wyk	Theunis Johannes	Maligent stomach disease	04.07.1902
Venter	Petrus Jacobus Johannes	Pneumonia	03.05.1902

WENTWORTH CONCENTRATION CAMP (16 recorded deaths)

Surname	Name	Cause	Date
Coetzee	Dirk Jacobus	Convulsions and prematurity	20.04.1902
Erasmus	Jacobus E	Pneumonia	20.07.1902
Jacobs	Maria Catrina	Laryngitis	26.05.1902
Kemp	Johanna	Bilateral pneumonia	01.08.1902
Kolbe	Maria Esther	Gastroenteritis	14.07.1902
Kriek	Annie	Enteric fever and bronchitis	03.06.1902
Lambrecht	Johannes Christiaan	Inanition	03.06.1902
Loog	Hendrik Cornelius	Dentition and diarrhoea	05.07.1902
Schutte	(unchristened)	Meningitis and inanition	14.04.1902
Smit	Hendrina Cecilia	Meningitis	13.05.1902
Steyn	Gabriel Petrus	Infantile convulsions	23.04.1902
Van Eeden	Casper Jacobus Hermanus	Meningitis	27.04.1902
Van Rensburg	(unchristened)	Stillborn and inanition	22.05.1902
Van Straten	Johanna Aletta	Heart disease	08.04.1902
Venter	Johanna Elizabeth	Heart disease	04.07.1902
Visser	Frans Jacobus	Heart disease	05.07.1902

123. NAR, SOP 32: letter CP Schulz to superintendent, Umbilo, 6.5.1902.

124. *The Tick* (2), 12.6.1902, p.3.

125. *The Tick* (3), 26.6.1902, p.1.

126. *The Tick* (3), 26.6.1902, p.1.

127. *The Tick* (1), 5.6.1902, p.1.

128. *The Tick* (1), 5.6.1902, p.1.

129. *The Tick* (2), 12.6.1902, p.3.

130. *The Tick* (3), 26.6.1902, p.4

131. PAR, P 5389: *Umbilo Camp. General Scheme for reception and subsequent distribution of ex-prisoners of war*, p.10.

132. NAR, SOP 33: letter war office to the general officer commanding, Natal, April, 1902.

133. NAR, SOP 32: note SOP Natal to camp commandant, Umbilo, 26.5.1902.

134. *The Tick* (1), 5.6.1902, p.1.

135. *The Tick* (1), 5.6.1902, p.1; *Natal Mercury*, 26.6.1902.

136. *The Tick* (2), 12.6.1902, p.3.

137. *The Tick* (1), 5.6.1902, p.1.

138. *Natal Mercury*, 26.6.1902.

139. NAR, GS Preller collection, A.787. 62: diary of C Röcher, p.109.

140. DAR, 3/DBN 8/1/111/3/2: letter granting E Suleman permission to erect a stand, 21.4.1902.

141. *The Tick*, (1), 5.6.1902; *The Tick*, (2), 14.6.1902; *The Tick*, (3), 26.6.1902.

142. NAR, CS 226: document on employment of men in the Umbilo camp, 14.1.1903.

143. NAR, SOP 34: note Colonel RM Ireland to HA Coddington, 5.9.1902; note HA Coddington to Colonel RM Ireland, 7.9.1902.

144. NAR, SOP 35: statement by Hendrik Bredenham 5.12.1902; NAR, SOP 35: note WR Saunders to Captain McHardy, 24,12,1902; NAR, SOP 35: letter Captain McHardy to the Natal police, Sydenham, 26.12.1902.

145. *Natal Mercury*, 19.9.1901.

146. NAR, SOP 29: memorandum SOP to HM Bousfield, 24.2.1902.

147. NAR, SOP 34: description of staff attached to the Umbilo camp, 8.8.1902.

148. NAR, SOP 33: note Lieutenant Colonel HTW Allatt to the press censor, Durban, 15.7.1902; NAR, SOP 33: particulars of a POW who slipped out from Umbilo camp on 16 June 1902.

149. NAR, SOP 33: letter W Dunn & Co. to the commandant Durban, 16.6.1902.

150. NAR, SOP 33: letter Lieutenant Colonel HTW Allatt to general officer commanding, Middelburg, 24.6.1902.

151. PAR, GH 545: telegram general officer commanding, Natal to HE McCallum, 12.6.1902; NAR, SOP 33: letter provost marshall to SOP Natal, 9.7.1902.

152. PAR, SOP 33: letter Lieutenant Colonel HTW Allatt to prime minister, 14.6.1902.

153. NAR, CS 100: letter colonial secretary to military secretary, 4.7.1902.

154. NAR, CS 95: letter private secretary to Lieutenant Colonel HTW Allatt, 13.1.1902; NAR, CS 95: telegram Lieutenant Colonel HTW Allatt to imperial chief commissioner office, 4.6.1902.

155. NAR, CS 148: letter military secretary to colonial secretary, 2.10.1902.

156. PAR, GH 707: translation of telegram sent to the Boers by the Boer generals, 2.7.1902; NAR, SOP 33: Dutch copy of the telegram, 4.7.1902.

157. PAR, SOP 33: letter SOP Natal, to DAAG. Natal, 10.6.1902.

158. PAR, GH 546: telegram general officer commanding, Natal to governor, 20.6.1902.

159. NAR, Ploeger collection, A 2030 51: circular, F. 20

160. NAR, SOP 33: letter Lieutenant Colonel HTW Allatt to provost marshal, 7.7.1902.

161. PAR, GH 563: telegrams SOP to camp superintendents, 25.8.1902.

162. NAR, GH 563: telegrams DAAG to the governor, 19.8.1902, 13.09.1902, 22.10.1902; NAR, GH 563: list HE McCallum to Milner, 17.9.1902.

163. PAR, GH 563: telegrams SOP to governor 29.11.1902, 4.12.1902, 3.1.1903, 6.1.1903.

164. PRO, WO 108/155: final recommendations for civilians, 3.6.1902.

165. NAR, CS 226: documents regarding employment for POWs in the Umbilo camp, 14.1.1903.

166. PAR, PA 5389: *Umbilo Camp. General Scheme for redistribution and subsequent distribution of ex-prisoners of war*, passim.

167. NAR, SOP 34: telegram provost marshal, Pretoria to SOP Umbilo, date unknown; telegram chief ordnance officer to SOP, Umbilo, 20.8.1902.

168. PAR, GH 564: letter HE McCallum to Milner, 17.9.1902.

169. NAR, SOP 34: letter general manager, NGR to assistant quartermaster general, Durban, 25.8.1902.

170. PAR, PM 32: letter acting general manager of the NGR to the secretary of the prime minister, 1.9.1902.

171. PAR, PM 32: memorandum W Bonham to HE McCallum, 26.8.1902.

172. PAR, PM 32: letter acting general manager of the NGR to the secretary of the prime minister, 1.9.1902.

173. NAR, SOP 35: memorandum station master Umbilo to DAAG, 14.11.1902.

174. NAR, SOP 35: letter Captain AA McHardy to Lieutenant Radford, 14.11.1902.

175. NAR, GH 563: telegram SOP to HE McCallum, 26.8.1902.

176. PAR PM 32: telegram DAAG to prime minister, 7.9.1902.

177. NAR, SOP 34: letter HA van Bart to SOP, Cape Town, 17.7.1902; NAR, SOP 34: letter SOP, Cape Town to SOP, Natal, 23.7.1902.

178. NAR, SOP 35: letter Major FA Tyler to the commandant Durban, 24.6.1902.

179. NAR, SOP 35: telegram Captain W Bonham to SOP 16.9.1902.

180. NAR, GS Preller collection, A. 787, 62: diary of C Röcher, p.201.

181. PAR, PM 33: letters Captain AA McHardy to attorney-general, 6.10.1902 and 15.10.1902; PAR, PM 33: note secretary of the prime minister to DAAG 31.10.1902.

182. PAR, PM 36: note secretary of the prime minister to SOP, 12.01.1903.

183. DAR, 3/DBN A 1/1/1: report Durban corporation town report on liabilities, 1903.

184. PAR, MJPW 129: letter deputy mayor to minister of justice, Pietermaritzburg, 17.6.1902.

185. PAR, NCP 8/1/10/6/20: Indian immigration report, 1902/1903

CHAPTER 8

COMRADES IN QUIETUS: DEATHS OF VOLUNTEERS AND BOER PRISONERS OF WAR
Brian Kearney and Johan Wassermann

One of the inevitabilities of war is death. Death during the Anglo-Boer War did not occur only on the battlefields but also in various hospitals, in camps and by accident. Regardless of how these deaths came about, all casualties, Boer and British alike, had two factors in common: they paid the ultimate price for a war which was not of their making, and they left family and friends behind who had to deal with the emotional and financial trauma that follows in the wake of death.

Durban volunteer deaths and compensation

There are numerous comprehensive accounts of the actions and behaviour of the Durban volunteers and Boer commandos at the war front. Their experiences are usually described en masse, excepting in the case of individual acts of heroism. However, some archival documentation exists which provides us with brief glimpses into the lives, backgrounds and family life of individual volunteers and soldiers. These documents are invariably concerned with their capture, sickness, wounds or death and the consequences for those whom they left behind. The following accounts were probably microcosms of the greater community experience.

Accidents certainly interrupted the lives of some volunteers and one such recorded event illustrates a number of dimensions in the life of a volunteer even before the war began. Surgeon Lieutenant AW Hall and other members of the Durban Light Infantry (DLI) were participating in revolver practice at the regimental range on a Saturday in September 1899. At the conclusion of the exercise, Private Gadsby ejected the expended cartridges from the revolver, or thought he had, when one exploded, lacerating his hand and hitting Hall in the right thigh. Carelessness in counting the number of shots fired caused the accident and perhaps the fact that several volunteers, including officers, used the same weapon to practise with, also contributed to the mishap. Hall had been in charge of the training session and, after the incident, he was removed to the Berea Hospital in Kensington House, Musgrave Road, where he was treated by Dr Sam Campbell. Not wishing to be regarded as an idler, Hall offered his services to his regiment for any duties which could be carried out while in hospital. He reported the accident to Colonel Royston, the commandant of volunteers:

> I received a bullet wound in the right thigh – which pierced the thigh from within outwards – passing just behind the bone – at the junction of the middle and lower thirds of the femur ... I hardly expect to be able to ride in less than six weeks or two months ... The practice was conducted with the greatest care and each man present having fired twelve shots we were about to leave the range when Sergt. Clinton finding he had 12 more cartridges, I loaded the revolver myself and fired six more shots myself – after which Private Gadsby took the pistol to fire the remaining cartridges. He did so – or thought he did ...[1]

Lieutenant Hall at some later stage joined the Natal Volunteer Medical Corps (NVMC). In the *Natal Volunteer Record* he is included both in the 'roll call' list of the DLI as Surgeon Lieutenant AW Hall and in the 'honours roll' of the NVMC.[2] He died of enteric as did many of his colleagues. No evidence has been found of any compensation which his family may have received.

Volunteer compensation laws

In May 1900, the Natal parliament established a select committee appointed to 'consider and report upon the provisions to be made for the Widows and Dependents of Volunteers falling in action or dying of disease or wounds received on active service'.[3] The committee under the chairmanship of Advocate Morcom reported in June and noted that 83 volunteers had already died by that date, including three commissioned officers. One was a major whose widow had been awarded a pension of £140 per annum, another a lieutenant whose mother received a pension of £60 per annum and the third was a quartermaster, whose widow would be given £52, with an additional £12 for each of her three children.

Volunteer compensation laws had existed in the Colony of Natal since 1872 and provided for various categories of compensation for death or wounds,[4] catering for widows, children or dependent women and, in line with the regulations for the British army, the scale of compensation depended on the rank of the soldier. The most recent legislation was that of 1895. In making various recommendations, the select committee based their suggestions on the following factors:

> (a) Cognisance should be taken of the fact that the cost of living in Natal is higher than in England, and
> (b) the cost of education is also higher.
> (c) The length of time during which the volunteers had been on active service should be taken into consideration and the probability of their having to cross the borders, should be borne in mind.
> (d) It was considered important that encouragement should be given to the volunteer force.

The principle employed in determining compensatory pensions or gratuities was that they were to be calculated 'as if the said Officers came under the provisions ... as Officers in Her Majesty's Army' and eight recommendations were passed into legislation.

To receive any of the recommended compensations was not to be easy as evident in the cases of Ogelsby and Welch, which had been finalised before the release of the select committee report. The first case concerned Mrs Oglesby, the mother of a member of the DLI, Lieutenant JD Oglesby, who had died at Estcourt on 8 May 1900. The documentation which describes this case illustrates the degree of thoroughness employed in the investigation into the family circumstances of a dead volunteer and the reasonably equable application of the regulations and principles by government ministers and officials. Volunteer Paymaster Owen, requested Grant, the DLI bandmaster, to provide details of the family. Oglesby had a married brother who worked as a bookkeeper for a confectionery company. His mother was widowed and lived in Manning Road with her two daughters, and the three were entirely dependent on her unmarried son. Originally Hime recommended to the attorney-general that in the light of this information, she be awarded an annual allowance of £60. Had she been a widow, she would have been awarded a full allowance of £104, plus a gratuity of £310 5s, as if he had been a member of the regular army. But in the case of a mother, the officials 'had been left a free hand', and so when the matter came before the ministers for debate, they eventually agreed on the pension originally granted, plus a 'half allowance by way of gratuity'.[5]

Before volunteering, Private R Welch had worked as a clerk in the Smith Street branch of Steel, Murray & Co. General Merchants. He had probably had to leave the family farm in Umzinto to seek work in Durban. His father, aged 59, who had once been 'well-to-do', had suffered as a result of the rinderpest which had destroyed all his cattle and a locust invasion which had decimated his crops. Welch senior had long been widowed and was 'suffering from rheumatism and dyspepsia'. In addition, Private Welch had to provide support for an ailing aunt and two young sisters aged 13 and 14. Prime Minister Hime confirmed these family circumstances through the magistrate in Umzinto, who also noted that Welch had been paying £3 per quarter for his sisters' schooling and also for their clothing and that, since his death, they had been sent to a cheaper school. It was agreed to pay the sisters the 'usual half pension and half gratuity', and the attorney-general advised that instead of appointing trustees Welch senior be paid the money and that he account to the magistrate for its use.[6]

60

Your Committee therefore recommend that the provision which should be made for the widows and dependents of Volunteers falling in action or dying from disease contracted or wounds received on active service be on the following scale :—

(a) That the pensions awarded to the widows of Volunteer Officers shall be calculated as if the said Officers came under the provisions above stated as Officers in Her Majesty's Army. Provided that a Lieutenant or Second Lieutenant's ordinary pension in the above list shall be read as if the amount were £52 and not £40.

(b) That the pension awarded the widow of any member of a Volunteer Force shall not be less than £52 per annum.

(c) That the compassionate allowance for each child being a son under 18 years of age or a daughter under 21 years of age shall not be less than £12 per annum.

(d) That an addition of 33 1-3rd per cent. be made to all pensions and allowances calculated on the basis of the above paragraphs (a), (b), (c).

(e) That a year's gratuity calculated on the rate of pay of which the Volunteer Officer or member was actually in receipt when killed or wounded shall be granted in addition to pension to the widow of such deceased Officer or Member.

(f) That the sum payable to a widow may be paid to female relatives dependent on any member of the Volunteer Force who shall be unmarried.

(g) That a receipt by a widow on account of her husband's services of any other pension, charitable provision or charitable allowance from the public, shall not affect her claims to pension under the Volunteer Laws of the Colony.

(h) That the above recommendations be made applicable to all widows, children, and female dependents whose cases have been dealt with or are under consideration in connection with all members the Volunteer Force called out on active service in September, 1899, or at any time during the present campaign.

Signed on behalf of the Committee,

W. B. MORCOM,
Chairman.

Committee Rooms,
  Legislative Assembly, Natal,
    5th June, 1900.

Second Avenue, Greyville with humble wood and iron cottages with front verandas (LHM).

A working-class family and cottage on the lower Berea (KCL).

Victims of the armoured train incident at Chievely

An unusual and interesting case of compensation concerned the mother of Private Z Espeland, a Norwegian, of C company of the DLI, who probably thought that gaining 'colonial experience' and 'doing well' were two good reasons to volunteer to serve in a foreign conflict and thereby establish himself in colonial society. Espeland had been killed in action in the armoured train disaster at Chievely on the 16 November 1899. Extensive correspondence worked its way up from the adjutant of the DLI, through the paymaster of the volunteer forces eventually reaching the prime minister's office.[7] The volunteer and war relief committee, under the attorney-general made a grant to his mother, Mrs Inger Jacobsen, who lived in Fjellestad near Farsund in Norway. According to Egeland, a Durban timber merchant, Espeland had not been married and his mother 'a widow in poor circumstances was mainly depending on him for support'. The Scandinavian community in Durban was small and fairly close, thus Egeland had known Espeland and his younger brother who resided with a certain Hansen in North Street, Greyville. Furthermore Egeland told the volunteer paymaster that his own parents lived close to Espeland's family in Fjellestad, and that he had 'requested his father to break the news to Mrs Jacobsen. He also mentioned that he thought she would be entitled to an amount sufficient for her maintenance for life under the Volunteer Law besides getting a share of money subscribed for berieved [sic] volunteer relatives'.[8] Espeland's brother wrote to Lieutenant Owen of the DLI and told him that his sibling had been apparently serving an apprenticeship with a Lieutenant Flood of the DLI (who was, no doubt influential in getting him to volunteer) and that money had been sent home regularly; as their father, Captain Jacob Jacobsen-Espeland, had died some ten years before, which had left their mother destitute. He wrote:

> She has been supported by my brother, she being without means and was entirely depending on him. As I have not been very successful and able to do much when he was doing well and has gained Colonial experience and being a good tradesman as Lieutenant Flood DLI will, whom he served his apprenticeship with, bear out. His death is therefore all the more a terrible blow to my mother and I can only hope that the Natal Government in whose service he died a soldier's death will provide for her. I have no means and have been out of employment for the last two months.[9]

The volunteer and war relief committee made a grant to Mrs Espeland in February 1900, but it took until May to verify her circumstances. Attorney-General Henry Bale, chairman of the committee, recommended that the British legation in Stockholm, Sweden, should supply them with an accurate assessment of her conditions. This course was pursued by Governor Hely-Hutchinson in March, but the query had to be routed through Joseph Chamberlain's office, then sent to the foreign office, then the British consul general, Charles Dundas in Christiania, and

finally to Vice-Consul Sundt at Farsund. The response naturally took until June to reach Natal and confirmed her situation, mentioning that she owned a small house which had been mortgaged up to its full value, and that she had no other means of income. Dundas also confirmed that she had already received a sum of £60 from the Natal Armoured Train Relief Fund.[10]

The wives of DLI men involved in the armoured train incident were granted relief, albeit over an extended period of time. Private King was taken prisoner at Chievely in November 1899, and it was only in March 1900 that his wife, Bella King, eventually received £30 assistance from the Armoured Train Relief Fund, in addition to the 27s 6p she received regularly from her husband's pay. Since she was in Aberdeen, Scotland, this was made possible through the services of a Captain Macneal at the Castlehill Barracks, and a Mr Cheyney of Durban, who held power of attorney for King.[11]

Volunteer victims of disease

Not all volunteers died in action on the front lines and one suspects that the military authorities may have deliberately sent certain men home when sick or injured in order to avoid being blamed for their deaths. One DLI soldier, Private William Horsley of First Avenue, Greyville, had been sent home from Estcourt with a sprained ankle, but later died of enteric fever on 7 July 1900, raising a question as to the real reason for his withdrawal from the front. Horsley had resigned from the NGR on volunteering. Like his father, who had been a fireman, then an engine driver and then an instructor, he joined the railways as an apprentice blacksmith in the Durban workshops. He had given over his nine shillings per day to his mother to help with the upkeep of the home, and to help provide for his three sisters and one brother. One sister had 'met with a misfortune', the particulars of which were not revealed. In addition, he had also given his full volunteer pay to his mother. Captain Molyneux of the DLI did not think that the case came within the government scheme of compensation and he advised that an application for compensation be turned down. However, when the matter came before Prime Minister Hime, he requested further information on the family circumstances and specifically why Horsley had given over his wages to his mother. Molyneux then wrote to Horsley senior requesting further details and, on 10 July 1900, in his absence Mrs M Horsley responded:

> My husband being away at Volksrust I have to answer these questions myself. First I will state I have had a family of eleven children, 5 I have lost, 6 I have alive, of whom 1 son and 1 daughter married. 4 I have at home at present which are 3 girls and 1 young son. My young son which is home is very delicate suffers from heart and kidney disease which we are afraid will never be very much help to himself or us in the home. My late son William was apprenticed at 15 years of age to the Railway when he received 9/- per week for the first year and a rise as usual every year after that. At the time he was called away to the front he was receiving 9/-per day which he gave me [his mother]. Why he gave it, was because he was a good son and wanted to help the home and do some good for me. We are not well off, we have had so much trouble bringing up the family which has kept us poor and has taken all our means to keep us. I have received all my son's volunteer money and he told me if anything happened to him while on active service I should receive a pension which I am sure I am entitled to. As regards Mr Horsley's occupation, he was first a fireman on the NGR and then a driver and at present he is Local Instructor. His age is 51 years and I myself am the same age. As regarding my late son's disease the doctor says he had contracted it at the front. I have enclosed the certificate to you from the doctor.

Once again Molyneux advised against compensation, arguing that the family lived in their own house and that Horsley's father ought to be drawing good pay from the NGR. However, Mrs Horsley responded:

> ... I am very sorry to hear your Government cannot entertain my claim for compensation ... I cannot accept your reply as final as I feel sure if the case came under the notice of the Government they would most surely consider it. I have been myself to the Colonial Secretary in PM Burg and he advised me to make a fresh statement ... My late son William Horsley has been a great assistance in my home and through his death I have sustained a very great loss and assistance, all through being forced away by Government for active service, and now Government say they cannot entertain my application for compensation. Others have had it in Durban who are better off than myself ...[12]

Again the request was turned down by the commandant of volunteers, Royston, but a very determined Mrs Horsley requested to see him in Pietermaritzburg. Somehow she managed to bypass Royston and, late in August 1900, Prime Minister Hime noted that Horsley had been to see him in Pietermaritzburg to present her case and, in particular, to argue that she had been 'to considerable expense in connection with his [her son's] illness and funeral expenses'. He recommended that she be granted a sum of £25 as compensation. Perhaps this was a relatively small amount but she may be regarded as an excellent example of a determined mother who persisted until she received what was due to her.

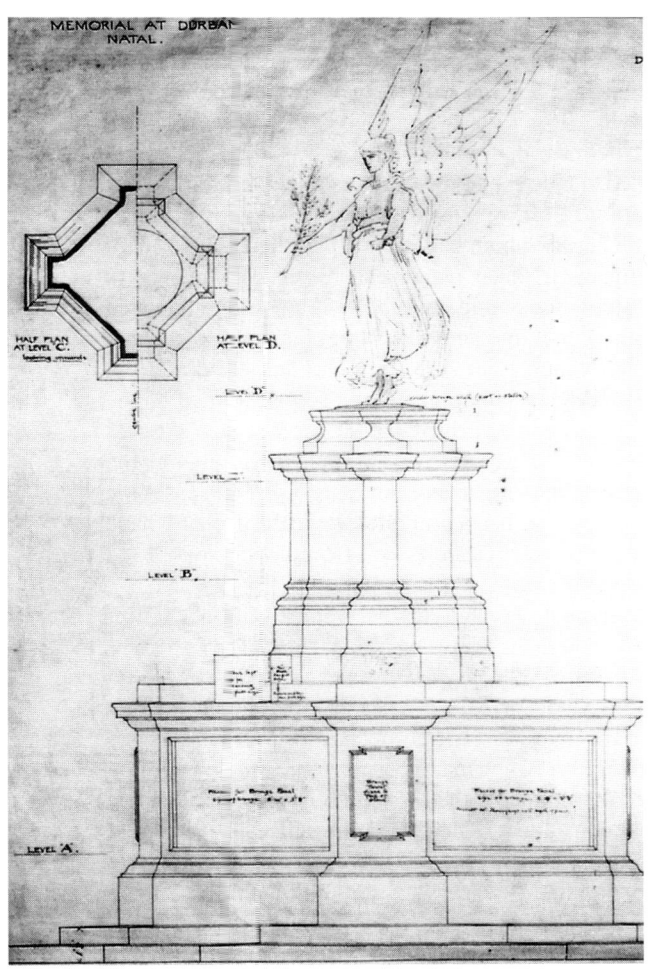

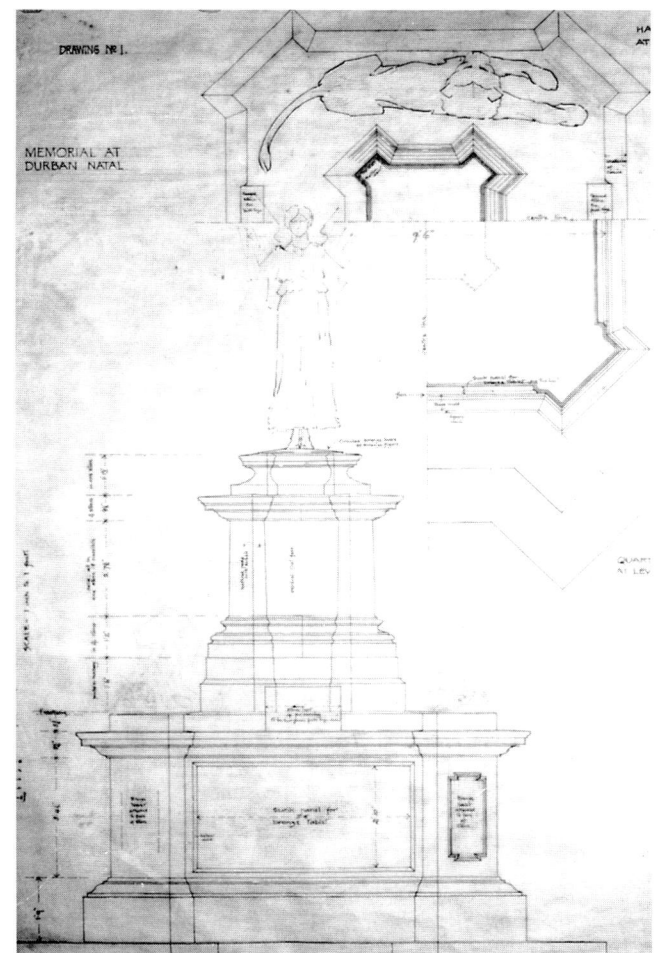

Design drawings for the Volunteer Memorial by Hymo
Thorneycroft, 1904 (City Architect's archives).

Volunteer Memorial town gardens (PAR).

When the DLI returned to Durban a bugler, EWD Ashdown, arrived home ill with enteric fever. According to the records, 'This man was sick when leaving Dundee but it was thought [to be] a passing indisposition only. On arrival in Durban he was worse and was taken home where he now lies.' He died a few days later, aged 19 years and two months. Ashdown had joined the DLI as a boy some four years before. Dr Addison confirmed that he had contracted enteric fever on active service. Within the application made for compensation initiated by the adjutant of the regiment, it became clear that the family was in difficult circumstances: his father contributed very little, being 'away from Durban and of weak intellect'. For six months at a time Mrs Ashdown would not receive a penny. The family was living with her mother in Leopold Street and included Ashdown's three sisters, Elizabeth Alice (20), Natalia Minerva (17) and Violet Cooper (14). The two elder girls earned £2 10s per month from teaching. Bugler Ashdown had been apprenticed to Mason & Atkinson, ironmongers, where he had earned £6 per month, 'the whole handed to his mother'. The authorities were persuaded by these facts and Mrs Ashdown was granted a half pension and a half gratuity.[13]

It is not known how Private G Francis, who lived and worked in Cape Town, landed up in Natal and became a member of the DLI. After contracting enteric fever, he was returning to Cape Town in May 1900, on the hospital ship *Dunera*, when he died. The Soldiers' Christian Association in Cape Town became involved in tracking down his wife and child. The secretary of the association, Will Gordon Sprigg, located the bereaved Francis family, who were also known by the surname Drake, and, in September, arranged for compensation for Mrs Florence Edith Francis by issuing a Natal treasury draft of £147 2s 4d. It was fortunate that the late Francis had worked for a board member of the association, who had his interests at heart.[14]

Private AR Sturgeon, also of the DLI, died of pneumonia in the Dundee Hospital on 6 July 1900. His widow, who lived at 410 Point Road, was asked for her marriage certificate in order to benefit from the pension payout. The process was, however, fairly long winded as in January 1901, the Durban attorneys, Shepstone and Wylie, requested that payments be made to her half-yearly at her request. They also informed the colonial treasury that she was about to leave for Australia, where in April of that same year, the treasury of the State of Victoria acknowledged making arrangements for her to be paid £69 6s 8d per annum.[15]

It seems not all Durban volunteers who died received compensation. If a member of the regular volunteers such as those belonging to the DLI left the regiment at the end of a period of service or on the disbandment of the local regiments in October 1900, and thereafter joined another corps, any claims for compensation seem to have been forfeited. Such was the case of Charles Berry, who had served as a private in the DLI until 8 October 1900, and at some later stage joined the Prince of Wales Light Horse where he became a commissioned officer. It is not known how, or when, he was killed, but a query was directed to the commandant of volunteers on 13 May 1901, regarding the validity of his mother's claim to a pension and gratuity. Molyneux, who had by now risen to the rank of major, replied from the commandant of volunteers' office that 'no

Sir Albert Henry Hime

Hime was the prime minister of Natal for the duration of the Anglo-Boer War. He had been born in Wicklow in Ireland on 29 August 1842, was educated at Trinity College in Dublin and had entered the Royal Engineers in 1861, from which he retired as an honorary Lieutenant Colonel in 1883. He became the colonial engineer of Natal in 1875 and a member of the executive and legislative councils in 1876. On Natal gaining responsible government in 1893, he retired. He was elected as a member of the legislative assembly for Pietermaritzburg in 1897 and became minister for lands, works and defence between 1897 and 1899. He took over as prime minister from the dying Henry Binns in 1899, while at the same time retaining his other ministry.

Captain William Henry Arthur Molyneux

Molyneux had served in the Natal military police during the Anglo-Zulu War and thereafter in a number of clerical posts in the civil service, reaching the position of sergeant-at-arms in the legislative assembly in 1893. He was appointed district adjutant in the volunteer department in 1895, then acting staff officer in May 1900, and finally volunteer paymaster in April 1901.

Natal Volunteer joining an Imperial Irregular Corps would be entitled to pension or gratuity under our Colonial Act, nor would his mother or other relative'.[16]

Burials, exhumations and reinterments of Durban Volunteers

In early 1900, after the major engagements in Northern Natal, the Natal government agreed to free railway transportation for the remains of deceased volunteers which were to be moved from their hastily made places of burial on the battlefields to cemeteries in Durban. A certain local undertaker, JE Wade of 51 Queen Street, appears to have monopolised this particular market.

But the free carriage was only one facet of the problem, for Wade soon ran into the thorny issue of who actually could give authority for the removal and reinterment of the bodies. In the process of attempting to remove the remains of Alex Adrain of the NNV, George Thomas of the NMR and Charles Beaumont of the Natal Police from where they had been buried at Intombi Spruit, he fell headlong into the usual dispute between the civil and military authorities. In April 1900, General Buller telegraphed Hime saying that:

> ... I find now that the Colonial Secretary wrote as follows on the 27th March to Mr. Wade an undertaker in Durban – begins – I am directed to convey to you the necessary authority for the removal of these bodies subject of course to the approval of the local authorities – ends. Mr. Wade applied to the Colonial Secretary for authority to exhume the bodies of certain Volunteers who were buried at Intombi Spruit Cemetery and bring them to Durban for reinterment. I was not aware of this ...

Hime responded to the effect that he had never given anybody permission to remove the body of any person. Wade thereupon requested, and received the necessary authority from the chief of staff, Ladysmith, for the removal of the bodies. The only condition applied was that the names of the deceased volunteers who were to be moved should be supplied.[17]

Robinson, who was one of the section leaders of the ambulance corps which had been active at Spioenkop, had been killed during the action. In June 1900, Wade again sought permission for an exhumation and reinterment and his request to the colonial authorities was passed on to General Wolfe-Murray. The general objected strangely and strongly:

> Unless further particulars are forthcoming, I think the proposal highly objectionable. I do not think that undertakers should be permitted to go burrowing into the graves on battlefields in a promiscuous fashion, as appears to be proposed. I must ask that the Civil Government (if my view is concurred in) will support

me in this view, and I will ask that Mr. Wade be informed that upon reconsideration the Natal Government does now object ... the burial places upon the battlefields in Natal will remain after the large Military force in Natal moves away; and the control of those burial places will cease – and, in my view, has already ceased – to be in military hands – I can conceive of no more unfortunate state of affairs than that it should become generally known that interference with these burial places is not a matter in which the Civil Government concerns itself. If no hindrance is to be placed in the way of indiscriminate search for the bodies of persons interred in these places, I feel we may have intolerable scandals ... I am writing to Mr. Wade forbidding him to proceed till I receive fuller information ... may we not ask that the same protection be afforded to the remains of those who, through no fault of their own, have had to be buried where they fell, beyond the pale.

Thus Wolfe-Murray passed the responsibility back to the Natal government but, nevertheless, made a stand. Charles Smythe, the colonial secretary, explained that he had misunderstood the point and that the colonial authorities would give permission only if the military authorities were in consensus. He agreed that there should be no indiscriminate disturbance of graves on the battlefields, but argued that since Natal was still under martial law 'the battlefields are, at the present time, solely under the control of the Military Authorities'. He also used the opportunity to request that the question of whether the military or the civil authorities were responsible should be settled at once. It is to be presumed that Wade, in spite of the controversy surrounding the matter, was finally granted the permission which he sought and that Robinson's remains were returned to his home town.[18]

The death of Boer prisoners of war in Durban

Shortly after the outbreak of the Anglo-Boer War, the first Boer POWs passed through Durban harbour. By 1903, thousands of these prisoners had been deported and had returned via Durban. Of these numerous POWs passing through Durban approximately 22 died in the city. Their names can be obtained from the honours roll at the and of this publication.

The first Boer POW to die in Durban was the 49-year-old HJ Odendaal of Bethlehem in the Orange Free State, who passed away on 4 May 1901. Odendaal probably died in hospital, of an unknown cause, as he was not buried at sea but in the West Street Cemetery at site 12 in block 33.[19] The second recorded death was that of 22-year-old Carl Johann de Villiers of Eerste Geluk, Heilbron in the Orange Free State. De